A Companion to the Victorian Novel

Blackwell Companions to Literature and Culture

This series offers comprehensive, newly written surveys of key periods and movements, and certain major authors, in English literary culture and history. Extensive volumes provide new perspectives and positions on contexts and on canonical and post-canonical texts, orientating the beginning student in new fields of study and providing the experienced undergraduate and new graduate with current and new directions, as pioneered and developed by leading scholars in the field.

A COMPANION TO

THE VICTORIAN NOVEL

EDITED BY **PATRICK BRANTLINGER**
AND **WILLIAM B. THESING**

Blackwell
Publishing

350 Main Street, Malden, Massachusetts 02148-5018, USA
108 Cowley Road, Oxford OX4 1JF, UK
550 Swanston Street, Carlton South, Victoria 3053, Australia
Kurfürstendamm 57, 10707 Berlin, Germany

First published 2002 by Blackwell Publishers Ltd

Library of Congress Cataloging-in-Publication Data

A companion to the Victorian novel / edited by Patrick Brantlinger and William B. Thesing.
p. cm. – (Blackwell companions to literature and culture)
Includes bibliographical references and index.
ISBN 0-631-22064-X (hb : alk. paper)
1. English fiction – 19th century – History and criticism – Handbooks, manuals, etc.
2. Literature and society – Great Britain – History – 19th century – Handbooks, manuals, etc.
3. Great Britain – History – Victoria, 1837–1901 – Handbooks, manuals, etc. I. Brantlinger,
Patrick, 1941– II. Thesing, William B. III. Series.
PR871 .C643 2002
823'.809 – dc21
2002022768

A catalogue record for this title is available from the British Library

Set in 11 on 13 pt Garamond 3
by SNP Best-set Typesetter Ltd., Hong Kong
Printed and bound in the United Kingdom by T. J. International Ltd, Padstow, Cornwall
For further information on
Blackwell Publishing, visit our website:
http://www.blackwellpublishing.com

Contents

Acknowledgments

We have worked at a distance, but very well together on this project since the spring of 1999. Our greatest debt is to Andrew McNeillie at Blackwell for first suggesting such an important enterprise to us. He has been unfailingly generous with his time and advice during work on this book. We are also grateful to the excellent staff at Blackwell Publishing, including Alison Dunnett, Emma Bennett, Laura Montgomery, and others who worked on our book. Gillian Bromley did a superb job of copy-editing; Randy Miller compiled an excellent index.

We have been fortunate to receive intellectual, moral, and financial support at our two universities. At Indiana University, we express our gratitude to the faculty and students of the Victorian Studies program, especially Donald J. Gray, Andrew Miller, and Joss Marsh, as well as to the Lilly Library and its superb staff. At the University of South Carolina, several graduate research assistants helped with xeroxing, mailing, and filing chores: we are especially grateful to Leean Hawkins, Jamie Ridenhour, and Amy Smith. Steve Lynn and William Richey have been very supportive with various types of research assistance. Colleagues David Cowart, Patrick G. Scott, and Meili Steele, and the various graduate student members of the USC Nineteenth Century Club, have offered useful suggestions concerning the project. The fine staff of the Thomas Cooper Library offered helpful assistance.

Finally, we are grateful to our excellent and efficient contributors for their outstanding essays that make the volume so successful. Our thanks go especially to our wives – Ellen Brantlinger and Jane Thesing – for their support and encouragement over the years. We also appreciate the patience and love of our children.

Patrick Brantlinger and William B. Thesing

The Contributors

John Bowen is a Reader in the Department of English and Director of the Centre for Victorian Studies at Keele University. He is the author of *Other Dickens: Pickwick to Chuzzlewit* (2000) and has edited Dickens's *Barnaby Rudge* for Penguin. He is a member of the editorial board of the *Journal of Victorian Culture*.

Patrick Brantlinger is former editor of *Victorian Studies*. Among his books are *Rule of Darkness: British Literature and Imperialism, 1830–1914* (1988) and *The Reading Lesson: The Threat of Mass Literacy in Nineteenth-Century British Fiction* (1999).

Joseph W. Childers teaches English at the University of California, Riverside. He is the author of *Novel Possibilities: Fiction and the Formation of Early Victorian Culture* (1995) and co-editor of *The Columbia Dictionary of Modern Literary and Cultural Criticism* (1995).

Deirdre David is Professor of English at Temple University in Philadelphia. She is author of *Fictions of Resolution in Three Victorian Novels* (1982), *Intellectual Women and Victorian Patriarchy* (1987), and *Rule Britannia: Women, Empire, and Victorian Writing* (1996).

Ian Duncan, Professor of English at the University of California, Berkeley, is the author of *Modern Romance and Transformations of the Novel: The Gothic, Scott, Dickens* (1992), editions of Walter Scott's *Rob Roy* and *Ivanhoe*, and articles on Ruskin's quarrel with fiction and on Edinburgh as a Romantic metropolis. He is completing a book on the novel in Romantic-era Scotland.

Kamilla Elliott is Assistant Professor of English at the University of California, Berkeley. She specializes in the interdisciplinary study of literature and film, with an emphasis on Victorian literature and film. Her book, *Rethinking the Novel/Film Debate*, is forthcoming from Cambridge University Press.

Hilary Fraser is Dean of Arts and Humanities at Canterbury Christ Church University College and Adjunct Professor of the University of Western Australia. She is author of *Mediating Gender: Femininities, Masculinities, and the Victorian Periodical Press* (with Judith Johnston and Stephanie Green, forthcoming), *English Prose of the Nineteenth Century* (with Daniel Brown, 1997), *The Victorians and Renaissance Italy* (1992), and *Beauty and Belief: Aesthetics and Religion in Victorian Literature* (1986). She currently works on Victorian women art historians.

Regenia Gagnier is Professor of English at the University of Exeter, where she teaches Victorian studies, especially the *fin de siècle*, social theory, feminist theory, and inter-disciplinary studies. Her books include *Idylls of the Marketplace: Oscar Wilde and the Victorian Public* (1986); *Subjectivities: A History of Self-Representation in Britain, 1832–1920* (1991); an edited collection, *Critical Essays on Oscar Wilde* (1992); and *The Insatiability of Human Wants: Economics and Aesthetics in Market Society* (2000). She is currently writing about nineteenth- and twentieth-century models of individualism in the transatlantic context.

Winifred Hughes is the author of *The Maniac in the Cellar: Sensation Novels of the 1860s* (1980), as well as articles on Victorian fiction and poetry. She is book review editor of *Victorian Literature and Culture*.

Anne Humpherys is Professor of English at Lehman College and The Graduate Center, City University of New York. She is author of *Travels into the Poor Man's Country: The Work of Henry Mayhew* and of articles in various volumes and journals on the nineteenth-century press, Victorian popular culture, the Victorian novel, Dickens, and Tennyson.

Audrey Jaffe is the author of *Vanishing Points: Dickens, Narrative, and the Subject of Omniscience* (1991) and *Scenes of Sympathy: Identity and Representation in Victorian Fiction* (2000). She is a former member of the English Department at Ohio State University.

Christopher Keep teaches in the English Department at the University of Western Ontario. He has published on topics ranging from "The Cultural Work of the Type-writer Girl" to theories of embodiment in hypertext fiction and virtual reality. He is currently researching a book concerning the emergent information economy of the nineteenth century.

John Kucich, Professor of English at the University of Michigan, is the author of *Excess and Restraint in the Novels of Charles Dickens* (1981), *Repression in Victorian Fiction* (1987), and *The Power of Lies: Transgression in Victorian Fiction* (1994), as well as the co-editor, with Dianne Sadoff, of *Victorian Afterlife: Postmodern Culture Rewrites the Nineteenth Century* (2001).

Joss Marsh is an Associate Professor of English at Indiana University. Her book *Word Crimes: Blasphemy, Culture, and Literature in Nineteenth-Century England* appeared in 1998; she owes her interest in visual culture, on which she has published articles in media as diverse as the *Times Literary Supplement* and *Select* rock magazine, in part to membership in a three-generation film-making family.

John R. Maynard is Professor of English at New York University. He has published a biography, *Browning's Youth* (1974), and is a long-time member of the Biography Seminar in New York. His other work includes studies of Victorian literature and sexuality – *Charlotte Brontë and Sexuality* (1984) and *Victorian Discourses on Sexuality and Religion* (1994) – a book on contemporary Browning criticism (*Re-viewing Browning*, 1999), and a study of reader theory (work in progress). Since 1990 he has been co-editor of *Victorian Literature and Culture*.

Kelly J. Mays, an Assistant Professor of English at the University of Nevada, Las Vegas, has published articles on Chartist poetry, working-class autobiography, and nineteenth-century reading practices and serves as an editor of the *Norton Introduction to Literature*. She is currently completing a study of representations of reading and literacy in nineteenth-century Britain.

Renata Kobetts Miller received her Ph.D. from Indiana University. Her dissertation, "Setting the Stage: Victorian Culture, Theater, and the Suffragettes" (2001), demonstrated that the centrality of actresses in the suffragette movement derived from the importance of the theatrical woman as a figure of artifice and public influence in Victorian culture.

John R. Reed is Distinguished Professor of English at Wayne State University. He has published widely on nineteenth- and twentieth-century British literature and culture. His most recent scholarly book was *Dickens and Thackeray: Punishment and Forgiveness* (1995). He is currently at work on a book-length study of the armed services in nineteenth-century British literature and culture.

Lewis C. Roberts teaches Victorian literature and children's literature at Indiana University. He is the author of "Disciplining and Disinfecting Working-Class Readers in the Victorian Public Library" (*Victorian Literature and Culture*, 1998). He is currently working on a book about Victorian literacy, material culture, and publishing practices, as well as researching the role of children's literature publishing in the nineteenth-century British marketplace.

Jonathan Rose is Professor of History and convenor of the graduate program in Book History at Drew University. He is author of *The Intellectual Life of the British Working*

Classes (2001), and he edited *The Holocaust and the Book: Destruction and Preservation* (2001). Co-editor of the journal *Book History*, he is also the founding president of the Society for the History of Authorship, Reading and Publishing (SHARP) and a past president of the Northeast Victorian Studies Association (NVSA).

Cannon Schmitt, the author of *Alien Nation: Nineteenth-Century Gothic Fictions and English Nationality* (1997), teaches Victorian literature and culture at Duke University.

Hilary M. Schor is Professor of English at the University of Southern California. She is author of *Scheherezade in the Marketplace: Elizabeth Gaskell and the Victorian Novel* and *Dickens and the Daughter of the House*, and of articles on Victorian fiction and culture. Her current project explores realism, gender, and the culture of curiosity.

F. S. Schwarzbach is Professor and former Chair in the Department of English at Kent State University. His most recent publications include an edition of Dickens's *American Notes* (1997), as well as essays on Harriet Shelley, Dickens as a travel writer, and the cultural significance of Staffordshire figurines.

James Richard Simmons, Jr., Assistant Professor of English at Louisiana Tech University, is the author of a number of published articles and reviews which have appeared in *Brontë Society Transactions*, *Victorian Studies*, *English Language Notes*, and *The Dickensian*. He also has a forthcoming book, *Factory Lives: Four Nineteenth-Century Working Class Autobiographies*.

Jeffrey L. Spear is an Associate Professor of English at New York University. He is the author of *Dreams of an English Eden: Ruskin and his Tradition in Social Criticism*. His current project is a study of Victorian literature and visual culture with the working title *Lines of Sight*.

William B. Thesing, Professor of English at the University of South Carolina, has written or edited several books, including *The London Muse* (1982), *English Prose and Criticism, 1900–1950* (1983), *Conversations with South Carolina Poets* (1986), *Victorian Prose Writers before 1867* (1987), *Executions and the British Experience* (1990), *Critical Essays on Edna St. Vincent Millay* (1993), *Robinson Jeffers and a Galaxy of Writers* (1995), *Victorian Women Poets* (1999), and *Caverns of Night: Coal Mines in Art, Literature, and Film* (2000).

Athena Vrettos, Associate Professor of English and Director of Graduate Studies at Case Western Reserve University, is the author of *Somatic Fictions: Imagining Illness in Victorian Culture* (1995) and recent articles on Victorian theories of habit and déjà vu. Currently, she is working on a book titled *Mental Economies: Victorian Fiction, Psychology, and Spaces of Mind*.

Introduction

Patrick Brantlinger and William B. Thesing

The aim of this *Companion* is to provide contextual and critical information about the entire range of British fiction published during the Victorian period. It offers students, teachers, and general readers at all levels original, accessible chapters written from current critical and theoretical perspectives. In part I, each chapter provides an overview of one central context or issue, including the publishing world, education, social class and economics, nineteenth-century psychology, race and empire, religion, science, technology, the law, gender and women's rights, the fine arts, and the theater. In part II, the chapters survey the various forms of the Victorian novel: Newgate novels and detective fiction, historical fiction, the sensation novel, autobiographical fiction, Victorian versions of Gothic romance, regional fiction, industrial and "condition of England" novels, fiction for children, and science fiction. Part III deals with the reputations and canonization of such major authors as Charlotte Brontë and Charles Dickens; Victorian, modern, and postmodern theories applied to Victorian fiction; postmodern rewritings of Victorian novels; and film and television adaptations. The detailed and, we hope, conveniently constructed index will enable cross-referencing and study of a broad spectrum of authors, novels, themes, and controversies. Bibliographies following each chapter offer both a list of "References" detailing works cited directly in the text and a list of "Further Reading" containing helpful recommendations of recent criticism and scholarship that, while diverse and innovative, are accessible to the general reader.

In his consideration of prose fiction as a "rational amusement," Anthony Trollope declared: "we have become a novel-reading people, from the Prime Minister down to the last-appointed scullery maid." Indeed, not only was one of Britain's great Prime Ministers, William Gladstone, a novel-reader; so was Queen Victoria, despite an education from which novels were banned – and another of her great premiers, Benjamin Disraeli, was a novel-writer. John Sutherland estimates that between 1837 and 1901 some 60,000 novels were published in Britain – roughly 20 percent of all book production – and that these figures perhaps double if religious tracts and magazine serials that did not appear in bound volumes are added. Further, some 7,000 Victorians "could legitimately title themselves 'novelist'" (Sutherland 1989: 1). In studying Victorian culture, no matter from what disciplinary perspective, it is difficult not to feel that it was all novels, or at least that it was all in novels.

In part because of the very dominance of the novel in Victorian culture, novel-reading was as controversial as television-watching is today. For example, although we now take for granted that libraries should have novels in their collections, for the Victorians, whether or not the first public libraries should acquire works of fiction was hotly debated. During the parliamentary hearings on the Library Act of 1850, there was much testimony that libraries, together with schools and literacy in general, would wean working-class readers from booze and crime. But opponents sometimes turned that argument around. In his history of public libraries, Thomas Greenwood cites a number of commentators who alleged that libraries encouraged idleness, and one who even declared he would "rather see a young man hanging about a public-house than spending his time in these places" (quoted in Greenwood 1891: 82). If they offered novels, public libraries were frequently also said to encourage romantic fantasies (and, hence, sexual misbehavior) in female readers. Thus, another opponent of libraries invoked the figure of the "Female Quixote": "Many are the crimes brought about by the disordered imagination of a reader of sensational . . . rubbish, whilst many a home is neglected . . . owing to the all-absorbed novel-reading wife" (quoted in Greenwood 1891: 82).

The phrase "Female Quixote" comes from Charlotte Lennox's 1752 novel of that title. As early as the 1600s, novel-reading was often identified as a female activity, especially hazardous for impressionable young women. In the 1700s, many of the customers of the so-called circulating libraries were women, and many of the books they read were novels. As private businesses, the early circulating libraries could not be accused of squandering public money, but they were often accused of undermining public morality. In Richard Sheridan's 1775 play *The Rivals*, novel-reading turns the head of Lydia Languish, causing Sir Anthony Absolute to say that "a circulating library in a town is an ever-green tree of diabolical knowledge."

Despite such objections, novels became one of the mainstays of nineteenth-century publishing. Increasing demand did lead to the writing of a lot of trashy novels – the sort published by the Minerva Press, for example. These include the Gothic romances parodied by Jane Austen in *Northanger Abbey*, featuring Catherine Morland as Female Quixote. Besides Ann Radcliffe's *Mysteries of Udolpho*, which Catherine reads, most of the titles mentioned by her novel-neurotic friend, Isabella Thorpe, were published by the Minerva Press. Among those on Isabella's list are *Midnight Bell*, *Necromancer of the Black Forest*, and *Horrid Mysteries* – all of them, to use Isabella's term of high praise, "horrid novels."

Much of the fiction produced between the 1760s and 1830s was condemned not because it had any serious purchase on the world, but for just the reverse reason: because it was frivolous entertainment. Evangelicals, Quakers, and some other religious groups prohibited novel-reading within their flocks, and prohibitions also came from sober, secular utilitarians such as James Mill — and the caricature of the utilitarian pedagogue, Mr. Gradgrind, who prohibits fiction in Dickens's 1854 novel *Hard Times*. Thomas Carlyle held that novel-reading was usually a waste of time, an opinion also expressed by later social critics including John Ruskin, Matthew Arnold, and William Morris.

These hostile attitudes affected even the greatest novelists, who before George Eliot, at least, had trouble taking their own imaginative productions seriously. Thus, most of Thackeray's early works are mock-novels, parodies of other people's fiction, as in his "Novels by Eminent Hands" series for *Punch*. Thackeray also mocked himself: a key metaphor for his 1847 masterpiece, *Vanity Fair*, is that of the puppet show — the novel as mere child's play. Thackeray also recalled how, as a "lazy, idle boy," reading a good novel seemed to him as "sweet and delicious as the raspberry open-tarts of budding boyhood" — not much different from the "intellectual gingerbread" condemned by an eighteenth-century critic. And Trollope, Thackeray's great emulator, declared that the public consumed novels "as men eat pastry after dinner, — not without some inward conviction that the taste is vain if not vicious." At least Thackeray's and Trollope's gustatory metaphors do not treat novels as poisonous — just fattening.

Despite the anti-novel attitudes even of novelists, by the 1840s novel-reading was growing more socially acceptable. One reason has to be the sheer imaginative pleasure of reading a good novel. Another is that many novels without the least hint of impropriety were readily available — novels by Jane Austen, of course, and by such lesser lights as Fanny Burney and Maria Edgeworth. Also crucial were Sir Walter Scott's phenomenally popular "Waverley" novels, approved reading in some households from which all other novels were banned. Ironically, perhaps the most important single factor in the growing respectability of fiction was a circulating library. Established in 1842, Mudie's Select Circulating Library dominated the trade in novels down to 1894. It did so both by sanitizing fiction and by guaranteeing publishers predictable sales of first editions, just so long as these came in the standard format of the famous three volumes or "triple-decker." After its library run was over, a popular novel was typically reprinted in a single-volume edition. Although many novels first appeared in monthly parts or as serials, and only later in bound volumes, between the 1840s and the 1890s most first editions came in three volumes, priced out of the range of the average reader, who was thus forced to subscribe to Mudie's. For decades, triple-deckers cost 31s. 6d. each; but anyone who paid a guinea a year to Mudie's could borrow a volume at a time, or, for an additional guinea, all the books she wanted.

Mudie's really was "select," moreover, even censorious. Charles Edward Mudie personally screened novels before buying them from the publishers to make sure that they would not, as Dickens's Mr. Podsnap puts it, "bring a blush to the cheek of the young person," especially the female young person. Novelists often grumbled about Mudie's dominance, though they put up with it. Thus, in 1860, George Eliot wrote to her publisher, John Blackwood, that there should "be some authors and publishers strong enough to resist his tyranny, which threatens to thrust poor books down the throats of the public, and to strangle good ones" (quoted in Griest 1970: 65). But both Eliot and Blackwood were delighted when Mudie's bought large quantities of *Felix Holt* and *Middlemarch*. Mudie's Mrs. Grundyism, though constraining what novelists could say (especially about sex), helped make novel-reading an acceptable family activity for many Victorians.

From the first decades of the nineteenth century, there was great concern about how the working class in particular was using or abusing its gradually increasing literacy. Continuing James Catnach's tradition of downscale street literature – "broadsides" such as gallows confessions – Edward Lloyd and the Salisbury Street publishers produced hundreds of "penny dreadfuls" or "bloods." Melodrama, Gothic horror, violent crime, and sexual titillation were the main ingredients, as in Thomas Prest's *Sweeney Todd* and *Varney the Vampire*. These elements, coupled with radicalism, characterize the novel that may have been the biggest bestseller of the Victorian era, and was certainly the most-read work of English fiction by Indian readers prior to World War I. This is G. W. M. Reynolds's multi-volume *Mysteries of London*, first published in penny numbers in the mid-1840s. Imitating Eugène Sue's *Mysteries of Paris*, Reynolds provided a muckraking tourguide of London's underworld and nightlife, with illustrations of muggings, burglaries, brothels, "boozing kens," and even loaded dice. Throughout, the message is that the corruption of the aristocracy reaps its just punishment from the criminal brutality of the poor. Reynolds did a considerable amount of poaching – if not outright plagiarism – from Dickens, even down to illustrations. But, then, perhaps Dickens returned the favor: a key figure in *Mysteries* is the Resurrection Man or grave robber, whose grisly trade is pursued several years later by Jerry Cruncher in *A Tale of Two Cities*. Further, Dickens's late novels – *Bleak House*, *Little Dorrit*, *Our Mutual Friend* – all belong to the "urban mysteries" genre (see Maxwell 1992).

Through the 1840s, novels and novel-reading gained in respectability. Trollope recalled that, when he was growing up in the 1820s, "the families in which an unrestricted permission was given for the reading of novels were very few, and from many they were altogether banished." But Trollope's success – a rags-to-riches story resulting, as he proudly announced in his 1883 *Autobiography*, in a fortune of £70,000 – is obvious evidence of changing attitudes toward fiction. Dickens's rags-to-riches story was even more spectacular, and also abetted the sense that prose fiction was a substantial, respectable kind of writing, if not precisely great literature on the order of the Greek and Roman classics.

For both commercial and artistic reasons, upscale novelists were anxious to control how their work was circulated and interpreted. Dickens and many others were keen advocates of stricter copyright laws. They were also frequently reviewers and critics of each other's work, and sometimes influential evaluators for publishers. Dickens, Thackeray, Trollope, Eliot, and other novelists also edited journals – and, in Dickens's case, owned them as well. After an early editorial stint with *Bentley's Miscellany*, in which both *Jack Sheppard* and *Oliver Twist* first appeared, and a brief attempt at his own fiction journal, *Master Humphrey's Clock*, Dickens established *Household Words* in

1850 and, nine years later, *All the Year Round*. He serialized his own novels – *Hard Times* in *Household Words*, *Great Expectations* in *All the Year Round* – as well as other authors', including Elizabeth Gaskell's *North and South* and Wilkie Collins's *The Moonstone*.

Beginning with *The Pickwick Papers*, Dickens's novels first appeared either as weekly or monthly part-issues or as serials, wonderfully illustrated by George Cruikshank, Hablot Browne, John Leech, and other artists. Much as we value these today, in Gaskell's *Cranford*, Miss Jenkyns, worshipper of Dr. Johnson, peers down her nose at Captain Brown's delight in the part-issues of *Pickwick Papers*: "I consider it vulgar, and below the dignity of literature, to publish in numbers," she says; to which the Captain responds: "How was [Dr. Johnson's] Rambler published?" By 1870, however, part-issuing was giving way to serialization and triple-deckers.

Another way Dickens tried to control his fiction is evident in his public readings, which allowed him both to strike a theatrical posture and to make direct contact with his readers. And he kept up a steady correspondence with fans, sometimes altering the course of a part-issue or serial according to their reactions. The assiduity with which Dickens and other Victorian novelists cultivated forms of intimacy with their readers bespeaks anxiety about what Wilkie Collins called, in an 1859 essay, "The Unknown Public" – that is, the anonymous masses, who were consuming novels in ways the novelists could not control or even know. And, of course, mediating between the novelists and the ever-growing reading public were publishers, reviewers, book-sellers, and Mudie's, as well as smaller circulating libraries.

Through the mid-Victorian decades, many of the alternatives to Mudie's triple-deckers continued to be viewed as more or less disreputable. There were, for instance, the so-called "yellowbacks," predecessors of our own paperbacks; frequently transla-tions or reprints, from the midcentury onward they were sold at railway stalls by Mudie's chief competitor, W. H. Smith – and consequently were also known as "railway novels." In the 1870s, Matthew Arnold wrote of "the tawdry novels which flare in the book-shelves of our railway stations, and which seem designed . . . for people with a low standard of life." When original fiction appeared in this format, it was typically by minor authors. Like *Mysteries of London*, the yellowbacks bordered, at least in their cheapness, on the even more disreputable "penny dreadfuls" and "shilling shockers," which were increasingly aimed at boy readers and which continued to be roundly condemned by those who worried about copycat crimes or the prospect that you become what you read. ·

The popularity of "penny dreadfuls," with their often criminal heroes, led to a number of endeavors in the 1860s and 1870s, typically by the religious, to provide adolescent readers with more wholesome fare. These include much of the great out-pouring of imperialist and military adventure fiction for boys that begins with Captain Frederick Marryat in the 1830s. The Religious Tract Society founded *The Boys' Own Paper* in 1879, and by 1900 there were twenty-three such journals. Novels like R. M. Ballantyne's 1858 *The Coral Island* and G. A. Henty's 1884 *With Clive in India* aimed at inculcating patriotism and pluck in the boy reader, who was definitely not supposed to be the loafing office boy of the public libraries. The emergence of fiction directed at both boys and girls is also an indication of increasing specialization in publishing.

Of the many protests by novelists against Mudie's "tyranny," the angriest came from George Moore in his 1885 pamphlet, *Literature at Nurse*. After Mudie rejected his first novel, *A Modern Lover*, Moore fought back, declaring that the "strength, virility, and purpose" of English literature was being "obliterated to suit the commercial views of a narrow-minded tradesman":

> literature is now rocked to an ignoble rest in the motherly arms of the librarian. That of which he approves is fed with gold; that from which he turns the breast dies like a vagrant's child; while in and out of his voluminous skirts run a motley and monstrous progeny, a callow, a whining, a puking brood of bastard bantlings . . .

Those "bastard bantlings," of course, include many examples of what we now study and revere as great Victorian novels. Moore's assault on Mudie's and its three-volume system did not single-handedly cause its demise, though he contributed to that result. In 1894, after negotiating with W. H. Smith and others, Mudie's abandoned the three-volume format. This led to a slow decline for Mudie's, but also to an expansion of alternatives for novelists, pointing the way toward literary modernism and "December 1910" when, as Virginia Woolf famously declared, "human character changed."

One-volume novels, unmediated and unblest by Mudie's, rapidly became standard after 1894. Shorter forms of fiction came to the fore, as in H. G. Wells's science fiction and Arthur Conan Doyle's Sherlock Holmes stories. With the renewal of Gothic romance in such works as Robert Louis Stevenson's *Dr. Jekyll and Mr. Hyde*, Oscar Wilde's *Picture of Dorian Gray*, and Bram Stoker's *Dracula*, came as well, especially in the 1890s, versions of Zolaesque naturalism, as in George Moore's *Esther Waters* and the novels of George Gissing, Thomas Hardy, and Arthur Morrison. Naturalism also influenced the "new woman" fiction of that decade, as exemplified by Sarah Grand's *The Heavenly Twins* and *The Beth Book*, Gissing's *The Odd Women*, Mary Augusta Ward's *Marcella*, and George Egerton's *Keynotes*. There were also new forms of elite publishing such as *The Yellow Book*, produced by John Lane's Bodley Head Press. Associated with aestheticism and the so-called decadent movement, *The Yellow Book* foreshadowed modernist "little magazines" as venues for experimental, avant-garde fiction and poetry.

At the end of the century, in "The Decay of Lying," Wilde mocks the ongoing controversy over the moral effects of reading the hundreds of popular crime stories that were published throughout the Victorian era as "penny dreadfuls" and "shilling shockers." Vivian declares that "Life imitates art far more than Art imitates Life":

> The most obvious and the vulgarest form in which this is shown is in the case of the silly boys who, after reading the adventures of Jack Sheppard or Dick Turpin, pillage the stalls of unfortunate apple-women, [and] break into sweet-shops at night . . . The

boy-burglar is simply the inevitable result of life's imitative instinct. He is Fact, occupied as Fact usually is, with trying to reproduce Fiction, and what we see in him is repeated on an extended scale throughout the whole of life.

As Wilde understood, nothing more clearly indicated the worrisome centrality of novels to modern culture than the many efforts to control their production, dissemination, and indeed inclusion in the first public libraries. In Wilde's play *The Importance of Being Earnest*, Algernon says, "it is absurd to have a hard-and-fast rule about what one should read and what one shouldn't. More than half of modern culture depends on what one shouldn't read." In other words, nothing better promotes a form of culture than attempts to curtail or censor it. *Madame Bovary, Nana, Jude the Obscure, Ulysses, Lady Chatterley's Lover* – the list of novels made famous partly because they were subjected to censorship is a long one.

For many reasons, the Victorian novel has influenced and will continue to influence modern and now postmodern culture and society. We believe that this *Companion* will enhance the understanding and appreciation of that pervasive influence, as well as of individual works by Dickens, Thackeray, the Brontës, Trollope, Eliot, Hardy, and many other Victorian novelists.

REFERENCES

Greenwood, Thomas (1891), *Public Libraries: A History of the Movement and a Manual for the Organization and Management of Rate-Supported Libraries* (London: Cassell).

Griest, Guinevere (1970), *Mudie's Circulating Library and the Victorian Novel* (Bloomington and London: Indiana University Press).

Maxwell, Richard (1992), *The Mysteries of Paris and London* (Charlottesville: University Press of Virginia).

Moore, George (1976), *Literature at Nurse, or Circulating Morals: A Polemic on Victorian Censorship*, ed. Pierre Coustillas (Hassocks, Sussex: Harvester). (First publ. 1885.)

Sutherland, John (1989), *The Stanford Companion to Victorian Fiction* (Stanford: Stanford University Press).

Trollope, Anthony (1979), "Novel Reading," in John Olmsted, ed., *A Victorian Art of Fiction: Essays on the Novel in British Periodicals, 1870–1900*, 3 vols. (New York: Garland), 111–30. (First publ. 1879.)

PART I
Historical Contexts and Cultural Issues

1

The Publishing World

Kelly J. Mays

In his 1883 *Autobiography*, Anthony Trollope describes his fifth novel, *Barchester Towers* (1857), as his "first real step on the road to substantial success" as a novelist (1980: ch. 6, 105). For Trollope, the novel represented such a step for one simple reason – he received for it more money than he had received for any previous manuscript. Associating, if not equating, literary with economic "success," Trollope gives a great deal of attention throughout the *Autobiography* to the terms of his contracts for various works, and concludes with a table of his earnings. As a result, Trollope's *Autobiography* not only contains a wealth of information about the business of Victorian novel-publishing, but also communicates much about the matter-of-fact manner in which one mid-Victorian novelist accepted both his role as a producer of goods in a competitive marketplace and the values of that marketplace. For Trollope, there seems to be no tension between literary and economic value – the "good" novel is simply the novel that yields the most in the marketplace, the "successful" author he or she who most effectively exploits the market.

Though the *Autobiography* is in many ways a unique document, the vision of literature and authorship it sets forth was arguably the dominant one throughout much of the Victorian period. Proudly declaring himself a "prose labourer," for example, a character in Thackeray's *Pendennis* (1848–50) echoes Trollope when he insists, "capital is . . . the bargain-master. It has a right to deal with the literary inventor as with any other" (1986: ch. 32: 355). Such a vision did much to shape the practices of producers, distributors, and consumers of fiction in the Victorian period, as well as the form and content of the novel.

As Trollope recognized, however, this picture of the "prose labourer" and his publisher as professionals whose success depended upon "industry," "perseverance," and a keen business sense would have been anathema to both earlier and later generations. On the one hand, while the tremendous popularity and profitability of Scott's "Waverley" novels did much to inspire and shape the efforts of Victorian novelists and publishers, Scott saw himself as a professional only because he was a lawyer, referred to publishers as mere "retailers," and refused to acknowledge for most of his life that he wrote novels; instead, he bankrupted himself in the effort to use the funds raised through his (secretive) labors as a novelist to become a landed gentleman. On the other hand, the generation of writers coming of age at the time Trollope's *Autobiography* was published were no less horrified than Scott likely would have been by the vulgarly commercial attitudes it reflected. In Thackeray's *Pendennis* it is the heroic George Warrington who describes himself as a humble "prose labourer," and it is setting out to "earn [his] bread" "with [his] pen" that helps to turn Pendennis himself from "worthless idler and spendthrift" to hero (1986: ch. 32, 357). In George Gissing's *New Grub Street* (1881), however, it is the unheroic Jasper Milvain who declares, "Literature nowadays is a trade . . . your successful man of letters is your skilful tradesman" who "thinks first and foremost of the markets" (1998: ch. 1, 8–9). As this suggests, any account of Victorian publishing must distinguish between the 1830s through the 1870s – the era of Trollope, Thackeray, Charles Dickens, and George Eliot – and the 1880s and 1890s – the age of Gissing, George Moore, Walter Besant, and Marie Corelli.

*

During the era that began with Scott and ended with George Eliot, publishing became a major, multi-million-pound industry that both benefited from and contributed to the more general economic and technological developments of the Victorian period. Early in the century, publishing remained a traditional, exclusive affair: books were expensive luxuries produced in small editions designed for the wealthy and discriminating few by a close-knit group of long-established publisher–booksellers who co-operated to keep newcomers out of the trade. Readers purchased new novels from the few booksellers scattered throughout the country or from traveling peddlers, or borrowed such volumes from local circulating libraries that charged high yearly subscription rates. However acquired, such books were still printed much as they had been in Gutenberg's time.

Starting with Scott, all of this began to change. While new novels remained expensive, Scott's tremendous popularity helped to reveal hitherto undreamed-of possibilities in terms of both the size of the potential audience for fiction and the profits to be made from it. While early in the century novels were printed in fairly small editions of 500–750 (and while the norm for first editions remained fairly low throughout the century), Scott's novels sold in the tens of thousands: 1,000 copies of his first novel, *Waverley* (1814), sold within a few weeks, and 2,000 more were purchased within three months; by 1829, 40,000 "cheap editions" had been sold. More importantly, the numerous "Waverley novels" that followed sold equally well: the first printings of *Rob Roy* (1818) and *Ivanhoe* (1820) sold 10,000 copies each, while 7,000 copies of *The Fortunes of Nigel* (1822) sold on the morning of publication (Altick 1999: 292). When Scott's publisher, Archibald Constable, failed in 1826 for around £250,000, leaving Scott himself £120,000 in the red, the very size of their debts revealed just how large the potential profits and the potential risks were in the high-stakes game of fiction publishing – a lesson reinforced by the fact that Scott eventually published his way back to solvency.

While the example of Scott and Constable helped to effect radical changes in the thinking and practice of publishers, theirs was an ambivalent legacy: for if it encouraged authors and publishers to see fiction as an avenue to fortune and fame, it also demonstrated that one might instead easily write or publish one's way to the poorhouse. Partially for this reason, Victorian publishing came to be characterized by an odd blend of daring speculation and cautious conservatism. That odd blend became most apparent in the way that successful innovations tended to become orthodoxies: if a particular type of novel or a particular publishing format proved successful, then authors and publishers tended to ride the wave until readership and profits ebbed.

If such were the long-term effects of the Scott–Constable debacle, its short-term effects were to chase from the field of fiction publishing what one writer in 1852 called the "old easy-going race" of established publishers, thus making way for a new generation characterized by a "busy spirit of enterprise and competition" (quoted in Barnes 1964: 122). Of the eight family-owned houses that dominated early and mid-Victorian novel publishing, only Longman's dated back to the eighteenth century, while just two – Blackwood's and Smith, Elder – had published books before the Constable failure. The rest – Chapman & Hall, Bentley, Macmillan, Bradbury & Evans, and Tinsley – were all recent arrivals on the scene, establishing their businesses in the thirties, forties, or even fifties. These publishers were also remarkably young when they first achieved positions of influence and prominence: the brothers Macmillan had only fifty-five years between them when they published their first book in 1843; and in 1836, when Chapman & Hall published Dickens' *Pickwick Papers,* the combined ages of the three young men barely totaled seventy (Sutherland 1976: 10). Publishers like Chapman & Hall and novelists like Dickens thus quite literally represented a new generation.

The "busy spirit of enterprise and competition" that drove these young publishers made them remarkably active managers who negotiated directly with authors, printers, and booksellers; solicited, read, and often commented elaborately on manuscripts; and encouraged writers to undertake particular topics, genres, and formats and to steer clear of others. As a result, individual publishers did much to shape the content and form of Victorian fiction and even of particular novels. While Charles Lever's first novel – *The Confessions of Harry Lorrequer* (1839) – was still being serialized in the *Dublin University Magazine*, for example, Richard Bentley was one of four publishers to make overtures to the young novelist, offering both a contract for his next novel and advice about what subjects he should tackle and how he should treat them. Lever eventually took Bentley's advice, making an Irish officer the hero of his next novel, *Charles O'Malley* (1841), and mixing sentiment with comedy in a way he had not done previously (Gettmann 1960: 156). Though more seasoned writers might enjoy more freedom, they were often (and often quite happily) subject to influence of a more subtle kind. Dickens's contract for *Martin Chuzzlewit* (1843–4), for example, echoed others of the period by requiring that the novel be "in form, size and price, precisely similar to the *Pickwick Papers* [1836–7] and *Nicholas Nickleby* [1838–9]" – language through which Chapman & Hall tacitly encouraged the novelist to stick to a popular and profitable formula (quoted in Sutherland 1976: 77). If, at its best, such advice could help a novelist to find both voice and audience, it also helped to ensure that particular types of fiction – the "silver-fork" novel, the historical romance, nautical and military novels, etc. – tended to come into vogue, dominate the market for several years, and then disappear rapidly as readerly interest and profits declined (Gettmann 1960: 59). Many mid-Victorian novelists eagerly sought out the advice of publishers, whom they saw as partners in the enterprise of producing novels that might prove popular with readers.

Though popularity was prized for many reasons, one of them was undoubtedly the unprecedented economic benefits into which it translated. While the £100 advance he received for *Barchester Towers* seemed significant to the young Trollope because it equalled his yearly salary as a Post Office official, by the 1860s he was earning as much as £3,200 per novel (Trollope 1980: 363–4). Even such receipts, however impressive, did not put Trollope on the top rung of the earnings ladder: the single largest payment for a novel in the nineteenth century seems to have been the £10,000 that ex-Prime Minister Benjamin Disraeli received for *Endymion* in 1880, and Dickens – who left an estate of £93,000 upon his death in 1870 – earned £9,000 from the first edition of *Dombey and Son* (1846–8); between 1876 and 1879, George Eliot made £9,000 from *Daniel Deronda* (Jones 1974: 154); and, over the course of his career, Thackeray earned back, through writing, an amount equivalent to the £20,000 inheritance he lost early in life through bad investments. Publishers, too, reaped the benefits: at his death in 1891, George Routledge left an estate of £94,000, while George Bentley four years later bequeathed his family almost £86,000 (Gettmann 1960: 152). Those associated with Longman's left behind even bigger legacies: Thomas Longman III nearly £200,000, Longman partners Thomas Brown and Bevis Green £100,000 and £200,000 respectively (Briggs 1974: 10). Still, as Royal Gettmann rightly points out, such legacies seem small when compared to the multi-million-pound fortunes amassed by the manufacturers, bankers, and top professionals of the day, and the average novelist could not hope to realize anything like the small fortunes earned by a Dickens or a George Eliot. Between 1830 and 1850, Bentley paid an average of £250 per novel, and throughout the century organizations such as the Royal Literary Fund (est. 1790) and the Guild of Literature and Art (created by Dickens and Edward Bulwer-Lytton in 1851) sought to help the ever-increasing tribe of impoverished writers. Yet the prospect of riches encouraged unprecedented numbers of people to try their hand at writing and led would-be writers to privilege fiction over every other genre.

While the concern with popularity and profitability might seem mercenary, there was something profoundly democratic about the respect for ordinary readers it implied. As novelist Wilkie Collins insisted, "I don't attach much importance to the reviews . . . But the impression I produce on the general public of readers is the lever that will move anything" (quoted in Sutherland 1976: 46). Such a view also involved seeing an author's success as a matter less of inherent "genius" than of, in Trollope's words, "industry" and "perseverance." By this scheme, every reader's opinion of a work – expressed, in part, through their willingness to buy it – is granted equal value, while every author – no matter how well-born or well-connected – must compete on what is theoretically a level playing field.

One of the most obvious ways in which this concern for "the general public" shaped Victorian fiction was through publishers', editors', authors', and reviewers' enforcement of an unwritten set of rules governing fictional propriety. While these rules obviously forbade the direct representation of anything even vaguely sensual or sexual, they also enforced certain ideas about (among other things) gender, class, and British character. This was the case in part simply because of the way authors, publishers, readers, and reviewers tended to justify such unwritten rules by referring to the (imagined) sensibilities and susceptibilities of the distinctively English "young lady": nothing, in other words, should appear in a novel that a middle-class British father would be ashamed to read aloud to his family or that might make his young daughter blush. While Thackeray mildly protested such restrictions in the preface to *Pendennis* and Dickens ridiculed "Podsnappery" in *Our Mutual Friend* (1864–5), in practice they, like other early and mid-Victorian novelists, agreed with Margaret Oliphant that the "very high reputation" of "English novels" (as opposed, particularly, to French ones) rested on their peculiar "sanity, wholesomeness, and cleanness" – qualities that derived from, and encouraged, "that perfect liberty of reading which is the rule in most cultivated English houses" (1867: 257). While later generations saw such prudery as requiring a sacrifice of artistic freedom, of realism, and even of moral range, one of its more positive effects was to train Victorian novelists in the fine art of allusively and symbolically representing the darker, more sensual aspects of human experience.

Another upholder of these unwritten rules and a major force in the world of Victorian publishing was Charles Edward Mudie, proprietor of Mudie's Select Circulating Library (est. 1842). Mudie's role was vital for many reasons, one being the way the library widened the audience for fiction by allowing readers to borrow as many novels as they wanted (one volume at a time) for a yearly fee of one guinea – two-thirds the cost of a single three-volume novel. Mudie's became so popular and respected a Victorian institution that its proprietor could single-handedly ensure the success of a given novel by choosing to include it in his "Select" Library. As Margaret Oliphant remarked, Mudie's thus did "more . . . than any other agency in existence to make a name, or at least to ensure a sale," and "patronage of Mudie was a sort of recognition from heaven" (1897: 457–8). Mudie's patronage, like a reviewer's praise, ultimately depended as much on moral qualities as on literary ones: among the novels banned from Mudie's on moral grounds were George Meredith's *The Ordeal of Richard Feverel* (1859) and George Moore's *A Modern Lover* (1883).

While allowing readers to borrow rather than buy helped widen the audience for fiction, Mudie's also paradoxically helped to ensure that fiction *had* to be borrowed rather than bought by cementing the Victorian publishing industry's 73-year-long dedication to the expensive three-volume novel. The "triple-decker" or "three-decker" was the prime instance of Victorian publishers' tendency to turn innovations into orthodoxies: in this case, the innovation was the 1821 publication of Scott's *Kenilworth* in three volumes at the price of 10s. 6d. per volume, or one-and-a-half guineas (31s. 6d.) for the whole. While Scott and his publisher chose this format only because it suited, and ensured the profitability of, this particular novel, format and price alike remained the standard ones for fiction until the 1890s. So much an institution did the three-decker become that publishing contracts assumed that every novel would conform to the format; the publisher Bentley informed an author in 1883 that a novel consisted of 920 pages with twenty-one and a half lines on each page and nine and a half words in each line (Gettmann 1960: 232). Though publishers occasionally produced one- or two-volume novels, early and mid-Victorian authors found it difficult to get short manuscripts accepted or to get adequate payment for them, and thus tended, like publishers, to accept that a novel was by definition three volumes long.

Though Mudie's profited from this format, given that borrowers had to pay for three subscriptions if they wanted to take out all three volumes of a given novel simultaneously, the dominance of the three-decker was ensured largely because it rendered fiction an economically safer venture for publishers and authors: publishers were ensured a profit on a relatively small edition; often sold the bulk of an edition before publication day (thanks to the practice whereby Mudie's and other libraries and booksellers "subscribed" for a certain number of copies of a novel before its release); and thus could afford to pay authors a sizable sum upfront. As John Sutherland notes, such a system was good insofar as it required many fewer sales than it would today to render a novel "a reasonable source of income to author and publisher" and thus "encouraged [publishers] to take risks because . . . [they] had a kind of built-in insurance against loss" (1976: 16). It also encouraged authors and publishers to produce as many novels as possible, since they depended on relatively small profits from many novels rather than on huge profits from any one.

Several other factors conspired to keep the price of new novels high. Prime among these were taxes on paper and on print advertisements. Though both taxes were reduced in the 1830s, they remained a considerable expense until they were finally abolished outright – the tax on advertisements in 1853, that on paper in 1861. The cost of advertising itself, which might range anywhere from £20 to £300 per novel, remained an important budget item. Before the arrival of the railways in the 1830s and of cheaper rates for parcel post in 1852, another major expense was the cost of conveying books to readers and booksellers outside London, the center of Victorian publishing. An equally important, if more amorphous, factor was middle- and upper-class readers' deeply ingrained prejudice against "cheapness" – for such readers, owning expensive books or subscribing to Mudie's brought a kind of respectability and prestige that could not be gained through the purchase of "cheap" novels.

For all of these reasons, the expensive three-volume novel produced in relatively small editions of 750–1,000 remained the standard from 1821 to the 1890s; but Victorian publishers and authors found three ways (besides the circulating library) to reduce the price of new fiction and to expand its audience, while maintaining its respectability. The first of these, part-publication, was yet another accidental innovation-turned-tradition. In this case, the innovators were Chapman & Hall, who in 1836 (only six years after establishing their business) hit upon the idea of issuing a monthly series of sporting plates accompanied by text written by the young journalist Charles Dickens. Though the novice publishers didn't necessarily envision the ultimate product as a novel, that's precisely what they got in *The Pickwick Papers*. And since, by the end of its run in November 1837, the novel had reached a circulation of 40,000 and paid its publishers a total of £14,000, its long-term result was yet another Victorian institution: thereafter, all but two of Dickens's major novels, four of Thackeray's, and many of Trollope's were initially published just as *Pickwick* had been – in twenty monthly parts, each costing 1s. and consisting of thirty-two pages of text accompanied by two illustrations. Thus the total cost of a novel, if bought in parts, was only £1.

Dickens also helped popularize a second means of bringing fiction to more readers at a lower cost: serialization in magazines. Magazine serialization of new fiction began in the 1830s, and by the 1840s serials were a common feature of half-crown monthlies, but the real take-off of this format came in the 1850s and 1860s with the founding of weekly magazines such as Dickens's *Household Words* (1850–9) and *All the Year Round* (est. 1859), and of monthlies such as *Macmillan's* (est. 1859) and Smith, Elder's prestigious *Cornhill* (1860–1975), first edited by Thackeray. Designed for family reading, such magazines offered one or two illustrated serials by the best-known authors, plus a wealth of other material, for the same 1s. price previously demanded for a novel "part" alone. As a result, such magazines reached as many as 100,000 readers and became the initial publishing venue for many of the major works of Collins and Trollope, George Eliot and Elizabeth Gaskell.

Third and finally, two new kinds of reprint series appeared. The first of these – collected editions of popular novelists' previously published works – began with Smith, Elder's publication, in 1844, of the collected works of G. P. R. James at a mere 8s. per volume. This formula was imitated and cheapened in the next few years, the most famous such series being Chapman & Hall's cheap editions of Dickens and Bulwer Lytton (both published in parts at 1½d. each and thus at around 2s. 6d. to 4s. per novel). The second type of series, usually called "libraries," reprinted the works of several different authors. The earliest successful venture of this kind was Bentley's "Standard Novels," launched in 1831, and in the 1840s such series proliferated in ever-cheapening forms: in 1847, Bentley reduced his "Standard Novels" from 6s. to 5s. per volume and in 1849 to 3s. 6d. or even 2s. 6d.; in 1852 he supplemented that series with a new shilling-a-volume "Railway Library" designed to compete with the phenomenally successful series of the same name launched in 1848 by Routledge, a newcomer in the field of publishing.

These new or revived publishing formats reinforced rather than undercut the three-volume system. For serialization in parts or in a magazine was almost always followed up by publication of the three-volume "library" edition and in due course by various one-volume "cheap" editions, each format reaching a distinct group of readers. Thus, even after *Great Expectations* sold well enough as an *All the Year Round* serial to dramatically boost the weekly's flagging sales, Chapman & Hall immediately sold off their 3,750-copy library edition and went on to produce five more editions in the following year (Sutherland 1976: 38).

Such formats had a range of effects. For one, the tendency to publish a single author or even a single novel in many different, often overlapping formats guaranteed that the work of the most popular Victorian authors had a unique kind of omnipresence. From January 1860 to July 1867, for example, readers were offered an installment of one new Trollope novel or another in some form every month, while the movement from serialization to ever-cheaper volume editions meant that both the old and new works of a popular novelist were constantly before the public, giving him "a kind of total and continual existence for the readers of his age" (Sutherland 1976: 37). If such omnipresence helped tighten the already (theoretically) close relationship between author and reader, so, too, did serialization, insofar as it allowed readers to communicate their responses to a novel as it unfolded – if only by choosing whether or not to buy the next installment. Such responses were very much attended to, on occasion actively shaping the direction that particular novels took – especially in the case of those writers who, like Dickens, not only published but wrote their novels in installments, keeping only one or two stages ahead of the publisher. The prominence of Sam Weller in *Pickwick Papers*, for example, can be attributed to the increase in sales that followed his introduction in Part 4, while the rehabilitation of Miss Mowcher at the end of *David Copperfield* (1849–50) resulted from readers' negative comments about the way Dickens had portrayed her in early installments. For readers, serialization made the reading of particular novels a collective experience of national and even international proportions – ensuring that a fictional event like the death of Little Nell was experienced nearly simultaneously by thousands of widely dispersed readers.

The combination of serialization and three-volume publication also did much to give the Victorian novel its distinct shape. On the one hand, the length of the three-decker encouraged prolixity. As Gissing observed, the need to fill out three volumes, as much as the insistence upon moral certainty, inspired early and mid-Victorian novelists to write "with profusion and detail . . . to tell everything, & leave nothing to be divined" (quoted in Gettmann 1960: 254). On the other hand, serialization required that such prolixity be complemented by tightness of construction when it came to the parts. More generally, the system required Victorian novelists to think in terms both of multiple small parts and of a very large whole in a way unique in literary history.

The innovations in format and pricing that led to the proliferation and cheapening of both novels and periodicals were made possible by a host of technological developments, including the mechanization of paper-making (after 1807) and of printing (after 1814), and the various refinements that improved the quality and lowered the cost of the illustrations accompanying every Victorian serial. Perhaps most important of all was the development of stereotyping, which ensured that publishers did not have to pay to have a given work set up in type every time they wished to reprint it. This made it possible to print more copies if and only if demand warranted it (rather than risking a huge initial print run) and to print the same text in a variety of different formats (serial installments, library and cheap editions, etc.) without resetting type. Equally vital were technological developments unrelated to the book production process itself. By far the most important of these was the railway, which by the 1850s provided a reliable, fast, and cheap book transport and distribution system. Thanks to the periods of leisure forced on railway passengers and to the establishment of W. H. Smith bookstalls in most stations, the railways also helped spawn all the cheap series (often, fittingly enough, called "Railway Libraries") that began to appear in the late 1840s and 1850s.

Law, as well as technology, played a part. As previously noted, the cheapening of magazines and books in the mid-Victorian period was enabled, in part, by the repeal of taxes on paper and advertising. From the point of view of both authors and publishers, however, developments in copyright law were even more crucial. Domestically, the most important events were the passage, in 1814, of an act that set the term of copyright at twenty-eight years or the remainder of the author's life, and, in 1842, of another act that extended the term to the author's life plus seven years or a total of forty-two years, whichever was longer. Internationally, the situation was much more problematic. For most of the century, nothing either barred American or European publishers from reprinting a British novel or required them to compensate the novel's author or publisher. While a combination of legislative acts and treaties secured British authors some right to copyright protection on the continent at midcentury, British authors enjoyed no US copyright protection until century's end. An 1854 Act of Parliament exacerbated the unfairness of this situation by enabling American authors to secure British copyrights for their work by simply being present in Britain or any of its dependencies at the time of publication. Before 1854, however, American authors had as few rights in Britain as British authors had in America, and British publishers greatly profited from this situation. In 1852, for example, British publishers realized a fortune by selling over a million copies of Harriet Beecher Stowe's *Uncle Tom's Cabin* without paying its author a penny.

However uneven its protection, copyright was obviously of fundamental importance to the publishing enterprise since it secured to both authors and publishers the economic benefits of their investments. Nevertheless, many Victorian novelists continued the long-standing practice of selling their copyrights to a publisher for a fixed sum. While some did so because they couldn't afford to wait for potential profits, others chose this type of contract because they felt, as Trollope did, that "a lump sum down was more pleasant than a deferred annuity" and that such an arrangement gave the publisher more incentive to promote the work (1980: 109). Still others agreed with Gaskell that the very simplicity of this kind of contract ensured good relations between author and publisher; in her words, "short agreements make long friends" (quoted in Gettmann 1960: 79). Such contracts did not directly reward the author for sales, however, and on occasion a publisher made a great deal of money on a work for which the author had been paid very little. At the same time, high sales on one novel usually ensured that its author could demand a higher price for the copyright of his or her next work, and it was in this manner that Trollope's price per novel increased, over time, from £100 to £3,000.

The number of authors who chose to sell their copyrights declined as the century progressed and as the long-term value of copyrights became more obvious. As a result, novelists increasingly opted for one of three other types of contract. The first of these entailed leasing a copyright to a publisher for a certain time period or for certain specified editions. George Eliot, for example, turned down Smith, Elder's offer of £10,000 for the copyright of *Romola* in favor of a £7,000 contract that returned the copyright to her after six years. A second type of contract required that publisher and author split any profits that accrued after the deduction of costs and a 5–10 percent publisher's commission. Since profits were usually split equally or with the advantage going to the author, this arrangement was theoretically the most fair, yet it was one that many authors mistrusted because of the ease with which a publisher could "pad" accounts. Third was publication on commission, a type of arrangement favored, on the one hand, by established authors certain of success and, on the other, by publishers unwilling to risk money on unknown authors. Such a contract required the author to pay the entire cost of production and promotion; granted the publisher a certain percentage (usually 10 percent) of gross receipts; and guaranteed any remaining profits to the author. In 1871, Thomas Hardy published his first novel, *Desperate Remedies*, on these terms, eventually losing £15 of the £75 advanced to Tinsley. But if Hardy's is the classic case of an unknown author losing financially by such a bargain, the case of Mrs. Henry Wood demonstrates how a novelist or her heirs could benefit. After her death in 1887, her son arranged with Bentley to produce a cheap edition of her works on commission. The publisher lost £2,700 on the venture; Wood's heirs realized over £35,845 (Gettmann 1960: 115).

As Mrs. Henry Wood's case demonstrates, women as well as men could find fortune and fame as novelists in the Victorian period. Though the number of women able to achieve success may have declined as the century progressed, writing fiction remained the nineteenth-century woman's surest route into the literary profession. Thus, of the nineteenth-century women writers listed in the *Cambridge Bibliography of English Literature*, one-third are described as "novelists" and 50 percent as "children's writers"; only 14 percent are labeled "poets" and a mere 3 percent specialists in such fields as philosophy, history, or economics. The same source suggests men were much more evenly distributed across the literary field, 25 percent being poets, 14 percent novelists, 14 percent critics and essayists, 11 percent children's writers, and 8 percent philosophers (Cross 1985: 167). Such figures imply that women's tendency to write fiction was as much a matter of necessity as of choice, a reflection of the way assumptions about femininity circumscribed the kinds of experience and expertise to which women could lay claim. The novelist-heroine of Emily Morse Symonds's *A Writer of Books* (1898) becomes "depress[ed]" when she compares herself to male novelists: for while "They had drunk deep of the cup of life, and wrote of that they did know; . . . she, a girl, . . . had gained all her knowledge at second-hand" (Symonds 1999: 32). Getting knowledge of certain kinds only, if at all, at "second-hand" did much to determine the kinds of fiction women wrote. The historical romances that dominated the literary marketplace in the 1830s, for example, were written almost wholly by men, women finding "writing about battles and skirmishes both difficult and uncongenial" because they "could not draw on a vast supply of manly knowledge acquired on the playing fields and in the club-rooms" (Cross 1985: 179).

Women's lack of access to "club-rooms" also made it difficult for them to forge the intimate relationships with publishers enjoyed by male writers. For clubs of various kinds played a vital role in the publishing world. At one end of the spectrum were formal, exclusive, and expensive clubs. These included clubs composed largely of "men of letters" – the Athenaeum (founded in 1824 by, among others, Walter Scott), the Literary Union Club (founded in 1831 and later transformed into the Clarence), and the Garrick (1831) – and clubs organized on more general, often political, lines. Thackeray, for example, frequented the Garrick and Reform clubs, introducing publisher George Smith into the latter, while Harrison Ainsworth ensured Bentley's election to the Conservative (Sutherland 1976: 85). At the other end of the spectrum were the many small, convivial groups who met together periodically at particular taverns. Charles Lever noted the importance of these groups and gatherings when he described the negative effects of living abroad: "You would scarcely believe," he wrote, "how much I have sacrificed in not being a regular author of the Guild of Letters – dining at the Athenaeum – getting drunk at the Garrick" (quoted in Sutherland 1976, pp. 85–6).

For a variety of reasons, then, the Victorian world of publishing was, in practice, less a fully democratic "republic of letters" than a "guild" whose membership reflected the gender and class inequities of Victorian society at large. While at least some middle-class women overcame the odds, working-class people were almost wholly excluded. Analyzing a sample of 840 nineteenth-century British authors, Richard Altick found that "10.6% were born into the nobility and gentry, 86.3% into the middle class, and only 3.1% into the working class" (1962: 394).

*

As we have seen, the early and mid-Victorian novel was the product of a sense of community and of shared interests and ideals among publishers, circulating librarians, booksellers, authors, and readers. That sense was guaranteed both by similarities in background and experience and by widespread acceptance of certain ideas about fiction and life. Not least among these was a remarkable degree of faith in the virtues of entrepreneurial capitalism and free trade, particularly in creating a (theoretically) meritocratic system in which individual industry, talent, and good conduct inevitably met with appropriate acclaim and financial reward. This faith led the government to strengthen copyright protections and to repeal taxes that inhibited literary free trade and led readers, writers, and publishers both to equate popularity, economic success, and literary quality and to value novels that themselves reinforced that faith by ultimately meting out to their characters the appropriate rewards and punishments.

In the eighties and nineties a number of forces combined to threaten that sense of community and consensus. Radical changes in the practice and the ethos of publishers, authors, and readers, and in the form and content of the novel, both resulted from and caused that breakdown. For contemporaries, a key event was the passage of the 1870 Education Act, which they believed vastly increased the size of the novel-reading public. In 1899, Walter Besant estimated that whereas the English-speaking reading public had numbered around 50,000 in 1830 it was, by the 1890s, more like 120 million (Cross 1985: 206). Though such estimates are factually inaccurate, they reflect a view widely promulgated in the 1890s. More importantly, the perceived increase in the size of the reading public was seen to entail an increase in diversity that rendered it impossible any longer to envision that public either as a culturally homogeneous group or as one that shared the same background and values as those seeking to reach it through the written word.

Through a variety of means, the publishing industry worked to capitalize on, and foster, the increase in readership. New three-volume novels were more quickly reprinted in cheap editions; the price of the latter fell lower; and the pace of novel production accelerated as never before, the number of new "adult" novels published per year rising from around 516 in 1874 to 1,315 in 1894 – the equivalent of 3.5 novels per day. The number of "juvenile" novels also increased dramatically as publishers vied for the custom of the Board schools and their students. In 1875, 188 juvenile novels were issued; between 1875 and 1885 an average of 470 were published each year (Keating 1989: 32).

However high such figures, they underestimate the total amount of new fiction being produced in the late Victorian period insofar as they ignore the vast quantities appearing in periodicals, which were themselves being produced in ever-greater quantities at ever-cheaper rates. The number of newspapers produced in the British Isles increased from around 1,609 in 1875 to 2,504 by 1914, while between 1875 and 1903 the number of magazines leapt from 643 to 2,531 (Keating 1989: 34). Three innovations in the late Victorian periodical market were particularly important. First was a new breed of high-quality monthly miscellany, including the influential *English Illustrated* (1883) and *Strand* (1891). Distinguished by their large size and their lavish use of illustrations and – by the mid-1890s – photographs, such magazines were aimed at the suburban middle-class family whose members' diverse needs and interests they fulfilled by offering both juvenile and adult fiction; puzzles and games; and "light" informational articles. This successful formula ensured sales well beyond those of the family magazines of earlier days: the *Strand*, which featured serial novels and Conan Doyle's Sherlock Holmes stories, reached an estimated worldwide audience of well over three million people by century's end (Keating 1989: 156). Second, and even more popular in every sense of the word, was a new type of penny weekly, the first and most notorious being *Tit-Bits from All the Most Interesting Books, Periodicals and Newspapers in the World* (1881). As its title suggests, *Tit-Bits* reprinted brief extracts from other publications, but it also, after 1889, included new serial fiction. As Conan Doyle insisted, *Tit-Bits* and its many imitators deliberately aimed at the audience created by the 1870 Education Act, readers "who were not sufficiently educated to study the deepest and thickest volumes" (quoted in McDonald 1997: 145). By the close of the 1890s, *Tit-Bits* enjoyed sales of over a million per week in Britain alone. Third was the increase in newspaper publication of both serials and short fiction made possible by the arrival of syndication – the system whereby a central agency or "fiction bureau" purchased the serial rights to a fictional work which it then sold to provincial newspapers throughout the country.

These developments had many and profound effects. On the one hand, the expansion of the audience and the multiplication of publication venues could afford authors more opportunities, more money, and an unprecedented kind of celebrity. (All the more so since the new magazines often featured stories about authors.) Since contracts with fiction bureaus, for example, were not only lucrative in themselves, but also covered only serial rights, novelists could negotiate separately for other forms of publication and thereby increase the overall amount they received for a given novel. Also, since both the new-style periodicals and the fiction bureaus sought out short fiction as well as serials, novelists could now supplement the income derived from novel-writing by writing less labor-intensive short stories.

Two other developments enabled novelists to capitalize more effectively on their "bestseller" status. (The 1890s invented the term "bestseller," which denoted both the popular novel and the author who could be counted on to produce one.) The first of these developments was the royalty contract, which guaranteed the author a fixed percentage of the sale price of a book published in volume form. A type of contract virtually unknown in Britain before the 1880s, the royalty contract became quite common thereafter. Second was the 1891 passage of a US International Copyright Act that enabled British novelists to contract for American as well as British editions of their work. At least some emerging young writers found the new opportunities available in the 1890s distinctly exhilarating; as one of them, H. G. Wells, remembered in his 1934 autobiography, "there was [more] opportunity, more public, more publicity, more publishers and more patronage" (quoted in Keating 1989: 31).

These innovations also had their potential downsides. To some, the proliferation of novels and authors created a competition so intense that it resembled a Darwinian struggle for survival. Publishers were no less subject to that struggle than novels and novelists, thanks to the emergence of a host of new competitors – men such as William Heinemann and John Lane who were as young, enterprising, and brashly innovative as the heads of the older houses had been when they started out earlier in the century. By century's end, both Bentley and Tinsley had succumbed to the competition, while Chapman & Hall survived mainly on the profits they continued to realize from

Dickens's novels – so much so that when Arthur Waugh became head of the firm in 1902 he was warned that "If it wasn't for Dickens . . . we might as well put up the shutters to-morrow" (Waugh 1930: 102).

Such competition required publishers to devote ever-larger sums to devising ever-more splashy types of publicity and encouraged authors to promote themselves by granting interviews and getting into the gossip columns. Novelists were thus led to become avid participants in a cult of celebrity that was encouraged by, and itself encouraged, the illustrated magazines; periodicals devoted specifically to literary news and gossip, including the *Bookman* (founded 1891) and *The Times's Literature* (1897); books such as *The Art of Authorship* (1890) and *Homes and Haunts of Famous Authors* (1906); and bestselling novels about novelists and the publishing world, such as Besant's *All in a Garden Fair* (1883), Rudyard Kipling's *The Light that Failed* (1890), Gissing's *New Grub Street* (1891), and Marie Corelli's *The Sorrows of Satan* (1895).

The diversification of publishing vehicles and contract types made the business aspect of the novelist's job both more important and more complex. Though the late Victorian novelist still had the option of simplifying her business dealings by selling her copyright, she was more than ever likely to pay dearly for that decision. If, for example, the then-unknown Rider Haggard had stuck with his original decision to sell *King Solomon's Mines* (1886) outright for £100, he would have sacrificed the additional £650 he made in the first year through a royalty agreement, not to mention the royalties he received for years thereafter (Keating 1989: 16).

Although publishing as an industry and authorship as a profession were by the 1880s more lucrative, more complex, more respectable, and in certain ways more "modern" than ever before, this new publishing world was one in which the various branches of the trade began to see themselves more as competitors than as allies. Symptomatic of this mood was the creation of organizations representing each publishing-related profession – the Society of Authors (founded by Walter Besant in 1884), the Associated Booksellers of Great Britain and Ireland (1895), and the Publishers' Association (1896). Such organizations testified to the increased prominence and respectability of these professions, but they also demonstrated the increasingly antagonistic character of relations among the industry's various players. For while the primary goal of the Society of Authors was to lobby for better copyright protection (a goal as beneficial to publishers as to authors), the Society represented itself as helping authors win what was conceived as a battle with publishers who would, if they could, always profit at the author's expense.

Also reflecting the increasing complexity of the business of authorship and the increasing hostility between authors and publishers was the rise to prominence of the publisher's reader and the literary agent. Strictly speaking, neither of these professional intermediaries was an entirely new phenomenon in the eighties and nineties. Publishers had employed men and women to read, evaluate, and even revise manuscripts since the late eighteenth century; Dickens had, in fact, met his future "agent" John Forster when the latter was employed by Chapman & Hall as a reader. Yet the publisher's reader became a more powerful and prominent figure in the final decades of the century as unsolicited manuscripts multiplied and as publishers' readers lifted the veil of anonymity that had traditionally protected them in order to cultivate intense personal and professional relationships with individual novelists – as Chapman & Hall's George Meredith did with the young Hardy in the late 1860s and as Edward Garnett did with Joseph Conrad in the 1890s. As such relationships suggest, while readers were employed by the publisher and while they helped to make the relationship between publisher and novelist less direct than it might once have been, their work did not necessarily imply any antagonism between the interests of the two.

In these terms, the case of the literary agent was very different. Again, this was not because literary agency was an entirely new phenomenon. Not a few early and mid-Victorian novelists had asked trusted friends to intervene in, or even take full responsibility for, negotiations with publishers, as Dickens did with Forster and George Eliot with G. H. Lewes. What was new in the late Victorian period was, first, the appearance of professional agents – men like A. P. Watt and J. B. Pinker, who made careers and fortunes out of representing many authors in exchange for a fixed percentage of the profits – and, second, the fact that so many novelists now employed agents. By 1893, A. P. Watt's long list of clients included Besant, Conan Doyle, Haggard, Hardy, Collins, and Kipling. Publishers, for their part, saw literary agency not as one among many symptoms of the increasingly antagonistic relations between themselves and authors, but as a major cause – destroying, Heinemann insisted, the "free and intimate intercourse between author and publisher" (quoted in Hepburn 1968: 80).

Whether or not the rise of literary agency destroyed the "free and intimate intercourse between author and publisher," it did, in practice, sever the business aspects of the novelist's craft from the creative. In this way, literary agency facilitated the development of an opposition between "business" and "art," between economic and literary value, that would have made little sense to earlier generations. Thus, while some late Victorian novelists agreed with Trollope that the literary marketplace rewarded the writer who, in the words of Gissing's Jasper Milvain, "thinks first and foremost of the markets," they strongly disagreed with Trollope's conviction that writing for the market meant writing well. Indeed, Gissing's *New Grub Street* largely reverses mid-Victorian logic by portraying Milvain's tradesmanlike attitude as a sign of his *lack* of artistic and moral integrity, and the ultimate popularity and financial success of his work as an equally sure sign that its "literary value" is, in the words of one character, "Equal to that of the contents of a mouldy nut" (ch. 14, 181). In *New Grub Street*, true artists like Edwin Reardon and Harold Biffen "never as[k themselves] what [they] should get for [a] book" but do the work "for its own sake" (ch. 15, 202). Yet their idealism dooms them to poverty and early death.

Such attitudes were often accompanied by an altogether new sense of estrangement from ordinary readers. Where mid-Victorian novelists had highly valued those readers' responses, late Victorian novelists like Gissing had little faith in the discriminating powers of "the reading multitude" (ch. 27, 376), the "quarter-educated" products of "the Board schools" (ch. 33, 460). As a result, such writers prided themselves on appealing not to the masses, but to those few who could be counted on to share similar backgrounds, experiences, and values – what Edmund Gosse called, in a letter to Hardy, "your own confrères," "the serious male public" (quoted in McDonald 1997: 7).

This hostility toward "the reading multitude" also expressed itself in rebellion against the traditional rules governing fictional propriety and in a conviction that the novelist who followed such rules, like the novelist who wrote for money, would inevitably – as Hardy wrote – "belie his literary conscience" (1967: 130). That Gosse described the ideal audience as a *male* public was no accident. For, just as the reticence of early and mid-Victorian fiction was justified with reference to the (imagined) needs and susceptibilities of *female* readers, so those late Victorian writers who advocated greater openness saw themselves as championing literary "virility." Such, for example, were the claims made on behalf of the Rabelais Club, founded in 1880 by Besant and drawing to its fold Hardy, Meredith, and Robert Louis Stevenson. Dedicated, in Hardy's words, to promoting "virility in literature," the club was named for an author believed to exemplify that manly frankness (Keating 1989: 266).

These authors tended to reserve their greatest hostility for Mudie – the man whom they saw as the greatest "profiteer" of the literary trade and as the representative of the feminized "reading multitude" – and for the three-decker, the literary form Mudie's library did so much to sustain. Despite the fact that *New Grub Street* was published in three volumes, it portrays the three-decker as "A triple-headed monster, sucking the blood of English novelists" (ch. 15, 203). The same argument and the same virulent language appear in *Literature at Nurse; or Circulating Morals* (1885), a pamphlet by George Moore, whose novels had been excluded from both Mudie's and W. H. Smith's on moral grounds. *Literature at Nurse* attributes the qualitative decline (or devolution) of English fiction to Mudie's "feminine" concern with morals and "tradesmanlike" interest in profit:

> the character for strength, virility, and purpose, which our literature has always held . . . is being gradually obliterated to suit the commercial views of a narrow-minded tradesman . . . literature is now rocked to an ignoble rest in the motherly arms of the librarian . . . in and out of his voluminous skirts run a motley and monstrous progeny, a callow, a whining, a puking brood of bastard bantlings. (Moore 1978: 18)

As this suggests, the three-decker increasingly came to be seen as a novel not just of a certain length, but of a certain kind – one that was old-fashioned not only because it had dominated since Scott's day, but also because its form and content enforced traditional attitudes and reflected the dominance of "business" over "art." Not surprisingly, then, a novel of only one or two volumes seemed to many artistically, morally, and socially radical – embodying the choice of "art" over "business," the fidelity to ambiguous "truth" rather than the specious certainty that came of adhering to traditional beliefs, values, and fictional formulas. Gissing told a friend in 1885, "It is fine to see how the old three-vol. tradition is being broken through . . . Far more artistic, I think, is the . . . method, of merely suggesting . . . – hinting, surmising" (quoted in Gettmann 1960: 254).

Gissing's confidence that the "old three-vol. tradition" was dying in 1885 turned out to be justified. Yet its death, like its long life, was ultimately the result of economic rather than artistic imperatives. The very pace of novel production had created various problems for the circulating libraries. If one multiplies the number of novels published per year by the three volumes that comprised each, one can begin to appreciate the basic storage problem confronting Mudie in the final decades of the century. Where, after all, was Mudie to keep all these volumes, particularly if he wanted to offer borrowers non-fiction and older, as well as newer, fiction? A partial solution to the storage problem – and much of Mudie's income – came from selling extra copies of novels as their popularity waned. Such sales had been possible and profitable, however, only while Mudie's remaindered library editions did not have to compete with cheaper editions – while, that is, there was sufficient lag-time between publication of library and cheaper editions. That lag-time decreased greatly as the century progressed, while a host of factors conspired to exacerbate Mudie's problems: the cost of the library edition remained high, while the cost of cheaper editions fell; the pace of novel production ensured that any one novel's window of popularity grew ever narrower; and the number of Mudie's patrons declined as the result of competition from the free libraries founded in accordance with the 1850 Public Libraries Act. Ironically, then, even as Moore attacked Mudie and the three-decker, Mudie was himself coming to see the three-volume novel as an economic hindrance. Such complaints turned into action after Charles Mudie's son, Arthur, took control of the business. In 1894, he announced that Mudie's would cease dealing with any publisher who did not drastically reduce the price of library editions and wait one year before publishing cheap editions. Since producing three-volume novels on such terms would, as he recognized, spell economic disaster for publishers, his edict ensured the swift demise of the three-decker: the year Mudie issued his decree, British publishers produced 184 three-deckers; in 1895, fifty-two; in 1897, four (Feather 1988: 155).

Though Moore and others had once envisioned the three-decker's demise as an answer to the artistic novelist's prayers, its ultimate effect was to increase competition. It did so, in part, by making the individual author more directly dependent on the patronage of the public and on the advertising and cultivation of celebrity so essential to gaining and sustaining that patronage. Effectively, it widened the gap between the "bestseller" and the novel(ist) with small public appeal.

Not all writers agreed with Moore or Hardy about the meaning and effects of such developments: the breakdown of the sense of community and consensus that had characterized the world of early and mid-Victorian publishing divided late Victorian novelists from one another as much as it divided novelists from publishers, librarians, and readers. In 1895, for example, Edmund Gosse defended publishers and booksellers against the Society of Authors, arguing that literature's real enemy was the "greedy," Milvain-like novelist who sought only money and "celebrity" (quoted in McDonald

1997: 15). For some, Besant's Society itself encouraged that mercenary approach to art by implying "that the end of literature was the making of money" (quoted in McDonald 1997: 33). Other writers, however, saw the situation quite differently, Arnold Bennett, for one, attacking the Gosse-like "tendency to disdain the public, and to appeal only to artists" (quoted in McDonald 1997: 93).

The many novels about novelists published in this period bring to life these competing views. While, for example, *New Grub Street* depicts the popular novelist as an inauthentic, inartistic, and rather heartless panderer to popular ignorance and prejudice, Marie Corelli's *Sorrows of Satan* (1895) attacks the presumptions of self-styled literary artists like Gissing himself. For Corelli represents a fictional novelist who views "the public [as] an 'ass'" as literally selling his soul to the devil (Corelli 1996: ch. 15, 139), while making her hero the popular female novelist Mavis Clare. *Sorrows* thereby envisions popularity as both the result and sign not of pandering to the audience but of elevating it, which Mavis Clare does by writing novels that uphold the traditional values and beliefs undermined by self-styled "artists" like Gissing. Taking direct aim at such artists, Corelli has the novel's "fallen woman" declare, "my vices have been encouraged and fostered . . . by most of the literary teachers of my time" (ch. 36, 334), while Mavis Clare's novels alone "give me back my self-respect, and make me see humanity in a nobler light" (ch. 17, 162). Like most early and mid-Victorian novelists, in other words, Corelli envisions popularity as a sign both of literary merit and of moral conscientiousness.

In some sense, then, the divisions within the late Victorian publishing world boiled down to a conflict between those who continued to uphold the beliefs and values that had shaped the ethos and practice of the early and mid-Victorian publishing world and those who instead embraced very different ideas and ideals. The fact that the latter closely resemble our own views of business and art, literary and economic value, popularity and artistry, makes it very tempting for us to see them as somehow true or noble in a way that Corelli's are not. But both visions are no more and no less than visions – two of the many conceptualizations of the literary marketplace that struggled for dominance in the late Victorian period. While that struggle produced literary masterpieces such as *New Grub Street* and *Jude the Obscure*, equally masterly novels such as *David Copperfield* and *Middlemarch* were instead the products of a publishing world organized around a quite Corelli-like vision of the business of fiction.

See also EDUCATION, LITERACY, AND THE VICTORIAN READER; MONEY, THE ECONOMY, AND SOCIAL CLASS; TECHNOLOGY AND INFORMATION: ACCELERATING DEVELOPMENTS.

REFERENCES

Altick, Richard (1962), "The Sociology of Authorship: The Social Origins, Education, and Occupations of 1,100 British Writers, 1800–1935," *Bulletin of the New York Public Library*, 66, 389–404.

Altick, Richard (1999), "Publishing," in Herbert Tucker, ed., *A Companion to Victorian Literature and Culture* (Oxford: Blackwell), 289–304.

Barnes, James J. (1964), *Free Trade in Books: A Study of the London Book Trade since 1800* (Oxford: Clarendon).

Briggs, Asa (1974), "Introduction: At the Sign of the Ship," in Asa Briggs, ed., *Essays in the History of Publishing in Celebration of the 250th Anniversary of the House of Longman, 1724–1974* (London: Longman), 1–28.

Corelli, Marie (1996), *The Sorrows of Satan* (Oxford: Oxford University Press). (First publ. 1895.)

Cross, Nigel (1985), *The Common Writer: Life in Nineteenth-Century Grub Street* (Cambridge: Cambridge University Press).

Feather, John (1988), *A History of British Publishing* (London: Croom Helm).

Gettmann, Royal A. (1960), *A Victorian Publisher: A Study of the Bentley Papers* (Cambridge: Cambridge University Press).

Gissing, George (1998), *New Grub Street* (Oxford: Oxford University Press). (First publ. 1891.)

Hardy, Thomas (1967), "Candour in English Fiction," in Harold Orel, ed., *Thomas Hardy's Personal Writings* (London: Macmillan), 125–33. (First publ. 1890.)

Hepburn, James (1968), *The Author's Empty Purse and the Rise of the Literary Agent* (London: Oxford University Press).

Jones, Annabel (1974), "Disraeli's *Endymion*: A Case Study," in Asa Briggs, ed., *Essays in the History of Publishing in Celebration of the 250th Anniversary of the House of Longman, 1724–1974* (London: Longman), 141–86.

Keating, Peter (1989), *The Haunted Study: A Social History of the English Novel 1875–1914* (London: Secker & Warburg).

McDonald, Peter D. (1997), *British Literary Culture and Publishing Practice 1880–1914* (Cambridge: Cambridge University Press).

Moore, George (1978), *Literature at Nurse; or Circulating Morals* (New York: Garland). (First publ. 1885.)

[Oliphant, Margaret] (1867), "Novels," *Blackwood's Edinburgh Magazine*, 102, Sept., 257–80.

Oliphant, Margaret (1897), *Annals of a Publishing House: William Blackwood and His Sons, Their Magazine and Friends*, 2 vols., 2nd edn. (Edinburgh: Blackwoods).

Sutherland, J. A. (1976), *Victorian Novelists and Publishers* (Chicago: University of Chicago Press).

Symonds, Emily Morse ["George Paston"] (1999), *A Writer of Books* (Chicago: Academy Chicago Publishers). (First publ. 1898.)

Thackeray, William Makepeace (1986), *The History of Pendennis* (London: Penguin.) (First publ. 1848–50.)

Trollope, Anthony (1980), *An Autobiography* (Oxford: Oxford University Press). (First publ. 1883.)

Waugh, Arthur (1930), *A Hundred Years of Publishing, Being the Story of Chapman & Hall, Ltd* (London: Chapman & Hall).

FURTHER READING

Dooley, Allan C. (1992), *Author and Printer in Victorian England* (Charlottesville: University Press of Virginia).

Feltes, N. N. (1986), *Modes of Production of Victorian Novels* (Chicago: University of Chicago Press).

Griest, Guinevere (1970), *Mudie's Circulating Library and the Victorian Novel* (Bloomington and London: Indiana University Press).

Hamer, Mary (1987), *Writing by Numbers: Trollope's Serial Fiction* (Cambridge: Cambridge University Press).

Patten, Robert L. (1978), *Charles Dickens and his Publishers* (Oxford: Clarendon).

Seville, Catherine (1999), *Literary Copyright Reform in Early Victorian England: The Framing of the 1842 Copyright Act* (Cambridge: Cambridge University Press).

Shillingsburg, Peter (1992), *Pegasus in Harness: Victorian Publishing and W. M. Thackeray* (Charlottesville: University Press of Virginia).

Tuchman, Gaye with Fortin, Nina E. (1989), *Edging Women Out: Victorian Novelists, Publishers, and Social Change* (New Haven: Yale University Press).

2

Education, Literacy, and the Victorian Reader

Jonathan Rose

In the 1970s Rolf Engelsing posited that there had been, around 1800, a Reading Revolution, the literary counterpart of the Industrial Revolution. He identified a general shift from religious to secular reading; from collective to individual reading; from intensive and repeated reading of a small canon of texts to extensive and rapid reading of an ever-increasing flow of ephemeral literature, particularly newspapers and magazines. Engelsing developed his historical model in the context of Protestant Germany, but it serves even better to explain the transformation of the reading public in nineteenth-century Britain.

The scale of this revolution is apparent in statistics of print, which indicate exponential growth on every front. In 1780 there were only 76 newspapers and periodicals in England and Wales; but between 1800 and 1809 154 new ones were founded, and the number of new titles per decade rose to 968 in the 1830s, 1,639 in the 1860s, and 3,423 in the 1890s. The steam press, introduced by *The Times* in 1814, could print up to 2,500 sheets per hour, ten times the output of a hand press. The nation's first rotary press was installed in 1856 by *Lloyd's Weekly News*: by 1904 its presses were churning out 55,000 32-page papers per hour. Composition was accelerated by the Linotype, first installed by a newspaper in 1889. The press was free to reach a new audience after the fourpenny newspaper duty was dropped to a penny in 1836 and abolished altogether in 1855. Before 1853 there was only one successful provincial daily, the *Liverpool Telegraph and Shipping Gazette*. By 1870 there were 60 in England alone; by 1900, 171. The total circulation of all London newspapers, just 56,000 in 1837, jumped to 410,000 by 1874 and 680,000 in 1887.

Publishing trade journals reported only about 300 book titles issued annually in the first years of the century, surging to nearly 3,000 by 1842 and about 8,000 by 1897. (Since the journals undoubtedly missed some titles, the actual totals were somewhat higher.) In the period 1814–46 religion accounted for 20.3 percent of all book titles published, fiction for only 16.2 percent; but by the early 1870s the proportions were reversed, and by 1901 religion trailed fiction by 8.6 to 33.0 percent. As late as 1873, the ratio of secular to religious magazines was 60:40, but by 1902 it was 80:20.

British paper production amounted to 11,347 tons in 1800, nearly 40,000 tons in 1837, 100,000 tons in 1861, and nearly 700,000 tons in 1901. That expansion was made possible by technological innovations, notably the Fourdrinier papermaking machine, introduced early in the century. Esparto (by midcentury) and wood pulp (around 1880) afforded cheaper substitutes for rags, and the paper duty ended in 1861. By 1895 the *Glasgow Herald* was paying only 1¼d. for a pound of paper, down from 8½d. in 1845. The blizzard of paper was in part associated with the democratization of British politics: the Conservative Party, which printed only 42,000 pamphlets and leaflets in 1872, had to produce 12 million to reach the expanded electorate twenty years later.

Meanwhile, the Victorians were building an information superhighway for the rapid transmission of written and printed documents. In 1839, when the average cost of mailing a letter was 6d., the Post Office delivered 76 million items. The penny post was introduced the following year, and by 1914 deliveries had risen to 3.5 billion items. Per capita deliveries rose from four letters per year in 1839 to sixty in 1900, the greatest volume of any country in the world. The halfpenny postcard, introduced in 1870, was used for the kind of quotidian communications and appointment-making that would later be done over the telephone. In 1863 London was served by as many as twelve deliveries a day and (except for some middle-class resorts) received more mail per capita than any other part of the kingdom. Northern industrial towns like Wigan, Burnley, and Oldham had the fewest deliveries, indicating that the working classes were slow to develop the letter-writing habit. Before the penny post, a laborer might occasionally receive a letter, but he often had to find someone to read it to him and compose a reply. By the end of the century most working people knew how to write, after a fashion, though the writing they had been taught in school usually consisted of copying and penmanship, not the art of composing a letter. The penny post made possible the organization of nationwide trades unions, which used the service to communicate with local branches. It called into existence a new weapon of democratic politics: the mass mailing, first used effectively by the Anti-Corn Law League. It revolutionized marketing and distribution for every sector of the economy, especially the book trade.

Thus far the statistics are hard and clear; but when we address the question of literacy, we find ourselves on somewhat marshier ground. There is no common standard, no universally recognized borderline separating the literate from the illiterate. Some Victorians seem to have understood that: for example Leonard Horner, first Warden of London University, who in 1837 filed this report on 2,000 factory children in Manchester:

Of the 2000	186	did not know the alphabet	(9%)
	372	knew the alphabet only	(18%)
	509	knew words of one syllable only	(25%)
making	1067	who could not read	(54%)
	322	read the Testament with difficulty	(16%)
	611	read it with ease	(30%)

Writing literacy generally lagged behind reading literacy. Some of those who could sign their names in the marriage register could write nothing else, but signage is probably the best indicator we have of the ability to read. By that measure, two-thirds of all Englishmen and half of all Englishwomen were literate at the beginning of Victoria's reign, a level about equal to that of France and somewhat lower than that of Germany, Scandinavia, and the United States. In fact, the English literacy rate had not changed much since 1750, but in the Victorian era it rose rapidly. By 1884 women were actually more literate than men in southern England, but less literate in the north, in D. H. Lawrence's Nottinghamshire, and in Thomas Hardy's west country. In 1901 the signage rate for both sexes approached 100 percent, but only for marrying couples, who were usually young adults. Among older people there was still some residual illiteracy. And there were always those, like the mother of Labour Party stalwart Aneurin Bevan, who learned to read in school and then, preoccupied with daily chores, simply lost the ability through disuse.

It is often assumed that industrialization made a literate workforce necessary. In fact, in 1841 only 27.4 percent of male workers and 7.4 percent of female workers held jobs where literacy was required or likely to be useful: and those proportions had risen to just 37.2 percent and 15.4 percent by 1891. For the working classes, literacy was used primarily for leisure. In the second half of the century, their real incomes rose by 80–100 percent, their work hours decreased, and they could buy an ever-expanding array of cheap newspapers and magazines. All these factors – more money, more time, more printed matter – made it ever more worthwhile to learn how to read. The rise of literacy, then, was driven more by popular demand than by compulsory education, which was not universal before 1880.

Many parents paid a few pennies a week to send their children to "dame schools." This was a generic term for working-class private schools, which were not always run by women. Before compulsory education, anyone could set up as a schoolmaster and take in fee-paying pupils, and this was often a last resort for men crippled in industrial accidents. Victorian inspectors warned that most dame schools were hopelessly inadequate, often nothing more than child-minding services. Some modern historians have attempted to rehabilitate these schools, arguing that (in stark contrast to church-run schools) they offered more individualized instruction without religious indoctrination. Obviously many working-class parents preferred them, though the church-run schools generally charged lower fees, which were waived entirely for the poorest families. But nearly all memoirs written by dame-school alumni agree that they carried out little effective teaching, and few expressed any regret when they disappeared in the wake of the 1870 Education Act. "I am afraid her spelling and pronunciation were sadly wide of the mark," a shoemaker recalled of his teacher. "Hymns, I remember, she called humes, and bishops bushups – the number 6 she spelled s-i-c-k-s, and so on. But learning was a secondary consideration; to be kept out of harm's way and from troubling our parents were the main considerations."

Day schools for the working classes were also provided by the British and Foreign School Society, a mainly Nonconformist body founded in 1807, and the National

Society, established by the Church of England in 1811. These church-run schools taught children to read their Bible but not how to express themselves on paper. An intimate knowledge of the Holy Land was drilled into pupils, but there was rarely any other instruction in geography. Only in 1833 did Parliament agree to subsidize these voluntary schools; and six years later, to ensure that the taxpayers' money was properly spent, a government inspectorate was created. At first the inspectors could do little to improve education. They could only prod failing schools by filing critical reports, which were likely to provoke furious reactions from their Anglican or Dissenting sponsors. But some inspectors (notably Matthew Arnold) were eventually able to use their positions to agitate for school reform. In 1846 Parliament created a program to train pupil–teachers, thus opening up a new (though ill-paid) profession to the brightest working-class children. Under the 1870 Education Act sponsored by W. E. Forster (Matthew Arnold's brother-in-law), National and British schools continued to receive subsidies, but elected local boards were now empowered to levy rates and create nonsectarian schools. Not until 1891 were all school fees abolished.

The early National and British schools used methods of reading instruction that were "older than printing," as David Vincent observed: "A medieval schoolmaster would not have found himself out of place in the early-nineteenth-century classroom" (1989: 76). In primers pupils first learned the alphabet, then lists of syllables ("ba ab ca ac"), then one-syllable words, and finally longer words, often arranged in sentences expressing pious sentiments. Change came with the development of a corps of school inspectors, who could recognize and publicize the inadequacy of the system. Beginning around 1850, they pressed schools to switch to the "Look and Say" method, which first taught children actual monosyllabic words in simple sentences, and then showed them how these words were constructed. At the same time there was a general shift in the direction of a more secular curriculum, with school readers replacing the Bible as standard classroom texts. This trend was accelerated by the Revised Code of 1862, which introduced (over protests from Matthew Arnold) a "payment-by-results" system. Government subsidies to schools were now partly linked to results in examinations in reading and writing, a reform designed to promote the effective teaching of basic literacy. In the 1850s some schools tried to encourage the reading habit by introducing more advanced pupils to *Pilgrim's Progress*, *Robinson Crusoe*, and *The Swiss Family Robinson*. English literature was more firmly established in the curriculum after the 1882 Mundella Code, which mandated Shakespeare, Milton, "or some other standard author" for Standard VII.

Late Victorian elementary schools represented a marked improvement over their predecessors, according to oral history interviews with their graduates. Two-thirds of them had unambiguously happy memories of their schools and their teachers, while only a few were thoroughly unhappy. The 1870 Education Act resulted in the construction of hundreds of Board schools. Today they may strike us as decrepit "brick cubes," but at the time they were brand new and seemed palatial to their pupils. Their state-of-the-art heating, lighting, and plumbing fixtures were certainly not available in the homes of the poor – or in the drafty halls of the elite public schools, for that matter. Classes were large, discipline was strict, and instruction was still largely by rote. But the teachers were often from working-class backgrounds themselves, and understood what their children needed. They still treated history as a succession of kings and battles, and geography was a matter of memorizing place names. But they often taught English literature brilliantly, going well beyond the prescribed curriculum. Edgar Wallace was prepared for his career as a stupendously popular novelist by a "big yellow barracks" of a school, where his teacher read aloud from *The Arabian Nights*:

> The colour and beauty of the East stole through the foggy windows of Reddin's Road School. Here was a magic carpet indeed that transported forty none too cleanly little boys into the palace of the Caliphs, through the spicy bazaars of Bagdad, hand in hand with the king of kings . . . There were golden days – poetry days. We learnt the "Inchcape Rock," . . . and Casabianca, and Brave Horatius, and so by degrees to the Master. I learnt whole scenes of *Macbeth* and *Julius Caesar* and *Hamlet*, and could – and did – recite them with gusto on every and any excuse.

Nevertheless, not everyone was in favor of universal literacy. While liberal reformers argued that a well-read proletariat would be more productive and law-abiding, conservatives pointed to the threat of radical literature, and warned that penny dreadfuls were promoting juvenile crime. Once near-universal literacy was achieved, literary men complained loudly and often that compulsory education had created a "quarter-educated" reading public, interested only in *Tit-Bits*, horseracing results, and trashy novelettes. Arthur Conan Doyle was more optimistic about the audience he wrote for: Sherlock Holmes hailed the Board schools as lighthouses of knowledge, "out of which will spring the wiser, better England of the future."

In fact the Board schools created a working class that read novels and Sunday (if not daily) newspapers, a working class that was beginning to organize a Labour Party. Centuries-old rural folklore and superstitions gave way to at least a passing familiarity with national political issues, major world events, and Darwin's theory of natural selection. At the beginning of Victoria's reign, most laboring-class families owned a Bible and very few other books. "Books were a luxury in a decent home," recalled a mechanic who grew up in Bingley (quoted in Vincent 1982: 110). "A cottage library in a fairly well-to-do family would seldom exceed half-a-dozen volumes": typically *Pilgrim's Progress*, Captain Cook's *Voyages*, works of popular divinity such as Philip Doddridge's *Rise and Progress of Religion in the Soul* and *News from the Invisible World*, and a couple of volumes of magazines. Even in homes that had books, there was very little actual reading. "The Bible, is laid by on its peaceful shelf," observed plebeian poet John Clare, "and by 9 cottages out of 10 never disturb'd or turn'd to further than the minute's reference for reciting the text on a Sunday." In contrast, Lady Bell's sociological study of Edwardian Middlesbrough found that three out of four working men read newspapers, and more than one out of four read books, though their wives were less likely to be active readers. In 1837 a penny might buy a broadside reporting some gruesome crime. Sixty years later it could buy Longfellow, Arnold, Morris, or any one of the sixty "Penny Poets" volumes published by W. T. Stead, with 5,276,000 copies in print. A substantial minority of working men, and a smaller proportion of working women, were taking advantage of cheap reprints to educate themselves in classic literature.

Literacy was not an unmixed blessing: as H. G. Wells protested in *Tono-Bungay* (1909), it gave rise to mass-market advertising, which duped millions into buying worthless patent medicines. But in 1853 printer Charles Manby Smith argued that the London billsticker was teaching the masses how to read, free of charge:

> His handiwork stares the public in the face; and it is a sheer impossibility for a lad who has once learned the art of reading, to lose it in London, unless he be both wilfully blind and destitute of human curiosity. To thousands and tens of thousands, the placarded walls and hoardings of the city are the only school of instruction open to them, whence they obtain all the knowledge they possess of that section of the world and society which does not lie patent to their personal observation. It is thence they derive their estimate of the different celebrities – in commerce, in literature, and in art, of the time in which they live, and are enabled to become in some measure acquainted with the progress of the age. (quoted in Rose 2001: 391)

Indoor reading was facilitated by the repeal of the glass tax in 1845 and the end of the window tax in 1851 – the year, significantly, of the Crystal Palace. But at that point most working-class homes still lacked gas lighting, relying instead on candles and rushlights. Even in 1901, more middle-class homes were lit by kerosene lamps than electricity.

Readers were also hampered by the paucity of libraries. A succession of parliamentary measures, starting with the Public Libraries Act of 1850, allowed towns to levy rates to support museums and libraries. But many localities were slow to exercise this option; opponents warned that free libraries would be a tax burden and a haven for layabouts. Only 23 new public libraries were set up between 1851 and 1862, and then, after a lull, another 98 between 1868 and 1886. In 1885 they still served only 25 percent of the population in England, 15 percent in Wales, and 8 percent in Scotland. Before that date London had only two tax-supported libraries, one of which was the Guildhall Library (founded 1828). The Glasgow Corporation did not begin to develop a library system until 1899, though the privately endowed Mitchell Library had been serving the city since 1877. The real burst of expansion came between 1886 and 1918, when library authorities in Britain mushroomed from 125 to 584, the majority of them assisted by grants from Andrew Carnegie. Yet even by 1911, they covered only 62 percent of England's population, 50 percent of Scotland's, 46 percent of Wales's, and 28 percent of Ireland's. Closed stacks were another obstacle. No public library allowed its patrons to browse its shelves until 1894; the borrower had to consult an indicator to find out if a particular book was available, and then ask a librarian to fetch it, a system which many less-educated readers found confusing and intimidating.

Yet an 1876–7 parliamentary survey of 37 public libraries found that their users were mainly working-class – as many as 81 percent of them in the case of Leeds. At the Liverpool Free Library, one observer noted in 1858, "the larger proportion of solid reading is amongst the really working classes, the lighter literature more among young men in offices and shops" (Picton 1858). History and general literature accounted for fully 40 percent of loans (only 34 percent were novels), with Macaulay's *History of England* among the most frequently borrowed volumes. At the Portsmouth Free Public Library in 1887–8, the largest category of new borrowers (except for students) was shipwrights, with factory hands not far behind. The shipwrights accounted for 10 of the 23 borrowers of Ganot's *Physics*, while a volume of Aristotle was loaned out to a bootmaker, a carpenter, a compositor, two domestic workers, two drapers, two fitters, a gold-beater, a painter, a pastry-cook, two shipwrights, a shop boy, a smith, a tailor, and a warehouseman. One laborer borrowed *Dombey and Son*, *A Tale of Two Cities*, *The Old Curiosity Shop*, George Meredith's *Harry Richmond*, *Reminiscences of Abraham Lincoln*, and J. R. Green's *Short History of the English People*. A domestic servant took *East Lynne* and *Lady Audley's Secret*, but also *The Mill on the Floss* and a life of Harriet Martineau.

Even where there were no public libraries, the masses might still have access to books. Apprentices and house servants were sometimes allowed (and often not allowed) to use their employers' personal collections. Many Sunday schools, church schools, and parishes maintained modest libraries, usually (but not always) limited to religious literature. In the interest of keeping their workers sober and respectable, some employers provided workplace libraries; these were fairly common in the coalfields of Durham, Northumberland, and south Wales.

England also had 610 mechanics' institutes in 1851, with 102,050 members and a total stock of 681,500 volumes. (By comparison, there were only 25 institutes in Ireland, with 4,005 members and 57,500 volumes.) Because the mechanics' institutes had an odor of philanthropic paternalism, and often banned controversial literature, working men often preferred to organize their own libraries and reading rooms. In 1848 (for example) some Carlisle weavers, interested in the wave of revolutionary activity then sweeping across Europe, clubbed together to buy newspapers. A year later the group had about 300 members and a 500-volume library, all crammed into a room 22 feet by 14 feet. A larger permanent home was obviously necessary, and in December a magnificent new Elizabethan-style library was opened. But it was built only with substantial middle-class assistance, and its rulebook insisted "that party politics and controversial religion are shut out from all meetings of the institution." As it came to resemble a conventional mechanics' institute, its members melted away. But this was only one of more than 24 reading rooms organized between 1836 and 1854 by Carlisle working men. Some of them offered classes in reading and writing, and they undoubtedly contributed to the growth of literacy, which in one Carlisle parish rose from 64.85 percent in 1831 to 92.60 percent in 1871.

Indeed, the working classes provided themselves with reading matter through a host of self-help institutions. There were temperance groups, such as the Bury Abstinence Society, which had a library of 204 volumes in 1854. There were trades unions, such as the Alliance Cabinet Makers' Association: in 1879 its 1,500-volume library included Dickens, Scott, Carlyle, Macaulay, Thackeray, Bulwer-Lytton, Marryat, and Lord Brougham. Evidently the cabinet makers were thoroughly respectable, for they stocked hardly any radical literature: nothing by atheist Charles Bradlaugh, and only an occasional volume by Tom Paine. Of the 900 branches of the Working Men's Club and Institute Union in 1903, 500 maintained libraries with a total of 187,000 volumes. The Cooperative movement, inspired by Robert Owen, devoted a portion of its profits to libraries, which in the 1860s and 1870s outnumbered public libraries.

While free libraries were still scarce, the middle classes resorted to using commercial circulating libraries. C. E. Mudie created by far the largest lending library in the country, acquiring more than 170,000 volumes a year in the 1860s, when the Liverpool Free Library had a total stock of only 49,277 books. The firm of W. H. Smith realized that railways not only revolutionized book distribution but created wholly new audiences for books and new sites for reading. In 1848 Smith's opened its first railway bookstall at Euston Station: by 1902 there would be 1242 of them. They sold cheap fiction reprints ("yellowbacks") to travelers and, starting in 1860, they served as branches of a vast circulating library system.

By the 1890s Mudie's and Smith's served (respectively) 25,000 and 15,000 subscribers. Both firms banned novels by George Moore, who denounced them for emasculating Victorian fiction. In fact, only a third of Mudie's collection was fiction: still, he accounted for a large share of the first-edition novel market, so publishers and authors had to conform to his standards, which in turn reflected the standards of his middle-class customers. An annual subscription to Mudie's and Smith's was only a guinea: a three-volume novel cost half as much again to purchase. For that reason, Gladstone observed in 1852, his affluent friends rarely bought books, relying instead on their circulating libraries.

For scholars and professional intellectuals, there was the British Museum's Department of Printed Books. In 1837, when Anthony Panizzi became keeper of the department, it was poorly funded and staffed. The library had long been entitled to copies of every copyrighted book, but Panizzi was the first to enforce the policy seriously. He compiled an alphabetical catalogue of the collection, and designed the great circular Reading Room, which was opened in 1857.

Dissatisfaction with the British Museum drove Thomas Carlyle to organize the London Library in 1841. It was a proprietary library, where members paid entrance and annual subscription fees and could borrow books. It soon attracted nearly 500 subscribers, mainly professional men, politicians, and authors, along with a few women. Those early members included W. E. Gladstone, Charles Darwin, George Grote, John Stuart Mill, Giuseppe Mazzini, and Henry Hallam.

The most difficult question historians of reading must confront is absolutely basic: Who read what, and how? Though the borrowing records of the London Library and a few other collections have been preserved, scholars have only begun the laborious work of quantifying reading tastes. Sales records are reasonably good for some Victorian authors (notably Dickens) but spotty overall. (Hermann Goering and Winston Churchill must share the blame for those gaps: during the Second World War the Luftwaffe destroyed many publishers' archives, while others were patriotically donated to scrap-paper drives.) Richard Altick has drawn up lists of Victorian "bestsellers," but he honestly admits that these sales figures are neither complete nor entirely reliable (Altick 1998: 381).

Simon Eliot (1992) has approached the question by studying public library catalogues. A sampling of 28 libraries between 1883 and 1892 reveals that the most widely stocked novelist was Mary Elizabeth Braddon, with a total of 2,254 volumes, followed by Walter Scott (1,948), Mrs. Henry Wood (1,812), Charles Dickens (1,638), Edward Bulwer-Lytton (1,417), Anthony Trollope (1,389), R. M. Ballantyne (1,310), Margaret Oliphant (1,255), Wilkie Collins (1,159), Charlotte Yonge (1,110), James Payn (1,108), Harrison Ainsworth (961), Jules Verne (922), Walter Besant (885), William Black (760), Ouida (438), H. Rider Haggard (400), R. D. Blackmore (351), Robert Louis Stevenson (329), Mark Twain (297), and Rhoda Broughton (284).

In *Edging Women Out* (1989), Gaye Tuchman and Nina E. Fortin argued that the Victorian publishing industry was biased against women novelists, but these figures indicate that they could hold their own in the public library stacks. Half of the 28 libraries carried none of the risqué works of Ouida, suggesting that they had banned her novels. (If so, she may have been more popular than her numbers suggest.) Though G. W. M. Reynolds was one of the best-selling novelists of the previous generation, a total of only four copies of his works could be found in all these libraries. No doubt respectable librarians made sure that his sordid fiction was banished from their shelves, but his absence cannot be blamed entirely on bourgeois morality. In fact, he had gone out of fashion on all levels of society; a few years later his works could be found in only one of 20 Welsh miners' libraries, where the colliers themselves controlled acquisitions.

More recently, Troy Bassett and Christina Walter (2001) have used monthly reports from bookshops published in the *Bookman* magazine to reconstruct a bestseller list for the final decade of the century. Bassett and Walter acknowledge that their list may be no more accurate than the *New York Times* bestseller list today (both are based on reports from a selective and somewhat unrepresentative sample of bookstores), but the *Bookman* might offer us the best estimate we will ever have. Its lists suggest that four genres of fiction were especially popular in the 1890s. First, there was the "Kailyard school" of sentimental Scottish stories, such as J. M. Barrie's *The Little Minister* and Ian Maclaren's *Beside the Bonnie Brier Bush*. Historical romances (Arthur Conan Doyle's *The White Company*, Stanley Weyman's *A Gentleman of France*, Anthony Hope's *Rupert of Hentzau*) sold equally well, as did religious fiction (Mrs. Humphry Ward's *Helbeck of Bannisdale*, Marie Corelli's *The Sorrows of Satan*, Hall Caine's *The Christian*). Thus far the late Victorian literary diet seems predictably bourgeois, but there was also a strong demand for subversive "new woman" fiction: Sarah Grand's *The Heavenly Twins*, Grant Allen's *The Woman Who Did*, and (despite its devastating critical reception) *Jude the Obscure*. The bestseller lists also featured nonfiction that addressed (in the wake of Darwin) questions of religion and evolution: Henry Drummond's *The Ascent of Man*, A. J. Balfour's *The Foundations of Belief*, and Benjamin Kidd's *Social Evolution*.

The ten authors that appeared most often on the lists were, in descending order, S. R. Crockett, Marie Corelli, Rudyard Kipling, Ian Maclaren, Stanley Weyman, Robert Louis Stevenson, Arthur Conan Doyle, J. M. Barrie, Mrs. Humphry Ward, and E. T. Fowler. Although (or perhaps because) he was banned from some public libraries, and Henry Vizetelly had been jailed in 1889 for publishing him, Emile Zola ranked fourteenth on the combined lists. He was by far the most popular foreign author, well ahead of Mark Twain.

The Bassett–Walter list permits us to do what most bestseller lists do not: break down sales by region. Here it becomes apparent that the Victorian reading public was quite heterogeneous, that literary tastes could vary even among different neighborhoods of the same city. While one east central London bookstore sold mainly religious fiction and nonfiction, a west central London shop found plenty of buyers for avantgarde literature: George Moore, Thomas Hardy, George Gissing, *The Yellow Book*, *The War of the Worlds*, *The Ballad of Reading Gaol*, Huxley on evolution, Bernard Shaw's plays, *Fabianism and the Empire*, Joseph Conrad's *Tales of Unrest*. Meanwhile, in the Lancashire mill town of Burnley, a shop catering to a working-class clientele reported selling more than 20,000 copies of the works of Silas Hocking – more than one volume for every five inhabitants. As one might expect, regional literature found ready buyers in Scotland and Ireland, with one important difference: whereas Scottish authors like Barrie, Robert Louis Stevenson, Ian Maclaren, and (even at this late date) Walter Scott were selling well throughout the kingdom, Irish literature usually could find a market only in Ireland.

We may also turn to Edward Salmon's 1888 survey of the reading habits of 790 boys and just over 1,000 girls, all aged 11 to 19 and mainly middle-class. When the boys were asked their favorite authors, the clear winner was Charles Dickens with 223 votes, followed by W. H. S. Kingston (179), Walter Scott (128), Jules Verne (114), Frederick Marryat (102), R. M. Ballantyne (67), Harrison Ainsworth (61), William Shakespeare (44), Mayne Reid (33), Edward Bulwer-Lytton (32), Charles Kingsley (28), and Daniel Defoe (24). (Some respondents named more than one author.) Their favorite books were *Robinson Crusoe* (43 votes), *The Swiss Family Robinson* (24), *The Pickwick Papers* (22), *Ivanhoe* (20), *Boys' Own Annual* (17), the Bible (15), *Tom Brown's Schooldays* (15), Henry Cockton's *Valentine Vox* (13), F. Anstey's *Vice Versa* (12), F. W. Farrar's school story *St. Winifred's* (11), *The Arabian Nights* (10), Charles Kingsley's *Westward Ho!* (9), and *Oliver Twist* (9).

None of these results is unexpected, but the girls' responses contain some surprises. Their best-loved authors were Charles Dickens (355), Walter Scott (248), Charles Kingsley (103), Charlotte Yonge (100), William Shakespeare (75), Mrs. Henry Wood

(58), Elizabeth Wetherell (56), George Eliot (50), Edward Bulwer-Lytton (46), Hans Christian Andersen (33), H. W. Longfellow (32), A.L.O.E. (Charlotte Maria Tucker) (32), F. W. Farrar (27), Hesba Stretton (27), Grace Aguilar (23), Jules Verne (22), W. M. Thackeray (20), the Brothers Grimm (20), Mrs. O. F. Walton (20), W. H. G. Kingston (19), and Whyte Melville (18). Astonishingly, their favorite book was Kingsley's rip-roaring novel *Westward Ho!* (34 votes), trailed by Elizabeth Wetherell's *The Wide, Wide World* (29), the Bible (27), Mrs. O. F. Walton's *A Peep Behind the Scenes* (27), Diana Mulock Craik's *John Halifax, Gentleman* (25), *David Copperfield* (22), *Little Women* (21), *Ivanhoe* (18), Grace Aguilar's *The Days of Bruce* (16), Charlotte Yonge's *The Daisy Chain* (13) and *The Heir of Redcliffe* (12), and Scott's *Kenilworth* (12). More than 70 percent of the girls' votes were cast for male authors, and about half for books written by men. Although Jules Verne, W. H. G. Kingston, and Whyte Melville are generally typed as boys' authors, they were more popular among girls than Louisa May Alcott, Mary Elizabeth Braddon, Harriet Beecher Stowe, Elizabeth Gaskell, or Charlotte Brontë. No one voted for the other Brontë sisters or Jane Austen. The girls in the survey rated the *Girls' Own Paper* their favorite magazine, but the *Boys' Own Paper* took second place.

The apparent explanation for these findings is that many Victorian girls found "girls' stories" vapid and saccharine. In Kingsley and other thrilling writers, they found the blood and thunder they craved. "Girls as a rule don't care for Sunday-school twaddle," observed one young woman; "they like a good stirring story, with a plot and some incident and adventures – not a collection of texts and sermons and hymns strung together, with a little 'Child's Guide to Knowledge' sort of conversation" (Salmon 1888: 21–31).

Where Jonathan Culler and many feminist critics have asked "how a woman might read," Kate Flint (1993) has shown that the question is unanswerable. The reading tastes of Victorian women were strikingly heterogeneous and not all that different from those of Victorian men. Reading manuals presumed to steer young ladies toward wholesome literature, and not all of them were produced by men. From Mary Wollstonecraft's *Vindication of the Rights of Woman* (1792) to contemporary monographs in cultural studies, feminists have warned that romantic fiction insidiously indoctrinates women in patriarchal values. Flint notes the condescension here: the assumption, common to many fathers and feminists of the nineteenth and twentieth centuries, that women are "'naturally' more susceptible to being manipulated by their reading matter" than men, and cannot safely roam through a library without warning signs. This is a prejudice based on no careful study of actual Victorian women, who in fact could be serious, self-directed, and adventurous readers. Jeanne Peterson (1989) has described the rigorous and far-ranging self-education pursued by the women of the upper-middle-class Paget family. Lillian Faithfull's mother studied and annotated Buckle's *History of Civilisation* and John Seeley's *Ecce Homo*. Mary Cholmondeley remembered that her mother "read and was deeply interested in books on hydraulics, astronomy, anything that had a law behind it, and was bitterly disappointed that her children refused to be interested in these – to her – entrancing subjects." Upon finishing school in 1857, Louisa Martindale plunged into Schiller's *Wallenstein* (Coleridge's translation), Froude's *History of England*, *The Bible and Modern Thought*, Butler's *Analogy*, Bancroft's *American Revolution*, Rollin's *Ancient History*, and Locke's *Essay Concerning Human Understanding*. In a single diary entry (18 January 1874) sixteen-year-old Beatrice Webb recorded that she was reading Shakespeare and the German novelist Ludwig Tieck, in addition to translating Goethe's *Faust*, which she considered "far more powerful than Tasso." Considering the ossified curricula of the ancient universities, one might well conclude that Victorian women were better off educating themselves. Meanwhile, girls with less intellectual tastes could identify passionately with the rugged heroes of H. Rider Haggard, G. A. Henty, and Alexandre Dumas.

In the Salmon survey very few boys voted for women authors, a fact open to three possible interpretations. Either (a) these young men did not like female novelists, or (b) they were ashamed to admit that they liked them. We must also bear in mind that the survey was limited to adolescents; perhaps (c) only a mature masculine sensibility could acquire a taste for *Lady Audley's Secret* and *East Lynne*. In the Welsh miners' libraries of the early twentieth century, Mrs. Henry Wood, Marie Corelli, and Mary Elizabeth Braddon were among the most widely stocked novelists, exceeded only by Dickens, Scott, and Haggard. No doubt they were read by the colliers' womenfolk – but only by them? How then do we explain seaman Frank Bullen, who reported that his shipmates were reduced to tears by Mrs. O. F. Walton's *Jessica's First Prayer*? Another sailor whiled away the long hours at sea with bound volumes of the *Family Herald* and other women's magazines, which he passed around to his shipmates. "They like 'em better than anything. They're the most popular things on the ship," he explained. "I read to prevent myself thinking" (McAleer 1992: 30). And when the 1909 Churchill Committee investigated reading tastes in prison libraries, Mrs. Henry Wood was by far the inmates' favorite.

Victorians of all classes recorded their reading experiences in diaries and memoirs, and these documents testify to the amazing variety of the nineteenth-century literary diet. Gladstone's diaries describe his reactions to *Jane Eyre* ("a very remarkable but jarring book"), *Uncle Tom's Cabin* ("scarcely denies exaggeration"), Froude's *Nemesis of Faith*, and large helpings of pornography. The poorer classes could be equally random in their reading, if only because they had to take whatever came to hand. "The difficulty was to get hold of books," explained a Salisbury Downs farmer. "The only ones in our house were the Bible, a few thin Sunday School prizes, which were mostly very pious publications, one or two more advanced theological works, and a Post Office Directory for 1867, which volume I read from cover to cover" (quoted in Rose 2001: 372).

Working people could also borrow books from neighbors, rescue them from trash heaps, patronize twopenny used-book stalls, or purchase reprints, which became cheaper with every passing decade. Thus they had some access to the classics, but not new books, which were simply too expensive. Henry Mayhew reported that a London bookstall sold working men mainly eighteenth-century literature: *Rasselas*, *The Vicar of Wakefield, Peregrine Pickle, Tom Jones*. Welsh miner Joseph Keating read Swift, Pope, Fielding, Richardson, Smollett, Goldsmith, Sheridan, Keats, Byron, Shelley, and Dickens – every one of them a dead author. "Our school-books never mentioned living writers," he explained; "and the impression in my mind was that an author, to be a living author, must be dead; and that his work was all the better if he died of neglect and starvation" (quoted in Rose 2001: 121). The great exception here was American literature: because the United States did not sign an international copyright agreement until 1891, Cooper, Longfellow, and Harriet Beecher Stowe were readily available to English common readers in an array of cheap editions.

Even books that were read by everyone might be read very differently in different social strata. *Pilgrim's Progress* was passionately devoured even by the most disadvantaged, including gypsies and prison inmates. But the latter might read a radical political message into Bunyan's allegory, which was certainly not the intention of those who stocked prison libraries. Bored children, denied any secular books on Sundays, often read Christian's adventures as a thrilling penny dreadful. Whatever the teachings of clergymen, Sunday school pupils found in the Old Testament action heroes as thrilling as anything in Charles Kingsley, not to mention sexual information they could read nowhere else. *Uncle Tom's Cabin* was probably the bestselling novel of the century: in its first year, numerous competing editions sold 1.5 million copies throughout the empire, according to one unverifiable estimate. But middle-class journals (notably the anti-abolitionist *Times*) worried that the novel might inflame working-class audiences. They had reason to worry, given the audience response to a stage version performed in a north Wales mining village:

> *Uncle Tom's Cabin* played absolute hell with our emotions. We felt every stroke of the lash of the whip. It cut us to the quick, heart and soul. In the audience some people wept unashamedly like the Greeks of old who considered it manly to give vent to their feelings when moved. Others with obvious effort restrained themselves by the exercise of great control from rushing on the stage, taking the whip out of the hand of the cruel task master and giving him a taste of his own medicine. One or two were only repressed with the reminder that it was on the stage – and not in real life. Not so Mrs. Whalley. In the middle of the sixpennies . . . she was loudly sobbing, looking up and calling out, "Oh, oh" as each lash discordantly cut the air and Tom's poor body. At one juncture her grief was awful to behold and as she was sympathetically escorted out to the back . . . she was still sobbing and crying and would not be comforted. (quoted in Rose 2001: 383)

In his lifetime, Dickens was hugely popular among middle-class readers: in book form *The Pickwick Papers* sold 140,000 copies and *Nicholas Nickleby* more than 100,000 by 1863. His reputation fell after his death in 1870, when critics began to write him off as a cheap, melodramatic, early Victorian caricaturist. Nevertheless, his sales continued to climb ever higher: working-class readers could now acquire his works very cheaply or entirely free, given away by merchants as premiums to attract customers. At the Loveclough Printworks Library, Dickens accounted for 10 percent of all loans in 1892–3. From 1900 to 1906 two million of his books were sold by Chapman & Hall. Neville Cardus, a Manchester laundryman's son, read in the *Athenaeum* that Dickens was *passé* and then discovered that the local public libraries had loaned out every one of his books. While the elite reviews dismissed Dickens as cartoonish, common readers like Cardus found him grippingly realistic:

> It was scarcely a case of reading at all; it was almost an experience of a world more alive and dimensional than this world, heightened and set free in every impulse of nature . . . David Copperfield so often behaved and thought as I behaved and thought that I frequently lost my own sense of identity in him. (quoted in Rose 2001: 112–13)

Readers of all classes just as frequently lost themselves in school stories, which were anything but realistic. The actual public schools still devoted most of their classroom time to thrashing Greek and Latin into captive pupils, making few concessions to the sciences or English literature. Halls and baths were usually unheated, and refectories served up a starvation diet. Corporal punishment occasionally drove boys to suicide, and probably accounted for Gladstone's and Swinburne's fixation on flagellation, which happened to be the most overworked theme in Victorian pornography. But the fictional public school was a high-minded exercise in character-building, and life followed art remarkably far. Fans would adopt the slang, mannerisms, and moral codes of their favorite schoolboy characters. Dr. Thomas Arnold never introduced games to Rugby, but after reading *Tom Brown's Schooldays* (which ran through 52 editions from 1857 to 1892) many thought he had, and by the 1890s every public school had made sports compulsory. The *Boys' Own Paper*, launched in 1879, swiftly attained weekly sales of 200,000, mainly on the strength of school stories by Talbot Baines Reed. The correspondence columns reflect a readership that cut clean across socioeconomic lines. The magazine was popular at Wellington College, and was read by 68 out of 84 younger workers at the Technical Department of the Post Office in Scotland. Its fans included Australians, New Zealanders, adults (e.g. a Norfolk clergyman and a sergeant in the Royal Engineers), messenger boys, more than a few girls, and two princes of the realm (Edward and George).

The Victorian reading public was not limited to the United Kingdom. Britain exported £445,000 worth of printed books in 1854, a third of them to Australia. In 1861, when 24.6 percent of Englishmen and 34.7 percent of Englishwomen were illiterate, the figures for colonists in Victoria were 11 and 22 percent. When Anthony Trollope visited Australia in the 1870s, he was duly impressed by the proliferation of libraries and their well-thumbed copies of Macaulay, Scott, Bunyan, Tennyson, and Dickens. At the time public libraries in Victoria held one volume for every four inhabitants, while in the mother country the ratio was closer to one volume for every twenty people. In Australia as in England, boys devoured public-school stories, Mrs. Henry Wood was stupendously popular, working-class autodidacts diligently pursued the classics, and the middle classes patronized circulating libraries (Samuel Mullen's was Melbourne's equivalent of Mudie's). Some complained that Australian readers were too much like British readers, so devoted to English literature that native authors could not gain a foothold. The syllabus for one Australian women's reading circle for 1903–5 was challenging and wide-ranging: Shakespeare, Darwin, Longfellow's *Evangeline*, both Brownings, *David Copperfield, Enoch Arden*, F. Marion Crawford's *The Crisis* (a novel of the American Civil War), Israel Zangwill's *The Children of the Ghetto*, Rosa Praed's *Nyria*, Marie Corelli, *Ivanhoe, The Cloister and the Hearth, Heroes and Hero-Worship*, and books about Japan and Siberia. But something is missing: the list includes only one book by an Australian (Mrs. Praed) and none that deals with Australia.

By 1864 Britain was selling £328,024 worth of books to India, bought both by colonists and by the small but growing community of Indians literate in English. Targeting this market, the London publisher Macmillan began its Colonial Library of cheap reprints in 1886. Though the novel as a genre was not indigenous to the sub continent, Indian readers embraced it enthusiastically. Their tastes in fiction, however, did not extend to Austen, the Brontës, Thackeray, Eliot, or Meredith. They much preferred authors who, in the minds of English critics, ranged from second-rate to downright trashy: G. P. R. James, Edward Bulwer-Lytton, G. W. M. Reynolds, F. Marion Crawford, Marie Corelli. None of them could be called social realists, but "realistic" portrayals of English society were hardly meaningful to Indian readers. These novelists offered instead the kind of fantasy, romance, melodrama, and moralizing that suffuse traditional Indian poetry, epics, and religious literature: hence their mode of storytelling was quite familiar to Indian readers. For much the same reason – and because they satirized European civilization from a non-European perspective – *Gulliver's Travels* and *Rasselas* also found a following in India.

"Interactive" has become the great cliché of the internet era, but print literature also provokes and is shaped by reader feedback. In this sense, Victorian literature was highly interactive. With the serialization of novels, writers and publishers could track the response to an unfolding story through the sales and reviews of its monthly parts – and they could use that knowledge to make midcourse corrections. When Charles Reade's *Hard Cash* alienated the readers of *All the Year Round*, Dickens gently persuaded him to wind it up. Frederick Marryat cut back *Poor Jack* from an announced twenty installments to twelve, and his next novel, *The Children of the New Forest*, was sunk after one episode. One popular but now-forgotten Victorian genre was the confession album, which invited the owner to record answers to a series of personal questions, often relating to qualities sought in a member of the opposite sex. Victorian newspapers, especially local newspapers, were to a large extent written by their readers: letters to the editor may be our most reliable indicators of public opinion and audience response before the Gallup Poll. It is difficult to think of any popular late Victorian paper that did not invite its readers to submit entries to literary competitions: Scotland's *People's Journal*, with a huge working-class following, relied heavily on such contributions.

Like the industrial revolution, the reading revolution had an uneven impact, transforming British society as a whole while leaving certain traditional practices intact.

Collective reading of newspapers, a necessity when they were expensive and illiteracy was widespread, naturally declined over time, but in 1901 bits from the evening papers were still read aloud in many kitchens and parlors. And "intensive reading" did not come to an end, in spite of the surging deluge of print. Matthew Arnold closely and repeatedly studied the *Bhagavad Gita*, and Mark Pattison was still capable of reading a magazine article on English poetry five or six times over. Even when free-thinking working men abandoned the Bible, many of them turned to some secular text and read it just as religiously. Often it was Shakespeare or Ruskin – or, in the case of V. S. Pritchett's uncle, *The Anatomy of Melancholy* ("Look it up in Burton, lad").

And not everyone welcomed the ever-rising tide of reading matter. In 1839, following the successful runs of *The Pickwick Papers* and *Nicholas Nickleby*, Dr. Arnold of Rugby warned his students that serialized novels, with their engaging plots and cliffhanger endings, were a dangerous distraction. He was already nostalgic for the pre-Dickens era. We were, he sermonized, much better off just a few years ago, when books were fewer, more costly, and not nearly so interesting.

REFERENCES

Altick, R. D. (1998), *The English Common Reader: A Social History of the Mass Reading Public, 1800–1900*, 2nd edn. (Columbus: Ohio State University Press).
McAleer, J. (1992), *Popular Reading and Publishing in Britain 1914–1950* (Oxford: Clarendon).
Picton, J. A. (1858), "Notes on the Free Library and Museum of the Borough of Liverpool," *Transactions of the National Association for the Promotion of Social Science*, 693–5.
Rose, J. (2001), *The Intellectual Life of the British Working Classes* (New Haven and London: Yale University Press).
Salmon, E. (1888), *Juvenile Literature as It Is* (London: Henry J. Drane).
Tuchman, Gaye with Fortin, Nina E. (1989), *Edging Women Out: Victorian Novelists, Publishers, and Social Change* (New Haven: Yale University Press).
Vincent, D. (1982), *Bread, Knowledge and Freedom: A Study of Nineteenth-Century Working Class Autobiography* (London: Methuen).

FURTHER READING

Altick, R. D. (1989), *Writers, Readers, and Occasions: Selected Essays on Victorian Literature and Life* (Columbus: Ohio State University Press).
Bassett, T. J. and Walter, C. M. (2001), "Booksellers and Bestsellers: British Book Sales as Documented by *The Bookman*, 1891–1906," *Book History*, 4, 205–36.
Black, A. (1996), *A New History of the English Public Library: Social and Intellectual Contexts, 1850–1914* (London: Leicester University Press).
Borchardt, D. H. and Kirsop, W. eds. (1988), *The Book in Australia* (Melbourne: Australian Reference Publications).
Brantlinger, P. (1998), *The Reading Lesson: The Threat of Mass Literacy in Nineteenth-Century British Fiction* (Bloomington: Indiana University Press).
Burnett, J., ed. (1984), *Destiny Obscure: Autobiographies of Childhood, Education, and Family from the 1820s to the 1920s* (Harmondsworth: Penguin).

Casteleyn, M. (1984), *A History of Literacy and Libraries in Ireland* (Aldershot: Gower).

Eliot, S. (1992), *A Measure of Popularity: Public Library Holdings of Twenty-four Popular Authors 1883–1912* (Oxford and Bristol: History of the Book – On Demand Series).

Ellis, A. (1971), *Books in Victorian Elementary Schools* (London: Library Association).

Flint, K. (1993), *The Woman Reader 1837–1914* (Oxford: Clarendon).

Gardner, P. (1984), *The Lost Elementary Schools of Victorian England* (London: Croom Helm).

Griest, G. L. (1970), *Mudie's Circulating Library and the Victorian Novel* (Bloomington and London: Indiana University Press).

Honey, J. R. de S. (1977), *Tom Brown's Universe: The Development of the English Public School in the Nineteenth Century* (New York: Quadrangle/The New York Times Book Co.).

Hurt, J. S. (1979), *Elementary Schooling and the Working Classes 1860–1918* (London: Routledge & Kegan Paul).

Jones, A. (1996), *Powers of the Press: Newspapers, Power and the Public in Nineteenth-Century England* (Aldershot: Scolar).

Joshi, P. (2002), *In Another Country: Colonialism, Culture, and the English Novel in India* (New York: Columbia University Press).

Kelly, T. (1973), *A History of Public Libraries in Great Britain 1845–1965* (London: Library Association).

Mitch, D. F. (1992), *The Rise of Popular Literacy in Victorian England* (Philadelphia: University of Pennsylvania Press).

Peterson, M. J. (1989), *Family, Love, and Work in the Lives of Victorian Gentlewomen* (Bloomington: Indiana University Press).

Vincent, D. (1989), *Literacy and Popular Culture: England 1750–1914* (Cambridge: Cambridge University Press).

3

Money, the Economy, and Social Class

Regenia Gagnier

In *The Theory of Moral Sentiments* (1759), Adam Smith describes a "poor man's son" who might be Bradley Headstone in Dickens's *Our Mutual Friend* (1864):

> The poor man's son, whom heaven in its anger has visited with ambition, when he begins to look around him, admires the condition of the rich . . . To obtain the conveniencies which these afford, he submits in the first year, nay in the first month of his application, to more fatigue of body and more uneasiness of mind than he could have suffered through the whole of his life from the want of them. He studies to distinguish himself in some laborious profession. With the most unrelenting industry he labors night and day to acquire talents . . . He endeavors next to bring those talents into public view . . . For this purpose . . . he serves those whom he hates, and is obsequious to those whom he despises. Through the whole of his life he pursues the idea of a certain artificial and elegant repose which he may never arrive at . . . and which, if in the extremity of old age he should at last attain to it, he will find to be in no respect preferable to that humble security and contentment which he had abandoned for it. It is then, in the last dregs of life, his body wasted with toil and diseases, his mind galled and ruffled by the memory of a thousand injuries and disappointments which he imagines he has met with from the injustice of his enemies, or from the perfidy and ingratitude of his friends, that he begins at last to find that wealth and greatness are mere trinkets . . . more troublesome to the person who carries them about with him than all the advantages they can afford him are commodious. (Smith 1984: 181)

Yet the fact that the poor man's son has wasted his life in emulation of the rich is not a tragedy in Smith but a comedy – a comedy called the wealth of nations, for "it is this deception," Smith says – the waste of life in pursuit of the wealth possessed by others – "which rouses and keeps in continual motion the industry of mankind," the building of commonwealths, the invention and improvement of the arts and sciences that "have entirely changed the whole face of the globe, have turned the rude forests of nature into agreeable and fertile plains . . . and made the great high road of communication to the different nations of the earth" (Smith 1984: 184). This is why Smith's other great work, *The Wealth of Nations* (1776), is a great work of irony. The Invisible Hand that was introduced in Defoe's *Moll Flanders* (1722) as the providential agency that blighted happiness had come in Smith to mean the selfish interest that led to social good. But in Dickens the schoolmaster Headstone's emulation of the wealth and repose of others that results in self-loathing and self-destruction is a tragedy: a life wasted from the obscure origins he psychotically lays before Eugene Wrayburn at their very first meeting. To some extent we can follow René Girard (*Deceit, Desire, and the Novel*, 1976) and Eve Sedgwick (*Between Men*, 1985) here, as well as Adam Smith and Thorstein Veblen (*Theory of the Leisure Class*, 1899), in seeing the schoolmaster's envy of Wrayburn as more significant than his object choice of Lizzie Hexam. That is, according to the theory of mimetic or triangular desire, Headstone wants Lizzie because Eugene wants her, and he wants to be Eugene. But within the iron cage of social class he can never be Eugene, only Rogue Riderhood, to whom he is bound in death as in an "iron ring" (ch. 66).

I

In the contrast between Smith's comedy and Headstone's tragedy we see that one man's or nation's wealth is another man's or nation's waste. *Our Mutual Friend*, which Dickens considered entitling *Dust*, is about the wasting of human life in the pursuit of wealth, not for its own sake, to be sure (the miser, in fact, has no place here), but, as Smith said very clearly in *The Wealth of Nations*, for the power it commands over others. It is about the power to transform the self (John Rokesmith or Harmon, Boffin or Bella) and the power to transform all social relations. In Trollope's *The Way We Live Now* (1875), the financier Augustus Melmotte determines the fates of the characters by his stock's spectacular rise and fall. Yet Melmotte himself is silent, inarticulate among Trollope's brilliant dialogues, almost without content. Representing the pure form of the power of credit to transform human lives, he retains a mysterious power, even when he all too humanly fails to trust his market and precipitously commits suicide. Corporate center of "the way we live now," hosting huge balls where his guests will not speak to him, Melmotte retains a social and emotional marginality, his power seen only in his effects on others. As the narrator remarks of Melmotte and his money: "the world was more than ordinarily alive because of Melmotte and his failures" (vol. 2, ch. 83).

In *Literature, Money and the Market*, the critic Paul Delany (2002) argues that the prominence of money in Victorian literature was obscured under modernism only to return under our contemporary neoliberalism: that modernism occluded money under elite notions of taste but that wealth returned to literature with a vengeance in the last decades of the twentieth century with novels and plays called, for example, *Money* (Martin Amis) and *Serious Money* (Caryl Churchill). The high visibility of money in Victorian literature that every student of the period marks had begun with developments from 1690 in the global colonial trade centered in London: banknotes, deposit banking, a central bank, insurance, government debt management, and the stock exchange (see Brantlinger 1996). The most famous passage on money's trans- formative power, the one that best shows the genuine shock that the Victorians experienced when they saw the extent to which money would transform all traditional hierarchical social relations, which called forth exclamations that all that was solid was melting into air, was Karl Marx's most famous piece of literary criticism. Marx cites Mephistopheles' speech in Goethe's *Faust* (1808):

> Six stallions, say, I can afford,
> Is not their strength my property?
> I tear along, a sporting lord,
> As if their legs belonged to me.
> (Marx and Engels 1978: 102–3)

Marx then cites gold, the "yellow slave" in Shakespeare's *Timon of Athens* (1623) that, in true Hegelian dialectic of master and slave, determines the master's value:

> This yellow slave will . . . bless the accursed;
> Make the hoar leprosy adored, place thieves
> And give them title, knee and approbation
> With senators on the bench: this is it
> That makes the wappen'd widow wed again.
> (Marx and Engels 1978: 103)

Marx's *explication du texte* goes like this (note that the misers have it all wrong: the issue is not the money's intrinsic value when it is hoarded but the social relations built into the exchange when it is given away). It is the lesson learned most dramati- cally by Heathcliff of *Wuthering Heights* (1847), but also by numerous other heroes of Victorian novels and plays, from Becky Sharp of *Vanity Fair* (1847) and Pip of *Great Expectations* (1861) to Wilde's *Ideal Husband* (1895).

That which is for me through the medium of money – that for which I can pay (i.e., which money can buy) – that am I, the possessor of the money. The extent of the power of money is the extent of my power. Money's properties are my properties and essential powers . . . What I am and am capable of is by no means determined by my individu- ality. I am ugly, but I can buy for myself the most beautiful of women. Therefore I am not ugly, for the effect of ugliness – its deterrent power – is nullified by money. I, in my character as an individual, am lame, but money furnishes me with twenty-four feet. Therefore I am not lame. I am bad, dishonest, unscrupulous, stupid; but money is honored, and therefore so is its possessor . . . I am stupid, but money is the real mind of all things and how then should its possessor be stupid? Besides, he can buy talented people for himself, and is he who has power over the talented not more talented than the talented? Do not I, who thanks to money am capable of all that the human heart longs for, possess all human capacities? Does not my money therefore transform all my incapacities into their contrary? (Marx and Engels 1978: 103–4)

Marx concludes that Shakespeare showed us two properties of money – "the transformation of all human and natural properties into their contraries" and the conversion of "my wishes from something in the realm of imagination into their sensual, actual existence – from imagination to life, from imagined being into real being. In effecting this mediation," he writes, "money is the truly *creative* power." In a recent book on the cultural meanings of money, James Buchan calls the money that converts wishes in the realm of imagination into their sensual, actual existence "frozen desire." Because money has the potential to fulfill any purpose and convey any desire, it becomes the absolute purpose and the object of the most intense desire. He cites the nineteenth-century philosopher Arthur Schopenhauer: "Other goods can satisfy only *one* wish and *one* need. Food is good only for the hungry, wine for the healthy, medicine for the sick, fur for winter, sexual love for the young, etc. They are all *goods for a particular purpose*, that is, only relative good. Money alone is the absolute good: for it confronts not just *one* concrete need, but Need *itself in abstract*" (cited in Buchan 1997: 31).

At the end of the nineteenth century, the philosopher Georg Simmel in *The Philosophy of Money* (1900) called money "the historical symbol of the relative character of existence," thereby characterizing the relativism of modernity. "There is no more striking symbol of the completely dynamic character of the [modern] world," wrote Simmel, "than that of money. The meaning of money lies in the fact that it will be given away . . . [I]t lives in continuous self-alienation from any given point and thus forms the counterpart and direct negation of all being in itself" (Simmel 1978: 510–11). For Simmel, the abstraction of money-value was profoundly tied to the increasing differentiation of modern individualism. Only money could satisfy the diverse needs of modern individuals in society; money was the symbol of the relativity of wants.

The development of money seemed to be an element in a profound cultural trend away from specific objects and essences toward symbols and abstractions. Amid a myriad of incomparable individualistic wishes, money alone could provide each person's sublime reification of desire into object: through its possession, the wishes or fantasies of modernity could be turned into material facts.

The increasingly influential principle of economizing strength and materials leads to more and more extensive experiments with representatives and symbols that have virtually no relation to what they represent ... The idea that life is essentially based on intellect [i.e., rational understanding, as opposed to emotion or feeling], and that intellect is accepted in practical life as the most valuable of our mental energies, goes hand in hand with the growth of a money economy ... The growth of intellectual abilities and of abstract thought characterizes the age in which money becomes more and more a mere symbol, neutral as regards its intrinsic value. (Simmel 1978: 151)

This abstract function of money – money as the abstraction of everyone's unique wishes – contributes not only to the fantasy lives of modern consumers but also to what Simmel calls "the psychological expansion of qualities" (1978: 228), or the displacement of money as means by the growth of money as end in itself. The fear of this displacement informs George Eliot's moralistic *Silas Marner* (1861), whose protagonist shifts his center of value from a miser's hoard to a golden-haired child.

No doubt, writes Marx, unwittingly explaining the tortured minds of Bradley Headstone, Uriah Heep (*David Copperfield* [1850]), and other figures of class hatred and *ressentiment* in Victorian literature, demand also exists for him who has no money; but his demand is a mere thing of the imagination without effect or existence for a third party and therefore remains for third parties like the Other Guv'nors or Eugene Wrayburn "unreal" and "objectless." The difference between effective demand based on money and ineffective demand based on my wish, or my need, or my passion, is the difference between being and thinking, between the imagined as it is outside me as a real object and the imagined which exists merely within my own fantasy. This money, which, as Marx says, mediates my life for me, also mediates the existence of other people for me. For me, he says, money is the "other person," that is, the other person will see me and acknowledge my wish, or my need, or my passion, to the extent that I possess the money.

Here money is not the miser's hoard, for the miser, like the poor man, lives only in his own imagination; his money does not mediate social relations for him (see the phantasmatic hoard, an illusion, "an hallucination," in Gissing's *Netherworld* [1889]). Once in circulation, however, money is a power of awesome creativity, capable of the creative destruction of all social relations: all that was solid was melting into air. Dickens said it less analytically but no less forcefully in the diatribe on shares in *Our Mutual Friend*: "Where does he come from? Shares. Where is he going to? Shares. What are his tastes? Shares. Has he any principles? Shares. What squeezes him into Parliament? Shares. Perhaps he never of himself achieved success in anything, never originated anything, never produced anything. Sufficient answer to all; Shares" (ch. 10).

In the dialectic of wealth and waste, waste is what happens to those who do not possess money's transformative power. Unlike money, which is the absolute good in that it can bestow on its possessor all other goods, waste is what nobody wants, what cannot be exchanged for anything else. If money is all dynamic, waste is entropy, stasis. The very year in which the 26-year-old Marx was studying the metaphysics of money in Goethe and Shakespeare, the 24-year-old Engels was observing waste in Manchester in his father's factory. While Marx gives us the image of creative power and force, of capital, Engels gives us the image of waste, as the destruction of workers' lives. In an essay on the Victorian sanitation officer Edwin Chadwick, Joseph Childers (1994) describes how in Chadwick a "logic of contiguity" transferred the physical environment in which the poor lived to their characters, and then metaphors of animalism and bestiality came to represent their degraded states. Childers here writes in the tradition of one of the great pieces of literary criticism of the twentieth century,

Steven Marcus's essay *Engels, Manchester, and the Working Class* (1974). Marcus drew our attention to how, in *The Condition of the Working Class in England*, Engels had traced the source of national wealth to the so-called "new towns" lying "near the commercial center[s]" (Engels 1968: 73).

Where Engels saw the factories that created "the Great Towns" of industrial England, he also saw workers' communities where "one privy served three hundred and eighty people" (1968: 74) and in which consequently "workers inhabit dwellings in which it is impossible to live in either cleanliness or comfort" (1968: 75). Influenced by psychoanalysis, Marcus was impressed to find that Engels had stumbled upon the material source of wealth as, literally, fecal waste: "Here [in a Salford Street called Hope]," Engels wrote,

> I found a man who seemed to be about sixty years of age living in a cow-shed. He had constructed a sort of chimney for his square-shaped hovel, which had no floor-boards, no plaster on the walls and no windows. He had installed a bedstead and here he lived although the rain came through the decaying roof. The man was too old for regular work, but he earned a living by removing manure and garbage with his handcart. Pools of filth lay close to his shed. (1968: 75)

Marcus comments:

> The old man has been productively used up and discarded as refuse; accordingly in his old age he sustains himself from refuse . . . I know of no representation of an industrial city before [Engels'] that achieves such an intimate creative hold upon its living subject. For anything that stands with it or surpasses it, one has to go to the later Dickens, to *Bleak House*, *Hard Times*, *Little Dorrit* and *Our Mutual Friend*. (Marcus 1974: 198)

Such are the blighted lives that, as Childers, Rosemarie Bodenheimer, Catherine Gallagher, and others have shown, became metaphorically mixed up with waste in middle-class minds like Dickens's in *Our Mutual Friend*.

II

The convergence in the city of money and waste helped to shift economic theory from production to consumption models. The second half of the nineteenth century saw a transition from notions of Economic Man as producer (Smith, Ricardo, Mill, and Marx) or reproducer (Malthus), to a view of Economic Man as consumer. To the student of culture, one of the most important insights of classical political economy was that the division of labor was the source of differences between people. People may or may not identify with a social or economic class; in Britain in the nineteenth century they often did, in the United States today they typically do not. But, as Smith showed in the early chapters of *The Wealth of Nations*, most people's subjective and objective identities are centrally related to whether they make nails, automobiles, books, contracts, breakfast, hotel beds, music, speeches, or babies. The fact that the division of labor also reflects major social divisions of race, gender, and ethnicity, and internationally reflects relations of domination and subordination between nations, is also crucial in establishing individual and collective identities, as Smith and the other political economists of the Scottish Enlightenment well knew.

Victorian political economists were concerned about the negative consequences of the division of labor. Mixing mechanistic and organic metaphors, Smith proposed government structures to ameliorate British workers' deterioration in what he called the social, intellectual, and martial virtues. Mixing market and virtue ideology, Mill feared that competitive individualism would drive out sympathy and altruism. And Marx and Engels, who criticized political economy while adopting some of its fundamental categories, put alienation and atomism at the centers, respectively, of working-class and bourgeois life. Despite their penchant for economic laws and the abstraction of a self-interested maximizer of material advantage called Economic Man, the political economists also believed that economic systems made kinds of people and that the division of labor, as John Ruskin said, also divided people from one another.

Being typically *progressive* rather than *developmental*, the classical political economists did not believe that markets were the end of history. Markets were taken as one stage of growth, but economic growth was no more an end in itself to them than beauty was to their contemporaries in aesthetics. Smith thought that free trade, if it ever happened (which he thought unlikely), would lead to world peace (the so-called doux-commerce thesis). Mill thought that once production reached a certain level, society's primary concern should be more equal distribution; indeed, he believed that the appropriate level of production had already been reached in 1871, a view which inclined him toward socialism late in his life. Political economy entailed a theory of social relations in a world in which scarcity was perceived to be a relationship of productive forces to nature, and markets were appropriate to but one stage of the development of those productive forces. Once society had *developed* its productive forces, humanity could *progress* ethically and politically.

Around 1871, economic theory began to shift its focus from the social, macroeconomic relations of population growth, landlords, entrepreneurs, workers, and international trade to the individual's subjective demand for goods. The labor theory of value, which had seen the human body and human labor as the ultimate determinants of price, was abandoned in favor of consumer demand. Value no longer inhered in goods themselves – whether the goods were grain or human labor – but in others' demand for the goods. Political economy's theory of the productive relations between land, labor, and capital thus gave way to the statistical analysis of price lists and consumption patterns. One of the corollaries of marginal utility theory, as it came to be called, was that consumer choice ceased to be a moral category; it did not matter whether the good desired was good or bad, just that the consumer was willing to pay for it. Value ceased to be comparable across persons; it became individual, subjective.

The theory of economics became more psychological than sociological. And, as we shall see, in the last quarter of the nineteenth century, so did the novel as a genre.

The psychological bias transformed the modern concept of scarcity. For Malthus and the early political economists, scarcity was a relation of productive forces to the earth, as in population growth and diminishing returns from agriculture. Under marginal utility theory, scarcity was relocated in the mind itself, as a consequence of the insatiability of human desires. Stanley Jevons, Carl Menger, and the other early theorists of consumption saw that as the basic needs of subsistence were satisfied, humankind's desire for variety in shelter, food, dress, and leisure grew limitlessly, and thus the idea of needs, which were finite and the focus of political economy, was displaced by the idea of tastes, which were theoretically infinite.

All this amounted to a noticeable shift in the concept of Economic Man. Under political economy, Economic Man was a productive pursuer of gain; for Jevons and Menger, on the other hand, Economic Man was a consumer, ranking his preferences and choosing among scarce resources. Significantly, *modern* man would henceforth be known by the insatiability of his desires, and the indolent races of savages – whether Irish, African, or native American (key examples throughout Victorian political economy) – needed only to be inspired by envy to desire modern man's desires, imitate his wants, to be on the road to his progress and his civilization. His modern nature, insatiability, was henceforth human nature itself. His mode, consumer society, was no longer one stage of human progress, but its culmination and end, the end of history. And here we begin to see the displacement of ideas of progress, which implied moral and political progress as well as economic growth, by ideas of development, which implied, by way of increasingly biological or organic analogies, only an inevitable trajectory toward high mass consumption (see Gagnier 2000).

In 1900, Simmel called his *Philosophy of Money* a sociology of the metropolis. Concerned with the social instability characterizing debt management and inflation, he analyzed the money economy not as capital or industrial relations of production but as circulation and consumption within the city, whose lifeblood was universal exchange and consumption. In contrast to political economy's emphases on production and efficiency, including a labor theory of value, Simmel saw consumption and exchange through money. It was to Simmel's theory that Walter Benjamin looked in his *Arcades Project* – the great attempt to construct the origins of modernity in mid-nineteenth-century Paris.

As it became clear that the possession and exchange of money would take the place of other, traditional forms of status and community, money was criticized because it negated not just its metal referent but all human capacities and therefore all social relations. "Cash payment," wrote Thomas Carlyle in "Chartism" (1839), his defense of the political movement for universal male suffrage and the economic survival of working men, "is the sole nexus between man and man" (Carlyle 1971: 199). Like other Victorians driven to political reaction by the total transformation overcoming them, he desperately recalls a time when capacities reflected intrinsic value:

And now what is thy property? That parchment title-deed, that purse thou buttonest in thy breeches-pocket? Is that thy valuable property? Unhappy brother, most poor insolvent brother, I without parchment at all, with purse oftenest in the flaccid state imponderous, which will not fling against the wind, have quite other property than that! I have the miraculous breath of Life in me, breathed into my nostrils by Almighty God. I have affections, thoughts, a *god-given capability to be and do*; rights, therefore – the right for instance to thy love if I love thee, to thy guidance if I obey thee. (Carlyle 1971: 194)

The problem for the Victorians was not whether the money was in the form of gold, beads, cash, check, or charge, but in the replacement of substantive properties with the properties money can buy. The problem was not that money was necessarily evil, for although Marx and Carlyle thought it an evil that the dishonest should appear honest and that the dishonorable should be honored, it was probably a good that the ugly should be made attractive, and that the lame should be made mobile.

The problem was not the essential or relative status of money, but that money had come to be the sole perspective through which human value could be judged, the sole nexus between people; that without money one did not appear at all except as ugly, lame, bad, dishonest, or stupid. Being human happiness in the abstract, money's acquisition could become an end in itself. Aristotle in the *Politics* foresaw the problem with money made from and for more money, calling usury "unnatural" and "incestuous": "The birth of money from money" in usury "is the most unnatural way of enriching yourself" (cited in Buchan 1997: 32). Dante followed Aristotle when he placed the usurers with the sodomites in Hell. The problem with money was the havoc it played with presumed natural social relations, not with the gold standard. People were either commodities, to have their value augmented by money, or creatures with capabilities to be and do, to love and be loved, to guide and be guided. Without that, the particular fetish in which the money, or the commodification of social relations, was embodied, was to little account. "Capital," as Marx said, "was not a thing, but a social relation between persons . . . Property in money, means of subsistence, machinery, and other means of production, do not yet stamp a man as a capitalist if there be wanting the correlative – the wage-worker" (Marx 1967: 766).

High Victorian fiction – variously called the industrial novel, social problem fiction, bourgeois or domestic realism – takes as its grand theme these social relations. The basic categories are the productive relations between the three real or imagined classes of their time (landowners, workers, and capitalist entrepreneurs) and their commodified objects of exchange (land, labor, and capital), resulting in rent, wages, and profits in domestic and colonial markets. For examples of early adaptation of the political economic categories in fiction, see Harriet Martineau's *Illustrations of Political Economy* (1832–5). From Jane Austen and Mary Shelley through Elizabeth Gaskell, George Eliot, the Brontës, Charles Dickens, William Thackeray, Anthony Trollope, and the rest, the fiction of social relations described landed aristocrats, entrepreneurs, and wage-earners. Whether the aristocrats were represented as stable pillars of the community (as in Trollope) or lazy and decadent (as in Bulwer-Lytton); whether the entrepreneurs were energetic (as in Gaskell) or cruel (as in Dickens); whether the wage-earners were docile and dependent (as in Eliot) or angry and seditious (as in Disraeli), depended on the political perspective of each novelist. But there is no doubt that the great novelists saw the world in terms of social groups or classes in contact and often in conflict, in which no private life, as George Eliot said in *Felix Holt, the Radical* (1866), was not determined by a wider public life. In most cases, this wider public life was determined by the socioeconomic or professional class into which one was born: in *Sybil* (1845) Disraeli called the rich and the poor "The Two Nations" – the book's subtitle – and set the conflict in the Chartist agitation of the 1840s. Despite the political volatility of ideas of welfare, "entitlements," transfer payments – or, in Victorian terms, whether the poor were "deserving" or "undeserving" – the greatest transfers of wealth in human history have not been from rich to poor but from parents to children. Historically, economic class was largely inherited.

The novelists' views of socioeconomic relations extended considerably beyond those of the political economists, who refused to acknowledge the arena of unpaid work, including much housework and care of dependants, or widespread but illegitimate work, such as prostitution. The novelists did not have so limited a view of the economy. Even the fiction of greatest psychological depth, like Charlotte Brontë's *Villette* (1853), finds economic relations constitutive of the psyche; the governess or teacher, whether Lucy Snowe, Jane Eyre, or Bradley Headstone, is confined by class as in an iron cage. To marry out of it, for Jane Eyre, is literally the stuff of fantasy. Or, as George Eliot said in *Middlemarch* (1871), "[T]here is no creature whose inward being is so strong that it is not greatly determined by what lies outside it" – the understanding behind historical fiction since Stendhal, Balzac, and Scott's *Waverley* (1814; see Lukács 1962).

III

Yet there were other theories of class than that of political economy, based in material relations. Fictional naturalism (see Auerbach 1953) followed scientific method, Darwinian evolution, or, in extreme form, eugenics, in biologizing class (see George Moore's *A Mummer's Wife* [1885] in particular and Gissing's novels generally, as well as much "new woman" and "aesthetic" fiction). Germanophile Matthew Arnold offered aesthetics or "culture" as a solution to anomie, anarchy, and class conflict. (*Culture and Anarchy* [1869; Arnold 1965] was subtitled *An Essay in Political and Social Criticism*.)

Arnold's fear was that the Enlightenment's individual, progressively regulating herself for the social good (the reasoning agent), was being undermined by economic rationality, the self-interested, self-maximizing individual of competitive market society – at its worst, hedonic consumer society, as people came to fear it in the course of the nineteenth century. Inspired by continental idealist philosophy, Arnold proposed the state "to control individual wills in the name of an interest wider than that of individuals" (Arnold 1965: 117). Because class egoism is as destructive to culture as individual egoism, Arnold develops a "principle" of the relation of the individual and social group to the state in the sections "Doing as One Likes" and "Barbarians, Philistines, and Populace." As the individual's warring passions must be harmonized by the regulating will, so the state's social groups must harmonize according to their "best selves" for the good of the whole. Like many Victorian social critics, Arnold admired the Germans for their commitment to duty, unity, and the state against Anglo-American individualism. Yet because of the rigidities of the British class system, he figures his state as an individual whose different capacities had to be harmonized. Thus a "hard middle class" that tended toward machinery (work and money) and fanaticism ("the one thing needful") needed the complementary aesthetic virtues of the aristocracy – "beautiful" ease, serenity, and politeness and their more "sublime" "high spirits, defiant courage, and pride of resistance" (pp. 125–34). For its part, the aristocracy needed the complement of ideas, lest its serenity degenerate, as it had under current conditions, to futility and sterility. The role of supporters of culture is to "hinder the unchecked predominance of that class-life which is the affirmation of our ordinary self and seasonably disconcert mankind in their worship of machinery" (p. 146).

Given that the problem is selfish individualism across classes, it is ironic that Arnold figures the social body as an individual relying on distinct capacities: the middle class provides muscle, the aristocracy provides external refinement, and the working class emotes. The term "Philistine," representing the self-satisfied pursuit of wealth, "gives the notion of something particularly stiff-necked and perverse in the resistance to light and its children; and therein it specially suits our middle class, who not only do not pursue sweetness and light, but who even prefer to them that sort of machinery of business, chapels, tea-meetings, and addresses from Mr. Murphy, which make up the dismal and illiberal life on which I have so often touched" (p. 140). For their part, the aristocratic Barbarians' culture "was an exterior culture . . . consisting principally in outward gifts and graces, in looks, manners, accomplishments, prowess" (p. 141).

Yet beneath these "divisions" in English society "is a common basis of human nature" (p. 148); and this universalism grounds Arnold's ideas, first, that competing individual interests can be harmonized, and second, that the state can operate like a self-harmonizing individual. Although Arnold himself has "for the most part, broken with the ideas and the tea-meetings of [his] own [middle] class," he feels a common humanity with the aristocracy whenever he hunts and with the working class whenever he acts impulsively, without restraint, or irrationally.

> I never take a gun or fishing-rod in my hands without feeling that I have in the ground of my nature the self-same seeds which, fostered by circumstances, do so much to make the Barbarian . . .
>
> Who, whether he be Barbarian or Philistine, can look at [the working classes] without sympathy, when he remembers how often . . . he has found in his own person

the eternal spirit of the Populace, and that there needs only a little help from circumstances to make it triumph in him untamably. (pp. 144–5)

Just as all classes share some commonality in human nature, each class provides a few who do not conform to its "Ordinary Self" but pursue perfection, "and this number is capable of being diminished or augmented . . . in proportion both to the force of the original instinct within them, and to the hindrance or encouragement which it meets from without" (p. 146).

In *Friendship's Garland* (1866–71), in which Arnold employed Europeans, especially Germans, to criticize British competitive individualism, he also used America to represent the democratic spirit of the age, the *Geist* behind which Britain lagged. The Americans had broken the mind-forged manacles, the iron cage, of class. They showed "a feeling for ideas, a vivacity and play of mind, which our middle class has not, and which comes to the Americans probably from their democratic life with its ardent hope, its forward stride, its gaze fixed on the future" (Arnold 1965: 30). "Arminius," Arnold's European mouthpiece in *Friendship's Garland* (and an ancient Teutonic hero beloved in *Volk* mythology), warns the British that the Americans "have got the lead" in equality and democracy as well as trade: "After 1815, we [Europeans] believed in [Britain] as nowadays we are coming to believe in America . . . unless you change, unless your middle class grows more intelligent, you will tell upon the world less and less, and end by being a second Holland" (p. 27). Yet just three years later, when Arnold wrote the last addition to *Culture and Anarchy*, the preface, he had come to fear democracy as much as selfishness. America's spirit of democracy had degenerated to massification. America now represented "that chosen home of newspapers and politics . . . without a general intelligence," only "partiality of interestedness," not the "totality" of vision that culture now had to stand in for (pp. 243, 252). Having begun in praise of American institutions that had escaped the iron cage of class, Arnold now recoiled from their perceived leveling and lack of distinction.

In the last essay he ever wrote, "Civilisation in the United States" (*Nineteenth Century*, April 1888), Arnold grants that the United States seems to have solved "the political and social problem" of "freedom and equality, power, energy, and wealth" (Arnold 1986: 489). He praises US institutions for being at the forefront of modernity and democracy, particularly in contrast to British class and hierarchy; he praises the United States for providing access to more of the comforts and conveniences of life; he praises them for dispensing with invidious titles like Esquire, whose only function is to distinguish gentlemen from working men; he praises American women for their freedom and self-confidence, which make them a source of pleasure to "almost everyone" (p. 494). But he rejects wealth and wider access to a rising standard of living – that is, he rejects purely economic notions of progress – as the measures of "Civilization":

Do not tell me only, says human nature, of the magnitude of your industry and commerce, of the beneficence of your institutions, your freedom, your equality; of the great

and growing number of your churches and schools, libraries and newspapers; tell me
also if your civilisation – which is the grand name you give to all this development –
tell me if your civilisation is *interesting*. (p. 495)

Arnold proceeds to define the sources of interestingness as distinction and beauty –
"that which is elevated and that which is beautiful" – both qualities which are associated precisely with the kinds of hierarchy and differentiation that the American
pursuit of the greatest happiness of the greatest number had ostensibly compromised.
With its constitutional ethos "glorifying the average man" and its irreverent press,
America to Arnold lacked a sense for distinction, for awe, and for respect. Arnold concludes his last published work with a stark contrast pointing out that America's genius
– its democracy and equality – was also its tragedy. Calling the British malady its
social distinctions, its "upper class materialised, middle class vulgarised, and lower
class brutalised" (pp. 503–4), he concludes that the American "predominance of the
common and ignoble, born of the predominance of the average man," was a malady,
too. Reifying and polarizing British hierarchy and American equality, Arnold rejected
them both in favor of German idealism.

While Marx's and political economy's fictional counterparts were industrial novels,
with their tense class relations rooted in the relations of production, Arnold's satiric
idealism found its counterpart in "silver-fork" fiction and the literature of the
gentleman, rooted in property, taste, and consumption. From the 1820s through the
1840s, silver-fork fiction, or the "fashionable novel," played to status anxiety rather
than class conflict, purportedly telling middle-class aspirants how the aristocracy
behaved while simultaneously providing models of a new, improved bourgeois gentleman (see Disraeli's *Vivian Grey* [1826], Thomas Henry Lister's *Granby* [1826],
Robert Plumer Ward's *Tremaine* [1825], and, the two exempla of the genre, Bulwer-
Lytton's *Pelham* [1828] and [Mrs.] Catherine Gore's *Cecil* [1841]). It is arguable that
the greatest example of status anxiety on the road to gentlemanliness was Pip's in
Great Expectations (1861).

Well trained in satire in the periodicals, Thackeray also provided better models of
the gentleman in *Vanity Fair* (1848), *Pendennis* (1849), and *The Newcomes* (1855), while
he anatomized the myriad "character" types of social distinction in the popular *Punch*
series that became *The Book of Snobs* (1846–7). In Mrs. Craik's (Dinah Mulock's) *John
Halifax, Gentleman* (1856), the epitome of the self-help genre, an endlessly invoked
"natural" gentleman feminizes everyone around him as he enlists his strength in the
protection and solicitude of others: class conflict is solved by unselfish paternalism.
In *John Halifax*, trade does not make the gentleman but the gentleman makes his
trade (Craik 1914: 33), though John's natural "business faculty, without which the
cleverest man alive can never be altogether a great man" (p. 97), and his "natural
propensity for facts and weakness for machinery" (p. 117), contribute their part to his
prosperity. Class divisions melt into air in the face of this chivalric masculinity, as
almost do gender divisions: the male narrator (technically of a higher class than John
Halifax) draws his homoerotic imagery from the biblical story of David and Jonathan

and proclaims his admiration for John "passing the love of women" (p. 161). Silver-fork fiction and the literature of the Gentleman tamed both the Barbarian aristocrat and the Philistine businessman, providing a model of the bourgeois man subordinating his self-interest to duty to family and state (Eliot's and Arnold's respective antidotes to selfish or competitive individualism).

IV

Silver-fork fiction, the literature of the Gentleman, and the great Victorian satires like *Vanity Fair* and *The Book of Snobs* show that money could also have the face of community, shared taste, and companionable likeness. In fact, there was a school of romantic theorists who did not, like Goethe's *Faust*, associate money with the work of the devil, of a diabolical alchemy that produced value out of nothing. These theorists had no interest in metallism, but rather saw money as social glue precisely because its referent was not gold but a social, communicative pact. According to the Germanicist Richard T. Gray, Adam Müller argued against the commonly held notion that paper money was a mere second-order representation of metallic money, and defended paper currencies and credit money against metallism. Indeed, he reverses this relationship, giving priority to the pledged word that makes metal into minted coin:

> Legal tender, in other words, is constituted not by any concrete value, by the worth of the precious metals from which it is made, but by the 'credit,' the faith, belief, and confidence placed in it and in the state that secures its value . . . Money, for Müller, is nothing other than the representative, the symbol, of this natural sociability, this solicitous co-dependence among human beings. (Gray 2000: 298)

This account makes perfect sense of the story that critic Jean-Joseph Goux tells of the abandonment of the gold standard in favor first of paper money, then of checks, then of credit cards. As geopolitical relations developed, the state-supported dollar or pound had become a more plausible repository of confidence than any mere lump of metal. Against Adam Smith's fear that paper currencies threatened to undermine "the commercial and moral fabric of European civilization" (cited in Gray 2000: 299), for these romantic predecessors of Marx and Dickens money could be liberating. Gray cites the German economist Johann Georg Busch's *Treatise on the Circulation of Money* (1780): "Wherever money is employed, no one is tied any longer to particular individuals in order to satisfy his needs from those individuals" (p. 301). Money allows individuals to be both autonomous and social. This is the theory of social mobility that leads to all the dreamers of Gissing's novels, as well as the hope of women, whose aspiration to enter the workforce as independent wage-laborers came in conflict with domestic ideology (see Gissing's *Odd Women* [1893] and *The Year of Jubilee* [1894], Hardy's *Jude the Obscure*, and the "new woman" fiction from the 1880s by Sarah Grand, Olive Schreiner, and George Egerton). Arlene Young (1999) has studied in detail the

socioeconomic aspirations of the so-called lower middle class – in Marxian language
the "petty bourgeoisie" – whose economic development by the second half of the
century began to produce identifiable tastes; indeed, the more English term "lower
middle class" connotes taste and status rather than relations of production.

Gray argues that Müller's theory of money derived from a romantic theory of
interpretive community developed by Novalis and others comparable to "symphi-
losophizing" or "sympoeticizing" as collective intellectual effort and production. It
was not until Major C. H. Douglas's theory of "Social Credit" sought to liberate
citizens from the status of producers into that of consumers by saturating the state
with credit that the community of economic activity reappeared so palpably. By then,
the poet Ezra Pound was confusing this idea of community with fascism (see Tratner
2001).

For Müller, property should not be private, hoarded, but should be a "hypermarket," a nexus of furious and incessant exchange, holding a community together. Müller
objected to classical political economy's reification of economic "facts" to the detriment of social relations, dynamic interdependencies, and reciprocal interactions. Gray
has called Müller's relativism, hyperactivity, and semiotics "postmodern"; but his
"romantic semiotics" refers at its deepest levels to social relations. Similarly, Simmel's
emphasis on urban exchange and consumption has been called postmodern compared
with political economy's emphasis on industrial production. The view developed here
is that distinctions between relative and absolute or essential value, between representation and presence, disappear when money is considered in terms of community
and communication.

Since the nineteenth century, monetary transactions have become disembodied and
dehumanized beyond Simmel's wildest dream of abstraction. The arbitrageur or
investment banker at the computer terminal is far removed from Adam Smith's transactions among the village butcher, baker, and brewer, or Marx's ugly rich man's transactions with prostitutes who make him feel handsome. The crucial point, however, is
that despite this abstraction of the economic transaction, the fundamental nature of
money as a mediator of social relations remains unchanged. Paul Delany cites Bernard
Shaw's *Widowers' Houses* (1892), which greatly influenced E. M. Forster's *Howard's End*
(1910), on how the money increasingly disappeared in the attenuations of rentier
culture throughout the period of modernism, though the social relations remained
just as nasty:

> Social status is proportional to distance from economic reality. At the bottom is . . . the
> despised Mr. Lickcheese . . . who squeezes the money out of the wretched slum-dwellers.
> Next comes Mr. Sartorius, who owns the buildings but never sets foot in them. At the
> top are Dr. Dench and his Aunt Lady Roxdale, who have not even troubled to find out
> where their comfortable private incomes come from. (Delany 2002)

Modernism's distinctions of taste were underwritten, according to Delany, by a powerful network of rentier capitalists. The hidden relations of modernism's rentier capital

may be contrasted with the great philanthropic families of Victorian Britain – the Wilberforces, Thorntons, Stephens, Cadburys, Rowntrees, Frys and Gurneys – and their counterpart in the great Victorian family romances.

In Marx's *Capital*, the secret of commodity fetishism was the hidden labor of the producer that was appropriated as profit by the capitalist. There were always waste and filth and pollution in the factories, but, at bottom, as long as there was a labor theory of value, the main concern from Chadwick to Engels to Dickens to Pater was human waste: the wasted lives of laboring people. The labor theory of value said that the cost of a commodity was the value of the labor power it took to produce it, plus the value of the laborer's wear and tear in the production process, plus the value of the laborer's family's subsistence; or as Marx said, the value of labor power was "the necessaries by means of which the muscles, nerves, bones, and brains of existing laborers are reproduced and new laborers are begotten" (Marx 1967: 572). The very *urban* Dickens who wrote *Our Mutual Friend* discerned in 1864, just as the labor theory was being officially abandoned as a theory of price, that a money economy could replace a productive economy.

After 1871, the literature of productive and reproductive social relations, the essence of high Victorian fiction, was giving way to the literature of consumption, taste, and preference located in the individual, culminating in the modern individual's "stream of consciousness." With the exceptions noted above, for example, in the naturalism of the *fin de siècle*, there was a tendency to move from sociology to psychology. We began this chapter with Adam Smith's *Theory of Moral Sentiments*. As long as economics made reference to sentiments, emotions, feelings of the body, as in the labor theory of value, one could talk of wasted lives. As political economy and then marginalist economics moved further away from sense, feeling, the pleasures and pains of labor or production, it became harder and harder to talk of wasted lives or to see the world from the standpoint or perspective of the worker. Today, when economics is commonly accepted as a branch of mathematics, abstracted from political economic social relations, it is almost impossible to do so. Chapter 1 of *The Theory of Moral Sentiments* is called "Of Sympathy," meaning sympathetic identification with others. That is gone now from economics. In *Middlemarch*, George Eliot used a grain of dust in the eye to represent the self: "will not a tiny speck very close to our vision blot out the glory of the world, and leave only a margin by which we see the blot? I know no speck so troublesome as self." Neoclassical economics, grounded in self-interest, takes no such critical perspective on the self. The self blots out relations with others as "each mind keeps as a solitary prisoner its own dream of a world" (from Walter Pater's *Renaissance* [1873]).

There are, however, a few political economists who, against the grain of contemporary methodological individualism, still tell stories of social relations. In a classic critique of precisely the linearity of progress in which all roads lead to modern mass consumption, *The Modern World System* (1974; 1980), the political economist Immanuel Wallerstein points out the difference between precapitalist xenophobia (hatred or fear of *external* others) and the institutional racism of the global division of labor. In Wallerstein's global economic system, the Anglo-European "core" demanded the surplus, while the nonwhite "periphery" supplied the labor. In what Wallerstein calls the "ethnicization of the world's workforce," "racism was the ideological justification for the hierarchy of the workforce and its highly unequal distribution of reward" (Wallerstein 1984: 78). While racism served to control direct producers, Western universalism – the scientific search for truth (realism) or, in Wallerstein's view, the West's self-interested rationalization – served to direct the bourgeoisies of peripheral states through the exaltation of progress (linear causal narrative). The complicitous notion of "meritocracy" (self-help) preserved the idea that individual mobility was possible without threatening the hierarchical allocation of the workforce. Thus capitalist racism buttressed the global division of labor and unequal distribution of surplus; universalism supplied the idea that there was but one road to progress (e.g. US-style mass consumption); and the ideology of meritocratic individualism allowed for the exception that proved the rule of domination. Wallerstein's is an organic account of the wealth of nations, of the global economy as one system of interdependent parts. For him, a professional Africanist, the West's master narrative of scientific and technological progress, which, with the help of racism, universalism, and meritocratic individualism, provided the siren's song of modernity, also masked the irrationality of endless wasteful accumulation at the Anglo-European core.

The institutional racism of the global division of labor appears in the othering relations of Victorian imperial fiction, including "imperial Gothic" (see Brantlinger 1988). In early Victorian fiction the bourgeois self had been threatened by Gothic images of the working masses (see the literature of crowds, as in *Barnaby Rudge* [1841], *Felix Holt* [1866], and even as late as *The Netherworld* [1889]); by the end of the century the masses might be the conquered populace of the empire. From the India of Wilkie Collins's *Moonstone* (1868) and Kipling's *Kim* (1901) to the West Indies of Charlotte Brontë's *Jane Eyre* (1847), the Arabia of Disraeli's *Tancred* (1847), and the Africa of Haggard and Conrad in the 1890s, fears of contamination from outside became confused with fears of psychological disintegration, "going native," unreason, or, more familiarly today, the unconscious within. The literature of degeneration (*Dr. Jekyll and Mr. Hyde* [1896], or *The Island of Dr. Moreau* [1896], or *Dracula* [1897]) provided the pessimistic image of entropy to contradict the high Victorian optimistic image of progress. What Chinua Achebe has called "the breakup of one petty European mind" (Achebe 1988: 257) came to be one emblem of the literature of the *fin de siècle* or decadence, the literature of sensation and psychology – Conrad's Mr. Kurtz in *Heart of Darkness* (1902), which can be effectively counterposed with the literature of social relations of the midcentury.

REFERENCES

Achebe, Chinua (1988), "An Image of Africa: Racism in Conrad's *Heart of Darkness*," in Joseph Conrad, *Heart of Darkness* (New York: Norton).

Arnold, Matthew (1965), "'Culture and Anarchy' with 'Friendship's Garland' and Some Literary Essays," vol. 5 of *The Complete Prose Works*, ed. Robert H. Super (Ann Arbor: University of Michigan Press).

Arnold, Matthew (1986), "Civilisation in the United States," in Miriam Allott and Robert H. Super, eds., *Matthew Arnold* (Oxford: Oxford University Press).

Auerbach, Erich (1953), "Germinie Lacerteux," in *Mimesis: the Representation of Reality in Western Literature*, trans. Willard Trask (Princeton: Princeton University Press).

Brantlinger, Patrick (1988), *Rule of Darkness: British Literature and Imperialism, 1830–1914* (Ithaca: Cornell University Press).

Brantlinger, Patrick (1996), *Fictions of State: Culture and Credit in Britain, 1694–1994* (Ithaca: Cornell University Press).

Buchan, James (1997), *Frozen Desire: An Inquiry into the Meaning of Money* (London: Picador).

Carlyle, Thomas (1971), *Selected Writings*, ed. Alan Sheston (Harmondsworth: Penguin).

Craik, Mrs [Dinah Mulock] (1914), *John Halifax, Gentleman* (Oxford: Oxford University Press).

Delany, Paul (2002) *Literature, Money and the Market: From Trollope to Amis* (Basingstoke: Palgrave).

Engels, Friedrich (1968), *The Condition of the Working Class in England*, trans. and ed. W. O. Henderson and W. H. Chaloner (Stanford: Stanford University Press). (First publ. 1845.)

Gagnier, Regenia (2000), *The Insatiability of Human Wants: Economics and Aesthetics in Market Society* (Chicago: University of Chicago Press).

Gray, Richard T. (2000), "Hypersign, Hypermoney, Hypermarket: Adam Müller's Theory of Money and Romantic Semiotics," *New Literary History*, 31/2, 295–314.

Lukács, Georg (1962), *The Historical Novel*, trans. Hannah and Stanley Mitchell (London: Merlin).

Marcus, Steven (1974), *Engels, Manchester, and the Working Class* (New York: Random House).

Marx, Karl (1967), *Capital*, vol. I, ed. Friedrich Engels (New York: International Publishers). (First publ. 1867.)

Marx, Karl and Engels, Friedrich (1978), *The Marx-Engels Reader*, 2nd edn., ed. Robert C. Tucker (New York: Norton).

Simmel, Georg (1978), *The Philosophy of Money*, ed. David Frisby, trans. Tom Bottomore (London: Routledge).

Smith, Adam (1984), *The Theory of Moral Sentiments* (Indianapolis: Liberty Fund). (First publ. 1759.)

Tratner, Michael (2001), *Deficits and Desires: Economics and Sexuality in Twentieth-Century Literature* (Stanford: Stanford University Press).

Wallerstein, Immanuel (1974, 1980), *The Modern World System*, 2 vols (New York: Academic).

Wallerstein, Immanuel (1984), *Historical Capitalism* (London: Verso).

FURTHER READING

Armstrong, Nancy (1987), *Desire and Domestic Fiction: A Political History of the Novel* (New York: Oxford University Press).

Bodenheimer, Rosemarie (1988), *The Politics of Story in Victorian Social Fiction* (Ithaca: Cornell University Press).

Childers, Joseph (1994), "Observation and Representation: Mr. Chadwick Writes the Poor," *Victorian Studies*, 37/3, 405–33.

Childers, Joseph (1995), *Novel Possibilities: Fiction and the Formation of Early Victorian Culture* (Philadelphia: University of Pennsylvania Press).

Eagleton, Terry (1975), *Myths of Power: A Marxist Study of the Brontës* (New York: Barnes & Noble; London: Macmillan).

Gagnier, Regenia (1986), "Dandies and Gentlemen," in *Idylls of the Marketplace: Oscar Wilde and the Victorian Public* (Stanford: Stanford University Press).

Gagnier, Regenia (1991), "Representations of the Working Classes by Nonworking-class Writers," in

Subjectivities: A History of Self-Representation in Britain, 1832–1920 (New York: Oxford University Press).

Gallagher, Catherine (1985), *The Industrial Reformation of English Fiction: Social Discourse and Narrative Form, 1832–1867* (Chicago: University of Chicago Press).

Goux, Jean-Joseph (1999), "Cash, Check, or Charge?" in Martha Woodmansee and Mark Osteen, eds., *The New Economic Criticism: Studies at the Intersection of Literature and Economics* (London: Routledge), 114–28.

Jameson, Fredric (1971), *Marxism and Form: Twentieth-Century Dialectical Theories of Literature* (Princeton: Princeton University Press).

Jameson, Fredric (1981), *The Political Unconscious: Narrative as a Socially Symbolic Act* (Ithaca: Cornell University Press).

Watt, Ian (1964), *The Rise of the Novel* (Berkeley: University of California Press). (First publ. 1957.)

Williams, Raymond (1973), *The Country and the City* (New York: Oxford University Press).

Woodmansee, Martha and Osteen, Mark, eds. (1999), *The New Economic Criticism: Studies at the Intersection of Literature and Economics* (London: Routledge).

Young, Arlene (1999), *Culture, Class and Gender in the Victorian Novel: Gentlemen, Gents and Working Women* (Basingstoke: Macmillan).

4

Victorian Psychology

Athena Vrettos

In the opening chapters of Arthur Conan Doyle's first Sherlock Holmes story, *A Study in Scarlet* (1887), Holmes explains to Dr. Watson his theory of mental structure:

> "You see," he explained, "I consider that a man's brain originally is like a little empty attic, and you have to stock it with such furniture as you choose. A fool takes in all the lumber of every sort that he comes across, so that the knowledge which might be useful to him gets crowded out, or at best is jumbled up with a lot of other things, so that he has a difficulty in laying his hands upon it. Now the skilful workman is very careful indeed as to what he takes into his brain-attic. He will have nothing but the tools which may help him in doing his work, but of these he has a large assortment, and all in the most perfect order. It is a mistake to think that that little room has elastic walls and can distend to any extent. Depend upon it there comes a time when for every addition of knowledge you forget something that you knew before." (ch. 2)

In Holmes's theory of finite mental space we can see a number of characteristic assumptions of nineteenth-century psychology – assumptions about how memory works; how mental energy functions in an economy of balance and exchange; how crowded minds can become disorganized and confused; how the mind should be used most efficiently; and how individuals can control, or even construct, the self. At the heart of Holmes's theory is a view of the mind as a system based on finite quantities of mental energy (here conceptualized in terms of space). This assumption, which was widespread in Victorian medical and psychological writings, arose from the application of the second law of thermodynamics – the conservation of energy – to explanations of mental activity. As it was loosely applied to philosophies of mind, the conservation of energy could describe a wide variety of relationships between mental processes that, in turn, shaped the most basic frameworks of consciousness. It could also describe the complex relationship between body and mind. Perhaps most importantly, it helped to shape the predominant emphasis on the material basis of the mind, or what was called "physiological psychology," in Britain in the second half of the nineteenth century. Physiological psychologists emphasized the direct correspondence between mental processes and neural processes, or mind and brain; in addition, they often followed Darwin in their view of the human mind as a product of evolution, subject to physiological principles and inherited structures that governed human behavior.

Holmes's theory is also striking for its competing assumption that the individual has the capacity to control his or her mental composition, and its recommendation of the careful management of mental resources. The "workman" who organizes his mental "attic" into an efficient "toolroom" for the accomplishment of future tasks exemplifies the philosophy of the Victorian self-help movement, which advocated the individual's power to gain control over emotions, ideas, and behavior, and to foster mental development. As Sally Shuttleworth has noted, the overlap between Victorian psychology and the ideology of the self-help movement helps explain the presence of conflicting psychological models in the nineteenth century, one emphasizing the individual as "a powerless material organism, caught within the operations of a wider field of force," the other emphasizing the individual as "an autonomous unit with powers of self-control" (1996: 28). In effect, we see both of these models in Holmes's brain-attic. While he conceptualizes the finite nature of mental space and the automatic forces responsible for jettisoning mental clutter, he simultaneously emphasizes the power of the disciplined individual to intervene in this process through the efficient organization of knowledge.

Sherlock Holmes is not the only character in Victorian fiction to discuss psychology. Numerous Victorian authors speculated about the workings of the mind through their characters, offering a range of metaphors for mental processes and portrayals of mental experience that drew upon and at times influenced psychological discourses of the period. Novelists such as Charlotte Brontë, George Eliot, Thomas Hardy, and Henry James are particularly notable for their interest in creating psychologically complex characters and intricate social relationships as components of their realism, but writers in other genres also contributed to popular understandings and theories of the mind. Sensation novelists such as Wilkie Collins, Mary Elizabeth Braddon, and Charles Reade explored prevailing theories of insanity, provoking debates about what constituted madness and raising the specter of false incarceration of the sane. Robert Louis Stevenson's *The Strange Case of Dr. Jekyll and Mr. Hyde* (1886) explored multiple personality at about the same time as psychologists were recording early case studies of this phenomenon. Capitalizing upon longstanding popular interest in mesmerism, and scientific debates about its causes, limitations, applications, and effects, George du Maurier's *Trilby* (1894) placed an evil mesmerist and his suggestible female subject at the center of its plot. Bram Stoker used this same psychological phenomenon to delineate and combat vampirism in *Dracula* (1897). Indeed, almost anywhere we look in Victorian fiction, we can see the influence of and interest in psychology, ranging from explicit engagements with contemporary philosophies of mind, to theories of character development that echoed popular self-help and advice manuals of the day, to fictional experiments with the more speculative branches of

Victorian science and pseudoscience – physiognomy, phrenology, and, later in the century, psychical research into telepathy, trances, ancestral memory, and other mysteries of the mind.

The term "Victorian psychology" is potentially misleading, however, insofar as psychology in the nineteenth century was not a coherent discipline, but rather a collection of works by writers who drew upon philosophy, social theory, evolutionary theory, physiology, neurology, alienism, and psychiatry. These writers also drew upon creative literature for insight into human behavior, motivation, and psychological development, and for examples or case studies of insanity and other abnormal mental conditions. When the psychiatrist Sir James Crichton Browne addressed the West London Medical-Chirurgical Society in 1895, he began his lecture on "Dreamy Mental States" not with his own case studies, but rather with a lengthy series of psychological examples from "many of our most eminent writers" in British fiction and poetry. He cited passages from Charles Dickens, Thomas Hardy, Sir Walter Scott, Coventry Patmore, Dante Gabriel Rossetti, Alfred Tennyson, William Wordsworth, and Samuel Taylor Coleridge (Crichton-Browne 1895: 1). William James similarly used examples from the writings of Dickens, George Eliot, and Jane Austen to discuss the association of ideas and the psychology of habit, and Darwin cited incidents from *Oliver Twist* and Elizabeth Gaskell's and Margaret Oliphant's novels to illustrate the role of heredity and habit in the expression of emotion (James 1959: 538–9; Darwin 1872: 241, 150, 80, 270). By drawing upon fictional and poetic examples, nineteenth-century psychologists paid tribute to the contributions of literature in the study of human psychology. They simultaneously blurred the boundaries between disciplines, borrowing from a variety of sources to chart out their intellectual and methodological terrain.

Although psychology began to emerge as a scientific discipline only in the late Victorian period, it was already divided into two fairly distinct fields of expertise and objects of study that had gradually gained influence throughout the century. The term "psychology" came out of the tradition of "introspective psychology," or mental philosophy based on self-observation. The study of insanity and other forms of abnormal psychology, or mental pathology, came under the rubric of alienism, which was considered a separate field for most of the century. However, these two branches of study overlapped in significant ways. Both fields confronted concepts such as selfhood, individual and social identity, the relationship between consciousness and the unconscious, and the rational boundaries of the human mind.

Psychological debates on these questions, in turn, filtered into popular understandings of human behavior through articles in popular journals and periodicals. For example, there were numerous articles on insanity that would have been available to nonspecialist Victorian readers. Dickens's *Household Words* reported frequently on the lunacy reform movement, and in 1852 Dickens recounted his own visit to St. Luke's Hospital for the insane poor. Articles discussing the definition, classification, and treatment of insanity also appeared in *Household Words* and other popular Victorian journals and periodicals. These widespread social debates about psychological subjects linked not only Victorian fiction and psychology, but also medicine, political economy, social policy, and the law.

Associationism, Physiological Psychology, and Victorian Realism

Although there were many strains of psychological discourse and debate throughout the nineteenth century, the predominant focus of British psychology was on the physiological basis of mind. Drawing upon the philosophy of John Locke and on the associationist psychology of David Hartley in the eighteenth century and of James Mill and John Stuart Mill in the early to mid-nineteenth century, physiological psychologists such as Alexander Bain, Herbert Spencer, William Carpenter, George Henry Lewes, Henry Maudsley, James Sully, and G. F. Stout, among others, sought to establish a scientific psychology that was comparable to the natural sciences and that emphasized parallels between body and mind.

Associationism was the philosophical model that structured the premises of most physiological psychology, and it was the most widely accepted account of how the mind functioned, not only among philosophers and psychologists, but also in the wider intellectual community of nineteenth-century Britain. It was taught in schools and universities, and it appeared in textbooks and encyclopedias. Furthermore, its account of how the mind worked reached wider middle- and working-class audiences through discussions of the formation of habits and reformation of character in popular Victorian self-help and advice manuals such as Sarah Stickney Ellis's *The Women of England* (1838) and Samuel Smiles's *Self-Help* (1859).

Associationist psychology, in its most basic form, held that the mind worked through the association of ideas, combining simple ideas in increasingly intricate ways to form complex ideas. Beginning as a blank slate, or tabula rasa, the mind received sensations, conceived ideas of sensations, and eventually associated those ideas on the basis of resemblance, contiguity, and causation. That is, ideas and events that resembled each other, that were contiguous with each other in time and space, or that seemed linked through cause and effect, became associated with each other in the mind. This process took place through the neurological mechanisms of the brain, though these mechanisms were defined differently with each successive generation of philosophers and psychologists. In the eighteenth century Hartley envisioned "neural vibrations;" in the early nineteenth century James Mill emphasized "mental chemistry;" and in the second half of the nineteenth century Bain and Lewes conceptualized such mechanisms as neural "pathways," "channels," "tracks," or "currents."

With the rising scientific emphasis on heredity in the second half of the century, physiological psychologists eventually merged associationist philosophy with theories of inheritance and evolution. Spencer's *Principles of Psychology* (1855) and Bain's *The Senses and the Intellect* (1855) and *The Emotions and the Will* (1859), along with the founding of *Mind* (the first British journal of psychology), were probably the most significant British contributions to physiological psychology in this period. Bain and

Spencer were among the first to apply Darwin's teachings to psychological issues. Spencer's work in particular combined associationist philosophy and evolutionary theory in an attempt to chart how the human mind continuously adjusted internal relations to external forces, thereby formulating a complex developmental model. Thus, by the late nineteenth century, associationists had ceased to subscribe to Locke's conceptualization of the mind as a tabula rasa; rather, associationism was linked to more deterministic theories to account for both the inheritance of internal structures and the subsequent development of human character, thought, and habits of behavior through the individual's interactions with his or her environment.

This developmental emphasis on the interaction between inherited characteristics of mind and social and environmental contexts particularly appealed to Victorian realists, in part because it offered an intricate model for portraying the psychological growth of characters and the social structures in which they moved. Psychology thus played a substantial role in the development of nineteenth-century literary realism – sometimes referred to as "psychological realism" – especially as two of the period's most prominent writers, George Eliot and Henry James, were particularly well versed in nineteenth-century psychology through their friendships and familial connections. Eliot's intellectual circle included both Darwin and Spencer, and she lived with George Henry Lewes, whose *Problems of Life and Mind* (1879) made important contributions to the field of physiological psychology. Many of Eliot's writings demonstrate the same psychological principles as we find in Lewes's work, and critics such as Gillian Beer and Nancy Paxton have shown how Eliot's fiction offered an ongoing dialogue with the work of Darwin and Spencer. To take just one example, we can see Eliot and Lewes delineating some of the same ideas about the formation of sympathy. When Lewes writes that we "see in many highly wrought natures . . . an habitual outrush of the emotional force in sympathetic channels" (1879: 387), he articulates the same psychological principle upon which Eliot draws to delineate Dorothea Brooke's highly wrought nature and her repeated attempts to make sympathetic connections with those around her in *Middlemarch*. This is, furthermore, the same principle that informs Eliot's narrative voice in her attempts to create habits of sympathetic identification in the reader. Eliot frequently frames her own psychological observations in the language of physiological psychology, as when, in *Adam Bede*, she delineates the problem of griefs that endure too long: "Our sorrow lives in us as an indestructible force, only changing its form, as forces do, and passing from pain into sympathy . . . we get accustomed to mental as well as bodily pain, without for all that, losing our sensibility to it. It becomes a habit of our lives" (ch. 50). Here Eliot describes emotion and its capacity for transfiguration in the language of physics – as a form of energy subject to exchange, but not eradication, in a larger mental economy. So enduring are the "forces" of mental activity that even pain can become habit-forming, shaping the terms of individual perception. To feel something intensely is to alter for ever one's mental structures – to reconfigure the categories through which all subsequent thoughts and emotions are produced. Each new experience remaps the contours of one's mental landscape. This emphasis on the adjustment of internal structures to external events exemplifies the central developmental precept of physiological psychology.

Henry James was similarly invested in Victorian psychology and interested in theories of mental structure and development. His brother William James, a professor of psychology at Harvard, was one of the most influential psychologists of the nineteenth century. Henry James's fiction routinely explores the complexity and nuances of social interactions, as well as the tangled desires and fears, habits and impulses that construct human character and motivate human behavior. James delineates his characters so as to give the impression of psychological layers that are only obscurely suggested to the reader, layers that seem to inform patterns of thought and action (or more often, in James, inaction). Thus, in describing Isabel Archer, James informs us that "the depths of this young lady's nature were a very out-of-the-way place, between which and the surface communication was interrupted by a dozen capricious forces" (*Portrait of a Lady*, ch. 4). This description of mental space, with its emphasis on "surface" and "depths," and the "forces" that help to structure them, corresponds to emerging theories about subconscious mental forces with which William James's psychological writings began to grapple at about this time.

Childhood Development and Character Formation

Nineteenth-century theories of childhood development also grew out of associationist philosophy, and they followed a similar historical and intellectual trajectory toward more deterministic and evolutionary accounts of human development. Drawing upon the philosophical writings of John Locke and Jean Jacques Rousseau, nineteenth-century psychologists emphasized the influence of environment, experience, and training in childhood development. Associationist philosophy was built on the theory, drawn from Locke, that experiences and habits acquired in childhood had a formative role on character, as well as on the structure and functioning of the adult mind. Writers of advice literature popularized this theory, placing tremendous emphasis on the proper moral training and management of children, and the careful development of their character, habits, and powers of reasoning. Middle-class parents increasingly had recourse to the numerous parenting manuals published in the nineteenth century for information about childhood development. While offering a range of specific (and sometimes idiosyncratic) advice about child-rearing, these manuals continued to embrace Locke's central argument that early training in habits of self-discipline was crucial to a child's development. They thus reinforced and popularized the notion that children's minds were shaped by their environment, both morally and physiologically.

Victorian views of childhood development were further influenced by utilitarianism through the philosophical writings of Jeremy Bentham and James Mill. Bentham and Mill and their followers emphasized the primacy of reason in children's mental development and advocated a rigorous educational curriculum, focused on subjects such as natural science, mathematics, political economy, and philosophy, to foster the development of the reasoning faculties. This utilitarian educational philosophy was parodied most famously by Charles Dickens in his portrayal in *Hard Times* (1854) of the Fact-bound schoolroom of Thomas Gradgrind as an educational "murder of the innocents."

While most developmental theories emphasized the receptivity and plasticity of the youthful mind, nineteenth-century psychologists also emphasized the ways in which early environment, experience, and training actually structured neural pathways, thereby determining subsequent patterns of thought and means of responding to the world. Although the Victorian self-help movement was predicated on the assumption that an individual could, through education and diligence, reform bad habits, reshape character flaws, and pursue self-improvement at any time of life, many psychologists argued that habits formed in childhood were particularly intractable, and could thereafter be reformed only temporarily or superficially, if at all. They became, in effect, the foundation of character. William James argued that "Habit . . . dooms us all to fight out the battle of life upon the lines of our nurture or early choice," and that "by the age of thirty the character has set like plaster, and will never soften again" (1984: 132–3).

These competing assumptions about mental flexibility and rigidity – about the capacity for self-control and self-improvement versus the determining role of mental physiology – became increasingly strained in the latter decades of the nineteenth century. As they debated the plasticity of the mind and the shaping force of habit, psychologists confronted questions about free will that were usually the province of literature, philosophy, and religion. It is not surprising, then, that we find many of the same questions about the psychology of habit raised in nineteenth-century fiction, debated in religious and philosophical journals, and employed in popular theories of character development. In the eccentric characters that pervade Dickens's novels, for example, we see Dickens employing contemporary theories of habit as a means of registering individuality. For Dickens, verbal, gestural, and sartorial tics form the very basis of characterization. In Matthew Pocket's unnerving habit of lifting himself up by the hair, Mr. Jaggers' obsessive washing of his hands, Mrs. Snagsby's chronic curiosity, and Uriah Heep's unctuous handwringing, Dickens delineates character through identifying habits of body and mind. At the same time, Dickens raises questions similar to those that concerned psychologists, philosophers, and religious writers, about both the stability of identity and the capacity for human change.

The possibility of self-determination and the limits of human growth and change became increasingly pressing issues in the late nineteenth century as evolutionary biology influenced accounts of psychological development and reinforced deterministic arguments about the mind. In the decades after Darwin's *The Descent of Man* (1871) and *The Expression of Emotion in Man and Animals* (1872), theories of child psychology increasingly emphasized the role of heredity and instinct. In these accounts, the mind was not a blank slate; rather, as William Preyer argued, it had already been written upon "before birth, with many illegible, nay unrecognizable and invisible marks, the traces of long-gone generations" (quoted in Steedman 1995: 85). Psychologists at this

time compared the emergence of instinctual behavior in children to the same process
in animals, and argued that the primitive psychological development of children
paralleled that of "savage races." Following evolutionary biologists, who argued that
in the development of all living organisms the individual organism repeats the
evolutionary stages of its genus – a theory also known as "ontogeny recapitulates
phylogeny" – psychologists such as Sully held that the psychological development
of the individual recapitulated the evolutionary development of the human species.
Recapitulation theories of child psychology fostered a view of children as primitive,
instinctual, and wild (and a corresponding view of "primitive" peoples as childlike).
Both were susceptible to, and in need of, civilizing influences. In this way, the application of evolutionary biology to theories of childhood development, while offering a
more deterministic model of the mind than earlier associationism, did not undercut
popular Victorian beliefs about the capacity for change and the need for children to
develop rational faculties and habits of self-control. Instead, child-rearing became a
matter of taming children's animal instincts, and re-inscribing on the developing
mind of the child the process and progress of civilization.

Representations of childhood in the Victorian novel did not always correspond to
the prevailing psychological theories of the day, and they were often infused with an
acute sentimentality that is largely absent from the psychological writings. Nevertheless, Victorian novelists subscribed to the predominant associationist accounts of
childhood, as we see most clearly in the popularity of the bildungsroman, or novel
of development (see chapter 16 by John Maynard in this volume). In these novels,
Victorian writers provided complex renderings of the emotional life and psychological development of children by tracing the growth of their characters from childhood
into adulthood. The protagonists of *David Copperfield*, *Great Expectations*, *Jane Eyre*,
Wuthering Heights, *The Mill on the Floss*, and numerous other Victorian novels, offer
compelling accounts of the relationship between past and present, and the emotional
intensity of childhood affections, resentments, desires, and fears. In Jane Eyre's angry
rebellion against her uncaring relatives, and the psychological terror of her punishment; in David Copperfield's romantic love for his mother and jealous hatred of his
sadistic stepfather; in Pip's excruciating self-consciousness about class inferiority; in
Maggie Tulliver's rebellions against Victorian gender codes and ineradicable affection
for her judgmental brother Tom, Brontë, Dickens and Eliot render accounts of childhood that are notable for their emphasis on emotional intensity and psychological
pain. In all of these instances, the powerful feelings and experiences of childhood shape
the adult character. Furthermore, the haunting power of memory (whether traumatic
or pleasurable) provides the link between childhood and adulthood. Memory formed
the basis for constructing "personal identity" – the feeling that "I am the same self
that I was yesterday" (James 1959: 332). While this continuity of the self was not,
James argued, a "metaphysical or absolute Unity," it was a fundamental psychological component of an individual's perceptual reality. It was this perceptual "reality"
that many nineteenth-century novels of childhood explored. Carolyn Steedman has
argued that in the nineteenth century the figure of the child and the memory of the

past that childhood embodied came to represent the interiority of the human psyche – the core of identity. Searching for the self in a lost past, writers located in childhood the modern concept of a self (1995: 4). By tracing the direct effects of childhood experiences on the formation of adult character, exploring the temporal continuity between different versions of the self, and probing the role of memory in the construction of consciousness and interiority, Victorian writers both participated in and contributed to this psychology of childhood.

Alienism, Insanity, and the Victorian Asylum

While nineteenth-century parenting manuals were instructing parents in the careful moral management of their children, and self-help manuals were encouraging their middle- and working-class readers to reform their characters through habits of self-discipline, Victorian alienists were increasingly using the same techniques to treat their lunatic patients. Michel Foucault and many revisionist historians of psychiatry following him have argued that the introduction of "moral treatment" of the insane in the late eighteenth and nineteenth centuries constituted a crucial epistemological shift in Western conceptualizations of madness. For Foucault, this involved a transition from external forms of discipline – the public spectacle of the chained madmen and madwomen of Bedlam – to the internal policing of the insane through the moral management of their behavior. The discourse of moral therapy, with its emphasis on surveillance of the insane and the internalization of this regulating "gaze," thus led to new techniques of social control (Foucault 1973). Though moral management of the insane was first introduced by William Tuke in 1792, it was not until the first half of the nineteenth century that it became the dominant model for treatment in state asylums in Britain. While the term could refer to a number of related forms of treatment, in effect, moral therapy consisted of the attempt to modify the behavior of the insane according to proper codes of conduct drawn from the middle-class home. It attempted to promote mental stability through prescriptive moral training and the promotion of self-regulation.

Like Foucault's, most nineteenth-century accounts of the social and medical treatment of mental illness emphasized (and mythologized) the striking contrast between eighteenth-century methods of incarceration and the rise at the turn of the century of a new system for treating the insane. Nineteenth-century commentators used this contrast primarily to celebrate the humanitarian progress embodied in the shift from the cruelty and neglect of eighteenth-century madhouses to the benevolence and concern of nineteenth-century asylums, which relied on more nuanced diagnoses, humane therapies, and reformed architectural accommodations for the insane. However, despite the power of this narrative, undercurrents of social anxiety challenged the effectiveness of moral therapy and the increasingly ambiguous ways in which insanity came to be defined. These concerns arose in response to new psychiatric theories that emphasized the permeable boundaries between sanity and insanity;

they also derived from new emphases on evolution, heredity, the power of the unconscious, and mental fragmentation or compartmentalization. As the boundaries between mental states appeared increasingly fragile, they seemed to heighten the potential for both inaccurate diagnosis and the abuse of incarcerative authority by Victorian alienists and private asylum keepers.

Popular understandings of insanity were reshaped in particular by two new diagnostic categories introduced in the first half of the nineteenth century: "monomania" and "moral insanity." "Monomania," a term introduced by the French psychiatrist Etienne Esquirol, denoted a condition in which a break in the psyche – a separation of the faculties of emotion, reason, and will – produced a singular fixation, or aberration, within a mind that was otherwise rational. Monomania posited a form of partial insanity in which the afflicted subject could appear to be entirely normal and sane in all areas of behavior except one. It thereby blurred the distinction between sanity and insanity, making it possible for one to appear sane to all observers and yet harbor the capacity for irrational behavior. There are numerous instances of monomania (both explicit and implicit) in Victorian fiction, and fictional monomaniacs ranged in their behavior from mild eccentricity to murderous violence. Anthony Trollope's *He Knew He Was Right* (1869) offers a striking portrait of a husband's pathological jealousy as mental fixation, constituting one of the most extended explorations of monomania in Victorian fiction. The term "monomania" made further appearances in novels ranging from Brontë's *Villette* (1853) to Braddon's *Lady Audley's Secret* (1862). Lady Audley repeatedly charges her nemesis, Robert Audley, of monomania because of his obsession with the disappearance of his best friend, thereby demonstrating how, by midcentury, monomania had come to signify, in common parlance, any form of mental fixation or repetition. Brontë's narrator Lucy Snowe uses the term in a similar manner in *Villette*, describing the six-year-old Paulina Home's obsessive devotion to and pining for her father as "betraying that monomaniac tendency I have ever thought the most unfortunate with which man or woman can be cursed" (ch. 2).

Monomania was also associated with isolated and inexplicable fantasies and acts of violence, particularly in courtroom psychiatric testimony. Simon During has discussed the role that monomania plays in both *Middlemarch* and *Daniel Deronda* (1876), emphasizing not only the strangely sensational eruptions of murder and murderous fantasies in the works of Britain's premier realist, but also the conceptual link that monomania posits (and Eliot enacts) between narrative disruption and psychic disruption. Eliot delineates the complexity of the human psyche by exploring actions and impulses that defy rational explanation. In this way, she offers "new conceptions of how individuals are known" (During 1988: 96).

In contrast to monomania, "moral insanity," a concept introduced in 1835 by James Cowle Prichard, described "a morbid perversion of the natural feelings, affections, inclinations, temper, habits, moral dispositions, and natural impulses, without any remarkable disorder or defect of the intellect or knowing and reasoning faculties, and particularly without any insane illusion or hallucination" (Prichard 1973: 16). Moral insanity was not an isolated fixation or break in an otherwise unified psyche, but rather a systematic "perversion" of the subject's moral character or temperament. As in monomania, the intellect and rational powers of mind remained intact, and thus both monomania and moral insanity conceptualized the mind as potentially fragmented, with certain parts that were diseased or dysfunctional and other parts that functioned according to normal, or rational, standards of behavior. Sally Shuttleworth has suggested that Miss Flite in *Bleak House* (1853) offers a good example of moral insanity in Victorian fiction (1996: 14). The diminutive madwoman, who hovers about Chancery Court waiting for the "day of judgment" to release her birds, and whose mind has been shattered by her interminable lawsuit, is nevertheless sane enough to escort Esther Summerson around London and to instruct Caddy Jellyby in domestic management. Ultimately, in both of these new diagnostic categories "[t]he border to be policed was not so much between self and other, as between the conscious and unconscious self" (Shuttleworth 1996: 35). In this way, psychiatric concepts of partial insanity came to be understood as patterns of mental behavior that almost any individual had the potential to experience. Concepts such as monomania and moral insanity thus charted the irrational capacities of rational minds.

In addition to new definitions of partial insanity, an increased emphasis on the hereditary basis of mental illness characterized nineteenth-century psychology, and in figures such as Lady Audley and Bertha Mason, the madwoman in the attic of *Jane Eyre* (1847), we find explanations of insanity that emphasize the force of heredity. Bertha comes "of a mad family; – idiots and maniacs through three generations. Her mother, the Creole, was both a mad woman and a drunkard" (ch. 26), and Lady Audley spends her life convinced that she is destined to inherit her mother's postpartum madness. In both instances, hereditary madness specifically passes from mother to daughter. While male lunatics were just as likely to be linked to hereditary forms of insanity, the larger number of women diagnosed with mental disorders in the nineteenth century seemed to indicate a specifically female propensity for madness. Elaine Showalter has claimed that madness came to be understood as a "female malady" in Victorian culture, allied with hysteria, and viewed as a product of women's greater tendency towards emotional excess and irrational behavior and thought. Similarly, members of "foreign" races and cultures often were associated with mental fragility and an increased hereditary tendency towards madness. The figure of Bertha Mason, with her Creole heritage, thus emblematizes the conjunction of Victorian theories of race, gender, heredity, and madness – a conjunction that Jean Rhys explores in her twentieth-century rewriting of Brontë's novel from the madwoman's perspective, *Wide Sargasso Sea*.

If madness was linked increasingly to heredity in the second half of the nineteenth century, it also was understood in terms of evolutionary theory and late Victorian theories of degeneration. Degeneration theory proposed that the human species was suffering from an intellectual, physical, and moral decline, and becoming increasingly enfeebled through everything from syphilis, insanity, epilepsy, feminism, radicalism, crime, and immigration to the stresses of modern civilization. In charting this steady decline toward racial suicide, degeneration both influenced and was influenced by a number of different branches of scientific and psychological theory, including social Darwinism and the eugenics movement. Degeneration was also linked to theories of atavism – the psychological reversion of an individual to more primitive human ancestry (see chapter 21 by Patrick Brantlinger in this volume). We can see this in Joseph Conrad's 1899 *Heart of Darkness*, through the atavistic descent of the imperialist Kurtz into savagery and madness in the African jungle. Evolutionary theory, degeneration, and madness were similarly linked in *Dracula* through the figure of the lunatic Renfield, who attempts to reproduce the trajectory of evolution by subsuming increasingly higher life forms and ultimately to link himself with the vampire, who feeds on human blood. But in Stoker's double twist of Darwinian logic, Dracula can be seen as either a degenerative, criminal throwback, or a terrifying specter of evolutionary superiority, enacting survival of the fittest by feeding upon British citizenry. In these and other late Victorian fictions of madness, the figure of the lunatic, like the vampire, came to represent the potential eruption of irrational forces in the human psyche – the "other" underlying the self. The lunatic thus became, for both nineteenth-century fiction and psychology, an emblem of the evolutionary past and its lurking presence in the human mind.

Mesmerism and Hypnotism

If the hereditary lunatic was afflicted by the "other" within, the mesmeric subject was seemingly possessed by another's will. Mesmerism raised parallel questions about the structure of the human psyche, but here the emphasis was on the power of one person to influence the body and mind of another. One of the most sensational Victorian fads, mesmerism reached its peak of popularity between the 1830s and 1860s, with a further revival of interest at the *fin de siècle*. It was widely practiced in the form of mesmeric experiments or séances and public lectures on the causes and effects of mesmeric trances, their curative powers, and their social implications.

"Animal magnetism," as it was first termed, had been introduced more than half a century earlier by Franz Anton Mesmer, a Viennese physician who speculated that a powerful magnetic fluid connected heavenly and animate bodies. Mesmer claimed he could manipulate this fluid in order to alleviate human suffering. The word "mesmerism" was adopted soon after as a derisory term to discredit Mesmer's theory and claims. But while the legitimacy of mesmerism was a subject of scientific and popular debate, the phenomenon itself captured the public imagination and spawned a remarkable number of practitioners and subjects. Associated, paradoxically, with both romantic mysticism and scientific rationalism, it gained numerous followers and subjects from the ranks of British writers, including Matthew Arnold, Charlotte Brontë, Elizabeth Barrett Browning and Robert Browning, Wilkie Collins, George Eliot, William Makepeace Thackeray, and Anthony Trollope. Another follower, Herbert Spencer, wrote articles for mesmeric journals, and both Charles Dickens and Harriet Martineau became adept practitioners of mesmerism, frequently putting their literary and non-literary friends into trances. Dickens even played Mesmer in an 1859 production of Elizabeth Inchbald's drama *Animal Magnetism* (Winter 1998: 404).

As a scientific phenomenon, mesmerism held a precarious status throughout the century, embraced by a number of prestigious medical practitioners, but eventually shut out from the scientific mainstream in Britain because it did not seem sufficiently scientific for disciplines that were newly establishing their authority and legitimacy. Nevertheless, mesmerism received considerable attention from the medical and scientific communities, and made frequent appearances in the wider intellectual and philosophical debates of the era. It raised crucial questions about free will, the connection between mind and body, the presence of invisible forces in nature, the relationship between consciousness and the unconscious, the power of human influence and suggestibility, the permeability of mental boundaries, and the reliability of memory. The curative potential of mesmerism was also the subject of fierce contention. Hoping to harness mesmeric phenomena in the service of medicine, the surgeon James Braid developed the practice of "hypnotism" in 1842. Braid claimed that the mesmeric, or hypnotic, trance was a product of human imagination and attention, rather than magnetic or electric fluids, and involved a voluntary suspension of the will. Although hypnotism, as either a diagnostic or a curative practice, continued to be viewed with considerable medical skepticism in Britain, by the early twentieth century Braid's term "hypnotism" had largely superseded "mesmerism," particularly in medical parlance. Furthermore, questions about suggestibility, imagination, and attention that marked Braid's reframing of the debate gained widespread currency in nineteenth-century psychological writings, even though the practice of hypnotism itself remained medically marginalized in England.

Mesmerism was also associated, as Alison Winter has noted, with disparities in social and sexual power. This was because, despite the tremendous variety in mesmeric practices and their proponents, mesmeric practitioners were most often of a different class and gender from their subjects. Fictional representations of mesmerism and hypnotism in the nineteenth century often emphasize these disparities of gender and class, as we see in both *Dracula* and *Trilby* — two of the most sustained literary explorations of hypnotism, and two of the most popular novels of the 1890s. In both works, mesmeric power is associated with male sexual authority and demonic force of will, and extends beyond the relationship between two individuals to delineate psychological power over wider populations. Stoker's novel is notable for investing both the vampire and its enemies with the tools of mesmeric authority; indeed, we can see the changing history and cultural associations of mesmerism and hypnotism re-enacted in the novel. Dracula's single-handed ability to overpower the will of others, his quite literal "animal magnetism" in commanding the animal world and transforming himself into bats and wolves, his mysteriously piercing eyes and the swirling confusion they produce in his subjects, all invoke the theatrical displays of popular mesmeric practitioners in the early decades of the century. Conversely, Dr. Van Helsing's careful medical deployment of hypnosis on one of Dracula's female victims, her participation as a voluntary subject, and his emphasis on the power of the unconscious mind in combating forces beyond human understanding, emphasize many of the popular associations of medical hypnotism after Braid. If Dracula threatens to unleash his powers on entire populations, envisioning an army of vampires asserting their will upon a supine populace, Van Helsing seeks to correct this threat by reframing hypnotism as an individual relationship between doctor and patient. The overwhelming popularity of both *Dracula* and *Trilby* suggests the powerful hold of mesmerism on the popular imagination, and of the questions it raised about sexual, racial, and class authority, psychological influence, and collective experience, nearly a century after animal magnetism was first introduced.

Physiognomy, Phrenology, and the Divided Mind

Like mesmerism, both physiognomy and phrenology were scientific, or pseudoscientific, theories introduced at the end of the eighteenth century that reached their height of popularity in the early Victorian period. Both physiognomy and phrenology were objects of scientific skepticism (and eventually refutation), and each had considerable influence on nineteenth-century fiction. Although different in substance, they shared the premise that external features of the body corresponded to internal features of the mind, soul, or character.

Physiognomy was introduced by John Caspar Lavater, who proposed that an individual's inner moral qualities were directly embodied in the features of the face, and that God had inscribed this relationship between body and spirit on the face of nature, available for the trained eye to read. Physiognomy proposed that knowledge of humankind could be gained through the senses, and particularly through careful visual observation of physical details. We can see traces of this theory – at least in its assumption that humankind is knowable through details of external form – later in the nineteenth century in fields such as evolutionary biology, medical psychiatry, and anthropometry. Physiognomy also appears in physical descriptions and analyses of fictional characters. In Charlotte Brontë's fiction, physiognomy provides an intratextual model for close reading. Jane Eyre's relationships with both Edward Rochester and St. John Rivers involve reciprocal readings of facial features and inner character, and Brontë establishes parallels between M. Paul's precise physiognomical analyses of Lucy Snowe's face and Lucy's own detailed visual and narrative penetrations of other characters in *Villette*. Lucy's intense and penetrating scrutiny becomes the model for the readerly scrutiny of Lucy's character that Brontë both encourages and demands. In this way, physiognomy becomes one of Brontë's structuring principles – a means of translating new psychological conceptions of selfhood into the realm of literary art.

Phrenology was introduced in the 1790s by the Viennese philosopher and scientist Franz Joseph Gall, but rather than focusing on external features of the face, it charted the propensities of human character through careful study of the shape of the cranium. Phrenology constituted one of the first attempts to identify the brain as the organ of the mind and to determine cerebral localization. Although phrenological charts of the skull, which were divided into over thirty propensities, senti-ments, and intellectual faculties, eventually were undermined by the failure of par-ticular parts of the brain to correspond to particular personality types or behavioral disorders, the theory of phrenology encouraged important research on cerebral localization. Unlike physiognomy, phrenology was a fundamentally materialist and secularist theory. It proposed that bumps on the cranium were part of a system of external signs that could provide information about individual character and the internal workings of the mind. Phrenology emphasized the mind's contradictions and competing energies, a view that was increasingly embraced by nineteenth-century physiologists and psychologists, and that furthered theories of the unconscious later in the century. Associated in the first half of the century with liberal ideology and secularism, phrenology appealed to a range of intellectuals, including Spencer, Lewes, and Eliot. Though many early adherents lost faith in the system as its exaggerated claims to reveal character fell into scientific disrepute, phrenology gained new groups of believers in the second half of the nineteenth century, as it became popularly associated with spiritualism and theosophical societies, spawning hybrid practices such as "phreno-mesmerism."

Many nineteenth-century novels contain passing references to "reading character" through the shape of another's skull or forehead, as well as assessments of personality that draw upon the phrenological "organs." Such details seem, on the one hand, to offer reassurance of the body's legibility as a system of signs; on the other hand, they reflect phrenology's emphasis on the competing and often contradictory forces gov-erning human character, and thus make such knowledge appear tantalizingly incom-plete. When, in *Villette*, Lucy Snowe describes Rosine as "a young lady in whose skull the organs of reverence and reserve were not largely developed" and studies Mme. Beck's "high and narrow" forehead, finding that "it expressed capacity and some benevolence, but no expanse," she invokes phrenological categories to interpret and predict human behavior (ch. 30; ch. 8). Both phrenology and physiognomy invite us to read internal character from external signs, but Brontë ultimately views the self as divided, contradictory, and subject to competing forces. That is, we are not offered certain knowledge of a character's essential nature, as Lavater's physiognomy proposed; rather, Brontë uses phrenology to reveal the complex relationships among different components of the human mind.

Ultimately, this emphasis on what Gall called "the double man within you" (1835: vol. 2, 43) helped to establish the groundwork for materialist and pluralistic concep-tions of the mind that informed later Victorian psychological research and fictional representations of self-division. Phrenology was only one of the earliest and most explicit of a number of theories that conceptualized mental multiplicity and frag-mentation. Mesmerism and hypnotism also posited a divided consciousness, as did theories of psychological development that found traces of evolutionary ancestry and primitive instincts in the modern psyche. William James argued that the "self" was really a multiplicity of "selves," a "mixture of unity and diversity," and he empha-sized the "rivalry and conflict of the different selves" (1959: 352, 309).

In Victorian fiction self-division could take many forms, ranging from the emphasis on warring mental faculties in *Villette* to Oscar Wilde's separation of body and soul in *The Picture of Dorian Gray* (1891) or Stevenson's reverie on the coexistence of good and evil in *Dr. Jekyll and Mr. Hyde*. Victorian novels are filled with doublings of characters – doppelgängers, alter egos, twins, portraits. Although these conventions originated in Gothic and romantic fiction, they took on increasingly psychological significance in the Victorian novel as doublings between characters became doublings within. As psychologists attempted to map the complex structures and layers of the mind, Victorian novelists similarly constructed fragmented, fluid, and permeable mental lives for their characters. In late Victorian writers such as Hardy and James, as well as Stoker, Haggard, Doyle, Stevenson, Wilde, and H. G. Wells, we find a range of psychic phenomena. Hardy's *The Well-Beloved* (1897) offers a sustained exploration of imagined metempsychosis, and James's *The Turn of the Screw* (1898) can be read as both a traditional ghost story and a disturbing exploration of sexual repression, hallucination, and child psychology. H. Rider Haggard's *She* (1886) includes reincarnation, telepathic communication, and supernaturally prolonged life, and Stoker's *The Jewel of Seven Stars* (1903) and his earlier short story "The Squaw" focus on reincarnation. Not only do we find increasingly complex renderings of consciousness and subjectivity in Victorian works of psychological realism, leading eventually to early modernist fiction that attempted to reproduce the "stream of consciousness," but we also find many of the more speculative psychological theories of the late Victorian period translating into popular gothic and fantasy fiction of the era. Together, over the course of the century, Victorian psychology and Victorian fiction challenged the unity and stability of the self and the coherence of consciousness. Both attempted to map the intricate structures and capacities of the psyche. In doing so, they helped to redefine both consciousness and identity, offering increasingly complex accounts of human behavior and expansive visions of the human mind.

References

Crichton-Browne, Sir James (1895), "Dreamy Mental States," *Lancet*, 3749, 1–5 and 3750, 73–5.

Darwin, Charles (1872), *The Expression of the Emotions in Man and Animals* (London).

During, Simon (1988), "The Strange Case of Monomania: Patriarchy in Literature, Murder in *Middlemarch*, Drowning in *Daniel Deronda*," *Representations*, 23, 86–104.

Foucault, Michel (1973), *Madness and Civilization: A History of Insanity in the Age of Reason*, trans. Richard Howard (New York: Vintage).

Gall, François Joseph (1835), *On the Functions of the Brain*, 6 vols., trans. W. Lewis (Boston: Marsh, Capen & Lyon).

James, William (1959), *Principles of Psychology* (New York: Dover). (First publ. 1890.)

James, William (1984), *Psychology: Briefer Course* (Cambridge, Mass.: Harvard University Press). (First publ. 1892.)

Lewes, George Henry (1879), *Problems of Life and Mind*, 2 vols. (London: Trubner).

Prichard, J. C. (1973), *A Treatise on Insanity and Other Disorders Affecting the Mind* (New York: Arno Press Reprints). (First publ. 1835.)

Shuttleworth, Sally (1996), *Charlotte Brontë and Victorian Psychology* (Cambridge: Cambridge University Press).

Steedman, Carolyn (1995), *Strange Dislocations: Childhood and the Idea of Human Interiority, 1780–1930* (Cambridge, Mass.: Harvard University Press; London: Virago).

Winter, Alison (1998), *Mesmerized: Powers of Mind in Victorian Britain* (Chicago: University of Chicago Press).

FURTHER READING

Cameron, Sharon (1989), *Thinking in Henry James* (Chicago: University of Chicago Press).

Castle, Terry (1988), "Phantasmagoria: Spectral Technology and the Metaphorics of Modern Reverie," *Critical Inquiry*, 15, 26–61.

Chase, Karen (1984), *Eros and Psyche: The Representation of Personality in Charlotte Brontë, Charles Dickens, and George Eliot* (New York: Methuen).

Cooter, Roger (1984), *The Cultural Meaning of Popular Science: Phrenology and the Organization of Consent in Nineteenth-Century Britain* (Cambridge: Cambridge University Press).

Dames, Nicholas (2001), *Amnesiac Selves: Nostalgia, Forgetting and British Fiction 1810–1870* (Oxford: Oxford University Press).

Hacking, Ian (1995), *Rewriting the Soul: Multiple Personality and the Sciences of Memory* (Princeton: Princeton University Press).

Kucich, John (1987), *Repression in Victorian Fiction: Charlotte Brontë, George Eliot, and Charles Dickens* (Berkeley: University of California Press).

Oppenheim, Janet (1985), *The Other World: Spiritualism and Psychical Research in England, 1850–1914* (Cambridge: Cambridge University Press).

Scull, Andrew, ed. (1981), *Madhouses, Mad-Doctors, and Madmen: The Social History of Psychiatry in the Victorian Era* (Philadelphia: University of Pennsylvania Press).

Taylor, Jenny Bourne (1988), *In the Secret Theatre of Home: Wilkie Collins, Sensation Narrative, and Nineteenth-Century Psychology* (London and New York: Routledge).

Vrettos, Athena (1995), *Somatic Fictions: Imagining Illness in Victorian Culture* (Stanford: Stanford University Press).

Vrettos, Athena (1999/2000), "Defining Habits: Dickens and the Psychology of Repetition," *Victorian Studies*, 42/3, 399–426.

5

Empire, Race, and the Victorian Novel

Deirdre David

Empire is itself the strangest of all political anomalies. That a handful of adventurers from an island in the Atlantic should have subjugated a vast country divided from the place of their birth by half the globe; a country which at no very distant period was merely the subject of fable to the nations of Europe; . . . these are prodigies to which the world has seen nothing similar. Reason is confounded. We interrogate the past in vain.

Thomas Macaulay, House of Commons, 10 July 1833

When Macaulay rose in the House of Commons in 1833 to support what he termed "the work of retrenchment" needed to cleanse the East India Company of inefficiency and corruption, the Indian empire, that strange political anomaly of which he speaks, was not yet the significant presence in the novel it was to become during the Victorian period. Although the moral laxity of East India Company officials had been satirized in plays such as Samuel Foote's 1778 comedy *The Nabob*, it was not until the 1840s that the British experience in India became a fully developed subject for the novel: John William Kaye's *Peregrine Pulteney; Or, Life in India* (1844), for example, outlined the material benefits enjoyed by English officers in the East India Company's army. Certainly, by 1833 Captain Frederick Marryat had begun publishing a string of adventure novels based on his naval experiences, and the racially different worlds of eighteenth-century Scotland and Norman England had been explored by Walter Scott in *Waverley* (1814) and *Ivanhoe* (1819). In general, however, the subjects of empire and race tended to be incidental in nineteenth-century fiction, despite the fact that in political actuality Britain's imperial reach and governance was anything but decoration. Beyond the expanding Raj, the English had settled in Australia and acquired Singapore, the Cape Colony, Malta, Ceylon, St. Lucia, and Guiana, the latter West Indian territories augmenting islands such as Dominica, St. Vincent, Grenada, and Tobago that had become imperial possessions over the previous two centuries. All these West Indian colonies were slave societies, a discomforting fact avoided in early nineteenth-century drawing-room conversation, if one takes Jane Austen's *Mansfield Park* as evidence.

When Edward Said's influential *Culture and Imperialism* was first published in Britain in 1993, popular journalists and Jane Austen fans were astonished at the suggestion Jane knew something about imperial power. Offering *Mansfield Park* as his example, Said argues that the comfort of an English gentleman's country house depended upon the income from an Antiguan sugar plantation: what "assures the domestic tranquility and attractive harmony of one is the productivity and regulated discipline of the other" (1993: 87). According to Said, Austen wrote *Mansfield Park* at a time just before "the great age of explicit, programmatic colonial expansion" got going in the Victorian period (p. 81), and he explores the issue of how a novelist such as Austen, little traveled, generally sequestered in the Hampshire countryside, might have seen herself and her work in the larger world. *Mansfield Park* was published in the summer of 1813, just before the beginning of what many historians term Britain's imperial century: a period of significant economic and political growth commencing with the defeat of the French in 1815 and ending with the defeat of the Boers in 1902. Nowhere in *Mansfield Park* are the words "empire" or "race" uttered. The sole moment when Austen ventures close to mentioning a significant source of Bertram wealth and social power comes with Fanny's shy questions to Sir Thomas about the slave trade: they are greeted with a "dead silence." For Said, this is a moment when "that other setting" (the empire) is avoided or resisted by those who profit from the unpaid labor of slaves. At the beginning of the great imperial century, then, in the finely measured social world of an Austen novel, empire was not a topic for polite conversation. Nor was it yet a significant subject of literary representation.

In his influential nomination of Walter Scott as the first historical novelist, Georg Lukács argues that at the end of the Napoleonic wars, Europeans began to see themselves as existing in a relationship of complex transformation with social and political events. Earlier, history tended to be perceived as colorful background for expressions of humankind's unchanging nature; but after 1815 European individuals developed an awareness that human progress emerges from conflict with social forces, that they were nationally and racially distinct from one another, and that they shaped, and were shaped by, historical forces. In a number of Scott's novels, awareness of races other than the Anglo-Saxon assists characters in gaining this historical consciousness. In *Waverley* (1814), the eponymous hero acquires this understanding through an incremental awareness of his national affiliation, of his identity as an upper-class Englishman venturing further and further north into the Scottish highlands and into the thick of political alliances between the Scots and the French just prior to the battle at Culloden in 1745. In *Waverley*, discovery of Anglo-Saxon and Scottish racial difference proves crucial to the attainment of individual and national consciousness.

Not unhappy to leave the feudal manor of his host, Baron Bradwardine, where he has survived many whisky toasts to the Jacobite cause, Edward Waverley traverses rough and stony landscapes, falls into numerous bogs, meets various Highland hags, is kidnapped by a Highland cattle thief, and finally arrives at the romantic hideaway of Fergus and Flora McIvor. He also encounters a ragtag army of lowlanders said to speak English no better than the negroes in Jamaica (p. 405). From the perspective of early nineteenth-century racial attitudes, the superiority of English gentry values is expressed through the rowdy feudalism of Baron Bradwardine, the sullen roughness of Scottish lowlanders, and the romantic posturing of the McIvors. With the definitive colonization of Scotland and the final defeat of separatist aspirations at Culloden in 1745 as its concluding historical events, *Waverley* relies on figures who create a disruptive "other" (Scottish/French rebellion against English law and order) so that, in turn, the cultural, economic, and political superiority of the colonizer may be asserted. Scott's description of the post-Culloden, war-ravaged landscape and his fine characterization of the loyal clansmen willing to die in exchange for the release of Fergus McIvor help to redeem *Waverley* from crude Anglo-Saxon propaganda, as does his sensitive effort to find a political middle way for Waverley between the Whig materialism of his father and the Jacobite/Tory romanticism of the Chevalier. An English family restores the gutted Bradwardine estate, and Waverley and his bride, Bradwardine's daughter, are installed as its new and distinctly more refined owners. To be sure, this marriage symbolizes racial fusion; but from the beginning of the novel Rose Bradwardine's delicate demeanor (in contrast to Flora McIvor's vibrancy) has made her seem more English than Scottish. *Waverley* legitimates Anglo-Saxon racial superiority and advances the triumph of English colonizing values, not in India or Antigua but just across the border from Cumberland.

As British imperialism gathered steam, fueled in part by the technological developments of the industrial revolution, empire and the related subjects of race and slavery became increasingly visible in the novel, principally for two reasons: the growing significance of Britain's geopolitical power in the lives of ordinary Victorian people and the formal commitment of the novel to social realism. The middle-class families who read newspaper accounts of successful conquests and travel, and missionary narratives sent home from imperial outposts, also read novels; they frequently had sons serving in civil and military outposts of empire, and daughters whose marriages to colonial officials and missionaries took them to Africa, India, and the West Indies. Quite simply, Victorian fiction began to register this enlarged awareness of imperialism. In Charles Dickens's *Dombey and Son* (1848), for example, the reader encounters multiple references to the empire. Major Bagstock, a purple-faced military relic, is said to have performed daring exploits in the Punjab and in the West Indies, and has returned to England in possession of a "dark servant" whom he showers regularly with verbal and physical abuse; Mrs. Pipchin, a sour childminder for colonial families, takes in sad little boys sent home from India, one of whom wistfully asks Florence Dombey if she can give him any idea of the way back to Bengal; and the House of Dombey is known throughout British possessions abroad, its offices situated just around the corner from East India House.

Dombey and Son is a novel deeply critical of the cold patriarchal attitudes practiced by Mr. Dombey and, by association, of the materialistic empire-building in which he and his House participate; as we witness the demolition of Dombey's financial might, founded on shipping various cargoes along Britain's trading routes, Dickens's moral rehabilitation of the withered Mr. Dombey may be seen to call, by association, for a rehabilitation of the unfeeling, commercial nature of imperialism. In *Dombey and Son* it is difficult to divorce a critique of domestic tyranny from a critique of oppression reinforced by race – to separate, say, Dombey's emotional abuse of his daughter from Major Bagstock's virulent attacks upon his "dark servant."

In his other novels, Dickens tends to deploy race and empire for formal convenience: to flavor a minor character or resolve intractable difficulties in the plot. In *David Copperfield* (1850), for instance, a feckless character named Jack Maldon is sent to India with the encouragement from his family that "The winds you are going to tempt, have wafted thousands upon thousands to fortune" (Dickens 1948: 244), a social fact attested to by Victorian calls for alteration in the laissez-faire attitudes that still dominated the East India Office, despite Macaulay's 1833 calls for reform. At the end of *Hard Times* (1854) a whimpering Tom Gradgrind, a miserable fellow who has betrayed the love of his sister, stolen money, and generally disgraced all around him, is shipped by his father "to North or South America, or any distant part of the world to which he could be the most speedily and privately dispatched" (Dickens 1955: 282–3). In common with a number of his literary contemporaries, Dickens finds the colonies of white settlement to be convenient repositories for characters difficult to integrate into English society. Just as, at the close of Elizabeth Gaskell's *Mary Barton* (1848), Mary and Jem Wilson depart for Canada accompanied by his querulous mother who hopes that "in them Indian countries" they will recognize the cherished qualities of her adored son, so at the end of *David Copperfield* Mr. Micawber takes his family to Australia. Armed with the knife of "a practical settler," he declaims on his departure, "The luxuries of the old country . . . we abandon. The denizens of the forest cannot, of course expect to participate in the refinements of the land of the Free" (Dickens 1948: 804). Lastly, as an instance of how thoroughly imperialism begins to penetrate the imagination of the Victorian novelist, consider the moment in Elizabeth Gaskell's *Cranford* (1853) – that most domestic of English domestic fictions – when a minor character, the washerwoman wife of a former sergeant in the 31st regiment of the East India Company army, relates a touching narrative to the ladies of Cranford of how she walked to Calcutta to get her one surviving child back to England.

As well as providing Victorian novelists with the plausible means of despatching characters from England, colonial governance in the West Indies and political control of large parts of India facilitated the fictional creation of racially defined figures. In William Thackeray's *Vanity Fair* (1847), for instance, we find Miss Swartz, "the rich woolly-haired mulatto from St. Kitt's" (Thackeray 1963: 14), who seems to communicate primarily with "yoops," who pays double at the finishing school attended by Amelia Sedley and Becky Sharp, and whom George Osborne refuses to woo, despite the materialistic encouragement of his father. In Thackeray's novel we also discover (to return to the India of *Dombey and Son*) that the East India Company has provided Jos Sedley, tax collector of Boggley Wollah in the Bengal division, with an income

culled from the revenues he has sent regularly to Calcutta. In *David Copperfield* we find
another nabob character, albeit a minor one: Julia Mills, bosom friend of David's first
wife, returns from India married to an "old Scotch Croesus, who is a sort of yellow
bear with a tanned hide," together with "a copper-coloured woman in linen" and a
"black man to carry cards and letters to her" (Dickens 1948: 875). An expanding
empire and racial difference enable the fictional existence of Miss Swartz, the "black"
servants of Major Bagstock and Julia Mills, and, of course, her "copper-coloured
woman."

The changing nature of attitudes toward race in the Victorian period has been
documented by a number of historians of European imperialism, many of whom
ground their analyses in the work of Victorian writers such as Robert Knox, Charles
Darwin, and Edward Burnett Tylor. Philip Curtin (1971) has pointed to the effects
of the industrial revolution upon European technology, and shown that whereas in
the eighteenth century an English sense of national superiority was grounded in
religious difference and general xenophobia, in the nineteenth century evidence of
supremacy in factory production, agricultural yield, and elaborate systems of transportation led to different explanations of expanding hegemony. Curtin points out that
the financial and industrial power created by mercantile capitalism (of the sort
enjoyed, say, by the House of Dombey) led to a belief that English supremacy
must be grounded in more than mere cultural and religious difference: Protestantism
and its accompanying work ethic, however admirable, were seen as insufficient
explanation for extraordinary economic growth in the Victorian period.

Curtin elaborates the way Victorians interpreted the global reach of empire and
attendant subjugation of millions of racially different peoples as indisputable evidence
of Anglo-Saxon racial superiority. For example, in *The Races of Men* (1850) Robert
Knox attributes all historical change to racial inequality (Knox 1969). England was
supreme in *all* things, not just in banking, shipbuilding, and insurance. This belief,
Curtin argues, led to the creation of a racially oriented view of human beings and
their civilizations, a kind of racial pyramid with Europeans on top. In a circular process
of ideological reinforcement, superior racial qualities must be the explanation for
phenomenal success; and that success, in turn, must be interpreted as evidence of
racial superiority. In sum, early Victorian thinking about race tended to shift from
construction of a hierarchy of societies based on differences in culture to invention of
a hierarchy based on differences in race.

Other historians of nineteenth-century imperialism have explored the significance
of evolutionary theory and early cultural anthropology in Victorian attitudes to
race. Douglas Lorimer (1978) has argued that, before 1860, ethnocentrism dictated
belief in cultural superiority, an attitude that sometimes grudgingly admitted the
possibility of a subjugated people being educated, or "civilized," so that it, too,
might conform to the superior norm; but that after 1859 belief in cultural and social
superiority began to derive its dubious authority from theories of biological difference,
popularly appropriated (and usually vulgarized) from Darwin's *Origin of Species*. In fundamental accord with historians such as Curtin and Lorimer who link the emerging

discipline of anthropology with imperialism and also point to the distortion of Darwin's ideas to advocate racial purity, Christine Bolt cautions that there is no demonstrable "*causal* relationship between racism, expansionism, and colonial policy" (1984: 146). Arguing that for some the ever-broadening span of Britain's empire was evidence of the divinely sanctioned superiority of the Anglo-Saxon race, and that for others the empire was first, foremost, and always a place to make money, she urges that Victorian attitudes to race must be seen as developing adjacently to expansion of the empire, and that they are always shifting in their relationship to imperialist hegemony.

In his introduction to the nineteenth-century volume of the *Oxford History of the British Empire*, Andrew Porter observes that at the local levels of imperial and colonial governance, the definition of races held enormous potential "for justifying rule, generating unity, and for establishing practices of political or administrative exclusion" (1999: 22). Porter sees racial superiority as taken for granted from mid-century onwards by the ordinary English Victorian person; it is this belief in racial superiority that helped cement the different parts of a wide-ranging geopolitical empire. From the outbreak of the Indian rebellion in 1857, via the Morant Bay riots in Jamaica in 1865 and the opening of the Suez Canal in 1869, through the first sitting of a Maori parliament in New Zealand in 1892, the ordinary Victorian found much evidence of "native" barbarism and Anglo-Saxon success in "civilizing" once "savage" peoples. Moreover, an Anglo-Saxon belief in the inevitable ascendancy of its own race received confirmation in what was seen as the equally inevitable extinction of indigenous peoples, either through cultural assimilation or through annihilation as the result of disease and war. Finally, Porter claims, the optimistic assumption that since human nature was everywhere identical, benevolent governance might trans-form barbaric cultures, also began to decline. In place of this optimism, Victorian people began to think more negatively about a racial world elsewhere, to believe that there must be permanent racial divisions. As a result, the English imperialist (missionary, teacher, colonial official, army officer) must fail in "civilizing" the savage.

Throughout the imperial century (1815–1902), the novel participated vigorously in the celebration, legitimation, and interrogation of imperialism and colonialism. Just as Britain's imperial wealth produced a middle-class prosperity that enabled the production and reading of novels, so Victorian novelists participated in the con-struction of imperialist wealth – not as crude agents of political ideology, but as unconscious agents in the complex, always changing interaction between political governance and cultural practice. In this way the cultural work of the Victorian novel in regard to empire was similar to that performed by the "social problem" or "indus-trial" novels of the 1840s. As Raymond Williams showed in *Culture and Society* (1958), social problem novels provided for their readers knowledge about industrial culture, about a world of working-class misery far removed from the secure space of the middle-class home. If an Elizabeth Gaskell novel informed a curious middle-class readership about the "knowable community" of back-street Manchester in *Mary Barton*, then Charlotte Brontë's *Jane Eyre* (1847), obviously not a work that claimed to be a historically faithful picture of Jamaica in the late 1820s, nevertheless, through Rochester's account of his torrid infatuation with Bertha Mason, conveyed a felt sense of the tropical West Indies. Like *Jane Eyre*, most of the novels discussed in this chapter map the domestic spaces invaded by empire and race and the foreign places where ideologies of empire and race acquired their material beginnings.

*

By the 1840s, the English had taken over Hong Kong, annexed the Punjab and Natal, and commenced construction of the vast railway system in India, all the while building domestically upon the technological advancements of the early nineteenth-century industrial revolution. Industrial culture became the subject of investigation, in both nonfictional and fictional texts, and a whole new discourse emerged for the education of the middle and upper classes. Working conditions in the factories and in the coal-mines became the subject of parliamentary commissions (the published results known popularly as Blue Books), dangerous sanitary conditions led to fearful official investigation, and writers of the 1840s such as Dickens, Elizabeth Gaskell, and Charles Kingsley began to give frightening life to the appalling state of things disclosed by governmental enquiry. This discourse of industrialization, in its deployment of images of empire and race, whether in Blue Book, political essay, or social problem novel, discloses how thoroughly imperialism had entered the domestic sphere.

R. W. Cooke Taylor, for instance, detailing his impressions of Manchester manufacturing districts in 1842, asserts that "the Anglo-Saxon race seems peculiarly qualified for carrying out the factory system." He finds in the English character "a steadiness of energy, and a coldness of temperament" that makes it especially suitable for bureaucratic management of industrial power (1968: 115). The Anglo-Saxon "coldness of temperament" to which he refers is contrasted with the fondness for drink and dissolute behavior frequently ascribed by parliamentary investigators to the working class, and particularly to the Irish immigrants who formed a large proportion of the population of factory "hands." Victorian writing about the Irish suggests that, for the middle classes, alien races were to be found not only in distant Africa: right in the heart of industrial Manchester one could see the unfortunate Irish. From the sixteenth-century English attempts to impose Protestantism on a Catholic population, through the 1800 Act of Union fusing England and Ireland, the potato famine of 1845–9, and the guerrilla warfare of the "Troubles," through recent political efforts to put an end, once and for all, to Sinn Fein and Orange resistance, the Irish have been (and continue to be) negatively stereotyped in English culture.

Probably the most sustained deployment of negative images of the Irish is to be found in an otherwise persuasive work of social investigation, Friedrich Engels' *The Condition of the Working Class in England* (1844). Engels' indictment of the hypocrisy and greed of the English bourgeoisie is punctuated by regular and racially marked descriptions of the Irish laborer and his family: they are all filthy drunkards, lazy potato-eaters, and rabble-rousers. In the discourse of industrial culture, this image of the drunken, dirty, and promiscuous Irish working class is often embroidered with fantasies of torrid sexuality. For example, a fellow-investigator of Cooke Taylor's, Peter Gaskell (no relation to Elizabeth Gaskell), likens the fetid, overheated atmosphere of the cotton mill to that felt somewhere in the tropics; in describing the deplorable conditions in which young working-class women in the mills are subject to a "stimulus of heated atmosphere," he declares that they are constantly surrounded by instances of "lasciviousness upon the animal passions" (Pike 1966: 280).

Thomas Carlyle's long essay "Chartism" (1839) travels between sympathy for the suffering Irish and rhetoric that so brutally captures the racism of the "Saxon" that one needs to read it very carefully to see that Carlyle is engaged in a satiric attack upon such racism. Labeling the Irish peasant a "Sanspotato" (a neologism that evokes English fears of class revolution in its similarity to "Sans-culotte"), Carlyle sympathetically (and accurately) attributes the miserable Irish economy to an oppression by the English so long practiced that the "Irish National character is degraded, disordered . . . Immethodic, headlong, violent, mendacious: What can you make of the wretched Irishman?" he asks sarcastically (Carlyle 1971: 169). What Carlyle makes of him in "Chartism" is a figure seen as racially inferior by an Englishman. Possessed of "wild Milesian features" and a "laughing savagery" (thus a descendant of the fabulous Spanish king said to have conquered Ireland around 1300 BC), he darkens the industrial towns, a threat to the "Saxon native" since he will do anything to secure potatoes (p. 171). In a fierce parody of the racism of the "Saxon" who, unlike the Irishman, "has not sunk from decent manhood to squalid apehood" (p. 171), Carlyle suggests how deeply a sense of racial distinctiveness pervaded all social classes in the late 1830s.

Charles Dickens, traveling in America in the 1840s and otherwise savagely critical of the racist brutality and injustice of slavery, a "bloody chapter" of history that must have a "bloody end" (Dickens 1957: 228), describes an Irish colony in the Catskills as completely "ruinous and filthy," despite the "means at hand of building decent cabins." These Irish immigrants (probably desperate refugees from their famine-ravaged land) are all "wallowing together" in a mess of pigs, dogs, pots, dunghills, vile refuse, rank straw, and standing water (p. 214). To Dickens, they form a racially repellent group. And Elizabeth Gaskell's *North and South* (1854) elaborates, albeit briefly, the crude racism excoriated by Carlyle. The Boucher family is doomed by virtue of an inherited Irish melancholia: the father kills himself and the mother lapses into morbid self-pity. As Margaret Hale, Gaskell's sensible and sensitive heroine, says to her father, Boucher lacked the conventional granite of the Anglo Saxon "northern people" – probably because of his "Irish blood" (p. 308).

One novel of the 1840s that is fully freighted with references to race and empire is *Jane Eyre*. Over the last decade or so, discussion of this text has been central in most analyses of the complex links between Victorian women and imperialism. In Jane, the Victorian reader would have found an ideal Victorian woman of empire, thoroughly imbued with the moral authority required of Britain's colonial governance, and granted the physical fortitude necessary to survive the climate, food, and generally non-Anglo-Saxon mode of existence to be found in India, Africa, or the West Indies. First, a confident self-alliance with a national authority produced through racial difference is found everywhere in Jane's thinking. Her sense of being English enables her to confide to the reader that there is no question about whether it is better "to be a slave in a fool's paradise at Marseilles . . . or to be a village schoolmistress, free and honest . . . in the healthy heart of England" (Brontë 1966: 386). She is a character who, through her moral perfection, physical strength, and celebration of Englishness, helps to construct English national identity, and as a symbolic emblem of impeccable colonial practices, she draws the red spaces on the map of empire. Without question she would have been entirely at home in India as the wife of a missionary had she succumbed to St. John's desire for her to accompany him on his journey.

Allusions to empire in *Jane Eyre* are both brief and sustained. Jane is too good, says Diana Rivers, to be "grilled alive in Calcutta" and should not go to India with St. John; in her campaign to resist Rochester's ardent courtship, Jane declares she will be not be hurried away in a "suttee" should he die before her; and in the most developed example of racialist imagery in the novel, an insane Creole woman from Jamaica grotesquely embodies English fears of, and fascination with, tropical passion. In Brontë's descriptions of Bertha Mason Rochester one finds the English fear of excitable dark races that is apparent in a virtually contemporaneous nonfictional text, Carlyle's "Occasional Discourse on the Nigger Question" (1849; see Carlyle 1905). Just as Brontë's novel presents Jane's idealized female morality as purifier of Rochester's tainted association with racial murkiness, so Carlyle's infamous essay offers Anglo-Saxon values to cleanse a reeking jungle desperately in need of a European clean-up.

Long after the abolition of slavery in all British territories in 1833, Carlyle's essay purports to render a speech given on the "Rights of Negroes" in the West Indies. Carlyle first evokes the dreadful conditions in Ireland to describe Demerara (not technically in the West Indies but grouped by Britain with the Caribbean plantations), an instance of how the pervasive racial stereotyping that sometimes characterizes imperialist writing allows one subjugated group to be interchangeable with another. The essay, with a wild rhetorical energy, claims that the black West Indian is destined for servitude, good for nothing better than lolling around with rum-bottle in hand, "no breeches on his body, pumpkin at discretion, and the fruitfulest region of the earth going back to jungle round him" (Carlyle 1905: 470). For the speaker of the essay, the West Indies have produced only "mere jungle, savagery, poison-reptiles and swamp malaria: till the white European first saw them, they were as if not yet created, − their noble elements of cinnamon, sugar, coffee, pepper black and grey, lying all asleep, waiting the white enchanter who should say to them, Awake!" (p. 484). Constructed as jungle so that the imperialist imagination evoked by Carlyle might then invent the lazy, drunken inhabitants of that jungle, the islands are, however, paradoxically not really in existence until the Europeans arrive.

Carlyle's fruitful jungle is not unlike Rochester's Jamaican inferno as he relates to Jane Eyre his narrative of tropical desire. Married off by his father to the daughter of a West Indian planter, Rochester initially finds his wife Bertha Mason exciting; but soon, as he tells Jane after his aborted attempt at bigamy with her, he finds Bertha's nature alien, her mind common, her character rife with "giant propensities." A figure both fascinating and loathsome to the Victorian sexual imagination, with a large frame, thick black hair, red eyes, and "swollen, dark lips," she is the frightful image of a degraded Jamaican black woman; but Bertha, of course, is not black. She is a Creole and, through Brontë's descriptions, made more terrifying by virtue of her racial similarity to a colonized West Indian. This "filthy burden" is finally despatched through the mechanisms of Brontë's plot and Jane can announce to her reader that she married Rochester – maimed, half-blind, but cleansed of his racially inflicted pollution. Interpreted until the last two decades or so by feminist critics as the sad story of a suffering governess, Brontë's novel is much more than that; it is also a powerful story about race and empire.

Any discussion of imperial invasion of domestic space must inevitably cope with Heathcliff – that dark, vengeful figure found wandering on the streets of the slave-trading port of Liverpool by his savior, Mr. Earnshaw. Who he is and what he is are the questions posed by Emily Brontë's *Wuthering Heights* (1847), and they are never satisfactorily answered, either by characters in the novel or by critics who write about it. Heathcliff's darkness, the mystery of his origins, his savage, even racially stereotyped behavior make him a symbol of the colonized, the racially oppressed. Some critics read Heathcliff as Irish, and if one recalls Carlyle's Milesian figures lurching savagely through the industrial towns, then it is easy to see Heathcliff salvaged from the Irish immigrant world by a kindly Yorkshireman. According to Terry Eagleton, by June 1847 300,000 destitute Irish had landed in Liverpool (Eagleton 1995: 3); this was at the height of the disastrous Irish famine, and it seems likely that Emily Brontë had images of ragged, grimy Irish children wandering the Liverpool streets in mind as she created her remarkable character. Nelly Dean, the primary narrator of the novel, in one of the moments when she attempts to console Heathcliff for the ill-treatment he receives from Hindley, tells him to come to the mirror and see that his father might have been an emperor of China and his mother an Indian queen. To be sure, this is a rather far-fetched racial mixture, but it indicates both the racial mystery of Heathcliff's appearance and the ready availability for Victorian novelists of racialist, exotic imagery.

*

By the 1860s, the infiltration of Victorian life by empire may be discovered in the sensation novel, a subgenre that became wildly popular. The sensation novel usually played, "sensationally," upon the reader's nerves and often took its plot material from "sensational" stories to be found in the Victorian equivalent of today's tabloid newspapers. Wilkie Collins's *Armadale* (1866), whose wildly complicated murder and revenge plot defies paraphrase, features a woman "of the mixed blood of the European and the African race, with the northern delicacy in the shape of her face, and the southern richness in its colour" (Collins 1977: 14), and also a dissolute Englishman who has passed "the greater part of his life in the West Indies" and has lived "a wild and a vicious life" (p. 9), like that pursued by Rochester when first in Jamaica. Of all his novels, Collins's *The Moonstone* (1868) is the most thoroughly shaped by imperial history. The theft in 1799 of a diamond from an Indian temple statue by a corrupt army officer sets the plot in motion. Starting with a moment of colonial violence, *The Moonstone* proceeds to trace the misfortunes of all who come in contact with the precious and religiously valuable gem. It is brought to England, shadowed for the following sixty years or so by various Indians, and, through the intelligent agency of a character named Ezra Jennings, finally restored to its rightful place. Jennings is a racial and cultural hybrid, the son of an Englishman and a woman, as he puts it, from "one of our colonies." Possessing a "gipsy darkness," his nose presenting "the fine shape and modelling so often found among the ancient people of the East" (Collins 1966: 371), he is a product of empire who imaginatively provides the gratifying ending wherein the diamond is restored to its original location and disruptive Indians who have invaded the domestic space of a Yorkshire country house are put back where they belong on Britain's imperial map.

Sensational journalism, a source of plots for novels such as *Armadale* and *The Moonstone*, often (now and in the Victorian period) depends on racial stereotypes, and earlier in the imperial century Dickens's *Oliver Twist* (1838), a sensationalistic novel with its headline-making story of a missing boy's adventures with a criminal gang, provided a controversial portrait of the quintessential stereotype in Victorian fiction: the Jew. In *Oliver Twist*, to be sure, one finds a regular array of stereotypical characters, ranging from the child-pilgrim Oliver, who although born in a workhouse speaks improbably in an upper-class English accent, through the fair domestic angel Rose Maylie and the bad-complexioned Monks with evil pitted into his face, to the Semitic red-haired devil Fagin, whom Dickens characterizes as "a crafty old Jew, a receiver of stolen goods." Fagin is first glimpsed by Oliver as "a very shrivelled Jew, whose villainous-looking and repulsive face was obscured by a quantity of matted hair" (Dickens 1949: 56). As Steven Marcus observes, he "flourishes in darkness and dissimulation" (1965: 75); gliding, creeping, and crawling, he is the devil, the serpent, the dirty Jew. Charged with antisemitism for such imagery, Dickens is said to have compensated for racial stereotyping with the portrayal of Riah in *Our Mutual Friend* (1865) – but Riah is as implausibly benevolent, spiritual, and unselfish as Fagin is excessively malevolent, greedy, and cruel. Each character in his own way is as stereotypically conceived as the other.

With the intellectual dedication that characterizes her life and work, in the early 1870s George Eliot studied Hebrew with an eminent Jewish scholar to prepare herself for the writing of *Daniel Deronda* (1876), a novel of English manners and the Jewish diaspora, one half devoted to the psychological misery of Gwendolen Harleth and the other to the journey to Jewish identity of Daniel Deronda. Her idealization of Jewish characters in this novel exceeds even Dickens's idealistic portrayal of Riah in *Our*

Mutual Friend. George Lewes, Eliot's lifelong companion, wrote to her publisher that the Jewish readership of *Daniel Deronda* will "constitute an energetic propagandist party, for never have [they] been so idealized and realized so marvellously before" (Eliot 1954–78: vol. 6, 224). In *Oliver Twist* and *Our Mutual Friend* the Jewish figures are minor, but in *Daniel Deronda* Jewish religious belief and daily life are central to Eliot's critique of English upper-class moral vapidity. Brought up as a privileged member of the English ruling class, Daniel Deronda discovers that he is Jewish, marries a Jewish woman, and goes off to Palestine. Well-intentioned as Eliot may have been in her portrayal of Jewish life in *Daniel Deronda*, she sometimes lapses into a racial stereotyping little different from that found, say, in Scott's *Waverley* at the beginning of Britain's imperial century, or, indeed, in *Ivanhoe*, where we encounter the Jewish usurer, Isaac, and the lively, dark heroine, his daughter Rebecca. Just as Scott's descriptions of Scots and Jews assist in a definition of English national identity generated by racial difference, so Eliot's descriptions of the Jews serve to define English cultural decay *and* English cultural superiority.

In an essay written some three years after the publication of *Daniel Deronda*, Eliot addressed the problem of antisemitism in English society through an analysis of medieval Christian notions about Jewish life. She declares that England must deal with the Jews because they will not go away: "our best course is to encourage all means of improving these neighbours who elbow us in a thickening crowd" (Eliot n.d.: 210). Mordecai, the Jewish visionary of the novel, although not the elbowing type, fanatically seeks to persuade Deronda of his unchangeable racial difference from the English. The only flaw in Mordecai's family is his father, Lapidoth, unattractively and stereotypically Jewish. "A foreign-looking, eager, and gesticulating man" with bushy curls and a prevailing interest in money, Lapidoth belongs more with the lower-class, East End Jewish family, the Cohens, whom Deronda meets in his wanderings in Whitechapel. This family is endowed by Eliot with all the negative racial markers of Jewish culture: they are noisy, greedy, and vulgar, and a prevailing interest in money seems to direct all their transactions. Headed by a pawnbroker father, they live in a world of small commerce – in some ways, to be fair, a world little different in regard to money from that inhabited by the upper-class, materialistic Christian characters in the novel. The significant difference is that Eliot's Jewish characters are racially one-dimensional, and the others, mostly ruling-class, are defined in multiple ways.

In addition to relying upon images of racial difference in *Daniel Deronda*, Eliot deploys metaphors of colonization in her depiction of the troubled psychological condition of its heroine, Gwendolen Harleth. Before her marriage to the sadistic Henleigh Grandcourt, Gwendolen reigns over a "domestic empire" where all revolves around gratification of her desires. Unlike Fanny Price in *Mansfield Park*, she is indifferent to the "conditions of colonial property" that are the source of her family's income (all she can bother to remember is that her grandfather made money in the West Indies). Gwendolen is sold in the upper-class marriage market to a man far more skilled in the management of subjugated individuals than she, someone who if he "had been sent to govern a difficult colony," would have claimed "it was safer to exterminate than to cajole" (ch. 48) – a sentiment anticipating Kurtz's claim in Conrad's *Heart of Darkness* that one must "exterminate the brutes." At a lunch party in Eliot's novel, conversation about the Morant Bay rebellion in Jamaica in 1865 discloses ruling-class attitudes toward empire: Grandcourt pronounces the Jamaican negro "a beastly sort of Baptist Caliban"; someone else remarks that the half-breeds are to blame for all the trouble; and Gwendolen's mother offers that her father had an estate in the West Indies. The rebellion in Jamaica (brutally suppressed by Governor Eyre) is as uninteresting to Gwendolen's mother as the American Civil War is to Gwendolen. Preoccupied with "how to make her life pleasant," she is unaware, observes the narrator, of how, in 1865, men have died in the Civil War and how Lancashire cotton workers have "stinted of bread" because of the northern blockade of southern ports. Gwendolen's wilful ignorance of a tragic war across the Atlantic, and thus of slavery, is an aspect of the complex psychological characterization that Eliot fashioned for her intellectually mature readers; such characterization is understandably missing from the juvenile adventure fiction popular toward the end of the imperial century. In the novels of H. Rider Haggard, for instance, we find that the influence of empire so elegantly woven into the lives of characters in *Daniel Deronda* is the very stuff by which an unsubtle masculine and national identity is defined.

Haggard's *King Solomon's Mines* (1885) and *She* (1887) constitute English national and masculine subjectivity through tropes of travel, hazardous adventure, and eventual mastery of the forces that both threaten and define male power. The racism of these novels is unembarrassed and extreme. "Rather different from the ordinary run of Zulus," the character who is named both Ignosi and Umbopa in *King Solomon's Mines* is described as "Scarcely more than dark"; he is a magnificent physical specimen, rightful king of the Kukuanas, who speak an old Zulu analogous to Chaucerian English and who are comically awed by false teeth, white legs, and firearms. Physically, the Africans in this novel do not even look African. More like exotic figures of Orientalist fantasy, the women have curly rather than "woolly" hair; their features are "frequently aquiline," their lips "not unpleasantly thick as is the case in most African races," and their manners are suitable for a "fashionable drawing-room" (Haggard 1989: 129). They would seem more at home in a Turkish harem than on the plains of what is now northern Zimbabwe. In *She*, the male natives are as magnificent as the warriors in *King Solomon's Mines*: "of a magnificent build," they have "thick black locks" rather than frizzy hair. Both novels legitimate the superiority of English culture: in *King Solomon's Mines* the trio of male adventurers sets the African kingdom to order by re-installing its rightful king, and in *She*, Ayesha's kingdom is a bad, unproductive empire ruled by a 2,000-year-old intellectual elitist, gifted chemist, and vegetarian clairvoyant. When the male force of decent imperialism reduces the empress of the Kingdom of Kor to a shriveled monkey, her empire of sterile, unproductive narcissism is wiped out.

In Haggard's romances, empire is fantastic setting, and race a glamorous or demonic marker; but for Joseph Conrad, writing at the end of the imperial century, empire and race are subjects of ambiguous and anguished representation. *Heart of*

Darkness (1899), one of the most frequently assigned literary texts in Anglo-American higher education, is taught from multiple critical perspectives: as a parable about the nature of good and evil, as a psychological journey of the individual to self-understanding, as an anticipation of the dislocation of moral certainties that emerges full-blown in British modernism, as a deeply self-reflexive interrogation of the conventions of Victorian realism, and, most of all, as a searing critique of imperialism. Conrad averred in 1917 that *Heart of Darkness* was the "spoil" he brought out of the center of Africa; it is also about the "spoil" of ivory for which Kurtz is famed and the "spoil" of Marlow's narrative, which he offers to his listeners on the yacht in the setting that frames his account. Marlow derives comfort from seeing large chunks of the world colored red on English maps of imperial territories; that he can feel this way signals his immersion in late Victorian imperial culture, however ironically he may view his situation. His sense of security rests upon English geopolitical power at the end of the nineteenth century. To say this another way, the privileged cultural milieu of civil discourse that fosters Marlow's ambivalence about imperialism – expressed in his observation that "The conquest of the earth, which mostly means the taking it away from those who have a different complexion or slightly flatter noses than ourselves, is not a pretty thing when you look into it too much" (Conrad 1946: 50–1) – was enabled by the military and civil forces that invaded and took over various territories around the world, ranging from chunks of Africa to small islands in the West Indies during the imperial century from 1815 to 1902. Imperialism is a nasty business, Marlow concedes, but the English do it better than others; scorning the Roman colonists in ancient Britain as mere "conquerors" bent on "a squeeze," not to "an unselfish belief in the idea" (p. 50), Marlow shows that it is not the English who leave dying "black shapes" to litter the earth in "all attitudes of pain, abandonment, and despair" (p. 55). It is Belgian imperialists (never named as such) who have brought natives from the interior to build the railway, who have let them fall sick and then left them to die. Speaking like the decent and unconsciously racist fellow that he is, Marlow undeniably stereotypes Africans; but the brilliance of *Heart of Darkness* is that it refuses a comforting, one-dimensional reading of imperial practices and attitudes to race.

If Marlow as a character and as a narrator is produced by English imperial governance, and if his attitudes toward race and empire are representative of a late nineteenth-century liberal new imperialism (skeptical, humane, tending to isolationism), then Rudyard Kipling's eponymous hero Kim is even more fully bred by empire, nurtured by empire, and finally employed by empire. The child of a nurse-maid in a colonel's family and a color sergeant in an Irish regiment, after his mother's death and his father's fall into opium addiction Kim becomes an imperial hybrid. He is a wild child of the streets who looks like an Indian but underneath is an Irish boy, not wandering the streets of Liverpool as Heathcliff might have done, but skipping along the glorious, vital length of the Great Trunk Road. There, he dives "into the Asiatic disorder" of India on the move: "India was awake, and Kim was in the middle of it, more awake and more excited than anyone." The plot traces his journey from sitting astride the gun in Lahore to his employment as seasoned and canny spy in the Great Game of imperial control of the northwest frontier played by Britain and Russia. Along the way he asks himself understandable questions about his own identity, is trained as a spy by spending his time in the back alleys of Simla, is apprenticed in surveying, is taught by Hurree Babu, and ends up high in the mountains of the frontier.

Kim was published at a time when another kind of fiction about India was also popular: that dealing with the Anglo-Indian female experience. Flora Annie Steele's *On the Face of the Waters* (1896), for example, evokes not the sheer fun of scampering around the back streets of Simla, but the terror of hiding, disguised as an Indian woman, in Delhi as the rebellion of 1857 takes place. Steele's novels, and those of Maud Diver and Sara Duncan, feature women who are exhausted by the imperial experience: worn out by the climate; desperately missing their children, sent off to English boarding schools; restricted to the life of the cantonment. In a sense, the experience of these female characters imaginatively suggests the general malaise that infected English attitudes to empire at the end of the imperial century. Its economy strained by the upkeep of that empire whose power so "confounded" Macaulay in 1833, Britain entered a period of domestic and foreign anxiety. Worries about activist "new women," declining birth rates, immigration from eastern Europe, and the likely degeneration of Anglo-Saxon racial supremacy unsettled things on the home front. In the realm of imperial and colonial rule, competition from other European imperial powers, restlessness in the colonies of white settlement, and the founding in 1885 of the Indian National Congress (which led, eventually, to the dismantling of the British Raj) all contributed to a sense that the imperial century was coming to a close. Indeed, another global empire was in the making. In Bram Stoker's *Dracula* (1897), a hearty Texan who has assisted in the elimination of that racialized monster, the Count, is praised by another character as follows: "If America can go on breeding men like that, she will be a power in the world indeed." At the beginning of the imperial century, the novel glanced briefly at Antigua when, in *Mansfield Park*, Sir Thomas Bertram must travel there to check on the family's sugar plantation; at the end of it, the Victorian novel looks across the Atlantic to marvel at the rapid growth of another empire, one born from discontent with the mother-country and destined to outdo her in terms of global power.

REFERENCES

Bolt, Christine (1984), "Race and the Victorians," in C. C. Eldridge, ed., *British Imperialism in the Nineteenth Century* (New York: St. Martin's), 126–47.

Brontë, Charlotte (1966), *Jane Eyre* (Harmondsworth: Penguin). (First publ. 1847.)

Carlyle, Thomas (1905), "Occasional Discourse on the Nigger Question," in *Critical and Miscellaneous Essays*, 3 vols. (New York: Funk & Wagnalls), vol. 3, 463–92. (First publ. 1849.)

Carlyle, Thomas (1971), "Chartism," in *Thomas Carlyle: Selected Writings*, ed. Alan Sheston (Harmondsworth: Penguin).

Collins, Wilkie (1966), *The Moonstone* (Harmondsworth: Penguin). (First publ. 1868.)

Collins, Wilkie (1977), *Armadale* (New York: Dover). (First publ. 1866.)

Conrad, Joseph (1946), *Heart of Darkness* (London: Dent). (First publ. 1899.)

Cooke Taylor, R. W. (1968), *Notes of a Tour in the Manufacturing Districts of Lancashire* (London: Frank Cass). (First publ. 1842.)

Curtin, Philip D. (1971), "Introduction," in *Imperialism* (New York: Walker).

Dickens, Charles (1948), *David Copperfield* (London: Oxford University Press). (First publ. 1849–50.)

Dickens, Charles (1949), *Oliver Twist* (London: Oxford University Press). (First publ. 1937–9.)

Dickens, Charles (1955), *Hard Times* (London: Oxford University Press). (First publ. 1854.)

Dickens, Charles (1957), *American Notes and Pictures from Italy* (London: Oxford University Press), 228–43. (First publ. 1842–6.)

Eagleton, Terry (1995), *Heathcliff and the Great Hunger: Studies in Irish Culture* (London: Verso).

Eliot, George (1954–78), *The George Eliot Letters*, ed. Gordon S. Haight, 9 vols. (New Haven: Yale University Press; London: Oxford University Press).

Eliot, George (1967), *Daniel Deronda* (Harmondsworth: Penguin). (First publ. 1876.)

Eliot, George (n.d.), "The Modern hep! hep! hep!" *Impressions of Theophrastus Such*, in *The Works of George Eliot* (Edinburgh: Blackwood).

Gaskell, Elizabeth (1973), *North and South* (London: Oxford University Press). (First publ. 1854.)

Haggard, H. Rider (1989), *King Solomon's Mines* (New York: Oxford University Press). (First publ. 1885.)

Haggard, H. Rider (1991), *The Annotated* She: *A Critical Edition of H. Rider Haggard's Victorian Romance*, ed. Norman Etherington (Bloomington: Indiana University Press).

Knox, Robert (1969), *The Races of Men: A Fragment* (Miami: Mnemosyne). (First publ. 1950.)

Lorimer, Douglas (1978), *Colour, Class, and the Victorians: A Study of English Attitudes toward the Negro in the Mid-Nineteenth Century* (Leicester: Leicester University Press).

Lukács, Georg (1962), *The Historical Novel* (London: Merlin). (First publ. 1937.)

Macaulay, Thomas (1967), "Government of India," in *Macaulay: Prose and Poetry*, selected by G. M. Young (Cambridge, Mass.: Harvard University Press). (First publ. 1835.)

Marcus, Steven (1965), *Dickens: From Pickwick to Dombey* (London: Chatto & Windus).

Pike, E. Royston, ed. (1966), *Human Documents of the Industrial Revolution in Britain* (London: Allen & Unwin).

Porter, Andrew (1999), "Introduction," in *The Oxford History of the British Empire: The Nineteenth Century* (Oxford: Oxford University Press).

Said, Edward W. (1993), *Culture and Imperialism* (New York: Knopf).

Scott, Walter (1998) *Waverley* (Oxford: Oxford University Press). (First publ. 1814.)

Thackeray, William (1963), *Vanity Fair* (Boston: Riverside). (First publ. 1847–8.)

Williams, Raymond (1966), *Culture and Society, 1780–1950* (New York: Harper & Row). (First publ. 1958.)

FURTHER READING

Brantlinger, Patrick (1988), *Rule of Darkness: British Literature and Imperialism, 1830–1914* (Ithaca: Cornell University Press).

Bristow, Joseph (1991), *Empire Boys: Adventures in a Man's World* (London: HarperCollins).

Chaudhuri, Nupur and Strobel, Margaret, eds. (1992), *Western Women and Imperialism: Complicity and Resistance* (Bloomington: Indiana University Press).

David, Deirdre (1995), *Rule Britannia: Women, Empire, and Victorian Writing* (Ithaca: Cornell University Press).

Hyam, Ronald (1990), *Empire and Sexuality: The British Experience* (Manchester: Manchester University Press).

Kiernan, V. G. (1986), *The Lords of Human Kind: Black Man, Yellow Man, and White Man in an Age of Empire* (New York: Columbia University Press). (First publ. 1969.)

Meyer, Susan (1996), *Imperialism at Home: Race and Victorian Women's Fiction* (Ithaca: Cornell University Press).

Perera, Suvendrini (1991), *Reaches of Empire: The English Novel from Edgeworth to Dickens* (New York: Columbia University Press).

Stocking, George (1987), *Victorian Anthropology* (New York: Free Press).

Viswanathan, Gauri (1989), *Masks of Conquest: Literary Study and British Rule in India* (New York: Columbia University Press).

6

The Victorian Novel
and Religion

Hilary Fraser

On the day she read the third episode of Elizabeth Gaskell's *North and South*, serialized in *Household Words* in 1854, Charlotte Brontë wrote to her friend that she liked it "well, and better and better each fresh number." Understandably, given the novel's focus on Mr. Hale's crisis of conscience in its early chapters, she takes its subject to be the Church of England rather than the Condition of England, as would later become apparent, and it is on this assumption that she comments:

> The subject seems to me difficult: at first, I groaned over it. If you had any narrowness of views or bitterness of feeling towards the Church or her Clergy, I should groan over it still; but I think I see the ground you are about to take as far as the Church is concerned; not that of attack on her, but of defence of those who conscientiously differ from her, and feel it a duty to leave her fold.

She concedes that "it is good ground," but warns that it is "still rugged for the step of Fiction; stony – thorny will it prove at times – I fear" (Wise and Symington 1980: 153).

This exchange between the novelist daughter of an Anglican clergyman (recently married to his high church curate) and the novelist wife and daughter of Unitarian ministers is of interest for a number of reasons. First, it gives a sense of the sectarian tensions that existed in mid-nineteenth-century Britain and frequently informed its fiction; it suggests that there was a recognized genre of Dissenting fiction which displayed the very narrowness and bitterness towards the established church, on the part of those who were themselves "everywhere spoken against" (Cunningham 1975), that Brontë was relieved to find absent from her friend's work. Second, as an intelligent critical response to a work in progress that was to evolve from one kind of novel into another, it demonstrates how hard it is to draw boundaries around a strictly conceived category of religious fiction. For, while there were indeed many novelists in the period who wrote with a distinctly doctrinal purpose, there were many too who, like Gaskell, included contemporary religious issues in their work but were more interested in the broader social issues with which they intersected; others (including Brontë herself) whose religious sensibility manifested itself in unorthodox ways; and others again (such as Anthony Trollope) who located their stories in ecclesiastical settings, but whose concerns were preponderantly worldly. Third, it is noteworthy that Brontë's remarks about the difficulties of rendering contemporary dramas of faith and doubt in a fictional form ironically reveal how heavily the language and codes available to the novelist in this period were freighted with religious signification. The rugged and stony path that she maps out for the writer of religious fiction draws upon a trope – that life is a journey, beset with trials, with a moral destination – which not only shaped Bunyan's *Pilgrim's Progress*, that crucial fictional prototype familiar to Victorian readers and writers alike, but was also to provide the organizing narrative framework for much of their own fiction, not least Brontë's own (Qualls 1982; Ermath 1997: 4).

This chapter will pursue the trajectories suggested by Brontë's response to Gaskell's novel in greater detail, and in so doing develop a sense of the complexity with which the Victorian novel articulated and helped produce the religious debates of the period. I will first briefly consider the principal religious denominations and movements and their status in Victorian England, the Acts of Parliament and laws that sustained the pre-eminence of the established church and their gradual removal, and the particular moments of crisis that marked the religious history of the century, before looking at a sample of those texts that may unequivocally be classified as religious novels, in that their primary objective was the fictional realization of spiritual and doctrinal battles. I will then cast my net more broadly, to examine that class of texts which is not narrowly polemical, but in which religious ideas and histories are given imaginative embodiment, and are in some way critical to the fictional effect. For example, the development of the novel as a genre can be said to have been profoundly affected by the beliefs, practices and spiritual narratives of evangelicalism, with its assertion of the unique importance of the individual and its focus upon self-examination, moral development, and conversion (Jay 1979: 7). Similarly, it is not hard to see how the novel might have been imaginatively informed by the beliefs of a secularized "religion of humanity," as the faith of the positivist followers of Auguste Comte was termed (Wright 1986), or by other religious perspectives – the Judaic, for example – which challenged the hegemony of a Christian world view. Moreover, during a period when the Bible itself was read as a kind of novel, in which might be found the origins of narrative, it is not surprising that the scriptures were frequently invoked to legitimate and give meaning to the Victorian novel, or that contemporary biblical hermeneutics influenced the typological use of symbolism, for instance, in the secular literary form (Landow 1980; Prickett 1996). Finally, I will turn to the larger question of the rhetoric and emplotment of Victorian novels, to consider how in the course of the century the prevailing "providential aesthetic" (Vargish 1985) came to be supplanted by a secular and historical narrative code. Here I will ask: What were the implications for narrative composition of the idea that there is "a sacred masterplot that organizes and explains the world" (Brooks 1984: 6)? And how was a loss of faith in such providential plots to manifest itself discursively in the way novels were framed and organized? To what extent was the ordering of narrative governed by teleology? Or dysteleology? How did God's plots come to be overlaid by Darwin's plots, or Kelvin's plots, or worse (Beer 1983; Ermath 1997: 45–6)? In this section, as in the first two parts of my discussion, I interpret my topic to include doubt and loss of faith as well as belief, and to encompass religious difference, both within and beyond the Anglican fold.

By adopting such a tripartite structure, I hope to suggest some of the different ways in which we might think about the crucial nexus between religion and the novel in Victorian England. For the rich and varied history and experience of religion in the period is of interest not only as an important context within which fiction was produced, as the historical background against which to understand the imaginative work, or even insofar as it supplies a variety of novelistic subjects and styles. It also profoundly affected the novel at the level of organization – its tropological form, the ordering of narrative – and this in turn became the bearer of cultural meaning. Narrative form itself offered modes of interpretation, explanation, and understanding that articulated and confirmed, or modified, or, in some cases, radically challenged religious orthodoxies. In such ways, novels actively participated in religious debate, in much the same way as social novels contributed to ongoing debates about the condition of England, and did not merely passively reflect it.

It is hoped that such an approach will enable an appreciation of the multiple ways in which religious history, ideas, and experience are inscribed in Victorian fictional texts. In the case of *North and South*, for example, even though finally Gaskell pays little attention to sectarian distinctions, and indeed the general tendency of the text is ecumenical, it is important that we understand something of the context of Mr. Hale's conscientious dissent from the doctrines of the Church of England, and of Fred Hale's position as a Roman Catholic, and of Bessy Higgins's Methodism. Gaskell's imaginative focus is, however, more on the connections between the Anglican clergyman's crisis of conscience at the beginning of the novel, as he struggles with his obligation to subscribe to the Thirty-nine Articles, and his daughter's crisis of conscience later in the novel, associated with the lie she tells in order to protect her brother, and it is helpful to know that this focus was likely governed by Gaskell's Unitarian belief in the importance of, as one reviewer of the novel noted, obeying "the truth, which is always invisible, and not the outward forms of truth, which are always imperfect" (Easson 1991: 358). Her preoccupation with the social, rather than the doctrinal, and her preference for realism rather than the transcendental, also aligns her with Nonconformism and evangelicalism. Furthermore, if, like the evangelicals, she put her faith in individual conversion, rather than in structural and legal reform or radical politics, as the key to the amelioration of the conditions of the poor in industrial England and the end of the class war between masters and men, this is because, as Elizabeth Ermath observes, "her vision . . . is informed by providential considerations not Marxist ones" (Ermath 1997: 33). And yet, as Ermath also notes, Gaskell is writing in a secular form, that of the serialized work of fiction, which, with its episodic form and cumulative effect, is a "publishing format [which] declares by its very nature the evolutionary possibilities of sequence" (p. 103). A historical plot is therefore palimpsestically imposed on the novel's providential plot. Such textual negotiations are inevitable when the sacred traffics in the secular, and similar maneuvers may be identified in other branches of religious art and literature in the nineteenth century, such as Pre-Raphaelite painting and Tractarian poetry. My purpose in this chapter is to tease out these tensions between the sacred and the secular as they occur in the particular arena of the novel.

I

In her famous article "Silly Novels by Lady Novelists" George Eliot makes honorable exception of both Elizabeth Gaskell and Charlotte Brontë as she catalogues the aesthetic crimes committed by contemporary female writers. She reserves her most acerbic criticism for the women who write religious novels – whether of the general "*mind-and-millinery* species," a meretricious composite of "the frothy, the prosy, the pious, or the pedantic" (Eliot 1963: 301); the "*oracular* species" (p. 310), "generally inspired by some form of High Church, or transcendental Christianity" (p. 317), of which she notes that "as a general rule, the ability of a lady novelist to describe actual life and her fellow-men, is in inverse proportion to her confident eloquence about God and the other world, and the means by which she usually chooses to conduct you to true ideas of the invisible is a totally false picture of the visible" (p. 311); or the "*white neck-cloth* species, which represent the tone of thought and feeling in the Evangelical party," which she describes as "a kind of genteel tract on a large scale, intended as a sort of medicinal sweetmeat for Low Church young ladies" (p. 317).

Eliot's taxonomy here, by which "silly" novels are classified as high church, evangelical, or broadly Anglican, provides a convenient framework for our analysis of religious novels that may be extended to include those which are neither silly nor by ladies. Indeed, Eliot herself was to produce profound fictional studies that focused upon the spiritual lives not only of individual members of these various groups within the Anglican fold, but also of Nonconformists, Roman Catholics, Jews, and doubters. She was well placed to do so, having been brought up as an evangelical, lost her faith, translated into English some of the most significant examples of the modern German biblical scholarship that proved to be so damaging to Victorian belief, and eventually become, like so many intellectuals of the day, a Comtean positivist, committed to a broadly ethical religion of humanity. Although in 1839, in the full fervor of her evangelical girlhood, she had denounced religious novels as "hateful" books, "monsters that we do not know how to class" (Eliot 1954–78: vol. 1, 23), there had been, of course, a venerable tradition of evangelical fiction since the turn of the century, when writers such as Hannah More and the Revd. J. W. Cunningham commanded a popular readership extending far beyond the circle of the elect. As Elisabeth Jay has shown in her expert analysis of Anglican evangelicalism and the nineteenth-century novel (Jay

1979), it was a tradition that was to exercise a significant influence throughout the century. Eliot's own first work of fiction, *Scenes of Clerical Life* (1858), was a sympathetic portrayal of Anglican evangelicalism which ably countered the pernicious effects of the trashier forms of low church fiction she pillories so mercilessly in "Silly Novels." Furthermore, there was not one of her subsequent novels that did not have a significant religious dimension. Given Eliot's own agnosticism, the pervasiveness of her concern with religion in her fiction may seem surprising. Indeed, more generally, it is extraordinary how many Victorian plots turn on matters of faith – which prompts the question: Why were religious issues considered to be such good copy for fiction?

It is no exaggeration to say that the established church was in crisis in the middle decades of the nineteenth century, and the drama of its embattled defence of its traditional rights and privileges was acted out on a very public stage, so that the ramifications of that crisis seemed to touch on the lives of every individual. The Anglican church was under attack both from without and from within. The theory of evolution, gathering momentum through the first half of the nineteenth century and fully articulated by Charles Darwin in *The Origin of Species* in 1859, contradicted the very essence of William Paley's argument from design, or natural theology, according to which evidence of God's creative hand was found in the ordered perfection of the natural universe, which had constituted the philosophical foundation of the Anglican faith. Simultaneously, the historicist biblical scholarship emanating from Germany exposed the unreliability of the gospel narratives, and accordingly undermined the scriptural foundations of the church. The combined impact of Darwinism, the so-called "higher" biblical criticism, and skepticism towards the authority and status of the church was nothing short of devastating, and many individuals felt a profound sense of spiritual dislocation in the face of the disappearance of God from their world (Miller 1975).

In the meantime, the privileged status of the established church was being eroded by a series of parliamentary and legal reforms. The Repeal of the Test Act in 1828, and Catholic emancipation in 1829, enabled non-Anglicans to enter Parliament, at which point the vulnerability of a church so closely identified with the secular authority of the state began to become apparent. Soon Jews were to gain access to parliamentary representation, when in 1835 the requirement to swear the Christian abjuration oath was removed. Although it was not until much later that the civil disabilities of non-Anglicans were entirely removed (it was not until 1837 that Dissenting chapels could be registered for marriage and 1880 that Dissenters were entitled to perform their own burial rites in parish churchyards; and – despite Gladstone's Universities Test Act of 1871 – it was nearly fifty years before the Oxbridge BD and DD degrees were open to non-Anglicans [Cunningham 1975: 19–20]), the Whig reforms that followed hard upon the 1832 Reform Act made the church aware that its spiritual authority was radically compromised by its established status. The reforms of the Irish church in 1833, although necessary and long overdue, provoked alarm among high church Anglicans because they constituted an intervention in church affairs by a civil government that depended on Catholic and

Dissenting votes. John Keble's delivery of his famous assize sermon on "National Apostasy" in Oxford on 14 July 1833 came to be seen as the inauguration of the Oxford Movement, which sought to restore in the public mind the sense that the Anglican ministry possessed a divine authority independent of the state and establishment.

The Oxford Movement, or Tractarianism as it was otherwise known from the "Tracts for the Times" on particular Anglican doctrines published under its auspices, brought about a much-needed theological renovation of the Church of England, under the charismatic leadership of such cultured and brilliant men as Keble and John Henry Newman. It also generated a new genre of fiction, in which handsome, passionate, but virtuous high church heroes, such as Charlotte M. Yonge's Sir Guy Morville in *The Heir of Redclyffe* (1853), experience interesting spiritual conflicts and do battle with the forces of evil in their romantic quest for spiritual perfection. However, the movement that was to be the savior of the Anglican church also turned out to be a further thorn in its side. Doctrinally, Tractarianism appeared to many to teeter on the edge of Romanism, and such suspicions seemed confirmed when a number of high-profile members of the Oxford Movement, most notably Newman himself in 1845, went over to Rome.

Newman was later to describe his conversion experience in his spiritual autobiography, *Apologia Pro Vita Sua* (1864), in a manner more grippingly dramatic than any novel, but in the meantime the romance of the charismatic Oxford don's spiritual crisis and his tortuous journey to Rome lent itself to fictional treatment by both Catholics, for whom Newman's heroic struggle with his conscience made him a perfect novelistic subject, and non-Catholics, warning against the dangers of being seduced by Rome. A number of novelists in this period explored the perilous attraction of Rome for those susceptible to its charms, from the relatively sympathetic Elizabeth Sewell to her anti-papist brother William, and from the urbanely aesthetic Benjamin Disraeli to the histrionic Elizabeth Harris. It was the latter's *From Oxford to Rome* (1847) that provoked Newman to write his conversion novel *Loss and Gain* (1848), whose hero Charles Reding follows his author's path from the dreaming spires of Oxford to Rome. Fears of the infiltration of popery were further fanned by the restoration of the Roman Catholic hierarchy in Britain in 1850. Cardinal Wiseman himself, the first Archbishop of Westminster, was to enter the fictional fray with his own *Fabiola; or, The Church of the Catacombs* (1854), a historical novel that inaugurated the Catholic Popular Library series under whose imprint Newman's *Callista: A Sketch of the Third Century* (1856) appeared. Newman's second novel was written in response to Charles Kingsley's anti-Catholic historical novel *Hypatia: or, New Foes with Old Faces* (1853), in an interesting fictional anticipation of the circumstances which prompted him to write the *Apologia*. Like the theological treatises of the day, these novels referred to the history of the early church as a crucial context for the religious debates of the nineteenth century.

But if Rome and the conversion plot provided one type of fictional scenario, loss of faith, or, more specifically, loss of faith in the dogmatic foundations of the Anglican church, provided another. Tractarianism had stirred up among all parties within the

Church of England questions about the articles of faith upon which their religion rested. In their sermons and essays, and in the Tracts for the Times, Newman, Keble, William Palmer, Hurrell Froude, and others had set themselves the task of exposing and correcting the general ignorance, even among its clergy, of the true nature of the Church of England, stressing its apostolic descent as the central article of faith upon which its authority was founded, and exploring the real meaning of the beliefs and institutions and sacraments which had been for so long simply taken for granted. Clergymen, in particular, were obliged to examine their consciences anew, to determine whether they could unreservedly subscribe to the Thirty-nine Articles; whether they did believe in the letter of the scriptures, the creeds, the doctrines of everlasting punishment and of baptismal regeneration. If the church felt on the one hand beset by papal aggression, and compelled to patrol the borders between High Anglicanism and Catholicism, it was also experiencing another kind of threat to its integrity from the other end of the spectrum. For the "broad church movement," led by such figures as Thomas Arnold and Benjamin Jowett, as its name suggests, sought to make the church more inclusive rather than exclusive, by relaxing the boundaries that divided Anglicanism from Dissent. Publications such as the controversial multi-authored *Essays and Reviews* (1860) attempted to reconcile the established church's position with the various intellectual movements by which it was assailed, to assimilate change rather than to retreat to the high moral and theological ground. As Jowett wrote from Oxford to a friend in 1861, defending *Essays and Reviews*, to which he had been a major contributor, against censure, "In a few years there will be no religion in Oxford among intellectual young men, unless religion is shown to be consistent with criticism" (Abbott and Campbell 1897: vol. 1, 345).

His fears were well founded. Even the broad church was not broad enough to accommodate the doubts of some Anglican clerics who, when forced by the general climate of "criticism," found that in all conscience they could not affirm their faith in the Thirty-nine Articles. Charlotte Brontë's misplaced expectation that Elizabeth Gaskell's hero was to be Mr. Hale, and that the plot was to center on his religious difficulties as a conscientious man of the Church, was entirely reasonable given the vogue for such novels in the period. The drama of personal intellectual and spiritual crisis – of severance from the church, and possibly loss of faith – and its devastating impact on families and communities was one that exercised a number of Victorian novelists throughout the period, from James Anthony Froude to Mrs. Humphry (Mary Augusta) Ward. The clergyman hero of Froude's *Nemesis of Faith* (1849), Markham Sutherland, resigns his living when he can no longer subscribe to the Anglican articles and creeds. Froude was later to provide a historical context for the crisis of faith experienced by his fictional hero and other doubters of his generation in an essay on "The Oxford Counter-Reformation," in which he described the state of the church before it was revolutionized by Tractarianism:

> It was orthodox without being theological. Doctrinal problems were little thought of.
> Religion, as taught in the Church of England, meant moral obedience to the will of

God. The speculative part of it was accepted because it was assumed to be true. The
creeds were reverentially repeated; but the essential thing was practice . . . About the
powers of the keys, the real presence, or the metaphysics of doctrine, no one was anxious,
for no one thought about them. (Froude 1899: vol. 4, 239–40)

Little wonder, then, that clergymen such as Sutherland, and later Robert Elsmere,
were so ill-equipped to cope with the profound theological questions raised by the
Oxford Movement on the one hand and the new biblical criticism on the other. Ward's
Robert Elsmere (1888) tells the story of an Anglican clergyman, married to a devout
evangelical churchwoman, who comes to have doubts about historical Christianity
and resigns his orders. He becomes a Unitarian and does mission work in the East
End of London, abandoning faith in the supernatural element of Christianity to concentrate on good works. His decision causes serious strains in his marriage, but he
and his wife are finally reconciled before his untimely death ends the novel. In proof
of the enduring popularity of the conversion plot even this late in the century, the
novel was an enormously popular bestseller. Its spectacular sales figures notwithstanding, Oscar Wilde's character Cyril, in "The Decay of Lying," sees its subject
matter and treatment as passé, remarking that "As a statement of the problems that
confront the earnest Christian it is ridiculous and antiquated . . . It is as much behind
the age as Paley's *Evidences* [published in 1794] or Colenso's method of Biblical
exegesis [which had caused a scandal in 1862]" (Wilde 1989: 221).

If Robert Elsmere finds refuge in Dissent, another eponymous hero, Mark
Rutherford, depicts the somewhat bleaker fate of the Nonconformist hero who loses
his faith. William Hale White's *The Autobiography of Mark Rutherford* (1881) cannot
be accused of being behind the age, but its author is writing in the 1880s with a
strong sense of the passing of a generation. At the beginning of *The Autobiography*,
the eponymous hero laments: "I feel increasingly that the race to which I belonged is
fast passing away, and that the Dissenting minister of the present day is a different
being altogether from the Dissenting minister of forty years ago" (White 1988: 9).
The retrospective mode of *The Way of All Flesh* (1903), Samuel Butler's brilliantly
satirical attack on Victorian evangelicalism, and its protagonist's insistence "on
addressing the next generation rather than his own" (Butler 1993: 429), similarly suggests a watershed, serving, as Elisabeth Jay argues, "to confirm for a new
generation the remoteness of Evangelicalism as a dominant force" (Jay 1979: 284).
At the end of his seminal study of Dissent in the Victorian novel, Valentine
Cunningham observes that, indeed, "the obsolescence of Nonconformity, as of
Calvinism, or Christian orthodoxy, or of Christianity itself, is continually and
widely affirmed," while "What the novelists envisage as viable alternatives are
offered instead" (Cunningham 1975: 278). Another way of thinking about this is
to suggest that, unlike writers such as Newman and Froude, for whom the pressing
intellectual, spiritual, and doctrinal questions of the day were the crucial imaginative
impetus of their work, and whose novels fall generically at the very boundaries of
fiction, to use George Levine's suggestive term (Levine 1968), the novelists to whom

Cunningham alludes saw their task as showing how religion operates in a broader social context.

II

There is an appreciable difference between those novelists who write about religion and its representatives from a close personal knowledge and those who write as outsiders. The hostility shown by William Hale White, whose background was Congregationalist, towards the Dissenters who turn away Mark Rutherford from his intended vocation, and by Samuel Butler, who was raised in an evangelical family, towards the evangelicalism from which Ernest Pontifex finally dissociates himself, is quite unlike that of writers who, knowing little of sectarian doctrinal differences, and of the varieties of evangelicalism and Dissent, often confused the two in undiscriminating generalized caricatures. Nevertheless, neither White nor Butler was as interested in doctrine as in the social and ethical behavior of his characters, and what this tells us about the real state of their souls. Their critical focus is the narrow-minded bigotry and the complacent hypocrisy of those, whatever their sectarian persuasion, who profess to be Christians. Elizabeth Gaskell's motive in *Ruth* (1853) is rather to offer a fictional delineation of exemplary Christian behavior, when she contrasts the attitude of a sympathetic Dissenting minister and his sister towards an abandoned single mother and her illegitimate child with that of the so-called Christians who condemn her as a fallen woman. Nevertheless, her concern is also with practice rather than doctrine. As Cunningham observes, "Mrs. Gaskell is ultimately less interested in her Dissenters as Dissenters than as Christians" (Cunningham 1975: 140).

Just as the social, economic, and political upheavals of the early Victorian period provoked many novelists to re-open the question of what constituted a true gentleman, in the context of the unprecedented class mobility which saw a wealthy self-made manufacturer like Gaskell's Mr. Thornton in *North and South* employing an impoverished former clergyman to give him tutorials in the classics, so the revolutions that had taken place in the church during the same period invited a similar interrogation of what it meant to be a Christian. Indeed, the two questions were not unconnected; for there were clear social distinctions drawn between, for example, evangelical Anglicanism and Dissent, and "low" and "high" church sympathies tended to correspond to lower and higher class positions. It was this fundamental re-evaluation of the qualities that made a person a true Christian that formed the real theme of many Victorian novels. Even when a novelist such as Anthony Trollope chooses an entirely ecclesiastical setting, as in the *Chronicles of Barsetshire* (1855–67), and a predominantly clerical cast, the clergymen are conspicuously untheological, barely religious even, in their preoccupations. Although the low church Mr. Slope and Mrs. Proudie are pitted against the old "high and dry" church group led by Archdeacon Grantly, Trollope is concerned less with the doctrinal struggles within the church that so exercised the more strictly religious novelists than he is with the behavior of individuals within such a powerful institutional structure as they jockey for influential and lucrative positions. The power struggles over who will be warden and who will be dean are a vehicle for his defense of such characters as the unheroic and flawed Mr. Harding, who nevertheless is represented as a man of conscience, possessing the unfashionable Christian virtues of meekness and humility.

As a consequence of this perceived need for a reappraisal of the real meaning of Christianity (in social and ethical, rather than in doctrinal terms), the plotting and characterization of the Victorian novel often invite readers to examine their prejudices, and to discover and affirm, along with the hero or heroine, an appropriate personal moral and spiritual value system by which to live in the modern world. Charlotte Brontë's *Jane Eyre* is one such novel, whose heroine undergoes an episodic spiritual journey through a typological landscape, from Gateshead, to Lowood, to Thornfield and beyond, in which she encounters a spectrum of religious types, from the sadistic and menacing Mr. Brocklehurst to the saintly and self-denying Helen Burns and the icily zealous, repressive St. John Rivers. Although Jane learns a degree of self-governance from Helen Burns, she can finally conform to none of these rather unattractive examples of evangelical practice. Rather, the aspect of evangelical faith that shapes Brontë's heroine in this and her other novels is its emphasis on the individual's personal relationship with God and capacity for making personal ethical judgments, even if they appear to conflict with the teaching of the church or seem out of step with contemporary societal values. Jane follows her conscience rather than submitting to any of those in whom spiritual or social or economic authority is vested.

The valorization of the individual in Victorian fiction is generally attributed to the fact that the novel as a form, in this its heyday, was underpinned by the ideological imperatives of bourgeois capitalism; but it also suggests how profound an impact evangelicalism had in this phase of the novel's formal development, both on the characterization of the intensely self-analytical protagonist and in providing a narrative structure. It is striking how many Victorian fictional protagonists are presented with serious ethical dilemmas to which organized religion can give them no answers, testing their integrity, and obliging them to develop an active ethical consciousness and identity that can enable them to function as independent moral agents in a complex social world. Jane Eyre herself has to make conscientious choices which span the extremes of entering an adulterous relationship with the man she loves and becoming the wife of a missionary she doesn't, and in this she is like other heroines who experience conflicts between love, or its failures, and duty, for which their formal religious education has given them no preparation, and who must undergo trials and reversals before finding salvation. The heroine of Anne Brontë's *The Tenant of Wildfell Hall* (1848), Helen Huntingdon, is obliged to negotiate her own independent path as a Christian woman trapped within a disastrous marriage. Her conscientious decision to leave her husband, taking their child with her when he is in danger of being corrupted by his father's debauchery, is one that conflicts with her duty to her marriage vows, and she meets with social disapprobation even when posing as a widow to avoid detection. Her decision to return to nurse her dying husband is similarly a matter of personal conscience; "Nothing persuaded her but her own sense of duty" (Brontë 1992: 430), her brother explains to the man who loves her. The same may be said of her part in wrestling to save her lost husband's soul. Her resolve to return when she did is justified by her later conviction of his salvation, "the blessed confidence that, through whatever purging fires the erring spirit may be doomed to pass – whatever fate awaits it, still, it is not lost, and God, who hateth nothing that He hath made, *will* bless it in the end!" (Brontë 1992: 456).

Spiritual crises are gendered in the Victorian novel; remaining true to her sacred marriage vows in the face of intolerable personal suffering is the burden of a number of fictional heroines. The eponymous Romola is persuaded to return to her husband Tito by no less a figure of patriarchal authority than Savonarola, whom she meets on the road out of Florence. "My daughter, you must return to your place" (Eliot 1999: 363), he urges; when she confesses that she can no longer love her husband, he rejoins: "My daughter, there is the bond of a higher love" (p. 369). She does return to Florence, but, like Jane Eyre and Helen Huntingdon, has too much spiritual independence to conform to the corporate authority of the church, and must act upon her own sense of what is right. Although her own first husband is not guilty of such heinous crimes as Tito, Dorothea Brooke, the heroine of George Eliot's *Middlemarch*, is similarly unhappy in her choice of partner and, in the absence of adequate spiritual guidance from the church, also has to draw on her own reserves of inner strength to survive her marital disappointments. The "English and Swiss Puritanism" and "meagre Protestant histories" that nurtured her youthful religiosity provided no resources for dealing with the adult woman's dilemmas. She must find the grounds for self-unity and belief, and indeed for self-transcendence, within herself, rather than in organized religion.

George Eliot is one of the novelists to whom Valentine Cunningham refers as offering what they envisage to be viable alternatives to historical Christianity in their fiction: "Eliot replaces a supernaturally sanctioned Christianity by its humanist 'essence'" (Cunningham 1975: 278). Nevertheless, she draws on traditional religious forms and language in her secular redefinition of Christianity for a despiritualized world. As Barry Qualls argues, "Each of George Eliot's novels is a spiritual biography or *Bildungsroman* focusing on Bunyan's question 'What shall I do?' and charting the 'civil war within the soul' . . . as answers are sought" (Qualls 1982: 141). Furthermore, his contention is, more generally, that many Victorian novelists were indebted to the cultural inheritance of the seventeenth-century Puritan tradition: to spiritual biography, emblem books, and the typological reading of scripture, all of which still formed a significant part of the cultural and imaginative life of Victorian England. Above all, he notes their indebtedness to the narrative form of Bunyan's *Pilgrim's Progress*: "Their plots are essentially his plot," he argues (p. 13).

Taking his title from *Pilgrim's Progress*, Thackeray makes his satirical play on Bunyan's text the organizing principle of *Vanity Fair* (1847), but the intertextual allusiveness to this tradition in other novels of the period is typically more indirect and subtle. Qualls traces the use of emblems such as the prison, the dunghill, the mirror, the labyrinth, the rescue of the shipwrecked pilgrim, and of other inherited religious ideas and forms by novelists such as George Eliot, Charlotte Brontë, and Charles Dickens. He sees the double focus of their sacred/secular scripture as its defining characteristic, and attributes the Victorians' need to underwrite their secular narratives of modern life with the emblems, parables, and plots of religious tradition to the very erosion of religious certainties in mid-nineteenth-century Britain that made theirs such a different intellectual and spiritual environment from Bunyan's:

> Lacking Bunyan's assurance, readers and writers held all the more tenaciously to his language. They were determined to shape the facts of this world into a religious topography, making a path towards social unity in this world an analogue to Christian's progress towards the Celestial City. They used "typological symbolism" because, as Hugh Witemeyer has said of George Eliot, "it offered a way of conferring spiritual meaning upon the representation of phenomenal experience, of affirming the existence of design while yet representing the integrity of history." (Qualls 1982: 12)

Intriguingly, one of the most powerful modern exemplars of Christian's progress towards the Celestial City in Victorian fiction is a Jew – Daniel Deronda. Judaism, like other non-Christian religions, is not well represented in the Victorian novel, with the Jew being either culturally stereotyped as cunning and rapacious (one thinks of Dickens's Fagin, for example) or impossibly idealized as poor but wise and good, or as a romantic and cosmopolitan protector/savior (such as Dickens's Riah and Disraeli's Sidonia). Even the Jewish poet and journalist Amy Levy, who in an article of 1886 on "The Jew in Fiction" had regretted that "there had been no serious attempt at serious treatment of . . . Jewish life and Jewish character" (Levy 1993: 17), was to produce a portrayal of upper-middle-class Anglo-Jewry in her novel *Reuben Sachs* (1888) that proved offensive to many readers both then and now. Part of her purpose in that novel was to offer a less idealized representation of modern Jewish life than she found in Eliot's novel, of which she wrote: "It was, alas! No picture of Jewish contemporary life, that of the little group of enthusiasts, with their yearnings after the Holy Land . . . As a novel treating of modern Jews, *Daniel Deronda* cannot be regarded as a success, although every Jew must be touched by, and feel grateful for the spirit which breathes throughout the book" (Levy 1993: 17).

Despite Levy's reservations, George Eliot does seek to challenge antisemitic prejudice and stereotyping in *Daniel Deronda* (1876), and to offer a serious account of Judaic religious history, faith, and culture. To this end, she presents us with a hero, the Daniel of the title, who, although raised as a Christian in an English aristocratic household, discovers his Jewish heritage, and increasingly seems emblematic of an ancient culture which offers redemptive hope for a degenerate and regressive English society. In so doing, she makes a genuine and courageous attempt to represent in fiction an alternative spiritual vision to the dominant Christian world view. Despite her good intentions, and her particular aim to demonstrate the "peculiar debt" and "peculiar thoroughness of fellowship in religious and moral sentiment" of Christians towards "the Hebrews" and other "oriental peoples" (Eliot 1954–78: vol. 6, 301–2), Eliot's deployment of Jews as a signifier of otherness – notably through her stress on Mordecai's Orthodox, patriarchal, and visionary Messianic faith, rather than on modern Reform Judaism – means that, as Reina Lewis argues, *Daniel Deronda* tends to replicate orientalist tropes of difference (Lewis 1996: 192; Brantlinger 1992). The hybridized Daniel, combining the best of Englishness and Christianity and of Judaism, remains separated from Mordecai, the unadulterated, unassimilable Jew. As Lewis points out, "The Jews in *Daniel Deronda* are often of a sort calculated to stay strange, unlike the Methodists in *Adam Bede* who, though strange to the villagers, are found to be familiar," and suggests that this is because "Mordecai's Kabbalistic vision not only offers a way to reconstruct society, but conveniently relocates nineteenth-century Jews in a spiritually glowing medieval past, thereby bypassing any of the difficulties associated with contemporary Jews with all their flaws" (Lewis 1996: 209–10). Amy Levy's fictional riposte reinforces Lewis's argument, when in *Reuben Sachs* a Christian convert to Judaism finds Jewish society so "little like the people in *Daniel Deronda*:"

> "Did he expect," cried Esther, "to see our boxes in the hall, ready packed and labelled *Palestine?*"
>
> "I have always been touched," said Leo, "at the immense good faith with which George Eliot carried out that elaborate misconception of hers." (Levy 1993: 238)

George Saintsbury wondered in his review of the novel for the *Academy* "whether the phase of Judaism now exhibited, the mystical enthusiasm for race and nation, has sufficient connexion with broad human feeling to be stuff for prose fiction to handle" (Carroll 1971: 374). But actually it is precisely through such historical and cultural displacements that religion continued to find a place in Victorian fiction, at least for an author like Eliot, who had lost her faith in historical Christianity. Reviewing *Daniel Deronda* in the *Spectator*, as it appeared part by part (29 January, 8 April, 10 June, 29 July 1876), R. H. Hutton found "more of moral presentiment, more of moral providence, and more of moral subordination to purposes higher and wider than that of any one generation's life" than in any of Eliot's earlier fiction. He concluded in his final unsigned review of the novel in the *Spectator* (9 September), when it was published in four volumes, that "The art of this story is essentially religious" (Carroll 1971: 366). But might not the overdetermined insistence of this and other Victorian novels on presentiment, providence, and higher purposes signify something other than confirmation of the religious certitudes that Hutton is so keen to find? Peter Brooks has suggested that:

> The enormous narrative production of the nineteenth century may suggest an anxiety at the loss of providential plots . . . The emergence of narrative plot as a dominant mode of ordering and explanation may belong to the large process of secularization, dating from the Renaissance and gathering force in the Enlightenment, which marks a falling away of those revealed plots – the Chosen People, Redemption, the Second Coming –

that appeared to subsume transitory human time to the timeless . . . And this may
explain the nineteenth century's obsession with questions of origin, evolution, progress,
genealogy, its foregrounding of the historical narrative as par excellence the necessary
mode of explanation and understanding. (Brooks 1984: 6–7)

This is something that Thomas Carlyle understood when he remarked on the
importance of linearity in narrative in his essay "On History." Narrative, he proposes,
"travels towards one, or towards successive points," thereby enabling a person to feel
part of a teleological historical order, and to "unite himself in clear conscious relation
. . . with the whole Future and the whole Past" (Carlyle 1896–1901: vol. 27, 88–9).
In his discussion of the ways in which plot generates meaning in the European bildungsroman, Franco Moretti distinguishes between this kind of teleological rhetoric,
whereby "events acquire meaning when they lead to *one* ending, and one only," and
its opposite, whereby "Meaning is the result not of a fulfilled teleology, but rather, as
for Darwin, of the total rejection of such a solution" (Moretti 1987: 7). The concluding section of this chapter will consider further the semantics of narrative form,
in particular how the rejection, or merely the loss, of a teleological and providential
aesthetic is represented in the fictional plotting of the late nineteenth-century novel.

III

In her important study of evolutionary narrative, Gillian Beer observes that "Fiction
in the second half of the nineteenth century was particularly seeking sources of authoritative organisation which could substitute for the god-like omnipotence and
omniscience open to the theistic narrator" (Beer 1983: 160). In *Daniel Deronda* George
Eliot still organizes her plot around the Judeo-Christian trope of the spiritual journey,
but this is in part because this was the only language available to her. Darwin himself
encountered the same difficulty when he had to articulate his theory of evolution in
a language that was permeated with natural-theological assumptions. It is a problem
encapsulated in the very title of his most famous work, *The Origin of Species*, in which
he actually challenges the prevailing belief in absolute origins and an originary first
cause with a theory of natural law and adaptation, and undermines the whole notion
of fixed species (Beer 1986: 212, 221). Gillian Beer notes that at first evolutionism
itself seemed "to offer a new authority to orderings of narrative which emphasized
cause and effect, then, descent and kin." However, she adds, as its implications became
more fully understood, "its eschewing of fore-ordained design (its dysteleology)
allowed chance to figure as the only sure determinant" (Beer 1983: 8).

These different orders of plot are legible in *Daniel Deronda* alongside that of the
pilgrim's journey. Clearly descent, kin, and causal sequence are important organiza-
tional principles of the novel, but they are not unproblematically so. Chance is a presiding theme, from the opening scene at the casino onwards; the narrative is ruptured
by sudden, unpredictable changes in fortune; the plot does not evolve in the ways that

we, or its characters, anticipate, and we are left with a sense of multiple possibilities, of narrative plurality and indeterminacy rather than singularity, fixity, inevitability. Although Moretti reads the novel as a quintessential example of teleological rhetoric and closure, of the "classification" principle rather than the "transformation" principle, its meaning lying in the finality of the hero's marriage to "not so much a woman, as a rigidly normative culture" (Moretti 1987: 7–8), *Daniel Deronda* is actually much more open-ended than he suggests. We do not know the outcome of Gwendolen's story, and neither do we know the future of the Zionist state to which Daniel dedicates himself (Beer 1983: 193). Indeed, the novel may be read as a critique of teleology. As Gillian Beer points out, "the book moves into that central problem focused by Darwinian theory: is there a foreknown or an ultimate plan? Is teleology itself a fiction? – do we self-protectively interpret as providence that which is chance?" (Beer 1983: 191).

Moretti judges *Daniel Deronda* to be a "disaster," and attributes its failure to the fact that "Eliot was tempted by the impossible, and tried to capture the essence of a new historical phase with the most significant symbolic form of the previous age" (Moretti 1987: 227). Ten years after its publication, another novelist began writing fiction that faced square-on the bankruptcy of the available symbolic forms, narrative codes, and language of Judeo-Christian tradition for the modern world. Thomas Hardy entirely repudiated the Puritan allegory and romantic quest narratives that sustained his Victorian predecessors. Plot in his fiction, "so careless of the single life" (Tennyson 1987: vol. 2, 371), is never providential. In his last and darkest novel, *Jude the Obscure* (1895), the ideologies of a Christian class society that underpinned so much mid-Victorian fiction – the belief in "self-help," for example, in both its worldly and its spiritual forms – are savagely critiqued, and the plots that the characters imagine for themselves are cruelly mocked. Jude Fawley's spiritual journey to Christminster is grimly parodic of Christian's to the Celestial City. Indeed, Jude's most obvious spiritual prototype is not Christian, but Job, his God a punishing Old Testament deity. His dying words, punctuated by the cheers of the revelers outside, are taken, with minor variations, from the Book of Job (3: 3, 4, 7, 11, 13, 18–20):

> *"Let the day perish wherein I was born, and the night in which it was said, There is a man child conceived."*
>
> ("Hurrah!")
>
> *"Let that day be darkness; let not God regard it from above, neither let the light shine upon it. Lo, let that night be solitary, let no joyful voice come therein."*
>
> ("Hurrah!")
>
> *"Why died I not from the womb? Why did I not give up the ghost when I came out of the belly? . . . For now should I have lain still and been quiet. I should have slept: then had I been at rest!"*
>
> ("Hurrah!")
>
> *"There the prisoners rest together; they hear not the voice of the oppressor . . . The small and the great are there; and the servant is free from his master. Wherefore is light given to him that is in misery, and life unto the bitter in soul?"* (Hardy 1998: 403)

The jarring, interpolated "Hurrah!"s, like parodic "Amens" in this litany of despair, mark an incursion of the satirical into the hero's final tragic encounter with his God in this world that would have been unthinkable to a previous generation. *Jude the Obscure* pushes the genre of the religious novel to its limits, and its hero's deathbed scene may be said to sound the death knell to the fictional form that in so many ways defined the central preoccupations of the Victorian age.

REFERENCES

Abbott, E. and Campbell, L. (1897), *The Life and Letters of Benjamin Jowett, MA*, 2 vols. (London: John Murray).

Beer, Gillian (1983), *Darwin's Plots: Evolutionary Narrative in Darwin, George Eliot and Nineteenth-Century Fiction* (London: Routledge & Kegan Paul).

Beer, Gillian (1986), "'The Face of Nature': Anthropomorphic Elements in the Language of *The Origin of Species*," in L. J. Jordanova, ed., *Languages of Nature: Critical Essays on Science and Literature* (London: Free Association Books), 207–43.

Brantlinger, Patrick (1992), "Nations and Novels: Disraeli, George Eliot, and Orientalism," *Victorian Studies*, 35/3, 255–75.

Brontë, Anne (1992), *The Tenant of Wildfell Hall*, ed. Herbert Rosengarten (Oxford: Clarendon Press). (First publ. 1848.)

Brooks, Peter (1984), *Reading for the Plot: Design and Intention in Narrative* (New York: Vintage; Oxford: Clarendon).

Butler, Samuel (1993), Michael Mason (ed.), *The Way of All Flesh* (Oxford and New York: Oxford University Press). (First publ. 1903.)

Carlyle, Thomas (1896–1901), "On History," in H. D. Traill, ed., *The Works of Thomas Carlyle*, centenary edn., 30 vols. (New York: Charles Scribner's Sons), vol. 27. (First publ. 1830.)

Carroll, David, ed. (1971), *George Eliot: The Critical Heritage* (London: Routledge).

Cunningham, Valentine (1975), *Everywhere Spoken Against: Dissent in the Victorian Novel* (Oxford: Clarendon).

Easson, Angus, ed. (1991), *Elizabeth Gaskell: The Critical Heritage* (London and New York: Routledge).

Eliot, George (1954–78), *The George Eliot Letters*, ed. Gordon S. Haight, 9 vols. (London: Oxford University Press; New Haven: Yale University Press).

Eliot, George (1963), "Silly Novels by Lady Novelists," in Thomas Pinney, ed., *Essays of George Eliot* (New York: Columbia University Press; London: Routledge & Kegan Paul). (First publ. 1856.)

Eliot, George (1999), *Romola*, ed. Leonée Ormond (London: Dent). (First publ. 1863.)

Ermath, Elizabeth Deeds (1997), *The English Novel in History 1840–1895* (London and New York: Routledge).

Froude, James Anthony (1899), "The Oxford Counter-Reformation," in *Short Studies on Great Subjects*, 4 vols. (London: Longman, Green & Co.).

Hardy, Thomas (1998), *Jude the Obscure*, ed. Dennis Taylor (London: Penguin). (First publ. 1895.)

Holstrom, John, and Lerner, Laurence, eds. (1966), *George Eliot and Her Readers: A Selection of Contemporary Reviews* (London: Bodley Head).

Jay, Elisabeth (1979), *The Religion of the Heart: Anglican Evangelicalism and the Nineteenth-Century Novel* (Oxford: Clarendon).

Landow, George (1980), *Victorian Types, Victorian Shadows: Biblical Typology in Victorian Literature, Art and Thought* (Boston: Routledge & Kegan Paul).

Levine, George (1968), *The Boundaries of Fiction* (Princeton: Princeton University Press).

Levy, Amy (1993), *The Complete Novels and Selected Writings of Amy Levy, 1861–1889*, ed. Melvyn New (Gainesville: University Press of Florida).

Lewis, Reina (1996), *Gendering Orientalism: Race, Femininity and Representation* (London and New York: Routledge).

Miller, J. Hillis (1975), *The Disappearance of God: Five Nineteenth-Century Writers* (Cambridge, Mass.: Belknap/Harvard University Press).

Moretti, Franco (1987), *The Way of the World: The Bildungsroman in European Culture* (London: Verso/New Left).

Prickett, Stephen (1996), *Origins of Narrative: The Romantic Appropriation of the Bible* (Cambridge: Cambridge University Press).

Qualls, Barry V. (1982), *The Secular Pilgrims of Victorian Fiction: The Novel as Book of Life* (Cambridge: Cambridge University Press).

Tennyson, Alfred (1987), "In Memoriam A. H. H.," in *The Poems of Tennyson*, ed. Christopher Ricks, 2nd edn., 3 vols. (Harlow: Longman). (First publ. 1850.)

Vargish, Thomas (1985), *The Providential Aesthetic in Victorian Fiction* (Charlottesville: University Press of Virginia).

White, William Hale (1988), *The Autobiography of Mark Rutherford and Mark Rutherford's Deliverance, edited by his friend Reuben Shapcott*, ed. Don Cupitt (London: Libris).

Wilde, Oscar (1989), "The Decay of Lying," in Isobel Murray, ed., *Oscar Wilde* (Oxford and New York: Oxford University Press, Oxford Authors series). (First publ. 1889.)

Wise, Thomas James and Symington, John Alexander, eds. (1980), *The Brontës: Their Lives, Friendships and Correspondence*, 2 vols. (Oxford: Blackwell). (First publ. 1932, 4 vols.)

Wright, T. R. (1986), *The Religion of Humanity: The Impact of Comtean Positivism on Victorian Britain* (Cambridge: Cambridge University Press).

FURTHER READING

Bebbington, D. W. (1989), *Evangelicalism in Modern Britain: A History from the 1730s to the 1980s* (London: Unwin Hyman).

Binfield, Clive (1977), *So Down to Prayers: Studies in English Nonconformity* (London: Dent).

Chadwick, Owen (1970), *The Victorian Church*, 2nd edn., 2 vols. (London: Adam & Charles Black).

Chadwick, Owen (1975), *The Secularisation of the European Mind in the Nineteenth Century* (Cambridge: Cambridge University Press).

Cosslett, Tess, ed. (1984), *Science and Religion in the Nineteenth Century* (Cambridge and New York: Cambridge University Press).

Fraser, Hilary (1986), *Beauty and Belief: Aesthetics and Religion in Victorian Literature* (Cambridge and New York: Cambridge University Press).

Hall, Donald E. (1994), *Muscular Christianity: Embodying the Victorian Age* (Cambridge: Cambridge University Press).

Hogan, Anne, and Bradstock, Andrew, eds. (1998), *Women of Faith in Victorian Culture: Reassessing the Angel in the House* (London: Macmillan; New York: St. Martin's).

Jasper, David and Wright, T. R., eds. (1989), *The Critical Spirit and the Will to Believe: Essays in Nineteenth-Century Literature and Religion* (London: Macmillan; New York: St. Martin's).

Jay, Elisabeth, ed. (1983), *The Evangelical and Oxford Movements* (Cambridge: Cambridge University Press).

Kreuger, Christine L. (1992), *The Reader's Repentance: Women Preachers, Women Writers, and Nineteenth-Century Social Discourse* (Chicago and London: University of Chicago Press).

Lightman, Bernard (1987), *The Origins of Agnosticism: Victorian Unbelief and the Limits of Knowledge* (Baltimore: Johns Hopkins University Press).

Mackillop, I. D. (1986), *The British Ethical Societies* (Cambridge: Cambridge University Press).

McLeod, Hugh (1996), *Religion and Society in England, 1850–1914* (London: Macmillan; New York: St. Martin's).

Maison, Margaret (1961), *Search Your Soul, Eustace: A Survey of the Religious Novel in the Victorian Age* (New York: Sheed & Ward).

Newsome, David (1966), *The Parting of Friends: A Study of the Wilberforces and Henry Manning* (London: John Murray).

Nockles, Peter Benedict (1994), *The Oxford Movement in Context: Anglican High Churchmanship, 1760–1857* (Cambridge and New York: Cambridge University Press).

Parsons, Gerald, ed. (1988), *Religion in Victorian Britain*, 4 vols. (Manchester: Manchester University Press/Open University).

Reardon, Bernard (1971), *Religious Thought in the Victorian Age: A Survey from Coleridge to Gore* (London: Longman).

Royle, Edward (1980), *Radicals, Secularists, and Republicans: Popular Freethought in Britain, 1866–1915* (Manchester: Manchester University Press).

Smart, N., Clayton, J., Katz, S. and Sherry, P., eds. (1985), *Nineteenth Century Religious Thought in the West* (Cambridge: Cambridge University Press).

Vance, Norman (1985), *Sinews of the Spirit: The Ideal of Christian Manliness in Victorian Literature and Religious Thought* (Cambridge: Cambridge University Press).

Wheeler, Michael (1990), *Death and the Future Life in Victorian Literature and Theology* (Cambridge and New York: Cambridge University Press).

Wolff, Robert Lee (1977), *Gains and Losses: Novels of Faith and Doubt in Victorian England* (New York and London: Garland).

Wolffe, John, ed. (1997), *Religion in Victorian Britain*, vol. 5: *Culture and Empire* (Manchester and New York: Manchester University Press).

7
Scientific Ascendancy
John Kucich

An enormous increase in the prestige and authority of science was, perhaps, the central intellectual event of the Victorian period. Although the pace of British technological innovation had been accelerating throughout the industrial revolution, the birth of what we now think of as modern science profoundly affected the Victorian cultural imagination. Not until the nineteenth century was the word "science" itself applied exclusively to study of the natural or physical world. Previously, any pursuit of knowledge might be called a "science," and observers of the physical world were often termed "natural philosophers." Over the course of the nineteenth century, however, science as a specialized field, as well as the branches and subdisciplines that comprise it, literally came into being. Chemistry separated itself from physics, to become its own branch of study; geology emerged from fossil-hunting and landscape description; and biology dissociated itself from natural history. Subdisciplines like embryology or seismology appeared, along with "bridge" disciplines such as biochemistry. This new disciplinary order does not merely reflect a professional redistribution of tasks and titles. It is symptomatic of Victorian science's powerful conceptual reorganization of the knowable world – cosmic, psychological, and social – as well as its introduction of astonishingly new models for understanding the nature of human life itself. It also signals, implicitly, a new conception of science's autonomy and its precedence among the types of knowledge. What is most striking about the birth of modern science in the nineteenth century is the tremendous impact science had on all aspects of Victorian intellectual life and culture. Looking back at the second half of the nineteenth century, Beatrice Webb wrote:

[W]ho will deny that the men of science were the leading British intellectuals of that period; that it was they who stood out as men of genius with international reputations; that it was they who were the self-confident militants of the period; that it was they who were routing the theologians, confounding the mystics, imposing their theories on philosophers, their inventions on capitalists, and their discoveries on medical men;

whilst they were at the same time snubbing the artists, ignoring the poets and even casting doubts on the capacity of the politicians? (Webb 1926: 126–7)

Webb's characterizations oversimplify the complexity of Victorian attitudes toward science, but they do capture the fundamental rearrangement of intellectual authority – as well as the widespread excitement – sparked by scientific advances. Educated Victorians, caught up in the sensational growth of science, often developed amateur passions for fossil-hunting, insect-collecting, seashell study, and the like. Victorian novelists, like other intellectuals, were profoundly influenced by the pace and the significance of scientific advances – although science's effects on literature were mixed, and sometimes even contradictory. Discrete scientific discoveries, of course, haunt the pages of Victorian novels (for instance, George Eliot's use of optics, in *Middlemarch* [1871], as in her famous analogy between "egoism" and the concentric rings produced by placing a candle on a scratched surface; or Wilkie Collins's fascination with the methods of forensic science in solving the mystery of *The Woman in White* [1860]). But Victorian science was forced to the surface of the novel, above all, by its revolutionary ideas about the history, nature, and processes of human life, as well as by the unprecedented popular accessibility of those ideas.

In particular, new scientific models brought rational knowledge into direct conflict with religion, igniting controversies that deeply engaged novelists. A series of scientific theories (primarily those of geology and astronomy in the first half of the century, and those of evolutionary biology in the second) put into question the biblical account of divine creation, and of human pre-eminence among species. George Eliot once claimed that "the supremely important fact" of the Victorian age was "that the gradual reduction of all phenomena within the sphere of established law, which carries as a consequence the rejection of the miraculous, has its determining current in the development of physical science. The great conception of universal regular sequence [is] the most potent force at work in the modification of our faith" (Eliot 1865: 55).

One of the most important links between scientists and novelists was their common attempt to replace religious conceptions of worldly order with rational models. Victorian fiction is a thoroughly secular form, rejecting appeals to, or instances of, divine intervention (with rare exceptions, such as Rochester's miraculous, telepathic communication with Jane at the end of Charlotte Brontë's *Jane Eyre* [1847]). While scientific authority often seemed to spring directly from its undermining of religious belief, the fact that many writers turned to science itself to provide a more secure source of moral and social unity is, perhaps, an even more telling sign of the prestige and power of science. All the same, Victorian science was itself wracked by debates between partisans of either "religious" or "value-free" methodologies, and, as a result, the secular models explored by novelists varied greatly in their philosophical implications.

The accessibility of Victorian scientific writing was an equally important factor in consolidating its social authority. Nineteenth-century scientific writing rarely departed from a rhetoric and vocabulary shared by the educated layman, and scientific books and essays were read avidly by non-specialists. In addition, for those readers who did not have the time to read lengthy works by, say, the evolutionist Charles Darwin, or the geologist Charles Lyell, well-informed popularizations of scientific work were authored by writers like Mary Somerville, or, late in the century, by the scientist–philosopher Thomas Huxley. Popularizations of science were also widely circulated in such magazines as the *Westminster Review*, the *Cornhill*, and the *Fortnightly Review*. These journals printed summaries of scientific theories and discoveries side by side with the latest fiction. In consequence, Victorian novelists were not only likely to be familiar with scientific ideas, but found their works competing directly with those of scientists for the attention of the educated reading public. In this competition, a facility with scientific thought was indispensable for novelists. The reviewer Edward Dowden claimed that

> the truest pedantry, in an age when the air is saturated with scientific thought, would be to reject [it] . . . Insensibility to the contemporary movement in science is itself essentially unliterary . . . The cultured imagination is affected by it, as the imagination of the men of Spenser's time was affected by his use of the neoclassical mythology of the Renaissance. (Dowden 1877: 360)

The cross-fertilizations between Victorian science and literature can be traced both ways, since scientists often invoked literary texts and metaphors. Scientists depended on magazine writing and the lecture circuit for their livings – before they overcame Anglican resistance, late in the century, to their enfranchisement in the universities – and this necessity alone compelled a clear, literate style. But many Victorian scientists also preserved a sincere respect for the values of literary culture. Both Huxley and the physicist John Tyndall declared that reading Thomas Carlyle had been formative at early stages of their careers; and Darwin frequently alluded to literary classics. The demands of popular accessibility, as well as a desire to prove their own cultural legitimacy, together with many scientists' liberal educations and philosophical beliefs – all helped produce a recognizably literary stylistics in scientific writing. Lyell borrowed rhetorical devices from Ovid, and the physicist James Clerk-Maxwell did the same with Tennyson. In "Matter and Force," Tyndall claimed that natural processes were best described by scientists through analogies – a rhetorical method he specifically linked with creative discourse: "You *imagine* where you cannot *experiment*" (Tyndall 1898a: vol. 2, 60). In the course of his Rede lecture in 1865, he declared: "the study of natural sciences goes hand in hand with the culture of the imagination" (Tyndall 1871: 46). Citing these profuse cross-fertilizations, George Levine (1987) has argued that Victorian literature and science cannot in any meaningful way be considered separate cultures.

Scientific and novelistic discourses shared epistemological principles, as well as philosophical attitudes and professional concerns. In this chapter I will consider, in turn, each of these three areas of convergence. To begin with the epistemological conjunction: its most obvious manifestation is the realist aesthetic of Victorian fiction. Victorian realists condemned instances of the poetic, the ideal, or the metaphysical in fiction, and promoted notions of "correspondence" between novelistic action and the facts of nature or psychology. As Charlotte Brontë's narrator put it in *The Professor* (1857): "Novelists should never allow themselves to weary of the study of real Life" (ch. 19). While they claimed fidelity to the real world, Victorian novelists did not naïvely believe their work presented unmediated reality. Rather, they saw themselves – much like scientists – to be engaged in a kind of controlled study of the world, almost as if the novel were a kind of laboratory experiment. In *Middlemarch*, for example, Eliot claims to explore "the history of man," showing "how the mysterious mixture behaves under the varying experiments of time" (Prelude), and the novel's section titles ("Two Temptations," "Three Love Problems") suggest a series of laboratory experiments. In France, Emile Zola would make the laboratory model explicit with his "experimental novels" and "naturalism." The general aesthetic ideals of Victorian fiction, as well as its moral values – detachment, self-denial, truthfulness – derive, in part, from experimental procedures. Like Victorian scientists, too, novelists were devoted to ordering through typology. According to Georg Lukács, Victorian novelists were trying, in particular, to represent character "types" that might model the range and coherence of human behavior: "The central category and criterion of realist literature is the type" (Lukács 1964: 6). The novels of Wilkie Collins, Charles Dickens, George Meredith, and others investigate obsessive character types, for example. Other writers were preoccupied with exploring medical pathologies, such as hereditary insanity (which is pivotal in the plots of both *Jane Eyre* and Mary Elizabeth Braddon's *Lady Audley's Secret* [1862]), or the physiognomic traits of criminal or otherwise perverse character types.

There were, indeed, a number of scientific ideas or metaphors besides typological classification that saved writers from naïve assumptions about objectivity – or what Thomas Hardy disdained as "copyism" (Hardy 1925: 87). In addition to dramatizing their ongoing exploration of the real world, or demonstrating the viability of typological systems, novelists shaped their work to formulate natural, sociological, or psychological laws. Victorian science systematically prioritized the hidden laws of nature it claimed to find at work beneath the confusing surface of physical appearances. Lyell's epigraph to *Principles of Geology*, for instance, came from John Playfair's *Illustrations of the Human Theory of the Earth* (1802): "Amid all the revolutions of the globe, the economy of Nature has been uniform, and her laws are the only things that have resisted the general movement" (Lyell 1837: v). Novelists such as Dickens, Eliot, and Anthony Trollope created fictional worlds whose orderliness and coherence depended on their fidelity to the laws of human interaction. Among other things, this emphasis on natural and social law helped render most Victorian fiction "conservative" in its stress on social stability, and on gradual rather than catastrophic theories of change – in contrast to the revolutionary disposition of romantic literature.

As a result of its search for foundational laws, the dominant structuring device of much Victorian fiction was detection. In the sensation fiction of Collins, Braddon,

Charles Reade, and others, or in the bestselling *Adventures of Sherlock Holmes* (1891) by Arthur Conan Doyle, detection often organizes both plot and thematic structures. The processes of detection absorbed novelists because detection depends on the existence of immutable laws that enable observers to link phenomena together within explanatory systems. Bertrand Russell has famously suggested that what both scientific and literary detection have in common is an idealization of logic – or, in his terms, of logical positivism: "The sense of reality is vital in logic, and whoever juggles with it by pretending that *Hamlet* has another kind of reality is doing a disservice to thought" (Russell 1919: 170). While writers such as Dickens (most famously in *Hard Times* [1854]) may have criticized scientists for dehumanizing social relations, he nevertheless consistently celebrated the deductive power of scientific intelligence through the investigative work of characters such as Inspector Bucket in *Bleak House* (1852) and the lawyer Jaggers in *Great Expectations* (1860). Dickens also defended the more implausible incidents of his fiction (notoriously, the spontaneous combustion of Krook in *Bleak House*) in scientific (or, in this case, pseudoscientific) rather than imaginative terms. In addition, Dickens practiced a kind of abstract sociological descriptiveness derived from science – also found in writers such as Trollope, Eliot, and Hardy. Instead of providing detailed physical descriptions of slums in *Bleak House*, for example, Dickens adopts an abstract rhetoric meant to convey both precision and comprehensiveness. But Dickens's deepest affinities with science are revealed through the increased presence of detectives and mystery plots in his novels after midcentury. Even his novels' absorption with familiar, everyday things is driven by a sense that ordinary things are not what they seem, and must be interpreted by those skilled in deductive abilities.

Finally, Victorian novelists borrowed from scientific methodology an insistence that formal procedures should be congruent with the phenomena observed. As George Eliot put it: "if I have ever allowed myself in dissertation or in dialogue [anything] which is not part of the structure of my books, I have there sinned against my own laws" (Eliot 1954–78: vol. 5, 459). For all these reasons, Victorian realism was the first aesthetic form in literary history to have systematically incorporated the methods, procedures, and analytical goals of science. It was also the first literary aesthetic to make epistemological methods drawn from science the basis for the formal principles of order within literary works.

The philosophical relationship between Victorian fiction and science (particularly, but not exclusively, their common renovation of theological beliefs) is deeply intertwined with the secular aspects of narrative form – experimental procedures, preoccupation with typologies, the formulation of natural laws, detection, structural correspondence – that Victorian fiction borrowed from scientific epistemologies. The most important philosophical link, which follows directly on secularization, is that novelists and scientists were both concerned to find an underlying congruence between natural order and human society. Their optimism about the possibility of such a congruence was expressed in a widely popularized nineteenth-century philosophy called "scientific naturalism," which was based directly on August Comte's system of philosophical "positivism." Naturalism, following the lead of Comte and the positivists, affirmed a harmonious relation between the structure of the human mind and that of the natural world. Its faith in such harmony paralleled that of romantic philosophy, although naturalism rejected the idealistic metaphysics of romanticism, which valued the unifying energies of the aesthetic imagination over rationality and objectivity. Positivism, which has been falsely caricatured as the naïve pursuit of objective truth, was primarily concerned to explain natural systems by articulating the rationality of natural laws. Faith in the shared rationality of both human observer and natural phenomena was the key to the positivists' rejection of theological or metaphysical models of understanding, without thereby opening the door to relativism, or to the potential solipsism of an ungrounded romantic imagination. To cite a familiar example, Darwinian theory illustrates the principles of positivism by asserting the regularity of natural law; by affirming the inextricability of human and natural order through logical deductions from empirical study; and by repudiating any purely imaginative will, divine or otherwise, in the regulation of evolutionary processes. Tyndall evoked the positivists' faith in a harmonious confluence of human and natural systems when he proclaimed, rapturously: "all our philosophy, all our poetry, all our science, and all our art – Plato, Shakespeare, Newton, and Raphael – are potential in the fires of the sun" (Tyndall 1898b: vol. 2, 131). Or, as Mill once put it, all knowledge of the world must begin with "the scientific view of nature as one connected system, or united whole, united not like a web composed of separate threads in passive juxtaposition with one another, but rather like the human or animal frame, an apparatus kept going by perpetual action and reaction among all its parts" (Mill 1963–75: vol. 10, 423–3).

Because it was so fundamentally optimistic about the rational basis in nature of human experience, positivism was a deeply reformist philosophy. It sought not merely to describe the harmonies between natural and human processes, but to prescribe the political changes that would help develop a social order conforming to these processes – a cause which the positivists identified with moral good. The progressive philosophical ambitions of positivism carried its influence beyond natural science itself, leading to important developments in psychology (Mill), sociology (Comte), ethics (Herbert Spencer), and language study (the Vienna circle). But positivists were more directly concerned with the progressive moral principles discoverable in natural order itself, and with the possibility of extrapolating social order directly from nature. Ultimately, they presented science not just as a methodology, but as itself the means of furthering social regeneration. As Mill put it: "The backward state of the Moral Sciences can only be remedied by applying to them the methods of Physical Science, duly extended and generalized" (Mill 1963–75: vol. 8, 833).

For Comte, and for his most dedicated advocates – among them Mill, Spencer, Frederic Harrison, George Henry Lewes, and John Morley – positivism became a kind of scientific religion, or what Comte himself called the "Religion of Humanity." It substituted innate human moral potentials for God as an object of worship. As a result of its faith in rational, impartial observation, and in the organic unity of nature and moral good, positivism explored social progress through the fundamental moral opposition of egoism and altruism. Positivism's chief moral goal was to demonstrate that altruism, with its tendencies toward objective sympathy and unbiased perception, was conducive to the social realization of nature's intrinsic order, while egoism was synonymous with faulty science. The moral mission of positivism, especially its exaltation of altruism, was reflected in all forms of scientific naturalism, even those that may have distanced themselves from certain positivist orthodoxies. Although the moral rhetoric shifts considerably, for example, a similar spirit might be said to inspire late Victorian and Edwardian sexology, which hoped, through the scientific exploration of human nature, to bring society into a candid, open conformity with sexual needs and thus produce both a moral and a physical utopia.

While some Victorian novelists (notably the early George Eliot) fully endorsed the positivist faith, many others struggled with the philosophical difficulties latent in positivist thought. For example, positivism often seemed to leave little room for human agency, since it subordinated human imagination to the inexorability of natural law. Darwinian evolution was probably the most striking instance of a theory that denied belief in human will as a force for change. Victorian evolutionists who clung to their faith in human agency sometimes sought refuge in the "intentionalist" theories of Chevalier de Lamarck, who argued that individual organisms grope toward beneficial change (as giraffes stretch their necks by continually reaching for food in high places, for example), and then pass their incremental progress on to their progeny through heredity – although Lamarckian theory was soundly discredited late in the century. In general, despite the pious respect scientists themselves often expressed for literature and the arts, positivism tended to leave the imaginative faculties in a decidedly secondary relation to truth. Strict Comtean positivists believed that art should faithfully represent a natural order that was actively knowable only through scientific observation.

These conflicts between the claims of science and the claims of human agency, will, and imaginative power became more and more pronounced over the course of the Victorian period, until, in the 1880s and 1890s, philosophers and novelists started to emphasize the intractable differences between science and aesthetics – differences later consolidated by modern writers' emphasis on the autonomy of the literary symbol (as in James Joyce's fictional "epiphanies," for example, or Oscar Wilde's enigmatic portrait of Dorian Gray), or on the self-referentiality of narrative worlds, such as Thomas Hardy's Wessex – not to mention the mythicized worlds of Joyce's *Ulysses* (1922) and Djuna Barnes's *Nightwood* (1937). But despite occasional satires of the most extreme versions of positivism – for instance, Dickens's ridicule of Thomas Gradgrind's reverence for "facts" in *Hard Times* – Victorian novelists generally sought to reconcile the optimistic social vision of scientific naturalism with their own affirmation of human will or imagination. Late Victorian naturalism – particularly the work of George Gissing and George Moore – drew on French naturalist theories, most fully developed by Emile Zola, to establish an objectively verifiable, synthetic relationship between the human imagination and natural law. But the more common approach among Victorian novelists was to attempt an adjustment of the balance between human creativity and scientific naturalism, in the pursuit of a social vision that was grounded in some concept of organic moral good.

George Eliot is the paramount instance of a novelist who struggled to adjust this balance. Over the course of her career, Eliot moved from being a disciple of Comte to believing that scientific naturalism should be modified to include the autonomous and uniquely human power of moral vision. Preoccupied as she was with the break-down of traditional moral systems (signified in her first novel, *Adam Bede* [1859], by the failure of moral leadership in Arthur Donnithorne, and the failure of maternal instinct in Hetty Sorrel), Eliot explored her characters' quests for an alternative per-sonal and social order – quests that, early in her career, conformed closely to scien-tific naturalism. *Adam Bede*, for example, is a transparent positivist allegory, in which Dinah Morris embodies nature's altruistic moral order, and serves as the reference point for the moral development of Adam himself: "Tender and deep as his love for Hetty had been . . . his love for Dinah was better and more precious to him . . . 'It's like as if it was a new strength to me,' he said to himself . . . 'For she's better than I am – there's less o' self in her, and pride'" (ch. 64). Through Adam, Eliot suggests that the sexual instinct itself (which is to say, nature) is the source of this "more precious" kind of human love, since Adam's moral development depends on the growth of his romantic love away from the narcissistic Hetty and towards the self-sacrificing Dinah. In these ways, the novel illustrates the dependence of social order on altruism, while it shows the aspiration toward altruism to have its source in biology, particularly in the sexual instinct.

In *Middlemarch*, however, Eliot satirizes her positivist figures, Lydgate and Casaubon, for their mechanical efforts to ground moral regeneration in the disciplines of biological science and cultural anthropology, respectively. Lydgate's quest for the "primitive tissue," like Casaubon's for the "key to all mythologies," is an attempt to discover natural ordering principles from which social and moral good might be derived. But *Middlemarch* frustrates these positivist quests, and suggests instead that attempts to reform society on moral grounds depend on desires that are intrinsically human, but that are representable only through art – not through science – and that do not depend on an infallible correspondence between individual effort and natural law. Rather than celebrating objective natural laws fully accessible to human obser-vation, Eliot stresses the intuitive and undefinable qualities of human moral vision, which gropes toward principles of natural and social order through imaginative experiment. One sign of this emphasis is Eliot's growing faith in symbolic language. In *The Mill on the Floss* (1860), Eliot had lamented that all language is saturated with metaphor: "intelligence so rarely shows itself in speech without metaphor . . . that we can so seldom declare what a thing is, except by saying it is something else" (bk 2, ch. 1). But in her later work, this lament is transformed into an affirmation of the organic potentials of symbolic language. Dorothea Brooke's prophetic role in *Middle-march* is to defend "desiring what is perfectly good, even when we don't quite know what it is" (ch. 39). Thus, too, the banner of political reform in *Middlemarch* is carried by an artist, an imaginative thinker – Will Ladislaw. One crucial aspect of this shift is that, in *Middlemarch*, the overtly taxonomic organization of human life that Eliot borrows from positivism (which is embodied in her specimen-like array of characters at similar life-stages: loving, dying, launching careers, etc.) is modified by an emphasis on human difference and originality. Following Darwin, who believed individual variation to be the motor of evolution, Eliot's companion George Henry Lewes wrote: "Let us never forget that Species have no existence. Only individuals exist, and these all vary more or less from each other" (Lewes 1862: 155).

From *Middlemarch* onwards, Eliot turned to the prophetic imagination of her individual protagonists for the expression of her faith in the moral regeneration of society, and resigned herself to the always incomplete but nevertheless progressive tendencies of that regeneration. Her faith in the organic potential of prophetic vision depended largely on her belief in the power of symbolic language to convey moral order. But she also affirms the indirect ways in which certain characters' imaginative vision aids in the moral transformation of others. In *Daniel Deronda* (1876), through Mordecai's transformation of Daniel, together with Daniel's transformation of Gwendolen, Eliot stresses the incremental moral progress generated by the prophetic seeker, rather than trying to uncover an ideal moral order, available either to rational human observation or to prophetic imaginative vision. Nevertheless, the incremental progress Eliot's characters achieve suggests that for her, within the social realm, human responsibility for evolutionary development has replaced the Darwinian principle of "natural selection." An emphasis on human responsibility for social evolution had, in fact, gained much currency in scientific circles during the 1870s and 1880s – in Darwin's own late work, *The Descent of Man* (1871); in the studies of the eugenicist Francis Galton; and in the preoccupation with scientific "prediction" that dominates the work of the mathematician William Clifford and others at this time.

Eliot's apostasy from strict positivist thinking also led to some degree of skepticism about the fulfillment of her protagonists' imaginative yearnings – a skepticism she shares with numerous late Victorian novelists. After all, Will's political career in *Middlemarch* is launched in "those times when reforms were begun with a young hopefulness of immediate good which has been much checked in our days" (Finale). Furthermore, Eliot recognizes in *Middlemarch* that the vastness of natural processes is a deterrent to any quest for large-scale social solutions – a demoralizing recognition that saturates much late Victorian fiction. "I . . . have so much to do in unravelling certain human lots," her narrator declares, "and seeing how they were woven and interwoven, that all the light I can command must be concentrated on this particular web, and not dispersed over that tempting range of relevancies called the universe" (ch. 15). The failure of Eliot's protagonists to realize social progress in their own lifetimes deeply qualifies their idealism, and the later novels do not express the unrestrained optimism of *Adam Bede. Daniel Deronda*, in particular, emphasizes the unknowability of past and future, especially in its unresolved debates about the future of Jewish nationalism. Eliot ultimately appears to believe, like Darwin, that we live in a world of mixed conditions, in which perfection is unrealizable, or is at least not dictated by some kind of natural design: "I believe . . . in no law of necessary development," Darwin declared in *On the Origin of Species* (Darwin 1988: vol. 15, 250).

The cautious optimism that survives in Eliot's late novels, however, does owe a great deal, ironically, to evolutionary theory. Eliot continually stresses the gradualist effects of human action, despite the inevitable incompleteness of the historical process at any given moment of time. Herbert Spencer's ideas about the completion of individual effort in the future progress of the human race as a whole greatly shaped Eliot's gradualist vision, as it did the gradualism of a number of other late Victorian writers – particularly the feminist Olive Schreiner, who, in a somewhat more melancholic key, stressed that the unrewarded efforts of her rebellious female protagonists would ultimately be redeemed by the painfully slow progress of sexual enlightenment in society at large. Late-century feminist fiction thrives on the belief in deferred evolutionary progress. Eliot's own gradualist hopes for ongoing, super-individual progress are inscribed into the very title of *Middlemarch*. In general, Eliot's various modifications of scientific naturalism do not add up to a rejection of positivism, since she continues to believe in the inherent, natural basis of human moral vision. Her modifications parallel those of William James's pragmatism – which, though growing out of positivism, nevertheless placed its faith in human intuition as a guide for scientific inquiry. They also parallel the less overtly intellectual attitudes of Dickens, whose moralistic affirmation of human interconnectedness, like Eliot's ideas about the human "web," also synthesized observed sociological fact with creative, moral imagination.

Among scientists, philosophical differences over the relationship between empirical science and imagination eventually divided logical positivists (who came to disavow the moral responsibilities of science altogether) from pragmatists, who, like Eliot, grew to see science as an instrument in service of deeper human intuitions of moral good. In the second half of the century, a few scientific dissidents protested against the amorality of positivism, or what the psychologist Frederic W. H. Myers described as the "new orthodoxy of materialistic science," which he saw as "too narrow to contain [human] feelings and aspirations" (Myers 1886: vol. 1, liv–lv). Henry Sidgwick, James Ward, Alfred Russel Wallace, James Martineau and other scientific thinkers disputed naturalism's tendency to refer all human experiences and values to rational laws – forming a loose group of thinkers that Frank Miller has termed "extranaturalists" for their secular belief in human potentials that remain beyond the reach of scientific analysis. The impact of these thinkers on Victorian science was negligible, but for late-century novelists, public debate over the conflicts between scientific and humanistic world views led productively in two contrary directions, which are each latent in the work of Eliot – her modified naturalistic meliorism, on the one hand; and her moments of doubt about the reconciliation of individual human agency and the social order, on the other. In exemplary ways, Meredith and Hardy take up the two sides of this issue, seeming to divide Eliot's vacillations between them.

Meredith adopted Eliot's more optimistic view of the gap between the existing social order and human desire, believing that, by nature, human beings are more inclined to altruism than to egoism, and that human prophetic imagination would eventually reform the social world in moral terms. In *The Egoist* (1879), Clara Middleton's choice of Vernon Whitford over Sir Willoughby Patterne is meant to demonstrate social evolution toward altruism – much like Adam Bede's love for Dinah. But, like Eliot in her later works, Meredith is also intent on demonstrating that science is not the only means to the discovery of natural right. It is Sir Willoughby who represents faith in science, and his smug objectivism is explicitly opposed to Vernon's humanistic training in philology. Meredith sees science, in fact, to be on the side of egoism – science teaches us only an "o'er-hoary ancestry," in claiming that self-interest underlies human motivation, but "poets . . . may be cited for an assurance that the primitive is not the degenerate: rather is he a sign of the indestructibility of the race" (ch. 39). Like Eliot, Meredith finds in symbolic language the prophetic potential to project a moral order that might harmonize human desire with reality: "The banished of Eden had to put on metaphors, and the common use of them has helped largely to civilize us" (ch. 27), he writes in *Diana of the Crossways* (1885). Seconding Eliot's endorsement of spiritual aspiration and prophetic vision, rather than passive, objective analysis of the order of external nature, Meredith has Clara's father proclaim, in *The Egoist*: "We know not yet if nature be a fact or an effort to master one" (ch. 44). Though Meredith's faith in human behavior was, like Eliot's, rooted in the organic force of human imagination, he seemed not to share her reservations about the fulfillment of that faith.

Meredith is one of the few late Victorian novelists to keep the naturalist faith alive, however, as the more tragic moods latent in Eliot's fiction seem to be echoed more and more strongly by late-century novelists. Darwin's theory of evolution, in particular, began to take a massive toll on any faith in the moral foundations of nature, as its implications became increasingly clear to late Victorian intellectuals. Two of the biggest obstacles to belief in organic social progress that Darwin presented were the apparent cruelty of natural selection and the seeming randomness of variation through mutation. Both argued against the old-fashioned concept of "design" in nature. Darwin himself confessed that "I cannot persuade myself that a beneficent and omnipotent God would have designedly created Ichneumonidae with the express intention of their feeding within the living bodies of caterpillars, or that a cat would play with mice" (Darwin 1896: vol. 1, 554–5). Certain philosophers of science, such as Arthur Schopenhauer and Eduard von Hartman, began to develop a scientific basis for such pessimism. They argued that natural selection could as easily lead to evolutionary degeneration as to social progress. Late-century ethnology, reflecting this view, began to assert that the primitive races inhabiting Britain's colonies were proof of such degeneration – provoking a heated debate among anthropologists about the trajectory of social evolution. Critics of imperialism, including many novelists, sometimes argued that contact with primitive races could only lead to white degeneration as well, and that the rapacity and moral compromises of colonialism were themselves evidence of such degeneration. Robert Louis Stevenson, Joseph Conrad, and Rudyard Kipling (in "The Man Who Would Be King" [1888], for instance) all sound this warning. Moreover, the apparent randomness of genetic mutation within evolutionary theory contributed to a widespread loss of faith in the biological and intellectual telos of human emergence itself, adding to the growing sense in late-century culture that science had succeeded only in demonstrating the frightening insignificance of humankind in the universe. Advances in biology, genetics, heat theory (particularly the second law of thermodynamics), atomic theory, and astronomy all reinforced this sense of human insignificance.

Hardy's novels are profoundly driven by such doubts about the significance of humankind in the universe. His pessimism may have had a number of overlapping causes, but it was fundamentally anchored in his conviction – bolstered by scientific theory, particularly Darwin's late works – that human life lacked cosmic purpose. Hardy's novels are infused with a sense of nature's incoherence: happiness, he wrote in *The Return of the Native* (1878), "grows less and less possible as we uncover the defects of natural laws, and see the quandary that man is in by their operation" (bk 3, ch. 1). This preoccupation appears quite clearly in his early novel, *A Pair of Blue Eyes* (1873), which features a famous scene in which the scientist Charles Knight slips over a cliff and hangs by his fingertips from the edge. Suspended helplessly, Knight finds himself directly opposite a fossilized trilobite staring back at him from the exposed rock. As he contemplates his own imminent death, Knight ponders the meaninglessness of evolutionary time and human development, as well as the grim reality of universal extinction: "He was to be with the small in his death" (ch. 22). St. Cleeve, the scientist hero of *Two on a Tower* (1882), touches on this dour view of man's position in the universe when he proclaims: "Until a person has thought out the stars and their interspaces, he has hardly learnt that there are things much more terrible than monsters of shape, namely, monsters of magnitude without known shape. Such monsters are the voids and waste places of the sky" (ch. 4).

Like those late Victorian scientists who bemoaned the randomness of evolution, Hardy's novels also brood on the workings of chance in creating human destinies – an emphasis that tends to undermine faith in the certainty of progress. In *Tess of the d'Urbervilles* (1891), to cite perhaps the most poignant instance, Angel Clare tragically misses an opportunity to meet the innocent Tess at a May Day dance long before she is despoiled by Alec d'Urberville; and, later, Tess's confession is regrettably – perhaps fatally – delayed when she accidentally slips her letter to Angel under the carpet at the threshold of his lodgings. Hardy's novels are full of the cruelties of chance, and they emphasize historical accident – in conformity with Darwinian theory. Events in his novels are never directed by benign forces, and his plots are inevitably tragic. As the narrator of *Tess* declares, "In the ill-judged execution of the well-judged plan of things the call seldom produces the comer, the man to love rarely coincides with the hour for loving. . . . [S]uch completeness is not to be prophesied, or even conceived as possible" (ch. 5).

One of Hardy's most pronounced breaks with the optimism of scientific naturalism was his inability to believe in the existence – or even the desirability – of altruistic love. Like Eliot, Hardy consistently shows love to be based in physical desire; but, unlike her, he demonstrates that this physicality undermines the altruistic moral fantasies of his characters. Hardy thus demonstrates the terrible, inevitable conflicts between biological desire and social order – a preoccupation that his work shares with much late Victorian and modern psychology, including the author of *Civilization and its Discontents* (1939), Sigmund Freud. Sexual desire is often frustrated by social order in Hardy's novels, while altruistic ideals are disrupted by the unwanted eruptions of sexuality. As Sue tells Jude in *Jude the Obscure* (1895):

> We went about loving each other too much . . . We said – do you remember? – that we would make a virtue of joy. I said it was Nature's intention, Nature's law and *raison d'être* that we should be joyful in what instincts she afforded us – instincts which civilization had taken upon itself to thwart. What dreadful things I said! And now Fate has given us this stab in the back for being such fools as to take Nature at her word! (pt 6, ch. 2)

Jude's and Sue's love for one another is demystified over the course of the novel: Jude discovers that sexual desire is not conflatable with either religious ecstasy or the pursuit of knowledge, as he had believed in his idealistic youth; and Sue discovers that her idealization of primitive sexual nature is incompatible with social pressures. Hardy's protagonists often discover that the idealized object of their desires is itself an illusion, or, worse, merely a projection of their own narcissism – which is, in fact, the theme of Hardy's allegorical final novel, *The Well-Beloved* (1897), as well as being one of the fundamental insights of psychoanalysis. Significantly, Hardy's lovers rarely produce children (or their children die young, as in the case of Jude and Sue) – a pointed irony at a time when the topic of sexual selection was widely discussed in both scientific and nonscientific circles. In all these ways, Hardy – like Freud – ironically completes the positivist project, identifying man with nature, but only to discover the monstrous dysfunctions of natural instinct and passion.

Hardy was one of many Victorian novelists to express despair about science's evident discovery of a cosmic misfit between humans and nature, although he was one of the few to make its scientific bases so explicit. H. Rider Haggard's colonialist adventure novels, for example, always revolve around a melancholy awareness of vanished civilizations, extinct races, and the meaninglessness of death – even if they do not cite scientific theories. Haggard's most famous novel, *She* (1887), is set amid the ruins of an ancient African civilization, where the conjunction of a semi-miraculous, originary natural force – the great Fire of Eternal Life – an epic sexual passion, and the roots of Egyptian (and, therefore, European) civilization produces only a tragic vision of sexual disharmony. Haggard's sexual tragedy is played out against the background of massive ruined sepulchers piled with the unthinkably vast remains of innumerable generations of the dead. Sharing Hardy's pessimism about innate human goodness, Stevenson's novels and stories – particularly *The Strange Case of Dr. Jekyll and Mr. Hyde* (1886), but including as well his more "innocent" boys' books – are haunted by the demonic impulses deep within human nature. Other late-Victorian novelists, such as Samuel Butler, author of *Erewhon* (1872) and *The Way of All Flesh* (1903), more closely resemble Meredith, in seeing nature as commensurate with human ideals. But much late-century fiction – including, most notably, the "new woman" fiction of Schreiner, Mona Caird, Sarah Grand, George Egerton, and others – shares Hardy's pessimism about the compatibility of human desire with either natural or social order. What is most striking about this pessimism, though, is how frequently it accompanies great respect for scientific discourses and methods. Many of Hardy's characters, for example, betray a reverence for scientific procedures in their striving for detached, objective observation – such as Gabriel Oak's lengthy inspection of Bathsheba Everdene in *Far from the Madding Crowd*, or Clym Yeobright's panoramic surveillance of various characters in *The Return of the Native*. This respect for scientific observation suggests a lingering, sometimes nostalgic hopefulness – in Hardy, and in other Victorian novelists as well – that detached, scientific knowledge of the world may yet lead to individual transformation of the relations of man and nature. Clym's apparent kinship with his natural surroundings in Egdon Heath – even if this kinship includes a sense of profound loss and disappointment – is perhaps the most fully realized expression of such hopefulness in Hardy's work.

Besides the epistemological and the philosophical impact that Victorian science had on fiction, its sudden increase in social authority fixed novelists' attention on a figure who might represent crises in the relationship between scientific knowledge and social melioration: the professional. Many of the conflicts novelists had over the social implications of scientific theory, as well as their resentments over science's burgeoning social prestige, were centered on their representation of professionals – primarily doctors and lawyers, but also clergymen, private investigators, and educators. All of these figures become increasingly prominent in fiction from midcentury onwards. To some extent, this prominence simply reflects a social fact: the growing professionalization of all phases of intellectual life in Victorian England. Early in the period, intellectuals usually regarded themselves as amateurs; but the development of a rigorous order of specializations within the natural sciences became the model for other areas of intellectual life as well. In the field of novel-writing itself, the Society of Authors – the first literary professional organization – was founded in 1884, and organized demands for stronger copyright laws, as well as other common concerns, increasingly inclined authors to regard themselves as a professional fraternity. Anthony Trollope's *Autobiography* (1883), long reviled by postromantic humanists, who scorned its unsentimental analogies between novel-writing and craftsmanship, and its scrupulous accounting of the economics of authorship, was one of the first celebrations of novelistic professionalism. But in the second half of the century, marketplace changes made it easier for many writers to see themselves as skilled producers and marketers of their own work. The rising mass market for novels, the growing middle-class reading public (expanded enormously by institutions such as Mudie's lending libraries, W. H. Smith's railway bookstalls, and reviewing journals), and technological publishing advances that reduced prices all contributed to the professionalization of the novelist (see chapters 1 by Kelly Mays and 2 by Jonathan Rose in this volume). Moreover, novelists imitated science's emphasis on professional rigor – both as a methodological approach (exemplified in the theories of narrative aesthetics that were publicly debated by Henry James, Stevenson, Hardy, and many other novelists of stature, and which resulted in great theoretical works like James's *Art of the Novel* [1934]), and also as a complex code of ethical and business principles. Novelists, however, unlike scientists, were never completely comfortable regarding themselves in professional terms. The clash between positivistic science and the more visionary tendencies we have seen in Eliot or Meredith became increasingly hard to avoid, as the scientific outlook began to shift away from the concerns with moral order and social melioration that had characterized scientific naturalism, and as novelists sought to reaffirm the romantic faith in imaginative autonomy that had lapsed during the mid-Victorian years, but that later seemed necessary to counter scientific pessimism.

The strongest symptom of uneasiness about the professionalization of fiction lies in the ambiguities surrounding professional characters in Victorian novels from about the 1860s onwards. The novels of Collins, for example, are marked by a rivalry and mistrust between scientific professionals and literary or artistic intellectuals. The plots of Collins's novels tend to revolve around the outwitting of pretentious scientific professionals by a broad collection of quasi-professional humanists – artists, writers, dilettantes, proto-bohemians – who manage to fuse scientific deduction with creative imagination in their quest to solve the central mysteries of the novels. In *The Woman in White*, doctors, lawyers, and professional spies like the villainous Count Fosco are overcome by the earnest and imaginative Walter Hartright, who blends a variety of marginally professional skills with his bedrock humanism, which is defined through his unifying commitment to both sexual love and truth. At various times an art teacher, draughtsman, journalist, and explorer, Hartright combines methodological rationality with creativity, in order to "present the truth always in its most direct and most intelligible aspect" (Preamble).

Yet Hartright, like all of Collins's protagonists, seeks legitimation in the very professional arenas he seems to challenge. Hartright composes his narrative, he tells us, in the form of a series of depositions, "as the story of an offence against the laws is told in Court by more than one witness – with the same object, in both cases" (Preamble). Collins's heroes seek ultimately to displace scientific professionals, not to discredit their authority. Similarly, Dickens manifests his ambivalence about professionals by dividing them melodramatically into the compassionate (usually doctors and policemen) and the inhuman (usually lawyers). Sometimes he creates ambiguous figures, like Jaggers in *Great Expectations*, who offers Pip a chillingly Darwinian vision of all the children in the world being "so much spawn, to develop into the fish that were to come to his net – to be prosecuted, defended, forsworn, made orphans, bedevilled somehow," but who then celebrates his professional competence to spare Estella: she is "one pretty little child out of the heap who could be saved" (ch. 51).

Hardy, more consistently condemnatory, often demystifies the figure of the pedagogue. Jude's mentor, Mr. Phillotson, inspires Jude with a dangerous intellectual idealism, only to emerge late in the novel as a figure of moral degeneration himself.

Throughout Victorian fiction, scientific professionals of various kinds are on trial. At the extreme, novelists virulently condemn professionals such as Tulkinghorn in Dickens's *Bleak House* and Dr. Downward in Collins's *Armadale* (1866) for embodying the social harshness and cruelty that science had seemed to discover in the natural world. But Victorian novelists more commonly dramatize a complicated ambivalence toward professionals. "New woman" novelists like Sarah Grand, for instance, both feared and craved professional knowledge – Grand's Dr. Galbraith in *The Heavenly Twins* (1893) is a disturbingly powerful "expert" on female hysteria, whose clinical treatment of his own wife remains mixedly coercive and therapeutic. At best, such figures can provoke Victorian protagonists to determine whether their imaginative powers can overcome the witheringly rational calculations of the professional himself – as is the case in most of Collins's novels. But at worst, as with Dr. Galbraith, or Stevenson's Dr. Jekyll, they express great anxiety about the conjunction of scientific knowledge and social power.

Competition in Victorian novels over the moral authority of professionals is, in part, an attempt to reveal the social self-interest of scientists. Victorian novels often reveal the professional to be an interested party in the scramble for social status, and intellectual dogma to be inextricable from social competition of the most vulgar kind. The exclusion of women from the ranks of the professionals is one of the most dramatic ways in which science's assumption of social power is discredited. Novels by Eliot, Collins, Charlotte Brontë, Elizabeth Gaskell, and others are full of frustrated intellectual women. Charles Reade's *A Woman-Hater* (1874) explicitly indicts the medical profession for excluding talented women. Arguably the most popular novel of the century, Ellen Wood's *East Lynne* (1861) compares the social ambitions and ascendancy of the middle-class male lawyer to the fall of his formerly aristocratic wife – gendering professional success as a displacement of women. Besides exposing the conspiracy against women that Victorian fiction often attributed to scientific professionals and their thirst for social power, novelists also tapped the ambivalent attitudes toward professional social authority deeply engrained in middle-class culture. The Victorian middle class vacillated between reverence for the professional as a kind of surrogate clergyman, who offered moral counsel and disinterested advice in the absence of religious certainty, and resentful contempt for him as an upstart servant. Professionals could thus be regarded either as powerful figures of authority or as dangerous usurpers. Novelists like Collins, with his ironically named Dr. Downward, or like Dickens, with his carnivalesque array of pettifogging lawyers and obfuscating quacks, drew on middle-class ambivalence toward the social status of professionals, and on middle-class paranoia about social aggression that paraded in the guise of erudite, often scientific knowledge.

Novelistic attempts from the 1860s onwards to expose the scientific intellectual as a class-bound, gender-bound figure may have supplemented the destabilizing of scientific certainties themselves towards the end of the century – particularly through the disorienting discoveries of late-century astronomy and quantum physics – in helping to diminish the tremendous social prestige science possessed throughout much of the Victorian period. In addition, the rebellion against rationality that characterizes much of modernism (whether in the microscopic attention to subjective processes in Joyce and Virginia Woolf, or in the deliberate intellectual absurdities of Jorge Luis Borges and, later, Thomas Pynchon) have also ensured that specific scientific paradigms would not dominate twentieth-century fiction as they once did that of the Victorian period. Yet the transformation of literature into a secular art form, one which proceeds from consistent methodological principles and which constitutes a distinct professional regime, has not been reversed. Rather, it characterizes the ongoing influence that Victorian science has had on the writing of fiction.

REFERENCES

Darwin, Charles (1896), *The Life and Letters of Charles Darwin*, 2 vols., ed. Francis Darwin (New York: D. Appleton & Co.).

Darwin, Charles (1988), *On the Origin of Species*, in *The Works of Charles Darwin*, 29 vols., eds. Paul H. Barrett and P. B. Freeman (New York: New York University Press). (First publ. 1859.)

Dowden, Edward (1877), "*Middlemarch* and *Daniel Deronda*," *Contemporary Review*, 29, 348–69.

Eliot, George (1865), "The Influence of Rationalism," *Fortnightly Review*, 1, 43–55.

Eliot, George (1954–78), *The George Eliot Letters*, 9 vols., ed. Gordon S. Haight (New Haven: Yale University Press; London: Oxford University Press).

Hardy, Thomas (1925), "The Science of Fiction," in *Life and Art* (New York: Greenberg).

Levine, George (1987), "One Culture: Science and Literature," in George Levine, ed., *One Culture: Essays in Science and Literature* (Madison: University of Wisconsin Press).

Lewes, George Henry (1862), *Studies in Animal Life* (London: Smith, Elder, & Co.).

Lukács, Georg (1964), *Studies in European Realism* (New York: Grosset & Dunlap).

Lyell, Charles (1837), *Principles of Geology: Being an Inquiry How Far the Former Changes of the Earth's Surface Are Referable to Causes Now in Operation* (Philadelphia: John I. Kay & Co.).

Mill, John Stuart (1963–75), *The Collected Works of John Stuart Mill*, ed. J. M. Robson, 33 vols. (Toronto: University of Toronto Press).

Myers, F. W. H. (1886), *Phantasms of the Living*, 2 vols. (London: Trubner & Co.).

Russell, Bertrand (1919), "Descriptions," in *Introduction to Mathematical Philosophy* (London: Allen & Unwin), 167–80.

Tyndall, John (1871), *On Radiation* (New York: D. Appleton & Co.).

Tyndall, John (1898a), "Matter and Force," in *Fragments of Science: A Series of Detached Essays, Addresses, and Reviews*, 6th edn., 2 vols. (New York: D. Appleton & Co.), vol. 2: 53–74.

Tyndall, John (1898b), "Scientific Uses of the Imagination," in *Fragments of Science: A Series of Detached Essays, Addresses, and Reviews*, 6th edn., 2 vols. (New York: D. Appleton & Co.), vol. 2: 101–34.

Webb, Beatrice (1926), *My Apprenticeship* (London: Longmans, Green & Co.).

FURTHER READING

Beer, Gillian (1983), *Darwin's Plots: Evolutionary Narrative in Darwin, George Eliot, and Nineteenth-Century Fiction* (London: Routledge & Kegan Paul).

Beer, Gillian (1996), *Open Fields: Science in Cultural Encounter* (Oxford: Clarendon).

Chapple, J. A. V. (1986), *Science and Literature in the Nineteenth Century* (London: Macmillan).

Cosslett, Tess (1982), *The "Scientific Movement" and Victorian Literature* (New York: St. Martin's).

Dale, Peter Allan (1989), *In Pursuit of a Scientific Culture: Science, Art, and Society in the Victorian Age* (Madison: University of Wisconsin Press).

Levine, George (1988), *Darwin and the Novelists: Patterns of Science in Victorian Fiction* (Cambridge, Mass.: Harvard University Press).

Rothfield, Lawrence (1992), *Vital Signs: Medical Realism in Nineteenth-Century Fiction* (Princeton: Princeton University Press).

Turner, Frank Miller (1974), *Between Science and Religion: The Reaction to Scientific Naturalism in Late Victorian England* (New Haven: Yale University Press).

8

Technology and Information: Accelerating Developments

Christopher Keep

Responses to the seemingly unceasing flow of new communication and transportation technologies in Victorian Britain varied from utopian promises that they would unite humankind in a spirit of universal brotherhood to apocalyptic fears that they would, in Carlyle's words, leave the world "one huge, dead, immeasurable Steam-engine, rolling on, in its dead indifference to grind [us] limb from limb" (1896: 133). But regardless of whether they were optimistic or pessimistic, commentators seemed to share one common perception: the train, the steamship, the telegraph, the typewriter, the linotype, and the gramophone, together with the myriad other technical marvels of the age, would serve to "annihilate space and time." The best-known instance of the phrase occurs in Marx's chapter on "Capital" in the *Grundrisse* (1857–8; Marx 1973), but it echoes across the period whenever new technologies are being discussed. It was already current by 1833, when the *Railway Companion* noted how the spread of railway lines across Britain had effectively eliminated "the bounds of space and time" (quoted in Freeman 1999: 78). The journalist Sydney Smith concurred, noting that with the advent of steam, "[e]verything is near, everything is immediate – time, distance, and delay are abolished" (quoted in Pearson 1934: 292). The idea was still very much present at the end of the century, when the electric telegraph service had begun to knit the globe into a vast communications network of land and submarine cables that stretched from London to Sydney, and from Newfoundland to Buenos Aires. Commenting on "The Intellectual Effects of Electricity" in an article from 1889, one writer notes that in the age of electric communications "the world is for purposes of 'intelligence' reduced to a village and the village gossip is discussed continuously without delay in every house." The result, he laments, is that "[a]ll men are compelled to think of all things, at the same time, on imperfect information, and with too little interval for reflection" (Anon. 1889: 632). Well before Marshall McLuhan would claim that television had transformed the world into a "global village," the Victorians were already confronting the sense that their new technologies had transformed space from a geographical quantity into a temporal one:

increasingly, distance was no longer measured in inches, yards, and miles, but in the hours, then minutes, and finally seconds required to traverse it. "The most salient characteristic of life in this latter portion of the 19th century," W. R. Greg concluded, "is its SPEED" (Greg 1877: 272).

Of course, the claim that the new technologies annihilated space and time is an exaggeration, one which is better understood as an index of the degree to which the train, the steamship, and the telegraph transformed the social sphere than as an accurate reflection of their material effects. It was not so much that space itself had disappeared or that clocks had ceased to tick, but that there were new ways of perceiving the nature of distance and duration. From a world in which the geographical horizons of the common person were often no wider than that of the parish in which he or she was born, and in which the rhythms of daily existence were largely measured by the rising and setting of the sun and the change of the seasons, the emerging technologies helped produce a sense of the increasing interconnectedness of the villages, towns, and cities of Great Britain; with the daily post and newspapers arriving on the trains, and charter companies such as that of Thomas Cook offering affordable package holidays to the middle classes, people had a much greater sense of belonging not only to a county or a region but to a nation, of being "British." As Benedict Anderson (1991) has noted, a nation is less a geopolitical reality than it is an "imagined community," that is to say, a constellation of cultural representations which allow individuals to identify their experiences as continuous with some shared ideal of an extended community. This ideal of Britain as a single, coherent, and unified set of values and experiences was in turn defined and amplified by the greater access to the colonies, whether through the daily telegraphic news that arrived from the far-flung outposts of empire or from the increasing opportunities for emigration made possible by the steamship. The necessary corollary of imperial space was standardized time, as the local differences in timekeeping gave way to the "universal standard time" set by railway companies in order to coordinate their complex schedules. The loss of regional timekeeping methods contributed to a loss of particularity and specificity; in their place came a sense of the increasing uniformity of culture, and of the need to "keep up" with the tremendous pace of change. Indeed, by the end of the century, many people had become, like Lewis Carroll's White Rabbit, obsessed by the notion of "clock time," constantly hurrying to stay ahead not of the seasons, but of the inexorable sweeping of the second-hand.

The harbinger of these new modes of perception, and that which came to symbolize their unrelenting progress, was the steam-driven locomotive. The first railroads were used to pull wagons of coal from the pit faces of mines. Modifying the early "atmospheric" engines of Newcomen and Watt, Richard Trevithick designed and built the first high-pressure steam engine to replace the horse-drawn wagons in 1804. Within two decades, George Stephenson introduced the first regularly scheduled steam freight trains between Stockton and Darlington, a distance of about 20 miles, and followed this success with the first passenger line in 1830, which ran between Liverpool and Manchester. The fact that the opening of the Liverpool and Manchester line was also witness to the first railway fatality, that of William Huskisson MP, who accidentally disembarked as the train was pulling away from a watering station, did not deter interest in the new means of transportation. "Railway Mania" quickly swept the nation, with hundreds of companies, many hastily formed and poorly capitalized, embarking on ambitious building projects that saw the spread of the railway into every corner of Britain. Battalions of engineers and workers spanned rivers with iron bridges, tunneled through hillsides, and ploughed through farmlands. As Sam Weller's father learns in Dickens's *Master Humphrey's Clock*, local establishments that depended on the carriage traffic that passed along the old roadways disappeared while new ones, such as the W. H. Smith bookstore chain that provided cheap reading material to the growing commuter market, quickly cropped up along the ever-expanding railway lines. By 1850, Stephenson's original 100 miles of track had grown to 6,600, operated by more than 200 separate companies, each employing its own equipment on tracks of a different gauge. Millions were made and lost during the boom periods, while passenger numbers soared from over 33 million in 1843 to a resounding 587,230,641 in 1880 (Newsome 1998: 30). By the century's end the railway had turned the map of Britain into a densely interwoven web of junctions, trunk lines, switching stations, loading yards, and passenger termini.

More than simply a technological achievement, however, the railway became a symbol of the new world of machines and industry. As Eric Hobsbawm writes, the word "railway" served as "a sort of synonym for ultra-modernity in the 1840s, as 'atomic' was to be after the Second World War. Their sheer size and scale staggered the imagination and dwarfed the most gigantic public works of the past" (1999: 89). And it was precisely as a symbol of modernity that the railway most often appears in the literature of the period. In Hardy's *Jude the Obscure* (1895), a novel for which the very table of contents reads like a train schedule with its starkly enumerated list of points of arrival and departure, Sue Bridehead warily consents to her cousin's entreaty to sit in the cathedral. " 'Cathedral? Yes. Though I think I'd rather sit in the railway station,' she answered, a remnant of vexation still in her voice. 'That's the centre of the town life now; the Cathedral has had its day!' " (Hardy 1985: 139). Sue's sense that the railway station has come to replace the church as the centre of modern experience was shared by many. Commenting on "the fantastic neo-gothic facade of the Midland Grand Hotel at St. Pancras" in London, one commentator claimed "that the railway termini and their hotels are to the nineteenth century what monasteries and the cathedrals were to the thirteenth" (quoted in Freeman 1999: 73). It is, however, just such faux medievalism that Sue seeks to escape in choosing the railway station. The nostalgic longing for the past and dutiful observation of custom and tradition are exactly that which will not only bar Jude from realizing his dream of becoming a scholar, but stymie her own attempts to live as a "new woman," one of those who, in Hardy's words, "does not recognize the necessity of most of her sex to follow marriage as a profession" (1985: xxxviii).

The speed and dynamism of the train seemed to many like Sue to represent a way of finally breaking free of the intense gravitational pull of history and convention. In

Mona Caird's *The Daughter of Danaus* (1894), another tale of an emancipated woman struggling to realize her life as an independent individual in the face of overwhelming familial and societal pressures to conform, Hadria Fullerton experiences her first real sense of liberation as she takes the train from her remote country village to the sea:

> The speed was glorious. Back flashed field and hill and copse . . . Back flew the iterative telegraph posts with Herculean swing, into the Past, looped together in rhythmic movement, marking the pulses of old Time. On, with the rack and roar, into the mysterious Future. One could sit at the window and watch the machinery of Time's foundry at work; the hammers of his forge beating, beating, the wild spars flying, the din and chaos whirling round one's bewildered brain; Past becoming Present, Present melting into Future, before one's eyes. To sit and watch the whirring wheels; to think "Now it is thus and thus; presently, another slice of earth and sky awaits" – ye Gods, it is not to be realized! (Caird 1989: 294)

Caird's breathless syntax, and, in particular, her seamless shifting from the past to present tense even as the train traces its passage from the England of "field and hill and copse" to the mystery of the unknown Future, celebrates the power of the train to break out of the Victorians' acute sense of historicity, that is to say, the belief, affirmed by both Darwin and Marx, that it is history that makes the individual and not the individual that makes history. The train acted as a powerful solvent to such bonds, blurring the distinctions between classes and genders, allowing the poor to mix with the rich, and men with women in ways that had been heretofore difficult to imagine.

The "glorious" speed in which Hadria exults was modest by contemporary standards. Despite bearing such formidable names as "Sirocco," "Wildfire," and "Dragon," early locomotives often averaged no more than 10 miles per hour and even by the end of the century 50 m.p.h. was considered very fast; Stephenson's *Rocket*, to which the hapless Huskisson fell prey, attained a top speed of only 28 m.p.h. Even so, the train dramatically diminished the time required to travel from place to place. A journey from the west of England to London that once required the better part of two days and several changes of carriage to complete could now be managed in less than six hours. As one commentator wrote in 1852, "the extremities of the island are now, to all intents and purposes, as near the metropolis as Sussex or Buckinghamshire were two centuries ago. The Midland counties are a mere suburb. With the space and resources of an empire, we enjoy the compactness of a city" (Williams 1852: 284). Such speeds, however, were not always welcome. Arnold, Carlyle, and Ruskin inveighed mightily against the quickening pace of life wrought by the train; the last-named warned his readers that only "a fool wants to shorten space and time; a wise man wants to lengthen both" (Ruskin 1904: 381). The concern not only for the rapidity of the train itself, but for its capacity to alter the landscape through which it passed, is amply evident in Dickens's famous description of Stagg's Gardens in his 1848 novel *Dombey and Son*. With the arrival of the railway, the quiet suburb of Camden Town has, in a matter of weeks, become unrecognizable:

There were railway patterns in its drapers' shops, and railway journals in the windows of its newsmen. There were railway hotels, office-houses, lodging-houses, boarding houses; railway plans, maps, views, wrappers, bottles, stands; railway omnibuses, railway streets and buildings, railway hangers-on and parasites, and flatterers out of all calculation. There was even a railway time observed in clocks, as if the sun itself had given in. (Dickens 1985: 290)

In stark contrast to Caird, Dickens, and many of his readers, saw the railway as the obliterator of a traditional way of life, of a model of social relations that valued continuity, custom, and community, and a more human speed of existence that allowed for careful adjustment to changing circumstances. It was part and parcel of what Arnold called "the strange disease of modern life," "with its sick hurry, its divided aims." As such, the railway often appears in Victorian novels as a force to be contested and resisted; but its very nature seemed to inspire a certain fatalism. The coming of the railway was to be lamented, but it could not be stopped, any more than one could stop the past giving way irrevocably to the future. In her 1872 novel *Middlemarch*, George Eliot drew on her own memories of the arrival of the surveyors for the London and Birmingham Railway in rural Warwickshire. While the field workers turn on the surveyors with hay-forks, hoping to drive them from the land before they could "cut Lowick Parish into sixes and sevens" (Eliot 1977: 599), the sage Caleb Garth intervenes, telling the hands, "Now, my lads, you can't hinder the railroad: it will be made whether you like it or not" (p. 604).

It was, however, precisely the inexorable nature of the railroad that made it so useful to novelists, providing them with a surprisingly effective means of resolving plotlines and dispensing with characters. Far from being a detriment to society, the mechanical force of the train, the very fact that it was an unthinking machine that destroyed everything in its path, also allowed it to be an instrument of justice, one which did not require the narrative difficulties of dramatizing an arrest and trial. Hence while Dickens decries the train as "a type of triumphant monster, Death" (1985: 354), it also provides him with a convenient and distinctly modern *deus ex machina*: Carker, the Machiavellian villain of *Dombey and Son*, receives his just deserts courtesy of a speeding locomotive before he can make off with Dombey's wife. Dickens's use of the locomotive as an instrument of death had the advantage of being corroborated by the almost daily reports of rail-related accidents. As Michael Freeman writes,

> when passengers were not anxious to be "in time," or scrambling for their luggage, they were worrying about the prospect of instant death. For with the railways came what has been described as the "technological accident" . . . When things went wrong, the power of the express train in the early railway era must have seemed lethal against a "peaceful, bucolic England of coach, plodding wagon or silently gliding canal boat." (1999: 84)

Far from disturbing the novel's carefully developed sense of verisimilitude, the demise of Carker seems to secure it, reaffirming the emerging sense of the arbitrary and unpredictable nature of modern life, and of its subordination to the forces of the industrial order. In her 1853 novel *Cranford*, Elizabeth Gaskell employs a very similar narrative device, and tips her hat to Dickens's influence, by relating how Captain Brown dies in a train wreck while reading the latest installment of the *Pickwick Papers*.

The capacity of the railroad to transform the nature of space and of time, and to introduce a sense of the deep interconnectedness that constituted the "imagined community" of Britain, was substantially aided by the advent of the electric telegraph. The earliest means of "writing at a distance" were the optical telegraphs operated by the Admiralty. Using a series of large semaphore towers, coded messages could be conveyed from the coast to inland stations in a matter of hours. The very success of these instruments prohibited the development of electric means of communication for many decades until its developers shifted their attention from the military to the railways. The first such device was patented by William Cooke, a former British army medical officer and commercial entrepreneur, and Charles Wheatstone, the chair of experimental philosophy at King's College, Cambridge, in 1837. Forming the Electric Telegraph Company, Cooke and Wheatstone arrived at an arrangement with the Great Western Railway Company, whereby the railway would get free use of the telegraph in exchange for permission to run their cables along its tracks and to send and receive messages paid for by the public. As telegraphic communication became increasingly popular, and profitable, competing firms soon flooded the market. By 1870, the original 13 miles of cable, extending from Paddington Station to West Drayton, had grown to 50,000, owned and operated, like the railways, by a profusion of private companies, each operating different equipment over different lines and using different code systems. To resolve the problem of transmitting messages over incompatible lines, the government did what it dared not do with the railway companies: it nationalized the myriad private telegraph companies and turned them over to the Postmaster-General, creating a single uniform system that spanned not only the nation but the world, creating what Tom Standage (1998) has called "the Victorian internet." With 1,000 post offices and 1,900 railway stations now acting as telegraph offices, the number of messages conveyed by the system skyrocketed from 7 million in 1869 (the last year under the private system), to 10 million in 1870; following the 1885 rate decrease to a halfpenny per word, this figure rose to 50 million by 1887, and to almost 90 million by the turn of the century.

The simultaneity of telegraphic communication, its ability to maintain an instantaneous and continuous contact between widely separated locations, was heralded as the miracle of the age. Lord Salisbury claimed that "it assembled all mankind upon one great plane, where they can see everything that is done and hear everything that is said" (quoted in Morus 1996: 13). Such an encompassing perspective was of particular importance to detective fiction. Telegraphs feature prominently in many of the Sherlock Holmes novels and short stories of Arthur Conan Doyle. Holmes, we are told in "The Adventure of the Devil's Foot," "has never been known to write where a telegram would serve" (Doyle 1986b: 419), and the great detective has regular recourse to the device as he attempts either to gather more information concerning his quarry or to prepare some trap to bring the villain to justice. As James R. Wright writes, "There was an urgency in every adventure. A criminal must be thwarted (wire to Mawsons, though it failed) or captured (wire to Forbes to arrest Joseph Harrison), an innocent must be protected (Violet Smith), or a mystery unravelled (Captain Crocker), which sends Holmes to the Post Office" (1996: 19). Detective fiction such as Doyle's, then, represented the telegraph not only as a means of gathering information, but as a means of extending the power of the law to every corner of the nation. In such fiction, the force of law, if not always of the government proper (Holmes prides himself on being the "world's first consulting detective" and much of the fiction turns on his superiority to the local constabulary), amounts to a pervasive, all-seeing eye, and the telegraph is its nervous system, transmitting that visual information back to London for prompt processing. By means of the services available to him in the post office conveniently located opposite 221B Baker Street, Holmes is able to be in several places at once, and to coordinate a complex variety of official (Scotland Yard) and unofficial (the Baker Street Irregulars) law enforcement agents. The telegraph thus emerges in these texts as an integral aspect of what Michel Foucault has described as the "panoptic" effect of power, in which the omnipresence of surveillance serves to compel the subject of the modern nation-state to take on the responsibility of watching herself. "What this machinery of surveillance," writes D. A. Miller in his study of Victorian detective fiction, "is set up to monitor is the elaborate regulation (timetables, exercises, and so on) that discipline simultaneously deploys to occupy its subjects. The aim of such regulation is to enforce not so much a norm as the normality of normativeness itself" (1988: 18). In celebrating the instrumentality of the telegraph in locating and incarcerating the criminal, Doyle's fiction does not simply reflect the Victorian fascination with new technology. It actively participates in producing the necessary illusion that the law is everywhere, that the panoptic eye sees all, and, what is more important, that the communications network of the modern state is a seamless whole in which each part is in constant and coordinated contact with every other part.

The centrifugal effect of the new communications and transportation technologies, that is to say, their capacity to consolidate and extend the imaginary community of the nation-state, were partly offset, however, by a reverse trajectory, a centripetal effect which resulted in the return to the metropole of previously expelled or foreign elements to trouble the integrity of Britain. The foremost agent of this centripetal energy, at least in the world of the Victorian novel, was the steamship. Concurrent with developments of steam power for the railways, naval engineers such as John Fitch and Robert Fulton in the United States began to experiment with adapting Watt's steam engine to the demands of water transport. The first transatlantic crossing by steamship was achieved in 1819, by an American vessel, the *Savannah*. A fully rigged wooden sailing ship, it was fitted with a pair of steam-powered paddle wheels and completed the voyage in twenty-nine days. In Britain, the most ambitious developer of the steamship was also its most forward-thinking railway engineer, Isambard Kingdom Brunel. Just as he championed the seven-foot "broad gauge" track for his

Great Western Railroad, and was also the first to enter into an agreement with Cooke and Wheatstone to develop their telegraph, Brunel pushed the envelope of ship-building. In 1837 he launched the *Great Western*, the first steamship designed specifically to make regular Atlantic crossings. It was followed in 1858 by the crowning achievement of the steamship age, the *Great Eastern*. With a displacement of 27,000 tons, and measuring nearly 700 feet from stem to stern, it was fully five times as large as any other vessel afloat, and could accommodate 4,000 passengers. For all that it was one of the great engineering feats of the era, the vessel failed to recoup its costs as a commercial vessel and fell into disuse before being called back into service to help lay the transatlantic telegraph cables across the ocean floor in 1866, succeeding where three earlier attempts in 1857–8 had failed. The *Great Eastern* was sold for scrap in 1888, but its sheer scale and size served as a powerful testament to the might of Victorian industrial achievement and of Britain's continuing domination of the seas.

While Victorian fiction contains many descriptions of voyages to the peripheries of the known world, such as Marlow's struggles to pilot his steamboat up the Congo river in Joseph Conrad's *Heart of Darkness* (1902), one of the most consistent motifs of the period is of the figure who employs the new means of transportation to return to Britain. In some cases, this return serves to bring about a happy reunion of lovers or some significant revelation that allows the narrative to come to closure. Like his role model, Dick Whittington, Walter in Dickens's *Dombey and Son* survives a ship-wreck to return to Florence. Similarly, in Charles Reade's *Hard Cash* (1863), the appar-ently lifeless body of David Dodd is returned to England, where it is discovered that he is not dead, but in a state of suspended animation following a mosquito bite at sea. But more common is the figure whose sudden and unexpected arrival brings consternation and conflict. In Dickens's *Great Expectations* (1861), for example, Abel Magwitch is transported to Australia after his brief interlude with Pip on the marshes along the Thames, only to return years later to announce that it was he, and not Miss Havisham, who has been Pip's secret benefactor. Magwitch's appearance fills Pip with apprehension, not just because the ex-convict has broken the law by traveling to his native land, but because he represents all that the young man has tried to suppress: his lowly birth, his vain hopes of winning Estella's heart, and his betrayal of the love and affection of Joe. In such narratives, the figure who returns is associated with death and destruction; drawn ever nearer by the speed of the steamship, the colonies represent the past that cannot be repressed, the inescapable reminder of some trauma that the novels' protagonists must face in order to resolve the narrative of self-development.

The figure who returns, however, was not limited to the nation's own expelled elements, its émigrés and transported convicts. In extending British power to the peripheries of the known world, the modern technologies of communication and transportation also brought the peripheries closer to the imperial center, and with them the fact of racial otherness. From the Creole "madwoman," Bertha Mason, who burns down the ancestral home of Mr. Rochester in Charlotte Brontë's *Jane Eyre*

(1847), to the Hindoo assassins who patiently plot the return of their stolen jewel in Wilkie Collins's *The Moonstone* (1868), and from Tonga, the monkey man who murders a former English army officer in Doyle's *The Sign of Four* (1890), to the Transylvanian count who preys on the blood of Englishwomen in Bram Stoker's *Dracula* (1897), the foreign agents responsible for the narrative action of so many Victorian novels enter the permeable space of the nation through the portals provided by the shipping industry. Such fantasies of foreign invasion, in which the purity of the body of the English nation-state has become infected by some eastern pollutant, are described by Stephen Arata as indicative of the period's anxieties concerning "reverse colonization." "In each case, a terrifying reversal has occurred: the colonizer finds himself in the position of the colonized; the exploiter becomes the exploited; the victimizer victimized. Such fears are linked to a perceived decline – racial, moral, spiritual – which makes the nation vulnerable to attack from more vigorous, 'primitive' peoples" (Arata 1990: 623). In the age of the steamship, it seemed increasingly possible that the empire might indeed strike back, that Britain was no longer immune to the very forms of invasion and infection that it exercised abroad.

The concerns for the way in which the new technologies deformed the social sphere of the nation, even as they seemed to offer a means of consolidating its reach, are especially acute in those texts which dramatize their effects on women. Telegraphy was one of the earliest professions, apart from the traditionally "feminine" occupations of governess, teacher, or nurse, that was open to middle-class women of good standing. In fact, the Central Telegraph Office, the "great brain" of the empire's communications system, was operated chiefly by women. Following experiments in the 1850s that showed women to be "more teachable, more attentive, and quicker-eyed" than the male clerks formerly employed, not to mention "sooner satisfied with lower wages" (Rye 1987: 334), the daughters of middle-class clerks and civil servants were increasingly recruited as telegraphists. Of the 1,240 instrument clerks employed in the Central Telegraph Office in 1874, 740 were women. The novelty of so many women gathered in one place, and with such responsibilities, never failed to elicit comment from reporters. In his 1877 article, "The Young Women at the London Telegraph Office," Anthony Trollope writes:

> The stranger . . . will think a great deal more about the young women than the telegraphy . . . To me [the chief attraction of the place] was the condition of the girls – their appearance, their welfare, their respectability, their immediate comfort, their future prospects, their coming husbands, their capabilities, their utility, and their appropriateness in that place – or inappropriateness. (1877: 379)

Earning their own incomes, living alone or in shared lodgings with other women, and operating the most advanced communications equipment yet devised, the women employed at the Central Telegraph Office confounded all the conventional associations of femininity with domesticity, servitude, and passivity. They were enigmas, as cryptic in their gendered identities as the coded messages which they transmitted through the electrical wires of their instruments. As such they elicited a kind of intense epistemophilia, a need or desire to know, to resolve their uncertain place within the ideological norms of gender. "Oh! – if only I could know what those two pretty girls in the distance were talking about!" laments Trollope. "Not from curiosity, but that I might judge somewhat of their inward natures, – whether they were good or bad, happy or unhappy, pure or impure" (1877: 379–80).

Trollope's fascination with and anxieties for the "inward nature" of the Telegraph Girl are evident in his 1877 short story of the same name. It tells the story of one of the Central Telegraph Office's female employees, Lucy Graham. Lucy takes great pride in the independence afforded her by her work; she has "taught herself to despise feminine weaknesses" (Trollope 1982: 71) and is disgusted by the idea that her occupation is little more than a "stepping-stone to a husband" (p. 75). Even so, Lucy worries that her profession will affect her nature as a woman. "She must begin life after what seemed to her a most unfeminine fashion, – 'just as though she were a young man,' – for it was thus she described to herself her own position over and over again" (p. 71). The impression that life as a telegrapher has masculinized the young woman becomes increasingly evident as Lucy takes in a fellow telegraph girl named Sophy as a room-mate. In time, Lucy discovers that "in truth she loved her," and increasingly adopts the role of husband to Sophy, jealously warning off prospective suitors, and financially supporting her when she falls sick (p. 77). Such strong overtones of homoeroticism are a feature of another literary representation of the secret life of the female telegrapher, Hardy's *A Laodicean* (1881). No common Post Office employee, Paula Power is the daughter of a "great railway contractor" (Hardy 1975: 62), and an heiress to the fortune he amassed in that pursuit. She lives in Stancy Castle, a crumbling medieval pile that has been partially modernized and outfitted with a private telegraph line. "'That looks strange in such a building,'" remarks the architect George Somerset, upon first seeing the cable. "'Miss Power,'" he is told, "'had it put up to know the latest news from town. It costs six pounds a mile. She can work it herself, beautifully . . . Miss Power was so interested in it at first that she was sending messages from morning till night'" (p. 64). As different as her social situation is from Trollope's Lucy Graham, however, Paula shares with her an uncertain sexuality. A "laodicean" is one who is lukewarm, and in this instance Paula's lukewarmness refers principally to her relations with men. Despite being vigorously courted by a pair of eligible bachelors, Paula seems more attached to her friend Charlotte. "'Now that's a curious thing again these two girls being so fond of one another,'" a neighbor remarks. "'[T]hey be more like lovers than maid and maid'" (pp. 78–9). Moreover, Paula, too, is described in distinctly masculinized terms, especially when she exercises in her private gymnasium. "'[T]here she wears such a pretty boy's costume,'" reports her maid, "'and is so charming in her movements, that you think she is a lovely young youth and not a girl at all'" (p. 193).

The uncertain and shifting gendered identities of these fictional female telegraph operators are perhaps indicative of the uncanny nature of telegraphic communication itself: the way in which it translates language into a series of electrical impulses that render the sender simultaneously present and absent, and her messages both legible and illegible. "There was something curious," Somerset reports upon watching Charlotte operate Paula's device, "in watching this utterance about himself, under his very nose, in a language unintelligible to him" (p. 71). Jay Clayton argues that the repeated association of the telegraph with same-sex desire is indicative of "the odd, still unassimilated position of the telegraph network in the regime of modernity" (1997: 229). Where twentieth-century communications technology is increasingly allied with the faculty of sight, and with a state of disembodiment, the development of the telegraphic "sounder," an instrument that allowed messages to be "read" acoustically as a series of long and short pulses, had the effect of enforcing a sense of "presentness:" the person sending the message seemed physically present in the room at the moment of communication. As Hardy writes, "The telegraph had almost the attributes of a human being at Stancy Castle. When its bell rang people rushed to the old tapestried chamber allotted to it, and waited its pleasure with all the deference due to such a novel inhabitant" (1975: 80). According to Clayton, such "intensification and immediacy, combined with a sense that distance has been internalized, brought inside the subject, resulting in a split but oddly augmented identity," gave to telegraphy a peculiar somatic dimension, a "queerness," which texts such as Trollope's and Hardy's register as a deep ambiguity in the sexual nature of their female characters (1997: 226).

Similar anxieties concerning the way in which technology transforms not only the nature of communications, but the identities of those who are in its employ, greeted the appearance of the typewriter. Machines for mechanical transcription had been devised in the early eighteenth century and were in limited circulation in Europe by the mid-nineteenth century, but it was not until 1874 that they were first mass-produced. It was in that year that the American gun manufacturer, E. Remington & Sons, began marketing a product patented by an amateur inventor from Milwaukee named Christopher Latham Sholes. Sales were slow at first, especially in Britain, where the business community was notoriously averse to change. Commercial and professional communications had heretofore been carried out by young men trained in the "clerk's hand," a highly formalized style of handwriting that was much prized. The typewriter introduced not only a method of transcription that challenged the primacy of the clerk's hand, but what Friedrich A. Kittler has described as an entirely new "discourse network," a writing system linking power, technology, and identity. In the discourse network of the modern era, the idea of the self as the source and origin of communication disappears: where once handwriting maintained and made visible the uniqueness and particularity of the individual, the typewriter severs the connection between self and utterance, introducing in its stead a form of writing free of any origin exterior to its own system. "Spatially designated and discrete signs," writes Kittler, "that, rather than increase in speed, was the real innovation of the typewriter. In place of the image of the word [in handwriting] there appears a geometrical figure created by the spatial arrangement of the letter keys" (1990: 193). The uniformity of the typewritten word makes it a suspect thing, an utterance that represents some prior essence, the person who speaks or writes, but effaces any visible signs of its relationship to that essence. Such anxieties gave rise to concerns for fraud, and the use of the type-writer in acts of subterfuge and impersonation. In Doyle's "A Case of Identity," for example, Sherlock Holmes discovers that the mysterious suitor of a young woman is in fact her own stepfather, who has maintained this elaborate charade by sending her typewritten letters in order to disguise his handwriting. Holmes ultimately concludes that "a typewriter has really quite as much individuality as a man's identity. Unless they are quite new, no two of them write exactly alike" (Doyle 1986a: 263). But the story nonetheless testifies to the fears concerning the new means of transcription and the threat it posed to the ideal of uniqueness that underlay the Victorians' conceptions of communication.

Commercial acceptance of the typewriter came as a result of the increasingly hier-archical organization of corporations and their greater need for an effective and effi-cient means of handling documents. While even the most expert clerk could transcribe only about forty words a minute, a good typist could manage sixty or more; in the typewriting contests that soon sprang up to test different models and methods of typing, speeds of one hundred words a minute were common and winners often clocked in well above one hundred and twenty, or approximately ten keystrokes a second. Such speeds, together with the greater regularity and clarity of typewritten communications, became necessary as businesses struggled to manage the masses of paperwork upon which vertically integrated operations depended. As Gregory Anderson writes, "The structure of the late-Victorian economy began to shift towards services, with more white-collar workers needed to run an increasingly urban society and to manage the external foreign trade and financial services sector focussed on the City of London" (1988: 4). Female clerical workers were an ideal solution to this problem: like the telegraph girls employed by the Post Office, they seemed willing to accept lower wages and the fact that the position of a typist, unlike that of the male clerk she came to replace, did not lead to opportunities for career advancement. Many women were willing to forgo such material compensation because typewriting allowed them to retain their class and gender status. With its piano-like arrangement of keys, and the need for a fineness of touch that recollected needlework, the type-writer could be associated with the conventional skills and attributes of middle-class femininity. As the author of one typewriting manual put it: "The type-writer is especially adapted to feminine fingers. They seem to be made for type-writing. The type-writing involves no hard labour, and no more skill than playing the piano" (Harrison 1888: 9). Typewriter manufacturers and businesses alike helped secure the association of femininity with typewriting; the former undertook to promote and train young women in the art of typing, largely as a means of selling more machines, while the latter established separate working spaces and elaborate social protocols designed to protect the gentility of female workers. As a result, the total number of women working as clerks, stenographers, and typists rose from about 2,000 in 1851 to 166,000 by the end of the century, by which time they accounted for 20 per cent of all white-collar workers in Great Britain (Zimmeck 1986: 154).

The Type-Writer Girl was more than a feature of Victorian workplaces and offices, however. She was also a popular figure in the cultural imaginary, appearing in novels, short stories, plays, music-hall routines, postcard illustrations and a host of other media as a fashionably dressed, well-educated, and often sexually adventurous symbol of the "new woman" (Keep 1997). Juliet Appleton, the protagonist of Grant Allen's *The Type-Writer Girl*, for example, depicts her life in distinctly epic terms: "I mean to sail away on my Odyssey, unabashed, touching at such shores as may chance to beckon, yet hopeful of reaching at last the realms of Alcinous" (1897: 17). To that end, she attends Girton College, trains herself to operate a typewriter, and moves to London. There she takes an apartment of her own and soon lands a job, and a prospective romance, with a dashing young London publisher. In her off hours, she takes up smoking, tours the countryside on her bicycle, and even spends a weekend living at an anarchist commune. Such radical pastimes are treated lightly by Allen who, writing under the pseudonym of Olive Pratt Rayner, is anxious to portray the Type-Writer Girl as little more than new wine in an old bottle. Far from breaking with the ideal of marriage and motherhood as the *raison d'être* of woman's life, Juliet's story seems largely to confirm it, with much of the narrative turning on the absolute and continuing necessity of "romance." "For, pretend as we will," she concludes, "the plain truth is this: woman is plastic till the predestined man appears; then she takes the mould he chooses to impose upon her. Men make their own lives, women's are made for them" (p. 138). The Type-Writer Girl emerges less as a harbinger of an independent and emancipated womanhood than as the slightly comical, even pitiable figure of the woman beset by the dilemmas facing her in the modern world.

Not all writers were quite so sanguine, however. The sheer number of young women entering the white-collar workplace evoked the possibility that many would choose a career over the sacred duties of matrimony and maternity. Moreover, there were fears that the willingness of women to accept a lower wage than male office workers would result in the displacement of the men who formerly occupied these positions, causing hardship to the families they once supported. Such views find expression in George Gissing's *The Odd Women* (1893), in which Mary Barfoot, the proprietor of a semi-charitable typewriting school for young women of good families, sums up the arguments against women in the workplace in a lecture to her student typists.

"They will tell you that in entering the commercial world, you not only unsex yourselves, but do a grievous wrong to the numberless men struggling hard for a bare sustenance. You reduce salaries, you press into an already overcrowded field, you injure even your own sex by making it impossible for men to marry, who, if they earned enough, would be supporting a wife." (Gissing 1977: 134)

Such arguments, however, fall on deaf ears. Unlike Allen's lovelorn Type-Writer Girl, the women in Gissing's novel are militant feminists, who see the typewriter as a weapon in a grand struggle for female emancipation. Mary tells her students:

"I don't care whether we crowd out the [male clerks who complain about the rising numbers of women office workers] or not. I don't care *what* results, if only women are made strong and self-reliant and nobly independent . . . Most likely we shall have a revolution in the social order greater than any that yet seems possible. Let it come, and let *us* help its coming . . . Let the world perish in tumult rather than things go on in this way!" (p. 136)

Such revolutionary sentiments serve to dramatize the distance between these women and the conventions of Victorian womanhood. As Kittler argues, "[m]achines do away with polar sexual difference and its symbols. An apparatus that can replace Man or the symbols of masculine production [such as the phallus-like pen] is also accessible to women" (1990: 351–2). Like Trollope and Hardy, Gissing depicts the most radical of his female information workers, Rhoda Nunn, in distinctly masculinized terms, as if her work has indeed "unsexed" her, as the women's critics claimed. She is described by the narrator as being of "an unfamiliar sexual type," whose countenance, on first view, "seemed masculine, its expression somewhat aggressive – eyes shrewdly observant and lips consciously impregnable" (1893: 20–1). And, like Lucy Graham and Paula Power, Rhoda shares her lodgings and her life with another woman in a manner that, as Sally Ledger has argued, has distinct overtones of homoeroticism (1997: 20).

The difference between Gissing's portrayal of women information workers and those of his predecessors, however, becomes evident in the contrasting trajectories of their romance plots. Trollope and Hardy ultimately join Allen in reaffirming the essential femininity of their heroines; Lucy's jealous response to Sophy's relationship with a friendly widower is revealed to stem from her own secret attraction to him, and the story closes with the two happily married and living in the provinces. Similarly, Paula's pronounced indecisiveness gradually dissolves and, after Somerset chases her to the continent and back, she too shows herself to be a conventional woman desirous of the love of a good man. Gissing's Rhoda Nunn courts such a romantic conclusion, coming perilously close to marrying Everard Barfoot, but the incompatibility of their ideological views ultimately undermines the relationship, and the novel closes with Rhoda reunited with Mary and the two planning to launch a new magazine to promote female equality. Abjuring the conventional closure of the romance plot, Gissing underscores the fundamental difference that the new technologies have made in the lives of Victorian women. No longer dependent on a male figure to give meaning and purpose to their lives, nor limited to the traditional female occupations such as governess or teacher, modeled on the ideal of woman's "nurturing" sensibilities, Rhoda and Mary set out to imagine a cultural identity for women as radically different as the typewriter and the telegraph were from handwriting.

As Gissing makes clear, the new technologies sent shock waves through the social formation of Victorian Britain, affecting the ways in which people conceived not only of themselves but of their relationships with one another both within and without the "imaginary community" of the nation. But there was a further, unforeseen consequence. In increasing the ease and the speed at which data might be transcribed and transmitted from place to place, the new technologies, together with advances in print technology such as the steam-powered rotary press and stereo lithography, also encouraged the production of ever more complex and numerous kinds of information. Victorian Britain was awash in printed materials: government Blue Books, geographical surveys, census statistics, and scientific reports, not to mention the daily newspapers, weekly gazettes, monthly magazines, quarterly reviews, penny dreadfuls, and part-issue novels, all clamored for the attention of the reading public. Paper production rose from 2,500 tons in 1715 to 75,000 tons in 1851, with per person consumption increasing from two and a half pounds annually in 1800 to eight and a half pounds in 1860 (Welsh 1985: 38). The result was a sense of cognitive overload, of there being simply more information than any one person could ever effectively know. As Thomas Richards writes, "If today we call this the 'information explosion,' it was because by the century's end many people had stopped using the word 'knowledge,' which always had something about it of a prospective unity emerging, and started using the word 'information,' with its contemporary overtones of scattered disjunct fragments of fact" (1993: 5). Under the pressure of such an outpouring of "information," the idea that there was an inherent structure and form to all knowledge, that there might yet be some "key to all mythologies" as Casaubon believes in Eliot's *Middlemarch*, seemed increasingly remote. In its stead came the regime of facts, that is, a granular, atomistic knowledge that privileged the local and specific over the global and totalizable and was thus eminently reproducible – which indeed made reproducibility the condition of its veracity: a fact was only a fact, only obtained to its factuality, by virtue of its repeatability. The cancerous proliferation of written documents deeply troubled the Victorian imagination, resulting in what Alexander Welsh has described as a "psychopathology of information in the play of consciousness" (1985: 36), an obsessive concern for the integrity of the information network that manifested itself, in texts such as Henry James's novella *In the Cage* (1898), in fantasies of postal intrigue and blackmail.

The curious nature of documents, their tendency not only to produce further documents, but to exceed the bounds of the information network in which they were produced, is the focus of much of Dickens's work. The Court of Chancery in *Bleak House* (1853) and the Circumlocution Office in *Little Dorrit* (1857) are monstrously ineffectual institutions that have become overwhelmed by the sheer surfeit of their documentation. As D. A. Miller writes, "[w]ith its endless referrals, relays, remands, its ecologically terrifying production of papers, minutes, memoranda, Dickens's bureaucracy works positively to elude the project of interpretation that nominally guides it." (1988: 67). But it is Stoker's *Dracula* that most effectively dramatizes the relationship between the new communication and transportation technologies and the unmanageable problem of "information." The novel has been popularized by its many film adaptations as a kind of Gothic romance set in a medieval castle in Transylvania. But most of its action is in fact set in London, and the novel shows a marked fascination with the new technologies: Mina Harker uses a manifold typewriter to transcribe and collate the various firsthand reports and documents that constitute the narrative; Jonathan Harker takes a Kodak camera, the first to use roll film, to document his trip to Transylvania; and Dr. Seward records his diaries on a wax cylinder phonograph, an instrument first patented by Thomas Edison in 1877, but not marketed until the late 1880s. Furthermore, Dracula travels to Britain in the hold of a steamship, and effects his escape by the same means, only to be tracked by an elaborate system of lookouts that employ the submarine telegraph to report his route. He is finally hunted to his lair in a breathless chase combining fast steamboats and a detailed knowledge of the local railway timetables.

This formidable array of modern technological prowess is pitted against an enemy that seems to model the very nature of information itself. Like information, the vampire absorbs all with which it comes into contact, assuming the energies of its readers as its own; it is a protean force, taking on a variety of shapes and forms at will; and it is, first and foremost, a process of reproduction, a way of making copies that are themselves copies of copies, and which seem to circulate – as the vampire's own international travels make evident – well beyond the bounds of their place of origin. Vampirism, as Jennifer Wicke has argued, is not so much the antithesis of typewriting as another form of it, a means of transcription and multiplication that is both the central problem of the text and the ostensible solution to that problem:

> The book is obsessed with all these technological and cultural modalities, with the newest of the new cultural phenomena, and yet it is they that shatter the fixed and circumscribed world the novel seems designed to protect through those very means . . . The same science, rationality and technologies of social control relied on to defend against the encroachments of Dracula are the source of the vampiric powers of the mass culture with which Dracula . . . is allied. (Wicke 1992: 476–7)

The contradictions at the heart of *Dracula* are also those of the relationship of the Victorian novel to the new information technologies of the period. Dictated to or transcribed by typists, printed by steam-powered presses, serialized in the weekly newspapers, advertised on broadsides and billboards, sold in railway bookstores, and read by the illumination of electric lights, the novel was as much a part of the new discourse network of the nineteenth century as the locomotive, the steamship, or the telegraph. It existed not in some space removed from the technological forces it sought to describe, but rather was contiguous with them, as much a cause of the "pathology of information" as a remedy to it. Hence, while the novels of the period are able to articulate the nature of the new forms of space, time, and identity that these technologies produced, and to provide telling critiques of their effects on society, they could not wholly distance themselves from those effects. The striking ambivalences of Dickens's treatment of the railroad as an agent of both destruction and justice, of Hardy's representation of the female telegraphist, or of Stoker's depiction of vampirism, are precisely those of a medium aware that the world it sought to represent had ceased to exist as a stable point of reference, either anterior or exterior to the economy of signs. Like Jonathan Harker at the end of *Dracula*, surveying the paltry evidence of his and his colleagues' struggles against the vampire, the Victorian novel looked out on the modern world only to discover that what remained was "nothing but a mass of type-writing" (Stoker 1995: 378).

REFERENCES

Allen, Grant ["Olive Pratt Rayner"] (1897), *The Type-Writer Girl* (London: C. Arthur Pearson).

Anderson, Benedict (1991), *Imagined Communities: Reflections on the Origin and Spread of Nationalism*, rev. edn. (London: Verso).

Anderson, Gregory (1988), "The White-Blouse Revolution," in Gregory Anderson, ed., *The White-Blouse Revolution: Female Office Workers since 1870* (Manchester: Manchester University Press), 1–26.

Anon. (1889), "The Intellectual Effects of Electricity," *Spectator*, 9 Nov., 631–2.

Arata, Stephen D (1990), "The Occidental Tourist: *Dracula* and the Anxiety of Reverse Colonization," *Victorian Studies*, 33, 621–45.

Caird, Mona (1989), *The Daughters of Danaus* (New York: Feminist Press).

Carlyle, Thomas (1896), *Sartor Resartus: The Life and Opinions of Herr Teufelsdrockh* (London: Chapman & Hall).

Clayton, Jay (1997), "The Voice in the Machine: Hazlitt, Hardy, James," in Jeffrey Masten, Peter Stallybrass and Nancy Vickers, eds., *Language Machines: Technologies of Literary and Cultural Production* (New York: Routledge), 209–32.

Dickens, Charles (1985), *Dombey and Son*, ed. Peter Fairclough (Harmondsworth: Penguin).

Doyle, Sir Arthur Conan (1986a), "A Case of Identity," in *The Complete Sherlock Holmes*, vol. 1 (New York: Bantam), 251–67. (First publ. 1892.)

Doyle, Sir Arthur Conan (1986b), "The Devil's Foot," in *The Complete Sherlock Holmes*, vol. 2 (New York: Bantam), 418–41. (First publ. 1917.)

Doyle, Sir Arthur Conan (1994), *The Sign of Four*, ed. Christopher Roden (Oxford: Oxford University Press). (First publ. 1890.)

Eliot, George (1977), *Middlemarch*, ed. W. J. Harvey (Harmondsworth: Penguin).

Freeman, Michael (1999), *Railways and the Victorian Imagination* (New Haven: Yale University Press).

Gissing, George (1977), *The Odd Women* (New York: Norton). (First publ. 1893.)

Greg, W. R. (1877), "Life at High Pressure," in *Literary and Social Judgments*, vol. 2 (London: Trubner), 262–88.

Hardy, Thomas (1975), *A Laodicean* (London: Macmillan).

Hardy, Thomas (1985), *Jude the Obscure*, ed. Patricia Ingham (Oxford: Oxford University Press).

Harrison, John (1888), *A Manual of the Type-Writer* (London: Isaac Pitman).

Hobsbawm, Eric (1999), *Industry and Empire: From 1750 to the Present Day* (Harmondsworth: Penguin).

Keep, Christopher (1997), "The Cultural Work of the Type-Writer Girl," *Victorian Studies*, 40, 401–26.

Kittler, Friedrich A. (1990), *Discourse Networks 1800–1900*, trans. Michael Meteer et al. (Stanford: Stanford University Press).

Ledger, Sally (1997), *The New Woman: Fiction and Feminism at the Fin-de-Siècle* (Manchester: Manchester University Press).

Marx, Karl (1973), *Grundrisse: The Foundations of the Critique of Political Economy*, trans. Martin Nicolaus (New York: Random House).

Miller, D. A. (1988), *The Novel and the Police* (Berkeley: University of California Press).

Morus, Iwan Rhys (1996), "The Electric Ariel: Telegraphy and Commercial Culture in Early Victorian England," *Victorian Studies*, 39, 339–78.

Newsome, David (1998), *The Victorian World Picture* (London: Fontana).

Pearson, Hesketh (1934), *The Smith of Smiths* (New York: Harper & Brothers).

Reade, Charles (1863), *Hard Cash: A Matter of Fact Romance* (Boston: De Wolfe, Fiske).

Richards, Thomas (1993), *The Imperial Archive: Knowledge and the Fantasy of Empire* (London: Verso).

Ruskin, John (1904), *Modern Painters*, vol. 3, in *The Works of John Ruskin*, vol. 5, eds. E. T. Cook and Alexander Wedderburn (London: George Allen). (First publ. 1843–59.)

Rye, Maria Susan (1987), "The Rise and Progress of Telegraphs," in Candida Ann Lacey, ed., *Barbara Leigh Smith Bodichon and the Langham Place Group* (New York: Routledge), 323–36.

Standage, Tom (1998), *The Victorian Internet: The Remarkable Story of the Telegraph and the Nineteenth Century's On-Line Pioneers* (New York: Walker and Co.).

Stoker, Bram (1995), *Dracula*, ed. A. N. Wilson (Oxford: Oxford University Press).

Trollope, Anthony (1877), "The Young Women at the London Telegraph Office," *Good Words*, 18, 377–84.

Trollope, Anthony (1982), "The Telegraph Girl," in Betty Jane Slemp Breyer, ed., *Anthony Trollope: The Complete Short Stories*, vol. 4 (Fort Worth: Texas Christian University Press), 69–105. (First publ. 1877.)

Welsh, Alexander (1985), *George Eliot and Blackmail* (Cambridge, Mass.: Harvard University Press).

Wicke, Jennifer (1992), "Vampiric Typewriting: *Dracula* and its Media," *English Literary History*, 59, 467–93.

Williams, Fredrick S. (1852), *Our Iron Roads: Their History, Construction and Social Influences* (London: Ingram, Cooke).

Wright, James R. (1996), "They Were the Very Models of the Modern Information Age," in Charles R. Putney et al., eds., *Sherlock Holmes: Victorian Sleuth to Modern Hero* (Lanham, Md.: Scarecrow), 16–24.

Zimmeck, Meta (1986), "Jobs for the Girls: The Expansion of Clerical Work for Women, 1850–1914," in Angela V. John, ed., *Unequal Opportunities: Women's Employment in England, 1800–1918* (Oxford: Blackwell), 152–77.

9

Laws, the Legal World, and Politics

John R. Reed

Law and Politics

The Victorian period saw great political changes. A strong monarchy was gradually transformed into a government dominated by Parliament. The right to vote was extended from a small group of landed individuals to the greater part of the male population. A land that had been primarily agricultural and rural rapidly became industrialized and highly urbanized as well, and many new laws had to be conceived to deal with these situations, especially laws regulating the relationships between manufacturing interests and the laboring classes. New laws sought to establish humane but economically and morally efficient ways of dealing with the indigent, and a severe and brutal criminal code was steadily modified in the direction of mercy and greater justice. During Victoria's reign enormous changes occurred in the political and legal realms, and these changes were reflected in the literature of the age.

A few years before Victoria came to the throne, a monumental legal victory was won by those interested in extending opportunities for participating in the political process. This was the First Reform Act of 1832. Agitation in favor of extending the right to vote had begun as early as the end of the eighteenth century and was active after the Napoleonic wars. A Bill to extend the franchise was introduced in Parliament in 1831, but was rejected by the House of Lords. The disappointment of the public was reflected in riots around the country, most notably in Bristol. The next year a similar Bill, redistributing and extending the franchise, was passed. What were called "rotten boroughs" or "pocket boroughs," because they were controlled by powerful aristocrats, were reduced in number, and large new cities, like Manchester, were awarded appropriate representation. It must be remembered, though, that although more people were granted the right to vote in 1832, voting remained public; the secret ballot was not employed until the national elections in 1874. Until then, a man had to be polled at a public venue and declare his vote out loud. As a result, intimidation was widespread. Merchants, tradesmen, and farmers who rented their land could not afford to displease the powerful families whom they served. Hence, although the First Reform Act benefited the comfortable middle class, in particular the merchant and manufacturing elements of that class, power remained largely in the hands of the great landowning families, who were mainly aristocratic.

The Second Reform Act, extending the franchise yet more widely, was passed in 1867, and the Third Reform Act, which approached the liberal ideal of universal manhood suffrage, was passed in 1884. This extension of the franchise did not affect women, who remained without the right to vote. Women had little overt power in the political structure of Victorian Britain, despite the presence of a queen on the throne. They might exert political influence in indirect ways, as Trollope's series of "Palliser" novels indicates, but they had no legal power. Although there was significant agitation for women's right to vote during the last quarter of the nineteenth century, women did not achieve that right until the Representation of the People Act of 1918, and even then it remained subject to a number of qualifications such as age and marital status.

During most of the Victorian period, two principal political parties vied for power: the Whigs and the Tories, the former generally associated with liberal views, the latter with conservative positions. But both parties were capable of taking uncharacteristic stands on particular issues, and both parties had their own radical and ultraconservative wings. Disraeli, for example, was a "radical" in the Tory party and Lord Cochran at an earlier date a "radical" in the Whig party. Nevil Beauchamp in George Meredith's *Beauchamp's Career* (1875) runs for Parliament as a Radical Liberal. In time a Liberal Party emerged as an independent entity. During the Victorian period, the queen was titular ruler of the nation, but the real work of governing fell to the Prime Minister and his Cabinet, and Parliament, made up of the permanent members of the House of Lords and the elected members of the House of Commons. Originally Parliament met during the months of May, June, and July, and these months also constituted "The Season" in London when the fashionable world met to amuse and entertain itself. This Season officially ended on August 12. By mid-Victorian times, and until the end of the century, Parliament was meeting from February through August. Upon occasion, Parliament might be required to prolong its season, and more rarely, even call a special session.

In the early part of the century, elections could be quite unruly, even violent. There was a good deal of verbal abuse and sometimes partisans, with the addition of hired ruffians, would resort to physical abuse as well. In the election contest between Millbank and Rigby in Disraeli's *Coningsby* (1844) the characters Magog Wrath and Billy Bluck typify this bought muscle, though they are depicted as controlling as much as inciting the adherents to the two sides of the contest. However, in George Eliot's *Felix Holt: The Radical* (1866), electioneering roughness fueled by alcohol leads to an outright riot. Dickens treated election-time corruption comically in the election at Eatanswill in *The Pickwick Papers* (1837).

Buying votes was commonplace to such a degree that it began to receive serious parliamentary attention early in the century, when a select committee of the House of Commons was charged with investigating election practices. The subject turns up frequently in the literature of the time. In Edward Bulwer-Lytton's *Pelham* (1828), the subject is evident in the name of the town in which the election campaign occurs – Buyemall. There are also lively election scenes in Bulwer-Lytton's *My Novel* (1853). Despite legislation designed to address the crime of buying votes, the practice persisted through the century. The Corrupt Practices Act of 1854 did not halt bribery, despite its elaborate descriptions of the various forms the illegal conveying of money or money value could take. Anthony Trollope sets *Doctor Thorne* (1858) in 1854 and seems to make a direct statement about the limitations of the Act. In this novel, Roger Scatcherd ignores the laws and wins the contest he has entered. On the other hand, he has a petition brought against him challenging the results of the election, is found guilty of paying electors, and is unseated. Trollope also refers to the practice in *Ralph the Heir* (1870–1) and *The Duke's Children* (1879–80); in the latter, the electors of Polpenno receive ten shillings apiece for their votes. Harold Transome in *Felix Holt* announces that he will have nothing to do with paying electors for their votes and loses the election.

Running for Parliament could be a costly endeavor in a contested election, and a candidate needed either deep pockets of his own or a wealthy sponsor. The issue comes up in Disraeli's *Coningsby*, where the title character needs the wealth either of his rich and aristocratic uncle or of a manufacturer to run for Parliament. He refuses to compromise his principles with the former, who then abandons him, but eventually finds support from the latter. Charles Egremont in Disraeli's *Sybil, Or The Two Nations* (1845) seeks help from his older brother, Lord Marney, to defray the expenses of a successful campaign. But even a candidate like Phineas Finn in Trollope's novel of that name (1867–9), though running unopposed, finds the expenses considerable. Most of the election campaigns described in fiction occur in smaller towns, as in George Eliot's *Middlemarch* and Robert Surtees' *Handley Cross* (1843) and *Hillingdon Hall* (1845), but some, such as those in Dickens's *Our Mutual Friend* (1865) and Trollope's *Can You Forgive Her?* (1865), take place in London.

From a modern point of view, the political situation remained unbalanced for much of the nineteenth century, favoring the propertied classes. The Combination Laws of 1799 and 1800 made the formation of labor unions illegal, but even after their repeal in 1824, which was followed by numerous strikes, resistance to the organization of labor continued. For example, whereas manufacturers could freely band together to make arrangements favorable to their businesses, various prohibitions made it difficult for laborers to organize in order to put pressure on owners to ameliorate working conditions, negotiate wages, and so forth. Gradual unionization did nevertheless take place, largely through occupation-specific groups, notably the coal-miners. The formation of the Trades Union Congress in 1869 signaled the establishment of a forceful union presence.

One powerful influence toward reform was the Chartist movement, which between 1838 and 1848 sought universal manhood suffrage; but in 1839 it failed in its objective of obliging Parliament to accept the working men's petition appealing for the vote and other reforms. Elizabeth Gaskell provides a vivid rendering of the hope and the resentment surrounding this episode through the character John Barton in her novel *Mary Barton* (1848). Alton Locke, in Charles Kingsley's novel of that name, is embittered and radicalized when he learns of the failure of the Chartist petition and determines to participate in the movement to give power to the working classes. In Disraeli's *Sybil*, the rejection of the Chartist petition leads to a riot by working-class men. A whole category of novels took up issues relating to laws affecting the working class, including Mrs. Trollope's *Michael Armstrong, The Factory Boy* (1839), Disraeli's *Sybil* (1845), Kingsley's *Yeast* (1851), and Gaskell's *Mary Barton* (1848) and *North and South* (1855). Dickens's *Hard Times* (1854) is one of the most famous of these novels that specifically discusses labor unions. Charles Reade's *Put Yourself In His Place* (1870) is centrally concerned with questions of trade union activities and George Gissing's *Demos* (1886) is partly so.

Of the many laws that found their way into the literature of the period, the New Poor Law of 1834 is especially significant. Prior to the passage of this law the poor were cared for out of the resources of local parishes, often under the supervision of a local minister. The New Poor Law was designed to separate the "deserving" from the "undeserving" poor, to withhold support from those who were not genuinely in need. It instituted a means test of need, which required that the household not be supportable on its own resources. If the head of a household applied for relief, all family members were regarded as paupers. The help provided was residence in a workhouse, where women and children were separated from men, meaning that families could not live together. At first these workhouses remained parish institutions, but soon they were consolidated into regional "union" workhouses. Those indigents who sought public assistance felt humiliated and abused by the mandated treatment. Though the New Poor Law's regulations were severe, local authorities often tempered that severity. Several novelists deal with the workhouses and the New Poor Law – none more critically than Dickens, whose Oliver Twist is born in a workhouse where conditions are severe and where Oliver is punished for requesting more gruel. Betty Higden in *Our Mutual Friend* is so horrified by the thought of being sent to the workhouse that she flees from her friends and acquaintances, exhausts herself, and dies. Frances Trollope's *Jessie Philips* (1843) concentrates vigorously on the terrible conditions in the New Poor Law workhouses.

Law and Money

There were great fears among the middle classes about losing money or falling into debt, and these were serious concerns for a good part of the century, since the penalties for indebtedness could be severe. Especially at the beginning of the century, the laws were quite hostile to insolvent debtors. Creditors could easily have such unfortunate individuals seized and taken to what were called sponging-houses, where they were confined for a short while pending their ability to come up with payment to one or more creditors. If the debtor could raise no such payment, he was soon conveyed to prison, there to remain until he or his friends could pay his debt or make arrangements with his creditors. In Thackeray's *Vanity Fair* (1848), Becky arranges for her husband, Rawdon Crawley, to be arrested for debt so that she can carry on her affair with Lord Steyne. She assumes that he will remain safely in the sponging-house at least overnight. But Crawley's relatives assist him; he is released the same day and comes upon Becky and her admirer alone, a discovery that separates the husband and wife.

There were three principal prisons for housing insolvent debtors. King's Bench was for gentlemen; the Fleet and Marshalsea prisons were for less respectable types. As the century progressed, new laws improved the circumstances of insolvent debtors. A law passed in 1808 allowed the release of prisoners after a year for a debt of less than £20, considering that length of incarceration sufficient punishment. It also no longer permitted keeping imprisoned those debtors who agreed to pay what they owed on being released; of course, when a debtor was released, the debt remained in force. An Act of 1813 created a Court for Relief of Insolvent Debtors, which provided the opportunity for debtors to petition for release. Popular sentiment continued to favor leniency toward insolvent debtors, and a series of new laws improved conditions until the Debtors Act and the Bankruptcy Acts of 1869 abolished imprisonment for debt and transferred jurisdiction for cases of debt to the Court of Bankruptcy, bankruptcy now being the available means for insolvent debtors to escape punishment. Dickens refers to cases of insolvent debtors often, most notably in *Little Dorrit* (1857), where William Dorrit has been confined so long that he has come to be a kind of aristocrat of the poor and is referred to as "the father of the Marshalsea." In *The Pickwick Papers*, Mr. Pickwick is imprisoned because he refuses on principle to pay a legal judgment against him for breach of promise. In *David Copperfield* (1850), Mr. Micawber is constantly in jeopardy of being arrested for debt.

There were innumerable ways of falling into debt, but a favorite mode, which permitted the debtor to remain an honorable character, was the unwise cosigning of someone else's bill of credit. This happens to the Reverend Mark Robarts in Trollope's *Framley Parsonage* (1861). The good man is in danger of losing his parsonage to the bailiffs until a wealthy lord pays the creditors and spares the Reverend's home and career. Another honorable way to lose wealth was to fail in business. The proud Mr. Dombey in *Dombey and Son* (1848) loses his fortune and his business through the machinations of his manager, James Carker. Though guilty of much bad behavior, Dombey honorably meets all of his debt obligations. Mr. Sedley similarly fails in business in *Vanity Fair*, and, in his former friend Mr. Osborne's eyes, drops out of the ranks of respectable society. In contrast to these honorable bankruptcies is financial indebtedness brought about through irresponsible behavior, most notably through uncontrolled financial speculation. Much speculation from midcentury on in Britain resulted from the rapid proliferation of joint stock companies and was driven by the railway boom largely symbolized in the figure of George Hudson, called the Railway King for the fortune he made and subsequently lost through shares in various railway companies. Robert Bell's novel, *The Ladder of Gold* (1850), models its main character on Hudson and examines in detail the speculation and panic surrounding the railway industry in the 1840s. Dickens denounces the obsession with shares in *Little Dorrit* and creates the fraudulent financier Merdle as an example of the dishonesty abroad in the world of investment; Trollope follows suit with the character Melmotte in *The Way We Live Now* (1870), who fraudulently raises money purported to be destined for an American railway scheme.

Throughout the century, new laws were enacted to counter the inventiveness of investment fraud and exploitation. Speculation is a frequent subject in the literature of the time. As early as Samuel Warren's *Ten Thousand A-Year* (1841) fiction was already dealing with fraudulent joint stock companies such as the "Gunpowder and Fresh Water Company" and the "Artificial Rain Company." In G. W. M. Reynolds's *The Mysteries of London* (1845), a "City Man" living by financial speculation is a pronounced villain. Thackeray incorporated financial investment significantly in *The Newcomes* (1855), and a land development swindle is important to the plot of Charles Lever's *Davenport Dunn: A Man of Our Day* (1859). The development of limited liability companies, through which debt responsibility was more widely distributed, diminished the likelihood of bankruptcy from failure.

One quite common way of acquiring wealth for those in the upper registers of society was inheritance, which is accordingly a major theme in Victorian literature. Primogeniture was the abiding rule of inheritance for the landed classes, which meant that the eldest son inherited the bulk of the family estate and saw to the welfare of the rest of the family, who became his dependants unless they had other sources of income. From the mid-seventeenth century a standard arrangement developed that came to be referred to as strict settlement. According to strict settlement, the nominal owner of the estate settled the property on his eldest son, leaving the estate in tail to that son's eldest son. This arrangement left the nominal owner and his eldest son life tenants of the estate with only limited power to change it. When the son's eldest son came of age, pressure was exerted for him to renew the strict settlement arrangements. Wives were protected financially by way of jointures. Younger sons and daughters would generally be provided for in modest ways. Under this system, women could inherit only if no male relative was available, unless other provisions were made in the marriage settlement. The case was different in lower levels of society, where inheritance was generally determined by will rather than legal instruments such as the strict settlement; hence, although legal assistance was still required, it could be quite modest. In these circumstances, women were as likely to inherit property as men. There were, in fact, many women who inherited money and property, and some of them were extremely wealthy, such as Dickens's friend and fellow philanthropist Angela Burdett-Coutts.

In novels, inheritance can serve many plot purposes. Sometimes it has to do with lost identity — as with Oliver Twist, who does not know that he is entitled to a portion of his father's estate and who is kept from that knowledge through most of his story by his evil half-brother, Monks. In Collins's *No Name* (1862), Magdalen and Norah

Vanstone do not inherit the family estate when their parents die in an accident because it turns out that their parents had never formalized their union through marriage. Magdalen seeks to regain the inheritance by devious means and is not successful, whereas Norah is patient and submissive and ultimately achieves honestly what Magdalen could not achieve through deception. She marries the man who has become heir to the Vanstone estate. Who is to receive the wealth associated with the Jarndyce and Jarndyce case is the oppressive question that hovers over all of the action of *Bleak House* (1853); eventually the case destroys Richard Carstone, as it has others, and ends with no money left, not even the wherewithal to settle costs.

Sometimes inheritance is at the core of a novel, as with Charlotte Yonge's *The Heir of Redclyffe* (1853) or Trollope's *Ralph the Heir* (1871). Inheritance is an important complicating issue in *Our Mutual Friend*, where marriage conditions have been attached to the inheritance by his son of old John Harmon's fortune. The son appearing to have been murdered, the fortune descends to old Harmon's faithful employee, Nicodemus Boffin. Young Harmon is not dead and ultimately comes into his fortune, but only after he has proved that he doesn't need it to prosper. Meanwhile Mortimer Lightwood's and Eugene Wrayburn's lives are held in suspension because they depend on patriarchal will, in the sense of both volition and testament. Inheritance similarly complicates the plot of Eliot's *Felix Holt*, in which the unpretending Esther Lyon discovers herself to be the heir to the Transome estate, a development that intensifies her problematic situation rather than simplifying it.

It is not uncommon for plots to begin with disinheritance, if only temporarily, to get a hero started off on his own. More often, inheritances are used to reward characters with both foreseen and unforeseen fortunes. The accidental discovery of Lord Ringwood's will near the end of Thackeray's *The Adventures of Philip* provides the titular hero with an appropriate bounty. Frequently an inheritance serves as a surprising salvation, as it does in *Jane Eyre* (1847), when Jane learns that her uncle in Madeira has willed her his fortune.

Real inheritance disputes occasionally prompted fictional renderings. In the notorious Tichborne Claimant case (1870–1) a man returned from Australia claiming to be the heir of a vast fortune and was accepted by his mother and others; but inexplicably he knew little of his own background and had neither the manners nor the bearing of his supposed aristocratic condition. His two trials were closely followed by the public. At last he was declared to be one Arthur Orton and was imprisoned for his attempted fraud. This case, which attracted considerable popular attention, moved novelists to exploit the theme, including Trollope in *Ralph the Heir*, Charles Reade in *The Wandering Heir* (1872), and Marcus Clarke in *For the Term of His Natural Life* (1875).

Usually inheritance plays a small role in a larger narrative, as with Uncle Featherstone's dangling his fortune before Fred Vincy to make him submissive to his will in *Middlemarch*. Mary Garth "saves" him by refusing to assist Featherstone, who is on his deathbed, in altering his will back to Fred's advantage. In *Dr. Thorne* (1858), Mary Thorne turns out to be the heir of Roger Scatcherd, to whom the Gresham family estate is deeply in debt. By marrying Frank Gresham, she saves the Gresham family lands and fortunes.

Intrigues, criminal or otherwise, are often coupled with inheritance plots. In Sheridan Le Fanu's *Uncle Silas* (1864), the eponymous character plans the murder of his own niece to inherit her fortune, but fails. In William Harrison Ainsworth's *Rookwood* (1834), legitimate and illegitimate members of the Rookwood family scheme for an inheritance. False heirs are familiar figures in the Victorian novel. A striking instance occurs in Warren's *Ten Thousand A-Year*, where the vain and incompetent Tittlebat Titmouse is declared the proper heir of the Aubrey estate, ousting Charles Aubrey's truly genteel, deserving, and responsible family in favor of this upstart lout, who misuses the money. The lawyers who have effected this fraud through forgery are eventually unmasked; one commits suicide and the other two are prosecuted and imprisoned. Tittlebat winds up in a lunatic asylum – and, of course, Charles Aubrey and his family resume possession of the estate. In Wilkie Collins's *The Woman in White* (1860), Sir Percival Glyde has Anne Catherick confined in an asylum because he fears she knows that he has appropriated his estate illegally, he having altered the record of his illegitimate birth. A false heir is also at the center of Reade's *A Terrible Temptation* (1871).

Law and Morality

Some aspects of life were complicated by moral or religious constraints. A man or woman unhappy in marriage, for example, found it difficult to end the union, because divorce required an Act of Parliament, both time-consuming and very costly. Dickens's *Hard Times* calls attention to this difficulty in the character of Stephen Blackpool, who is bound to a drunken wife and cannot free himself because he is a factory worker for whom divorce would entail an impossible expense. But even for those who could afford divorce, the conditions were not favorable for women. The Matrimonial Causes Act of 1857 made divorce a secular rather than an ecclesiastical issue, establishing courts for the purpose and making it somewhat less expensive, so that it became more accessible to those who were well-to-do but not wealthy. For the working class, even those who petitioned *in forma pauperis*, the cost was still prohibitively high – around £30. Prior to the 1857 Act, a petitioner had to succeed in obtaining from an ecclesiastical court a judgment of *mensa et thoro*, effectively a judicial separation where man and wife lived apart and the wife was supported but neither could marry again. Next he or she had to succeed with a case for damages against the spouse's lover in a court of Common Law. Only then could a Bill be presented first in the House of Lords and then in the House of Commons for a divorce *a vinculo matrimonii* that would permit both parties to remarry. This process could take three years and cost about £1,000, and in exceptional circumstances much more.

Despite improvements, divorce laws remained unfair, since a man had only to prove adultery, but a woman had to prove that her husband had been unfaithful and was also guilty of some other offense, such as physical brutality, incest, or rape. In George Meredith's *Diana of the Crossways* (1884), Diana Warwick lives apart from her husband after he falsely accuses her of having committed adultery with her friend Lord Dannisburgh – an episode based upon a real incident involving Lord Melbourne and Caroline Norton – but she cannot divorce him and lives in dread that he will compel her to resume her conjugal duties. A wife's property was vested absolutely in her husband at marriage unless both parties agreed to special arrangements. A wife separated from her husband had no right in common law to custody of or access to their children except with the husband's consent. In Trollope's *He Knew He Was Right* (1869), the husband hires a detective to provide information about his wife's misconduct, though the information is inconclusive. Adultery is not often a subject amenable to treatment in Victorian fiction, but Caroline Norton presented a tendentious case in her novel *Lost and Saved* (1863). Ironically, while novelists were discouraged from treating the themes of adultery and divorce, the front pages of the newspapers every day provided abundant information about the proceedings in the divorce courts.

The Married Women's Property Acts, the first of which was passed in 1870, slowly corrected the earlier law that conveyed all of a woman's property to her husband. Even before 1870, many women preserved some portion of their own wealth through marriage settlements. Another way in which women were discriminated against by law was the Contagious Diseases Acts of 1864, which could compel prostitutes suspected of being infected to undergo medical examination, but made no provision for a similar inspection of their customers, often members of the armed services living in barrack or port towns. Increasing public resistance, inspired by Josephine Butler's leadership, led to suspension of the Acts in 1883.

The Profession of Law

If the political world was almost all male, so were the professions, including the legal profession. Although many men who became lawyers attended Oxford or Cambridge first, these universities did not grant law degrees; to obtain such a degree, a man attended the Inns of Court or the Inns of Chancery (to become a barrister), or was apprenticed to a law firm (to become a solicitor). Solicitors sought clients and prepared legal cases; barristers were engaged by solicitors to present cases in court. Those who attended the Inns of Court and of Chancery "read for the law," which is to say they studied law, either on their own or with private tutorial help. The Inns of Court were associated with the common law, the Inns of Chancery with the Court of Chancery, which had been designed to temper common law, based on case-law precedent, with sympathy and fairness, and was therefore discretionary. It is for this reason that orphans and difficult property disputes came under its jurisdiction, as in *Bleak House*. It was also to this court that marriage settlements were assigned. Prospective barristers were obliged to take a certain number of dinners at the Inns of Court, which included Lincoln's Inn, the Inner Temple, the Middle Temple, and

Gray's Inn; these had the exclusive right to admit candidates to practice law as barristers.

Barristers were gentlemen with independent means or sources of financial support; solicitors were in a more doubtful social class. Mr. Vholes in *Bleak House* is a solicitor at the lower end of his social scale. Solicitors did not ordinarily argue cases in court, and barristers did not seek out clients – with exceptions such as the redoubtable Jaggers in Dickens's *Great Expectations* (1861). A barrister might aspire to be named King's (or Queen's) Counsel (KC or QC), which meant that he was a member of a select group of barristers appointed to be the crown's counsel. The highest order of barrister enjoyed the title of Serjeant. A barrister might also aspire to the Woolsack, a judgeship. In the church courts, which dealt chiefly with probate but also processed issues concerning marriage and divorce, the roles of advocate and proctor were roughly equivalent to those of barrister and solicitor. Their own separate inn of court was Doctors' Commons. David Copperfield is in training for practice there when his mentor, Mr. Spenlow, dies suddenly. The legal year consisted of four terms when the courts were in session: Hilary Term (January 11–31), Easter Term (April 15–May 8), Trinity Term (May 22–June 12), and Michaelmas Term (November 2–25). The period from July through October was known as the Long Vacation, when the courts did not meet.

The rules of the British courts had gradually been modified over the years before Victoria came to the throne. The rule excluding the accused from speaking in his own defense, for example, had been abandoned, but it was not until the end of the century that the accused in criminal proceedings was allowed to give evidence under oath. The normal case in a large town was argued before a panel of judges. Frequently, plaintiffs brought charges against individuals to a magistrate or justice of the peace, who was a significant man of the community but not necessarily trained in law, though he had the services of a clerk who was presumably conversant with legal details. Magistrates could adjudicate minor cases. Dickens gives examples of their incompetence in the municipal magistrate Fang in *Oliver Twist* and the provincial magistrate Nupkins in *Pickwick Papers*. In more serious cases, such as felonies, magistrates could bind culprits over for trial, which meant that they would either remain in jail until the quarter sessions or the assizes came round, or be let out on bail if their friends could provide assurances that they would appear for trial. In *Mary Barton*, Jem Wilson, charged with murder, must wait in jail to be tried at the Liverpool assizes because his is a serious felony and he has no friends with sufficient resources to offer bond. The assize courts were travelling groups of lawyers and judges who went "on circuit" twice a year, arguing and hearing cases in the county seats. The County Courts Act of 1846 replaced local and special courts with a new national system of county courts.

Law and Crime

In 1794 William Godwin published *Things as They Are, Or the Adventures of Caleb Williams*. In this tendentious novel, the law is represented as being the creature of hierarchical, largely aristocratic power, and legal institutions as the devices by which tyrannical authority preserves its power. Although attitudes changed markedly during the subsequent decades, distrust of law remained an abiding feature of the Victorian novel. The legal system was, to a large degree, disorganized and even incoherent. Legal principles were based upon precedent. During most of the century, criminal prosecution depended upon action initiated by the victim of a crime or by a magistrate, since there was no public prosecutor endowed with the power to bring charges against offenders. Victims of crimes were thus responsible for investigation, apprehension, and prosecution, using posters and newspapers to advertise rewards, and hiring semi-professional or professional detectives to assist them. In general the British resisted the establishment of a public prosecutor because they feared the erosion of personal freedom.

Trial scenes appear in quite a few Victorian novels. Felix Holt is tried for murder in *Felix Holt*, as are Phineas Finn in *Phineas Redux* and Jem Wilson in *Mary Barton*, the latter two unjustly. An interesting feature of several of these novels is the appearance of women in court. Women testify in *Felix Holt*, *Mary Barton*, Trollope's *Orley Farm* (1862) and *The Eustace Diamonds*, Reade's *Griffith Gaunt* (1866), and Mrs. Henry Wood's *Mrs. Halliburton's Troubles* (1862). Not all trial cases are for murder. *Orley Farm* and *The Eustace Diamonds*, for example, involve property. Collins wrote an entire novel entitled *The Law and the Lady* (1875), which includes the transcript of a fictitious trial. The novel consists of Valeria Macallan's efforts to clear her husband's name, which is tainted by the "Scotch Verdict" of Not Proven.

Enforcement of the laws became increasingly certain through the Victorian period. At the end of the Regency period there had been some 200 capital crimes on the books, but both professional practitioners and juries were reluctant to enforce the death penalty. Justice was seriously unequal during the first part of Victoria's reign: two individuals committing the same crime could receive wildly different punishments. Sir Robert Peel set about reforming the criminal code in 1827, and by 1837 the death penalty had been repealed for all crimes against property. One way of avoiding capital punishment was transportation to Australia. For many prisoners this was a dreadful prospect, but perhaps for others it was a matter of indifference or was even welcome.

In literature, the most famous case of transportation and illegal return is Magwitch in *Great Expectations*, but a harrowing account of what transportation could involve is Marcus Clarke's *For the Term of His Natural Life* (1875). The Penal Servitude Act of 1853 allowed transported convicts to be released on a revocable license called a ticket-of-leave. The Penal Servitude Act of 1864 permitted a policeman to arrest a ticket-of-leave man on suspicion and without a warrant and take him before a justice. Meanwhile, the Penal Servitude Act of 1857 abolished transportation as a punishment, substituting sentences of penal servitude instead. With a ticket-of-leave, a former convict could legally return to Britain, and many did. An instance in literature of a convict legally returned from transportation to Australia is Tom Taylor's very popular play *The Ticket-of-Leave Man* (1863).

It was not easy to catch criminals. In most areas in the early part of the century village watchmen or constables served this purpose as part of their general duty of keeping the peace. Sometimes provincial magistrates or influential gentlemen might employ small local police forces, and thief-takers might pursue criminals for advertised rewards. Much of the action against criminal offenders depended upon citizen efforts, often of the "hue and cry" variety. For example, in *Oliver Twist* Bill Sikes is hunted down by an outraged mob. In London there were also Bow Street Runners, House Patrol, and constables attached to the police offices at Bow Street, Wapping, and elsewhere. Peel reformed this system by establishing a professional Metropolitan Police force in 1829, eventually housed at the famous Scotland Yard. The County and Borough Police Act of 1856 finally made it obligatory for all local authorities to establish a police force, but many were slow to implement the law. The important court reforms effected by the Judicature Acts of 1873 and 1875 combined the common law, equity, and civil courts into a single High Court divided into three parts.

In 1842 the first professional detective force was created to facilitate a systematic method of detecting crime. Detectives generally worked under immediate police supervision, but they could be hired for private cases. Inspector Bucket in *Bleak House* works directly for the London police, whereas Sergeant Cuff serves at the bidding of Mrs. Verinder in Collins's *The Moonstone* (1868). Blathers and Duff in *Oliver Twist* are Bow Street Runners sent to investigate a crime outside London. Joseph Grimstone in Braddon's *Aurora Floyd* is sent to Yorkshire by Scotland Yard. Louis Trevelyan in Trollope's *He Knew He Was Right* (1869) hires a private detective to track his wife, whom he suspects of being unfaithful to him. Detectives were appearing frequently enough in fiction for James Fitzjames Stephen to attack such representations in an essay in *The Saturday Review* entitled "Detectives in Fiction and Real Life" (1864). But fictional detectives abounded, from Hawkshaw in *The Ticket-of-Leave Man* to that apogee of detecting power, Sir Arthur Conan Doyle's Sherlock Holmes.

Popular as detectives became in the latter half of the nineteenth century, they and the law were not always considered trustworthy or dependable. *The Woman in White* makes the point that law could never have achieved the justice that a few amateur detectives manage on their own. Similarly, in *The Moonstone*, Sergeant Cuff is sent away with the mystery of the Moonstone's disappearance unresolved. Only much later does Franklin Blake apply his and others' amateur methods to the solution of the mystery. A detective is invited to assist investigations in *Aurora Floyd*, but the main characters are already employing their own detective strategies. Robert Audley plays amateur detective in *Lady Audley's Secret* (1862) to uncover his putative aunt's criminal behavior.

The law itself often came in for strong criticism. In *Mary Barton* it is interpreted by the working-class characters as a tool of the rich. Dickens complained of the incompetence of Chancery in *Bleak House*. Young lawyers like Eugene Wrayburn and Mortimer Lightwood in *Our Mutual Friend* complain about not being able to build adequate careers in the law. Paul Clifford, as an accused criminal in Bulwer-Lytton's novel of that name, denounces the very judge who sentences him, a man who turns out to be responsible for Clifford's criminal career and his father to boot. And in William Johnson Neale's *Paul Periwinkle; or, The Pressgang* (1841), an innocent man is convicted and almost hanged for a murder on circumstantial evidence, but is rescued by a band of ruffians. The lawyers working on his behalf are so disgusted with British law and the legal profession that they decide to emigrate to the West Indies.

If the pursuit of criminals was not always professional, conditions were not good for the criminals when they were caught. Most places of incarceration, such as the watch house or house of correction, were makeshift, dirty, and unhealthy. Even a major London prison such as Newgate was unclean and crowded and allowed for very little time or room for exercise. Since a fair amount of Victorian literature is set in pre-Victorian years, there are references to outmoded forms of punishment, such as hanging criminals from gibbets in chains, drawing and quartering, and imprisoning in the hulks – that is, naval ships no longer in service but employed as prisons. The most famous reference to the hulks is in Dickens's *Great Expectations*, at the opening of which the convict Magwitch escapes from such a vessel but is recaptured.

During the Victorian period, new prisons were constructed on healthier principles. Newgate was rebuilt in 1795 and reconstructed between 1858 and 1861. Millbank opened in 1816 and Brixton in 1820. Tothill Fields was rebuilt in 1835 and the new prisons of Pentonville and Clerkenwell were completed in 1842 and 1849, followed by Wandsworth in 1851 and Holloway in 1852. Dartmoor, originally designed for prisoners of war, became a convict prison in 1850. In *Prisons and Prisoners* (1845), Joseph Adshead deplored the enormities of one kind or another that he discovered at many prisons, but approved the then new model prison at Pentonville. New systems of prison discipline were attempted as well, including the separate system, solitary confinement, and the silent system. Dickens was deeply interested in prison reform and visited prisons in Britain and the United States. He disapproved of some of the more lenient innovations and satirized them in the model prison where Uriah Heep and Littimer are confined at the end of *David Copperfield*. Charles Reade made the subject a central theme for his novel *It Is Never Too Late to Mend* (1856).

A whole subgenre of crime fiction developed early in the century, initiated by Bulwer-Lytton's success with *Paul Clifford* and *Eugene Aram*. This kind of fiction was called the "Newgate novel" after Newgate prison and *The Newgate Calendar*, which recorded the lives of notable criminals. William Harrison Ainsworth followed Bulwer-Lytton with two novels that incorporated the lives of eighteenth-century criminals. *Rookwood* (1834) includes some adventures of the notorious highwayman Dick Turpin, and the titular character of *Jack Sheppard* was famous for his escapes from prison. Dickens's *Oliver Twist* could easily be included in this subgenre.

Although the murder rate in nineteenth-century Britain was not high, there were always enough prominent cases in the news to keep the public entertained. The John Thurtell case, which involved the brutal murder of an associate, excited great attention in 1824. The Red Barn murder of 1833, in which John Corder murdered Maria Marten, the woman he loved, generated a great deal of public excitement and was quickly dramatized on the stage. One of the most gruesome cases was Daniel Good's murder and dismemberment of his lover. Maria Manning and her husband were found guilty in 1849 of shooting a man for his money and were hanged. Poisonings were always of special interest and had a significant effect on fiction. Three famous cases involved doctors, the most notorious being that of William Palmer in 1856, followed by those of Thomas Smethurst (1859) and Edward Pritchard (1865). The character Philip Sheldon in Mary Elizabeth Braddon's *Birds of Prey* (1867) could have been based on any or all of these practitioners.

Stage melodramas frequently employed murder as an element in their plots, often based on real crimes. But the novel also fitted murder into its narratives, from Bill Sikes's brutal bludgeoning of Nancy in *Oliver Twist* to Hortense's vindictive shooting of Tulkinghorn in *Bleak House* to Jonas Chuzzlewit's desperate murder of Montague Tigg in *Martin Chuzzlewit* to the mutual murder of Rogue Riderhood and Bradley Headstone in *Our Mutual Friend*. And these are just a few examples from Dickens. The gifted and otherwise admirable scholar Eugene Aram, in Bulwer-Lytton's novel of that name, lives a life haunted by the memory of a theft and murder he committed in the past. Tess Clare in Hardy's *Tess of the d'Urbervilles* (1891) is hanged for her murder of Alec d'Urberville. Other murders in novels were mentioned earlier in this chapter. Some murders are planned and not carried to fulfillment, as in Le Fanu's *Uncle Silas* and Mary Elizabeth Braddon's *Lady Audley's Secret*, where a bigamous wife incorrectly believes that she has murdered her first husband and unsuccessfully tries to murder the man who is tracing her secret, and in Wilkie Collins's novel *Armadale* (1866), where Lydia Gwilt attempts to suffocate Allan Armadale while he sleeps. Some homicides are inadvertent, but chargeable nonetheless, as with Felix Holt's killing of a constable during a riot in Eliot's *Felix Holt*.

Suicide and attempted suicide were classified as homicide, but were treated leniently in the legal system. In the early part of the century religious objections to suicide prevailed. Proven suicides could not be buried in sacred ground, though the old rule of burying a suicide at a public crossroad was rarely observed. After 1823 burial had to take place in a regular burial ground, but no religious ceremonies could be obtained for a *felo de se* until the Burial Act of 1880. Until 1882, the body of a *felo de se* was by law buried privately by the police between the hours of nine and twelve at night. Understandably, juries were reluctant to bring a verdict of *felo de se* since it would prevent Christian burial, allow forfeiture of the deceased's property to the crown, and nullify life insurance. A familiar trope in literature and the arts associates fallen women and prostitutes with suicide, especially by drowning. George Cruikshank's famous etching from the series entitled *The Drunkard's Daughter* shows a woman plummeting downward from a bridge, Thomas Hood's "The Bridge of Sighs" takes up the theme, and there is a notable scene in *David Copperfield* when David and Mr. Peggotty watch as the fallen Martha contemplates throwing herself into the Thames. But suicide could result from many motives and affected the respectable and disreputable alike. Lydia Gwilt commits suicide out of frustrated love in *Armadale*. Ralph Nickleby in *Nicholas Nickleby* (1839) commits suicide in a moment of remorse, and Jonas Chuzzlewit in *Martin Chuzzlewit* as a way to avoid public execution. Bankrupts occasionally exploited this route of escape from their troubles. The ruined Merdle in *Little Dorrit* takes this exit.

Another category of murder that was also treated with surprising sympathy was infanticide. On the one hand, ignorance and poverty were credible defenses against manslaughter or murder charges; on the other hand, forensic science was not adequately developed to conclude with any certainty in a large number of cases what the true cause of a child's death might be. An example was the "privy defense," in which the new mother claimed that she had discharged a fetus into the privy without being aware of what was happening until it was too late. The Offences Against the Person Act of 1803 declared infanticide a form of murder, but the mother was innocent until proven guilty. There were so many ways in which youngsters, especially in their first few months, could come to harm apart from infanticide that the population in general, and also lawyers, judges, and doctors, felt more sympathy than suspicion for mothers whose children died. There are few references to actual infanticide in Victorian literature. A notable exception is Eliot's *Adam Bede* (1859), where Hetty Sorrel leaves her child exposed to the elements, and is arrested, tried, and found guilty, though her execution is commuted to transportation. In Frances Trollope's *Jessie Phillips*, infanticide constitutes an important feature of the plot. The most notorious instance of infanticide in literature is Little Father Time's murder of his siblings and himself – "Done because we are too menny" – in Thomas Hardy's *Jude the Obscure* (1895). The baby farm in *Oliver Twist* and Dotheboys Hall in *Nicholas Nickleby* (1839) were reflections of real practices, the consequences of which were often fatal for the children involved, not because children were murdered outright, but because they were so badly treated. Similarly, abortion was scarcely mentioned in literature, though it is implied as a practice of midwives in Emma Caroline Wood's *Sorrow on the Sea* (1868) and as a service of the unsavory Doctor Downright in Collins' *Armadale*.

Dueling was illegal and nearly extinct in Britain by the time Victoria ascended the throne, but it remained a lively subject in fiction nonetheless. It was often treated comically, as in *The Pickwick Papers* more than once and in Thackeray's *Barry Lyndon* (1844), and it was a standard item in the military fiction of the time, most notably the early novels of Charles Lever. Harry Oaklands almost dies as the result of a duel in the generally lighthearted *Frank Fairleigh* (1850) by Frank E. Smedley. Duels figure prominently in many more serious novels of the time. A whole chapter is devoted to a duel in Robert Bell's *Ladder of Gold* (1850), and a duel is almost lovingly recorded in G. A. Lawrence's highly popular *Guy Livingstone* (1857). George Meredith has his titular hero seriously wounded in a duel in *The Ordeal of Richard Feverel* (1859).

Crimes against property, especially theft, occur frequently in Victorian fiction. Trollope founded the plot of *The Last Chronicle of Barset* (1867) on a supposed theft: the Reverend Josiah Crawley is suspected of stealing a check for £20 and is so absent-minded that he cannot explain how he came into possession of it. Ultimately he is exonerated, but the thought of a man of God being a thief gave the narrative a good deal of bite. More intriguing were stories where elegance and mystery were associated with theft. An outstanding example is *The Moonstone*, where the loss of a diamond forms the core of the entire novel. Disappearing diamonds are important in Trollope's *The Eustace Diamonds* (1872) as well. Mary Cholmondeley's *The Danvers Jewels* (1887) owes a good deal to *The Moonstone*, and includes a jewel theft and consequent mystery in an English country house.

One strange feature of the law involved lunacy. It was possible to have a person confined for lunacy on the evidence of a single individual – a member of the family or other concerned person with some degree of authority – supported by medical testimony. The subject of unjust confinement for lunacy figures prominently in the literature of the time. Henry Cockton shaped much of *The Life and Adventures of Valentine Vox, the Ventriloquist* (1840) around this subject, and he prefaced his novel with an attack on the system of private lunatic asylums. Thanks to the conniving of his brother, nephew, and bribed medical men, Grimwood Goodman is confined in a particularly brutal asylum. His nephew and brother hope to acquire his property. Goodman escapes, only to die soon after; his evil brother dies first by his own hand. Near the end of Captain Frederick Marryat's *Peter Simple* (1834), Peter is falsely confined in Bedlam as insane, though he is merely delirious from illness, as his grandfather, who has him committed, knows. Marryat remarks that it doesn't take much to establish a case of lunacy, but takes a great deal to reverse that decision. Peter is rescued when an acquaintance happens to visit Bedlam and recognizes him. False incarcerations for lunacy also occur in *The Woman in White*, Sheridan Le Fanu's *The Rose and the Key* (1871), and Charles Reade's *Hard Cash* (1863) and *A Terrible Temptation* (1870–1), the latter in particular denouncing abuses of lunacy certification, the former illustrating how difficult it was to extricate oneself from an asylum once committed.

A form of law that turns up frequently in the subgenres of naval and army novels is military law. Duels, though outlawed, are winked at by authorities in novels of this kind. But certain offenses, such as striking a superior officer, desertion, and others, are severely punished. Naval novelists such as Captain Frederick Marryat and army novelists such as Charles Lever objected especially to the alacrity with which senior officers and courts martial ordered flogging in particular.

There are many other forms of law that could be discussed here, including the whole range of regulatory law and administrative law, but, with the notorious exception of the Circumlocution Office in *Little Dorrit*, they do not often find their way into fiction. Similarly, though certain laws or the lack of them affected novelists and other writers, novelists infrequently incorporated them in their fictions. Dickens, for example, along with other authors, argued long and hard, but unsuccessfully during his lifetime, for an international copyright law, but he does not make the struggle a significant part of any of his novels. Similarly, the Obscene Publications Act (1857) made the treatment of certain subjects, such as adultery, more difficult for British novelists, but there is rarely any substantial reference to this or other censoring laws like it in their novels.

REFERENCES

Adshead, Joseph (1845), *Prisons and Prisoners* (London: Longman, Brown, Green & Longman).
Altick, Richard (1991), *The Presence of the Present: Topics of the Day in the Victorian Novel* (Columbus: Ohio State University Press).

Anderson, Olive (1987), *Suicide in Victorian and Edwardian England* (Oxford: Clarendon).

Barty-King, Hugh (1991), *The Worst Poverty: A History of Debt and Debtors*, with foreword by Sir Gordon Borrie QC (Wolfeboro Falls, NH: Alan Sutton).

Burn, W. L. (1964), *The Age of Equipoise: A Study of the Mid-Victorian Generation* (New York: Norton).

Emsley, Clive (1987), *Crime and Society in England, 1750–1900* (London: Longman).

Forsythe, William James (1987), *The Reform of Prisoners 1830–1900* (London: Croom Helm).

Fraser, Derek, ed. (1976), *The New Poor Law in the Nineteenth Century* (New York: St. Martin's).

Habakkuk, John (1994), *Marriage, Debt, and the Estates System: English Landownership: 1650–1950* (Oxford: Clarendon).

Horstman, Allen (1985), *Victorian Divorce* (London: Croom Helm).

Jay, Douglas and Snyder, Francis, eds. (1989), *Policing and Prosecution in Britain 1750–1850* (Oxford: Clarendon). (First publ. 1986.)

Radzinowicz, Leon (1948–68), *A History of English Criminal Law*, 4 vols. (New York: Macmillan).

Radzinowicz, Leon and Hood, Roger (1990), *The Emergence of Penal Policy in Victorian and Edwardian England* (Oxford: Clarendon).

Reed, John R. (1975), *Victorian Conventions* (Athens, Ohio: Ohio University Press).

Rose, Lionel (1986), *The Massacre of the Innocents: Infanticide in Britain 1800–1939* (London: Routledge & Kegan Paul).

Rose, Michael E. (1986), *The Relief of Poverty, 1834–1914* (London: Macmillan).

Rudé, George (1985), *Criminal and Victim: Crime and Society in Early Nineteenth-Century England* (Oxford: Clarendon Press).

Trodd, Anthea (1989), *Domestic Crime in the Victorian Novel* (London: Macmillan).

Wiener, Martin J. (1989), *Reconstructing the Criminal: Culture, Law, and Policy in England, 1830–1914* (Cambridge: Cambridge University Press).

FURTHER READING

Holcombe, Lee (1983), *Wives and Property: Reform of the Married Women's Property Law in Nineteenth-Century England* (Toronto: University of Toronto Press).

Leckie, Barbara (1999), *Culture and Adultery: The Novel, the Newspaper, and the Law 1857–1914* (Philadelphia: University of Pennsylvania Press).

Ousby, Ian (1976), *Bloodhounds of Heaven: The Detective in English Fiction from Godwin to Doyle* (Cambridge. Mass.: Harvard University Press).

Thesing, William B., ed. (1990), *Executions and the British Experience from the 17th to the 20th Century: A Collection of Essays* (Jefferson, NC: McFarland).

Thompson, F. M. L. (1988), *The Rise of Respectable Society: A Social History of Victorian Britain 1830–1900* (Cambridge, Mass.: Harvard University Press).

Thoms, Peter (1998), *Detection and its Designs: Narrative and Power in Nineteenth-Century Detective Fiction* (Athens: Ohio University Press).

10

Gender Politics and Women's Rights

Hilary M. Schor

Most readers of Victorian literature come to their understanding of nineteenth-century feminism and gender relations through one of its most powerful statements: the direct, challenging voice of Charlotte Brontë's heroine, Jane Eyre, when she stands upon the leads of Thornfield Hall and addresses her readers. "Anyone may blame me who likes," she admonishes us, "if then I longed for a wider sphere of vision . . ." And, as Jane Eyre herself tells us, she is not the only woman with such desire: "Many are doomed to a stiller lot than mine . . ."

Jane Eyre, and, in a much larger way, Charlotte Brontë, is doing more than speaking up for herself: she is addressing and *bringing into being* a class of speaking subjects: women. For it is as part of a class that she speaks of her feelings:

> Women are supposed to be very calm generally, but women feel as men feel; they need exercise for the faculties and a field for their efforts as much as their brothers do; they suffer from too rigid a restraint, too absolute a stagnation, precisely as men would suffer; and it is narrow-minded in their more privileged fellow-creatures to say that they ought to confine themselves to making puddings and knitting stockings, to playing on the piano and embroidering bags. It is thoughtless to condemn them, or laugh at them, if they seek to do more or learn more than custom has pronounced necessary for their sex. (Brontë 1987: 96)

To the first-time reader of Victorian fiction, this voice comes as somewhat of a surprise, given the powerful ideology surrounding women's roles in the middle of the nineteenth century. Women were expected to center their lives on home and family; they were expected to conduct themselves, indeed drape themselves, in modesty and propriety; they were expected to find the commands of duty and the delights of service sufficient, in fact ennobling, boundaries for their lives. Jane has been remarkable for her boldness in crossing borders throughout the novel, beginning the book with a negative statement ("there was no possibility of taking a walk that day . . .") and following it up directly with an assertion of what our mothers would always tell us was just "our opinion": "I never liked long walks. Dreadful to *me* was the coming home in twilight . . ." Far from echoing the commands of others, Jane Eyre is a heroine who does not fear speaking her own mind.

But the novel asks more from us than that we just enjoy the energetic resistance of its heroine: it asks that we think explicitly about the fate of an intelligent woman in the middle of Victorian England, trying to make sense of her own destiny; it asks that we understand the voice of a feminist narrator in the context of the larger discussion of women, gender roles, and the organized feminist movements of the nineteenth century. Such a discussion will lead us to consider not only the historical status and changing roles of women in the nineteenth century, but the centrality of women's social conditions to the plots, forms, and structures of the Victorian novel. I will begin by discussing *Jane Eyre* and the paradigms it created for understanding Victorian women and the choices they faced, then move on to the wider historical debates around Victorian women and to the many different kinds of realist novels which followed. No single question mattered more to the Victorian novel than what the nineteenth century considered "The Woman Question," and no other interrogation had more effect on the *forms* of the novel we still read today than the question Freud was to raise at the century's end, "What do women want?"

*

From its first publication, *Jane Eyre* has been taken seriously as both a literary and a social document, and it has been central to modern and postmodern rethinkings of Victorian gender questions, figuring importantly in the works of readers from Virginia Woolf to Adrienne Rich, Sandra Gilbert and Susan Gubar. I want to begin here with a fairly simple question: What is Jane Eyre's story, and in what ways does it reflect what we know of women's social, political, and economic situations in the middle of the nineteenth century? By the time we finish the novel, we can retell the heroine's story in historical terms. Jane Eyre is an orphan; the daughter of an upper-middle-class woman and her clergyman husband, she was born in an industrial city and, at her parents' death in a fever epidemic, was brought to the home of her far-wealthier uncle, John Reed, to be raised with her cousins John, Eliza, and Georgianna Reed. On his deathbed, John Reed asked his wife to promise to raise the orphan with their own children, and she has obeyed the letter but not the spirit of this agreement. She treats Jane as an outsider and a dependant, and allows the children to torment her as they please, leaving Jane vulnerable to the contempt even of the servants, for, as they and the children express it, Jane does not even work for her keep. After a fiery incident in which the sensitive girl attacks her cousin John and is locked in the Red Room with (she believes) the ghost of her uncle, she is offered a chance to go to school. Realizing (with the clever logic of a terrified child) that if her cousin John does not like school, she is likely to enjoy it very much herself, she chooses to begin life again at the Lowood Institution, where she survives a spartan, Christian education designed to make dependent children into independent women. In time, she becomes a teacher at the school, but, restless for at least a "new servitude," she advertises for a position as a governess, and walks off into the romantic plot which most of us remember as the "real" *Jane Eyre*.

The hardiness that Jane's family and education instill in her is at the center of her most explicitly feminist statement, the one she makes to her employer, Mr. Rochester, the one which provokes him to propose to her. When he has threatened to marry another, and to send her off as governess to the daughters of Mrs. Dionysius O'Gall at Bitternutt Lodge in Ireland, she cries out, "I am not talking to you now through the medium of custom, conventionalities, nor even of mortal flesh – it is my spirit that addresses your spirit, just as if both had passed through the grave, and we stood at God's feet, equal, – as we are!" She exclaims, passionately, "Do you think, because I am poor, obscure, plain, and little, I am soulless and heartless? If God had gifted me with some beauty and much wealth, I should have made it as hard for you to leave me, as it is now for me to leave you" (Brontë 1987: 222). This outburst not only wins her employer's respect, it incites him to a declaration of love and a marriage proposal – a trajectory of desire somewhat abruptly foreclosed when it is revealed that he is already married, to a madwoman locked upstairs; Jane's subsequent flight, and her struggles to find a new home, end in her discovery of unexpected cousins, her inheritance from a long-lost and recently deceased uncle, and her reunion with her beloved master, now free, blind, and crippled, but as loving as she (or any reader) could desire. Their subsequent marriage is a model of companionship and equality: "we talk, I believe, all day long; to talk to each other is but a more animated and an audible thinking." Jane's trials, and her quest for independence and a strong voice, have merged absolutely in Brontë's narration with her romantic quest, and the successful marriage to Mr. Rochester (in addition to restoring his eyesight and bringing them a son) marks the fulfillment of that demand for equality her first speeches made on us.

The romance plot is central to the novel's themes and its continuing popularity, but what must strike us first in reading the novel is Brontë's unerring social satire. Among her targets in the novel are spoiled children, spoiled boys (a special category), beautiful and pampered heiresses, and organized religion, best represented by a rigid cleric, Mr. Brocklehurst, who first appears as a phallic column in the middle of the Reed breakfast-room. As Jane moves through the repressive and criminally under-nourishing school for orphans, not only the religious structures that support it but the gender roles it supports come under attack; once she arrives at Thornfield Hall, she (or the novelist) excoriates the treatment of younger sons, the idiocies which pass for social conversation, the oppression of governesses, and the ridiculous idealization of children. But at the core of Brontë's critique of her society is a set of issues which we would identify now, and which were beginning to be identified in the years around the writing of *Jane Eyre*, as explicitly, and quite progressively, feminist: the education of women and the refusal to train them to take a serious role in society; the legal and property restrictions that kept women from assuming the independence that would make them full citizens; and a series of legal and imaginative restraints on women's lives, chief among them, paradoxically, the structure of marriage and the laws which supported it, which made women vulnerable to violence, imprisonment, and cruelty. For all its passionate romanticism, and its fairy-tale ending, *Jane Eyre* renders quite coolly the realities of Victorian women's lives, and the constraints women faced everywhere they turned in their society.

*

Charlotte Brontë was, of course, not alone in identifying these central limitations on women's lives: when Jane claims "many are condemned to a stiller lot than mine," that women "feel as men feel," that "they need exercise for the faculties and a field for their efforts as much as their brothers do," she is anticipating more explicit claims, and a series of feminist activities, carried forward in the 1850s and after. The arenas Jane identifies (education, law, property, religion, service, family) were all central to women's expanding roles in Victorian England. With the opening of Queen's College in 1848 and Bedford College in 1849, higher education became available to women, thereby preparing an important next generation of feminist theorists and activists. But such activity was already underway. In 1855, the remarkable Barbara Leigh Smith organized the first feminist committee, writing the pamphlet *A Brief Summary in plain Language of the most important Laws Concerning Women* and then submitting it through a friend to the Law Amendment Society, which drafted a resolution and a petition supporting the reform of the laws governing married women's property, laws which kept married women from owning property, acting as independent economic agents, protecting their wages, or writing wills without their husband's permission – permission which, astonishingly, the husband could revoke (invalidating the will) after the wife's death. The Bill was brought before Parliament in 1857, the year that first saw proposals for changes in the divorce and infant custody laws, laws which severely restricted women's access to any form of divorce and gave them few or no rights to their children after divorce. Like the Married Women's Property Bill, the Marriage and Divorce Bill was seen to present an absolute challenge to the sanctity, privacy, and order provided by marital and family relations – but to a modern reader of *Jane Eyre*, a critique of the laws which governed marriage, divorce, and women's separate property seems inevitable.

The Marriage and Divorce Act was passed in 1857. Reform of the married women's property laws had to wait several more decades – but the impulse which allowed Parliament even to consider these profound changes in domestic relations (in particular the laws which considered wives, under the principles of coverture, to be legally the possession of their husbands, without separate legal identity) exhibited itself throughout the 1850s, as women undertook a variety of activities which removed them from the sanctity of the domestic habitat, bringing them into new forms of employment and more radical questioning of the "conventionalities" against which Jane Eyre rails with such fictional authority. A variety of female philanthropic organizations sprang up which, though they had no explicit feminist ideas, nonetheless brought women into the public realm with a vengeance. And the group of women around Barbara Leigh Smith went even further, running a printing press, publishing *The English Woman's Journal*, and offering a series of widely attended and circulated public lectures on women, most famously Anna Jameson's lectures on "Sisters of Charity" and "Community of Labor," which proposed for women an active "sisterhood" which would offer them the "field" for their efforts that Brontë imagined. The center Smith established at Langham Place offers a picture of remarkable enthusiasm and imagination. Ray Strachey's *The Cause* gives a marvelous account of the radical questioning of social roles which went on in those years:

> Why should not women do law engrossing? An office was opened at once and filled with women workers. Why should not women be hairdressers, hotel managers, wood engravers, dispensers, house decorators, watchmakers, telegraphists? Out! Out! Let us see if we can make them do it! . . . And then there were the swimming baths in Marylebone, why were they not open to women? Did the manager say that women did not want to use them? Nonsense, of course they did. If thirty women came they would be opened? Very well, thirty women should come; and every Wednesday afternoon the young ladies trooped away from the office to help to stir the face of the waters. Nothing must be let slip, be it small or great, in the campaign they had begun to wage. (Strachey 1978: 96)

Strachey's account offers us a powerful feeling of transformation: the women are not only setting out to "stir the face of the waters," but to wage a campaign; these women are at war, with their culture and its expectations. The passage moves between its wonderful sense of precise detail (thirty women must troop away every Wednesday afternoon or the world will not change) and its broader charge, that the world itself must change to meet the demands of these women. The list-making technique so crucial to the novel, the very ordinariness that makes up everyday life ("hairdressers, hotel managers, wood engravers, dispensers, house decorators, watchmakers, telegraphists") becomes revolutionary when it becomes the provenance of women.

Fiction, of course, begins not with the ordinary but the anomalous; something which is entirely ordinary is not the business of the novel. By the same token, feminism as well begins with women who step outside of the ordinary; women who charge the world *not* to go on as it does. How, then, are novels to respond to the charge of feminism; the charge to place the anomalous heroine at their center? How can we connect the novel's attention to detail and reality to this larger question of how women are upending the order of the world? To address this question, we need to return to *Jane Eyre*, and to the many novels which came after it and responded powerfully to its challenges.

*

Jane Eyre has a far more complicated relationship to reality than most readers have noticed. True, Jane refers frequently to unvarnished physical reality to lend further credibility to her story. As she reminds us, she is plain; Mr. Rochester is not handsome; Grace Poole carries a pot of porter; Adele is an unremarkable child. But Jane also moves frequently to some plane of reality far beyond the laws of probability. Bertha Mason makes her first appearance looking like the "foul German spectre – the Vampyre," and her last ("as cunning as a witch") on the battlements of the great house; Jane and Rochester both await the fairies or the Gytrash (a mythical beast) by the side of the road; at the novel's climax, they communicate across England by some telepathic call, when Jane hears "wildly, eerily, urgently . . . the voice of a human being – a known, a loved, well-remembered voice – that of Edward Fairfax Rochester," and Rochester, in answer to his cry, hears "a voice – I cannot tell whence the voice came, but I know whose voice it was – repl[ying] 'I am coming: wait for me.'" When Jane returns to Rochester, the blind man kisses and caresses her, but only when she announces that she has a legacy from her dead uncle does he proclaim, "Ah, this is practical – this is real!" *Jane Eyre* makes a similar double claim on us, at once claiming the "practical" as "real" (much as we do, when we notice the congruences between its satire, polemic, and passion and the ongoing debates of Victorian feminists) and demanding that we take as real its visionary, Gothic, fairytale dark side. In this way, Jane's story partakes less of some absolute reality principle, and far more of fiction's other impulse, the impulse of "romance" in its many complicated senses: that of a wandering, episodic narration filled with uncanny occurrences, of the heroine's own romantic quest for fulfillment, and finally of the desire for another world elsewhere, the utopian impulses of Shakespeare's romances, which find their fulfillment in the green world of Ferndean Dell. There, the material demands (and realistic constraints) on Jane's story are displaced, making room for the Edenic landscape she creates with her husband; Jane Eyre, as character and as novel, flees not only temptation, but realism as well.

The question, then, is: What are we to do with the oddity of Charlotte Brontë's portrait of a midcentury woman of independence, one whose quest for love and desire for autonomy put her in conflict with most of the conventional thinking of her age, but whose outspoken statements of spirit and perversity (a word that other characters love to use about Jane) instead helped shape a very different midcentury discourse of feminism? Contemporary feminists are more likely to be drawn to the Jane who demands her rights and argues for her desires, but the novel does not remain exclusively in the realm of reason and argument. If we ask which is the real *Jane Eyre*, are we also asking what are the limitations of using any of the powerful Victorian women's novels as elements in a discussion of the nineteenth century's debates over gender? Or can we use precisely these seemingly anomalous literary techniques, the fraying of the realist fabric of *Jane Eyre* and the deliberate perversity of its heroine, as a way of rereading the Victorian novel and debates over the woman question?

I can begin to answer this question by taking a novel written only a few years after *Jane Eyre*, one in some ways very different from it in subject, tone and conclusion, but written by the contemporary woman novelist most caught up in the legend of Charlotte Brontë – and most pivotal in its creation. Elizabeth Gaskell, who was one of Brontë's closest friends and literary supporters (and eventually her posthumous biographer) formed her own literary reputation not by challenging expectations of gendered behavior (no one ever told one of her heroines that her behavior was "unfeminine" or "unnatural") but rather by taking her readers beyond other versions of middle-class conventionality: by lifting the veil on industrial poverty in the urban north of England, and by raising her voice in defense of those otherwise disenfranchised by their culture – workers, children, women. But these questions do not take us outside the framework of this chapter, for in all of her fiction, but particularly in her second industrial novel, *North and South* (1854–5), Gaskell responds directly to the questions *Jane Eyre* raised: What is a woman's proper sphere of duty? How can a woman of passion find her equal in a society which disapproves of strong women and their (romantic) ardor? Can a woman find her own way in patriarchal culture without inheritance, property, and the legal rights denied married women in particular? And how is a woman to balance romantic love with intellectual and spiritual independence?

The novel begins in a whirl of change: the heroine, Margaret Hale, lives with wealthy relatives in fashionable London, and as the book opens her elegant cousin's wedding is about to take place. Margaret, who is framed from the beginning as a heroine with a difference, her mouth "no rosebud with which to say 'yes, sir,' and 'no, sir,'" (Gaskell 1970: 48) resists the forms and conventions of such wealth and such femininity, preferring instead her family's simpler life in the small English village of Helstone, to which she will return after the wedding. But rather than being free to immerse herself in country, family, and good daughterhood, Margaret finds herself swept off by familial and historical change: when her family moves to Milton-Northern, a fictional city modeled after the industrial center Manchester, Margaret is caught up not only in the lives of the manufacturers and newly enriched mill-owners of "Milton," but in the daily toil and troubles of the workers who crowd the streets around her. She is drawn first to the groups of women, with their bright, quick faces and free banter; and then to the Higgins family, the father an industrial weaver and the daughter a worker in the factory, dying from inhaling the cotton fluff always flying in the air of the mill. Through her friendship with them, Margaret comes to understand the differences between "north and south," as well as the difficulties of communication between the mill-owners she meets in over-elaborate drawing rooms and the workers she meets in dark, drafty apartments.

The most revolutionary element of *North and South*, and the way in which it responds to the feminist demands for a "stirring" of the waters, is that these dramatic class differences and rapid historical changes become a central part of the romance plot, for Margaret's growing understanding of the transformations around her brings her into conflict with the powerful mill-owner whom her father tutors in the classics, and who comes to their home and comments on her accounts of the daily life of Milton. As Margaret comes to understand the history of John Thornton, and to follow his fortunes through the economic depression and subsequent workers' strike, she increasingly becomes a translator between him and the workers he can no longer understand – she comes to understand how, in the words of Bessy Higgins, "between the men and the masters," nothing will change for the better. Margaret herself becomes a bridge between the two classes who have lost the ability to listen to each other. But the social differences also provide a turning point in the romantic relationship between Margaret Hale and John Thornton, which occurs when Margaret races out in front of a crowd of furious striking workers to protect Thornton from their rage. Struck by a blow from a thrown shoe, she collapses in his arms, overcome by both pain and shame; as he carries her fallen body into the house he, like everyone who witnesses the scene, assumes she has been driven forward not by her desire to protect a weaponless man (as she has claimed) but by her love for him. While she denies this fiercely, and asserts her sense of justice and fairness as she rejects his proposal of marriage, the powerful suggestion of the novel is that it is the erotic bond between them that has driven her into the public realm – and, for a shocking moment, a woman's political action and her sexual desire force her far beyond her conventional sphere of activity. The rest of the novel will follow the lovers' growing understanding through a series of fairly conventional romantic misunderstandings, until the plot is resolved by the death of Margaret's parents and guardian, and her inheritance of significant amounts of property in Milton, which she proposes to rent to the now-impoverished John Thornton. Since an offer of low rents seems tantamount to a marriage proposal in the world of industrial England, he greets her offer by taking her in his arms and claiming her "presumptuously." All discussion of property and profits is foreclosed, we might claim, in the higher merger of north and south, master and worker, man and woman.

If the interweaving of the heroine's romance with social change is one important element of the novel, a different element, one which seems to respond even more directly to the debates of Victorian feminism, comes before the resolution of the marriage plot; and it is this development which makes Margaret Hale one of the most interestingly reflective heroines in Victorian fiction, one who takes very seriously the question of what she is to do with her life. In the long and painful chapters when she has lost her entire family and believes she has lost the chance to marry the one man who would have suited her, she "trie[s] to settle that most difficult problem for women, how much was to be utterly merged in obedience to authority, and how much might be set apart for freedom in working." Margaret, after this period of reflection, "fulfilled one of her sea-side resolves, and took her life into her own hands," for she has "learnt, in those solemn hours of thought, that she herself must one day answer for her own life, and what she had done with it" (p. 508). Gaskell allows her heroine not only a physical space for contemplation, but a moral space for claiming her own sphere of activity. Margaret takes full advantage of that freedom, moving among the poor people in London, where she has come to live, and making decisions about her own life, threatening, as she teases her aunt, to become "a strong-minded woman," an early Victorian euphemism for an active feminist. Like Jane Eyre, when she explains to Rochester that she has inherited money and intends to build her own house next to his and make her own way in the world, Margaret claims not only property but a fuller kind of personhood; unlike Jane, up until the last moments of the novel, she claims that personhood apart from any relationship (even that of a neighbor) to a man she loves, and when she goes back to him, it is in the role not of suppliant but of landlord, an interesting reversal of gender and class roles.

North and South, then, at once echoes and comments on the most interesting moves Jane Eyre made in its examination of the issues central to mid-Victorian feminism, particularly its questioning of what any individual heroine's life can encompass and what her proper (feminine or moral) role is to be; however, it also expands those issues in ways Brontë could not have foreseen. Margaret's curiosity about the world draws her in many ways further than Jane in exploration, and brings the novel more fully into a complicated social world; indeed, much of what draws Margaret to Thornton is that, through him, she can achieve access to a wider world in which to act and learn, and her movement beyond her class expands her feminism to include women workers and their families. It is this movement, the relationship between the curious heroine's exploration of a new world and her society's response to her transformative quest, which will mark the Victorian woman's novel for the remainder of the century.

*

It is remarkable how many of the great Victorian novels are obsessed with what now seem to us clearly feminist issues – Trollope in Can You Forgive Her?, with its question of women's property; Dickens in Little Dorrit, and the discussion of the married women's separate property debate; Collins's critique of the bastardy laws in No Name; and the host of fiction later in the century focusing on the figure of "the new woman," a sexually adventurous if not always a feminist freethinker. Here I will emphasize as a self-reflexive genre the novel of the intelligent woman making difficult choices – focusing on Margaret Oliphant's Miss Marjoribanks, George Eliot's Middlemarch, and George Gissing's The Odd Women, and tracing a trajectory from the 1850s to the turn of the century. These novels raise not only the problem of what the heroine is to do, but what we are to do with the heroine. Jane Austen notoriously remarked that in Emma Woodhouse she had created a heroine whom nobody but herself would like; and yet, surprisingly, this disclaimer may have proved more of a stimulant than a dissuader. From the beginning, Dorothea Brooke has baffled and irritated critics, Gissing's feminist heroine Rhoda Nunn seems to act intentionally to force her own unhappiness, and even more conventional novels like Miss Marjoribanks accentuate what Jane Eyre's critics identified as her "perverse" characteristics; in all these novels, the heroines confound both their fellow characters and their critics.

But that is in large part because the heroines are interrogating the limits of their world. Like Jane Eyre and Margaret Hale, the heroines of these books are testing hypotheses gathered from yet other books – like Dorothea Brooke, they not only fantasize themselves heroines, but imagine themselves able to reconcile the anomalies around them through their own actions. Their struggles suggest not only the difficulty of living a heroic life, "here – in England," as Dorothea fantasizes she will, but the tremendous power of the heroine's own fantasy life. For these heroines, as for Jane Eyre, their lives are constrained or misshapen by the very strength of their visionary leaps – it is the desire to live some more powerful romance of female destiny, to imagine some wider sphere of action, which precisely leads their plots into implausibilities, and their characters out of recognizable molds.

As the heroines do this, the novels themselves take on new problems of character. Where the earlier novels, like *North and South* in 1855 and *Miss Marjoribanks* in 1866, are able to rely on narrators who could essentially see the world through the eyes of their heroines, increasingly the complexity of the heroine's troubles, her difficulty in reconciling her view with the social order around her, make it harder to maintain a single focus. In *Middlemarch* (1871–2), George Eliot questions the possibility of the community seeing any of what Dorothea Brooke sees in marrying the dusty and undistinguished Edward Casaubon; written at the end of the century, after his own engagement with the feminist movement, George Gissing's *The Odd Women* (1893) attempts to make the "odd" (singular as well as single, or redundant) woman the center of his novel, even as his heroines pull against the convention of the romance plot. The attention to the heroine, far from being business as usual, creates what we can only consider disturbances in the fictional field, disturbances which mirror the increasing agitation of the movement for women's rights, the activities culminating in the violence and disruption of the suffrage movement, with riots in the parks, parades in the street, and the display of suffragists' bodies in the forced feedings in prisons following their hunger strikes. In what follows, I can only suggest the transformations which took place in the novels of the period – the way they responded to these challenges within the heroine's plot, and what that response tells us about the cultural anxieties and possibilities which surrounded Victorian feminism.

*

Although they span thirty years, and offer a variety of generic differences, ranging from the comic to the philosophical to the grimly ironic, these novels have more in common than first appears. *Middlemarch* and *Miss Marjoribanks* take place far from London; in both of them, villages or market towns offer the heroine at once less and more room for eccentricity than the hurried pace of an urban fiction. *Middlemarch* and *The Odd Women* both extend an unusual focus on the period after marriage, rather than on the marriage plot, and each offers an unusual picture of at least one truly disastrous marriage. And finally, each is connected with a powerful idea of reform, ranging from the great debate over the Reform Bill of 1832, which punctuates the action of *Middlemarch*, to the feminist movement of *The Odd Women*; even the more comic world of *Miss Marjoribanks* gets most of its energy from its heroine's efforts to reform the social life of the village of Carlingford, and the heroine's desire to find some wider arena for her managerial tendencies. In each of these novels, that is, the heroine's desire to find more for herself to do is linked powerfully to some crisis in social organization, some recognition that contemporary English society does not offer enough room for individual action.

It is George Eliot who provides the most interesting metaphor for the transformation of the heroine and her plot in a world shaken by feminism and its debates. In her last novel, *Daniel Deronda*, Eliot's narrator reflects on the way one woman's consciousness could intersect with world-historical events.

> Could there be a slenderer, more insignificant thread in human history than the consciousness of a girl, busy with her small inferences of the way in which she could make her life pleasant? – in a time, too, when ideas were with fresh vigor making armies of themselves, and the universal kinship was declaring itself fiercely: when women on the other side of the world would not mourn for the husbands and sons who died bravely in a common cause . . . a time when the soul of man was waking to pulses which had for centuries been beating in him unheard, until their full sum made a new life of terror or of joy. (Eliot 1967: 159)

Eliot's answer is clearly that the struggle of women for a fuller imaginative and moral life is, to borrow her historical analogy, its own Civil War. For Eliot, the transformation of the heroine (her desire to move beyond her world) is a form of evolutionary change, a world-historical moment in itself. But it is important to see the ways feminist debate, and the slender thread of "the consciousness of a girl," permeated novels which are far less self-consciously caught up in the transformations of society, however terrible or joyful – novels which nonetheless play out important elements of the plot of the self-conscious heroine.

One such novel, written between *North and South* and *Middlemarch*, and clearly drawing on similar concerns about women and cultural change, is Margaret Oliphant's *Miss Marjoribanks*, which rehearses in a comic register the issues we have been tracing in this chapter. *Miss Marjoribanks* begins, like so many nineteenth-century novels, with the death of the heroine's mother and the heroine's return to her native village, prepared to be a comfort to her father and the center of his home. To her dismay, Lucilla's father rejects her soggy overtures, returning her to her girls' school, where she promptly sets upon a course of study in political economy and household management, as if Oliphant were determined to take seriously, if not to politicize, the role of women in mastering domestic life. Lucilla's domestic management, when she does return to Carlingford, extends not only to managing the servants, redecorating the interior, and planning the gardens, but setting upon a course of musical evenings, social organization, and matchmaking, in the course of which she overcomes resistance from droopy widows, interfering clergymen, and balky servants. Above all, she herself resists the allures of the marriage plot until remarkably late in the book, and much of the comedy of the novel comes from our sense that Miss Marjoribanks will postpone marriage until everything else is arranged to her satisfaction, and then set upon a marriage that will seem absurd to everyone else and completely fitting to us – which is, of course, exactly what she does.

The prelude to Miss Marjoribanks' renunciation of her name (we might almost think, of her title) is, however, a remarkably serious set of passages, reminiscent of the reflections of Margaret Hale at the end of *North and South*. The questions she engages, of how a woman who has not successfully navigated the treacherous waters of the marriage plot is to make her way to a proper end, and of where the limits of self, society, and duty are then to be, suggests the way single women, or the possibility of female identity apart from social relations, haunted the Victorian imagination, and remained not only a social but a literary problem. Lucilla observes that she is in "the condition of mind" in which "the ripe female intelligence, not having the natural resource of a nursery and a husband to manage, turns inward, and begins to 'make a protest' against the existing order of society, and to call the world to account for giving it no due occupation – and to consume itself." Lucilla realizes that "her capabilities were greater than her work," and with no great work ahead of her, much of the world would be a "blank" – and herself a "blank" as well.

This sense of "call[ing] the world to account" for giving an intelligent woman "no due occupation" runs throughout the novels of the nineteenth century, from *Jane Eyre* to *Jude the Obscure* and *The Portrait of a Lady*, but nowhere is it more powerful than in the fiction of George Eliot, and nowhere more moving than in *Middlemarch*. That novel, in addition to its panoramic view of England at the time of the Reform Act, turns a harsh light on the inadequacy of female education, the ignorance in which men and women marry, the exclusion of women from science and new forms of knowledge, and (through the cruel will that Edward Casaubon writes to keep the widowed Dorothea from marrying his cousin, Will Ladislaw) the vulnerability of women to legal forms of restraint. But Dorothea Brooke's story, carefully placed as it is within the "study of provincial life," makes it difficult for readers to trace the difference between the social disabilities of women and the powerful force of Dorothea's own puritanical, vibrant imagination. Not until the end of the novel does George Eliot make more explicit her critique of the ignorance in which Dorothea (and Rosamond Vincy as well) had been raised:

> Among the many remarks passed on [Dorothea's] mistakes, it was never said in the neighbourhood of Middlemarch that such mistakes could not have happened if the society in which she was born had not smiled on propositions of marriage from a sickly man to a girl less than half his own age – on modes of education which make a woman's knowledge another name for motley ignorance – on rules of conduct which are in flat contradiction with its own loudly-asserted beliefs. While this is the social air in which mortals begin to breathe, there will be collisions such as those in Dorothea's life, where great feelings will often take the aspect of error, and great faith the aspect of illusion. (Eliot 1956: 612)

For Dorothea, whose highly charged if idiosyncratic reading has only sparked her imagination without giving her a clear idea of how she is to realize her vision of a better life, this education is the worst possible conglomeration of noble ideas and insufficient information; by the novel's end, her ardor has been poured into her marriage with Will, and the life they will lead in London, where he will be first a journalist and then a Member of Parliament, but the sense of frustration that follows her actions throughout the novel is hardly diminished:

> Many who knew her, thought it a pity that so substantive and rare a creature should have been absorbed into the life of another, and be only known in a certain circle as a wife and mother. But no one stated exactly what else that was in her power she ought rather to have done – not even Sir James Chettam, who went no further than the negative prescription that she ought not to have married Will Ladislaw. (Eliot 1956: 611)

As Dorothea herself says, on marrying Will, "I never could do anything that I liked. I have never carried out any plan yet"; the limit of her regret is "that there was always something better which she might have done, if she had only been better and known better," but the novel makes clear that in the "medium" in which we struggle, only these ("and sadder") sacrifices are possible, and the struggles through which Dorothea has passed can never really be understood by the community, the medium, in which she has lived. By the end of the novel both Dorothea and Lydgate, the two newcomers whose arrival began the novel, have been forced out of Middlemarch, into some more anonymous, if not more interesting, life.

The London to which Dorothea and Will Ladislaw turn, the world they hope to reform, is the world of Rhoda Nunn, the avowedly feminist heroine of George Gissing's *The Odd Women*. It is precisely against that anonymity, the silence surrounding women's despair, the "blank" that Lucilla Marjoribanks saw before her, that Rhoda Nunn rails. Faced with the quiet misery of society's "redundant women," she exclaims, "I wish girls fell down and died of hunger in the streets, instead of creeping to their garrets and the hospitals. I should like to see their dead bodies collected together in some open place for the crowd to stare at . . ." Redundant women are at the heart of *The Odd Women*, those banished from the world of Carlingford, its community and its comforting narratives. The novel traces the fortunes of three sisters, Alice, Virginia, and Monica, as they attempt to make their way after the death of their father, who has neglected to leave money to provide for their future. Alice and Virginia become governesses (Virginia also becomes a drunk), and the two slip further and further into not-so-genteel poverty; their beautiful sister Monica is taken up by a friend of their youth, Rhoda Nunn, who has joined with a wealthy woman, Mary Barfoot, in a movement to educate young women to useful professions, and, as she says, to give them the "training to self-respect." Monica, however, cannot resist the marriage proposal she receives from a courteous older man, Mr. Widdowson, and their marriage descends into a dark odyssey of jealousy and despair, at the end of which she dies, miserably, in childbirth, leaving her daughter to be raised by her sisters and Rhoda.

Romance is where Gissing best elaborates the social tensions which infuse all gender relations in the novel. Rhoda Nunn herself has fallen in love with Mary's cousin, Everard, only to be equally trapped by jealousy and mistrust, and finally chooses not to abandon her political mission, despite her strong attraction to him – but Rhoda is not the only character unable to fit easily into the romance plot. Widdowson struggles to understand Monica's desire for independence, and his baffled attempts to give her some freedom while refusing to see her as a person separate from himself are powerfully moving. Widdowson is explicitly a disciple of John Ruskin, following almost to the letter Ruskin's prescriptions on the greater simplicity and dependence of women, even as he senses that Monica might be both more intelligent and stronger than he is. But equally persuasive is Gissing's portrait of the economic and social restraints on equality between all men and women and on free choice in sexual relationships. The freethinking Everard Barfoot visits his old friend, Micklethwaite, who has waited seventeen years to marry his devoted fiancée. The two have grown old in the interim; they will now live, on a small income, in a small house, with her blind sister; only Barfoot, who will make a quite conventional marriage himself at the end of the novel, can afford sexual dalliance and a trophy-marriage. As the novel suggests, until economic relations are made more equitable, the power differences between men and women (and between upper-, middle-, and lower-class lovers) will remain all but unsurmountable.

None of these novels is exactly optimistic about relations between the sexes – and none is optimistic either about the possibility of autonomous individuality for its heroines. The very difficulty women have in these novels in realizing their often murky visions of another way of life renders them awkward, often unlikable characters, and has opened the novels to various critiques of their realism, their usefulness, even their aesthetic appeal; indeed, George Gissing seems determined at moments to make his fictional world as grim as possible. But there is a strong streak of utopian reform which runs through all these books. The energy that permeates some of the plots is part of this, as when Miss Marjoribanks marries her cousin Tom against expectations and with no great fortune; or when Dorothea Brooke marries Will Ladislaw, announcing tearfully that she will "learn what everything costs." There is a careful realism, a deliberate scaling down of expectations, at the end of these novels.

At the same time, the novels' social experiments translate into experiments with the conventions of realist fiction. Just as Jane Eyre broke the frame, addressing her readers directly to challenge their expectations for a woman's story, so the narrator of *Middlemarch* intrudes repeatedly, reminding us of the limits of knowledge and the failures of imagination which we bring to both social and literary interpretation. After that novel's long, reflective passages, and the even more remarkable introspections of *Daniel Deronda*, we can sense the fictional experiments of Henry James and Virginia Woolf hovering nearby, both novelists taking as their initial impulse the inner life of unexpected heroines. In a very different manner, Gissing experiments with the nature of fictional subjects: for Gissing and, curiously, even for Margaret Oliphant, individual consciousness gives way to a kind of collective or communal consciousness, one realized not through romantic love or even individual desire, but through collective action and particularly collective labor. Oliphant, like her predecessor Elizabeth Gaskell in *Cranford*, seems at times more interested in sketching the life of the town than in pursuing any traditional romance narrative: she plays with the marriage plot as if tempted to deflect closure, continuing instead to flirt with improbabilities.

Even more than the fictional improbability these changes leave in their wake, the novels hold out for readers the possibility of a different order of reality, a sense that the world (and individual consciousness) is moving forward. When Jane Eyre stood upon the leads of Thornfield Hall, she longed for a "power of vision" to take her beyond herself, to bring her in contact with lives she could not yet conceive; in a sense, that desire for a wider sphere has charged all of these novels with their imaginative as well as more mimetic force. At the end of her life, Charlotte Brontë wrote a painful letter to her friend, William Smith Williams,

> Lonely as I am, how should I be if Providence had never given me courage to adopt a career – perseverance to plead through two long, weary years with publishers till they admitted me? How should I be with youth past, sisters lost, a resident in a moorland parish where there is not a single educated family? In that case I should have no world at all: the raven, weary of surveying the deluge, and without an ark to return to, would be my type. As it is, something like a hope and motive sustains me still. I wish all your daughters – I wish every woman in England, had also a hope and a motive. Alas! there are many old maids who have neither. (quoted in Gérin 1967)

A vision much like this informs the end of *The Odd Women*, when Rhoda announces that her work is more successful than ever:

> "We flourish like the green bay-tree. We shall have to take larger premises. By-the-bye, you must read the paper we are going to publish; the first number will be out in a month, though the name isn't quite decided upon yet. Miss Barfoot was never in such health and spirits – nor I myself. The world is moving!" (Gissing 1977: 336)

The great, revolutionary cry of the novel was Mary Barfoot's, "When I think of the contemptible wretchedness of women enslaved by custom, by their weakness, by their desires, I am ready to cry, let the world perish in tumult rather than things go on in this way!"; the final message is a quieter if no less feminist response. Rhoda looks at Monica's infant, being raised by her aunts, and says, kindly, "Make a brave woman of her."

The relatively modest hope of "a brave woman" sounds a great deal like Charlotte Brontë's plea that "every woman in England" should have "a hope and a motive." But Charlotte Brontë went further, imagining herself not as the raven failing to find dry land, but as the dove returning to Noah's ark, having found a new world. In much the same way, each heroine in turn expands the limits of what her society, and the novel itself, could imagine. There may be no question more central to understanding the Victorians than the question these novels raised, "What do women want?" There is no more powerful answer than the one they give repeatedly, and what they ask of their fiction as well: More.

REFERENCES

Bodichon, Barbara, *née* Leigh Smith (1855), *A Brief Summary in Plain Language of the most Important Laws Concerning Women; Together with a Few Observations Thereon* (London: John Chapman).

Brontë, Charlotte (1987), *Jane Eyre* (New York: Norton). (First publ. 1847.)

Collins, Wilkie (1986), *No Name* (Oxford: Oxford University Press). (First publ. 1862.)

Eliot, George (1956), *Middlemarch: A Study of Provincial Life* (Cambridge, Mass.: Riverside). (First publ. 1871–2.)

Eliot, George (1967), *Daniel Deronda* (Harmondsworth: Penguin). (First publ. 1876.)

Gaskell, Elizabeth (1970), *North and South* (Harmondsworth: Penguin). (First publ. 1855.)

Gérin, Winifred (1967), *Charlotte Brontë: The Evolution of Genius* (Oxford: Clarendon).

Gissing, George (1977), *The Odd Women* (New York: Norton). (First publ. 1893.)

Jameson, Anna (1855), *Sisters of Charity: Catholic and Protestant, Abroad and at Home* (London: n.p.).

Jameson, Anna (1856), *The Community of Labour: A Second Lecture on the Social Employments of Women* (London: n.p.).

Mill, John Stuart (1970), "The Subjection of Women," repr. in Alice Rossi, ed., *Essays on Sex Equality* (Chicago: University of Chicago Press). (First publ. 1869.)

Norton, Caroline (1982), *English Laws for Women in the Nineteenth Century* (Chicago: Academy Press). (First publ. 1854.)

Oliphant, Margaret (1998), *Miss Marjoribanks* (London: Penguin). (First publ. 1866.)

Strachey, Ray (1978), *The Cause: A Short History of the Women's Movement in Great Britain* (London: Virago). (First publ. 1928.)

Trollope, Anthony (1972), *Can You Forgive Her?* (Harmondsworth: Penguin). (First publ. 1864–5.)

FURTHER READING

Armstrong, Nancy (1987), *Desire and Domestic Fiction: A Political History of the Novel* (New York: Oxford University Press).

Bodenheimer, Rosemarie (1988), *The Politics of Story in Victorian Social Fiction* (Ithaca: Cornell University Press).

Davidoff, Leonore and Hall, Catherine (1987), *Family Fortunes: Men and Women of the English Middle Class, 1780–1850* (Chicago: University of Chicago Press).

Gallagher, Catherine (1985), *The Industrial Reformation of English Fiction: Social Discourse and Narrative Form, 1832–1867* (Chicago: University of Chicago Press).

Gilbert, Sandra and Gubar, Susan (1979), *The Madwoman in the Attic: The Woman Writer and the Nineteenth-Century Literary Imagination* (New Haven and London: Yale University Press).

Holcombe, Lee (1983), *Wives and Property: Reform of the Married Women's Property Law in Nineteenth-Century England* (Toronto: University of Toronto Press).

Kent, Susan (1987), *Sex and Suffrage in Britain, 1860–1914* (Princeton: Princeton University Press).

Poovey, Mary (1988), *Uneven Developments: The Ideological Work of Gender in Mid-Victorian England* (Chicago: University of Chicago Press).

Showalter, Elaine (1977), *A Literature of Their Own: British Women Novelists from Brontë to Lessing* (Princeton: Princeton University Press).

Vicinus, Martha (1972), *Suffer and Be Still: Women in the Victorian Age* (Bloomington: Indiana University Press).

Vicinus, Martha (1977), *A Widening Sphere: Changing Roles of Victorian Women* (Bloomington: Indiana University Press).

11

The Other Arts: Victorian Visual Culture

Jeffrey Spear

To give at least some feeling for the range and complexity of Victorian visual culture I have contextualized a set of representative events and institutions, conducting a time traveler's tour with selected stops, from the founding of the National Gallery to the first photographic exhibit of the Linked Ring Brotherhood and the acceptance of photography as a fine art in the 1890s. Illustration and additional information about many works, events, and people mentioned here can be found on the internet at George Landow's Victorian Web site.

Going to the Pictures

England entered the nineteenth century as the only major European country without a national gallery of art. In 1777 the London radical John Wilkes proposed purchasing the collection of Horace Walpole for the nation, but the nation declined to bid against Catherine the Great. In revolutionary France, the Louvre became a public institution opening the former royal collection to all citizens. By contrast, the English did not nationalize the collection of their beheaded king, preferring to auction it off. After the Restoration, monarchs collected privately and made no show of it. In 1800 England's artistic capital was still largely in the houses of aristocrats and the landed gentry.

Calls for a national art gallery ran concurrently with reform movements intended to empower the propertied middle class at the expense of the landed, and with the need to forge a genuine British national identity out of the formal union of England, Scotland, and Wales, a need served by creation of public institutions and symbols. When the founder of Lloyd's of London, John Julius Angerstein, died in 1823, the state was offered the pick of his collection. Angerstein had been a friend and patron of Sir Thomas Lawrence, then President of the Royal Academy, and it was he who selected the thirty-eight paintings that began the National Gallery. Angerstein's house at 100 Pall Mall had been open to all art lovers. The government kept both the pictures and the policy in place, completing a posthumous social triumph for the Russian-born, self-educated, and, it was rumored, bastard Jew who despite his wealth and philanthropy had never been accepted in elite society (Duncan 1995: ch. 2).

It was only after passage of the 1832 Reform Bill that the government under Sir Robert Peel committed itself to the construction of a gallery to house the growing collection. On March 31, 1838, eight months into her reign, Queen Victoria opened the National Gallery of Art in the west wing of William Wilkins's building on Trafalgar Square. In the Gallery's first year 397,000 people of all social classes came to see the nation's 194 pictures. By 1844, when an outraged workman put his crutch through a *Leda and the Swan* in the style of Pier Francesco Mola, open access proved to be beyond challenge (Robertson 1978: 78–80; Taylor 1999: ch. 2). Painters favored by the donors – Raphael, Correggio, Titian, Tintoretto, Canaletto, Van Dyck, Rembrandt, Poussin, Rubens, Guido Reni and, particularly, Claude – were of interest to artists as well as the general public. First as Keeper (1843–7) and later as Director (1855–65), Sir Charles Eastlake made it his policy to "give preference to works of sterling merit that may serve as examples to the Artists of the Country" (Robertson 1978: 81).

It was under Eastlake, who was also President of the Royal Academy (1850–65), that the gallery moved beyond the gentleman's taste in Old Masters, adding medieval and early Italian Renaissance works. English art did not feature in this program, coming into the collection mostly by accident of donation – a circumstance resented in the east wing of the Gallery, home to the Royal Academy until the burgeoning national collection pushed it out in 1868. When J. M. W. Turner bequeathed his unsold works to the nation, he did so on the condition that two of his paintings, *Sun Rising Through Vapour* (1807) and *Dido Building Carthage* (1815), be hung between two of the Angerstein Claudes. It was a dramatic gesture, both tribute and challenge, the champion of the east wing laying claim to a place among the west wing's continental immortals for himself and on behalf of British artists.

The Royal Academy was the dominant institutional force in British painting throughout the nineteenth century. Its schools were the country's most prestigious, and the private view that preceded its May exhibition was a major social event marking the beginning of the London season. In its Victorian heyday the letters RA after a painter's name meant a good living and the chance of a fortune, even a knighthood. Because it had a royal charter and, though publicly housed, was self-funding, the Academy remained an exclusive club less subject to public pressure and parliamentary intervention than the schools and museums financed by the government (Fyfe 2000).

There were other venues in London, notably the Royal Institution; Edinburgh had the Royal Hibernian Academy (founded 1803); and there were exhibiting academies in other cities – but none had the Royal Academy's prestige. Academicians could exhibit up to eight works. Others submitted paintings for review by the Academy

Council. Although ten paintings were rejected for every one accepted, visitors were still confronted with over a thousand paintings hung side by side, floor to ceiling.

John Constable died in 1837. Turner, the other romantic titan, had his last popular success in the annual Exhibit of 1839 with *The Fighting Téméraire*, a painting that captures the early Victorian sense of being in a transitional period at once progressive and belated. The age of sail takes the shrouded form of the Trafalgar veteran, reduced to two thousand tons of towering dead weight, being towed up the Thames to the ship-breaker by a steam-driven, paddle-wheel tug that is all business. Echoing the blood-red Turnerian sunset, fiery smoke belches back from its stack, blowing over the vacant spot on the bowsprit where the Union Jack flew in 1805 when *Téméraire* saved Nelson's *Victory* from being boarded by the French (Egerton 1995).

Turner's contemporary David Wilke considered English taste to be more domestic than historical, and it was Wilke more than either Turner or the Academy's painter of classic nudes, William Etty, who had the most immediate influence. Genre paintings were Wilke's specialty, often sentimental rural scenes set in his native Scotland, and genre, that pre-eminently bourgeois mode, burgeoned as the art market shifted away from domination by the titled and well-born and toward new wealth and a middle class more willing to consider the merits of modern English painters for work other than portraits (Vaughn 1999: ch. 9).

The great age of fiction was also the age of narrative painting. Thomas Webster and a host of others painted carefully varnished scenes of village life in the Wilke manner. William Mulready added a brighter palate and a psychological element to the interaction of figures in country landscapes. Richard Redgrave ventured into social commentary in the 1840s with scenes depicting the plight of women that could have been taken from novels of the decade: a lonely governess, an exploited sempstress, a girl leaving home for domestic service, a servant cast out with her illegitimate infant. Narrative situations were adapted wholesale from the Bible, history and literature and extended into such subgenres as animal painting and the life and loves of the fairies. Fairy painting developed a "grotesquerie of the erotic" inherited from Henry Fuseli and William Blake that stimulated both fantasy art and research into folklore (Silver 1999: 3–32).

The tableaux of narrative paintings were akin to those staged in melodrama and fiction. All three arts drew upon a shared vocabulary of gesture and the "science" of physiognomy. The vocabulary of painting permeated Victorian criticism of fiction, which made frequent reference to portrait, landscape, sketch, touch, graphic delineation, color, light, and shadow – not to mention allusions to specific schools and painters. Novelists wrote dramatic scenes intended for illustration, sometimes collaborating directly with artists as Charles Dickens did with Cruikshank and "Phiz" (Hablot Browne). William Makepeace Thackeray had the advantage of collaborating with himself; his illustrations to *Vanity Fair* (1848) in particular have a dialectical relationship to the prose and form an essential part of the text. When George du Maurier turned to fiction he followed Thackeray's example. In *Trilby* (1894) he not only used illustrations to comment on his text, but fictionalized his days as an art student in the manner of Thackeray's *Paris Sketchbook* (1840).

Art and artists appear frequently in Victorian novels. Plots may turn on recognition of a portrait original, like Lady Dedlock in Dickens's *Bleak House* (1853); or the power of a painter to capture something essential about his subject; whether it is Lady Audley's secret in Mary Elizabeth Braddon's 1862 novel, or the dandy's soul in Oscar Wilde's *Picture of Dorian Gray* (1891). Wilkie Collins, the son of William Collins, an RA noted for rustic scenes featuring children, recreates his father's studio as the workplace of Valentine Blyth in *Hide and Seek* (1854), and Walter Hartright, the protagonist of *The Woman in White* (1860), is by profession at least a drawing master rather than a detective. But the Victorian novelist whose work is most imbued with the other arts is George Eliot. Eliot recreates the ekphrasitic, word-painting mode of Ruskinian art criticism so completely that readers are variously reminded of Venetian portraiture, Dutch or Pre-Raphaelite particularity, or the Turnerian sublime. Eliot created the equivalents of contemporary genre painting as well. The striking opening of *Daniel Deronda* (1876) is a high society example, its fifty or sixty men and women gambling in Leubronn recalling the like number depicted in William Powell Frith's *The Salon d'Or, Homburg* (1871).

Genre paintings were generally of suitable size for purchase and display in middle-class homes and could be bought through dealers. While wealthy individuals still became patrons, the percentage of pictures commissioned or purchased directly from the artist shrank through the century. Some painters did work on a massive scale, however, notably John Martin and Francis Danby, whose scenes of biblical miracle and catastrophe drew paying crowds in special exhibitions and had wide sales in mezzotint reproductions. Their combination of scale and commercial exposition reflected the influence of that unique blend of painting and popular entertainment: the panorama (Lambourne 1999: 160–7).

As the name implies, the panorama was a 360-degree, *trompe l'œil* painting that, when viewed from a center space, gave the spectator an illusion of being a witness to the depicted event from a commanding point of view. (In *Adam Bede* [1859] Eliot refers to Arthur Donnithorne's mental picture of himself as a model landlord over-seeing his estates as a panorama.) The display of a panorama required a specially constructed building. The most successful, Burford's on Leicester Square, lasted from 1823 to 1861, putting up two views a year in London, then sending them to exhibitors in the provinces.

The most sophisticated of these optical illusions was the stage designer Louis-Jacques Daguerre's double-effect diorama. Its viewing platform rotated moving spectators from scene to scene, each viewed through an aperture creating an illusion of depth. Gradual switching from front to back lighting created the impression of time passing. To produce the double effect, different scenes were painted on the front and back of a translucent canvas. The superimposition of complementary colors caused some figures to black out and others to appear as the lighting was shifted, suggesting motion. Daguerre's London Diorama opened in 1823 and lasted until 1851. He used the profits from the diorama business to support the experiments that led to the daguerreotype, the first commercially successful form of photography (Oettermann 1997: chs. 1–2).

"Pre-Raphaelite"

"Art Language from which we recoil with loathing."
Athenaeum (1850)

When the White Knight offers to sing Alice a song in *Through the Looking Glass* she has trouble distinguishing between what the song is, what it is called, what the name of it is, and what its name is called. Discussions of Pre-Raphaelitism have something of the same problem. Although the short-lived Pre-Raphaelite Brotherhood was organized in the revolutionary year of 1848, it no more overturned the Academy than the Chartists did the government. The PRB exhibited in 1849 without causing a particular stir, and if it had not been for the furor of 1850 Pre-Raphaelitism might now refer exclusively to those brilliant works that William Holman Hunt and John Everett Millais created by careful painting with sable brushes over a damp white ground. This technique created glowing pictures that, when hung next to conventionally toned paintings, seemed almost windows rather than canvases. It was a section-by-section technique that did not allow for correction without erasing. Only the prodigious Millais had the facility to produce more than a painting or two a year this way, and he abandoned the arduous technique in 1855 for more conventional means and more remunerative subject-matter. Only Hunt remained committed to both the technique and the rendition of biblical topics and moral subjects in realistic settings.

As for Dante Gabriel Rossetti, who had been the moving force behind the idea of a brotherhood and the source of its rebellious slang – the denigration of standard academic technique as "slosh," the search through streets and shops for "stunners" to paint – he did not risk rejection by the Academy. His *Girlhood of the Virgin Mary* in 1849 and *Ecce Ancilla Domini* in 1850 were shown a week earlier at the Free Exposition to relatively mild disapprobation. Nevertheless, he quit exhibiting publicly after 1850, and thereafter most of his work was done for private patrons. As a painter Rossetti's natural bent was quite different from that of Millais and Hunt. His genius was for surface, color, pattern, and texture: haptic rather than optic art (Gandelman 1991: 5–7). Had there been no controversy he might be better remembered as an early symbolist painter than as the link between two generations of Pre-Raphaelites, a term that makes English painting of the late nineteenth century seem more insular than it was.

The picture that in 1850 roused the *Times* and the *Athenaeum* to rage and Dickens to nearly apoplectic fury was Millais' *Christ in the House of his Parents*. This was indeed a radical painting. Millais translated the circumstances of the holy family into contemporary terms and depicted them as working-class people in a carpenter's shop.

To get Joseph's musculature right, Millais used an actual carpenter for a model. A Victorian working-class Joseph shaving planks with a metal plane directly challenged viewers who accepted anachronism in Renaissance painting without a thought. As if that were not enough, Hunt's and Millais' pictures recalled those Catholic Germans in Rome, the Nazarenes. (Their leader, Johann Overbeck, was the original of Naumann, the friend of Will Ladislaw who wants to paint the Casaubons on their wedding journey in *Middlemarch* [1872].) There was also a suggestion of figuralism – the stigmatic wound on the palm of the young Jesus, the flock of sheep visible through the open door – that, taken together with the now decoded PRB signature, seemed to have the whiff of Rome about it, triggering the anti-Catholic paranoia that was still a reflex of English Protestantism (Bowness 1984: 77–9).

The furor continued in 1851, focusing primarily on Millais' *Mariana*, whose moated grange with its altar and stained glass window was thought by some to have been decorated by a Puseyite if not an actual Romanist. The poet Coventry Patmore persuaded Ruskin to come to the defense of painters who were, after all, embodying some of his principles. He did so in two letters to *The Times*, though Ruskin provided his own genealogy of Pre-Raphaelitism. Having declared it the modern English school, Ruskin thereafter tended to label any contemporary painting he liked Pre-Raphaelite, and the term expanded to include landscapes by such artists John Brett and John Inchbold done with an almost scientific attention to geological and botanical detail.

Rossetti's work in the 1850s featured highly stylized watercolors of religious and Arthurian subjects. He attracted William Morris and Edward Burne-Jones as disciples when they were still Oxford undergraduates, relationships cemented in 1857 by the "jovial campaign," that lively but ill-fated attempt by Rossetti and his followers to paint Arthurian frescoes on the poorly prepared walls of the new Oxford Union. While Rossetti was the chief influence on the young Burne-Jones, his mature work treated draped figures after the manner of Botticelli, Mantegna, and Crivelli, inspiring a second generation of "Pre-Raphaelites" almost wholly distinct from the first in style and technique. Meanwhile, Rossetti went on to paint neo-Venetian oils of commanding and untouchable women like *Astarte Syriaca* (1877) that anticipate the *femmes fatale* of late-century symbolism.

When the modernist disdain for all things Victorian began to fade, the anti-establishment Pre-Raphaelites were among the first to return to favor and it was, again, tempting to make the movement seem as inclusive as possible. Pre-Raphaelite books and exhibitions reached back to incorporate immediate forebears like William Dyce and Ford Madox Brown, annexed wholly independent figures like J. W. Lewis because of the bright, jewel-like coloring of his oriental scenes, and reached forward to claim painters like the Italian-born J. W. Waterhouse, who did not stylize the female form in either the Rossetti or the Burne-Jones manner, and might well have painted nymphs and sirens as he did had no Pre-Raphaelite ever lived. The recovery of Victorian women painters over the last two decades has repeated the process.

Consequently, there is no fixed point at which Pre-Raphaelitism can be said to cease and the aesthetic movement and symbolism to begin.

The Great Exhibition of the Works of the Industry of All Nations

> There will be no 10th of April Chartism here – our Exhibition of '51 is better than a revolution.
>
> *Chambers Journal*, March 1, 1851

In 1851 just about everyone who could manage it visited the Crystal Palace: six million people in five months. Over four million of them came from outside London, double the usual number of travelers. Handling that traffic was a tribute to the new, high-speed, mass circulation of people and goods by railroad. The project's architect, Joseph Paxton, was not simply a builder of greenhouses, but a railway engineer; the great ferrovitrious sheds that still lie behind the public face of King's Cross and Paddington stations are architectural cousins of the Crystal Palace. The cruciform palace was constructed of standard cast and wrought iron pieces, none over 24 feet long or weighing more than a ton. They supported 900,000 square feet of glass panes that were at the time the biggest ever manufactured. The enclosed floor space was 772,824 square feet: room for nearly 14,000 exhibitors from around the world, featuring every-thing from raw materials and massive machinery for mining and manufacturing to fine arts and finished products for daily use. Prefabrication allowed the building to be erected in nine months; it also meant the palace could be taken down as scheduled and rebuilt in expanded form as a cultural center in Sydenham, south London, where it survived until 1936 when it was destroyed in a fire (Briggs 1988: ch. 2).

The patriotic effusions that accompanied the Exhibition were expressions not of simple self-satisfaction, but of palpable relief. Only three years earlier the government had feared that the mass demonstration by workers supporting the great Chartist petition might prove a prelude to revolution. Would it be safe to allow the classes that made the goods into the great glass house to see them? What about damage, crime, disease? Inclusiveness won out, and the general public were admitted at reduced price on "shilling days," albeit in combination with increased police surveil-lance. As in the case of the National Gallery, the mixed-class public proved orderly and self-regulating. That the queen on her way to open the Great Exhibition was able to move through a peaceful, cheering crowd in Hyde Park larger than that assembled by the Chartists seemed a triumph of good British citizenship before the eyes of the world (Miller 1995: 76–84).

The Exhibition itself was the very apotheosis of the fetishized commodity, a pro-liferation of goods without price tags (though exhibitors could state prices and offer advertising cards). Many pieces were fantasy objects made simply for display. Here, insofar as it can be located in one event, was the birth of the consumer economy, of merchandise and merchandising addressed more to desire than to need. Goods became spectacle, arranged by place of origin but divorced from the processes of production featured in earlier expositions. Airy and light, the vast enclosed space foreshadowed the department store and the commercial arcade (Richards 1990: 53–72; Bennett 1995: 80–6).

The British side of the exposition included areas displaying the materials and products of the country's overseas possessions. The East India Company's Indian Court, as befitting the grandest British territory, had 30,000 square feet largely devoted to raw materials, but with a considerable display of Indian fabrics, arts, and crafts. The official story was that free trade and more exchange of goods meant peace and reconciliation between nations, between classes, and between colonies and mother country. But even in 1851 there was a discordant note to be heard amid the liberal and nationalistic triumphalism, one that was underscored not only by the aesthetic superiority evident in some continental goods, but by Indian and more generally oriental design. Many thought the bulk of what the British manufactured to be technically ingenious but hideous to behold. Advances in casting iron, electroplating silver, molding *papier mâché* and the like meant that shape and decoration were no longer limited by the nature of the material, nor was the relationship between representation and schematization in the design of utensils or fabric or wallpaper well defined. Not everything that can be done should be.

The Great Exhibition was organized under the aegis of Prince Albert by that great advocate of regular system in the teaching of design, the artist-utilitarian Henry Cole. (Cole was the original of that government gentleman in *Hard Times* [1854] who informs Sissy Jupe that if one doesn't walk on flowers in fact one shouldn't represent them in carpets.) The extraordinary success of the exposition produced a £186,000 profit that was used to purchase land for what is now the complex of museums in South Kensington. Cole led the drive for a museum devoted to applied arts combined with a new home for the government schools of art and design (Frayling 1987: 29–43).

After the closing of the Great Exhibition, Cole's purchasing committee spent about half of its funds on examples of European manufacture, but it also spent another quarter, almost £1,300, on items from the East India Company exhibit. These purchases, with the addition of Islamic items from the exposition, became the core collection of the South Kensington Museum, predecessor of the Victoria and Albert. Cole's associate, Owen Jones, used the collection's samples of Indian fabrics along with Japanese and Islamic patterns in his influential *Grammar of Ornament* (1856) (Barringer 1998). Most current commentary on the Great Exhibition critiques the culture of commodity and empire; but it is worth recalling that the aesthetic debate stimulated by the exposition, the institutions it helped finance, and their methods of teaching, played a key role in the development of all aspects of design in the second half of the century, and enabled the emergence of the arts and crafts movement.

The Crystal Palace as reassembled in Sydenham was larger by three stories and nearly 100 acres, and dedicated to the amusement and instruction of the masses. It was the setting Disraeli chose in 1872 for his appeal to the newly enfranchised working class, invoking their pride in "an Imperial country." Gissing denounced the sad spectacle of its bank holiday crowds distracted by xenophobic games in *The Nether World* (1889). The Sydenham Palace was organized into courts featuring the architecture and culture of various civilizations, including replicas of famous monuments. Natural history displays featured the development of the human race, the nave enclosed trees of many climates, and the grounds contained the first model dinosaurs in a conjectured prehistoric setting (Crinson 1996: 62–4; Auerbach 1999: 200–13).

The Sydenham exhibits gave strong impetus to the idea of displaying cultures, not just isolated artifacts, moving special expositions into what had been the province of entrepreneurial showmen like William Bullock, whose Egyptian Hall had in the first half of the century featured everything from Indian nautch dancers to Laplanders, Aztec artifacts to Napoleon's carriage (Altick 1978: chs. 20–1). "Scientific" exhibitions of exotic cultures showed living examples of native peoples whose names and images had become known through the reproduction of ethnographic photographs (Maxwell 1999: ch. 1).

The power of the metropole was such that living examples could be imported wholesale. The Japanese village erected in London with royal patronage in the wake of the opening up of Japan is a case in point. It contained dwellings for more than a hundred Japanese, including twenty-six women and children; tea houses that served visitors; shops, a Buddhist temple, and a stage for dance, wrestling, and martial exercises. The villagers worked their trades before the public, but without offering the goods for sale until near the end of the exhibition (*The Times*, Jan. 10, 1884.) It was in Knightsbridge in 1884 and not on Honshu that W. S. Gilbert discovered the town of Titipu immortalized in *The Mikado*. Not content with taking tea-ceremony photographs, Gilbert had the Savoy management borrow a male dancer and a tea-house geisha, whose only English was "sixpence please," to teach his cast proper Japanese deportment. Antique armor imported for the sake of authenticity proved to be too small for the actors, and the Japanese silk costumes were mostly from Liberty's, but Miss Rosina Brandram performed the comic old maid Katisha in a genuine seventeenth-century kimono. "It is," as the Mikado says, "an unjust world" (Hibbert 1976: 172–8).

A Tale of Two Paintings

In 1858 the most popular mid-Victorian painter, William Powell Frith, exhibited *Derby Day*. The 40 in × 88 in canvas had taken him fifteen months to paint, but he could afford to put in the time. His first stylized slice of Victorian life, *Ramsgate Sands*, had sold to a dealer for 1,000 guineas and he had regular portrait commissions. To record the setting and suggest groupings, he employed photographer Robert Howlett, who set up his camera on the roof of a cab to record scenes at the 1856 Derby. Like most successful Victorian artists, Frith had a studio in his home, and a stream of professional models and volunteers came in and out almost like movie extras. He tried a professional acrobat from a Drury Lane pantomime for the painting's central scene, but he, curiously, found staying in one position too difficult, kept fainting, and had to be replaced by a professional model. *Derby Day* was commissioned by Jacob Bell for £1,500, with engraving rights reserved for the artist. The noted dealer Ernest Gambart bought those for another £1,500. On private view day, May 2, 1858, this painting of the event contemporaries called the English Carnival caused a sensation. When the Academy exhibit was opened to the public a guardrail had to be set up and a policeman assigned to keep back the crowds for the first time since Wilke exhibited his *Chelsea Pensioners* back in 1822 (Noakes 1978: 60–9).

Derby Day reflects the new confidence in social order after the successful mixing of the classes at the Crystal Palace. Reading from left to right, Frith depicts the exclusive Reform Club's tent, a thimble-rigger setting up his table while tempting a rube being warned away by his wife, and a boy whose pocket has been picked. At the center a group has formed around the acrobat, whose boy is looking with envy at a gentleman's picnic lunch. On the right, a flower girl offers posies to a swell while a gypsy offers to tell the fortune of a woman, possibly a kept woman, in a carriage; and so on. The painting is a cross-section of mid-Victorian society, with even the disorderly elements frozen in place for contemplation. Realizing he had a hot property on his hands, Gambart took advantage of the time he had possession of the painting for purposes of engraving to send it on a very profitable tour.

In 1857, the year before *Derby Day*, Emily Osborne's *Nameless and Friendless* had been accepted by the Royal Academy, but, obscurely hung, it was little noticed, though it did find a buyer in Lady Chetwyth. Born in 1834, Osborne remained single, apparently sustaining herself by painting historical and contemporary genre and landscape. Frith praised her work in his autobiography, and her career was the longest of any Victorian woman painter. She last exhibited in 1905. Frith's work may have fallen out of favor, but it has not passed not out of sight. Osborne's paintings have "begun to come to light in recent years, though she has had up till now no reputation to speak of" (Nunn 1987: 24). She has been, in other words, nameless, and *Nameless and Friendless* can be read as a parable about Victorian women as professional painters.

The picture features a young woman in mourning, who has come out of the rain into an art dealer's shop accompanied by a boy carrying an artist's portfolio. She wears no wedding ring. In all likelihood she is an orphan accompanied by her brother. She is nameless and friendless in the same sense as the orphaned speaker of Tennyson's *Maud* (1855): "Your father has wealth well-gotten, and I am nameless and poor." For the exhibition catalogue, Osborne provided a quotation from Proverbs 10: 15: "The rich man's wealth is his strong city." (The strong city of rich painters like Frith was the Royal Academy, whose selection committee passed judgment on Osborne's work.) As the dealer contemplates her small, framed canvas, the painter's eyes remain decorously downcast while she nervously twists the fringe of her shawl. In contrast, the boy is free to look intently at the dealer's face, trying to read his expression. By the door two men about town look up from a print of a pirouetting, bare-limbed ballet dancer, and turn their gaze upon the painter. The metonym Osborne sets up is so strong that some modern readings suggest that the men are literally recognizing her as the dancer, rather than reacting to the direct sale of her work, an act that places her at the margin of respectability. She is caught between being a producer and being an image, "from desiring subject to desired object" (Cherry 1993: 81). Osborne was a successful painter with her own studio. Two of her pictures were purchased by the queen. But without the imprimatur of those male-dominated institutions that through membership, acquisition, and cultural discourse sustained the value of an artist's work, Osborne fell into obscurity until the recovery and advocacy project of feminist art history made her work visible again.

While the Academy would hang a woman's painting, it would not make her an ARA – even though two of its founding members had been female; not even Elizabeth Thompson (later Lady Butler), whose Crimean War memorial *Roll Call*, like *Derby Day* before it, commanded a guardrail and a bobby to keep back the crowds, was deemed worthy (Nunn 1987: ch. 3). The Royal Academy did not accept a woman until 1922, when Annie Swynnerton was admitted to a much diminished institution. Attending Academy schools, however, was another matter, and women agitated for access. As part of their campaign, they attended the academicians' public lectures held in the RA's room. For Anna May Howitt, that room, with its easels and pictures, was a place she felt born to: "a freer, larger, more earnest artistic world – a world, alas! Which one's *woman*hood debars one from enjoying. I felt quite *angry* at being a woman; it seemed to me *such a mistake*" (Cherry 1993: 56).

Just as permission to undertake nursing training came more easily to women than access to the medical schools, so it was easier for women to enter the schools of design, even as students of painting, than to enter schools for artists as such, schools that often added injury to insult by charging them more than men. The key issue in both cases was the acceptance of women as professionals, but the symbolic issue was anatomy. There could be no equality in art training without access to a life class, to the study of the undraped body, just as being a doctor meant studying anatomy and having access to the bodies of patients. Women had to get such knowledge where they could by studying abroad or establishing their own schools.

Even after women were admitted to the Royal Academy schools in 1867, their petitions for a life class were made in vain until 1893, when a partially draped model was made available in a female-only class. When the Slade School was founded in 1871 under Sir Edward Poynter, a painter noted for classical nudes, it welcomed female students, but even there figure study was accomplished only in stages. Besides the issue of nudity, there was the question of social contagion. Most aspiring female artists came from respectable families; models were considered little better than prostitutes. While no woman came to grief by being in the same room with a model, many talented Slade women paired up with painters.

By the twentieth century the battle was won, but respectable women who painted the nude could still be alienated from their own bodies. "I was sixteen," wrote Nina Hamnet, "I drew from the nude at the Art Schools, but had never dared to look at myself in the mirror, for my grandmother had always insisted that one dressed and undressed under one's nightdress . . . One day, feeling very bold, I took off all my clothes and gazed in the looking-glass. I was delighted. I was much superior to anything I had seen in the life class, and I got a book and began to draw" (Gillett 1990: 191).

The Nurture of Gothic

On June 1, 1859, on a small lot in a run-down neighborhood off Oxford Street, after ten years of design, construction, and decoration, William Butterfield's All Saints, Margaret Street, was dedicated. Whether or not it was "the nineteenth century's most influential church" (Brooks 1999: 309), from its aggressive use of undisguised brick in polychromatic striations to the hard, vibrant, glazed brick, tile, and inlaid stone patterning of the interior, it aggressively deployed the essential elements of high Victorian Gothic. Butterfield's "streaky bacon" Gothic has been derided as ugly, even sadistic, with its clash of northern and southern influences, but it suited the purpose of his sponsors, the high church Ecclesiological Society, which was more interested in meaning, religious ritual, and the associations of old parish churches than in comfort or quietude. The contemporaries who compared All Saints to Millais' *Christ in the House of his Parents* had a point.

Ecclesiology began at Trinity College as the Camden Society, and could be considered the Cambridge Movement. Unlike the Oxford Movement, the Ecclesiologists were more interested in church aesthetics, in the proper settings and accessories for high church ritual, than in theology. They were never tempted by Rome. All Saints was to be their model church, the embodiment of the architecture that their influential journal, *The Ecclesiologist*, had been advocating in the 1840s. Indeed, a founder of the movement, the wealthy MP Beresford Hope, was active in both the financing and the interior decoration of All Saints.

At first the Ecclesiologists followed A. N. W. Pugin in favoring the revival of a particular English style, settling on fourteenth-century Middle Pointed, while setting aside Pugin's belief that Gothic was essentially Roman Catholic (Crook 1987: ch. 2). The shift to mixed motifs in All Saints expresses a different influence on Ecclesiology, an associational aesthetic derived from the Scottish "common sense" philosophers. Associationism predicates interplay between an object and the mental associations it stimulates in the observer, between the object's "expression" and the viewer's "imagination"; it is a theory more conducive to eclecticism than stylistic purity. (Hersey 1972: 10–13, 26–34, 104–22; Brooks 1999: ch. 9).

Fifteen hundred new parish churches were built between 1830 and 1860, along with their vicarages and schools. Associational eclecticism encouraged experiment with style and materials, so Gothic revival architects were well prepared to design the country houses and public buildings that were commissioned in substantial numbers in the decades of Victorian prosperity and imperial ascendancy.

Eclecticism survived the fashion for Gothic, as younger architects from the offices of George Street and Gilbert Scott revived an urban style based on Queen Anne (Crook 1987: ch. 5).

The mid-Victorian wave of construction created a demand for both ecclesiastical and domestic furnishings: everything from stained glass, painting, and sculpture, to chairs, wallpaper, and fabrics. It was to supply these needs in a harmonious way that William Morris founded his firm of artist decorators in 1861. Morris followed the practice of the Gothic revival architects in studying how traditional arts and crafts such as stained glass, furniture-making, tapestry, dyeing, and printing were done in order to ground modern work in those traditions. He followed Ruskin by defining art as "man's expression of joy in his labour" rather than in the artifact as such. But he split from Ruskin in placing his hope for unalienated labor and social redemption in a Marxist revolution.

Influenced by Morris, the ideology of the arts and crafts movement of the 1880s and 1890s was biased toward collectives, guilds or schools organized for the production, generally by hand, of objects of use and beauty true to the materials of their making, and against the class system and the oppression of workers. The aesthetes, while not forming a coherent movement, differed ideologically; being for the most part individualists, believers in art for art's sake, who followed Walter Pater's assertion of the autonomy of each art. As it happens, the pioneer of aestheticist design was another Gothic revival architect, E. W. Godwin, who moved from designing churches, to theatrical productions and costumes for his lover Ellen Terry, to wallpaper, textiles, and lacquered furniture based on a thorough study of Japanese design. He was also a clever and prolific writer. If any one person could be said to be responsible for the Victorian Japanese craze it was Godwin. He designed Whistler's London studio home and Oscar Wilde's "white room," and was the source for much of what those more famous aesthetes advocated in interior design (Lambourne 1996: ch. 8).

It would be convenient if there were a distinct formal difference between arts and crafts design and that of the aesthetes, but there is not. Names overlap in histories of both movements and both flow into the art nouveau of the 1890s as exemplified in the astonishing work in art, architecture, and design of the Glasgow four: Margaret MacDonald, Charles Rennie Mackintosh, Francis MacDonald, and Herbert McNair, who absorbed influences from both camps (Greenhalgh 2000). Their use of organic motifs abstracted from the flora of Scotland and their social commitment came straight from Ruskin, Morris, and their associates. The sinuous lines of their decorative paintings and book illustrations suggest Edward Burne-Jones, Walter Crane, and Aubrey Beardsley. Their furniture advances the spare design of Godwin (Neat 1994). Although they are best known for fully decorated architectural commissions like Mrs. Cranston's Willow Tea Rooms, one of which has been reconstructed for museum display (Greenhalgh 2000: 315), the symbolist painting and illustration of the MacDonald sisters and others of the "spook school," as they were called, have a significant place in the history of European graphic arts at the turn of the century. The Four decorated a room at the Vienna Secession Exhibition in 1900, and Glasgow artists were featured in German art magazines, influencing artists as well known as Gustav Klimt (Burkhauser 1990).

A Palazzo of Art

"The Grosvenor is really the only place."
Oscar Wilde, *Picture of Dorian Gray*

There is no institution more closely associated with the aesthetes than the Grosvenor Gallery. Its founders, the Lindsays, were friends with its core figures: Rossetti, Swinburne, Pater, Wilde, and Whistler. Sir Coutts was a baron, and Lady Blanch Lindsay a Rothschild heiress. Their social circle not only patronized the arts, they employed the new Queen Anne architects like Norman Shaw and the new interior decorators like Rhoda and Agnes Garrett and Mary Eliza Haweis, who compared the composition of a room to that of a picture. The reputation and authority of the Royal Academy were in decline. Alternative galleries like the Dudley were attracting important work, but were not innovative in displaying it. After a joint investment estimated at £150,000, the Lindsays' gallery opened on fashionable New Bond Street in 1877 (Denney 1996).

Artists exhibited by Sir Coutts' invitation. Among the works in the opening show at the Grosvenor were paintings by Albert Moore, the French symbolist Gustave Moreau, James Tissot, George Frederic Watts (the artist in residence at Little Holland House where the Lindsays had met), Whistler, and Burne-Jones, who invited his friend Ruskin to attend. Burne-Jones had cause to regret that invitation. While others, including Oscar Wilde, were uncomprehending and dismissive of Whistler's set of "Nocturnes," Ruskin reacted to the splatter effects on the surface of *Nocturne in Black and Gold: The Falling Rocket* (1877) by accusing Whistler of "flinging a pot of paint in the public's face." Whistler sued and Burne-Jones found himself in court defending his old friend in the uncongenial company of the Royal Academician Frith. Ruskin was not there to defend himself, having suffered an attack of the mania that ended his public life in the 1880s. Whistler made his case for the autonomy of the artist and the rejection of any criticism save that given by a practitioner in the art's own terms, but was awarded only a farthing in damages. Bankrupted by legal fees, he had to sell his Godwin house and spent most of the rest of his life on the continent where, to be sure, he was not without friends. His credo, the "Ten o'Clock Lecture" (1885), was translated into French by Mallarmé.

The association of the Grosvenor with the aesthetes, and the aesthetes with affectation, from George du Maurier's cartoons in *Punch* featuring Maudle the poet and that lank collector in aesthetic dress Mrs. Cimibue Brown, to Gilbert's amalgam of Whistler, Swinburne, and Wilde, the poet Bunthorne in *Patience* ("A greenery-yallery, Grosvenor Gallery, / Foot-in-the-grave young man"), have obscured both the range of the painting shown at the gallery and the influential way in which it was displayed. Entering through a genuine Palladian doorway imported from Venice, the visitor would find art hung as it might be in a great house. The works of individual artists were grouped together and spaced for easy viewing under the most modern lighting: first gas, then electric. Lady Lindsay saw to it that more women artists were displayed at the Grosvenor than at the Academy, and that women were treated as independent customers, adding a ladies' club and a restaurant so that respectable women could patronize gallery events without a male escort (Gillett 1996).

By reputation one would expect the Grosvenor to be exclusively the home of late Pre-Raphaelite, symbolist and aesthetic painting, including the academic nudes in classical settings then popular. But, just as the age of Pater and Wilde is also the age of Hardy and Gissing, so there was an emerging school of rural naturalism following the lead of Jules Bastien-Lepage, whose *Les Foins* (1878) was part of a Grosvenor retrospective in 1880. Sir Coutts hung such grim scenes as Sir George Clausen's *Winter Work* (1883) and Henry La Thangue's *The Runaway* (1887), in which two farm laborers come across a girl lying exhausted or dead in the tall grass. He also chose work of the Newyln school led by Stanhope and Elizabeth Armstrong Forbes, so called after the fishing village where they lived to paint the daily life of its workers (McConkey 1996).

The Lindsays separated in 1882, Lady Lindsay removing both herself and her capital from the gallery, which, given Sir Coutts' lavish spending habits, had to close in 1890. The Grosvenor Gallery "recreated the kind of aristocratic space in which picture galleries were first found" and in doing so influenced the design and amenities of future galleries and "later avant-garde exhibition halls" (Denney 1996: 36).

Forging the Linked Ring

The Linked Ring Brotherhood was formed to assert the primacy of art over technical innovation in photography's professional organizations. On November 7, 1893, in the manner of the Royal Academy's private view, the Links celebrated the opening of their first photographic salon with an invitation evening at the Dudley Gallery. Traditionally, photographs had been displayed floor to ceiling, but the salon was organized like a Grosvenor Gallery exhibit, so that each carefully framed print was clearly visible without bending or climbing. By contrast, the exhibits of the Royal Photographic Society from which the Links had seceded had the look of an auction house (Harker 1979: 104–5). Photography as a fine art had arrived at last. But what took so long? Looking back, we see artistic merit in early daguerreotypes and Fox Talbot's calotypes of the 1840s, and a golden age of photography before 1900. Far from being young rebels, the Links comprised most of the elite professionals of the time, including Henry Peach Robinson who had spent forty years composing photographs and writing eleven books in the cause of art photography.

In 1857 Oscar Rejlander, having developed a technique for "combination print-ing" (making a seamless print from multiple negatives), assembled a moralizing update of Raphael's *The School of Athens* entitled *The Two Ways of Life* (Industry and Dissipation). But his photographic imitation of history painting could not overcome preconceptions about his medium. Viewers were more interested in who those bare-breasted "dissipants" were and how they held their pose so long than in what they were supposed to represent (Gernsheim 1988). The fact that the photograph is a time print, an "indexical" sign preserving the image of a moment, became from the outset its defining characteristic. Given that the manipulation of images is almost as old as photography itself, the belief that photography is essentially a mechanical, impartial recording technology and photographic prints "true" requires a fetishistic disavowal of origins. It was against this powerful realistic bias that photographic art, whether in the form of carefully composed scenes or technical manipulations of the image, had to contend.

From the time the first ghostly image of someone else appeared in the mirror-like surface of the daguerreotype there has been something uncanny about photographs. Preservation of a person's lifelike image is also a reminder of the absence of the subject – even of death. Belief in the fidelity of the absent/present image could so repress knowledge of its production that "spirit photographs" produced by double exposure or photomontage were advanced as evidence of the afterlife at the same time that phantasmagoria and fanciful angelic visits created by the same techniques were being sold as novelties. Belief in the objectivity of the photograph suppresses its contin-gency, and that suppression is ideology in action.

With each technical innovation, photography reached further into Victorian life. While it seems clumsy in retrospect, the development of wet plate collodion nega-tives put prints of everything from funerary memorials to family portraits, *carte-de-visite* images of famous people and pictures of faraway places within reach of the average person. While the process itself was cumbersome and relatively expensive, many amateurs became accomplished photographers. Charles Dodgson's photographs of children, Julia Margaret Cameron's portraits, and Lady Clementina Hawarden's dra-matically lit studies of her older daughters in fancy dress and costumed for amateur theatricals hold their own against professional work (Haworth-Booth 1984: 118–32).

Officers serving in India were encouraged to document the country and its people, and enterprising officials there invented the photo identity card to keep track of Indians with claims on the government and to ensure that those sentenced to prison did not pay another to serve their time. With the rise of anthropology, the photog-raphy of indigenous peoples was systematized by shooting "natives" against measured grids and associating the images of individuals with the moral attributes of races, tribes, and classes (Edwards 1992). At home, Darwin's nephew Francis Galton mod-ified the combination printing that Rejlander and Robinson had developed to imitate history painting by superimposing images of individuals and printing them as "scientific" studies of racial, criminal, and mentally deficient types. Painters used photographs as an *aide-memoire*, but memories of nudes were soon sold more generally as erotica, and erotica quickly devolved into out-and-out pornography. The hyper-realism of the unmediated stereoscopic image became so identified with obscenity that some argue it contributed to the decline of that medium by 1900 (Crary 1990: 127).

With the development in the 1880s of roll film so fast that ordinary cameras could stop motion, still photography reached maturity as a medium. Almost anyone could own a camera and create visual history. An early form of photolithography had already displaced the woodblock as a medium for the mass production of illustrations, but with the invention of halftone printing, which was adopted by the *Graphic* in 1884, photographs could be readily reproduced in newspapers and magazines, displacing the graphic work of a realistic school of urban painters, notably Luke Fildes, Frank Holl, and Hubert von Herkomer.

Faced on the one hand with cheap cameras and roll film, making everyone a poten-tial photographer, and on the other with the rapid emergence of photojournalism, it is small wonder that the Linked Ring and like photosecessionists in Europe and the United States felt an urgent need to differentiate their own work by establishing pho-tography as a fine art. The popular taste for visual narratives that sustained Victorian genre painting and illustration was not dying out with the nineteenth century; rather, it was changing media. All that remained was to fulfill the promise of the optical devices that fooled the eye and the double-effect dioramas of the early century by capturing motion on fast film. When the aptly named Lumière brothers patented the Cinematograph camera/printer/projector in 1895, the age of Victoria added the missing element to what would be the visual agenda for the first half of the twentieth century.

REFERENCES

Altick, Richard (1978), *The Shows of London* (Cambridge, Mass.: Harvard University Press).

Auerbach, Jeffrey (1999), *The Great Exhibition of 1851: A Nation on Display* (New Haven: Yale University Press).

Barringer, Tim (1998), "The South Kensington Museum and the Colonial Project," in Tim Barringer and Tom Flynn, eds., *Colonialism and the Object* (London: Routledge).

Bennett, Tony (1995), *The Birth of the Museum: History, Theory, Politics* (London: Routledge).

Bowness, Alan, ed. (1984), *The Pre-Raphaelites* (London: Tate Gallery).

Briggs, Asa (1988), *Victorian Things* (Chicago: University of Chicago Press).

Brooks, Chris (1999), *The Gothic Revival* (London: Phaidon).

Burkhauser, Jude (1990), *Glasgow Girls: Women in Art and Design 1880–1920* (Edinburgh: Canongate).

Cherry, Deborah (1993), *Painting Women: Victorian Women Artists* (London: Routledge).

Crary, Jonathan (1990), *Techniques of the Observer: On Vision and Modernity in the Nineteenth Century* (Cambridge, Mass.: MIT Press).

Crinson, Mark (1996), *Empire Building: Orientalism and Victorian Architecture* (London: Routledge).

Crook, J. Mordaunt (1987), *The Dilemma of Style: Architectural Ideas from the Picturesque to the Post-Modern* (Chicago: University of Chicago Press).

Denney, Coleen (1996), "The Grosvenor Gallery as a Palace of Art: An Exhibition Model," in Susan Casteras and Coleen Denney, eds., *The Grosvenor Gallery: A Palace of Art in Victorian England* (New Haven: Yale Center for British Art).

Duncan, Carol (1995), *Civilizing Rituals: Inside Public Art Museums* (New York: Routledge).

Edwards, Elizabeth, ed. (1992), *Anthropology and Photography: 1860–1920* (New Haven: Yale University Press).

Egerton, Judy (1995), *Turner,* The Fighting Téméraire (London: National Gallery Publications).

Frayling, Christopher (1987), *The Royal College of Art: One Hundred and Fifty Years of Art and Design* (London: Barrie & Jenkins).

Fyfe, Gordon (2000), "Auditing the RA: Official Discourse and the Nineteenth-century Royal Academy," in Rafael Denis and Colin Trodd, eds., *Art and the Academy in the Nineteenth Century* (New Brunswick: Rutgers University Press).

Gandelman, Claude (1991), *Reading Pictures, Viewing Texts* (Bloomington: Indiana University Press).

Gernsheim, Helmut (1988), *The Rise of Photography: 1850–1880* (New York: Thames & Hudson).

Gillett, Paula (1990), *The Victorian Painter's World* (New Brunswick: Rutgers University Press).

Gillett, Paula (1996), "Art Audiences at the Grosvenor Gallery," in Susan Casteras and Coleen Denney, eds., *The Grosvenor Gallery: A Palace of Art in Victorian England* (New Haven: Yale Center for British Art).

Greenhalgh, Paul, ed. (2000), *Art Nouveau: 1890–1914* (London: V&A Publications).

Harker, Margaret (1979), *The Linked Ring: The Secession Movement in Photography in Britain, 1892–1910* (London: Heinemann).

Haworth-Booth, Mark, ed. (1984), *The Golden Age of British Photography* (Millerton, NY: Aperture).

Hersey, George (1972), *High Victorian Gothic: A Study in Associationism* (Baltimore: Johns Hopkins University Press).

Hibbert, Christopher (1976), *Gilbert and Sullivan and their Victorian World* (New York: American Heritage Publishing).

Lambourne, Lionel (1996), *The Aesthetic Movement* (London: Phaidon).

Lambourne, Lionel (1999), *Victorian Painting* (London: Phaidon).

Landow, George, The Victorian Web: http://landow.stg.brown.edu/victorian/victov.html

McConkey, Kenneth (1996), "Rustic Naturalism at the Grosvenor Gallery," in Susan Casteras and Coleen Denney, eds., *The Grosvenor Gallery: A Palace of Art in Victorian England* (New Haven: Yale Center for British Art).

Maxwell, Anne (1999), *Colonial Photography and Exhibitions: Representations of the "Native" and the Making of European Identities* (London: Leicester University Press).

Miller, Andrew H. (1995), *Novels behind Glass: Commodity Culture and Victorian Narrative* (Cambridge: Cambridge University Press).

Neat, Timothy (1994), *Part Seen, Part Imagined: Meaning and Symbolism in the Work of Charles Rennie Mackintosh and Margaret Macdonald* (Edinburgh: Canongate).

Noakes, Aubrey (1978), *William Frith: Extraordinary Victorian Painter* (London: Jupiter).

Nunn, Pamela Gerrish (1987), *Victorian Women Artists* (London: Women's Press).

Oettermann, Stephan (1997), *The Panorama: History of a Mass Medium,* trans. Deborah Schneider (New York: Urzone).

Richards, Thomas (1990), *The Commodity Culture of Victorian England: Advertising and Spectacle, 1851–1914* (Stanford: Stanford University Press).

Robertson, David (1978), *Sir Charles Eastlake and the Victorian Art World* (Princeton: Princeton University Press).

Silver, Carole G. (1999), *Strange and Secret Peoples: Fairies and Victorian Consciousness* (New York: Oxford University Press).

Taylor, Brandon (1999), *Art for the Nation: Exhibitions and the London Public 1747–2001* (New Brunswick: Rutgers University Press).

Vaughn, William (1999), *British Painting: The Golden Age from Hogarth to Turner* (London: Thames & Hudson).

12

Imagined Audiences: The Novelist and the Stage

Renata Kobetts Miller

Two of the most widely read Victorian novels, both written in 1847, likened fiction to theatrical performance. William Makepeace Thackeray's prefatory acknowledgment, "Before the Curtain," in *Vanity Fair* is a famous and early Victorian example of a novelist using the metaphor of stage performance in order to express an awareness of audience. This self-consciousness about performance enables the author to address his audience directly and to acknowledge that fiction is constructed in order to entertain and please. *Jane Eyre*, dedicated by Charlotte Brontë to Thackeray, similarly uses a theatrical figure of speech in order to instruct the reading audience intimately: "A new chapter of a novel is something like a new scene in a play; and when I draw up the curtain this time, reader, you must fancy you see a room in the George Inn at Millcote" (ch. 11). Thackeray's novel develops an ambivalent position toward dramatic performance: its heroine, the notoriously theatrical Becky Sharp, daughter of theatrical parents, is compellingly spunky and drives the novel's plot. But she is also meretricious, manipulative, and downright nasty. *Jane Eyre* disavows theatricality in the form of Rochester's former mistress, the inconstant French opera dancer Céline Varens, while valorizing a plain Jane, who insists, "I will not be your English Céline Varens" (ch. 24). These two works reveal not only how the stage provided Victorian novelists with a model for an intimate and immediate relationship with an audience but also the ambivalence that writers had toward the theater.

It has become a commonplace that British theater failed to attract the nineteenth century's strongest writers. In "Dramatic Grub Street," an article that appeared in *Household Words* on March 6, 1858, the novelist Wilkie Collins "responds" to a fictional reader's observation that British novelists do not write for the stage while, in France, the reader closes the books of "Balzac, Victor Hugo, Dumas, and Soulié" and goes to the theater to find "Balzac, Victor Hugo, Dumas, and Soulié again. The men who have been interesting and amusing me in my armchair, interesting me and amusing me once more in my stall" (Collins 1858: 265–6). Collins's dismay that the lack of pay accorded to playwrights prevented him from writing for the stage indicates his interest in writing for the theater. Michael Booth points out that "[e]ven the highest earnings of Victorian dramatists pale beside the sums paid to successful novelists" (Booth 1991: 143). Thus, when successful novelists turned to the stage, they were not motivated by financial gain. Collins's ploy of responding to a manufactured letter to the editor itself suggests the Victorian novelist's desire to address an embodied audience.

Theater historians, including George Rowell (1978) and Michael Booth (1991), emphasize the critical role of the audience in shaping Victorian theater, and it was partly this centrality of audience that both attracted and repelled novelists. Victorian novels manifest what Jonas Barish (1981) has called "the anti-theatrical prejudice," viewing art that is staged for an audience as inauthentic and corrupted by the audience's demands. But they are also "caught in the act," as Joseph Litvak (1992) puts it, in his argument that they enact theatrical performances for audiences even as they deny doing so. Adaptations of novels for the stage, revisions of plays as novels, representations of the theater in fiction, and their own stage performances allowed novelists to explore their relationship to popular reading audiences. These interactions with the theater provide us with an understanding of how novelists conceived of the place of the novel in relation to audiences, to other genres, and to Victorian culture.

Charles Dickens, the most famous and famously theatrical Victorian novelist, wrote about and for the theater, was involved with the actress Ellen Ternan, staged public readings of his novels, and, with Wilkie Collins, wrote and performed the play *The Frozen Deep*. In a speech to the Royal General Theatrical Fund on March 29, 1858, Dickens argued that "every writer of fiction, though he may not adopt the dramatic form, writes in effect for the stage." From the comic representation of Vincent Crummles's acting troupe in *Nicholas Nickleby* (1838–9) through Mr. Wopsle's overwrought performance that Pip and his friend Herbert Pocket attend in London in *Great Expectations* (1860–1), Dickens's interest in theater is evident throughout his fiction.

Although dedicated to the actor W. C. Macready, "as a slight token of admiration and regard," *Nicholas Nickleby* is not entirely admiring of playwrights. En route to Portsmouth to become a sailor, Nicholas is recruited by the theatrical manager Vincent Crummles for a variety of miscellaneous duties, including playwriting, and instructed to "introduce a real pump and two washing-tubs" because Crummles had "bought 'em cheap" (ch. 22). Dickens satirizes trends in stage "realism" in the person of Crummles, who says, "That's the London play. They look up some dresses, and properties, and have a piece written to fit them. Most of the theatres keep an author on purpose" (ch. 22). Nicholas must also write the play to accommodate the demands of various members of the company and meet a deadline of a few days. Writing, however, turns out to be translating a play from French, as was common in the period. The play that he translates is both absurdly sentimental and formulaic. When actors drop in on Nicholas in order to ensure that they have adequate parts, they do not blink at Nicholas's description: "But just as you are raising the pistol to your head, a clock strikes – ten . . . You pause, . . . you recollect to have heard a clock strike ten in your infancy. The pistol falls from your hand – you are overcome – you burst into tears, and become a virtuous and exemplary character for ever afterwards" (ch. 24). Dickens holds the playwright, as well as theatrical business structures, culpable for the state of the drama, and becomes trenchant in his criticism of "a literary gentleman . . . who had dramatised in his time two hundred and forty-seven novels as fast as they had come out – some of them faster than they had come out – and *was* a literary gentleman in consequence" (ch. 48). Michael Slater (1982) details the heated exchange that occurred between Dickens and W. T. Moncrieff, whose *Nicholas Nickleby and Poor Smike or The Victim of the Yorkshire School* opened at the Strand Theatre on May 20, 1838, before this passage appeared on June 1, 1839. In this stab at Moncrieff, Nicholas accuses a Victorian adapter:

> you take the uncompleted books of living authors, fresh from their hands, wet from the press, cut, hack, and carve them to the powers and capacities of your actors, and the capability of your theatres, finish unfinished works, hastily and crudely vamp up ideas not yet worked out by their original projector, but which have doubtless cost him many thoughtful days and sleepless nights; by a comparison of incidents and dialogue, down to the very last word he may have written a fortnight before, do your utmost to anticipate his plot – all this without his permission, and against his will; and then, to crown the whole proceeding, publish in some mean pamphlet, an unmeaning farrago of garbled extracts from his work, to which you put your name as author, with the honourable distinction annexed, of having perpetrated a hundred other outrages of the same description. Now, show me the distinction between such pilfering as this, and picking a man's pocket in the street: unless, indeed, it be, that the legislature has a regard for pocket handkerchiefs, and leaves men's brains, except when they are knocked out by violence, to take care of themselves. (ch. 48)

Yet Dickens is also satirical about critics who are nostalgic for earlier drama. Mr. Curdle, for example, says, "As an exquisite embodiment of the poet's visions, and a realisation of human intellectuality, gilding with refulgent light our dreamy moments, and laying upon a new and magic world before the mental eye, the drama is gone, perfectly gone" (ch. 24).

In addition to depicting actors, playwrights, and critics, Dickens examines the theatrical audience. In *Nicholas Nickleby*, the drama is determined by audience taste. Nicholas and the actress Miss Snevellicci secure audience members for her benefit performance by agreeing to their requests. In fact, Hablot K. Browne's illustration of "the great bespeak for Miss Snevellicci" depicts the audience as seen from the stage, rather than the action on the stage, suggesting the central importance of the audience to theatrical production. Similarly, in *Great Expectations*, Pip's description of Wopsle's *Hamlet* is devoted to recounting the running commentary provided by the audience. Pip characterizes the audience's role in the stage action: "Whenever that undecided Prince had to ask a question or state a doubt, the public helped him out with it. As for example; on the question of whether 'twas nobler in the mind to suffer, some roared yes, and some no, and some inclining to both opinions said 'toss up for it;' and quite a Debating Society arose" (ch. 31).

Novel-writing did not provide Dickens with the direct audience contact that he craved. In 1857, a year punctuated by performances of *The Frozen Deep* in his home, by a series of benefits for the family of the recently deceased playwright Douglas Jerrold, and by a performance of the play for Queen Victoria, Dickens corresponded with audience-member friends, replying to their responses. In a letter of July 8, he wishes that he were able to experience the same closeness with readers that he can with a theatrical audience, commenting on his performance of the central character:

> I cannot possibly have given you more pleasure through Richard Wardour, than you have given me through your appreciation of it. In that perpetual struggle after an expression of the truth, which is at once the pleasure and the pain of the lives of us workers of the arts, the interest of such a character to me is that it enables me, as it were, *to write a book in company* instead of in my solitary room, and to feel its effect coming freshly back upon me from the reader. With such a reader as you to send it back, it is a most fascinating exercise. (Dickens 1938: 859)

Despite the commonly held view that serial publication allowed Victorian novelists to gauge and respond to their audience's interests, Dickens experienced novel-writing as a "solitary" act. Paul Schlicke (1988) has traced how Dickens viewed popular entertainments, including the theater, as community-building events. Dickens enjoyed the collaborative nature of theatrical production, writing on 20 January 1857 about the "bond of union among all concerned" in the play (Dickens 1938: 829). After performances of *The Frozen Deep* in Manchester in August as part of the Jerrold benefit, Dickens, desperate for company, wrote to Wilkie Collins (August 29):

> Partly in the grim despair and restlessness of this subsidence from excitement, and partly for the sake of *Household Words*, I want to cast about whether you and I can go anywhere – take any tour – see anything – whereon we could write something together. Have you any idea tending to any place in the world? Will you rattle your head and see if there is any pebble in it which we could wander away and play at marbles with? We want something for *Household Words*, and I want to escape from myself. For when I *do* start up and stare myself seedily in the face, as happens to be my case at present, my blankness is inconceivable – indescribable – my misery amazing. (Dickens 1938: 873)

Dickens recognized the challenges of interacting with an audience. In his 1850 essay in *Household Words* "The Amusements of the People," he saw the performer involved in a power struggle with the audience. Discussing the Victorian spectacular theater, designed to enchant a working-class public that did not have the patience or skill to read novels, Dickens argues that theater is dependent on the audience and, thus, controlled and created by the audience's taste. Dickens, however, challenges the working-class audiences he describes in that two-part essay not only by observing them and turning them into a spectacle (as he does when he depicts such audiences in his novels), but also by urging that theater should be used for educational ends. In underscoring the theater's potential as a form of social control, Dickens exhibits a confidence in the possibility of morally influencing an audience – a confidence that pervades Victorian fiction. Although Wopsle's comment, in *Great Expectations*, that his Hamlet "is a little classic and thoughtful for them here, but they will improve, they will improve" (ch. 31), represents a naïve form of this belief, it also demonstrates the respect that Dickens had for audiences' critical abilities, since he lampoons Wopsle and the entire production.

In his 1858 *Household Words* article, Collins similarly emphasizes the audience's control over stage entertainment. The "reader" to whose letter Collins responds points out that theater managers, in contrast to publishers of novels, cater to the lowest tastes in the audience:

> I read at home *David Copperfield, The Newcomes, Jane Eyre*, and many more original authors, that delight me. I go to the theatre, and naturally want original stories by original authors, which will also delight me there. Do I get what I ask for? Yes, if I want to see an old play over again. But, if I want a new play? Why, *then* I must have the French adaptation, or the Burlesque. The publisher can understand that there are people among his customers who possess cultivated tastes, and can cater for them accordingly, when they ask for something new. The manager, in the same case, recognises no difference between me and my servant. (Collins 1858: 266)

Collins's argument that theater managers make no attempt to bring those with "cultivated tastes" back into the theater because "the increase of wealth and population, and the railway connection between London and the country, more than supply in quantity what audiences have lost in quality" (p. 269) has become the standard view of how Victorian theater was shaped by demographic and technological change. Collins goes on to execrate the lack of taste of this broad-based audience. Theater managers cater to a

> vast nightly majority . . . whose ignorant sensibility nothing can shock. Let him cast what garbage he pleases before them, the unquestioning mouths of his audience open, and snap at it. . . . If you want to find out who the people are who know nothing whatever, even by hearsay, of the progress of the literature of their own time – who have caught no vestige of any one of the ideas which are floating about before their very eyes – who are, to all social intents and purposes, as far behind the age they live in, as any people out of a lunatic asylum can be – go to a theatre, and be very careful, in doing so, to pick out the most popular performance of the day. (p. 269)

The "reader" suggests that the theater, if it sets its sights higher, can raise the expectations of its working-class audience: "It may be said, Why is my footman's taste not to be provided for? By way of answering that question, I will ask another: – Why is my footman not to have the chance of improving his taste, and making it as good as mine?" (p. 266). While Collins, like Dickens, believes that the playwright can improve audience taste, Collins also indicates that attracting a more discriminating audience is essential to improving the state of British theater. The theater became progressively more respectable over the course of the century, and, in the 1860s, began to pay playwrights more generously (Booth 1991: 144). These trends could explain why, in the 1870s, Collins began to enjoy success in adapting his own novels for the stage.

The power of the audience to shape drama led Elizabeth Barrett Browning to define poetry in opposition to the theater. The eponymous poet-heroine of the narrative poem *Aurora Leigh* (1856) explicitly comments on how she would not write for the stage because

> . . . whosoever writes good poetry,
> Looks just to art. He does not write for you
> Or me – for London or for Edinburgh;
> He will not suffer the best critic known
> To step into his sunshine of free thought
> And self-absorbed conception and exact
> An inch-long swerving of the holy lines.
> If virtue, done for popularity
> Defiles like vice, can art, for praise or hire,
> Still keep its splendour and remain pure art?
> Eschew such serfdom.
>
> (bk 5, ll. 251–61)

In contrast to poetry, drama

> Makes lower appeals, submits more menially,
> Adopts the standards of the public taste
> To chalk its height on, wears a dog-chain round
> Its regal neck, and learns to carry and fetch
> The fashions of the day to please the day,
> Fawns close on pit and boxes, who clap hands
> Commending chiefly its docility
> And humour in stage-tricks – or else indeed
> Gets hissed at, howled at, stamped at like a dog,
> Or worse, we'll say.
>
> (bk 5, ll. 269–78)

In her January 1857 review of *Aurora Leigh* in *The Westminster Review*, George Eliot weighs Barrett Browning's poem by noting the degree to which it avoids the action-oriented strategies of sensation fiction: "The *story* of 'Aurora Leigh' has no other merit than that of offering certain elements of life, and certain situations which are peculiarly fitted to call forth the writer's rich thought and experience. It has nothing either fresh or felicitous in structure or incident" (Eliot 1857: 406). Litvak argues that in *Daniel Deronda*, Eliot, mirroring her companion George Henry Lewes's criticism of the actor Salvini in *On Actors and the Art of Acting*, hierarchizes poetry, as a genre, over dramatic representation in order to criticize sensationalism, aligning her own writing with poetry rather than theater (Litvak 1992: 156–7). But even as she refused the theatricality of sensation, Eliot was not untheatrical. In addition to the theatricality of her own life, which Nina Auerbach (1986) and Rosemarie Bodenheimer (1994) have explored, Eliot's depictions of performing women suggest that the stage was important because it enabled female artists to establish relationships with public audiences, thereby playing a role in the public sphere.

In *Armgart*, a little-studied poetic drama published in 1871, Eliot focuses on the relationship between the diva opera singer Armgart and her audience. While the dramatic form of *Armgart* underscores the charismatic power of the performing woman, Eliot's novels focus on lives of women who are thwarted in their attempts to participate in public life. The novel's tendency to depict unexceptional lives is emphasized by Armgart's statement, after she has lost her talent:

> I read my lot
> As soberly as if it were a tale
> Writ by a creeping feuilletonist and called
> "The Woman's Lot: a Tale of Everyday:"
> A middling woman's, to impress the world
> With high superfluousness; her thoughts a crop
> Of chick-weed errors or of pot-herb facts,
> Smiled at like some child's drawing on a slate.
> ". . . Well, she can somewhat eke her narrow gains
> By writing, just to furnish her with gloves
> And droschkies in the rain. They print her things
> Often for charity."
>
> (sc. 5)

Eliot's elision of the literary character with which Armgart identifies and the author who writes about that character underscores how the performing woman serves as a figure for the female writer. The author Armgart describes is powerless because she has no talent. Eliot's depictions of professional theatrical women, however, demonstrate that, for talented women, interacting with an audience is an empowering alternative to a domestic life. Armgart's mentor, Leo, echoes Dickens and instructs her that, in order to gain power, she must "lift [her] audience / To see [her] vision, not trick forth a show / To please the grossest taste of grossest numbers" (sc. 1).

As a performer, Armgart differs from the female social performers in Eliot's novels, who pander to their audiences. A notable example is Gwendolen, in *Daniel Deronda*, whose "belief that to present herself in public on the stage must produce an effect such as she had been used to feel certain of in private life" is dashed by the professional musician Klesmer (ch. 23). David Marshall has demonstrated how Gwendolen's social life is an ongoing theatrical performance in which she performs, often self-consciously, expected roles (Marshall 1986: 196–8). In the social performances of

Gwendolen, Eliot reveals how little control women whose talents are limited to drawing-room entertainment are able to exercise over their audiences. While she expects to rule her husband, Gwendolen is ultimately controlled by his watchful gaze. The novel's juxtaposition of Gwendolen and the Alcharisi, Daniel's mother, contrasts the life of a woman who can perform only in social circles with that of a woman with the talent to act professionally. Because the Alcharisi, as John Stokes (1984) points out, is modeled after the French Jewish actress Rachel, Gwendolen's contemplation "on the question whether she should become an actress like Rachel" (ch. 6) demonstrates that it is the life of the Alcharisi that Gwendolen covets. Gwendolen's "questioning . . . whether she need take a husband at all – whether she could not achieve substantiality for herself and know gratified ambition without bondage" (ch. 23) reveals that her aspiration to perform on stage is motivated by the same desire for freedom voiced by the Alcharisi when she describes how pursuing a career as an actress allowed her to escape a confining domestic sphere and participate in the public world. The Alcharisi tells her son Daniel, whom she abandoned: "I cared for the wide world, and all that I could represent in it" (ch. 51).

Ultimately, Eliot emphasizes the need not only for a wide audience but for an awareness of and intimate connection with that audience. Just as the Alcharisi in *Daniel Deronda* is isolated and alone, in *Armgart* the wide scope of the performer's world leads to her inability to understand the individuals that comprise her audience. Walpurga angrily points out that the everyday performances of unexceptional women, including herself, went unnoticed by Armgart until she lost her talent:

> Ay, such a mask
> As the few born like you to easy joy,
> Cradled in privilege, take for natural
> On all the lowly faces that must look
> Upward to you! What revelation now
> Shows you the mask or gives presentiment
> Of sadness hidden?
>
>   (sc. 5)

Walpurga states that she prefers her own concealed misery to Armgart's inability to see beyond masks and sympathize with the thousands of individuals who were her audience.

Just as Eliot cautiously embraced theatricality, the sensation novels from which she distinguished her work possessed distinctions from theater, even though sensation novels were easily adapted into stage melodramas. In "Sensation Novels," an article in the May 1862 issue of *Blackwood's*, Margaret Oliphant comments on the emerging genre, which enjoyed its greatest popularity in the 1860s (see chapter 15 by Winifred Hughes in this volume). She describes a phenomenon of sensation in both the drama and the novel:

it is only natural that art and literature should, in an age which has turned to be one of events, attempt a kindred depth of effect and shock of incident. In the little reflected worlds of the novel and the drama the stimulant has acted strongly, and the result in both has been a significant and remarkable quickening of public interest. Shakespeare, even in the excitement of a new interpretation, has not crowded the waning playhouse, as has the sensation drama with its mock catastrophes; and Sir Walter [Scott] himself never deprived his readers of their lawful rest to a greater extent with one novel than Mr. Wilkie Collins has succeeded in doing with his "Woman in White." (Oliphant 1862: 565)

Sensation novelists such as Collins and Charles Reade enjoyed success as playwrights, and Mrs. Henry Wood's *East Lynne* (1861) and Mary Elizabeth Braddon's *Lady Audley's Secret* (1861–2) were tremendously popular in a variety of stage adaptations. The sensation novel was so melodramatic in its form that Adrienne Scullion, who refers to *East Lynne* as "the definitive melodrama of the late century" (Scullion 1996: lv), includes an adaptation of Wood's novel in the anthology *Female Playwrights of the Nineteenth Century*, even though the version that she presents was written by T. A. Palmer, a male playwright. It is because "the drama and sentiment of Mrs. Wood's narrative" was "fine fare for stage adaptation" that "its stage history is remarkably and spectacularly successful and, being international from the very beginning, is both extraordinary and labyrinthine." (For a detailed explanation of adaptations of the novel, including other titles those adaptations bore, see Scullion 1996: lxxiii–lxxiv.) The Palmer adaptation, as well as an earlier American version that first appeared at the Brooklyn Academy of Music on January 26, 1862 (see Bailey 1966), do not make substantial additions to the novel.

Sensation novels abound with characters who behave theatrically, and the novels themselves, with plots based on unmasking secrets, engage in theatrical concealment and display for their readers. *Lady Audley's Secret*, like many sensation novels, incorporates a theme of class mobility that lends itself to the Victorian theater's use of working-class characters as a foil to the activities of the upper-class figures. C. H. Hazelwood's 1863 adaptation of the novel opens with a dialogue between Phoebe, Lady Audley's servant, and Phoebe's coarse fiancé, Luke, whose blackmail of Lady Audley is critical to the play's action. Braddon's focus on unmasking provides an appropriate opportunity for the play to self-consciously reflect on self-representation, as it does in an exchange between Lady Audley and her husband:

Sir Michael.   My dear light-hearted wife, I don't believe you ever knew a moment's sorrow in your life.
Lady Audley.   Ah, my dear, we may read *faces* but not *hearts*.
Sir Michael.   And could I read yours, I'm sure I could see –
Lady Audley.   That which would change your opinion of me perhaps.
Sir Michael.   Not it, I warrant, for if ever the face was an index of the mind, I believe yours to be that countenance.

Lady Audley {aside}.   We may have two faces. *{aloud}* Bless you! Bless you for your
confidence!

(act 1, sc. 1)

The play's frequent use of asides underscores the ubiquity of secrets in a world of
superficial appearances.

Typical of sensation novels, *Lady Audley's Secret* is rich with incident and coincidence, which lend its plot to the incident-driven forms of stage melodrama.
Twentieth-century theater historians have noted, however, that adaptations of sensation novels did not merely follow melodramatic tastes but, in catering to "an
increasingly refined audience in the 1860s," changed Victorian drama:

> The link with the "problem play" of the 1890s is self-evident; and if [Oscar] Wilde,
> [Sir Arthur Wing] Pinero, and [Henry Arthur] Jones displayed a surer grasp of con-
> struction and subtler strain of dialogue than the journeymen who turned Miss Braddon's
> and Mrs. Wood's work into plays, they were no less dependent on the central figure of
> a "woman with a past." Lady Audley and Lady Isabel may therefore be regarded as the
> forebears of Mrs. Chevely and Mrs. Arbuthnot. (Rowell 1972: 233)

Differences between Braddon's novel and Hazelwood's stage adaptation reveal,
however, that melodramatic conventions altered the meaning of the story.

In contrast to Braddon's novel, which is structured as a detective story in which
the reader follows Robert Audley's discovery of evidence, Hazelwood's adaptation
employs melodramatic display. Rather than learning of how Lady Audley threw her
estranged husband down a well, for example, the audience witnesses the event.
Moreover, the play's use of spectacle includes the melodramatic depiction of clearly
defined good and evil; Lady Audley's asides reveal her calculated, self-serving deceit.
We learn, in the play, that she became a governess in order "to gain Sir Michael's
affections" (act 1, sc. 1). Braddon's novel, on the other hand, allows for a richer understanding of Lady Audley. Its emphasis on Robert Audley's emergence as a self-made
professional man against a backdrop of declining landed wealth calls attention to
how Helen Talboys (who becomes Lady Audley), under law, was denied the ability to
become self-supporting after being deserted by her husband. The Matrimonial Causes
Act of 1857, which would have enabled her to divorce her husband, had not yet been
passed when Helen abandoned her child in 1854 to assume a new identity, and the
Married Women's Property Bill, enabling married women to possess their own earnings, did not become law until 1870. Braddon's novel thus criticizes marriage and
property laws that governed women and provides a sympathetic view of the heroine
as a woman who was determined to survive on her own: "I looked upon this as a desertion, and I resented it bitterly – I resented it by hating the man who had left me with
no protector but a weak, tipsy father, and with a child to support. I had to work hard
for my living, and in every hour of labour – and what labour is more wearisome than
the dull slavery of a governess? – I realized a separate wrong done me by George
Talboys" (vol. 3, ch. 3).

Alexander Smith's review of the novel *No Name*, by Collins, in the *North British Review* in February 1863 demonstrates that sensation novels were expected to be more realistic than melodramas. His criticism that the novel's characters "have no representatives in the living world. Their proper place is the glare of blue lights on a stage sacred to the sensation drama," also suggests that the stage influenced Collins as a novelist (Smith 1863: 185). After initial failures, Collins began to achieve critical success adapting his own novels for the stage with *The Woman in White* in 1860, for which, despite his earlier complaints about the stage not paying well, he reaped generous financial rewards (Peters 1991: 333–4). Although the significant changes that he made to both *The Woman in White* (Peters 1991: 334) and *No Name* indicate that Collins saw the stage and the novel as distinct, Catherine Peters points out that the novella *Miss or Mrs?* and the novel *The New Magdalen* suffer because they "were written with dramatization in mind, with limited settings, exits, entrances, critical encounters between pairs of characters, and much dialogue" (Peters 1991: 337). If the sensation novel influenced the theater, the prospect of theatrical presentation also shaped sensation novels.

A letter that Collins wrote to Harper & Brothers on October 22, 1870 reflects the degree of his involvement with the stage, but not the complicated nature of that involvement: "I am, at present, occupied entirely in dramatic writing. My present state of my health does not, I am sorry to say, encourage me to confront the long-continued strain of another serial story" (Collins 1870). In an unpublished letter to W. H. Wills on November 21, 1862, most likely about *No Name*, Collins is anxious to defend his legal rights:

> Mr. Bernard is certainly giving me plenty for my money! I wish I could write chapters as fast as he writes acts. Perhaps you will kindly do the same with the MS of the play as it comes in, as was done with the dramatised version of *Great Expectations*? All I want, as you know, is my legal protection from the British Manager and Dramatist. (Collins 1862)

Even in writing his own plays, Collins was anxious to retain control over his work. Robert P. Ashley's chronicle of Collins and the American stage suggests that Collins became increasingly unwilling to allow plays to be staged without his involvement, right down to tutoring the actor playing Count Fosco in *The Woman in White* (Ashley 1954: 252). In his 1870 dealings with Augustin Daly, who produced adaptations of several of Collins's novels in New York, Collins asked that his name be removed from Daly's adaptation of *Man and Wife* because he did not want "his name linked with an adaptation over which he had no control" (Ashley 1954: 244). Long before Collins attempted to control the theatrical representation of his own work, he voiced his reluctance to rely on a theatrical troupe to present an author's work adequately. Penning a poetic prologue for a June 1849 amateur performance of Oliver Goldsmith's comedy *The Good-Natured Man*, Collins addresses the audience:

Shall I entreat you not to yawn or hiss?
Strive to delude you of your very senses,
And palm the players off on false pretences?
Are *you* an audience to be wheedled so?
Each eye before me looks an answering "No!"
Each eye assures me that I *act* aright,
Who plead not for the *actors* of to-night!
Judge them, – these people who have sent me forth; –
Judge them, my public, just by what they're worth!
If, largely stored with all they can desire
Of speeches lit with sparkling comic fire,
They can't reflect the humour of their Poet,
But mar his wit and meaning – let them know it!
Show them no mercy for their want of skill;
Yawn when you please, and hiss them – if you will!
Yet – as 'tis found in most mundane affairs
Some merit lurks innate – some merit's theirs.
Though firm resolved to leave your judgment clear,
To weigh their acting in its proper sphere,
Still in their favour somewhat I may say:
They've chosen well in choosing this night's play!
                                          (Collins 1849)

This sort of direct communication with an audience is what Collins desired. Like Dickens, he embarked on an American reading tour, although Collins was much less successful than Dickens in performing for audiences (Peters 1991: 365–6). Collins wrote for the stage to establish a connection with the audience but felt thwarted by the mediating position of actors. While acting can spoil a play, in his *Household Words* essay Collins wrote: "It is literature that makes the actor – not the actor that makes literature" (1858: 267).

Although the theater's self-consciousness about performance provided an appropriate medium for the sensation novel's patterns of deception and unmasking, it was for this reason that sensation novelist and playwright Charles Reade found the stage inadequate when he sought to establish the emotional authenticity of the heroine of his novel *Peg Woffington* (1853). Fascinated with the stage and with actresses, Reade revised the play *Masks and Faces* that he had co-authored with Tom Taylor the previous year. In a letter to the *Athenaeum* on January 15, 1853, responding to a review that questions the degree of collaboration between the two men, Reade explains:

"Peg Woffington" [the novel] was written for three reasons: – First, I was unwilling to lose altogether some matter which we had condemned as unfit for our dramatic purpose; secondly, the exigencies of the stage had, in my opinion, somewhat disturbed the natural current of our story; thirdly, it is my fate to love this dead heroine, and I wished to make her known in literature, and to persons who do not frequent the theatres.

It is partly because Peg, in Taylor and Reade's play, cannot convincingly display a genuine, unperformed self, that Reade felt compelled to revisit his fictional account of the eighteenth-century actress in a novel.

In both versions of the story, the urbane Sir Charles Pomander points out that the fact that Peg's performances off stage in the social world go undetected is evidence of her dramatic ability: "Peg is a decent actress on the boards, and a great actress off them" (act 1, sc. 1). Peg is consistently able to pass for a lady despite her lowly origins and, at one point in the plot, assumes the identity of Lady Betty Modish – a character in Colley Cibber's play *The Careless Husband* – in a social setting. Both novel and play attempt to reclaim Peg by asserting that she has an untheatrical emotional core. Peg's displays of emotion that signify her authenticity, however, remain suspect in a play that defines great acting as that which is indistinguishable from nature. The *Times* review (November 12, 1852) of the opening night of *Masks and Faces* underscores how artifice and authenticity are without meaning in a context in which everything is performed. Although the two female roles that the review describes are both performed by actresses, it lauds Mrs. Stirling for "[s]tepping gracefully from seriousness to gaiety, and [being] equally *natural* in both" as Peg, but touts "the girlish effusive manner which is very prettily *assumed* by Miss Rose Bennett in the character of Mrs. Vane" (emphasis added). Even as the review suggests that an actress, "natural" in playing another actress, can only "assume" the role of a non-theatrical woman, it points out that the "authentic" woman, Mrs. Vane, can be convincingly performed.

Reade's novel attempts to establish more firmly the genuineness of Peg's supposedly unfeigned emotions. Its omniscient narrator vouches for the authenticity of Peg's emotional signs, and an epilogue, unique to the novel, initiates her conversion from her stage life to a private life of charity and piety. The epilogue's claim that it is distinct from the "art" of the novel further expresses Reade's desire to achieve a realism that is free of convention and able to penetrate superficial performances. Reade's reclaiming of Peg also reflects the antitheatrical bias of fiction and the novel's emphasis on the real. Even before her conversion, Peg, in the novel, points out that the illusions provided by the theater are cheap substitutes for a genuine life. In the play, Peg's complaint that actresses are excluded from domestic pleasures suggests that the theater offers a modicum of consolation: "But what have we to do . . . with homes, and hearts, and firesides? Have we not the theatre, its triumphs, and full-handed thunders of applause? Who looks for hearts beneath the masks we wear?" (act 2). The novel emphasizes the shallow artifice of the theater in contrast to the real pleasures of the home: "And what have we to do with homes, or hearts, or firesides? Have we not the play-house, its paste diamonds, its paste feelings, and the loud applause of fops and sots – hearts? – beneath loads of tinsel and paint? Nonsense! The love that can go with souls to Heaven – such love for us? Nonsense!" (ch. 13).

Theater was a figure against which novelists outlined their own claims to realism. In her preface to *The Story of an African Farm* (1883), Olive Schreiner describes the stage as conventional and formulaic, in contrast to the realism of her novel. She notes

that the "stage method" of representation is satisfying to an audience, while her mode
of realism is not shaped by audience expectations:

> Human life may be painted according to two methods. There is the stage method.
> According to that each character is duly marshalled at first, and ticketed; we know with
> an immutable certainly that at the right crises each one will reappear and act his part,
> and, when the curtain falls, all will stand before it bowing. There is a sense of satisfac-
> tion in this, and completeness. But there is another method – the method of the life we
> all lead. Here nothing can be prophesied. There is a strange coming and going of feet.
> Men appear, act and re-act upon each other, and pass away. When the crisis comes the
> man who would fit it does not return. When the curtain falls no one is ready. When
> the footlights are brightest they are blown out; and what the name of the play is no one
> knows. If there sits a spectator who knows, he sits so high that the players in the gaslight
> cannot hear his breathing. Life may be painted according to either method; but the
> methods are different. The canons of criticism that bear upon the one cut cruelly upon
> the other.

The drama as an unrealistic, audience-pleasing genre is central also to George
Moore's claim to realism and construction of a hierarchy that, in ranking his own
novel above theater and sensation fiction, echoes Eliot's. In *A Mummer's Wife* (1885),
Moore contrasts his representation of the disastrous home life of an actress, the alcoholic Kate Ede, to her illusions of a theatrical life, a vision that leads her to leave her
quotidian, domestic life for an extramarital affair with an actor–manager and, ultimately, her own stage career. Moore indicts the melodramas that Kate's lover's troupe
performs, and the romantic and sensational literature that she has read. Citing C.
Haywood's 1960 article, Judith Mitchell identifies Kate as a reader of sensation fiction,
arguing that "Kate's favorite novel . . . bears a much closer resemblance to [Braddon's]
The Doctor's Wife than to Flaubert's [*Madame Bovary*]" (1987: 21). Moore cites these
works for fueling Kate's escapist imagination and preventing her from living within
the bounds of real, domestic life, which Moore's novel stakes as the territory of his
own stark realism.

   While the novel used theater to posit its own relative realism, theater became more
realistic. Allardyce Nicoll stresses nineteenth-century playwright T. W. Robertson's
role in bringing greater realism to the Victorian theater:

> The introduction of a real lamp-post and a real cab may have been thrilling; such pro-
> cedure may have made a distinct break with the conventional tradition of the past; yet
> little attempt had been made to harmonise these real objects with the spirit of the plays
> or methods of production . . . What Robertson did was to emphasize clearly the neces-
> sity of securing a complete harmony in performance, and of emphasizing what may be
> termed spiritual reality. (Nicoll 1959: 122)

Just as Moore employed the domestic life of an actress in order to claim realism,
T. W. Robertson's play *Caste* (1867) depicts the actress at home in order to under-

score a new form of realistic theater. Unlike earlier melodramas in which the action is staged in spectacular, outdoor, natural settings (the watery cave in Dion Boucicault's 1860 *The Colleen Bawn*, for example), the action of *Caste* occurs entirely in the domestic sphere, moving from the actress Esther's maiden home to her married home and back again, after she has been widowed, to her maiden home. Just as Moore contrasts the realism of his novel with sentimental fiction and melodrama, Robertson contrasts his depiction of an actress's home life with sentimental novels and plays. His heroine says, "Our courtship was so beautiful. It was like in a novel from the library, only better. You, a fine, rich, high-born gentleman, coming to our humble little house to court poor me. Do you remember the ballet you first saw me in? That was at Covent Garden. 'Jeanne la Folle; or, the Return of the Soldier'" (act 2). The melodramatic details of the play that Esther mentions – the groom's forced conscription on his wedding day, the madness of his bride when he is supposed dead, and his return (act 3) – and the unproblematic romance in the novel serve to underscore Robertson's relative realism. Although Robertson's play is also about a husband presumed dead in battle, it portrays Esther's struggle to support her son and gain acceptance from her husband's family.

Unmasking the performances of actors and actresses was a strategy that Victorian novelists repeatedly used to emphasize their own realism. The realistic novel's lack of illusion about the actor, however, is reversed in Oscar Wilde's aesthetic novel, *The Picture of Dorian Gray* (1890). Rather than employing disillusionment in order to make a claim for realism, it demonstrates how it is the real life of the actress that destroys the theatrical performance that the aesthetes adored. In Wilde's novel, the actress Sybil Vane kills herself in response to Dorian's demand that she present an aesthetic façade at the expense of what she perceives as her real self. She poisons herself with what Dorian's aesthetic mentor, Lord Henry Wotton, describes as "some dreadful thing they use at theatres. I don't know what it was, but it had either prussic acid or white lead in it. I should fancy it was prussic acid, as she seems to have died instantaneously" (ch. 8). According to John Scoffern, a chemist who wrote a series of articles in Mary Elizabeth Braddon's *Belgravia* magazine in 1867–8, white lead is a highly toxic substance "used to impart whiteness to the skin" (Scoffern 1867: 216). By killing herself, possibly with a cosmetic that contributed to the artifice of the theater, Sybil underscores the theme of the Sybil–Dorian plot: the incompatibility between lived feeling and theatrical performance. Dorian loves Sybil because she embodies theatrical roles:

> I do love her. She is everything to me in life. Night after night I go to see her play. One evening she is Rosalind, and the next evening she is Imogen. I have seen her die in the gloom of an Italian tomb, sucking the poison from her lover's lips. I have watched her wandering through the forest of Arden, disguised as a pretty boy in hose and doublet and dainty cap. She has been mad, and has come into the presence of a guilty king, and given him rue to wear, and bitter herbs to taste of. She has been innocent, and the black hands of jealousy have crushed her reed-like throat. I have seen her in every age and in

every costume. Ordinary women never appeal to one's imagination. They are limited to their century. No glamour ever transfigures them. There is no mystery in any of them . . . But an actress! How different an actress is! Harry! Why didn't you tell me that the only thing worth loving is an actress! (ch. 4)

Sybil, however, loses all talent for acting once she has experienced true love and, while her love kills her art, she employs a substance associated with theatrical illusion to kill herself.

Another *fin de siècle* novel, Robert Louis Stevenson's *The Strange Case of Dr. Jekyll and Mr. Hyde*, is a fitting place to end this consideration of the novel and the theater because of its immediate theatrical fame after publication in 1886. Many adaptations, in both Britain and the United States, vied for attention in the late 1880s, and these adaptations, which added female characters and romance plots to the male world created by Stevenson, shaped the proliferation of films that, in turn, shaped late twentieth-century popular impressions of *Jekyll and Hyde*. Recent adaptations are divided in the sources that they take as inspiration. While David Edgar's 1991 play and Valerie Martin's 1990 novel *Mary Reilly* (and its 1996 film adaptation) return to the original text in order to recast Stevenson's plot, the musical by Leslie Bricusse, Steve Cuden, and Frank Wildhorn that opened at Broadway's Plymouth Theatre on April 28, 1997 bears a stronger resemblance to Victorian theater.

Like Collins, Stevenson was both supportive of the staging of his novel and concerned about maintaining control. Thomas Sullivan's play *The Strange Case of Dr. Jekyll and Mr. Hyde*, with Richard Mansfield in the title role of both Jekyll and Hyde, opened in London at the Royal Lyceum Theatre on August 4, 1888 after touring American theaters (Geduld 1983: 193). It billed itself as the "Sole Authorized Version," in contrast to another adaptation which opened at the Opera Comique two days later with Daniel Bandman in the split lead role, and a third version which was due to open at the Theatre Royal, Croydon, but was canceled because it violated copyright laws (as reviews in the *Graphic* on August 4, 1888 and in the *Sunday Times* on July 29, 1888 reveal). Stevenson pledged his support for Sullivan's play and received royalty checks directly from Mansfield. On July 18, 1886, Stevenson wrote Sullivan, "I am sure . . . that *Jekyll* will be in good hands; and I have no doubt (as you say) that the venture can do me only good. I wish you all success in what appears to me a difficult undertaking." Stevenson also wrote to the New York *Sun* on March 12, 1888 in order to clarify a misunderstanding regarding the adaptation, stating, "The version is fully authorized by me" (Stevenson 1923).

The novel itself expresses a similar uneasiness about the theater. The subject-matter that lent itself so easily to the stage is itself a criticism of a monstrous need for coherent self-representation, since Jekyll creates Hyde in order to separate "extraneous evil" from his "just" self. Although the novel famously appears to predict its future on the screen – Utterson sees a story about Hyde in "a scroll of lighted pictures" – it characterizes the theater as a frivolous pleasure to be renounced. Utterson "was austere with himself; drank gin when he was alone, to mortify a taste for vintages; and though he enjoyed the theatre, had not crossed the doors of one for twenty years." When spoken on stage, as it was in Edgar's 1991 stage adaptation, this line underscores the uneasiness of the novel's character in finding himself in the theater.

Just as Utterson would feel awkward entering a theater and, at the same time, enjoy the pastime that he had forsworn, Victorian novelists took guilty pleasure in the stage and its audience. While some novelists grappled with concerns about audience control over art and constraints that prevented artists from connecting with their audiences, others employed the theater's audience-pleasing conventionality as a point of contrast for defining the novel's aesthetic and cultural role (or, in the case of Wilde, to embrace theatricality). The theater, as a mode of considering the relationship between artist and audience, was critical to Victorian novelists' definition of the novel as a genre and to their understandings of their own work within that genre.

REFERENCES

Ashley, Robert P. (1954), "Wilkie Collins and the American Theater," *Nineteenth-Century Fiction*, 8, 241–55.

Auerbach, Nina (1986), *Romantic Imprisonment: Women and Other Glorified Outcasts* (New York: Columbia University Press).

Bailey, J. O. (1966), *British Plays of the Nineteenth Century: An Anthology to Illustrate the Evolution of the Drama* (New York: Odyssey).

Barish, Jonas (1981), *The Antitheatrical Prejudice* (Berkeley: University of California Press).

Bodenheimer, Rosemarie (1994), *The Real Life of Mary Ann Evans: George Eliot, her Letters and Fiction* (Ithaca: Cornell University Press).

Booth, Michael R. (1991), *Theatre in the Victorian Age* (Cambridge: Cambridge University Press).

Collins, Wilkie (1849), "Prologue, written by W. Wilkie Collins, June, 1849, on the occasion of an amateur performance, (at 38, Blandford Square,) of Goldsmith's Comedy, 'The Good-Natured Man'" (New York: Pierpont Morgan Library).

Collins, Wilkie (1858), "Dramatic Grub Street: Explored in Two Letters," *Household Words*, March 6, 1858, 265–70.

Collins, Wilkie (1862), Letter to W. H. Wills, November 21, Autographs Miscellaneous English (New York: Pierpont Morgan Library).

Collins, Wilkie (1870), Letter to Harper and Brothers, October 22, Harper Collection, MA 1950, R–V (New York: Pierpont Morgan Library).

Dickens, Charles (1938), *The Letters of Charles Dickens*, ed. Walter Dexter, vol. 2 (London: Nonesuch).

[Eliot, George] (1857), Review of *Aurora Leigh*, *Westminster Review*, 67, 306–10.

Geduld, Harry M. (1983), *The Definitive Dr. Jekyll and Mr. Hyde Companion* (New York: Garland).

Haywood, C. (1960), "Flaubert, Miss Braddon, and George Moore," *Comparative Literature*, 1, 138–55.

Litvak, Joseph (1992), *Caught in the Act: Theatricality in the Nineteenth-Century English Novel* (Berkeley: University of California Press).

Marshall, David (1986), *The Figure of Theater: Shaftesbury, Defoe, Adam Smith, and George Eliot* (New York: Columbia University Press).

Mitchell, Judith (1987), "A New Perspective: Naturalism in George Moore's *A Mummer's Wife*," *Victorian Newsletter*, 71, 20–7.

Nicoll, Allardyce (1959), *Late Nineteenth Century Drama*, vol. 5 of *A History of English Drama 1660–1900*, 6 vols. (Cambridge: Cambridge University Press).

[Oliphant, Margaret] (1862), "Sensation Novels," *Blackwood's Edinburgh Magazine*, 91, 564–84.

Peters, Catherine (1991), *The King of Inventors: A Life of Wilkie Collins* (London: Secker & Warburg).

Rowell, George, ed. (1972), *Nineteenth Century Plays* (London: Oxford University Press).

Rowell, George (1978), *The Victorian Theatre: 1792–1914*, 2nd edn. (Cambridge: Cambridge University Press).

Schlicke, Paul (1988), *Dickens and Popular Entertainment* (London: Unwin Hyman). (First publ. 1985.)

Scoffern, John, MB (1867), "Cosmetics," *Belgravia*, 4, 208–16.

Scullion, Adrienne (1996), *Female Playwrights of the Nineteenth Century* (London: Dent; Rutland, Vt.: Charles E. Tuttle).

Slater, Michael (1982), "Introduction" and notes to Charles Dickens, *Nicholas Nickleby* [1839] (Harmondsworth: Penguin).

[Smith, Alexander] (1863), "Art. VI. – Novels and Novelists of the Day," *North British Review*, 38, 168–90.

Stevenson, Robert Louis (1923), *Four Letters from Robert Louis Stevenson Concerning the Dramatization of Dr. Jekyll and Mr. Hyde* (Pretoria: privately printed; Parrish Collection, Princeton University Library).

Stokes, John (1984), "Rachel's 'Terrible Beauty': An Actress among the Novelists" *English Literary History*, 51, 771–93.

FURTHER READING

Auerbach, Nina (1990), *Private Theatricals: The Lives of the Victorians* (Cambridge, Mass.: Harvard University Press).

Axton, William F. (1956), *Circle of Fire: Dickens' Vision and Style and the Popular Victorian Theater* (Lexington: University of Kentucky Press).

Brooks, Peter (1985), *The Melodramatic Imagination: Balzac, Henry James, Melodrama, and the Mode of Excess* (New York: Columbia University Press).

Carlisle, Janice (1981), *The Sense of an Audience: Dickens, Thackeray, and George Eliot at Mid-Century* (Athens: University of Georgia Press).

Franklin, J. Jeffrey (1999), *Serious Play: the Cultural Form of the Nineteenth-Century Realist Novel* (Philadelphia: University of Pennsylvania Press).

Garis, Robert (1965), *The Dickens Theatre: A Reassessment of the Novels* (Oxford: Clarendon).

Hadley, Elaine (1995), *Melodramatic Tactics: Theatricalized Dissent in the English Marketplace, 1800–1885* (Stanford: Stanford University Press).

Meisel, Martin (1983), *Realizations: Narrative, Pictorial, and Theatrical Arts in Nineteenth-Century England* (Princeton: Princeton University Press).

PART II
Forms of the Victorian Novel

13

Newgate Novel to
Detective Fiction

F. S. Schwarzbach

In the winter of 1838–9, the recently crowned British queen was reading Charles Dickens's popular new novel, *Oliver Twist*. Evidently she was much taken with it – so much so that on New Year's Day 1839 she discussed it with Lord Melbourne, the Prime Minister and her intimate companion. She spoke of "the descriptions of 'squalid vice' in it; of the accounts of starvations in the Workhouses and Schools," and a few days later she pressed him to read it. He deferentially promised to do so, and in April, he admitted he had read half of the first volume, but then apparently had stopped. The queen reports him as explaining, "It's all among Workhouses, and Coffin Makers, and Pickpockets . . . I don't like that low debasing style; it's all slang; it's just like *The Beggar's Opera*; I shouldn't think it would tend to raise morals; I don't like that low debasing view of mankind." He continued, "I don't *like* those things; I wish to avoid them. I don't like them in *reality* and therefore do not like to see them represented" (Esher 1912).

Perhaps Melbourne was concerned that his monarch – a young, unmarried woman, queen though she was – was reading such a "low" book. And, knowing of Melbourne's own reputation as having been a leading rake in his day – after a spectacularly stormy marriage to Lady Caroline Lamb, later mistress of Byron, and his own role in two well-publicized divorce cases – one might be tempted to accuse him of hypocrisy, in that his own history might well have brought a blush to any maiden's cheek. Yet Melbourne appears to have been quite sincere: in fact, since Victoria had long finished reading the novel, the damage to her must already have been done.

Rather, Melbourne was taking a view that is very typical of one strand of the seemingly never-ending Victorian public debate about crime fiction, and Victoria a view characteristic of its opposite. She would seem to be taking the part of many novelists and readers in judging that crime was an exciting subject and crime fiction (to use the modern phrase) a good "read." He argues, in company with many reviewers, clergymen, and (one suspects) parents of young women, that writing about crime and criminals has a negative effect upon morals – presumably on the morals of the lower classes, by glamorizing the life of crime, and on the morals of the upper classes, by inuring them to moral squalor.

There was some urgency to this argument about crime fiction in large part because there was (or seemed to be) so much crime about. For example, Henry Mayhew, a great compiler of extraordinary metropolitan lists, opened the fourth volume of *London Labour and the London Poor* (1861) with a classification of all of the "workers" and "non-workers" of the city, the latter category further subdivided into "those who cannot work" and "those who will not work." The second group includes vagrants and tramps, beggars, cheats, prostitutes, and thieves; within that last group, there are those who use violence, those who plunder by manual dexterity, those who plunder by stealth, and so on. The stealthy include "Drag Sneaks," "Snoozers," "Till Friskers," "Area Sneaks," "Dead Lurkers," "Snow Gatherers," and "Cat and Kitten Hunters" – the last term describing those who steal pewter and pint pots from area railings where they were left to be collected by potboys from the public houses.

A modern reader of Mayhew might be forgiven for assuming that Victorian London was in the midst of a virulent and nearly uncontrollable epidemic of crime. Of course, crime, like the middle classes, seems always to be on the up. The long Victorian era was one in which there was constant alarm in the press and Parliament about rampant criminal activity, and (as in the present time) there seemed to be no end to schemes to reform prisons and the law and to make punishment more effective. Indeed, in 1810 the Home Office had begun compiling annual statistics about crime; but the science of statistics was yet in its infancy, and how to interpret the data (and their insufficiencies) was no simple matter.

Certainly, during the long reign of Victoria many types of reported crimes went up more sharply than the overall increase of population, but such phenomena might as easily have been the result of better reporting as of an increase in villainy. As policing improved, more crimes may have been reported simply because people had more faith in the efficacy of the constabulary. Moreover, it was only in the 1870s that anything like modern policing extended to all of Britain's cities, towns, and shires. Contemporaries, no less than modern scholars, struggled amid these uncertainties to determine if the widespread perception of a crisis of crime was just that, perception, rather than actuality.

In every decade of the queen's long reign, there was a seemingly endless succession of politicians, moralists, journalists, and public servants complaining that crime was on the rise and that, unless some solution were found, civilized life as they knew it would cease utterly to be possible. (Current consensus among historians is that violent crime rates steadily decreased.) But there is no need to determine whether crime was indeed on an upward trend between the 1830s and the 1890s – what matters is that it was widely believed to be increasing, and it was commonly accepted that no one in London or the other major cities was wholly safe from robbery, fraud, or worse.

The novel is probably the most topical of all literary genres, and so one would expect that this belief in a crime "crisis" would be represented in contemporary fiction.

It is rather a challenge to try to think of a Victorian novel that does not in some way turn on criminal activity. Writers such as Dickens, Wilkie Collins, Charles Reade, or Edward Bulwer-Lytton are almost too easy to categorize in this manner, so let us begin with a novelist rarely associated with crime as a subject – George Eliot. Eliot was always considered the most serious of the bestsellers of the third quarter of the century; she was far more intellectual, for example, than Dickens, who often courted sensation. Yet in her very first novel, *Adam Bede* (1859), a woman is found guilty of child murder and sentenced to the gallows; *Silas Marner* (1861), her second, turns on a false accusation of theft and as well as a genuine theft; in *Romola* (1863) there are Tito's many crimes and his murder by Baldassare; Felix Holt in the novel of that name (1866) commits manslaughter and is sent to jail; in *Middlemarch* (1872) we have Bulstrode's murder of Raffles; and, in *Daniel Deronda* (1876) there is Grandcourt's monumental abuse of his young wife and her ambiguous involvement in his fatal drowning. So even Eliot's fiction seems to be saturated with lurid crime.

Given the emphasis in Victorian fiction on crime, and in particular on murder, it comes as something of a shock to learn that the number of executions for murder averaged only about ten a year for most of the century. This suggests that the relationship between crime – particularly murder – and the novel in this period is not simply one of reflection, in which fiction transparently displays the concerns of the day. Indeed, if that were so, one could play this "reflecting crime" game quite well at the birth of the modern English novel in the early eighteenth century: Defoe, Richardson, and Fielding provide material enough for several monographs on the subject. This effort might well lead only to the time-honored observations that depicting goodness is boring but wickedness is quite interesting, and that innocence virtually demands that a corrupter rise up to sully it. The more interesting question is not what links the Victorian obsession with crime to the long novel tradition, but what is distinct about it.

I

On the morning of May 7, 1840 Londoners awoke to read in the papers that a peer of the realm, 72-year-old Lord William Russell, had been found brutally murdered, evidently by his valet, 21-year-old Bernard François Courvoisier. Courvoisier had slit his master's throat with a straight razor: he was reported as saying that Russell had been complaining about his work, and so, dreading that he would lose his "character" and with it all chance of further employment, he murdered his employer, threw a towel over his face, rifled the room to make it appear that it had been burgled, and went to bed. But what was most shocking of all was that he had alleged in a confession (one of several) that he had been inspired to the deed by reading William Harrison Ainsworth's *Jack Sheppard* (1839–40), probably the most notorious of the Newgate novels. Courvoisier was clearly unstable, and in other confessions he said nothing about Ainsworth's novel. But this twist in the crime was too good not to be true, and it provided moralists of every stripe an occasion to condemn popular fiction about crime as glorifying the characters of criminals and simultaneously encouraging the lower orders to indulge in the same activities.

The so-called "Newgate" novel was a development of the preceding decade. Contemporaries seem to have used the name of the well-known prison to describe fiction that centered on crime, criminals, and lower-class life almost upon the appearance of the first important work in the genre, Edward Bulwer-Lytton's *Paul Clifford* (1830). Bulwer-Lytton had throughout his career the uncanny knack of writing fictions that capitalized upon a popular fashion just as it was emerging, and in *Paul Clifford* it almost seems as if he were writing a how-to manual for the would-be Newgate author. Set the story back in the previous century; open the action with spectacularly foul weather; introduce a child who is low-born and either an orphan or as good as one; have him corrupted into a life of crime; portray several thieves' dens and if possible a hideout in a cave; sprinkle the dialogue with low-life slang; add a plot twist involving shady doings by the high-born (usually, unknown to all, a near relation of the protagonist); and finish with the central character managing against all odds to display true gentlemanliness, marry an heiress, and reform on or just before the last page.

Bulwer-Lytton adds to this mix two distinctive features: his penchant for dropping into improbably high-blown style (the novel's first words – "It was a dark and stormy night" – have, thanks to Charles Shultz, become notoriously synonymous with bad writing), and his radical political agenda, which impelled him to demonstrate that "laws are of but two classes; the one makes criminals, the other punishes them." Paul Clifford is an orphan, but he has a stepmother who tries to keep him honest; despite her efforts, he is wrongly accused of a crime and unjustly imprisoned for it: thus he is *made* a criminal. Ironically, he is blessed naturally with high spirits, courage, and intelligence that might well have led to a distinguished career in, say, the military, but instead he is forced to use those gifts as a highwayman (and a very successful one he is). In a preface of 1840, Bulwer-Lytton attacked "a vicious Prison-discipline, and a sanguinary Criminal Code, – the habit of corrupting the boy by the very punishment that ought to redeem him, and then hanging the man, at the first occasion, as the easiest way of getting rid of our own blunders." In the novel, he eschews a narrow adherence to his stern moral, and allows Clifford (having been sentenced to death by his own father) to escape the gallows by transportation to America, later to be joined by his intended bride who brings with her a substantial fortune.

The great success of *Paul Clifford* was followed by that of *Eugene Aram* (1832), in which Bulwer-Lytton used a "true life" murder. A reclusive scholar, Aram falls in love with an innocent country girl, to the dismay of her cousin who loves her. The cousin's father had disappeared many years before, and in the full flush of rejection the cousin goes off to solve the riddle of the disappearance, only to discover incontrovertible evidence that his father had been murdered by Aram. Though Aram is hanged in the end, Bulwer-Lytton seems to flirt with the notion that the murder is justified: the victim is as thoroughly dissipated and wicked as a man could be, and Aram intends to use the money stolen from the dead man to support his scholarly pursuits, leading thereafter an exemplary, blameless life. Aram sees himself as the victim of a fate he cannot resist; if Bulwer-Lytton faults him at all, it is for succumbing to the power of his own rationalizations divorced from any moral sense. (Later, Bulwer-Lytton rewrote the novel, muting its subversive force by making Aram only an accomplice to the crime, not the murderer.)

It was almost inevitable that works such as these would be seen as glorifying criminals if not actually encouraging crime, but Bulwer-Lytton still kept some socially redeeming purpose visible, if only faintly. In contrast, Ainsworth's *Rookwood* (1834) had no scruples at all about glamorizing its featured criminal, the well-known highwayman Dick Turpin. The main plot of the novel concerns a complex struggle between the legitimate and (apparently) bastard heirs of the cursed Rookwood line, and Turpin is really only a minor character in this typical romance-cum-melodrama plot, but his magnificent feats of criminal derring-do, his bravery, his gentlemanly behavior toward his victims, and, above all, his horsemanship result in his stealing the show. What apparently most captivated readers was Ainsworth's recreation of Turpin's famous ride from London to York on his favorite horse, Black Bess, at the end of which the noble steed expires. The real Turpin ended his career neck in noose, but in *Rookwood*'s penultimate chapter he escapes a crowd of pursuers, one of whom exclaims that he is not sorry to see him go free, stating boldly, "He's a brave fellow, and I respect courage wherever I find it, even in a highwayman."

The popularity of these novels led to a series of attacks by reviewers, principally in *Fraser's Magazine*, whose editor, William Maginn, had been parodied ruthlessly by Bulwer-Lytton in *Paul Clifford*. Other reviewers of Bulwer-Lytton's novels, at least at first, were reasonably balanced in their judgments, though from the beginning there were comments about the propriety of criminal subjects. But Maginn went after him with both barrels, faulting him both for his liking for low subjects and for "awakening sympathy with interesting criminals . . . wasting sensibilities on the scaffold and the gaol." Ainsworth was associated with the *Fraser's* set, and so for a time he escaped their pillory, but reviewers in other journals attacked *Rookwood* in similar terms. (The Bulwer–*Fraser's* feud continued for the better part of two decades, long after Maginn left the editorship in 1836.)

The Newgate craze (and the criticism of it, so far mainly provided by *Fraser's*) might well have faded, but it was revived in the late 1830s by the appearance in the same magazine, *Bentley's Miscellany*, of two very successful crime novels. They were Dickens's *Oliver Twist* (1837–8) and Ainsworth's *Jack Sheppard* (1839–40), both illustrated brilliantly by George Cruikshank. The first reviews of Dickens's book (the first of his works to strike reviewers as a "novel" in the conventional sense) were for the most part quite favorable, and as yet none noted the Newgate connection – perhaps because the opening installments featured Swiftian satire of the Poor Law. But after that the subject matter of *Oliver Twist* is classic Newgate territory, featuring Fagin's gang of thieving street urchins, the burglar Bill Sikes and his prostitute companion, Nancy, and the stage melodrama villain, Oliver's half-brother Monks. The plot involves robberies, burglaries, murder, and enough criminal activity to fill several jails with convicts, as well as spectacular death scenes for Sikes and Fagin, the latter in Newgate itself. Despite this, it is not difficult to see why Dickens was treated differently: he is simply so much better a writer than Bulwer-Lytton or Ainsworth that it is more difficult to find a hook on which to hang sharp criticism. The association of Dickens with the Newgate school gathered strength only in the year after the novel concluded, with a review in the *Quarterly* and with Thackeray's parodic anti-Newgate novel, *Catherine*, which appeared in *Fraser's* from May 1839 to February 1840.

Jack Sheppard, which was already appearing as Thackeray wrote his anti-Newgate tract, is set in the time of the real and quite infamous thief-catcher Jonathan Wild, who appears as one of its several fiendish villains; it tells the story of two apprentices, one noble and good and the other, Jack himself, obviously headed for the gallows. The plot is difficult enough to follow, but mainly involves aristocratic foul play, and Jack himself is transformed in the course of it from a mere ruffian to a diamond in the rough. (Cruikshank's depictions of Jack show his features becoming progressively less brutish and more refined.) His escapes from several places of confinement, including Newgate itself, are the narrative high points, and they at least rise to the level of a genuine page-turner. The judgment of a writer in the *Standard* – "rubbish, balderdash, twaddle, and vulgarity" – seems apt enough now. But *Jack Sheppard* had the benefit of being dramatized several times even as it was coming out in *Bentley's*, and it was soon selling even better than had *Oliver Twist*.

The novel's success called forth a flurry of attacks, and Courvoisier's widely reported statement that he had been inspired by it seemed to be the final provocation: such a direct link between a crime novel and a criminal act seemed incontrovertible proof of the corrupting influence of Newgate fiction. The *Examiner* stated bluntly, "If ever there was a publication that deserved to be burnt by the common hangman it is *Jack Sheppard*." The book was never burned in this manner, but Dickens now felt sufficiently tarred by the Newgate brush to respond with a new preface to *Oliver Twist* early in 1841 in which he disassociates his own work from the school (meaning, it would seem, principally Ainsworth) by claiming a high moral purpose in showing the degraded lives of criminals, warts and all. Dickens's account of what he had intended in the novel must be taken with a grain of proverbial salt: his interest in social reform and his sense of his role as a leading public figure had grown in the years since he had written it, and he was eager to recast the novel as the sort of book he would have liked it to be rather than what it was. Still, the Newgate moment had passed, and though crime and criminals feature in many fictions of the late 1830s and the early 1840s (such as Frederick Marryat's astonishingly nasty *Snarleyyow, the Dog Fiend* [1837] and Dickens's own *Barnaby Rudge* [1841]), writers were unwilling to provoke firestorms of critical abuse by dwelling on low life in quite the same way. Even when Bulwer-Lytton later returned to a criminal subject in *Lucretia* (1846), he wrote not about a lower-class villain but about the high-born eponymous villainess, a poisoner whose crimes were modeled on those of the notorious and gentlemanly Thomas Wainewright.

II

Of course, the Newgate novel did not arise spontaneously as a mere fad and just as spontaneously disappear. Bulwer-Lytton, as we have noted, had that gift for locating the popular pulse, and clearly with his crime novels he touched on a genuine nerve in the reading public. Indeed, that modern critics speak of the Newgate "novel" but contemporary critics of Newgate "fiction" is an interesting point – the 1830s were a time when distinctions between various fictional forms were still fairly fluid, and the later rise to eminence of the novel had yet to occur. So while it is true that "legitimate" novels rarely turned to criminal subjects before 1830 (though there are well-known exceptions, such as William Godwin's *Caleb Williams* [1794] and James Hogg's *Confessions of a Justified Sinner* [1824]), the boundaries between "high" and "low" fiction, while certainly present in the minds of many readers, were less sharply defined than we might think. Part of the reaction against the Newgate school was based partly on the fear of downward slippage into lower literary and cultural forms. For example, *Jack Sheppard* was dramatized so often and so successfully that the Lord Chamberlain banned further stage adaptations, lest the laboring classes be incited to further murders *à la mode de* Courvoisier. Dickens too suffered the compliment of being dramatized and imitated endlessly, and several theatrical versions of *Oliver Twist* graced the boards, beginning even before the novel was completed. The imitations, sometimes with names removed from the original only by the substitution of one or two letters (e.g. *Oliver Twiss*) were definitely geared toward lower-class readers, and some were reputed to have been quite successful commercially.

Dickens touches on this popular "low" tradition of crime writing in *Oliver Twist* itself, when in chapter 20 he has Fagin provide Oliver with a book about crime in hopes that it will corrupt his so-far inviolable morals: "It was a history of the lives and trials of great criminals . . . The terrible descriptions were so real and vivid, that the sallow pages seemed to turn red with gore; and the words upon them, to be sounded in his ears, as if they were whispered, in hollow murmurs, by the spirits of the dead." Though Dickens may be acquitted of mining such tales himself, both the established authors and their downmarket competitors drew from such sources, notably the so-called *Newgate Calendar*, which from 1773, in various editions, continuations, and imitations, and under various titles, provided accounts of famous criminals and lurid crimes. An even older tradition that flourished into the 1840s was that of the broadsheets (one-page, crudely illustrated penny publications) that specialized in sensational crimes and gallows confessions. Several in the 1840s were said to have achieved sales of a million or more. There also developed in that same decade "penny dreadfuls," eight-page double-column installments of bloody melodramatic and Gothic fiction, usually with woodblock illustrations to match. The most famous of their authors was G. W. M. Reynolds, whose scintillating, violent, and prurient *Mysteries of London* began life in 1845 and ran in one form or another until 1855. Later, in the same vein, came "shilling shockers": cheap one-volume novels with the same types of lurid and sensational subjects.

Roughly at the same time, the popular press was being transformed by the advent of cheap newspapers and magazines. During the years between the French wars of the 1790s and the Reform Bill in 1832, the government had been determined to keep the prices of periodicals high, to discourage the radical press from reaching what Edmund Burke had called "the swinish multitude." However, after 1832 the duties on paper and the tax on newspapers began to fall, while printing technologies (stereo-type and the steam press) made it increasingly possible to print long runs of daily journals. The 1840s brought a flood of cheap illustrated magazines, including the long-lived *Illustrated London News*, some of which made crime reporting a regular feature. Then, in the 1850s, with the final abolition of the "knowledge" tax on the press, came cheap dailies, including the first penny paper, the *Daily Telegraph*. Their pages too were filled with details of the latest crimes, both serious and trivial.

Newgate fiction was in part a political phenomenon as well as a matter of popular appetite. The contemporary interest in crime was related to the turmoil that preceded the Reform Bill, and the newly reformed parliaments of the 1830s devoted a great deal of attention to studying and remedying the worst features of English criminal law. Gradually the number of hanging offenses was reduced; effective police forces were established in the metropolis (after 1828), and then in other cities and the coun-ties; and criminal courts and procedures were rationalized and made less inherently biased against those accused.

This was one face of reform; another, however, driven by the same urge to create administrative order and generate fiscal efficiency, led to the New Poor Law of 1834. The radical (but hardly humanitarian) principle enshrined at the heart of the new welfare system was that of "less eligibility": in other words, the workhouse should offer assistance, but conditions there must seem less favorable than those available to the lowest-paid fully employed laborer. Otherwise, the workhouse would distort the labor market, encouraging workers to lounge about at the expense of ratepayers, driving up wages artificially for those who were willing to work. Such a system might have been at least theoretically justifiable were conditions minimally decent for those employed at the bottom of the wage ladder, but they were not. The result was that the workhouses were in de facto competition with the marketplace for casual labor to provide the most miserable lodging and rations possible that might not absolutely kill their inmates (at least, not too quickly): hence the scene in Dickens's novel in which Oliver asks for more.

The demise of Newgate as pure sensation came about in part because the same interest in crime flowed into a different channel, that of social reform. The Newgate novel per se declined in the 1840s, a decade when deep economic distress and social dislocation generated a flood of fiction ostensibly devoted to social problems, often termed the "condition of England" novels (see chapter 19 by Richard Simmons in this volume). These tended to focus on the plight of the poor, usually (though not invariably) the urban poor, and upon the miserable conditions they endured in the workplace and in their homes. These fictions would seem to be quite distinct from the Newgate line in that their aim was not merely to shock but to shock with a high-minded, reformist end, namely, the improvement of the condition of the masses.

Yet the lines that divide one genre from the other are not distinct. After all, Newgate novelists had tended to justify their efforts as social realism, meant to portray the misery and horrors of the life of crime as a deterrent (though whom it would deter is not immediately evident). Moreover, the same logic applied to the social causes of criminal behavior that served as underpinning for the Newgate school – that horrifying conditions made the honest poor turn to crime – would in a different, highly politicized context seem more an argument for the radical reform of the whole political system than merely of the criminal code and the prisons.

As Raymond Williams noted in *Culture and Society* (1958), the condition of England novel also tends to follow another logic, one that leads from legitimate protest to illegitimate violence. Thus, in Elizabeth Gaskell's *Mary Barton* (1848), the reader is shown with great sympathy how impoverished (in every possible way) are the lives of factory workers in Manchester; the "hands" finally strike, but almost immediately their apparently justified protest turns to violence when the son of the leading cotton-spinner is murdered. The Newgate antecedents of Gaskell's tale now revive with a fury, as the narrative quickly becomes a novel of crime – complete with the wrongful arrest and trial of an innocent ex- and future lover of Mary and the revelation of her father, John Barton, as the perpetrator of the foul deed. So too Benjamin Disraeli's *Sybil* (1845), Dickens's *Hard Times* (1854), and Gaskell's *North and South* (1855) begin as novels sympathetic to the working man's protests, but end by condemning him for succumbing to the temptation to act for himself, taking action that inevitably is violent and illegal.

There is, however, a clear difference of mood between a novel like *Oliver Twist* and what may be the finest of the social protest novels, Dickens's *Bleak House* (1852–3). Oliver himself, though a workhouse orphan, is distinguished (as George Orwell sharply noted) by his Oxbridge accent and his moral purity, both, apparently, a function of his heredity (illegitimate though he is) rather than his environment. Though he is assailed by criminals right and left, only a very dim-witted and gullible reader would wonder seriously whether he were going to wander from the primrose path. If Oliver has an analog in *Bleak House*, it is Jo, the crossing-sweeper, a boy so ignorant that he does not even know that St. Paul's is a church, so poor that when he is given a sovereign he cannot spend it because everyone assumes he's stolen it, and so bereft of community that his relationship to his fellows is summed up best by the policeman's constant reminder to "Move on." Jo too manages to avoid a life of crime – but not a ghastly death from an epidemic disease contracted from the very air of the slum that is not so much inhabited as infested by poor wretches such as himself. Oliver ends his life in genteel rustic seclusion, surrounded by his happy family, while all the criminals who threatened him are hanged or transported; Jo dies unable to receive even the comforts of religion, while the social villains (slum landlords, lawyers, politicians, etc.) who caused his death continue to lead seemingly respectable lives in comfort.

There are other novels of the late 1840s and the 1850s that, like *Bleak House*, aim at more comprehensive attacks on society for breeding crime and criminals, including Douglas Jerrold's *St. Giles and St. James* (1845–7), Charles Kingsley's *Alton Locke* (1850), and Augustus Mayhew's *Paved with Gold* (1858), whose subtitle – *The Romance and Reality of the London Streets* – suggests its purported focus (though it falls short of the latter and declines too much into the former). These novels borrow heavily in plot details and mood from Reynolds's *Mysteries* and its many imitators, often featuring twinned lower-class and aristocratic heroes to demonstrate that the former are driven to crime and then punished severely while the latter indulge in criminal pleasures and usually go scot-free in the end. Reynolds intended that his fiction should work in the cause of his Chartist politics, but in all of these tales of London crime the atmosphere of mystery, which seems to grow from the very paving stones of the labyrinthine city streets, inevitably becomes the principal focus. This is nowhere more so than in *Bleak House* itself, where the often mysterious relationships of all of the major characters to the endless Chancery suit of Jarndyce *v.* Jarndyce become intertwined with the mystery of the family relationship of Esther Summerson, Lady Dedlock, and Nemo, as well as the mystery of the murder of lawyer Tulkinghorn.

III

The urban mystery novel spawned two related offspring in the late 1850s: the sensation novel and the detective novel. The sensation novel literally burst onto the scene with Wilkie Collins's *The Woman in White*, serialized in Dickens's new weekly, *All the Year Round*, in 1859–60. Critics coined the term to describe fiction by Collins as well as by such authors as Mary Elizabeth Braddon, Charles Reade, Sheridan Le Fanu, Mrs. Henry Wood, and even Dickens himself, that featured sensational events (bigamy, arson, murder, insanity), sudden turns of plot (shipwrecks, murdered characters reappearing, inheritances won and lost), sexual misadventures, and an atmosphere of heightened suspense and tension throughout. To be sure, Dickens had pioneered this territory (as often he did) in *Bleak House* by placing at the center of the plot Lady Dedlock's premarital affair with Captain Hawdon and by basing the character of the murderess, Hortense, on the celebrated and recently hanged Maria Manning. But it was only with a flood of such fiction starting in the early 1860s that the reviewers took note.

The sensation novel attracted its fair share of vilification from the reviewers, not merely because it traded in sex and crime, but also because such subjects were being written about by women. Wood's *East Lynne* (serialized from January 1860) contains frequent authorial apologies for its subject-matter and adulterous heroine, but not so Braddon's first great bestseller, *Lady Audley's Secret* (1862). This novel features an anti-heroine who marries bigamously, deserts her child, murders (or so she thinks) her first husband, burns down a hotel to keep her previous crimes secret, and ends her short but intense life locked in a private madhouse. This pudding of secret crimes (many of them based on recent events widely reported in the press), illicit sex, and a female villain is typical of many of Braddon's imitators. (Her first readers, no doubt, would have been more shocked to know that Braddon was involved in an adulterous "marriage" to her publisher even as she was writing.)

However, no one was better at exploiting and sensationalizing the indeterminate relationship between newspaper fact and magazine fiction than Collins. Indeed, Collins was an effective borrower of events in his own life, famously so in the *Woman in White*, the germ of which was the author's own encounter on the streets of London with a mysterious woman so dressed. In Collins's *No Name* (1862), one of the principal characters, Magdalen, reads a newspaper report of the confession of a horrible murder and finds herself fascinated by it: no wonder, since she is about to marry a man she does not love with the express purpose of driving him to his death so that she can recover from him her family's fortune, which he has inherited through a legal technicality. The import here is quite clear – bizarre crimes may be the stuff of fiction, but reality is always ready to play a trump card. Later, Magdalen's victim, in her toils, remarks, "Very strange! . . . It's like a scene in a novel – it's nothing like real life." Those terms, "novel" and "real life," were increasingly interchangeable in sensation fiction.

Collins was masterful at using the grab-bag of tricks he developed to blur the line between the realm of the novel and the realm of everyday life. While his name is most often associated with the sensation school, he had begun to incorporate crime and psychological analyses of criminal characters in his fiction as early as 1852, with his third novel (and the one that started his reputation in earnest), *Basil*. The protagonist, who declines to embarrass his ancient and wealthy family by revealing his surname, recounts in the form of an autobiography the sordid tale of his falling in love at first sight during a ride on an omnibus, proving (if nothing else) that public conveyances are dangerous places for high-minded young men who sit opposite attractive young women. Margaret Sherwin, the woman who takes his fancy, is a shopkeeper's daughter, and eventually Basil persuades himself that he has charmed her and bribed her father into consenting to their marriage. Married they soon are, but (by the father's demand) they are to live apart for a year, at the end of which Margaret runs off to an assignation with Mr. Sherwin's head clerk, Mannion, who, by the sort of coincidence to which Collins was partial, is a sworn enemy of Basil's father. Margaret dies of a fever, but Mannion, whom Basil has disfigured horribly in a fight, persecutes the hero relentlessly until he finally manages to kill himself by falling off a cliff. No one lives happily ever after.

Merely to summarize the narrative gives no real sense of anything except its creakiness. (Collins got better at plotting by watching over the shoulder of the master, Dickens, whose intimate friend he became a few years later.) But Collins manages to give the novel the aura of plausibility through the first person narration – indeed, no reader, one suspects, is as thick as Basil in failing to detect that Margaret and Mannion are in cahoots long before their intrigue is consummated. The novel also features letters between various characters, some of them quite minor, as well as first-hand accounts by others, that fill in gaps in the narrative. This was the technique Collins was to perfect in *The Moonstone* (1868), which is made up entirely of individuals' accounts of what happened to them at particular points in the history of the theft of the diamond of that name.

It is in chapter 5 of *The Moonstone* that one of the characters famously exclaims, after hearing of a conspiracy of Indians to recover the diamond, "Who ever heard the like of it – in the nineteenth century, mind; in an age of progress, and in a country which rejoices in the blessings of the British constitution?" But this is an exclamation that might just as well burst from the lips of half a dozen characters in any Collins novel from *Basil* onward; indeed, it is the signature moment of shock of every sensation novel – not that there is wickedness in the world, but that *this* particular wickedness is happening in quiet, respectable, middle-class, law-abiding England.

Collins always exploits that sense of shock that ordinary people experience at the discovery of strange, wicked behavior in their back yards. For if one of one's own business associates, friends, or even family, secretly may be a villainous vixen or murderous madman, how is one to escape? What is worse, in normal circumstances, their wickedness is wholly invisible. (How often does a character observe in a sensation novel that the criminally insane look just as normal as do you or I?) But it is well to recall that the Victorian era was one of increasing professionalization; and, almost as if this sense of hidden peril in everyday life required a specific type of professional man to emerge, one did – the detective, the professional skilled at making invisible evil stand forth in the clear light of day.

The detective appears first in the novel of urban mystery, in such figures as Nadgett in Dickens's *Martin Chuzzlewit* (1844), probably the first private eye in British fiction, and Inspector Bucket in *Bleak House*. No doubt, as the professional and efficient police forces of London and Paris came into being around midcentury, it was inevitable that detectives would find their place in fiction. But the figures who solved mysteries in many of the novels of the 1850s and 1860s most often were amateurs pressed into service because they were participants in the circumstances of the plot. Perhaps borrowing from the French (especially Emile Gaboriau), Collins in *The Moonstone* introduced Sergeant Cuff of Scotland Yard, who brings his superior powers of observation and his powerful intellect to bear upon the disappearance of the huge diamond. The crimes prominent in novels of following years are different, however – usually less violent and often involving financial or other frauds, such as those depicted in Dickens's *Our Mutual Friend* (1865), Reade's *A Wandering Heir* (1872) – based on the celebrated Tichbourne case – and Anthony Trollope's *The Way We Live Now* (1875).

From Collins's Cuff to Arthur Conan Doyle's Sherlock Holmes was a journey of only a few steps. Detectives were everywhere in bestselling fiction in the 1870s and 1880s; even Trollope, who claimed not to write sensation fiction, has one in *He Knew He Was Right* (1869). But in the 1890s, with the ascendance of Doyle and his many imitators and competitors, detective fiction dominated the magazines, especially *The Strand*, founded in 1891 and priced at only sixpence, and where most of the Holmes stories were published. Holmes appeared first in the short novel, *A Study in Scarlet*

(1887), but it took Doyle a few years to realize what a spectacular property he had invented; it was in the short stories of the following decade that Doyle's intellectual sleuth came truly into his own. The story of Doyle trying and failing to kill off Holmes so he could get on with his more serious writing is well known, but such was the public appetite for detection that the magazines were filled with a seemingly endless parade of other master investigators, private and public, many coming in pairs like Holmes and Watson, and all of them solving similar mysteries – jewel thefts, missing persons, purloined documents (often treaties of state), and, of course, murders.

IV

Why did the figure of the detective become so ubiquitous and so popular? The answer, in part, is that the continuing Victorian obsession with the detection of crime is also connected to deeply rooted anxieties about identity in a modern urban society. The fear that in the new, socially heterogeneous milieu of the modern city it becomes nearly impossible to tell the true gentleman from the impostor is a feature of urban culture as early as the Elizabethan and Jacobean period; Jonson's city comedies invariably turn on this theme. But the Victorians realized quite early on that they were living in (to borrow the title of an 1843 book by Robert Vaughan) *The Age of Great Cities*: between 1801 and 1901, the population of London grew from a million to over six and a half million; the number of English cities housing 50,000 or more inhabitants grew from five to an astonishing forty-nine. The modern urban social revolution intensified the need to find some way to mark visually the criminal element.

That the trained eye could pick out the criminal from the crowd was a recurring trope in crime fiction. For example, in *Eugene Aram* Bulwer-Lytton had observed:

> In men prone to cruelty, it has generally been remarked, that there is an animal expression strongly prevalent in the countenance . . . The bull-throat; the thick lips; the receding forehead; the fierce, restless eye, which some one or other says reminds you of the buffalo in the instant before he becomes dangerous, – are the outward tokens of the natural animal unsoftened, unenlightened, unredeemed.

That Aram himself has the noble brow and refined profile of the natural scholar does not seem to be a counter-argument to this confident assertion. The new science of phrenology, invented in the Regency period, was a similar effort to use appearance to diagnose character: it purported to discern moral and intellectual tendencies inherent in the brain by the shape of the skull. It is almost impossible to read any Victorian novel without coming across confident descriptions of one or more criminal types or moral laggards, whose shifty eyes or thick brows all but scream out their owners' true nature. Later, social Darwinist thinkers (such as the Italian criminologist Cesare Lombroso) seemed to provide a more convincing scientific rationale for identifying criminal traits, which were seen either as holdovers from primitive races or, in the

1890s, as signs of the degeneration of the race through prolific overbreeding by defective types.

As Britain's empire grew, and as London and other large cities became magnets for very obviously foreign immigrants (the Irish in the first half of the century, east European Jews in the last decades), concerns grew about the purity of the race and about the lax morals and below-par intelligence of newcomers. Just as the comfortable classes reinforced their own sense of social identity by distinguishing those on the streets who were very visibly "other," so too did the political community seek to establish a distinct English (or at times, a more catholic British) national identity. In this light, the common practice of having foreign villains in crime novels (Jews and Frenchmen were especially popular, but Indians and Chinese get served as well) begins to seem less absurd. After all, we determine our communities of whatever type not only by identifying our commonalities but by stigmatizing those who are (or seem to be, which in this process is much the same thing) different. Thus, whenever the reader comes upon a stereotypical red beard and nasal accent, its owner is marked as what he is (a Jew) and what he isn't (English), and these markers, whether they apply to Fagin in the 1830s or Svengali in George du Maurier's *Trilby* in the 1890s, suggest criminal behavior as well.

The rise of detective fiction, then, cannot be considered in isolation from the general Victorian interest in crime, and that interest in turn must be seen as related to a tangled web of social and political problems and concerns. Moreover, the fictional focus on crime betrayed an even deeper anxiety about human nature. Until fairly recently, the conventional view of Victorian society was of an era smug in the confidence of its own superiority. Progress, material and moral, was the byword. Victorians were proud of this progress, and they could adduce many evidences to support their pride: rising population, increasing wealth, growing democracy, and the world's greatest empire. Yet, as any number of commentators observed, the great towns and cities of Britain that represented the pinnacle of the nation's achievement also were hotbeds of crime, vice, and depravity – and none more so than the very heart of the empire, London.

The work of fiction that perhaps comes closest to articulating this truth and to confronting the deep social fears associated with it is Robert Louis Stevenson's *The Strange Case of Dr. Jekyll and Mr. Hyde* (1886), published virtually at the same moment as the first appearance of Sherlock Holmes. This short novel is told first from the perspective of two conservative London professional men, Lanyon and Utterson, who come to believe that a low criminal named Hyde is blackmailing their respected friend, Dr. Jekyll. Hyde is so much the primitive troglodytic criminal type that even his mere presence causes a strong reaction of revulsion in any who encounter him; soon, however, he is also linked positively to several horrible crimes, including a completely senseless murder. Then, in a stunning reversal, Jekyll's posthumous narrative reveals that he *is* Hyde; or, more accurately, that through his experiments he has concocted a potion that releases the evil side of his nature and he *becomes* Hyde. Latterly, Hyde has come to dominate the pair, and the transformations begin to happen unpredictably without the drug. The only way out for Jekyll, in the end, is suicide, taking Hyde to the grave with him.

The inescapable conclusion is that within each of us is a primitive, violent, and, if not immoral, at least amoral savage, only waiting for the right moment to escape. This conclusion is similar to the ethos of a flood of "East End" fiction in the 1880s and 1890s. The vast, densely populated, and very poor districts of London's East End had become the focus of much attention in these decades as repositories of squalor, immorality, and crime, and just as the condition of England novels of the 1840s had explored the factory districts, the new wave of social realism (influenced strongly by Emile Zola) offered "slices of life" for middle-class readers. Examples of the genre are Walter Besant's *All Sorts and Conditions of Men* (1882), George Gissing's *Demos* (1886), and Arthur Morrison's *A Child of the Jago* (1896); despite their differences, all tend to focus on crime as the inevitable result of living in such miserable conditions. No one, it would seem, can survive an East End life without at the very least declining into a life of petty crime. And, in the same manner, the race itself might be declining into a more primitive state.

The fears about the decline of civilization and the resurgence of savagery typical of both detective fiction and social realism were so pervasive and uncontrollable that they could not be confined to fictional subgenres: they surface almost everywhere in the 1890s, in such diverse texts as du Maurier's novel of bohemian life in Paris, *Trilby* (1894), and Bram Stoker's tale of horror, *Dracula* (1897), both of which were runaway successes.

Trilby begins with a loving evocation of *la vie de bohème* in the Latin Quarter of Paris. But the jolly fellowship of three British art students and Trilby, a half-Irish, half-French artist's model, disintegrates when one of them falls in love with Trilby. The notorious villain of the piece is Svengali, a mysterious Jewish musician who uses hypnotism to transform Trilby (possessed of a thrilling voice but tone-deaf) into the greatest opera singer in Europe and his lover as well. Svengali is depicted as the base, groveling representative of an inferior race, yet his power seems irresistible; though Trilby is rescued after Svengali's death, she quickly dies, as does the artist who loves her still.

If there is a message in this farrago of stereotypes, it is that the promiscuous mixing of races, particularly more primitive races from the inferior stock of eastern Europe (Svengali's original home), threatens to undermine an England proud of, but uncertain of how to sustain, its global ascendancy. In its own way, *Dracula* promotes the same message: the Transylvanian count's invasion of England is accomplished mainly through the seduction of vulnerable English women, and his goal is to create a vampire army that will conquer all of Europe.

Such concerns about the purity of blood and savagery are also central to another subgenre classic of that same decade, a magazine tale published in *Blackwood's* in 1899, not long before Queen Victoria died and the era that already bore her name came to a close. This was Joseph Conrad's *Heart of Darkness*, a would-be adventure yarn ostensibly about the misbehavior of high-minded whites set loose in the Congo on the joint missions of trading with and civilizing the natives. Despite the very different subject-matter, traces of detective fiction, particularly of Doyle's tales, are to be found throughout Conrad's narrative. Marlow, the narrator, is very much a literal-minded Dr. Watson type; Kurtz, the hero–villain, is a super-rational, Holmes-like, universal genius, larger than life; he even resembles Holmes physically. The overall narrative structure is also similar, in that the story is told after the "mystery" of Kurtz has been solved, his crimes revealed, and his punishment (extra-legal, as so often in Doyle) meted out. The tale is filled with clues, as well, that emerge slowly and often without their true significance being known at first, like the round knobs on poles that on closer examination turn out to be human skulls. There is even a red herring in the form of writing that Marlow thinks is in code, but in fact is Russian written in Cyrillic characters.

These superficial likenesses, perhaps traces of Conrad's attempts to produce commercial fiction for a magazine audience, are interesting enough; more noteworthy is the deep thematic resonance with the dark, urban milieu of the *fin de siècle* detective story. The casual reader of *Heart of Darkness* might well believe that Conrad locates savage behavior and the "heart" of human evil in the primitive jungles of equatorial Africa. Yet a reader trained to analyze clues carefully, as the inimitable Holmes himself does, might note that the savagery here is perpetrated not by the natives but only by the whites, and also that it is they who seem to lose all moral restraint. Even the cannibal crew on Marlow's rickety river steamer have more self-control than the white "pilgrims," since they resist what Marlow thinks must be a great temptation to turn their employers into dinner.

Conrad provides more than a few clues that link Africa to London: despite the exotic subject-matter, the tale opens and closes in the Thames estuary just east of the city, with the evening sky dominated by "the monstrous town" and its "lurid glare." Marlow's constant talk of "darkness" no doubt also would have recalled for contemporary readers the titles of two relatively recent bestsellers, Henry Morton Stanley's *In Darkest Africa* and "General" William Booth's *In Darkest England*, both published in 1890.

Booth plays upon Stanley's sensational reports of the Congo and the primitive tribes that inhabit it to ask if England too were not breeding its own moral pygmies. Booth relied on both his own experience founding the Salvation Army and the reports collected by Charles Booth (no relation of his) in *Labour and Life of the People* (1889), which revealed that a huge proportion of London's residents lived hopelessly far below what we would term the "poverty line," with no chance of improving their condition, and that for many of the poorest crime was an inevitable way of life. Indeed, in the heart of London's East End, General Booth found "colonies of heathens and savages" as full of vice and pagan practice as any discovered by the great African explorers.

Ironically, at the beginning of the Victorian era, it had been common as well to refer to the inhabitants of London's slums as savages, although the comparisons then made were most often not to Africans but to North American Indians (as, for example, by Dickens in *Bleak House*). Certainly, the focus of crime fiction changed dramatically over the course of Victoria's long reign, from the criminal rookeries of the Newgate novel to the elegant drawing rooms of the detective tale. Yet the pervasiveness of metaphors of savagery indicate continuing and profoundly deep anxieties about the physical and mental condition of the lower classes, about the connections between class, race, and crime, and about the efficacy of the social order to withstand assaults from "below."

REFERENCES

Esher, Viscount (1912), *The Girlhood of Queen Victoria: A Selection from Her Majesty's Diaries between the Years 1832 and 1840*, vol. 2 (London: John Murray).

Vaughan, Robert (1843), *The Age of Great Cities: or, Modern Civilization Viewed in its Relation to Intelligence, Morals, and Religion* (London: Jackson & Walford).

Williams, Raymond (1958), *Culture and Society, 1780–1950* (Harmondsworth: Penguin).

FURTHER READING

Boyle, Thomas (1989), *Black Swine in the Sewers of Hampstead: Beneath the Surface of Victorian Sensationalism* (New York: Viking).

Brantlinger, Patrick (1998), *The Reading Lesson: The Threat of Mass Literacy in Nineteenth-Century British Fiction* (Bloomington: Indiana University Press).

Collins, Philip A. (1964), *Dickens and Crime* (London: Macmillan).

Hollingsworth, Keith (1963), *The Newgate Novel, 1830–1847: Bulwer, Ainsworth, Dickens, and Thackeray* (Detroit: Wayne State University Press).

Hubin, Allen J., ed. (1994), *Crime Fiction II: A Comprehensive Bibliography, 1749–1990* (New York: Garland).

Hughes, Winifred (1980), *The Maniac in the Cellar: Sensation Novels of the 1860s* (Princeton: Princeton University Press).

Kalikoff, Beth (1986), *Murder and Moral Decay in Victorian Popular Literature* (Ann Arbor: University Microfilms International Research Press).

Leps, Marie-Christine (1992), *Apprehending the Criminal: The Production of Deviance in Nineteenth-Century Discourse* (Durham: Duke University Press).

Maxwell, Richard (1992), *The Mysteries of Paris and London* (Charlottesville: University Press of Virginia).

Miller, D. A. (1988), *The Novel and the Police* (Berkeley: University of California Press).

Most, Glenn W., and Stowe, William W., eds. (1983), *The Poetics of Murder: Detective Fiction and Literary Theory* (New York: Harcourt Brace Jovanovich).

Porter, Dennis (1981), *The Pursuit of Crime: Art and Ideology in Detective Fiction* (New Haven: Yale University Press).

Shaw, W. David (1990), *Victorians and Mystery: Crises of Representation* (Ithaca: Cornell University Press).

Thomas, Ronald R. (1999), *Detective Fiction and the Rise of Forensic Science* (Cambridge: Cambridge University Press).

Thoms, Peter (1998), *Detection and its Designs: Narrative and Power in Nineteenth-Century Detective Fiction* (Athens: Ohio University Press).

Trodd, Anthea (1989), *Domestic Crime and the Victorian Novel* (London: Macmillan).

14

The Historical Novel

John Bowen

By rights, the historical novel should be one of the glories of the Victorian age. Almost every major novelist of the period, with the exception of the Brontës, made at least one attempt on the form: not only Dickens, George Eliot, Gaskell, Thackeray, and Hardy, but also such unlikely candidates as Trollope, Gissing, Wilkie Collins, and Conan Doyle. They were supplemented by a legion of lesser names, often enormously popular in their day, including Edward Bulwer-Lytton, G. P. R. James, and William Harrison Ainsworth, as well as the more surprising figures of Walter Horatio Pater, John Henry Newman, and Cardinal Wiseman. Even the poet Swinburne was tempted to co-author a historical tale for children. No form of novel-writing in the period had more prestige, and of none were hopes higher – hopes of dignity, seriousness, and moral insight; historical novels should have flourished in what was a deeply sympathetic environment. Victorians were acutely aware of the past, and "in almost every area of Victorian intellectual life, one encounters a preoccupation with ancestry and descent, with tracing the genealogy of the present in the past, and with discovering or creating links to a formative history" (Gilmour 1993: 28). But if one important strand in nineteenth-century culture was its historicism, Victorian thought was also drawn to the search for the transcendent and that which could resist the power of time. It was in response to the conflict of those two impulses that the most important Victorian historical fiction was created.

Literature of the nineteenth century had a complex and fruitful relationship to the writing of history, which grew in the course of the century into a professionalized discipline, on the one hand drawn to literary models and forms of writing, on the other seeking to distance itself from the merely "literary." There were historians, most notably Thomas Carlyle and Thomas Babington Macaulay, who were major literary figures in their own right, and whose works were devoured by a public eager for history. Indeed, "it was to the narrative and descriptive precedents of the novel, and particularly the work of Scott, that he [Macaulay] most turned for examples of what a modern historian might accomplish" (Burrow 1981: 36). Historical novels, however, were by no means a matter for the elite. Together with the Gothic and the tale of terror, the historical novels of Walter Scott and Ainsworth were major influences on working-class and popular literature in the earlier decades of the century, and sales of historical fiction were very high: nearly 80,000 sets of Scott's Waverley novels were bought between 1829 and 1849 and, later in the century, a reprint of Charles Kingsley's *Westward Ho!* sold a remarkable half a million copies (Altick 1957: 383, 385). It is not surprising that the historical novel has recently been described as "the most successful form of the century," its "key genre" (Moretti 1999: 33, 38).

Yet for all that it was produced in such a propitious climate, much historical fiction of the period can only be judged to fail, often quite spectacularly. There are many examples of bad writing in Victorian historical novels, a disease that can affect the greatest writers as well as the least. Here, for example, is the opening to one of the most popular of earlier Victorian historical novels, Ainsworth's *Windsor Castle*:

> In the twentieth year of the reign of the right high and puissant King Henry the Eighth, namely, in 1529, on the 21st of April, and on one of the loveliest evenings that ever fell on the loveliest district in England, a fair youth, having somewhat the appearance of a page, was leaning over the terrace wall on the north side of Windsor Castle, and gazing at the magnificent scene before him.

This is by no means the worst opening to a historical novel (that honor probably belongs to Bulwer-Lytton), but in its cliché, hyperbole, and pseudo-grandeur, it epitomizes the problems so many writers experienced of creating a plausible narrative voice able easily to mediate an accurate sense of period to a modern audience. Too often, the narrators of these works lose their narrative dynamic in a stifling scholasticism or romanticization.

A passage from a more ambitious novel by a much greater novelist, George Eliot's *Romola*, shows different difficulties:

> "Good-day, Messer Domenico," said Nello to the foremost of the two visitors who entered the shop, while he nodded silently to the other. "You come as opportunely as cheese on macaroni. Ah! You are in haste – wish to be shaved without delay – *ecco!* And this is a morning when every one has grave matter on his mind. Florence orphaned – the very pivot of Italy snatched away – heaven itself at a loss what to do next. *Oimè!* Well, well; the sun is nevertheless travelling on towards dinner-time again; and, as I was saying, you come like cheese ready grated."

Eliot's attempt to create a viable, idiomatic speech for a fifteenth-century Florentine results in a radically implausible mix of Italian exclamations and stagy English. Freighted with learning, Eliot's novel is constantly undercut by its repeated failures to create credible, vivid dialogue. This problem was not Eliot's alone; indeed, the greatest difficulty of writing historical fiction is that of creating a flexible yet authentic historical idiom for periods and countries that have to be imagined, not seen or heard.

Historical novels thus often suffer by comparison with those set in a contemporary, or near-contemporary, setting; and critics of almost all persuasions and theoretical views agree that Victorian attempts at the genre are, for the most part, inert, implausible, and dull. For Raymond Williams, for example, it is in their novels of contemporary life, "rather than in the fanciful exercise of a *Romola* or *A Tale of Two Cities*, that . . . novelists learned to look, historically, at the crises of their own time" (Williams 1984: 14). More brutally, an employee of his publishers asked Anthony Trollope as he delivered the manuscript of *The Three Clerks* (1857): "I hope it's not historical, Mr Trollope? Whatever you do, don't be historical; your historical novel is not worth a damn." Only Dickens's *A Tale of Two Cities* (1859) and Robert Louis Stevenson's *Kidnapped* (1886) have lived on in popular appreciation and culture. Unlike its continental rivals, the English novel boasts no unquestioned masterpiece of historical fiction – no *War and Peace* (1869) or *Charterhouse of Parma* (1832); the writing that sought to master history has often been buried by it.

Two names dominate the story of the historical novel, both enabling and disabling their successors: Walter Scott and György [George] Lukács. At the beginning of the Victorian period, the novel was dominated, overawed almost, by the achievement of Scott, who had been, by some distance, the most successful of all novelists writing in English and had raised the novel to a new seriousness and dignity. Although Maria Edgeworth's *Castle Rackrent* (1800) has claims to be the first historical novel in English, it was Scott's *Waverley; Or 'Tis Sixty Years Since* (1815) and its many successors that formed the model for his Victorian rivals. So influential was his work that one can find the influence of no fewer than five Scott novels in Dickens's *Barnaby Rudge* (Schlicke 1999: 508), for example. The sequence of "Waverley" novels – *Waverley*, *Guy Mannering* (1816), *The Antiquary* (1816), *Old Mortality* (1816), and *Rob Roy* (1817) – formed a model of a national epic, in which the fates of Scott's often strangely passive heroes become entangled in the civil wars and conflicts of eighteenth-century Scotland, and created the seminal conjunction of "the historical fiction of the modern imperial nation-state in relation to the sentimental formation of the private individual" (Duncan 1992: 5). Scott's reputation, which remained high until the 1880s, has suffered since, and the Victorians' frequent pairing of him with Shakespeare now seems hard to understand. However, the sheer range and generic inventiveness of Scott's work ensured that his influence was omnipresent, both in the depiction of recent national history and, through *Ivanhoe* (1819), on the many varieties of Victorian medievalism. His is a definitive role: the span of two generations and of events passing beyond living memory marked in the "sixty years since" of *Waverley*'s title have almost universally been taken as the necessary aesthetic and political distance that a truly historical novel requires.

Lukács' 1955 masterpiece *The Historical Novel* performs a similar role for modern critics of the form. Historical fiction is a problematic genre without clear boundaries or identity, so that many influential accounts of the novel, such as those of Mikhail Bakhtin and Raymond Williams, almost entirely neglect it. Lukács, by contrast, argues that the ability of the novel to comprehend the scope and possibilities of human lives within their historical context is its greatest achievement, and this argument creates a powerful and strikingly coherent history of the depiction of class struggle and national self-formation in fiction through the clash of representative individuals and social forces. For Lukács, the historical novel is an essentially secular form, in which the masses play a significant role; its task is to reveal the essential and causal links between the historical setting of the novel and the events and characters depicted in it. What makes a novel historical is the "derivation of the individuality of characters from the historical particularity of their age," so that the precursors of Scott "are historical only as regards the purely external choice of theme and costume" (Lukács 1969: 15) – that is to say, not historical at all – and his successors, for the most part, purveyors of mere historical spectacle. For all its philosophical ambition and authority, then, *The Historical Novel* provides a very odd map of the historical novel in Britain. After Scott, only Thackeray is treated at any length; Dickens's historical fiction is dismissed, and Stevenson, Gaskell, and George Eliot are not even mentioned. For Lukács, the English historical novel is Scott alone, and he is not English; the rest, with the exception of Thackeray, embody a merely external use of history. Among English Victorian novels it is hard to find one that conforms to his criteria; indeed, in many cases they explicitly and self-consciously question or subvert the Hegelian assumptions that underpin Lukács's model. They are often concerned not with the secular but with the force of the transcendent in history; they establish relationships that are not dialectical or even causal; they emplot their narratives not as epic but as satire, Gothic, or romance.

Lukács, like almost all critics of the genre, composes the canon of the historical novel through a number of exclusions, of which the most important is that of the large number of novels that are set some twenty or thirty years earlier than the date at which they are written: George Eliot's *Middlemarch* (1872) centers on the events leading up the Reform Bill of 1832; Charlotte Brontë's *Shirley* (1849) is concerned with the Luddite agitation of 1811–12; Dickens's *Great Expectations* (1860) takes place between 1807 and 1826. These works, set a generation or so earlier than the time of their writing, are not usually treated as historical novels, even though they are saturated in historical understanding and sense of period. It may be that the barrier between them and historical fiction "proper" is an unnecessarily restricting one. It is certainly the case that many of the Victorians' most successful enquiries into the nature of lives lived within history take place outside historical fiction strictly defined: it seems misleading too strongly to separate off, for example, Eliot's *Adam Bede* (1859), set at the turn of the century, or Thackeray's *Vanity Fair* (1848), which finds its protagonists on the skirts (and at times in the thick) of the battle of Waterloo, from their respective authors' more properly historical *Romola* (1863) and *Henry Esmond* (1852). Indeed, the ways in which the Victorians thought of their relationship to the past are remarkably various. John Burrow has described some of the ways in which time was figured in the period as:

bounded and catastrophic or endless; and, in its most profound and least perceptible ways moving at a pace too gradual for the eye to measure directly. Also history as reassuring, as judgmental and punitive; as directional or as repetitive; as drama, plotted and portentous, or as indifferent; as governed by the same rhythms as the natural world, or as crucially distinct from it; ending with a bang; ending with a whimper; not ending. (Burrow 2000: 198)

We can detect versions of all of these very different views of time and temporal change in the novelists of the period, and this should guard us against seeking for some elusive essence or common property or (like Lukács) a "classic form" of the historical novel. On the contrary, it is a hybrid and dynamic form of writing which changes substantially over the course of the century. It borders on, is touched by, and infiltrates many other forms: romance and Gothic in particular, but also melodrama and farce, satire, romance, and tragedy. It can be close to Christian apologetics in Wiseman and Newman, to parody and pastiche in Thackeray, to autobiography in Pater's *Marius the Epicurean* (1885), to topographical and tourist literature in Ainsworth, to juvenile fiction, and indeed to historical writing proper.

There was no shortage of candidates to be Scott's heir after his death in 1832, but three figures in particular – Ainsworth, Bulwer-Lytton, and G. P. R. James – are the most important, all of them well-established and successful writers of historical romance at Victoria's accession in 1837. Edward Bulwer (later Bulwer-Lytton), already the author of the influential historical novels *Devereux* (1829), *Paul Clifford* (1830), *The Last Days of Pompeii* (1834), and *Rienzi* (1835), "was generally considered as England's leading novelist" (Sutherland 1988: 389) when the young queen came to the throne. His two properly Victorian historical novels are *The Last of the Barons* (1843) and *Harold, The Last of the Saxon Kings* (1848), set at major historical turning-points in the fifteenth and eleventh centuries respectively. Bulwer's reputation has not fared well over the years and he is probably now best known for the much-parodied beginning of *Paul Clifford* (1830), "It was a dark and stormy night . . . ," and the annual Bulwer-Lytton prize for the worst opening sentence to a novel. There is no doubting Bulwer's ambition to create something more than historical romance, but this often manifests itself in intrusive and pedantic narration, clotted with esoteric knowledge and explanatory footnotes. Although Bulwer saw clearly the formal opportunities and challenges which Scott's work had thrown up, and worked hard to be both historically accurate and relevant to contemporary life – *Harold* is in a way a "condition of England" novel – his reach almost invariably exceeds his grasp. Fettered by self-consciousness, he "seems to have been incapable . . . of letting his characters move in a world which they at least take for granted" (Sanders 1978: 52).

Bulwer is often paired with Ainsworth; but whereas Bulwer aims at creating a kind of national epic and in consequence binds his novels hand and footnote, Ainsworth is a more fluent, not to say facile, writer, with none of Bulwer's "philosophical" ambition. He was happy to blend history with Gothic and other elements. In the 1830s, he was a star of the magnitude of Dickens and in many ways a model for the younger writer, pioneering what Rosemary Mitchell has called the "picturesque history" (Mitchell 2000: 15) which dominated much of the early Victorian perception of the past. Historical fiction then existed within a wider culture in which the visual was as significant as the textual, so that Ainsworth's novels were often effectively full-scale collaborations with his illustrators, most usually George Cruikshank (1792–1878). Cruikshank, indeed, claimed the credit for the initial idea of Ainsworth's *The Tower of London* (1840), which centers on the brief reign of Lady Jane Grey, and played a very full role in its conception and execution (Patten 1996: 137–8). A copiously illustrated early edition of Ainsworth with more than a hundred illustrations integrated into the text offers a radically different reading experience from that of a later edition without pictures. At times, indeed, Ainsworth's novels resemble a hybrid of novel and tourist guide: the entire third book (some forty pages) of *Windsor Castle* is devoted to a history of the castle, without even a gesture to further the story which encloses it, and the novel has several maps, and indeed even an index.

Ainsworth is interested in the historical picturesque, but he is equally drawn to the sublime and moments of surpassing power, grandeur, or horror. Indeed, it is the moment that matters in an Ainsworth novel – a particular effect or sensation – rather than the causal links between such moments, which are often vestigial or nonexistent. His are centrifugal texts, whose different elements – topographical, historical, Gothic, supernatural – are constantly threatening to fall apart into their constituent elements, with the consequence that they often fail to provide the bare minimum of coherent characterization and plotting, "at once a triumph for the picturesque historical vision and an indication of its limitations when carried to extremes" (Mitchell 2000: 85).

Ainsworth was in many ways the most faithful of Scott's successors, producing, over a long career, forty or more historical romances long after their peak of popularity in the 1830s and early 1840s had passed; yet even his productivity yields to that of G. P. R. James, the most prolific but also the most derivative of early Victorian historical novelists, the author of countless works from *Richelieu* (1829) onwards. Capable of writing as many as three full-length novels a year, often through heavy borrowing from Scott, he remained popular and successful for several decades: the midcentury cheap reprints of the Parlour and Railway Libraries carried forty-seven different titles by James, whereas his nearest rival, Bulwer-Lytton, was represented by a mere nineteen (Simmons 1973: 9).

The most successful and interesting of the earlier attempts to follow Scott is Charles Dickens's 1840 *Barnaby Rudge*, his tale of the anti-Catholic Gordon Riots of 1780, the greatest urban riots in modern British history. Owing a good deal both to Scott and to Ainsworth in its London setting and its use of Gothic and picturesque effects, it is marked by Dickens's characteristic inventiveness and energy, as well as a more coherent plot than those of Ainsworth. Nevertheless, it was a comparative failure both critically and with the public, and Dickens did not attempt historical fiction again until nearly two decades later, with *A Tale of Two Cities* (1859), which yoked the structures of stage melodrama to the events of the French Revolution to provide in the death of the redeemed Sydney Carton the best-known and most often-parodied ending in Victorian fiction. At the heart of *A Tale of Two Cities*, or rather beneath its layers of lost and embedded narratives, are the figure and voice of a nameless woman who has been abducted and, it seems, raped. She has been so traumatized by these terrible experiences, which follow the manslaughter of her husband, that she can speak only three phrases which are hysterically and endlessly repeated. The revelation of this incident, which is the inaugurating moment of the events that the novel narrates, occurs quite late in the book. We learn of the nameless woman neither through her own voice nor through that of the omniscient narrator, but from the written testimony of Dr Manette, set down during his long imprisonment in the Bastille. She dies shortly afterwards, and plays no active or direct part in the events of the book; yet the novel would not exist without her, for if she had not been abducted, then the entire sequence of events that follow would not have taken place and her sister Mme. Defarge, the embodiment of revolutionary terror, would not have been so vengeful, so long have implacably opposed the aristocracy or so long plotted their destruction. Within the terms of the novel, without this near-silent woman's abduction and rape, the French Revolution would not have taken place.

The greatest influence on Dickens's view of the public and political events of revolutionary France was undoubtedly the work of Carlyle, the dominant voice of Victorian history in its early decades. Indeed, Dickens once said that he was reading Carlyle's *The History of the French Revolution* (1837) – a book which Oscar Wilde later called "the greatest novel of the nineteenth century" – "for the 500th time." Other writers were less sympathetic to Carlyle's convulsive and apocalyptic view of history. Charles Reade, for example, explicitly repudiated Carlyle's emphasis on the importance of the heroic, world-shaking individual in his tale of "men and women of no note [who] do great deeds, speak great words, and suffer noble sorrows," in the now comparatively neglected *The Cloister and the Hearth* (1861), which was for many Victorians one of the century's great fictional achievements and its most important historical novel. It is a lengthy, meandering story of the conflicting claims of domesticity (the hearth) and the religious life (the cloister) in the lives of Gerard Eliassoen and Margaret Brandt, the parents of the great humanist scholar Erasmus (1466?–1536). Like George Eliot's *Romola*, which began publication the following year, Reade's story is concerned with the epochal cultural and social changes in Europe that the later nineteenth century would call the Renaissance; its mixture of sensation and sententiousness has not worn well, and the novel lacks the conceptual and narrative coherence that its topic deserved. Equally ambitious and unsuccessful was Anthony Trollope's third novel, *La Vendée* (1850), which, like Balzac's earlier *Les Chouans* (1829), concerns the royalist uprising or counter-revolution in western France in 1793. Trollope's most neglected work, it is a belated homage to Scott (who had translated its major source), but, like many novels of the period with foreign or exotic settings, it is overly dependent on its sources and fails to connect in a dynamic way the private fates of the novel with the revolutionary events of its setting.

Like Reade, William Makepeace Thackeray also deeply distrusted Carlyle's emphasis on history as "the biography of great men," but was much more successful in creating a counter-vision of ironic narration. Indeed, Thackeray was in many ways the most profoundly engaged and intelligent of all Victorian writers of historical fiction: *The Memoirs of Barry Lyndon* (1844), *The Virginians* (1857–9), *Henry Esmond* (1852), and even *Vanity Fair* (1848) are all in one sense or another historical novels, each of which deeply ironizes both the events it deals with and the motives and actions of its characters. From the beginning of his career, Thackeray marked his distance from many of the dominant Victorian discourses of history. In an early review essay, for example, he wrote with characteristically melancholy insight:

> the dignity of history sadly diminishes as we grow better acquainted with the material which composes it. In our orthodox history-books the characters move on as a gaudy playhouse procession, a glittering pageant of kings and warriors and stately ladies . . . Only he who sits very near to the stage can discover of what stuff the spectacle is made. The kings are poor creatures, taken from the dregs of the company; the noble knights are dirty dwarfs in tin-foil; the fair ladies are painted hags with cracked feathers and soiled trains. One wonders how gas and distance could have rendered them so enchanting. (quoted in Mitchell 2000: 202)

This use of a theatrical metaphor to undermine the picturesque and heroic in history was followed by his very funny parodies in *Punch* of Scott, Bulwer ("Sawedwadge-orgeearllittnbulwig"), and G. P. R. James, which marked Thackeray's distance from their grandiloquence and pretension. His own fiction is saturated with an irony that both reflects and anticipates a wider cultural change as the century progressed, from "the representation of history in terms of eventfulness, even of a catastrophic, apocalyptic kind, to the subtler representation of it as a kind of sedimentary process, whose longer-term significance . . . could only be perceived retrospectively and therefore necessarily ironically" (Burrow 2000: 198). *Barry Lyndon*, for example, is cast in the form of the autobiography of an eighteenth-century Irish scapegrace and bully narrating, as he dies in the Fleet Prison, his adventures in the Seven Years War. He is a gambler, deserter, and spy who nevertheless insists throughout his deeply unreliable and darkly ironic narration on his heroism, nobility and valor.

It is another fictional self-portrait, though, that of *Henry Esmond* (1852), which is Thackeray's historical masterpiece. Set in the late seventeenth and early eighteenth centuries, from the time of the Glorious Revolution to that of the Young Pretender, it subverts many of the conventions of eighteenth- and early-nineteenth-century fiction: significantly, there are no illustrations to the book, but its material form is that of an authentic eighteenth-century memoir, complete with period typeface and spelling. Its opening pages set a tone of sophisticated anti-heroism:

> I have seen in his very old age and decrepitude the old French King Lewis the Four-teenth, the type and model of king-hood — who never moved but to measure, who lived and died according to the rules of his Court-marshal, persisting in acting through life

the part of Hero; and, divested of poetry, this was but a little wrinkled old man, pock-marked, and with a great periwig and red heels to make him look tall – a hero for a book if you like . . . but what more than a man for Madame Maintenon, or the barber who shaved him, or Monsieur Fagon, his surgeon?

Thackeray, unlike almost all his contemporaries, did not try to reinforce the authority of fiction with that of history, but to subvert and relativize the reliability of both, the effect being not to give the novel greater reality and truthfulness but, as J. Hillis Miller puts it, "to make historical narrative seem phantasmal, fictional" (Miller 1982: 108). Playing off the very different truths and deceptions of history and of memory, both in Esmond's strangely Oedipally inflected romance and the political vicissitudes of England, this work has strong claims to be the most successful of all Victorian historical novels.

Henry Esmond's successor *The Virginians* (1859) continued the story of the Esmond family in the American revolutionary wars, but has found far fewer admirers. Indeed, Britain's imperial history figures more rarely in fiction than might be expected, although there are a number of interesting Irish historical novels, including several "National Tales" published in the early decades of the century, some works set in the Cromwellian period, and a spate of writing later in the century commemorating the 1798 rebellion. The most important group of novels, however, concerned with the history of territory then under British sovereignty are those of Philip Meadows Taylor, best known for his *Confessions of a Thug* (1839). His historical novels set in India deal with major military turning-points in the history of India: *Tippoo Sultaun* (1840) with the late eighteenth-century Mysore wars; *Tara, A Mahratta Tale* (1863) with the imposition of Mahratta rule in the mid-seventeenth century; *Ralph Darnell* (1865) with the conquests of Clive of India in the 1750s; and the posthumous *A Noble Queen* (1878) with the late-seventeenth-century siege of Ahmednagar. More typical of historical fiction concerned with the Empire, however, is Kingsley's *Westward Ho!* (1855) which, in its tale of Elizabethan brutality and derring-do, as Patrick Brantlinger observes, "offers as its central themes the racist and sexist tautology that informs much writing about the Empire throughout the nineteenth century: the English are on top of the world because they are English" (Brantlinger 1988: 44).

National identity in Britain, as Linda Colley has argued, is profoundly linked to religious identity (Colley 1996). The re-establishment of the Roman Catholic hierarchy in England in 1850 occasioned a spate of public controversy which was in part played out in historical fiction. The most important of this group of novels are Kingsley's *Hypatia, Or New Foes with an Old Face* (1853), set in early fifth-century Alexandria; John Henry Newman's *Callista, A Sketch of the Third Century* (1856); and Nicholas Wiseman's best-selling *Fabiola, or The Church of the Catacombs* (1854), set in fourth-century Rome. Kingsley's *Hypatia* brings together four important strands of historical fiction of this period: Romans, religion, race, and sex. There had been many novels set in ancient times since Bulwer's success with *The Last Days of Pompeii* in 1834, and both Wilkie Collins and George Gissing, for example, were tempted to write uncharacteristic works concerned with the fall of the Roman Empire: Collins's laborious *Antonina, or The Fall of Rome* (1850), set in the fifth century as the Gothic hordes descend on Rome, and Gissing's unfinished *Veranilda* (1903), set a century or so later. The growing religious controversy of the 1850s following the "Papal Aggression" scares of that decade gave the history of the early church a particularly controversial significance, in which the nineteenth century could find suggestive analogies for some of its own most pressing spiritual concerns: religious and sectarian difference, celibacy, vocation and conversion, as well as the overarching question of the relation of the historical and the transcendent. Rome also possessed, like Britain, a great and ethnically diverse empire, and Kingsley's *Hypatia*, like Collins's *Antonina*, is centrally concerned with racial difference and the opposing qualities embodied in the conflicts of the Romans, Greeks, Jews, and wandering Goths of the story. More surprisingly today, perhaps, is how bold *Hypatia* is in its willingness to link religious insight and erotic experience, a tendency which becomes, as Stephen Prickett has argued, "one of the most powerful – indeed, potent – images of nineteenth century fiction" (Prickett 1996: 225): Kingsley's violent and sensual story climaxes with Hypatia, a beautiful young neoplatonist philosopher, stripped naked and torn to pieces by monks under an enormous image of Christ.

The immediate response to Kingsley's polemically anti-Catholic novel was the founding by Cardinal Wiseman of the Catholic Popular Library; its first publication was Wiseman's own *Fabiola*, which had great international success. Like Kingsley's, it is a violent book, although with none of his opponent's eroticism. Set at the time of the persecutions of the church before the reign of the Emperor Constantine, it depicts many gruesome martyrdoms, which are described in a simultaneously detached and detailed manner. More important than Wiseman's own rather pedantic novel was his success in persuading Newman, the most important religious thinker of the century, to follow *Fabiola* with his own second novel, *Callista*. It is, like Wiseman's and Kingsley's novels and indeed George Eliot's slightly later *Romola*, a story of the spiritual journey of a beautiful young woman; in *Callista*'s case, the conversion and eventual martyrdom of a Greek maker of pagan images living in the third century. Newman's novel has clear continuities with his theological and other writings, both in its deep knowledge of the life of the early church and in its essentially historicist view of Christian revelation. Austere in its doctrine, but written with a dryly donnish humor, it makes suggestive analogies between the spiritual and public life of ancient north Africa and that of the nineteenth century. At the heart of the story is the essentially solitary tale of Callista's complex and lengthy process of conversion, written with a sympathy inflected throughout by Newman's own long travail of faith.

Steeped in the same questions – of religious faith, vocation, and self-sacrifice – is the most ambitious and challenging of all Victorian historical novels, George Eliot's *Romola*. When it appeared in 1863, Eliot was already the author of three works set in the eighteenth century: *Scenes of Clerical Life* (1858), *Adam Bede* (1859), and *Silas Marner* (1861); but these, despite their setting, express relatively little sense of

historical change. As John Goode remarks of *Adam Bede*, "there is very little sense of
the historical actuality of the vast upheavals in rural life which typify the 1790s. The
suggestions of historical change are marginal . . . Time itself, in fact, is primarily a
cyclical process" (Goode 1995: 45). Set in late fourteenth-century Florence, *Romola*
charts the movement of its eponymous heroine, a young and beautiful Florentine
woman, to spiritual enlightenment following her marriage to, and betrayal by, her
husband, the selfish and corrupt Tito Melema. Burdened with the results of Eliot's
formidable drive for historical accuracy, the novel has a complex relation to Victorian
understandings of historical process and to Eliot's own social thought. Eliot sees the
private life of the book as linked to its public events in an essentially organic way:
"as in the tree that bears a myriad of blossoms, each single bud with its fruit is dependent on the primary circulation of the sap, so the fortunes of Tito and Romola were
dependent on certain grand political and social conditions which made an epoch in
the history of Italy . . ." By homology, both political and personal, the novel is concerned with the relation between obedience to and rebellion against the culture of the
past. Romola's father Bardo, like the Catholic Church in the book, is blindly buried
in the past, whereas her immoral husband Tito breaks free from any historical obligation into a self-asserting egotism, which is paralleled on a public level by the fanat-
ical rebellion of Savonarola against the ecclesiastical hierarchy; these conflicts are
explored in Romola's internal divisions of loyalties and needs. Yet, for all the novel's
ambition and at times power, Eliot seems unable to create a historically grounded and
fictionally credible solution to the ethical and historiographical questions the novel
sets itself; its later chapters, in which Romola, free finally of the book's literal and figurative fathers, becomes a "Visible Madonna" to the inhabitants of a plague-stricken
village, leave Florence altogether for a dream-like state and place, seemingly outside
time.

Eliot's great admirer, Elizabeth Gaskell, whose *Sylvia's Lovers* was published in the
same year as *Romola* (1863), was also deeply concerned with the relationship between
the demands of personal desire and those of public duty. This tale of the impact of
the press-gang on a remote North Yorkshire fishing town and the conflicting claims
of the two lovers of the title for the hand of the novel's heroine takes great care with
its provincial location and the creation of a historically and linguistically accurate
world within which its characters can live. It anticipates Hardy's *The Trumpet Major*
in its use of a regional setting to focus a wider history; but whereas Hardy finds
comedy and even farce in his tale of the Napoleonic Wars, Gaskell's is a much bleaker
novel, which she called "the saddest story I ever wrote." Gaskell is concerned not with
the grand historical and political events of the period but with their impact on provincial, lower-class lives; Sylvia is the daughter of a small farmer, her lovers a "specksioneer" or harpooner on a whaling ship and an assistant in a drapery shop. Public
events impinge only as loss and suffering: Charley the specksioneer is press-ganged,
Philip the draper volunteers for war and is wounded to the point of being unrecognizable by his wife, and Sylvia's father is hanged for his attack on the press-gang. The
most important scene of public military history is set at the siege of Acre, at which,

as in Dickens's *A Tale of Two Cities*, one lover heroically saves the life of his rival. This chapter is written in a style that contrasts sharply with the detailed realism of the bulk of the book, drawing on melodrama and exoticism in its characterization of the essentially male romance of war. Although the chapter is often thought to be an artistic failure, Gaskell may be here attempting an unsettling of public history through a consciously artificial and distancing style which punctures the narrative conventions of the novel, just as the violence of war has ruptured the continuities of its characters' lives.

Sylvia's Lovers appeared at the peak of the production of historical fiction in the 1850s and 1860s, decades which also saw the appearance of *Henry Esmond*, *The Virginians*, *Callista*, *Romola*, *Antonina*, *Fabiola*, *The Cloister and the Hearth*, *La Vendée*, *Westward Ho!*, *A Tale of Two Cities*, and a host of lesser works. This spate came to an end with the publication of Kingsley's *Hereward the Wake* in 1865, after which, with the exception of R. D. Blackmore's Exmoor romance *Lorna Doone* (1869), no significant historical novels appeared until the 1880s, when they were revived in a very different form, as "philosophical romance." The first of these came from the most surprising of sources: the invalid son of a Birmingham chemical manufacturer, J. H. Shorthouse (1834–1903), who in 1880 privately published his *John Inglesant* after its rejection by a number of publishing houses. This quietly authoritative study of a secular saint caught in the religious and military conflicts of the English Civil Wars avoids many of the faults of its precursors by focusing much of the novel through Inglesant's consciousness. Despite the risky strategy of including cameo appearances by John Milton, Thomas Hobbes, Charles I, and a host of lesser seventeenth-century luminaries, Shorthouse nevertheless creates a plausible sense of period and character, achieved at least in part through the incorporation (or plagiarism) of authentic seventeenth-century sources. Together with Thackeray's *Henry Esmond*, it is the most successful of Victorian novels set in the key decades of national self-formation of the seventeenth century, registering with a deep inwardness the claims of religious conscience in an era of bloody civil and military conflict.

The most significant philosophical romance of the period was Walter Pater's *Marius the Epicurean* (1885), which resembles the novels of Newman and Wiseman in its concern with spiritual life at the time of transition between epochs of faith, yet differs strikingly from them. Although Marius, a second-century Roman torn between Christianity and the pagan belief of his forebears, is treated after his death as a Christian and a martyr, the novel is studiedly unclear as to whether either status is deserved. It is, by any standards, a very strange historical novel with little interest in plot, dialogue, or, outside of Marius himself, characterization. Formally and generically hybrid, its narration is punctuated by explanations, historical glosses and "anachronistic" references to later events and knowledge. Yet such interruptions are integral to Pater's historical vision, for his stories are always "the narration of an interruption, a destructive interpolation in a closed society . . . when something ancient comes back, repeats itself, is reborn out of its time" (Miller 1998: 183). *Marius* multiplies the temporal layers and perspectives of its story in a consciously antidialectical view of history, which constantly reveals the labor of scholarship on which its narrative rests. Depicting as it does the contemplative life of a passive hero in an undramatic history, it disturbingly enacts a point-by-point reversal of what had been the distinguishing marks of earlier Victorian historical novels.

In contrast to these more hieratic works is William Hale White's ("Mark Rutherford"'s) *The Revolution in Tanner's Lane* (1887), the story of the involvement of a Nonconformist printer, Zachariah Coleman, in the radical politics of the early nineteenth century through his friendship with the French revolutionary exiles Jean Caillaud and his daughter Pauline. Following the assassination (possibly by Pauline) of a government spy, the first part of the novel culminates in the Manchester "Blanketeers" march of 1817 and the subsequent hanging of Caillaud and imprisonment of Coleman. The novel then suddenly shifts to the 1840s and the story of Coleman's and his daughter's involvement in a "revolution" in the provincial Dissenting chapel of Tanner's Lane. In a limpid and understated manner, eschewing metaphor and figurative language, White writes a kind of "history from below," sympathetically focusing on the struggles of radical Dissenters and republicans in order to understand why there was no revolutionary upheaval in Britain in the earlier nineteenth century. Formally innovative, the novel creates a complex set of analogies between the two seemingly unconnected parts of the book as White, anticipating later historians, explores the relation between English Dissenting radicalism and the political inheritance of the French Revolution. It is probably the most underestimated of all Victorian historical novels.

Following the lead of Gaskell and of Blackmore's *Lorna Doone*, the 1880s also saw the rise of the provincial historical novel, of which the most important example is Thomas Hardy's *The Trumpet Major and Robert his Brother* (1880). It is that most unusual of things, a funny Hardy novel, in which the forces that in his work are usually destructive of human life and happiness, in particular sexual fickleness and unfaithfulness, have an essentially comic resolution. There is little attempt to establish causal links between the historical events and the lives of the characters, for historical process is here seen as a mass of contingencies and chances. History in the shape of the press-gang may come knocking on the door, but Bob (the Trumpet Major's brother) promptly escapes through the window, although he then immediately volunteers for what he has just been trying to evade. The novel shows little interest in the grand narratives of political history, creating a world of inconsistency and chance, in which all erotic and affective relationships are unstable and shifting. There could not be a less Lukácsian or Hegelian view of history, for Hardy will not allow any historicism, any sense of development or pattern of change, to shape his story: "History," he wrote in a notebook, "is rather a stream than a tree. There is nothing organic in its shape, nothing systematic in its development." *The Trumpet Major* is a quietly moving tale, with a subdued pathos as we are periodically reminded of the deaths that await these characters seemingly so vividly alive. History figures as oblivion, the dark ground against which the comedy of the story is played out. For all its charm and humor, it is an essentially elegiac novel, with one of Hardy's most poignant endings in which the Trumpet Major leaves the story "with a farewell smile on the doorstone, backed by the black night . . . and went off to blow his trumpet till silenced for ever upon one of the bloody battlefields of Spain."

It is Robert Louis Stevenson, however, who is the most important writer of historical fiction of the eighties and nineties. We see in Stevenson's work a reprise of many of the central concerns and tropes of his forerunners in its interest in the force of the transcendent and spiritual within the material world, in Scottish history and its relationship to the dispersed and unstable national identity that is "Britishness," in historical conflict as familial rivalry, in the eruption of Gothic material within the essentially realist claims of history, in empire and the creation of adventure stories for boys and young men. The unfinished *Weir of Hermiston* (1888) is the most directly Scott-like in its opening evocation of the Scottish Covenanters, its late eighteenth-century Edinburgh and provincial Scottish settings, and its mediocre hero, Archie Weir, trapped under the crushing weight of his father's legal and paternal authority. But it is *The Master of Ballantrae: A Winter's Tale* (1889) that is Stevenson's great achievement in this field. Set in the Jacobite rebellion of 1745, the novel begins with an aristocratic Scottish family fatefully deciding to divide its political loyalty to safeguard the future of the house: the Master of Ballantrae, James Durie, is sent to support the Stuart pretender while his brother Henry stays at home professing loyalty to the Hanoverian crown. James is thought to have been killed, but, as in *Sylvia's Lovers*, the supposedly dead man returns, bringing into being a set of conflicts – erotic, fraternal, political, and ultimately metaphysical – resolvable only by death. Revitalizing historical fiction with the Gothic elements it had increasingly tried to eschew, *The Master of Ballantrae* plays out its manichean conflicts on a progressively widening stage, from Scotland via India and Rome to the wilderness of North America. It is a fitting end to the Victorian historical novel, at once a summary of much that precedes it and an extension into new and dangerous ground.

The 1890s also saw the growth of future-oriented fiction, such as William Morris's *News from Nowhere* (1891) and H. G. Wells's *The Time Machine* (1895), which explored in a different temporal dimension many of the same questions of historical change and development that were at the heart of historical fiction (see chapter 21 by Patrick Brantlinger in this volume). The first decade of the twentieth century saw the appearance of Rudyard Kipling's remarkable *Puck of Pook's Hill* (1906) and *Rewards and Fairies* (1910), which shaped in important ways many twentieth-century acts of historical imagining. But it is worth pausing to register the sheer scale of Victorian achievement in this area. Jonathan Nield's still useful 1902 *Guide to the Best Historical Novels and Tales*, for example, lists over a thousand Victorian historical novels, set in every century from the first to the nineteenth, and ranging in subject-matter from seventeenth-century Dutch colonists in America to the persecution of the Albigenses – and this is a mere selection from a much vaster body of work. Nield's list displays in graphic form the sheer energy and variety of Victorian interest in the past, including the Victorians' determination to find in history analogies and significance for their own time. It is true, of course, that since Nield's work the historical novel has suffered: first by being overpraised and overvalued, through what John Sutherland calls its "pernicious respectability . . . for school study and examination" (Thackeray 1970: 514), and then from a later condescension. It is also undoubtedly true that there is a great deal of bad historical fiction. But we should not be too hasty to condemn writing that does not yield readily to us, for its resistance offers a salutary reminder of the Victorians' distance from ourselves. When we read Victorian novels, we are often misled into thinking how close that age is to our own; but when we encounter historical fiction of the period we recognize something equally powerful: the nineteenth century's strange otherness, the mark of its and our own historicity. The last great Victorian historical novel, Stevenson's *The Master of Ballantrae*, ends with buried treasure and someone thought to be dead who might in fact be more alive than he seems. It is an appropriate metaphor for the historical novel.

REFERENCES

Altick, Richard D. (1957), *The English Common Reader: A Social History of the Mass Reading Public* (Chicago: University of Chicago Press).

Brantlinger, Patrick (1988), *Rule of Darkness: British Literature and Imperialism, 1830–1914* (Ithaca: Cornell University Press).

Burrow, John (1981), *A Liberal Descent: Victorian Historians and the English Past* (Cambridge: Cambridge University Press).

Burrow, John (2000), "Images of Time: From Carlylean Vulcanism to Sedimentary Gradualism," in Stefan Collini, Richard Whatmore and Brian Young, eds., *History, Religion, and Culture: British Intellectual History 1750–1950* (Cambridge: Cambridge University Press).

Colley, Linda (1996), *Britons: Forging the Nation 1707–1837* (London: Vintage).

Duncan, Ian (1992), *Modern Romance and Transformations of the Novel: The Gothic, Scott, Dickens* (Cambridge: Cambridge University Press).

Gilmour, Robin (1993), *The Victorian Period: The Intellectual and Cultural Context of English Literature 1830–1880* (London and New York: Longman).

Goode, John (1995), "*Adam Bede*," in Charles Swann, ed., *Collected Essays of John Goode* (Keele: Keele University Press). (First publ. in Barbara Hardy, ed., *Critical Essays on George Eliot*, London: Routledge & Kegan Paul, 1970.)

Lukács, George (1969), *The Historical Novel* (Harmondsworth: Penguin). (First publ. 1955.)

Miller, J. Hillis (1982), *Fiction and Repetition: Seven English Novels* (Cambridge, Mass: Harvard University Press).

Miller, J. Hillis (1998), *Reading Narrative* (Norman: University of Oklahoma Press).

Mitchell, Rosemary (2000), *Picturing the Past: English History in Text and Image* (Oxford: Clarendon).

Moretti, Franco (1999), *An Atlas of the European Novel 1800–1900* (London: Verso).

Nield, Jonathan (1902), *A Guide to the Best Historical Novels and Tales* (London: Elkin Matthews).

Patten, Robert (1996), *George Cruikshank: His Life, Times, and Art*, vol. 2: *1835–1878* (Cambridge: Lutterworth).

Prickett, Stephen (1996), *Origins of Narrative: the Romantic Appropriation of the Bible* (Cambridge: Cambridge University Press).

Sanders, Andrew (1978), *The English Historical Novel 1840–1880* (London: Macmillan).

Schlicke, Paul, ed. (1999), *The Oxford Reader's Companion to Dickens* (Oxford: Oxford University Press).

Simmons, James C. (1973), *The Novelist as Historian: Essays on the Victorian Historical Novel* (The Hague: Mouton).

Sutherland, John (1988), *The Longman Companion to Victorian Fiction* (London: Longman).

Thackeray, William Makepeace (1970), *The History of Henry Esmond*, ed. John Sutherland and Michael Greenfield (London: Penguin). (First publ. 1852.)

Williams, Raymond (1984), *The English Novel from Dickens to Lawrence* (London: Hogarth). (First publ. 1970.)

FURTHER READING

Bann, Stephen (1984), *The Clothing of Clio: A Study of the Representation of History in Nineteenth-Century Britain and France* (Cambridge: Cambridge University Press).

Bann, Stephen (1990), *The Inventions of History: Essays on the Representation of the Past* (Manchester: Manchester University Press).

Bann, Stephen (1995), *Romanticism and the Rise of History* (New York: Twayne).

Beer, Gillian (1983), *Darwin's Plots: Evolutionary Narrative in Darwin, George Eliot and Nineteenth-Century Fiction* (London: Routledge & Kegan Paul).

Crosby, Christine (1991), *The Ends of History: Victorians and "The Woman Question"* (London: Routledge).

Culler, A. Dwight (1985), *The Victorian Mirror of History* (New Haven: Yale University Press).

Dennis, Ian (1997), *Nationalism and Desire in Early Historical Fiction* (London: Macmillan).

Fleishman, Avrom (1971), *The English Historical Novel: Walter Scott to Virginia Woolf* (Baltimore: Johns Hopkins University Press).

James, Louis (1974), *Fiction for the Working Man* (Harmondsworth: Penguin). (First publ. 1963.)

Lascelles, Mary (1980), *The Story-Teller Retrieves the Past: Historical Fiction and Fictitious History* (Oxford: Clarendon).

Levine, Philippa (1982), *The Amateur and the Professional: Victorian Historians and the English Past* (Cambridge: Cambridge University Press).

Reilly, Jim (1993), *Shadowtime: History and Representation in Hardy, Conrad and George Eliot* (London: Routledge).

Schramm, Jan-Melissa (2000), *Testimony and Advocacy in Victorian Law, Literature, and Theology* (Cambridge: Cambridge University Press).

Shaw, Harry E. (1983), *The Forms of Historical Fiction: Sir Walter Scott and his Successors* (Ithaca: Cornell University Press).

Viswanathan, Gauri (1998), *Outside the Fold: Conversion, Modernity, and Belief* (Princeton: Princeton University Press).

White, Hayden (1973), *Metahistory: The Historical Imagination in Nineteenth-Century Europe* (Baltimore: Johns Hopkins University Press).

15

The Sensation Novel

Winifred Hughes

Throughout the 1860s and into the following decade, the so-called "sensation novels" were exactly that – a literary and cultural phenomenon that took the newly expanded novel-reading public by storm. Unheard-of before 1860, they were suddenly every-where with their equivocal heroines, titillating secrets, and highly spiced plots. As one reviewer put it for *Fraser's Magazine* in 1863, "A book without a murder, a divorce, a seduction, or a bigamy, is not apparently considered worth either writing or reading; and a mystery and a secret are the chief qualifications of the modern novel" (Anon. 1863b: 262). It goes without saying that the sensation novels were controversial and provocative, quite deliberately so, and that they were all the rage in their day. It should be no less clear that "sensation," that buzzword of the 1860s, was not merely the disparaging nickname of a minor subgenre but a pervasive mode of confronting and processing hidden fears, anxieties, and obsessions behind the dominant Victorian cultural institutions.

To contemporary readers and literary historians alike, the sensation novel has seemed at once instantly recognizable and hard to define with any precision. Critics, in fact, are still arguing that it "is not really a distinct genre" (Cvetkovich 1992: 14). The term was coined, on the analogy of "sensation scenes" on the stage, in response to the unprecedented wave of bestsellers inaugurated by Wilkie Collins's *The Woman in White* (1860), Mrs. Henry Wood's *East Lynne* (1861), and Mary Elizabeth Braddon's *Lady Audley's Secret* (1862). What these novels, and countless imitations, had in common was the desire to create a sensation in every sense of the word. They sold sensationally – *East Lynne* went on to become the single top-selling novel of the entire nineteenth century, with *Lady Audley* not far behind – while provoking heated debate in the periodical press and in private drawing-rooms. Not only did their plots involve fictional characters in sensational situations, they had designs on the reader's body as well, appealing directly to the senses and stimulating, according to various re-viewers, such physiological reactions as creeping flesh, shocked nerves, teeth on edge, elevated blood pressure, and even sexual arousal. Sensation is at bottom a "somatic experience," to borrow D. A. Miller's phrase (1986: 96), and thus not amenable to rational control. "The appearance of the Victorian sensation novel in the 1860s," says Ann Cvetkovich, "marks the moment at which sensations became sensational" (1992: 13). Contemporaries frequently analyzed the vogue in the language of pathology, as a "diseased appetite" (Mansel 1863: 483) or certifiable mania which had infected, even depraved, its legions of readers.

The definitive feature of the sensation genre – underlying all the disparities between Wood's tearjerkers on the one hand and Charles Reade's hard-hitting "novels-with-a-purpose" on the other – is the trend to domestication of crime, secrets, and illicit sexuality. Unlike the Gothic romance of the 1790s or the Newgate novel of the 1830s, from both of which it was partly derived, the sensation novel dispensed with the traditional Italian castles or underworld hideouts to locate its shocking events and characters firmly within the ordinary middle-class home and family. Henry James was not the only reviewer to remark on the innovation of exploiting "those most mysterious of mysteries, the mysteries which are at our own doors." Instead of removing its readers from their daily lives to distant or exotic locales, the sensation novel brought them closer to grim reality by bringing them closer to home and to themselves. As James continued, "What are the Apennines to us, or we to the Apennines? Instead of the terrors of 'Udolpho,' we were treated to the terrors of the cheerful country-house and the busy London lodgings. And there is no doubt that these were infinitely the more terrible" (1921: 110). Or, as H. L. Mansel observed in the *Quarterly Review*, "it is necessary to be near a mine to be blown up by its explosion" (1863: 488). The implication was that mid-Victorian readers wanted to be blown up and that only contemporary settings were sufficiently explosive. "We are thrilled with horror, even in fiction," said Mansel, "by the thought that such things may be going on around us and among us" (p. 489). The most apparently respectable neighbor might turn out to be a serial poisoner; the most angelic of women, at least a bigamist and potentially a cold-blooded killer.

In the typical sensation novel, the middle-class home, which remained at the core of so much of Victorian culture, could no longer be counted on to function as a refuge from horrors or from the brutalities of an encroaching urban and industrial society. In fact, home was more likely to be the scene of the crime. Not only had it been invaded by mystery and violence, by impostors like Braddon's Lady Audley, but its very foundations were rooted in secrecy and criminality. As the sensation plots unfolded, Victorian middle-class existence was exposed as terrible in itself, in the very cheerfulness of its country-houses and bustle of its lodgings. "It is on our domestic hearths," protested a reviewer for *Temple Bar* in 1870, "that we are taught to look for the incredible. A mystery sleeps in our cradles; fearful errors lurk in our nuptial couches; fiends sit down with us at table; our innocent-looking garden-walks hold the secret of treacherous murders; and our servants take £20 a year from us for the sake of having us at their mercy" (Anon. 1870: 422). Crime became a matter of routine – no longer an aberration but the norm, even in respectable middle-class families. The proliferation of secrets came to imply that everybody had one, and that everybody else was down on his or her knees at a keyhole trying to ferret it out. Every spouse was primed to play the role of spy, especially in the wake of the Divorce Act of 1857, and every servant, the role of blackmailer. "According to Miss Braddon," complained another observer in the *North British Review*, "crime is not an accident, but it is the business of life" (Rae 1865: 104). The reader herself, by merely opening a sensation novel, could hardly escape being implicated in its questionable morality and guilty knowledge, becoming in effect an accessory to its secrets and crimes.

At the center of the home, inevitably, there was a woman – wife and mother, the proverbial angel in the house. At the center of the sensation novel was the same woman, who ran the household, often quite efficiently, while dabbling in bigamy, adultery, or murder on the side. The figure of the adventuress, much more prominent than in previous fiction, began to blur into that of the heroine. The other characters, and often the reader as well, could no longer tell the difference between the feminine ideal and the bigamist's fraudulent imitation of it without the detective's inside information. Or, as Braddon repeatedly suggested, there might be no difference to detect; all Victorian women were forced to be role-players, only more so the closer they came to enacting the ideal. Lady Audley's performance is impeccable, and she protests with some justice that she is only doing what women were trained to do when she uses marriage – in her case, more than once – to advance her social and economic position. The women in sensation novels were direct descendants of Thackeray's Becky Sharp, herself suspected of murder, who had earlier realized, "It isn't difficult to be a country gentleman's wife . . . I think I could be a good woman if I had five thousand a year." And her successors *were* good women, as long as no one threatened to unearth their secrets.

Like Becky as well, they tended to be active rather than passive, no longer the terrified and imprisoned victims of stage melodrama or the Gothic tradition. Sensational women act for themselves, without waiting for the sanction or assistance of men. That action, for some Victorian critics, was in itself already tantamount to crime. As E. S. Dallas argued, "When women are thus put forward to lead the action of a plot, they must be urged into a false position. To get vigorous action they are described as rushing into crime, and doing masculine deeds" (1866: vol. 2, 297). In earlier fiction and melodrama, the heroine was under assault by the villain with the handlebar moustache; in fact, the whole moral balance between good and evil hinged on the contest between them. By the 1860s, she was under assault by the novelists themselves as they reinvented her, no longer depicting her as an icon of sexual purity, whose sole function was to defend her virginity from the villain's seduction or violence. The sensation heroine, without ceasing to be heroine, began to represent equivocation, or moral ambiguity, rather than absolute certainty. Braddon's Aurora Floyd could elope with her father's groom, contract a bigamous remarriage, and still end up "unspeakably beautiful and tender, bending over the cradle of her first-born." Collins's Mercy Merrick in *The New Magdalen* (1873) could finish her career as a prostitute by masquerading as a respectable lady and legally marrying a clergyman. Even Trollope's Lady Mason, in the novel he was tempted to call "The Great Orley Farm Case," proved herself a heroine of the sixties by keeping her secret for more than two decades and by actually being guilty of forgery although twice acquitted in court. These plots, by no means atypical, register a major shift in the qualifications for the heroine in popular fiction.

The secret activities of women – fantasized or feared by mid-Victorian novelists and their extensive readership – were seen as posing a potentially devastating threat to the middle- or upper-class home and hearth. Braddon's Robert Audley realizes that unmasking his uncle's wife will result in the destruction of Audley Court and everything it stands for. As he warns Lady Audley, he is willing to destroy her home in order to save it: "I . . . shall level that house to the earth and root up every tree in these gardens, rather than I will fail in finding the grave of my murdered friend." The alternative to this root-and-branch work, offered in sensation novels of the *Aurora Floyd* or *New Magdalen* prototype, was to reinstate the heroine as angel, even after lapses that would earlier in the century have been socially, if not morally, unforgivable. The larger consequence was to re-establish the middle-class home on some other basis than what Margaret Oliphant called woman's "one duty of invaluable importance to her country and her race which cannot be over-estimated – and that is the duty of being pure" (1867: 275). Critics like Oliphant saw the reinstatement of the fallen or tarnished heroine as far more destructive than Robert Audley's leveling of the erstwhile domestic paradise. "It is easier, in fact," the *Christian Remembrancer* admonished, "to turn nun, hospital nurse, or sister of mercy, to take up and carry through the professed vocation of a saint, than to work out the English ideal of wife, mother, and presiding spirit of the house, after any wide departure from custom and decorum" (Anon. 1863a: 364). If the feminine ideal was more stringent than that of sainthood, no wonder the sensation novelists were castigated for undermining it and for threatening to topple the cherished institutions of home and family.

Matter-of-Fact Romance

In criminalizing the Victorian home, the sensation novels succeeded in defamiliarizing it. Characters and readers could no longer take it comfortably for granted; instead they were forced to become increasingly suspicious of whatever looked most familiar and ordinary. In literary terms, the sensationalists were engaged in picking at the apparent seamlessness of the mainstream realist novel as well as that of the Victorian culture and society it purported to represent. The narrative method they developed can be summed up in Charles Reade's all-purpose subtitle, "A Matter-of-Fact Romance." The "matter of fact" came from both the conventions of domestic realism and the sometimes incompatible standards of popular journalism. "Romance" was a catch-all term for the remnants of Gothic and Newgate, along with abundant infusions from stage melodrama. The result was a patchwork genre, lacking both the narrative coherence and the social cohesion that appeared so effortless – and so thoroughly naturalized – in the mainstream novel. The sensation novel, on the contrary, was drawn to borderlands; it compulsively blurred and transgressed boundaries and knocked down established barriers. Its generic instability at once reflected and encouraged a prevailing thematic instability and an attitude of ambivalence toward its unconventional materials.

When Anthony Trollope was writing his *Autobiography* in the mid-1870s, he seized on the methods of sensationalism to distinguish between the two major strains of Victorian fiction: "Among English novels of the present day, and among English novelists, a great division is made. There are sensational novels and anti-sensational, sensational novelists and anti-sensational, sensational readers and anti-sensational. The novelists who are considered to be anti-sensational are generally called realistic." Although Trollope identified himself as realistic and his friend Wilkie Collins as sensational, he argued that the opposition between them was all a mistake, arising from "the inability of the imperfect artist to be at the same time realistic and sensational. A good novel should be both, and both in the highest degree." The sensation novelists certainly tried to be both. They purposely avoided dependence on the impossible or the supernatural even in their most far-fetched scenarios, while at the same time cultivating the outer fringes of human experience. As Collins explained in the preface to *Basil* (1852), "I have not thought it either politic or necessary, while adhering to realities, to adhere to every-day realities only."

The sensation novelists regularly cited the daily newspaper as the source for their matter of fact, and their plots were often taken from actual crimes or abuses. Collins, for example, incorporated details from the notorious 1860 Road murder case into *The Moonstone*, while numerous "bigamy novels" alluded to the highly publicized Yelverton trial of 1861. Reade crusaded throughout his career against reported conditions in prisons and lunatic asylums. Much of the lurid tone of sensation fiction came directly from the increasingly extensive crime and courtroom reports in the popular press during the 1850s and 1860s, and the new emphasis on investigative reporting that grew up along with them. Mansel in the *Quarterly Review* identified the sensation genre with what he called "the Newspaper Novel, a class of fiction having about the same relation to the genuine historical novel that the police reports of the 'Times' have to the pages of Thucydides or Clarendon" (1863: 501). The sensation novelists could hardly have objected; they saw themselves much more as documentary reporters on the immediate temper of the times than as historians taking a longer-term view. Nor were they afraid of blurring the lines between fiction and journalism, since they were generally willing to forgo literary verisimilitude in favor of improbable fact. The sensation novels, like the popular press, were permeated with the sense that crime, violence, and illicit sexuality were daily occurrences, the sense that there would always be more to fill the crime columns of the next morning's paper. It was the basic premise of the sensation genre that human life, even in Victorian middle-class society, was less tame, less ordinary, less predictable than its readers may have liked to suppose.

At the same time, in order to substantiate this claim, the sensationalists deliberately invaded the fictional territory of the most domestic of realists. After three volumes of bigamy, blackmail, and murder, Braddon could still describe her own

Aurora Floyd (1863) as "this simple drama of domestic life." Like Braddon's, other sensation novels tended to be set in interior domestic spaces – drawing-rooms and boudoirs – or in the adjoining grounds, all described in exhaustive detail. With plots involving detectives, whether amateurs like Robert Audley or professionals like Sergeant Cuff in *The Moonstone* (1868), the most trivial of details – laundry lists, mailing labels, and the like – assumed the status of clues or circumstantial evidence. The novels typically built up a thickly layered material context for their crimes and secrets. Braddon and Wood, in particular, delighted in lavish minutiae of dress, furnishings, jewelry, and trinkets. And the character types who inhabited these cluttered Victorian interiors were themselves familiar from domestic fiction – the apparent angel of the hearth, the governess, the lawyer, the banker, the Trollopean country squire. Heroes and villains alike tended to be ordinary and prosaic, more Amos Bartons than Schedonis. The shock effect depended, more often than not, on the plight of such average, respectable citizens caught up in sensational circumstances beyond their ability to control.

If the conventions of domestic realism governed setting and character, romance asserted itself primarily through the element of plot, the more outlandish and convoluted the better. Contemporary reviewers referred to the genre as the "novel of incident" or "plotting novel," as opposed to the realist "novel of character," which was always considered more serious and more purely literary. Sensational characters were seen not only as diminished but as perfunctory, mere pegs on which to hang unexpected events. Sensational plots were seen as overriding character, breaking it down into weakness and inconsistency. E. S. Dallas extended these assumptions when he analyzed the philosophical underpinnings of sensation narrative in terms that looked forward to late-century naturalism: "We may like to see men generally represented as possessed of decided character, masters of their destiny, and superior to circumstances; but is this view of life a whit more true than that which pictures the mass of men as endowed with faint characters, and as tossed hither and thither by the accidents of life?" (1866: vol. 2, 293). For the sensation novelists – groping toward the secrets contained by the realist novel, determined to disrupt its celebrated equipoise – plot meant accident rather than logic, coincidence rather than consequence. Action and event, both what had happened in the secret past and what would happen next, were valued as ends in themselves. Suspense was screwed to the sticking point, and crisis became narrative routine. Plots often felt like roller-coaster rides, exploding in multiple climaxes or "sensation scenes," such as the first apparition of the Woman in White and, later in Collins's novel, the parallel appearance of Lady Glyde standing beside her own tombstone. In a review for *The Times*, Dallas remarked of Collins's plot, "There are in this novel about a hundred cats contained in a hundred bags, all screaming and mewing to be let out" (Page 1974: 98). Climax or revelation rarely seemed final, as secrets kept unraveling within secrets. In general, the novels gave the impression of leaving too many catless bags strewn behind them, too many loose ends ever to be completely tied up. Even if the detective succeeded in cracking particular crimes, there was a lingering feeling that nothing important had really been resolved.

If plot eclipsed character, it took precedence over narrative voice as well. In the "novel-with-a-secret" (Tillotson 1969: xv) there was obviously no place for the familiar, omniscient narrator of realist fiction, whose reliable commentary provided a framework for discrete episodes and revealed the inner workings of character. The sensational narrator had no choice but to withhold secrets from his readers, unless he could be ignorant of what was going on in his own text. In either case, as Patrick Brantlinger has pointed out, the sensation novels eroded narrative authority. The narrator was no longer trustworthy, perhaps no longer omniscient; like the reader, he became complicit in crime or, if he hoodwinked the reader, even criminal himself. If there was a mastermind behind the sensational narrative, that mind was morally ambiguous at best. If not – for example, in Collins's multiple first-person narratives, recounted by eyewitnesses as in a courtroom trial – then there could only be a structural and moral vacuum where the omniscient narrator had once predominated. In the telling of the tale, as well as in what was told, the sensation novels worked to sabotage the premises of Victorian realism, along with those of middle-class morality.

The primacy of plot, with the accompanying "diminution" of the narrator (Brantlinger 1982: 19), resulted in what Reade, well before Henry James, called "dramatic fiction" (Phillips 1919: 128), in which the narrative moves forward through action and dialogue, without authorial analysis or interference. Many of the sensation novelists were actors or playwrights, most were smitten with the stage, and the genre interacted quite openly with contemporary theater. Not only were the best-selling novels routinely dramatized, often pirated; their authors borrowed plots and techniques from the mid-Victorian "sensation dramas," stage spectaculars that became increasingly elaborate and more technically sophisticated during the sensation decade. Both plays and novels tapped into what has been termed "the melodramatic mode" by a half-century of critics from Wylie Sypher to Peter Brooks and Elaine Hadley. For Sypher, writing in the 1940s, "melodrama is a characteristic mode of 19th Century [*sic*] thought and art" (1965: 260) in which schematic oppositions – whether good and evil or the Marxist dialectic – culminate in crisis or revolution. Fifty years later, Hadley reformulated melodrama in terms of "the newly paradigmatic presence of its defining features throughout nineteenth-century English society" (1995: 3). The melodramatic mode, far from being simply the mechanism of inferior art, represents at the deepest level a pervasive way of thinking, feeling, organizing, and "acting out" (Brooks 1976: 12). With its emphasis on extremes and on moral absolutes, melodrama attempted to penetrate the dense surface of modern reality and to evoke what Brooks has called "the moral occult," the hidden "domain of operative spiritual values" (p. 5) and of underlying mystery. The appropriate melodramatic method is excess, heightening, over-the-top exaggeration – a kind of emotional hit-and-run. In Eric Bentley's suggestive phrase, "melodrama is the Naturalism of the dream life" (1965: 223). In its purest form, it operates in much the same way as the Freudian subconscious, projecting both deep-seated fears and wish-fulfillment.

These methods and preoccupations of nineteenth-century melodrama, which appeared in their rawest form on the popular stage and in the penny dreadfuls, were appropriated wholesale in the sensation novel – only to be radically altered or subverted. The "moral" became ever more "occult," in the sense of strained and eso- teric, as sensation characters were thrust into extreme dilemmas by the return of sup- posedly dead spouses or by the pressure of obscure moral and legal technicalities. The melodramatic framework of certainty and moral absolutes was replaced by ambiva- lence and equivocation. In popular melodrama, the audience could count on the villain to be double-dyed in villainy and the heroine to be infallibly chaste or at least to die of her sin. They could count on poetic justice. In the sensation novel, these traditional verities were reconfigured or even contorted. At the end of Reade's *Griffith Gaunt* (1866), which Dickens refused to defend in court, the hero's bigamy is undone simply by killing off his illegitimate child and redistributing his wives into happy, conven- tional marriages. As the twists of plot kept pushing the envelope further and further, the sensation genre became a site of contested values and attitudes. Its hallmark was the contest itself – the ongoing social and cultural construction – rather than any attempt at clear resolution.

Like stage melodrama, the sensation novel was a product of Victorian mass culture, which it helped, in turn, to define. Contemporary critics denigrated its status as commodity, produced in accordance with "the market-law of demand and supply" and with no higher goal than immediate sales. "A commercial atmosphere," sniffed Mansel, "floats around works of this class, redolent of the manufactory and the shop. The public want novels, and novels must be made – so many yards of printed stuff, sensation-pattern, to be ready by the beginning of the season" (1863: 483). Mansel blamed this state of affairs on the need to fill up the rapidly proliferating weekly and monthly periodicals, circulating libraries, and railway bookstalls of the period. Like hair tonic, gewgaws, or fashionable yard-goods, novels were made to be bought and sold, even if not actually read, on a mass scale. Publishers had to compete with each other, as well as with purveyors of more purely material commodities, and so resorted to dispensing "something hot and strong" (Mansel 1863: 485) for the refreshment of the literary consumer or passerby.

As Mansel's disdain indicates, there was a substantial class dimension to the critical outpouring against the fad for sensation. The most readily available source of hot and strong fiction was the flourishing penny press, that subliterary world of cheap and literally unbound serials aimed at, and often produced by, the lower and working classes. Not only were the sensation novels popular below stairs, bringing disparate classes together over the same printed page, their authors rarely scrupled to borrow both methods and raw materials from "penny dreadfuls" and "shilling shockers." Critics found the sensation plots more appropriate for *Reynolds's Miscellany* or the *London Journal* than for the standard three-volume novel. They sounded their alarm at the spectacle of what they termed "kitchen literature" infiltrating the middle-class drawing-room and capturing the mainstream market. The defining conventions of sensation fiction, like those of theatrical melodrama, had originated and developed outside middle-class control. The sensation novels were the first truly popular best- sellers, the first to reach below the middle classes for plots and thematic concerns as well as for a portion of their readership. The work of M. E. Braddon provides a direct link between the two classes of sensationalism; she got her start in the penny press and continued to turn out anonymous thrillers well after her stunning mainstream success. As she confessed in a letter to her mentor, Edward Bulwer-Lytton, "the amount of crime, treachery, murder, slow poisoning, & general infamy required by the Halfpenny reader is something terrible." The only apparent difference between this "piratical stuff" (Wolff 1974: 11) and the novel proper was quantitative – specifically, the number of dead bodies allowed. Braddon's fictional sensation novelist, Sigismund Smith in *The Doctor's Wife* (1864), finally makes a hit with "a legitimate three-volume romance, with all the interest concentrated upon one body." Judging by the publishing sensation of novels like Braddon's and Sigismund's, the interest in bodies was universal and transcended class. Notwithstanding the carping of critics and the moral dictates of Mrs. Grundy, there were plenty of Trollope's "sensational readers" at all levels of Victorian society.

Sensational Plots and Motifs

Universally recognized as the archetype of the sensation novel, Wilkie Collins's *The Woman in White* performed a function both innovative and transitional. It was also self-consciously textual, and in this respect played a crucial role, at once formal and thematic, in the high-speed evolution of the genre. Taking his cue from such sensational ur-texts as Bulwer-Lytton's *Eugene Aram* (1832) with its middle-class criminal-hero, and Charlotte Brontë's *Jane Eyre* (1847) with its eruption of madness and threat of bigamy, Collins rummaged around in the old bag of Gothic and melodramatic tricks, transposing them to the everyday domestic scene and deconstructing them as he did so. The wicked baronet, vestige of the class animus of popular melodrama, is exposed as a mere pasteboard figure in Sir Percival Glyde, who self-destructs before the hero can get at him. The really dangerous villain, Count Fosco, still Italian as in Anne Radcliffe's Gothic but newly polished and domesticated, exerts his fascination over victims and opponents alike while studiously avoiding any actionable crimes. It is Fosco who embodies the narrative's counter-voice in his compelling reversal of the heroine's copybook morality and his unmasking of society's own criminal complicity. "I say what other people only think," he tells Lady Glyde, and in fact Collins's plot works itself out not as providential design but precisely on the Count's amoral and relativistic terms. The middle-class hero, Walter Hartright, must learn to use Fosco's methods and operate outside the defective "machinery of the Law" in order to defeat him. The heroine is still cast in the role of victim, but Collins splits her in three – the half-sisters Laura Fairlie (later Lady Glyde), Marian Halcombe, and Anne Catherick, the Woman in White. Fosco's conspiracy against them turns on the threatened loss of identity, both social and psychic, that was about to become an overarching preoccupation of the sensation genre. While Laura and Anne change places, their frail sense of self broken down by the neo-Gothic claustration of lunatic asylum, decayed mansion, and tomb, Sir Percival and the Count are themselves revealed as impostors who have elaborately constructed their own fraudulent identities. Disguise and mistaken identity, insanity and the return of the dead alive – all became endemic in the spate of novels that followed in the footsteps of *The Woman in White*.

Collins's most famous innovation, though not quite so unprecedented as he claimed, was the strategic deployment of multiple, sometimes conflicting first-person narrators. Their collected narratives not only undermined the whole notion of omniscience or any single trustworthy interpretation of events, they did so by being self-consciously "written." The struggle for power in the novel becomes a struggle for the control of texts. Sir Percival secretly writes on the blank space in a marriage registry and tries to force his wife to sign damaging legal documents. Anne Catherick composes anonymous letters and traces words in the sand. Fosco stunningly violates the private text of Marian's diary, so that the reader is compelled to realize he has been reading it, in effect spying on it, along with the villain. Hartright copies and then effaces the inscription on the tombstone. He admits all the names are pseudonyms, including his own. Even as general editor, Hartright has only partial control over the ordering of narratives and no ultimate power to censor his enemies' texts. As Walter Kendrick has pointed out, Hartright himself inevitably deceives the reader, and the novel as a whole remains "a landmark of ambivalence" in raising the fundamental, anti-realist question of "whether the language of any text might not generate the reality it pretends to imitate" (1977: 35).

Collins's hero is a professional artist and not so unlike the sybarite, Frederick Fairlie, in being very much aware of what he refers to as "my own sensations." Hartright experiences events primarily in terms of the inarticulate, often subconscious process of receiving and registering stimuli. The fateful likeness between Laurie Fairlie and the Woman in White initially makes itself known as "a sensation, for which I can find no name." The word "sensation" itself, which reviewers were about to canonize as a literary term, recurs repeatedly in the opening section of the novel, as though Collins were offering it for their consideration. Filtering it through Hartright's artistic temperament, Collins aestheticizes sensation, aligning himself with the sensibility of De Quincey's earlier "aesthetics of murder" or Pater's later cultivation of aestheticism's "hard, gemlike flame." By self-consciously formulating these aesthetic and textual issues, Collins helped to make them generally available for other sensation writers. In Collins's novels, the reader can perceive the formal and philosophical framework behind all the popular pyrotechnics.

The first of the women's sensation novels, Ellen Wood's fabulously bestselling *East Lynne*, focused relentlessly and lingeringly on the painful sensations of a new kind of popular heroine, "at once transgressive adulteress and suffering victim" (Cvetkovich 1992: 97). Wood's guilty Lady Isabel Vane suffers just as intensely as the innocent Laura Fairlie, with the difference that she leaves her marriage voluntarily, rather than being decoyed away, and bears her lover an illegitimate child, rather than living with him as a childlike sister. The most original twist is that she abandons a good marriage with an almost too perfect hero (middle-class) for the purely lustful attractions of a murderous cad (another baronet). The plot of *East Lynne* seems to suggest that middle-class marriage in itself, even under the best of circumstances, is intolerably difficult and stifling. Lady Isabel's anguished repentance is undercut by the equally anguished vision of marriage as something that has to be "borne," a "trial" to be endured if not escaped: "Lady – wife – mother! . . . Whatever trials may be the lot of your married life, though they may magnify themselves to your crushed spirit as beyond the endurance of woman to bear, *resolve* to bear them; fall down upon your knees and pray to be enabled to bear them; . . . bear unto death." Instead of bearing the common lot of married life, Lady Isabel dooms herself to bearing the agony of her sensational return, disguised and disfigured, as the hired governess to her own aban-doned children. Wood was one of the first novelists to probe the emotional implica-tions surrounding the recent changes in divorce law, generating sympathy for the cast-off wife, however erring herself, who was separated from her children and forced to watch her former husband showering caresses on her legal replacement. As Mrs. Oliphant realized, much to her chagrin, "there is not a reader [herself included?] who does not feel disposed to turn her virtuous successor to the door and reinstate the suffering heroine" (1863: 170).

At the same time, Lady Isabel herself, like Wood and her mass audience, contin-ues to accept the inflexible moral and social code behind her devastating punishment. If there were any remote chance that the fallen woman could be reinstated, her predica-ment would not be so wrenching – or so safe to indulge in. All she can do is to die, like countless stage adulteresses before her, in the hope of spiritual if not social redemption. The reader, meanwhile, has had no choice but to identify with the adul-teress in her orgy of self-inflicted emotion. Gothic or melodramatic fear and trans-gression have been internalized; Lady Isabel has more to fear from herself and her own compulsions than from any external agency. Murder in *East Lynne* is a minor and per-functory subplot. Wood clearly aimed at producing the primal sensation of her readers' tears, rather than spine-tingling chills or excitements. If, as Ann Cvetkovich suggests, Wood systematically repressed the underlying social and economic causes for women's suffering, she ended up privileging women's weeping for its own sake. *East Lynne* reliably delivered both a good read and a good cry for at least two generations of novel-readers and theater-goers while still comfortably upholding what Wood's narrator considers "the ordinary rules of conduct and propriety."

East Lynne's qualified daring in demanding sympathy for the repentant adulteress was almost immediately eclipsed by the appearance of M. E. Braddon's *Lady Audley's Secret*, widely denounced as "one of the most noxious books of modern times" (Rae 1865: 96). Unlike Wood, Braddon consistently turned conduct and propriety upside down. Her heroines were unrepentant. The electrifying portrayal of her delicate, fair-haired lady-with-a-secret exposed the Victorian feminine ideal as both deliberately constructed and potentially murderous. Lady Audley perfectly embodies it. Unlike Wood's Lady Isabel, she is satisfied with the conventional domestic role and shows a natural aptitude for playing it. Nor is she subject to the usual sexual temptations; although she marries twice for social advantage, she remains a passionless child-woman in the approved Victorian manner. But there is something sinister in her very loveliness and conventionality. Lady Audley's half-finished portrait – a precursor to Dorian Gray's – betrays the underside that Braddon found to be inseparable from the feminine ideal. When that ideal is thoroughly aestheticized – as it is by Braddon's anonymous pre-Raphaelite painter, as it may have been in male fantasies – it reveals dimensions unsuspected by Lady Audley's ordinary associates: "No one but a pre-Raphaelite would have painted, hair by hair, those feathery masses of ringlets . . . . No one but a pre-Raphaelite would have so exaggerated every attribute of that delicate face as to give a lurid brightness to the blonde complexion, and a strange, sinister light to the deep blue eyes. . . . It was so like, and yet so unlike." As Lady Audley herself was so like and so unlike the typical Victorian heroine. Underneath all her babified femininity, Lady Audley was not just fallen but actively criminal. When she pushed her inconvenient first husband down an abandoned well, when she set fire to an inn where her blackmailer and her accuser lay asleep, Braddon's "beautiful fiend" succeeded in resetting the parameters for sensational womanhood.

The last of Lady Audley's multiplied secrets, and the explanation for the rest of them, is her supposed insanity, inherited from her equally feminine mother. Like Collins, Braddon shows female identity as radically unstable, but she does not show it as passive. Lady Audley invents her various selves and aliases, even insisting on her own identity as a madwoman, until her nephew finally locks her up in a Belgian sanitarium under the blatantly falsified name of "Madame Taylor." Far from marking her as unique or deviant, Lady Audley's intermittent madness is seen in the text as a universal human condition, from which not even the hero or the reader can feel safely immune: "There is nothing so delicate, so fragile, as that invisible balance upon which the mind is always trembling . . . Who has not been, or is not to be mad in some lonely hour of life? Who is quite safe from the trembling of the balance?" When Robert Audley, the self-appointed amateur detective, begins to suspect his aunt as a bigamist and murderer, he wonders if he might not be suffering from "monomania." As he proceeds to unmask her, he feels more and more like a criminal himself, until he almost trades places with the woman he has smuggled out of the country, almost becomes a Gothic conspirator confining her in his dungeon: "He felt as if he had carried off my lady, and had made away with her secretly and darkly." If we are all subject to Lady Audley's madness, Braddon suggested, might we not also be capable of her crimes? As Braddon's reviewers maliciously hinted, her scandalous plots were not so far removed from her life; she had a secret of her own in her liaison with the publisher John Maxwell and their five illegitimate children. Maxwell's legal wife, confined to a lunatic asylum, was all too real. Collins and Reade, as well, cohabited with women who by that very fact disregarded the customary restraints of Victorian convention.

The sensation novelists made the assumption that any society so much obsessed with respectability and appearances as their own was bound to be peopled by impostors of varying degrees. And, given the rigid double standard in sexual matters, which put Braddon in a much more precarious position than her male colleagues, women became the most likely offenders. *East Lynne* and *Lady Audley's Secret*, however divergent their attitudes toward conventional morality, served to open the floodgates for the fictional portrayal of women as criminal or sexually passionate or both. In her second straight bestseller, *Aurora Floyd*, Braddon recapitulated the memorable plot of her first, but this time with a heroine who approximated the stereotype of the villainess instead of a villainess who fit the feminine ideal. After *The Woman in White*, Collins felt free to dispense with the victimized heroine for the scheming Magdalen Vanstone of *No Name* (1862) and the depraved ex-convict Lydia Gwilt of *Armadale* (1866). In both novels, the traditional moral framework behind melodrama and Gothic fiction has finally collapsed, allowing what U. C. Knoepflmacher has called the "counterworld" (1975: 352), previously articulated by the unscrupulous Fosco, to take over entirely. Collins replaced the dramatic conflict between the forces of good and evil with the literal plots and counterplots of individual con artists, forgers, and sharp practitioners, unencumbered by any moral allegiance of their own. Charles Reade, meanwhile, not only rushed through the sensational breach but widened it with his graphic scenes of violence and frank depiction of women, both deviants and approved heroines, in states of sexual arousal. In *Hard Cash* (1863), originally serialized in Dickens's *All the Year Round*, his reformist exposé of private lunatic asylums exploded in a surrealist orgy of derangement, sexual predation, and sado-masochistic brutality. In *Griffith Gaunt, Or Jealousy*, Reade permitted his heroine, after a decade of marriage, to be nearly seduced by a young Italian priest, while his hero suffers from amnesia long enough to impregnate a bigamous second wife. Reade's sensation scenes transported the genre to its extreme verge and beyond, as he repeatedly lost all control over his explosive fictional materials and his own obsessions. Looking back now at his undigested mélange of newspaper reports, propaganda, and surprising sexual explicitness, it is hard to believe that his major novels were Victorian bestsellers. Among the lesser-known novelists associated with the sensation genre were Sheridan LeFanu, whose *Uncle Silas* (1864) strayed beyond the sensational into the supernatural; Ouida (Marie Louise de la Ramée),whose society novels, especially *Strathmore* (1865), had sensational elements; and Rhoda Broughton, who patented her own brand of the spirited, sensuous heroine in such bestselling works as *Not Wisely but Too Well* and *Cometh Up as a Flower* (both 1867).

It was primarily in the treatment of female characters and of illicit sexuality that Charles Dickens, friend to Collins and literary idol to Braddon and Reade, parted company with the sensationalists of the 1860s. Yet Dickens found himself in the odd position of being both forerunner and imitator of the sensation vogue. His Newgate novel, *Oliver Twist* (1838), while sanitizing Nancy's role as a gangster's moll, brought the underworld of fences and pickpockets into dangerous alignment with the upwardly mobile middle classes. *Bleak House* (1853), though not entitled "Lady Dedlock's Secret," sympathetically dramatized the sufferings of the fallen woman before exacting the traditional penalty of death for her sin. Although Dickens objected to Collins's tendency to stick to the plotline, rather than "play[ing] around it here and there" (Page 1974: 128), it has become a critical commonplace that the tighter plotting and criminal secrets of his late novels, *Great Expectations* (1861) and *The Mystery of Edwin Drood* (1870), can be partly traced to the influence of Collins and the sensation genre. By the 1860s, Dickens had separated from his wife of more than twenty years and embarked on his own double existence with the young actress Ellen Ternan, but he never felt comfortable venturing into the fictional arena of bigamy and moral equivocation. When he was asked to testify on Reade's behalf in a libel suit, Dickens expressed his unequivocal distaste for the "impurely suggestive" passages in *Griffith Gaunt*, particularly the central situation of bigamy and remarriage (Hutton 1892: 140).

During the final decade of Dickens's life, "sensation" in all its ramifications was undeniably in the air – a prominent element of the Victorian cultural and literary climate. It was not unusual for contemporaries to generalize from a popular fictional genre to an all-inclusive "age of sensation" (Anon. 1874: 142). Beneath the celebrated equipoise of midcentury, currents of a gathering uneasiness made themselves felt. Commentators like Margaret Oliphant connected the sensation novel with a retreat from the era of national self-congratulation and unqualified belief in progress, both moral and technological, that had been characterized by the Great Exhibition at the opening of the previous decade. Oliphant's series of articles in *Blackwood's* registered a mood of lost faith under the shocks of renewed war, particularly the Crimean War and the American Civil War, and of social change. "We who once did, and made, and declared ourselves masters of all things, have relapsed into the natural size of humanity before the great events which have given a new character to the age . . . It is only natural that art and literature should, in an age which has turned to be one of events, attempt a kindred depth of effect and shock of incident" (1862: 564–5). At the same time, an emerging discipline of modern psychology attempted to grapple with the fundamental questions of identity, consciousness, sexuality, and madness. The sensation novels resonated with a new anxiety, not only about the social institutions of marriage and family, but about the nature of the psyche as well. The individual self, the moral will, were perceived to be under attack not only from without but from uncontrollable forces within. The sensation novel functioned as something of a Pandora's box within this larger context, collecting and then releasing what the culture found most disturbing about itself.

As a literary fad, the sensational appeared to be inescapable. Its lurid coloring tinged even the work of the major realists. Trollope's darker novels of the 1860s and 1870s tended to gravitate toward literal crime and secrets as well as a more pervasive sense of corruption and moral degeneration. *Orley Farm* (1862) featured a sympathetic criminal as heroine. In *The Eustace Diamonds* (1872), Trollope wanted to have it both ways, at once cashing in on the vogue for sensation and mocking its trademark devices. The Lizzie Eustace plot closely parodied that of Collins's recent bestseller, *The Moonstone*, in which the heroine was suspected of stealing her own jewel and a professional detective had to be called in. In Trollope's version, Lizzie actually does steal her diamonds and contemplates falling in love with the detective Major MacIntosh. In the end, she marries a bigamist. Trollope's subplot was more straightforwardly melodramatic, centering on a sensational heroine, Lucinda Roanoke, who "would shoot a fellow as soon as look at him"; instead of murdering her intended husband, she avoids his unwanted caresses by going violently insane on their wedding day.

George Eliot, as well, was drawn to the plight of the strong-willed, respectable heroine with a guilty secret, in her novel of the mid-sixties, *Felix Holt, The Radical* (1866). The powerfully portrayed Mrs. Transome has not only committed adultery with a social inferior but produced an illegitimate heir to the Transome estate. Reviewers did not hesitate to link Eliot's sympathy for the fallen woman with that of the ordinary run of sensation novelists: "And here, we regret to say, Miss Braddon and George Eliot join hands, Lady Audley and Mrs. Transome being true twin-sisters of fiction" (Page 1867: 178). Eliot's later novel *Daniel Deronda* (1876) centered on a murder that was not prevented rather than one actively committed. Gwendolen Harleth, like Braddon's Lady Audley and Aurora Floyd, knows what it is to wish her husband dead. But Eliot internalizes the sensation; as Ann Cvetkovich puts it, "Eliot . . . retains her respectability as a high-culture novelist by converting sensational events into sensational psychological dilemmas" (1992: 129). Similarly, Henry James, another highbrow realist, translated his longstanding fascination with melodrama, both on stage and in popular fiction, into something more socially and aesthetically acceptable. "The melodrama of external action," still viable in his early novels, gave way increasingly to what Peter Brooks has termed "the melodrama of consciousness" (1976: 157). If sensation drama and the sensation novel worked by projecting dream, anxiety, and subconscious desire into a world of high-voltage action, the realists pushed that action back into the moral and psychological arena.

The major novelist most identified with melodrama of both varieties is Thomas Hardy, whose first published work, *Desperate Remedies* (1871), was a full-fledged if spectacularly unsuccessful sensation novel. Underneath the stock machinery of crime, clues, and illegitimate offspring, the young Hardy discovered his affinity for the typical sensation themes of thwarted or illicit passion, irresolute heroines, and multiple spouses or lovers. His Cytherea Graye, pursued by two lovers who represent constant types in Hardy's fiction, prefigured Tess caught between Alec d'Urberville and Angel Clare. Throughout his novelistic career, cut short by critical outcry in the 1890s, Hardy escalated the same controversies originally joined by the sensation novelists. When he gave *Tess of the d'Urbervilles* its provocative subtitle *A Pure Woman*, he was continuing and extending their campaign to redefine the popular heroine. Tess's "desperate remedies," like Lady Audley's and Lydia Gwilt's, included murder. In the chaotic sensation universe of accident and coincidence, Hardy also discovered a way of articulating his own sense of cosmic indifference to the human desire for a moral and meaningful world order. With Hardy, and after Hardy, the transgressive preoccupations of sensation fiction became those of the modern novel.

Meanwhile, the direct line of the sensation genre, following the influential example of *The Moonstone*, narrowed into the detective story proper. In fact, the sensation novel was one of the last bestselling subgenres that attempted to span both the high-culture and mass markets. Its controversial formulations played a role in the late-century split between the two sets of novelists and readerships. The original texts of the 1860s and 1870s, spurned or forgotten by the critics, remained in circulation among ordinary readers and theatrical audiences. The dramatized versions of Wood's cautionary tale of adultery became a repertory perennial and guaranteed money-maker for provincial theaters – hence the watchword, "Next week, *East Lynne*!" – and eventually a source for the new century's silent films. James Joyce's *Ulysses* (1922) placed the novels on the secondhand bookstalls of Dublin in 1904, still sensational enough to be passed around among Molly Bloom's acquaintances. Molly herself is familiar with all three of the major sensationalists from forty years before: ". . . she gave me the Moonstone to read that was the first I read of Wilkie Collins East Lynne I read and the shadow of Ashlydyat Mrs. Henry Wood Henry Dunbar by that other woman [Braddon] I lent him afterwards . . ."

Critical Approaches to the Sensation Novel

Having excoriated the sensation novel in reviews and skewered it in parodies, critics and academics largely ignored the whole phenomenon for the better part of the succeeding century, relegating it to obscure footnotes and unpublished doctoral dissertations. The sole book-length exception – Walter C. Phillips's monograph of 1919, *Dickens, Reade, and Collins, Sensation Novelists* – took a literary-historical approach, centering its discussion on Dickens and the male sensationalists and finding more confraternity among them than probably existed. Shorter treatments tended to classify the sensation genre as a precursor of the detective novel. It was revived as a serious object of academic criticism in its own right only with the advent of feminism and popular literature studies. The seminal text for both was Kathleen Tillotson's 1969 introduction to her edition of *The Woman in White*, entitled, still somewhat apologetically, "The Lighter Reading of the 1860s." Within the next decade or so, articles and book chapters became more frequent, leading to the publication of Winifred Hughes's *The Maniac in the Cellar: Sensation Novels of the 1860s* (1980), as well as important biographies and critical studies of Collins and Braddon. From the 1970s on, the major sensation novels were widely reprinted in paperback, often with valuable scholarly introductions, and they began to appear as standard fare in college and graduate-level courses. Only Charles Reade, the subject of a full-scale critical biography by Wayne Burns in 1961 and of scattered journal articles since then, has stubbornly resisted attempts at revival and reprinting. The 1990s brought renewed attention to the sensation novel from the perspectives of theory and gender studies. Ann Cvetkovich's book *Mixed Feelings: Feminism, Mass Culture, and Victorian Sensationalism* (1992) represents the most fully theorized approach. Cvetkovich skillfully negotiated the contradictions among Marxist and feminist criticism and post-structuralist theory, all the while relating Victorian constructions of feeling and sensation to a contemporary "politics of affect" and the literature of AIDS. For both Cvetkovich and D. A. Miller, the sensation novel offered fertile ground for

Foucauldian analysis. By the end of the twentieth century, it no longer seemed "minor"
or peripheral but essential to our understanding of the mid-Victorian period – and
central as well to many of our own critical debates. Current criticism of the genre,
not unlike the outraged Victorian response, functions as a gauge of our own compulsions and preoccupations. The sensation novel is still a site of contested values and
attitudes; critics, like its original readers, still find themselves drawn to its raw energies and transgressive proclivities. Its texts inevitably raise the issues most persistently
addressed by feminists and cultural historians.

The overarching debate in criticism of the sensation novel has concerned the
relative extent of its subversion of official Victorian verities and its opposing impulse
to containment or repression of those subversive tendencies. Pioneering critics, especially feminists, were inclined to emphasize the sensation novel's transgressiveness in
matters of female sexuality and gender roles. Elaine Showalter, in *A Literature of their
Own*, read the women's sensation novel in terms of feminine protest and discontent,
even "hostility towards men" (1977: 160). For Showalter, the sensational secrets of
the 1860s were less those of individual crimes than the larger "secrets of women's
dislike of their roles as daughters, wives, and mothers" (p. 158). "As every woman
reader must have sensed," she argued, "Lady Audley's real secret is that she is *sane*
and, moreover, representative" (p. 167). Not even Lady Audley's literal containment
in a madhouse could entirely undermine the novel's primary function as an outlet for
women's anger and fantasies of revenge. Later critics have focused more broadly on
what Lyn Pykett has termed "gender anxiety" (1992: x), analyzing the sensation
novel's blurring of boundaries between masculine and feminine in such salient
instances as the gender-bending androgyny of Collins's Marian Halcombe or the
homosocial relationship between George Talboys and Robert Audley.

Recent criticism has also looked more extensively at the novels' countervailing
strains of conservatism, most often as embodied in the endings. The sensationalists'
reliance on normative conventions of marriage or repentant death has been seen as
undoing or trying to undo all the earlier transgression and rebellion. In Miller's striking phrase, the moral of the sensation tale lay in "its ultimately fulfilled wish to
abolish itself: to abandon the grotesque aberrations of character and situation that have
typified its representation, which now coincides with the norm of the Victorian household" (1986: 107). Finding both conservative and "subversive elements" in *Lady
Audley's Secret*, Cvetkovich undertook to show how "affect" could be used politically
on either side: "The availability of both readings is testimony to the impossibility of
separating the mechanisms of subversion and recuperation or designating a particular
literary text intrinsically liberatory or reactionary" (1992: 55). In more purely literary
terms, Walter Kendrick had earlier pointed to the sensation novel's "double urge
towards conventionality and innovation, taking full advantage of its sensationalism
but at the same time demanding that it be read as if it were realistic" (1977: 22).

At its best, the genre's inherent doubleness or ambivalence, both formal and
thematic, enabled it to evade the strictly formulaic quality of much popular literature,
fruitfully complicating its appeal to scholars as well as mass-market consumers. What

a culture considers "sensational," what gives it the creeps, can tell us a good deal about it. So can its idea of entertainment, and the sensation novel was above all entertaining. Victorian reviewers may have felt obliged to fulminate against it in the upscale periodicals, but they also confessed their reluctant fascination with its Lady Isabels and Count Foscos. Tennyson, the Poet Laureate, was a grateful devotee of Miss Braddon; Thackeray and Edward FitzGerald found they couldn't put down *The Woman in White*. Over the course of a decade, the sensation novel provided a favorite target for *Punch*, which ran its own rambunctious serials under titles like "Mokeanna; Or, The White Witness: A Tale of the Times" and "Chikkin Hazard" (a take-off of Reade's *Foul Play?*), while citing such intriguing nonexistent texts as "Nobody's Nephew" and "Lady Disorderly's Secret." Disorderly it may have been, in both literary and cultural terms, but that was the secret of its unexpected mid-Victorian ascendancy.

REFERENCES

Anon. (1863a), "Our Female Sensation Novelists," *Christian Remembrancer*, 46, 209–36; repr. in Littell's *Living Age*, 78, 22 Aug., 352–69.

Anon. (1863b), "The Popular Novels of the Year," *Fraser's Magazine*, 68, Aug., 253–69.

Anon. (1870), "Our Novels. The Sensational School," *Temple Bar*, 29, July, 410–24.

Anon. (1874), "The Sensation Novel," *Argosy*, 18, 137–43.

Bentley, Eric (1965), "Melodrama," in Robert W. Corrigan, ed., *Tragedy: Vision and Form* (San Francisco: Chandler), 217–31. (First publ. in Eric Bentley, *The Life of the Drama*, New York, Atheneum, 1964.)

Brantlinger, Patrick (1982), "What Is 'Sensational' about the 'Sensation Novel'?," *Nineteenth-Century Fiction*, 37, June, 1–28.

Brooks, Peter (1976), *The Melodramatic Imagination* (New Haven: Yale University Press).

Burns, Wayne (1961), *Charles Reade: A Study in Victorian Authorship* (New York: Bookman).

Cvetkovich, Ann (1992), *Mixed Feelings: Feminism, Mass Culture, and Victorian Sensationalism* (New Brunswick: Rutgers University Press).

Dallas, E. S. (1866), *The Gay Science*, 2 vols. (London: Chapman & Hall).

Hadley, Elaine (1995), *Melodramatic Tactics: Theatricalized Dissent in the English Marketplace, 1800–1885* (Stanford: Stanford University Press).

Hughes, Winifred (1980), *The Maniac in the Cellar: Sensation Novels of the 1860s* (Princeton: Princeton University Press).

Hutton, Laurence, ed. (1892), *Letters of Charles Dickens to Wilkie Collins* (New York: Harper).

James, Henry (1921), "Miss Braddon," in *Notes and Reviews*, with preface by Pierre de Chaignon la Rose (Cambridge, Mass.: Dunster House), 108–16. (First publ. in *The Nation*, Nov. 9, 1865.)

Kendrick, Walter M. (1977), "The Sensationalism of *The Woman in White*," *Nineteenth-Century Fiction*, 32, June, 18–35.

Knoepflmacher, U. C. (1975), "The Counterworld of Victorian Fiction and *The Woman in White*," in Jerome H. Buckley, ed., *The Worlds of Victorian Fiction* (Cambridge, Mass. and London: Harvard University Press).

[Mansel, H. L.] (1863), "Sensation Novels," *Quarterly Review*, 113, April, 481–514.

Miller, D. A. (1986), "*Cage aux Folles*: Sensation and Gender in Wilkie Collins's *The Woman in White*," in Jeremy Hawthorne, ed., *The Nineteenth-Century British Novel* (London: Edward Arnold).

[Oliphant, Margaret] (1862), "Sensation Novels," *Blackwood's Edinburgh Magazine*, 91, May, 564–84.

[Oliphant, Margaret] (1863), "Novels," *Blackwood's Edinburgh Magazine*, 94, Aug., 168–83.

[Oliphant, Margaret] (1867), "Novels," *Blackwood's Edinburgh Magazine*, 102, Sept., 257–80.

Page, H. A. [A. H. Japp] (1867), "The Morality of Literary Art," *Contemporary Review*, 5, June, 161–89.

Page, Norman, ed. (1974), *Wilkie Collins: The Critical Heritage* (London and Boston: Routledge & Kegan Paul).

Phillips, Walter C. (1919), *Dickens, Reade, and Collins, Sensation Novelists* (New York: Columbia University Press).

Pykett, Lyn (1992), *The "Improper" Feminine: The Women's Sensation Novel and the New Woman Writing* (London and New York: Routledge).

[Rae, W. Fraser] (1865), "Sensation Novelists: Miss Braddon," *North British Review*, 43, Sept., 92–105.

Showalter, Elaine (1977), *A Literature of their Own: British Women Novelists from Brontë to Lessing* (Princeton: Princeton University Press).

Sypher, Wylie (1965), "Aesthetic of Revolution: The Marxist Melodrama," in Robert W. Corrigan, ed., *Tragedy: Vision and Form* (San Francisco: Chandler), 258–67. (First publ. in *The Kenyon Review*, 10/3, Summer 1948.)

Tillotson, Kathleen (1969), "The Lighter Reading of the Eighteen-Sixties," introduction to Wilkie Collins, *The Woman in White* (Boston: Houghton Mifflin).

Wolff, Robert Lee (1974), "Devoted Disciple: The Letters of Mary Elizabeth Braddon to Sir Edward Bulwer-Lytton, 1862–1873," *Harvard Library Bulletin*, 22, Jan., 5–35; April, 129–61.

FURTHER READING

Altick, Richard D. (1970), *Victorian Studies in Scarlet* (New York: Norton).

Boyle, Thomas (1989), *Black Swine in the Sewers of Hampstead: Beneath the Surface of Victorian Sensationalism* (New York: Viking).

Heller, Tamar (1992), *Dead Secrets: Wilkie Collins and the Female Gothic* (New Haven and London: Yale University Press).

Loesberg, Jonathan (1986), "The Ideology of Narrative Form in Sensation Fiction," *Representations*, 13, 115–38.

Mitchell, Sally (1981), *The Fallen Angel: Chastity, Class and Women's Reading* (Bowling Green: Bowling Green University Popular Press).

Peters, Catherine (1991), *The King of Inventors: A Life of Wilkie Collins* (London: Secker & Warburg).

Pykett, Lyn (1994), *The Sensation Novel: From* The Woman in White *to* The Moonstone (Plymouth: Northcote).

Rance, Nicholas (1991), *Wilkie Collins and Other Sensation Novelists: Walking the Moral Hospital* (Basingstoke and London: Macmillan).

Taylor, Jenny Bourne (1988), *In the Secret Theatre of Home: Wilkie Collins, Sensation Narrative, and Nineteenth-Century Psychology* (London and New York: Routledge).

Trodd, Anthea (1989), *Domestic Crime in the Victorian Novel* (London: Macmillan).

Wolff, Robert Lee (1979), *Sensational Victorian: The Life and Fiction of Mary Elizabeth Braddon* (New York and London: Garland).

16

The Bildungsroman

John R. Maynard

To consider the bildungsroman is necessarily to pose questions of genre. What are we doing when we apply a term such as the awkwardly still half-foreign (German) "bildungsroman" (sometimes capital B, sometimes italicized) to novels as diverse as George Eliot's *The Mill on the Floss*, Dickens's *Great Expectations*, or Joyce's *Portrait of the Artist as a Young Man*? What happens when we add, as most commentators on the genre do, a thesaurus entry full of cognate terms for the same characteristics of certain novels? Genre, the kind of literature, is a creation of criticism, though not necessarily of professional literary critics. Whenever we identify some qualities that make two works of art resemble each other and give the works possessing these qualities a name, we have produced a genre. Any number can play; there is no limit to new suggestions.

But, once *in* play, genre becomes history; it becomes part of culture. Some terms are proposed, used a few times, wither and die. They aren't useful ways of thinking of the works of art in question; or they don't keep uncovering interesting new examples. Others prosper, greatly, finding more and more readers interested in the qualities of the art proposed by the genre name. They help us think, talk, write about the work that seems to fit; eventually they even provide models for what kind of writing new writers say they are attempting – though as often as not these writers play with, or even parody or burlesque, the genre they take as a common heritage, much as a jazz musician riffs on a known tune.

In this case the awkward term "bildungsroman" (to reduce its foreignness, used advisedly throughout this chapter as an Englished word, lower case b, plural with s), first applied to Goethe's early work *Wilhelm Meister's Lehrjahre* (1795–6, Englished by Thomas Carlyle as *Wilhelm Meister's Apprenticeship*), to indicate its focus as a novel (*Roman*) about human development and formation (*Bildung*) has experienced mainly positive growth. Used as early as 1803 (by a Karl Morgenstern, German critic in Estonia), then revived and widely promoted by Wilhelm Dilthey in 1870 and 1906, it came into broader use only in the twentieth century, first in German studies and then, later, as a common term in English. Adopted first in English in the *Encyclopedia Britannica* in 1910, it has become the lead term to describe a larger and larger class of the novel. In this case, we may even wish to conclude that its Germanness, and its closeness to and distance from cognate meanings in English (something obviously about building and romance), has allowed it to serve well as an open-ended marker for novels that seem especially to epitomize the openness of the novel itself. As a genre marker we may even think of it as acting as a kind of cluster, a central term that allows by its polysemination, as it becomes variously translated, a variety of terms – not so much sub-subgenres as alternative focuses of the bildungsroman itself. The conception of the bildungsroman genre not only keeps expanding as a set of possible meanings but also tends to process and colonize other genres, repeating in a kind of multiplying *mise en abîme* the original processing of genre by the aggrandizing novel form itself. If in its central concern the bildungsroman is about the individual's situation in each coming generation, it really comes close to the normal concerns of the novel itself.

Not so fast, some traditional Germanists have cried. The name – *Bildungsroman* – is ours, they say; it applies to a few specific novels (Goethe's and a very few others by major authors: Novalis, Tieck, or E. T. A. Hoffman) in a historically specific place and period (the conservative German states, long before the development of a unified Germany, immediately after the French Revolution). The play of debate in German studies has featured those who would prefer to limit the term to a few examples, or even to the one, Goethean case (Sammons [1981] finds none!) and let it die. (See also Kontje 1993 for a useful summary of German scholarship, profoundly caught up in the radical political changes of the twentieth century.) Such purists begin to question – interestingly – whether even the model from Goethe fits the definition. They fight a losing battle against the broadening usefulness of the term, but their point is not unimportant. Rather than accepting their claims to maintain a binary in which there is one privileged, true *Bildungsroman* and an army of base pretenders, we may deconstruct and say there are many versions of novels about growing up in which Goethe and his immediate successors occupy only one (if an honored) place. A generic term either grows, expands, transplants – or contracts and dies. More important, we begin to see that Goethean moment better by viewing it not as originary and unique but as a crystallization, fostered by the great powers of the early German writers, of situations and forces at work before and after it. Social change puts Goethe's hero Wilhelm Meister in a special position: a middle-class person aspiring to the culture of the upper classes, unsure of his relations to tradition as it has been controlled by the aristocracy; a person seeking in a life in the theater a full education to all he might be as a conscious human. The person having to adjust his life around a new social situation will be virtually a universal component of the bildungsroman. The solution: a group of aristocrats known as the Society of the Tower, unknown to him, supervise what he experiences as his own freely chosen development. The model fits well the passive role of the German bourgeoisie of the time, when little civil power was being shared with them, but it also reminds us of Michel Foucault's famous use of

Bentham's prison panopticon as a model for the relations between power and the individual.

While some German critics have found (and some have denied finding) in the development of Meister's consciousness the assertion of an ever-growing aesthetic awareness (aesthetic awareness is said to offer a sense of inward control to its possessor, thus compensating for failure of outward power), a broader perspective allows us to see such concerns with education and individual self-consciousness as only one episode in modern educational movements stemming from the eighteenth century (see Barney 1990) and virtually universal romantic ideas of expanding consciousness. There is doubtless in this one version of bildungsroman some especial emphasis on wholeness and organic unity, with even a premonition of Hegelian ideas of mounting dialectically over one's earlier conscious selves; but in other ways this apparently limited tradition has been opened by criticism to many of the concerns we find in the broader history of works about growing up. Goethe's text especially has justified its fame and that of its creator by regularly provoking new interpretations. When we look for the true bildungsroman we find that even there, in the place of Germany's great classical writer, there is no there there. The generic name functions not to lead us to pure origins (and thank God, for these would be pure Aryan origins, as Nazi exploiters of the tradition of course recognized, though German critics after World War II have repudiated these obscene formulations) but to search among the manifold penumbra of generated meanings, among the strings of significations leading to significations, some of the ways in which different novels have been usefully compared. What packages of significance have been gathered into the portmanteau term "bildungsroman"?

First, a brief list of alternate terms for the tradition, some of which I shall return to in looking at different focuses of significance: novel of growing up, novel of growth, novel of education (*Erziehungsroman*), novel of development (*Entwicklungsroman*), novel of self-development, novel of socialization, novel of formation, novel of youth, novel of initiation, novel of paideia, novel of adolescence, novel of culture, novel of self-culture. The common connector of all these terms seems to be something about youth growing up and coming of age. But it would be a mistake to take that for a final generic descriptor. It is merely the lowest common denominator. Each term may reduce to that, but includes also some particular focus by which we could explore a set of novels: one grouping and calling attention to works about education, another about the development of the artist, another about the development of religious or sexual sensibility. The variety here is striking: while some few German critics were trying to hold this term to one manifestation of interest in growing up in one group of people at one time, writers, and then their critics, were filling every available space. The ensemble offers double benefit: a panoply of the various directions the novel itself has taken – for this genre concerns such a belt of human experience of such centrality that few novels are not at least implicitly involved with it; and also a taxonomy of the ways that youth, growing up, and society have been conceived. In both cases we feel the restless, sweeping movement of change tremendously at work. The Russian

critic Mikhail Bakhtin, who saw the novel itself as emerging out of a master change
from epic and from hierarchical and permanent social structures to speak for times
of irresolution and controversy, found that central site of change highlighted in the
bildungsroman (see Bakhtin 1986).

Since 1796, the forces of change, commercialism, and capitalism, the growth of a
world politics and a world economy, have kept changing the world incredibly – with
the growing person forced to live out in her or his life the gaps that endlessly emerge
between old and new. In its great variety the bildungsroman gives us access to most
of the important ways people have represented, conceptualized, and created discourses
about growing up in such a dynamic, disturbing period – one that seems to be
accelerating and to which we really cannot see an end.

Let's begin at an extreme from the proposed German archetype: the women's bildungsroman – one of the liveliest areas of critical thinking in the past thirty years as
feminist criticism, perhaps the greatest long-term growth area in our literary thinking
in the late twentieth century, has rethought what had seemed a genre about men
growing up. Wilhelm Meister is a young man, and so were the rest cited as heroes in
the work of the German masters. (True, Hoffman's comic hero is a cat; but still a
tomcat.) Feminism asks: What about her growth to maturity? Here the going is tricky;
we can't quite say that she, unlike the male, gets derailed by issues of love and marriage, with confusion over whether growing up is merely taking a place in another
family, because certainly male heroes regularly run aground, as Meister does himself,
on problems of personal relations. But we can say that these seem almost universal
problems for heroines of the female bildungsroman: to marry threatens to end any other
development in favor of a peculiar female destiny; not to marry seems, until feminist
rethinking mainly in the twentieth century, a failure in itself. It is thus no surprise that
Maggie Tulliver, in George Eliot's *The Mill on the Floss* (1860), seems unable to come
to a conclusion about the men in her life or indeed the direction of her life entirely: the
narrator solves her perplexity in a way (drowning in the arms of her brother) that for
most readers seems only to return her to the problem her growing up had been trying
to solve. If this awkward, apocalyptic solution is special to this novel, the problem is
virtually universal – and it is just as clear at the end of the century in Sarah Grand's
recently rediscovered *The Beth Book* (1897). How does a girl proceed on a path of gender
performance as prescribed by her society without crippling either her education or her
prospects for a career when adult? Maggie comes quickly into conflict over the "female"
tasks she is expected to learn and do and over the separate and very unequal education
offered her – in comparison to that offered her brother. Although Victorian women
could cross from the so-called "separate sphere" of women – home, children, women's
social world – to the career world of men (George Eliot herself, unlike her heroine,
became a successful intellectual and writer; Charlotte Brontë prospered as a writer,
though in *Jane Eyre* [1847]) she gave her heroine an inheritance and isolating marriage
to Rochester instead of a career of schoolteaching or missionary work), novels of
growing up show no simple paths to careers right into the end of the century. Beth
finally finds her own way as author and public speaker, but choosing to develop her

natural bent was no easier for her than it was for Maggie to pursue her interest in classics or for Dorothea Brooke (*Middlemarch*, 1872) hers in social action. If some traditional enthusiasts for the classical German bildungsroman thought it might be about the development of a secure identity for its male subject, writers on the female bildungsroman are sure that, for the female subject, it is not. By highlighting the conflicting scenarios for education and adult roles, the novels stress the difficulty of obtaining any single identity. The female bildungsroman is in effect always already deconstructing ideas of stable, unified identity – which should not establish a binary opposition, with all males as stable, resolute, linear, and coherent on the other side (see Fraiman 1993, who does tend to stereotype the male bildungsroman, and Fuderer 1990 for a review of research on the female bildungsroman).

Some final points here. We should not ghettoize representations of women as only about their femaleness so that we can't, for instance, see *Middlemarch* as about problems in female and male education or *Jane Eyre* as about religion. Conversely, we can find useful comparisons between works that are clearly female bildungsromans and works that may not at first seem to fit the class mainly because of their multiple focus in the tradition of multistrand Victorian novels: for instance, Esther Summerson's pathetic (in both senses) narrative in Dickens's *Bleak House* (1853) or the history of Gwendolen Harleth in *Daniel Deronda* (1876), or even the famous stories of Becky's and Amelia's shaky starts in life in *Vanity Fair* (1848). Finally, there are many works that can legitimately be seen as female bildungsromans that remain largely unknown to canonical, nineteenth-century novel study (Fuderer 1990: 33–44 offers a useful list). These include the novels of Geraldine Jewsbury, friend and even protégé of Goethe's translator Carlyle, whose *Zoe: or the History of Two Lives* (1845) and *The Half Sisters* (1848) are regularly cited in the critical literature but rarely read in courses or by individual readers. Given the centrality of their issues of growing up female to feminist concerns, this neglect seems unfortunate.

Despite stereotypes of socialized and unified males in feminist criticism, masculinist criticism and the deconstruction that hovers behind it has been excavating a much less coherent version of male identity, and this in turn allows us to resee the male bildungsroman as a genre about male identity. Even Meister has been subject to refocusing as a much more anxious, more passive, much less coherent male. Dickens's David Copperfield, in the novel of that name (1850), is perhaps the best-known hero of a Victorian bildungsroman; with his fixation on his mother, his unresolved hero-worship, his ambivalence in face of two object choices, and his inability to present his career as more than a shell of success, he epitomizes the issue. How could we mistake him for a comfortable, stable, male identity? Without Agnes, his tentative adult personality, put together with marine tar (or blacking polish), angel cake, and murdstones, can hardly hold together. Victorian heroes and their authors seem unclear whether males are supposed to exemplify passive, gentlemanly, or even Christ-like self-control and self-sacrifice or manly self-reliance and marketplace competitiveness. Pip in Dickens's *Great Expectations* (1861) finds that his model gentleman, Herbert Pocket, might as well have his hands in his when he goes to fight the rough young blacksmith. It will be a sign of Pip's ultimate gentility that he retreats from aggressive room-at-the-top manhood to meet his convict's vulgar but not unloving self-sacrifice with his own Christ-like vulnerability. Recurrent recourse to Christian ideals of self-sacrificing manhood, the traditional *Bildung* of imitation of Christ, is a principal wedge that destabilizes Victorian maleness. In the end, Pip at least is given a career and thus a social role; but his world, and most Victorian bildungsromans, bring males to the non-identity of gentlemanly *dolce far niente* that the society valued most highly. Thackeray can't seem to let Philip (of *The Adventures of Philip*, 1862) develop, as he seems to be doing, into a specific social role where he might, as the saying goes, earn a living for himself, but must shower him with inheritance and the highly prized nebulosities that the grand old name of gentleman carried with it. When H. G. Wells, unusually, offers the history of an engineer's soul, he hardly creates a stable identity. George Ponderevo, with his entrepreneur uncle Teddy and the entire world of *Tono-Bungay* (1909) – that snake-oil cure that made financial section history – is on a rocket trajectory and heading for social and personal disaster. George's unstable, edgy personality infects everything he does, from his ambitious, ineffective romance to his casual murder of a fellow human. He passes us, like a dangerous ship in the night, a male with a role but without any soul.

The adage, taken as another pole in the gender binary of feminist criticism, is that love for (Victorian) man is only a pastime but is the center of a woman's existence. But sex/love lives hardly seem something that male protagonists determine easily and then put snugly away into their secure male identities. We might think a portrait of a male possessed and destroyed by love such as that of Dr. Lydgate in *Middlemarch*, in which the medical researcher succumbs to his worldly wife's material needs as male to female spider, is the exception, the work of an intellectual woman able to cast an especially analytical eye on human aspirations and their enemies. But consider some of the prominent male authors. If Dickens's David Copperfield is finally rescued and stabilized by the love of a "good" woman, his near-shipwreck by the child-woman Dora occupies a much larger emotional space in the novel. Similarly, Pip of *Great Expectations* never escapes his obsession for his unanswering star Estella; if he thinks he helps cure and absolve the similarly obsessed Miss Havisham, most readers think he comes closer to raping/embracing her in the climactic fire scene, as if to underline their common participation in love's dangerous negative forces. Which ending is the right one, readers also still ask? Neither, of course: he gets the girl; he doesn't get the girl. His psyche has indelibly chosen the wrong girl; so either way he loses and we must think of his successful life as still a permanently unhappy one. Samuel Butler's *The Way of All Flesh* (published posthumously, 1903) leads the hero, badly damaged by his will-defeating upbringing, ineluctably to the conclusion his narrator has known all along: passive brotherhood alone can keep a male from suffering impossibly from the very life-force that the author so wished to celebrate. Damage from the controlling intimacies of his mother has left him unable to choose wisely (as he found in his lustful attack on a prim young lady he mistook for a prostitute, or in his mistakenly idealistic marriage to his mother's alcoholic maid). And, to take one final case, George

Meredith's Richard Feverel (*The Ordeal of Richard Feverel*, 1859) falls in love with a fine woman, who loves him in return; yet he is deeply compromised by his sexual drive when his scientifically controlling father keeps him from his bride, and his young life ends in a jealousy-charged duel.

Few Victorian writers would write in any explicit way about the experience of growing up gay; indeed, it remains unclear to what extent, if at all, they were aware of such a concept before specific words for a same-sex desire or identity were invented late in the century. Most often we sense the presence of such desire as further disturbance in the narrative drive toward one simple, settled identity. David Copperfield is a case in point, seeming to find in his aberrant but much admired friend James Steerforth a place of emotional disturbance. It seems almost useless to speculate on his author's involvement in such feelings. Dickens certainly spent a great deal of his fabulous energy and time on his male friends. As Eve Kosovsky Sedgwick (1985) has suggested, such homosocial "buddy" bonding conceals a repressed desire that is dangerous because repressed, disturbing to any simple identity formation because a real desire. Like Birkin at the end of D. H. Lawrence's *Women in Love*, David ends still wishing that it had been possible to have Steerforth as well as Agnes. Meredith's Feverel virtually marries his sweetheart in a triangular ceremony with his best friend. The author perhaps does not understand the many triangulations that lead Feverel from his marriage bed to desire a worldly woman pointed out to him by upper-class swells or to end up following male companionship to his death. In Butler's *The Way of All Flesh*, Ernest Pontifex similarly seems to choose bachelorhood as a way of being with men, above all in a cozy relation to his also bachelor narrator Overton, who seems to celebrate each failure in Ernest's heterosexual attempts. For the author, the way of his flesh was to share a woman on a regular basis, though not on the same day, with a good friend.

Walter Pater has been identified as an author who attempted to offer at least hints and promises of same-sex affinity or desire. His *Marius the Epicurean* (1878) certainly focuses on Marius' strong feelings for the poet Flavian and even for the attractive Christian heterosexual Cornelius, but it is little different from the other works mentioned above in suggesting only a general emotional field stirred to life by male–male associations. Only with Oscar Wilde's *The Picture of Dorian Gray* (1891) does the canonical bildungsroman offer a more clearly gay identity formation. Interestingly, it is anything but a performance of an originary gay identity, though Wilde is sometimes taken as the first father of gayness. Rather, he too seems to present a homosocial world, though one much more satisfied with itself, in young Dorian's relation to his two male mentors. The stress is not upon Dorian's possible homosexuality, which here may be read as a coded version of his illicit life, but on his particular *Bildung* in the sense of identity formation. Dorian has no parents and seems the perfection of youth almost as a generic: the beautiful young man. His identity exists as the desired of others, first of the loving painter Basil Hallward, who worships his beauty but also creates it for Dorian, gives him this identity by objectifying, even commodifying it on the canvas; then of Lord Henry Wotton, who shows Dorian how to fashion himself by demonstrating how easily he can remake and manipulate his identity. Wilde gives us a perspective on why the formation of identity has been so tentative in stories of female and male growing up. Identity, to use the term that Judith Butler has explored so well, seems to be not a heritage that one owns but an act one learns to perform. In this formulation, identity comes last, its manifestations first; it comes last as a conceptualization of a set of practices. And they in turn almost inevitably display more diversity than the identity ultimately formed, so that each formation is stricken already with its own confusion. Identity is always a fiction – in the bildungsroman a fiction about a fiction. But Victorian writers make us aware of its status as fiction in their fictions about identity; they show its excessive ordering and inevitable failure to order, even as they tell its tale.

The tale of female same-sex desire in the nineteenth century lacks even as clear a plot as Wilde's, and it is further troubled by our difficulty in perceiving differences between homosocial relations and lesbian ones, which tend to be confused on either side of the sexual line: as the Victorians took them, desiring relations among women are merely strong friendships; as we sometimes too readily take them, they represent same-sex bonding as bisexuality. Dickens's Esther, whose self-presented *Bildung* is half of the massive novel *Bleak House*, has her greatest frisson not with her father/lover Jarndyce, nor with the Dr. Woodcourt she marries, but listening at the door of her dear Ada Carstone, recently married, a frisson that connects to her uncannily romantic response to glimpses, alive and dead, of her estranged mother. We won't know what to make of desire prompted by jealousy – Dorothea's of Rosamond's hold on Will Ladislaw in *Middlemarch*, or Sue Bridehead's of Arabella, leading her to Jude's bed in Hardy's *Jude the Obscure* (1895); triangulation opens the possibility of same-sex interest behind the emotional charge. Because the construction seems incomplete in the text, it does not easily allow a sorting out of desires into identities. In all cases our reading will of course promote construction or deconstruction of identity formations; the Victorian bildungsroman doubtless takes on in my implied readings here much less of the form of settled development of identity for either heterosexual representations or homosexual ones. Indeed, the picture begins to look more a diverse, truly queer one, with each identity taking a form that combines some broadly represented social characteristics with an undertow of opposing qualities: the result may not be something new under the sun, but it is an individual identity. A strength of the Victorian novel generally, from Dickens's eccentrics to Wilde's exotics, is its ability to represent distinct identities for individuals that are more than mere shadows of their society's codes.

So far the focus has been on one traditional major topic in the bildungsroman, roughly equivalent to that of identity. The frequent characterizations of the bildungsroman as a genre committed to humanistic affirmations about the security and permanence of an essential human nature are false – though there have been those, including Nazi critics of the 1930s, who tried to identify the genre with a set of traditional or radically conservative ideas of a frozen, eternal human nature. But the form allows, indeed it is one of its strengths that it provokes, an open discussion about the nature of human nature. This discussion has two topics that are inevitably the focus of attention, namely the relation between the individual and her society and the nature of the individual's psychology. Each can be such a major focus in individual novels or in criticism that it becomes a defining approach to the genre, a way of reseeing it as intensely about one or the other.

To the extent that the bildungsroman is seen as about the integration of the individual into society it will focus on the issue of how much the individual is a product and creature of society and, more specifically, on the ways in which he or she should be read as an allegory of the society's condition. Obviously, the more the individual is seen as necessarily in sync with that condition, the more clearly may the allegory seem to be readable. The simplest conception that can be applied here is the Marxist one: the individual represents the rise or emergence of a class and is thus understood as a marker for broader changes in society. Usually this is seen as about the development of a middle class, thus paralleling theories such as Ian Watt's classic one of the entire rise of the novel as a bourgeois genre. As a critical approach this obviously has limited utility. We can see a character such as Tom, Maggie's brother in *The Mill on the Floss*, as a counter for the middle class as it takes on the prerogatives of the upper class (private tutorial education) and becomes determined, in Tom's own body, to rise to positions of power in society. Focus would then be on the relation to the aristocracy, though here perhaps, unlike in *Wilhelm Meister*, already industrialized England offers great play for the middle class; in place of established aristocrats we have indeed mainly higher strata of the middle class, the sons of lawyers or mill owners. The presence of such a well-developed commercial and industrial society has even led Franco Moretti to conclude that its English form offers little variety in its portrayal of character. If character mirrors society and the society is frozen in its middle-class existence, then there will be little real play in characters. These will be more like fairytale characters, who simply get tested and found adequate (positive to middle-class values of prudence and hard work) or unacceptable (negative to those values). The story is one of "classification"; the hero even in an eighteenth-century work such as *Tom Jones* is merely tested and then takes a rightful place. Somewhere there may be a process of social self-recognition by the hero who may, like Jane Austen's Emma, find her proper place in society (Moretti 1987: ch. 4).

This critique is valuable in calling attention to the frequent use of fairytale motifs and screens in bildungsromans. Jack or Little Red Riding Hood, the bad fairy godmother and the sleeping beauty, seem inevitably to lie behind the plot structures of works about growing up, there for comparison or to offer ironic contrasts with real life. But the overall image, of an unchanging society and plots that come out where they begin, is not a promising model for a major tradition of the bildungsroman in an England changing so fast; and indeed, the critic much prefers what he finds in great continental versions of the genre, in Balzac or Stendhal. It also seems false to the comic and social scene in which it builds its system, at least for representative voices of the middle class in Victorian authors or heroes. A better model, one that Moretti in fact uses for worlds elsewhere, is perhaps that first suggested by Bakhtin.

Bakhtin saw the novel generally as about a special moment in the relation between the individual and society, when there is sufficient disagreement in society to develop individuals that are little cosmoses in conflict within a larger world of conflict. The bildungsroman is for Bakhtin an epitome of this change and conflict; its hero "emerges along with the world and he reflects the historical emergence of the world itself. He is no longer within an epoch but on the border between two epochs, at the transition point from one to the other. This transition is accomplished in him and through him" (Bakhtin 1986: 23–4). This re-renders the character as allegory not of a class but of the very movement of history itself. It allows us to see a character in the same conflict as the broad social scene. Pip of *Great Expectations* is an allegory not just of the rising bourgeoisie, even out of working-class origins, but of the conflict of values in his changing society. We have only contradiction: the solidity but also solidarity of Joe, a blacksmith who is a figure both of working-class strength and of petty bourgeois prudence; the entrenched manipulation of the upper-class figures, where Compeyson the betrayer behaves much as Miss Havisham the betrayed or the equally predatory poor genteel relatives; the hulking violence and very rough justice of laborer Orlick; the monstrous bourgeois distance and precision of lawyer Jaggers and his only half-human assistant Wemmick; the working-class warmth, generosity, and violent vulgarity of Pip's convict Magwitch. Such a cast of characters plays notes up and down and around the social scale of a society where everyone and everything is in motion – old religious order topsey-turvey from page two on, everyone swept through with aspirations toward aspiration in a universal struggle for survival and, that secured, for snob points. In this world all troubled by change, Pip, like George Ponderevo, the engineer of destruction and change in *Tono-Bungay*, is both portent and enactor, the dupe of the bitch-god success but also a young man who knows the value of good education and standard English. Like the society itself, he embodies contradictory impulses to move up in class to great expectations and also to be loyal to the world of working class, petty bourgeois, or convict abjects.

Later in the nineteenth century, especially after Matthew Arnold's *Culture and Anarchy* (1869) and the aesthetic movement that followed had constructed an ideal of aesthetic culture open through broad education, particularly in the humanities, the play of class was often made even more monstrous by focus on disparity between class position and education. If George Ponderevo finds wealth and position to match his education in the sciences at the new Imperial College, Hardy's Jude Fawley, or the less well known Godwin Peak of George Gissing's *Born in Exile* (1892), find that cultivation only ironizes their failure to rise in class: they have the education, sometimes the aspirations of an upper-middle-class person or, even better, an aristocrat, but not the life (for a Marxist reading of such novels, see Alden 1979). And, as with Pip, their culture is a knife that can turn in their hands, exposing in them the vulgarity and indifference to others that are the usual furniture of rooms at the top. Jude's fine Latin is set against the superficial sophistication of the Christminster students, but he is nonetheless permanently on the outside, the possessor of the university's culture but not an inhabitant of its rooms.

In its concern with how persons are products of society, the bildungsroman is usually close to another special generic identity, the novel of education (German *Erziehungsroman*, a term still foreign). This other name for the bildungsroman (one of so many, as I have suggested) focuses our attention on the way in which education mediates the placing of individuals in class positions. It is both the way in which society tries to shape the individual and fix her place in society and also the wild card that can produce sports such as Jude or even offer, as Arnold dreamed, a different selfhood for all. Education is regularly narrated and also frequently thematized in the bildungsroman. If some novels explore the open possibilities, as also the dangers of education's radical potential, many try to find some way both to acknowledge the shaping force of education and to neutralize its de-individualizing force. Just as a later thinker such as Michel Foucault can spend a brilliant career exploring the oppressively controlling relations between discourse and social control, all in the hope of asserting and promoting individual resistance, so novelists often write of education's force while opposing it. From *Tom Jones* forward, the English bildungsroman especially looks with suspicion on educators and their philosophies. It doesn't like system, as the satirical look at utilitarian education in Dickens's novel about education and society, *Hard Times* (1854), shows. Novelists fear systems will stamp or cut out, often cut down humans; it prefers what it images as natural growth. The opposition appears, of course, in our term "culture" – another translation of *Bildung* – which can have alternate meanings of organic or functional growth. George Meredith, who sets his hero Richard Feverel in a lush natural landscape where he falls happily and "naturally" in love with a local beauty, writes his hero's ordeal as one of education: the suffering and ultimate extinguishing of a fine young growth by his father, that scientific humanist, and his system of education.

We have come to be suspicious of such binaries as "nature versus culture." They seem to deny, as more radical studies of class and education such as Hardy's *Jude* do not, the necessity of education in one form or other. No education: wolf man, as most of these authors knew; no education: more likely replication of present social types by the informal education of growing up in a society. They also seem to us to perform a kind of romantic sleight of hand, in which ideologies – here positions on what kind of humans education should turn out – are hidden rather than exposed. Wordsworth's charming "The Child is father of the Man; / And I could wish my days to be / Bound each to each by natural piety" seems suspiciously unclear. Piety to oneself may seem only to promise more of the same, the unexamined life not worth living, a life of pious conventionalities or even "natural" inertia and conservatism.

The Victorian bildungsroman reflects and reproduces this cultural ambivalence about education's force – one clear enough in Victorian foot-dragging on developing universal education. Just as we fear and admire our power to reshape the biological nature of humankind, they feared their own power over the DNA of social construction, education itself. The bildungsroman under its hat as novel of education also brings us back to the initial question of individual and society: are individuals made by society through education? What is individual enough about the individual to keep its substance through the smelting, alchemical process of education? Though many of our recent cultural theorists and historians have been attracted by the view that all is social construction, writers of bildungsromans were regularly interested in the individual's individuality. Some, such as George Eliot in *Middlemarch*, might seem to agree with sophisticated theorists and historians of today who would argue that individuals' special qualities are the result of the infinitely complicated spinning out of various threads in the pattern of culture. But more often novelists preferred to reify the individual. It is not quite that they find a self-determined and determining essentially good core in the individual. They often seem to carry into secular discussion traditional ideas of original nature inclining to sin. Even Pip, product of the essentially secular Dickens, for instance, grants he was self-corrupted at a very early age. Their point is rather that there is some core that takes responsibility for the individual, both in moral decisions and in cultural determinations – what we might call lifestyle decisions. Not society, not education, not fashion, not commodification should rule in that core but something inalienable: the individual's moral character, personality, or, at least eccentricity.

When we look at the novels from this point of view we are interested to find their frequent violations of their own ideology. Dickens's Esther may seem destined, despite all the hard knocks of her psychic life that make her seem lost like her own doll, to harvest credit and rewards for her core character, the sturdy housekeeper. But the premise of her world is that failure of education, human existence in the terrible poverty of Tom-All-Alone's, puts individuals terribly at risk. Everywhere noble pearls are found in the dung heaps – witness even Jo the crossing sweeper, truly the wolf-boy of the urban jungle with virtually no culture put into him, no capital of education to re-render him as human, no *Bildung* at all. But Jo, the text tells us, is the exception we can bear to look at; behind him everywhere are the street Arabs who terrorized Victorian society with their ignoble savagery. Thackeray's Pendennis (of the novel of that name, 1850), natural lad of virtue despite his society upbringing, lives in a world, another vanity fair, in which place and wealth are the empty signs that all chase without even hope of attaining satisfaction. Who, Thackeray asks us, can really be free of vanity fair and call their soul their own?

From the dawn of the novel in the late seventeenth century, as it agglomerated varying textures of prose discourse and narration (see Barney 1990), there were liaisons between the bildungsroman focused on education and more abstract theories of education. The danger to the novel was always that of pedantry; riding a thesis, we all feel, will not do for a novel. Yet novels can well accommodate a good deal of such ideological material. There were, of course, obviously didactic fictional lives, even some broad categories – Rousseauist, as in the work of Richard Edgeworth and Thomas Day, *Sandford and Merton* (1783–6), or evangelical moralizing like that of Mrs. Sherwood. But these are monitory tales, not attempts at full young lives. In novels, lessons of education, what to do and also what not to do to shape humans, could provide a central set of ideas for a work. Here is a British tradition of a novel of ideas. Though that genre is often thought of as exclusively a French or Russian tradition, it is in fact very much present as a debate about the central social/political issues raised by education. Charlotte Brontë had been a teacher herself, had fallen in love with a French teacher, and makes the heroes of her first novel, *The Professor* (1857), and the last, *Villette* (1852), proceed to complete their educations by becoming educators themselves, with very strong opinions about education, in these cases rather right-wing views of the difficulty of making any impression but a momentary one on "naturally" dull or frivolous students. We may disagree, and we may question other novels' belief in anti-system as the supreme good in education. But we are led into a dialogue on the educational issues placed before us. And this in turn shades into the broader meaning of education implied in novels of education, that they do not just plot an organic, predetermined unfolding in an individual but offer a long set of interaction points where education, formal or informal, leads the individual to some new identity. The extreme is Pater's *Marius*, which can be seen as offering even a veiled tribute to the Greek ideal of many-sided humanistic education through personal (for the Greeks, sexual) inspiration (see Dowling 1994 for an interesting general history of the revival of the Greek idea of *paiderastia* in Victorian England). Pip or Henry Esmond in Thackeray's historical bildungsroman of that name (1852) learn to subdue their pursuit of false female stars and in this broad sense of learning they too demonstrate a theme that is everywhere in the Victorian bildungsroman: that the protagonist's life will change to his or her benefit proportional to the shape of his or her learning curve. That tribute to education even novels most invested in organic ideas and images for growth will grant. *Tom Brown's Schooldays* (1856), Thomas Hughes's novel celebrating the system of moral education in the Rugbeian public school of Matthew Arnold's father Thomas, shares with Butler's *The Way of All Flesh*, with its utter contempt for that tradition, a structure in which even systems of education are presented as topics for education, subjects where the hero comes to learn and understand important points that go beyond the system itself: the Arnoldian concern with moral leadership, the Butlerian dislike for moral prigs and too-earnest types altogether.

Taken as a form that encourages its readers to think about education as they see it thematized and conceptualized, the bildungsroman as novel of education oddly opens up the possibility of individual freedom in the place of social control of the individual. We may read Hughes and his subjects as prigs, or, conversely, condemn Butler's frivolous concerns with money and emotional distance. The bildungsroman in its other major phase, as the novel concerned with the motivations and psychology of the individual, may on the other hand paradoxically seem to deny freedom to the growing individual. It has become customary to see the Victorian period as the heyday of a middle-class invention of self-determining rational man, a working model of the Cartesian individual able to separate himself not only from external cultural and societal direction but even from any needs of his body or psyche. I use the male pronoun deliberately here because the assumptions about the Victorians were about males, with females often defined as those not quite able to attain to such rational independence. In this view one expects the bildungsroman to reflect this presumed spirit of the age, to be in effect a novelistic version of the work of such a bestselling non-fiction writer as Samuel Smiles, author of *The Lives of the Engineers* (1863), exemplary biographies of successful persons, as well as the first how-to-get-ahead book (and perhaps still the most serious and thoughtful) *Self-Help* (1859).

What must be most striking, when we turn from such works that do suggest an ideology of rational independent man to novels about people's development, is the degree to which they do not offer such a psychology of rational self-sufficiency. Novels seem rather to anticipate the twentieth century's fascination with the individual's irrational, uncontrolled psychology. Freud said that he found most of his ideas about a psychological system that works in complex fashion within each individual in the work of creative writers before him. Scholars have returned the compliment and found sources for character motivation in the psychologies of the Victorians, especially those of the pseudo-science of phrenology, a science like psychoanalysis in that it attempted a rational explanation of the apparently unrational behavior of people. Charlotte Brontë's Jane Eyre burst upon the literary scene of the time precisely because she seemed to offer such truth to psychology. The angry young woman, like so many angry young women and men since, was at least in touch with her anger and later as in touch with her desire. Brontë portrays a world of characters variously at risk of emotional or mental disturbance, most notably the famous Bertha in the attic but also the Reed sisters and Mrs. Reed. Jane herself has a kind of breakdown experience as her anger cools in the Red Room, one that has attracted Freudian, Jungian, and Lacanian interpretations of her strange self-alienation as she sees herself in the mirror in that large, cold, sexy red room and undergoes a fit of terror at an apparition. Jane's task in life will be not so much education – which is easy for this bookish, bright spirit – but managing her emotions, which can turn so dangerous to her. At Lowood school the resentment that her friend Helen Burns is so weirdly able to turn from inburning hell to heaven leaves Jane rather searching for appropriate ways to express her anger or assert her self-respect. And her mental state becomes dangerous as she feels herself yielding to her emotions for Rochester and yet feels the ground is not solid under her. She learns lessons of psychology: to eschew relationships that do not have an emotional ground floor (as with Rivers), to value her independence even in a relationship based on a deeper emotional vibration. The point is that her life path is most especially a story of emotional and psychological self-management and maturation. Jane, Freudians will say, has a healthy ego, and yet its health lies not in mere rationality but in her ability to order her emotional house and even to learn when to listen, and when not to listen, to her careful conscience.

The form of this fundamental plot for a bildungsroman, once observed, is easily seen everywhere in the Victorian novel of growing up: obviously in women's lives, where, as with Jane, Victorian ideas of woman rather authorized focus on emotional development and where, as with Jane, Lucy Snowe of *Villette*, or Maggie of *The Mill on the Floss*, especial sensitivity to the need for self-sufficiency can provoke conflict within other emotions. Maggie's development fails because the author sends a flood that drowns her; but most readers see a failure to advance her emotions beyond her fixation on her past and family, a pattern we became familiar with in the twentieth century because of Paul Morel's notorious turn toward death and his dead mother in Lawrence's *Sons and Lovers*. *Villette*'s Lucy, by contrast, has steered her recessive, hidden engine of borderline emotions dating from severe childhood loss away from madness and even away from the tender trap of religion into a safe commitment to one man and to a profitable career; it is rather her fiancé who is overwhelmed in literally deep waters, a savior to her in her need for emotional development who cannot save himself. Even Dickens's Esther Summerson narrates her life as a difficult process of managing emotions, from her initial use of her doll to control her sense of loss to her dangerous scenes with the mother who, still alive, wanted to be dead to her. Center of order in the bleak world she inhabits, she finds it helps her manage her emotions to organize and manage a household.

But the male heroes of the Victorian bildungsroman can also be seen to be facing a difficult development into their emotions. David Copperfield's Oedipal conflicts over feelings about his mother and stepfather are, as so often, written out even in that ogre's name, Murdstone. His alternate instincts to fight males or submit to them, as he does to Steerforth, are the poles of his difficult and always tentative emergence as a grown male. Self-determination is more the ability to balance such conflicting inner feelings than to exercise rational control. Even male figures who seem at the rational pole of personalities – the detached and indifferent Ernest of *The Way of All Flesh* or the engineer George Ponderevo of *Tono-Bungay* – are as much studies in emotional as in intellectual development. Ernest must meet his deeper self, which emerges as a kind of place of what he desires as opposed to what others have wished him to desire, before he can begin to create a life independent of his controlling and guilt-provoking parents. George's intellectual development into a Royal Society scientist and top aeronautic and naval engineer is plotted against his difficulty in reaching his emotions; he seems an emblem of his world – a fine mind that cannot get its bearings in a world also out of control. Frenetic activity, a hopeless love affair, suggest life as a manic episode and a development that comes only to disconnection and violence – a very familiar pattern for the new century.

Two further avenues open up for criticism here. One is a more technical application of one or another psychology: usually an excavation of some kind of more immediately meaningful subtext embedded in the mass of ordinary life detail that the genre presents. Pip, in *Great Expectations*, for instance, has been subject to a great deal of analysis in which the violent workman Orlick is connected to his own apparent passivity; the madwoman Bertha, in *Jane Eyre*, or the *crétin* in *Villette*, have been seen as emblems of the main characters' repressed feelings of rage (Jane) or helplessness (Lucy). To a Lacanian, young Jane's confrontation with her image in the mirror may symbolize her break out of a prolonged imaginary stage and the opening up of symbolic distance through language. The game is endless and we all may play; the condition is only that the approach seems genuinely interesting, allowing us to work again on these well-known tales of growing up with our latest tools of insight.

I will note below how a technical development in narrative of childhood, an intense, virtually stream-of-consciousness train of memory, allows inner analysis of how the mind works. But even in more traditional narrative there is enough formal discussion of psychology to allow a criticism that tries to discuss protagonists' growth in abstract, quasi-philosophical, psychological terms. Here we find discussion of an emerging self-understanding, of self-discovery, of the development of a moral will that separates men from boys; women from girls, too, though the discussion is more often gendered male. The discussion is often based on a kind of faculty psychology, with different functions given names (as indeed they are in Freud, but the Victorians more often thought of faculties as known to the subject). Perhaps the most influential work focusing on this kind of analysis is also one of the most original, a work deeply inscribed in the German tradition: *Sartor Resartus* (1833/1838), not only by the translator of *Wilhelm Meister's Apprenticeship* but set in Germany – another account of the apprenticeship to life of a brilliant person, in this case also quizzical. As a work that deliberately parodies and sometimes burlesques the German tradition in order to set forward a broad approach to life and history, it is, if considered a bildungsroman at all, a unique example of the philosophical one. With such a focus it naturally schematized the psychology of the philosopher-in-the-making, Teufelsdröckh. Psychology here is interlarded with cultural history. Teufelsdröckh lives through what Carlyle categorizes as a romantic period infected by Byronic love, in which he finds himself will-less and drifting; but eventually some will develops and he opens the door to his future success by a decisive act of will: he stands up and protests against his own drift into existential nothingness – a force that he characterizes as universal and ideal, the devil within – even as he locates it in the zeitgeist. Carlyle's psychology is as infested with religious language as a stray dog with fleas, but that language is nebulous and allusive, whereas the stress on will is decisive. Teufelsdröckh and his author's famous imperative, "Work now," comes from the Bible, but the need for will, not the theology of the night, is what we hear. Carlyle was of course incredibly influential on two generations of Victorian writers. But if there is much talk of work and will, of self-understanding and discovery in the bildungsroman, there seems a healthy skepticism about characters' ability to prosper by bootstrapping exercises of will and self-awareness. A still religious, if very diversely religious, society recalled that it is God's not man's will that counted. St. John Rivers in *Jane Eyre*, Murdstone in *David Copperfield*, Magwitch in *Great Expectations*, along with fathers in Meredith's *The Ordeal of Richard Feverel* and *The Adventures of Harry Richmond* or in Butler's *The Way of All Flesh* are regularly seen, even in this age of willful class mobility and aggressive economic development, as too anxious to take charge and make their will prevail.

We would expect coming to reason or to the age of reason to be the normal goal of the bildungsroman, but this quality, the traditional one separating men from the apes as well as the boys, is also treated with some suspicion. Meredith here might be the writer who most sees the tragic history he offers as a result of failure of real brain, but even there false reasoning, of the sort father Austin Feverel does so well, seems hardly to be distinguished from the right reason. Feverel's *Pilgrim's Scrip*, his collection of aphorisms, seems often at the abstract level not so different from those of the narrator, so that the text that calls for more brain often seems to confess that it wouldn't know it if it saw it. Meredith's own psychology, as enunciated in his poem "The Woods of Westermain," called for a blending of powers, including what he calls blood, a more elemental and unconscious force, in the successful personality. And Ernest Pontifex dreads nothing more, because so distorting, than his mother's reasonings together on the sofa.

I suggested at the beginning of this chapter that the bildungsroman can best be understood as a series of possible genre screens to be opened under the main screen (to use a metaphor that would have entirely baffled our nonetheless technically advanced Victorians). Having suggested some of the large ways of thinking about the genre, I want now to suggest, without implying any limit to further suggestion, some other focuses of the genre or, to shift this only a bit from the work to the criticism, some other generic focuses. The broad concerns I have been looking at so far may seem suspiciously close to being a description of the Victorian novel in general. Here it will seem that the bildungsroman bleeds out into so many other kinds of the Victorian novel that it also has no identity of its own but simply marks a life segment of that genre. This has a good deal of truth in it; yet it also can be useful to call attention to the peculiar issues concerning growth, education, development, or, most simply, youth, in these kinds of novels. For instance, Carlyle's philosophical bildungsroman also touched on a language of religion. So we can speak, more or less narrowly, about a religious bildungsroman overlapping the Victorian genre sometimes treated as the religious novel. I cannot with each such focus go through the qualification I presented with the bildungsroman in general. Suffice it to say that in each case there will be advocates of a more or less rigorous and narrow definition of the genre. So some will limit it to works such as Newman's *Loss and Gain: The Story of a Convert* (1848), detailing its *Bildung* hero Charles Reding's education and religious life at Oxford, while others will include *Wuthering Heights* (1847) or *Middlemarch*. In either case, the overlap is especially significant for the bildungsroman because religious traditions of thinking about determining events in life are especially prominent, even in bildungsromans that one would not think of as mainly religious in orientation. Jerome Buckley, among others, long ago sensitized us to the centrality of conversion in lives of Victorians — a moment in a lifetime offering a singular discontinuity from what was represented as life before (see Buckley 1974). Teufelsdröckh's life is narrativized into major meanings by his conversion episodes. Bildungsroman heroes, male and female, regularly plot their lives by such inner apocalpyses, and as skepticism about religion grows these are often meaningful moments of deconversion, such as Butler's Ernest experiences, as does Joyce's twentieth-century Stephen Daedalus, as a liberation from controlling tradition. Even that focus reminds us, however, how much Victorians conceived of their lives in religious terms, so that failure of religion was still a central life event. Similarly, secular lives, as much as religious, could be patterned on parallels to plots in the religious myths of the culture; this was often seen as a specific tradition of interpretation called typology. Hardy's *Jude the Obscure*, for instance, leads Jude down into Christminster as a kind of typing of Christ's progress to the cross; he, named after the possible relation of Christ, rewrites, in secular, hopeless terms, the hope-giving mission of the savior.

Or the bildungsroman may overlap with the historical novel, as it does in its origins in Walter Scott's *Waverley* (1814), where history is sighted through the eyes of a young man coming into his maturity. That hero is usually subordinated to the brilliant characters cast out of history itself, so that the hero as historical ephebe is a way of placing us in history, offering in effect a window. Where there is more considerable focus on this novice's way of seeing the world, the result is what we have in the great Victorian historical bildungsromans, George Eliot's *Romola* (1863), set in Savonarola's Florence, and Walter Pater's ancient Roman *Marius*: namely, a new focus on sensibility. We come to know the protagonist and her or his life less as action, more as rich awareness of the flow of personality and history. How interfoliated generic identities of Victorian novels can be is suggested by the religious coordinates also present in Romola. Her passivity is compared to the religious typology of the Virgin Mary, suffering but strong; in *Marius*, the possibility of conversion, rather than its attainment as plot, suggests religion transmitted into sensibility.

Or the bildungsroman can be seen as overlapping novels that voyage out in space rather than time, exotic novels, novels of pre-postcolonial cultural intersections. Rudyard Kipling's *Kim* (1901) has the vigor and excitement of boys' adventure novels earlier in the century, such as those of Frederick Marryat, combined with the concerns over a quest for identity (and also, again, for a religious way in life) of so many bildungsromans. It balances concern with its very active young hero and its use of him as a window into cultural intersections. Kim, like his author, lives out as a kind of dual cultural citizenship the contrasting ethos of imperialist and colonized. We experience through him both the joy of multiplied personalities allowed in such a hybridizing context and the anguish over finding a mature identity equal to his complexity. Of course, this crisis only restates in terms made bolder by the obvious cultural clash the crises of identity of working-class heroes in the bildungsroman, whose development, as we have seen, divides them from the culture of their class origins. Similarly, the regional bildungsroman, which we see beginning in the Scottish context of Mrs. Oliphant or in the Irish context of James Joyce, heralds the major development of the bildungsroman in the twentieth century in its preoccupation with convolutions of emerging identity based on conflicting ethnic and natural identities. Other interesting cases are Amy Levy's story and novel based on the experience of Jews in England, "Cohen of Trinity" and *Reuben Sachs: A Sketch* (1889).

A similar central focus on the difficulty of developing any clear identity occupies the bildungsroman as art novel, a novel about an artist growing up, here sometimes given the German term *Künstlerroman*. Just as the romantic poem (Wordsworth's *Prelude*) or prose work (De Quincey's *Confessions of an English Opium Eater*) leads us to experience the special destiny of the artist, the bildungsroman of the artist usually ends up positioning its subject outside society. If *David Copperfield* seems to hide David's difference in his extreme alienation and sensitivity as a child, novels in the late nineteenth century and especially in the twentieth – Joyce's *Portrait of the Artist as a Young Man* (1916) – portray growth as leading to an apocalypse of rejection of societal identity. Stephen Daedalus will not serve his society in his adult self and will, rather, forge some new identity. But he will be less the model of a new self for his society than a type of the émigré artist, driven into pluricultural identities by his art as Kim is by his birth. And art, the life of the artist, comes to stand for the aspirations of the late nineteenth- and twentieth-century bourgeoisie to create themselves as radically individual and separated from their actual lives.

There are many other liaisons we could establish between the bildungsroman conceived as an independent genre and other ways of grouping similarities in the Victorian novel. One could speak of a country or pastoral novel as bildungsroman, with the rich texturing of *The Mill on the Floss* developed by modeling the intensity of vision on return to familiar childhood places. And we would observe the inevitable break of the idyll with the transition to maturity, something Thomas Hardy accomplishes as violent accident and rape early in *Tess of the d'Urbervilles* (1891). Or we could find the sensation novel in the bildungsroman, especially in *Great Expectations* in the sudden violent episodes of Pip's life and its incessant immersion in the world of matrimonial betrayal and crime. Or we could look in more detail at the connections between bildungsroman and myth or fairytale already noted. Although for a long time critics have taken relatively little interest in genre, tending to see it as a formal and somewhat barren area of enterprise, multiplication of genres within the bildungsroman proves a dynamic, mobile, and imaginative critical activity: it shows us in this major case how vitally novelists played off each other, revoicing themes, subject-matter, and ideologies from earlier work to create their own new vision of human formation. Formation is, after all, the creative reworking of the wealth of the past for the new creations of the present; genre in the bildungsroman well models that major theme of historical existence.

Critical discussion of the bildungsroman has, as we have seen, sometimes itself seemed to become frozen or fixated on formal issues of definition. And otherwise it has seemed mainly concerned with thematics. Concerning individual authors there has been a great deal of speculation, understandable to our natural curiosity about sources of art but not finally very useful, on the extent of overlap between the author's biography and his or her fiction. All this has led to a certain assumption of second-class status in the craft of the bildungsroman, as if its primary focus were on content, on that massive interest in presenting the novel, as Henry James famously put it, as a great pudding filled with the various stuff of life – the hotter off life's stove the better. This is entirely wrong in respect of the place of the bildungsroman in the history of style in the novel, where it has encouraged innovation rather than conservative repetition. This was especially true in the Victorian period, where important approaches that we think of as part of the modern novel of the next generation were first being developed.

Perhaps the most salient approach in fact comes early in the Victorian novel, and has not elicited a great deal of recognition. It is a place where romantic poetry, with its new concern with perception and consciousness, feeds into prose writing. One finds it in the perceptual conversation poems of Coleridge and in the famous spots of time in Wordsworth, which begin to find in memory a way to render both the intensity of particular experience and the subjective impact of such experience on the mind. One finds it in prose in De Quincey's *Confessions*, where childhood experience is relived first in detail recalled from memory and then again as a fantasia of the narcotized but tremendously self-receptive consciousness. Childhood allows both Wordsworth and De Quincey a focus on sensuous experience, a lifting of adult inhibitions to seeing and responding freshly. Since that time, this has been, of course, a truism in our ideas of childhood, but its consequences for prose style are large. Where in the novel do we find this recourse to a poetic intensity of rendered perception drawn out of childhood memory? First, perhaps, in *Jane Eyre*, where, as in the red room scene already discussed, the narrator Jane is taken back to the dangerous sensuous force of that childhood trauma. Visual intensity, for instance Jane's vision of Mr. Brocklehurst as a kind of black pillar, allows a way of moving the reader from shared perception to shared consciousness – in this case, of this man as moral rapist. With Brontë's *Villette*, we can see that her choice, as with Jane, of first-person narration, is further opening the way to a fluid internalized narrative, especially as we follow the memory of Lucy Snowe, a very inward-turned person with a concomitantly developed consciousness. The great scene in the summer park seems almost to allude to De Quincey, with its drug-inflected intensity of sensuous awareness and simultaneous dream-like consciousness.

We find poetic intensity, above all, in that household staple, *David Copperfield*, where David takes us back through memory to incredibly detailed and vital, sensuous memories of childhood. Perceptual stream and inner stream of consciousness, the former developed in romantic prose, the latter in the *Tristram Shandy* (1760–7) of Laurence Sterne or in the free indirect narratorial style of Jane Austen, here combine seamlessly. Proust may have learned from John Ruskin's similarly rich stream of description, but his memory stream of perception and consciousness above all fulfills what homely Jane and David began, and indeed what Esther's narrative in *Bleak House* well continues. Virginia Woolf's sense, seventy-five years later as she reviewed *Ulysses*, that there was a danger of being lost within an endless stream of consciousness, applies to this kind of novel masquerading as autobiography that first allowed such writing. It threatens to offer us a too subjective vision in which we are lost in one person's viewpoint, as we are, say, in De Quincey. Victorians had discovered a wonderful new style for intense representation in the bildungsroman and then also developed ways to stabilize it. The most obvious and in many ways the most continuously productive was the rather apparent one of combining different voices and perspectives from the time of first person narrator and the time narrated. Readers find it sometimes hard to distinguish the two in *Jane Eyre*, where the narrator often seems to blend with the younger self she recalls; mature Jane seems somehow not always able to distinguish herself from young Jane – which gives her both her vitality and sometimes also her attractive freshness and unattractive naïveté. Lucy seems to me to play complicated, even intricate games of early and later point of view; there has been much interesting critical discussion of this stylistic issue in *Villette*. *David Copperfield* moves from young to mature perspectives but at the risk of reducing the older David to a mealy-mouthed degradation of his younger self. But Dickens's great novel *Great Expectations* is (among other reasons) so good just because it works a much more effective solution to this problem. Pip the narrator keeps being with us as a running double perspective, able to move with wonderful dexterity from sensuous detail and fresh impression of childhood (recall the opening scene of Pip's typographical family and the steeple turned upside down) to a measured, humorous and ultimately moral (though rarely moralizing) perspective. The two play off as a style of wit and shifting viewpoint: childhood is pitiful or comic, tragic or just natural – moving from one to the other with a flip of point of view.

Other approaches were tried; George Eliot's narrator in *Mill*, sharing Maggie's memories but not her end; Butler with his similar use of sympathetic Overton, a kind of voiceover into whose tone Ernest grows as he matures so that we have a kind of long, persuasive dialog between mature view and developing Ernest; Dickens's interleaving of Esther's intense first-person narrative with a global, poly-perspectived journalist/philosopher narrator; Meredith's ironic, distanced narrator who can ventriloquize various character perspectives with his free, indirect, and certainly baroque style. In his elaborate concern for making conscious through the versatile narrator the fullest apprehension of the state of the protagonist, both as he sees himself and as others see him, Meredith presages the bildungsroman as it developed within the aesthetic movement: brilliantly in Pater's brief study *The Child in the House* (1894), and methodically in his interesting if somewhat overwritten *Marius the Epicurean*. This historical bildungsroman uses the historical narrator to voice and expand possibilities of awareness not even technically possible for his pre-Christian character: figures that are used as types for the secular evolution of human consciousness; epiphanic enlargements of understanding that are for our continued *Bildung* even more than for that of Marius. After this, and building on Meredith and Pater, there awaits us the glorious mixture of stream of consciousness, shifting with each era of the maturing person as Melville's Pierre had, combined with the objectification of parodied narratives in Joyce's *Portrait*. From the more conventional first try in Stephen Hero, the life of the artist has been crystallized as a gallery of lives in art. And Woolf's highly stylized bildungsroman of England, *Orlando* (1928), lies right around the corner.

In the critical language offered us by Bakhtin, the bildungsroman is intensely about dialogism: it faces an emerging modern world without easy cultural baggage securely stowed away; it works upon experience itself and rapidly splinters its apparently unitary perspective into two or multiple perspectives, in an ongoing argument about meanings and language. By the same token it keeps expanding and complicating its formal repertoire, almost an epitome of the novel itself as it developed. It introduces a variety of styles, from Pip's fairytale overlays to Joyce's kaleidoscopic style emporium, that quickly move to modernist devices of perspectivism, montage, and parody/burlesque.

Because it starts with the new, with an attempt to capture in form and language the path that an individual has followed, the bildungsroman has no standard ending.

It is not, as some have argued, about happy amalgamation into an existing society. It presumes a changing, usually cosmopolitan and diverse context, and it plots a similarly complicated individual. The end may be tragic regression (as in *The Mill*, *Feverel*, *Dorian Gray*, or even *Tono-Bungay*); it may suggest uneasy integration into a society not easily accepted, as in Dickens, with increasing anxiety from *David Copperfield* to *Great Expectations*, or to Thackeray's *Pendennis* or Meredith's *Adventures of Harry Richmond*. It may only offer the hero (here often a woman) a possible niche in a dangerous world, as Brontë's *Jane Eyre* and *Villette*, or Grand's *The Beth Book* – where Beth is able to exit her bad marriage – or in Butler's passive hero's moneyed recession from his world.

Finally, the bildungsroman's very flexibility and diversity allowed it to pick up and try out devices for meaning. Intense childhood moments naturally become spots of time, epiphanies of the way things might be (romantics) or of how they are stuck (Joyce). Use of storytale and fairytale overlays for childhood allow big, magical meanings as a symbolic structure linking mundane details of life; equally often, traditional religious stories, as we have seen, are used to shape new meanings. In the long poem of a growing life, lyrical, odic interludes, to use Karen Kligerman's useful term, are placed to raise the entire experience to a higher consciousness. New discourses and vocabularies of learning, from psychology to educational theory to anthropology and sociology, are quickly brought into the bildungsroman in the authors' regular quest for new language to explain new experience.

The bildungsroman, epitome of the restlessly growing art that has been the novel as it moves out to new experience, is similarly indicative of the novel's flexible quest for new forms, temporary places to settle before moving on. One could hardly find a better place to begin a broader study of the Victorian novel.

References

Alden, Patricia (1979), *Social Mobility in the English Bildungsroman: Gissing, Hardy, Bennett, and Lawrence* (Ann Arbor: UMI Research).

Bakhtin, Mikhail (1986), "The Bildungsroman and its Significance in the History of Realism," in *Speech Genres and Other Late Essays* (Austin: University of Texas Press), 10–59.

Barney, Richard A. (1990), *Plots of Enlightenment: Education and the Novel in Eighteenth-Century England* (Stanford: Stanford University Press).

Buckley, Jerome Hamilton (1974), *Season of Youth: The Bildungsroman from Dickens to Golding* (Cambridge, Mass.: Harvard University Press).

Dowling, Linda (1994), *Hellenism and Homosexuality in Victorian Oxford* (Ithaca: Cornell University Press).

Fraiman, Susan (1993), *Unbecoming Women: British Women Writers and the Novel of Development* (New York: Columbia University Press).

Fuderer, Laura Sue (1990), *The Female Bildungsroman in English: An Annotated Bibliography of Criticism* (New York: Modern Language Association).

Kontje, Todd (1992), *Private Lives in the Public Sphere: The German Bildungsroman as Metafiction* (University Park: Pennsylvania University Press).

Kontje, Todd (1993), *The German Bildungsroman: History of a National Genre* (Columbia: Camden House).

Moretti, Franco (1987), *The Way of the World: The Bildungsroman in European Culture* (London: Verso/New Left).

Sammons, Jeffrey (1981), "The Mystery of the Missing Bildungsroman; or What Happened to Wilhelm Meister's Legacy," *Genre*, 14, 229–46.

Sedgwick, Eve Kosofsky (1985), *Between Men: English Literature and Male Homosocial Desire* (New York: Columbia University Press).

FURTHER READING

Abel, Elizabeth, Hirsch, Marianne and Langland, Elizabeth, eds. (1983), *The Voyage In: Fictions of Female Development* (Hanover: University Press of New England).

Ariès, Philippe (1962), *Centuries of Childhood: A Social History of Family Life* (New York: Vintage). (First publ. 1960.)

Banerjee, Jacqueline (1996), *Through the Northern Gate: Childhood and Growing Up in British Fiction, 1719–1901* (New York: Peter Lang).

Beebe, Maurice (1964), *Ivory Towers and Sacred Founts: The Artist Hero in Fiction from Goethe to Joyce* (New York: New York University Press).

Coveney, Peter (1967), *The Image of Childhood*, rev. edn. (Baltimore: Penguin).

Ellis, Lorna (1999), *Appearing to Diminish: Female Development and the British Bildungsroman, 1750–1850* (Lewisburg: Bucknell University Press).

Hardin, James N., ed. (1991), *Reflection and Action: Essays on the Bildungsroman* (Columbia: University of South Carolina Press).

Howe, Susanne (1905), *Wilhelm Meister and his English Kinsmen* (New York: Columbia University Press).

Redfield, Marc (1996), *Phantom Formations: Aesthetic Ideology and the Bildungsroman* (Ithaca: Cornell University Press).

Steedman, Carolyn (1995), *Strange Dislocations: Childhood and the Idea of Human Interiority, 1780–1930* (Cambridge, Mass.: Harvard University Press; London: Virago).

Swales, Martin (1978), *The German Bildungsroman from Wieland to Hesse* (Princeton: Princeton University Press).

17

The Gothic Romance in the Victorian Period

Cannon Schmitt

Let Charles Dickens's *Oliver Twist* – which appeared in serial publication beginning in 1837, the year of Victoria's accession to the throne – stand as unlikely initiator and exemplar of the Gothic romance in the Victorian period. I write "unlikely" because this first proper novel (rather than collection of impressions and picaresque tales, such as the earlier *Sketches by Boz* and even *Pickwick Papers*) by the man whose name was to become almost synonymous with Victorian fiction clears a space for the sort of story it seeks to tell by condemning romance of all sorts as dangerous misrepresentation. In a preface added to *Oliver Twist* in 1841, Dickens makes that condemnation while defending his controversial choice to depict criminals without the usual embellishment:

> What manner of life is that which is described in these pages, as the everyday existence of a Thief? What charms has it for the young and ill-disposed, what allurements for the most jolter-headed of juveniles? Here are no canterings on moonlit heaths, no merry-makings in the snuggest of all possible caverns, none of the attractions of dress, no embroidery, no lace, no jack-boots, no crimson coats and ruffles, none of the dash and freedom with which "the road" has been time out of mind invested. The cold wet shelterless midnight streets of London; the foul and frowsy dens, where vice is closely packed and lacks the room to turn; the haunts of hunger and disease; the shabby rags that scarcely hold together; where are the attractions of these things? Have they no lesson, and do they not whisper something beyond the little-regarded warning of an abstract moral precept?

The immediate reference is to Edward Bulwer-Lytton's *Paul Clifford* (1830) and other Newgate novels that endow the life of the outlaw with a glamour not simply false but, as a consequence, fatally attractive to "the young and ill-disposed" – to potential criminals who are also, or so Dickens seems to think, potential readers. The larger quarrel, though, is with romance and the literature of misrepresentation more generally, and in this Dickens takes his place as one of the exponents of the realist aesthetic so pervasive in the Victorian novel. George Eliot, more programmatic and thoroughgoing a realist than Dickens, puts forth her own credo in the seventeenth chapter of *Adam Bede* (1859): "I would not, even if I had the choice, be the clever novelist who could create a world so much better than this, in which we get up in the morning to do our daily work, that you would be likely to turn a harder, colder eye on the dusty streets and the common green fields – on . . . real breathing men and women." The differences between Dickens and Eliot, *Oliver Twist* and *Adam Bede*, are significant: whereas Dickens justifies the portrayal of unvarnished criminality as the surest means to point a moral, Eliot advocates making the novel an accurate mirror as the best way to fit (or at least not to unfit) readers for sympathy with their fellow humans. Both authors and both novels, though, hold in common an assumption about the deleterious effects of distorting the world in the process of depicting it.

All this seems to show how *Oliver Twist* cannot possibly be considered a romance, much less serve as an exemplary instance of Victorian Gothic – since the Gothic for most of the nineteenth century incarnated misrepresentational fiction *par excellence*. Indeed, nearly everything about this novel appears to militate against characterizing it as Gothic: its deployment of a narrative of development that follows a young protagonist from naïveté and isolation to understanding and belonging; its direct, unmediated engagement with topical social questions such as the New Poor Law of 1834; its unifying and universalist narrative voice; and of course its commitment to showing things "as they are." Nevertheless, I have begun my account of the Gothic romance in the Victorian period with *Oliver Twist* because elements of the Gothic and other genres from which Dickens wishes to distance himself persist in this novel, and do so precisely in the service of the realist imperative that would appear to banish them.

We can see how this works by noting, for example, that the novel's seventeenth chapter opens with an attack on another denigrated art form, stage melodrama, for its tendency to "present the tragic and the comic scenes, in as regular alternation, as the layers of red and white in a side of streaky bacon." Despite the imputation that melodrama's abrupt and metronomic movements from tears to laughter and back again betray a hopeless artificiality, the narrator proceeds to assert that "the transitions in real life from well-spread boards to death-beds, and from mourning weeds to holiday garments, are not a whit less startling" – and then to effect such a transition himself. As melodrama functions here, so the Gothic elsewhere: when what Dickens takes to be "real" defies expectation, when it threatens to seem incredible by the lights of his readers' daily experience or refutes the comfortable assumptions fostered by that experience, he enlists the Gothic. Despite its apparent absurdities, that is, not the least of which is, as with melodrama, its marked conventionality, the Gothic appears uniquely capable of realizing on the page certain key aspects of the world Dickens aspires to render.

One aspect of that world prominent in Dickens's corpus from first to last is the menacing incomprehensibility of Victorian urban space. A direct line can be drawn from the architecture of the eponymous castle of Ann Radcliffe's *The Mysteries of*

Udolpho (1794) to the labyrinthine streets, hidden byways, and nightmarish pockets of squalor that distinguish Dickens's London. A hallmark of the Gothic in its pre-Victorian heyday is the role played by a topography disorienting to characters and readers alike. Horace Walpole's *The Castle of Otranto* (1764), Radcliffe's *Udolpho*, Charles Robert Maturin's *Melmoth the Wanderer* (1820), and dozens of similar productions chronicle the tribulations of imperiled heroes and heroines whose plight is made all the more dire by virtue of their imprisonment in strongholds full of secret chambers connected by byzantine passageways. As Mikhail Bakhtin indicates when he names "the castle" the Gothic's distinctive chronotope, or literary fusion of space and time, the apparently perverse spatial qualities of medieval fortresses in these novels carry a specific temporal resonance, suggesting premodern, feudal oppression and irrationality (1981: 246). In Walpole, Radcliffe, Maturin, and others, architectural antiquity and opacity give the lie to Enlightenment beliefs about clarity, rationality, and progress. Literally difficult to find one's way around in, the Gothic castle in its initial incarnation metaphorically signals the uncertainties of epistemology – of the possibility of knowing others and, especially, of knowing the self.

Thomas De Quincey, in the autobiographical essays that constitute his *Confessions of an English Opium Eater* (1821; revised and expanded, 1856), was the first to exploit this Gothic convention to body forth the streets of nineteenth-century London. De Quincey stresses the difficulty of navigating those streets, the *terrae incognitae* they conceal, and above all the likelihood of losing touch with others in them. Such a textual transformation of London into the site of Gothicism reaches an apogee with G. W. M. Reynolds's sprawling *Mysteries of London* (1845–8). As early as *Oliver Twist*, though, Dickens inherits and puts to use this mode of representing Britain's largest metropolis. As I have suggested above, he does so in part because for him the Gothic reveals the truth (or one of the truths) of London, a truth ironically conveyable only by way of patently conventional literary devices. Thus, to adduce merely one example, in a pivotal scene Oliver, while on an errand to repay the trust of the man who has saved him from life among a gang of thieves, takes an accidental wrong turn and soon finds himself recaptured by two of the gang and "dragged into a labyrinth of dark narrow courts."

This brings us to the denizens of those narrow courts, and especially to that chief of thieves, Dickens's Fagin. Radcliffe and her contemporaries set the action of their novels in a nearly manichean world of good and evil in which the role of the villain is most often occupied by rapacious (and, generally, southern European – a curious national-geographical specificity about which I will say more shortly) aristocrats, selfish men driven by their own passions and contemptuous of restraints either internal or imposed by society. Existing outside the pale of the civilized (if sometimes by virtue of being overcivilized – civilized beyond civility), such characters necessitate for their portrayal a particularly overwrought language that renders legible their unbridled appetites by verbally painting a physiognomy to match. Similarly, Fagin, whose Jewishness and criminality stand in for the more literal foreignness of earlier Gothic villains, comes to life in passages that dehumanize him even as they suggest that he is of a piece with the city that provides him refuge: "As he glided stealthily along, creeping beneath the shelter of the walls and doorways, the hideous old man seemed like some loathsome reptile, engendered in the slime and darkness through which he moved: crawling forth, by night, in search of some rich offal for a meal." The logic of Dickens's novel requires such lurid moments of characterization, even if our final sight of Fagin distractedly awaiting execution tempers them and the manicheism they imply.

As embodied in *Oliver Twist*, then, the Gothic romance in the Victorian period may be considered a paradoxical and even a parasitical entity. Condemned in the name of a new and better representational practice, the Gothic nevertheless remains necessary for the successful pursuit of that practice. Whence the persistence of the Gothic language of confusion, nightmare, and numinous malevolence in the works of a great many Victorian authors otherwise committed to varieties of realism – not only novelists such as Dickens, Elizabeth Gaskell, and (demonstrably if more rarely) George Eliot but also, remarkably, journalists and sociologists. Both Friedrich Engels, in *The Condition of the Working Class in England in 1844* (1845), and Henry Mayhew, in *London Labour and the London Poor* (1851–2), for example, borrow from the Gothic in their accounts of those unprecedented products of mass urbanization and industrialization, the proletariat and lumpenproletariat. In all these instances, the unreal, outmoded, and avowedly spurious textual world of haunted and unnavigable castles, ineffable horrors, and monstrous dukes and viscounts is pressed into the service of conveying the all-too-real, modern, and painfully insistent extratextual world of a growing and restless population of the poor, increasingly crowded cities, external disciplines imposed by industrial capitalism and legal strictures on poverty, and internal disciplines attendant upon a society deeply riven along lines of race, class, and gender. Thus we arrive at a first definition of the Gothic romance in the Victorian period as paradox: rejected as laughably conventional, a byword for artifice, the Gothic is at the same time incorporated as a form of writing particularly well suited to representing a new and refractory actuality. This mode of existence of the genre continues right through to the end of the nineteenth century, as the Gothic continues to provide one of the means to represent in fiction not only new elements of the social and political world but also what were conceived of as previously hidden or inaccessible realities, chief among them psychological interiority, sexual deviance, and scientific discoveries – particularly those suggesting that humans, despite their apparent differences from the rest of the animal kingdom, evolved from earlier and other forms of life.

Before leaving *Oliver Twist* behind it will be useful to venture a second definition of Victorian Gothic as paradox and parasite: initially concerned with the past and, by the 1830s, itself thought of as belonging to a bygone era, the Gothic remains, haunting later literary forms such as the realist novels mentioned above in the shape of an anachronism. The contortions and qualifications of the title of this chapter – "The Gothic Romance in the Victorian Period" – are necessary because the Gothic belongs at the outset (and, narrowly defined, perhaps properly) to the late eighteenth and early nineteenth centuries. The most well-known Gothicist, Ann Radcliffe, published *The*

Italian (her last novel, with the exception of the posthumously published *Gaston de Blondeville* [1826]), in 1797. Temporally and ideologically, Radcliffe's work occupies a liminal position between the Enlightenment's rejection of the past as barbarous and romanticism's adoption of the antiquarian turn back to the past (together with the individualist turn inward to the self) as the watchword for a movement. By 1837, at the outset of the Victorian era, the Gothic as an important literary phenomenon might be said to be already a dead letter, safely buried along with the rest of the Georgian and Regency tumult the Victorians sought to put behind them throughout the long period of consolidation and modernization under Victoria's rule that was to last until her own death in 1901. To speak of the Gothic romance in the Victorian period, then, is to speak of something that should have disappeared but that somehow nevertheless remains or returns. And this is right insofar as it enables an understanding of Victorian Gothic not only as a mode of representing the new but also as a textual location in which the old can persist or recur. Organized around secrets and mysteries, emplotting concealments and discoveries of information as much as of space, the Gothic puts past and present in communication with one another in ways not so readily achieved outside its pages. Consider Walpole's *Otranto*, often taken to be the first Gothic romance in English: easily lost in the ludicrous details of a colossal helmet dropping from the sky and the endless ramifications of Otranto's subterranean corridors is the story of the sins of the past refusing to stay in the past, rising up to punish those who continue to benefit from them in the present. And this, too, finds its place in *Oliver Twist*, which tells of an orphan who nonetheless cannot escape the legacy of his parentage and of a criminal relentlessly tormented by the memory of his own crime.

Dickens continued to exploit the potentiality of the Gothic to convey the shock of the new as well as the shocking persistence of the old: in *Bleak House* (1854), in which both the Chancery and Dedlock plots chart the ways in which history can burden the present; in *Great Expectations* (1861), the title of which alludes to the promise of a legacy but whose various characters suffer the ruin of their hopes; in ghost stories such as "The Signalman" (1866), a tale that casts anxieties about that technological novelty, the railway, in the form of uncanny premonitions and repetitions; and in many other works produced over the more than thirty years during which he was an active writer. But it is not until the very end of his career that the Gothic in Dickens achieves something of an apotheosis – in *Our Mutual Friend* (1865), the last of his novels to be published during his lifetime, and in the unfinished and posthumously published *The Mystery of Edwin Drood* (1870).

The London of *Our Mutual Friend* is like that of *Oliver Twist* only more so: a city of bewildering complexity, strewn with trash heaps, polluted rather than cleansed by the waters of the Thames, and overrun not with gangs of thieves but with what seems in many ways worse, speculators and *nouveaux riches* living out lives of superficiality and soulless hypocrisy. The "mutual friend" of the title, John Harmon, sets the plot in motion when he resolves to allow the false report of his death to go uncorrected and live on in disguise as John Rokesmith: "And so busy had he been all night, piling and piling weights upon weights of earth upon John Harmon's grave, that by that time John Harmon lay buried under a whole Alpine range; and still the Sexton Rokesmith accumulated mountains over him, lightening his labour with the dirge, 'Cover him, crush him, keep him down!'" Although Harmon does not narrate the novel, it is largely his Gothic coign of vantage from beyond the grave that renders possible the text's mordant critique of the corruptions of London society in the 1860s (the same corruptions later savaged by Anthony Trollope in *The Way We Live Now* [1875] – in part by way of his own Fagin-like villain, the foreign swindler Melmotte).

As for *The Mystery of Edwin Drood*, Gothic conventions thoroughly pervade this final fragment of Dickensian narrative: the inexplicable disappearance and probable murder of Drood himself (whence the title); the persecution of Drood's fiancée, Rosa Bud, by his uncle, John Jasper; opium visions; cathedral crypts – all these aspects of setting, character, and plot closely echo Gothic fiction of nearly a century earlier. So exaggerated is this Gothicization that the representational possibilities of the genre seem close to being emptied out, rendered null by virtue of sheer ubiquity. And this would in one sense be appropriate insofar as the principal cultural work accomplished in this incomplete novel – influenced in this regard and others by Wilkie Collins's *The Moonstone* (1868) – has to do with its overturning of the moralized national-racial topography that stands as one of the Gothic's uglier legacies. But if *Edwin Drood* explodes easy associations of the English John Jasper with virtue and the "foreign" Neville Landless with vice and danger, it also suggests that Jasper's murderous hatred is at least in part a result of contamination by the foreign in the form of that "oriental" panacea and poison, opium – the same drug that sent De Quincey wandering the streets.

In moving without interruption from *Oliver Twist* to *The Mystery of Edwin Drood*, however, I have elided more than a quarter-century of literary production during which Victorian Gothic of a different but no less significant sort developed. Not coincidentally, I have also remained largely in London. If, as the work of De Quincey, Reynolds, and Dickens attests, Britain's capital city and largest metropolis proved especially amenable to representation by means of the Gothic, this should not be allowed to obscure the fact that the isolated settings that characteristically play such a large role in the work of Radcliffe and her contemporaries have their own avatars in the Victorian era. Indeed, one way to understand the appeal of the Gothic for such authors as Emily and Charlotte Brontë is to note the degree to which isolation at once constitutes, precipitates, and resolves the crises of their heroines – whether that isolation is thought of as resulting from the limitation of those heroines' experience to provincial life far removed from the teeming social realm of London (or even from the industrial centers of Manchester and Birmingham) or as inherent in their defiant insistence upon the incommensurability of their own abilities and aspirations with the situations in which they find themselves.

To turn to Emily Brontë's *Wuthering Heights* (1847) from a reading of, for instance, Dickens's *Our Mutual Friend* is forcibly to feel a tremendous narrowing of focus. The former's small cast of characters, made to seem still smaller by virtue of the repetition of names from one generation to the next, appears to exist at an insuperable distance from any sort of larger national life. Those characters' isolation borders on imprisonment – Lockwood, the novel's frame narrator, at first reads their savage and incomprehensible manners as "the consequence of being buried alive" – and it requires only the entrance on the scene of Heathcliff, an earlier incarnation of Dickens's Neville Landless rescued from the streets of Liverpool, virtually to transform the Heights and the Grange into Udolphesque ruins. Isolation, too, proves a necessary condition for the tale of their lives to be told: Lockwood finds himself listening to Nelly Dean's account of Heathcliff's arrival and its disastrous consequences for the Lintons and the Earnshaws only after he himself has been entrapped by weather and illness. If the narrative that Lockwood constructs from that account and his own subsequent observations chronicles the likelihood of an end to ruins, of a rejuvenation that, as Fredric Jameson has argued, would effect an impossible reconciliation of "the immemorial (and cyclical) time of the agricultural life of a country squiredom" with "the alien dynamism of capitalism" (1981: 128), it also features what many critics have taken to be the definitive contribution of *Wuthering Heights* to the history of the novel in English: namely, a lexicon and syntax, both largely indebted to the Gothic, for the construction of inner life as powerful and irrational. As demonstrated by the portrayal of Heathcliff as vampire, fiend, and ghoul, and of Catherine as insistently plaintive ghost, nothing but the Gothic seems capable of conveying the preternatural strength of these characters' identity with and desire for one another.

The harnessing of Gothic trappings to the task of constructing psychological interiority as a realm of intensity and strangeness was to receive decisive development in the work of Emily's sister Charlotte Brontë. As Robert B. Heilman writes of her work, "that discovery of passion, that rehabilitation of the extra-rational, which is the historical office of Gothic, is no longer oriented in marvelous circumstance but moves deeply into the lesser known realities of human life" (1958: 123). Charlotte Brontë's *Jane Eyre* (1847) provides something like the quintessence of a narrative designed to make palpable those "lesser known realities." The novel takes the form of a bildungsroman in which the protagonist and narrator, Jane herself, tells the tale of rebellion against her outcast, orphaned state and the subsequent search for some sort of belonging, achieved finally in her marriage to Rochester and, as a consequence, her (admittedly muted) entry into the landed gentry. A Gothic figure intervenes at various moments to retard this nineteenth-century pilgrim's progress: Rochester's "mad" wife Bertha Mason, brought back from Jamaica and imperfectly imprisoned in the third story of his ancestral mansion. A living embodiment of the sins of Rochester's own past who refuses to be silenced or forgotten, Bertha Mason also functions as a doppelgänger for Jane, literalizing the fears of oppression to which she gives voice via the language of enslavement. Bertha Mason, that is, externalizes in the narrative that which Rochester and Jane are understood to hold within: his guilt and her fears manifest themselves in the person of the madwoman, and their union cannot take place until the exorcism of that guilt and those fears by way of Bertha's self-immolation.

So far in my discussion of the Brontës I have allied the Gothic in their work with a new kind of psychologism in the novel, a rendering of characters as castles, their forbidding or simply blank façades concealing unsuspected depths within. As Dickens draws upon the Gothic to represent in fiction London's sinister streets, I have been arguing, so Emily and Charlotte Brontë draw upon it in order to portray the equally tortuous, incomprehensible, and potentially dangerous alleys of the mind. To attend seriously to Heathcliff's often-mentioned resemblance to a "dark-skinned gypsy," to Bertha Mason's origins in the West Indies, or (in a more figurative register) to Jane's repeated references to herself as a member of an "anathematized race," however, is to recognize a different function of the Gothic in *Wuthering Heights* and *Jane Eyre* – namely, that of providing an avenue for engagement with another strange world conceived of as a reservoir of intensity and irrationality, an outer rather than an inner world: the other country.

The Gothic's association with foreignness can be traced back to the beginnings of the genre. Early Gothic novels were themselves often treated as texts of foreign origin. Walpole's claim in the preface to the first edition to have translated *The Castle of Otranto* from a sixteenth-century Italian manuscript, while clearly aiming at verisimilitude, also establishes an un-English provenance for the text. William Wordsworth, in the "Preface" to *Lyrical Ballads* (1800), estranges Gothics (those "frantic novels") by including them with "sickly and stupid German Tragedies, and deluges of idle and extravagant stories in verse" – all types of reading material destructive of the sensibilities of the English common reader (1991: 249). Further, while almost invariably set abroad, late eighteenth- and early nineteenth-century Gothics trade in varying degrees of xenophobia – despite or perhaps precisely because of the fact that they are usually peopled with characters who are all (villains, heroes, and heroines alike) nominally foreign. During the period of the French Revolution and the Napoleonic Wars, which corresponded to the height of the genre's popularity in England, Gothic portrayals of continental and especially Catholic depravity engaged in a displaced manner with the terrors across the Channel – representing the continent as the scene of atrocities in order to define what it was to be English against a caricatural version of things French, Italian, or Spanish. As I suggested above in connection with *The Mystery of Edwin Drood*, this binary opposition between domestic and foreign, which elevates Englishness by contrasting it with demonic versions of other nationalities, stands as a lamentable but enduring legacy of early Gothics. When De Quincey comes to write about a Malay he encounters in the Lake District, or Emily Brontë about a fictional Liverpudlian foundling who may be a Spaniard or a lascar or even an American but who at any rate is certainly not an Englishman, the Gothic provides ready means for doing so.

Charlotte Brontë's *Villette* (1853), like *Wuthering Heights* and *Jane Eyre*, deploys a Gothic demonization of the foreign. Like *The Mystery of Edwin Drood*, though, it also features an urgent anxiety about the consequences of that deployment. Lucy Snowe's desires – the insistence of which gave Matthew Arnold reason to denounce the novel for containing and fomenting nothing but "hunger, rebellion, and rage" (quoted in Allott 1974: 201) – cause her to flee England, a country in which she suspects those desires can never be met, for Labassecour, Brontë's fictionalized version of Belgium.

Appealing for the promise of freedom it holds out, Labassecour also repels because of its Catholic, continental ways, manifested by characters who, in their secrecy, hypocrisy, and self-interested scheming, rival even those officers of the Inquisition to be found in Radcliffe's *The Italian* or, especially, Maturin's *Melmoth the Wanderer*. This is just to say that Labassecour, as the other country, plays a dual role in the novel: at moments the locus of desire and liberation, at other moments it functions as a metonym for all that is to be feared and reviled. Corresponding to and to some degree resolving the contradictions of the double role of the foreign in the text is a similar doubling of the Gothic, which serves as a vehicle for giving fictional shape to the marvelous or frightful ways of Labassecour while, at the same time, providing the means to represent Lucy Snowe's interiority. *Villette* associates the foreign land with the psychological world of its English protagonist by invoking the Gothic to represent both. This association, which at times amounts to an identification between the two realms, importantly qualifies what might otherwise appear to be a merely xenophobic representation of the continent: the same means that serve to represent the sinister ways of Catholicism also give shape to the unknown but valorized depths of an English-woman's mind. Further, as in *Jane Eyre*, the complex nexus of Gothicism, women, inner life, and the foreign provides an opening on to history, in this case the European nationalist revolutions of 1848. In *Villette*, those revolutions, evoked through passages about Labassecour's own struggle for independent nationhood, are both ridiculed and understood to parallel the hard-fought independence of Lucy Snowe.

Although not usually considered to belong to that subgenre, certain aspects of *Wuthering Heights*, *Jane Eyre*, and *Villette* closely resemble "sensation fiction," a type of novel that came into being in the early 1860s with the publication of three texts in close temporal proximity to one another: Wilkie Collins's *The Woman in White* (1860), Mrs. Henry Wood's *East Lynne* (1861), and Mary Elizabeth Braddon's *Lady Audley's Secret* (1862). In a review essay titled "Miss Braddon," Henry James identified Collins's distinctive contribution to the English novel, and by implication that of sensation fiction as a whole, as the domestication of the Gothic:

> To Mr. Collins belongs the credit of having introduced into fiction those most myste-rious of mysteries, the mysteries which are at our own doors. This innovation gave a new impetus to the literature of horrors. It was fatal to the authority of Mrs. Radcliffe and her everlasting castle in the Apennines. What are the Apennines to us, or we to the Apennines? Instead of the terrors of "Udolpho," we were treated to the terrors of the cheerful country-house and the busy London lodgings. And there is no doubt that these were infinitely the more terrible. (1865: 593)

Such an innovation may seem just as fairly credited to Dickens and the Brontës, whose novels feature English "terrors" as far from that "everlasting castle in the Apennines" as anything to be found in Collins. Attention to the reception history of sensation fiction, however, confirms that, regardless of the extent to which it had been antici-pated, it was widely perceived as a radical departure. Moreover, while it was popular with the reading public, professional critics found in that departure something not simply novel but also threatening. A representative judgment is that of H. F. Chorley, who, in a review of Collins's *Armadale* (1866), averred that sensation fiction and its popularity were evidence of "a period of diseased invention" in the world of British letters (1866: 732). Further, as was the case with earlier incarnations of the Gothic, the "invention" represented by sensation was seen to be "diseased" because of its supposed foreign origins. As one reviewer commenting on Collins's *No Name* (1862) put it: "[Sensation] is a plant of foreign growth. It comes to us from France, and it can only be imported in a mutilated condition" (quoted in Page 1974: 134–5).

Collins's *The Moonstone* can serve as an example of what was new about sensation as well as what may have been objectionable. Although framed by a "Prologue" and an "Epilogue" set in India, and so at the outset and the conclusion enlisting that geographical displacement characteristic of 1790s Gothics, the novel's main action occurs in England. Anticipating in this regard various aspects of Dickens's *The Mystery of Edwin Drood*, *The Moonstone* deploys the full complement of Gothic conventions: malevolent aristocrats and dangerous foreigners, a threatened young woman, labyrinthine pathways both on country estates and in the seedier parts of London, nightmarish visions brought on by opium use. This marks a certain innovation at the level of plot and setting insofar as it brings, as in James's account, mystery and terror home, from lonely fastnesses in Italian mountains to a "cheerful [English] country-house" and "busy London lodgings." But the more striking innovation occurs not in what is narrated but in the narrating itself, or, more precisely, in the narrative medium. Modeled on the taking of depositions from witnesses at a trial, the narrative strategy of *The Moonstone* requires that each character relate, in the first person, only that part of the action in which he or she was directly engaged. An attempt to heighten suspense, this strategy also has the effect of taking novelistic realism to a higher level. Eschewing the synoptic gaze and homogenizing voice of a single authorial narrator, Collins's novel elevates character, and particularly the shaping (and often distorting) lens of characterological interiority, in ways that follow from the work of the Brontës and anticipate modernism.

Attention to the narrative strategy of *The Moonstone* should not obscure, however, the equally important contribution made by the novel's plot, a contribution bound up with the question of empire. The novel takes its title from a gem sacred to a Hindu god but stolen by a Briton during the successful siege of Seringapatam, a victory of historic importance for the expansion of the British empire in India. Brought home to England, the Moonstone brings with it a curse, a conspiracy, and eventually a murder. The domestic mystery and terror to which James calls attention are here shown to be imports from the imperial periphery. Collins is careful to undermine the invidious national and racial distinctions that might be inferred from such plotting by casting as his villain the English gentleman Godfrey Ablewhite and as one of his heroes Ezra Jennings. The product of a union between an Englishman and a woman from an unspecified British colony, Jennings is maligned and mistrusted by the provincials among whom he finds himself working, but uniquely able and willing to provide the solution to the mystery at the center of the action. Nevertheless, the novel's consistent portrayal of Indian artifacts — from opium to illuminated manuscripts to the Moonstone itself — as alluring but potentially dangerous cannot help but reinforce an older Gothic structure of opposition between a domestic world constitutive of the normative and a foreign one that, by means of its decided difference, threatens the domestic (and, in doing so, brings it into high relief).

From this perspective, *The Moonstone* takes its place as one of the earliest instances of what Patrick Brantlinger has termed "imperial Gothic," a "blend of adventure story with Gothic elements" developed in conjunction with the frenzy of pan-European imperialist activity during the latter part of the nineteenth century known as the "new imperialism" (1988: 227). Anticipated by *Jane Eyre* (and even *Wuthering Heights*, if we imagine Heathcliff's origins to be imperial), this type of fiction importantly modifies the Gothic's longstanding concern with the foreign. Where once Italian aristocrats or Catholic monastics incarnated all that was disturbingly un-English, now that office is carried out by natives of non-European lands, from the witch Gagool in H. Rider Haggard's African adventure *King Solomon's Mines* (1885), to the Egyptian priestess of Richard Marsh's *The Beetle* (1897), to the three indefatigable Brahmins who will stop at nothing to recover their sacred gem in *The Moonstone*. Most examples of "imperial Gothic" differ from *The Moonstone*, though, in one crucial particular: they are usually set abroad, in imperial rather than domestic space. Looking back at the history of the Gothic over the course of the nineteenth century, we can see that this new exploitation of foreign settings constitutes a return, but a return with a difference. Early Gothics take place abroad, occasionally (as in William Beckford's *Vathek* [1786]) in non-European space but more characteristically on the European continent. In the middle of the nineteenth century, the Gothic is brought home to England, as in Dickens's Gothic London or sensation fiction's domestic terrors. Toward the end of the century, with "imperial Gothic," the genre goes abroad again. But the movement is not cyclical so much as dialectical: the foreign space "returned to" is in fact a different space, that of empire rather than Europe. Conflating stereotypical and ethnographic accounts of the ways of non-Europeans with a purely fantasmatic sense of the possible customs of very "other" others, *fin de siècle* "imperial Gothics" engage with the dangers and difficulties of empire at the moment of Britain's greatest commitment to the acquisition of territory.

Exemplary in this regard is Haggard's *She* (1887). As with so many Victorian fictionalizations of Africa, the novel exploits the continent chiefly as a stage upon which Europeans pursue their own ends. Like *Otranto*, the story is one of the persistence of the past — embodied, in this case, in Leo Vincey's quest for vengeance against a "White Queen" who killed his ancestor millennia before. In the prelude to the encounter between Leo and that murderous Queen, *She* presents us with a familiar version of Africa as the realm of cannibals and big game. But these altogether predictable elements of the novel are undone, or at least made more complicated, by the presence at the heart of the dark continent of the woman Leo has left England to find, "She" herself. Immortal by virtue of having bathed in a magic column of light, ruling absolutely over a different and much "lower" race amidst the ruins of a once-great civilization, and possessed of wisdom and intelligence commensurate with her immense age, She problematizes the convenient notion of Africa as so barbarous as absolutely to require European settlement and development. Moreover, her vision of seizing power over all the regions of the globe evokes an empire sufficiently reminiscent of the British empire (with Victoria, another White Queen, at its head) as to cast a shadow over any unequivocal acceptance or approbation of imperialism. As the narrator, Holly, speculates: "In the end [She] would, I had little doubt, assume absolute rule over the British dominions, and probably over the whole earth, and, though I was sure that she would speedily make ours the most glorious and prosperous empire that the world has ever seen, it would be at the cost of a terrible sacrifice of life." The immediate pertinence of such a statement, which has to do with marking the difference between such an empire and the one ruled over by Victoria, is at least partially ironized by the implication that the British empire cannot be disassociated from the one Holly envisions: in his account it is not only "ours," "glorious and prosperous," but also made possible by "a terrible sacrifice of life."

Along with this defamiliarization of British imperialism in *She* comes the suggestion that England itself is not free from the strange and unfamiliar. Consider Holly, the Cambridge don who narrates the novel: almost the first thing we learn about him is that his looks are sufficiently ape-like to confirm the "monkey theory," which is to say Charles Darwin's claim, put forward in *The Descent of Man, and Selection in Relation to Sex* (1871), that "man is descended from a hairy quadruped, furnished with a tail and pointed ears, probably arboreal in its habits" (vol. 2, 389). Holly, in his simian appearance, signals the possibility of atavism, of a return to bestial origins. As the novel plays out, though, not Holly but She herself suffers this fate: stepping once more into the column of light that has given her immortality, She inadvertently achieves the undoing of its effects. Aging two thousand years in a matter of minutes, the once-great queen shrivels and dies, but not before, in a penultimate moment of hideous mockery or (depending upon one's predilections) high camp, "turning into a monkey." A notable Gothic element of *She*, horror of the possibility of atavism informed so many other late Victorian novels that it would be fair to refer to something like a Darwinian Gothic. The term captures, at any rate, some of the salient elements of several works published near the end of the century, including H. G. Wells's *The Time Machine* (1895) and *The Island of Dr. Moreau* (1896), both of which posit beings neither human nor animal but something in between, and Robert Louis Stevenson's *The Strange Case of Dr. Jekyll and Mr. Hyde* (1886), an enduringly influential version of the fantasy of regression.

In Wells's novels, creatures that are not-quite-not-human belong to worlds safely distant from the late Victorian Britain of the novels' author and readers. *The Time Machine*'s sheep-like Eloi and predatory Morlocks inhabit a barely recognizable London of the distant future, while *The Island of Dr. Moreau*'s terrible results of vivisection struggle against degeneration into animalism on the isolated Pacific island of the title. The first remarkable feature of *The Strange Case of Dr. Jekyll and Mr. Hyde* is that Hyde's brutal crimes are carried out in the midst of the well-populated streets of London, bright even at night ("street after street, all lighted up as if for a procession"). In this Hyde may remind us of Fagin in *Oliver Twist*; but the telling difference is that for Dickens's novel fully to resemble Stevenson's the former would need to reveal, in some harrowing final moment, that Oliver and Fagin are in fact one and the same – a conceptual impossibility that suggests just how far the Gothic, and with it the understanding of human beings and their vicissitudes, has traveled in the intervening half-century. For the really troubling feature of Stevenson's tale is, of course, not simply the mere existence of someone like Hyde but rather the implication that we are all Hydes, that like Jekyll's professional success or philanthropy our own public selves are nothing but masks for an inner beastliness.

In quite a different way, the possibility of English characters harboring something alien within governs another late Victorian Gothic, Oscar Wilde's *The Picture of Dorian Gray* (1891). Like Jekyll, Dorian Gray embraces a split between a public and a private or an outer and an inner self; unlike Jekyll, however, he never imagines the former as anything but a cynical necessity, a ruse to allow him to pursue his unspecified crimes or sins without fear of suffering the consequences. That the portrait he keeps locked away registers those consequences and is eventually transmogrified by them into something so awful that he is driven to destroy it and, with it, himself is finally less interesting than that what he does to merit this fate – those crimes and sins just alluded to – remains unspecified. Given Wilde's own later trial and imprisonment for sodomy, the temptation to identify what his character does with homosexuality – in the language of the day, "the sin that dare not speak its name" – is palpable. And this would be consonant with what I have written above about the vocation of the Gothic in allowing for the representation of new or previously hidden realities. But positively to make such an identification would seem to be precisely what the text will not allow: the novel's construction around perhaps unspeakable but at least unspoken acts repeats an earlier Gothic obsession with ineffability, the implications of which must remain just that – implications and not certainties.

Another novel in which clandestine connections between men are at issue, and the text with which I will close this survey, is Bram Stoker's *Dracula* (1897). The central European count of that name, a reprise of the villainous continental aristocrats of an earlier iteration of the Gothic, most famously preys upon women. He himself, however, articulates the purpose of that predation as a way to reach other men. Addressing the group of men who band together to repel his invasion of London, Dracula says: "'Your girls that you all love are mine already; and through them you and others shall yet be mine – my creatures to do my bidding and to be my jackals when I want to feed.'" As Dorian Gray's picture reveals his unspecified crimes, or as Hyde incarnates Jekyll's hidden desires, so Dracula speaks that which the novel that bears his name constructs as the repressed truth of Van Helsing and company's gentlemanly union, as well as of their zealous interest in tracking down the peculiar foreigner in their midst: if not necessarily veiled homosexual longing, then certainly that "homosocial" cementing of relations between men that, as Eve Sedgwick (1985) contends, must cleanse itself of the taint of homosexuality by passing by way of women – something in this case accomplished literally, as the blood of these men passes from them through Lucy Westenra to Dracula himself.

As compelling as it may be, however, to read Dracula as a man among men, and so *Dracula* as a textual enactment of the drama of homosociality, such an interpretive move risks missing the ways which this decadent aristocrat is portrayed not just as un-English but as inhuman. This marks a crucial difference not only from *The Picture of Dorian Gray* but also from the Gothic as practiced by authors such as Ann Radcliffe. In Radcliffe's *The Mysteries of Udolpho*, Signor Montoni and his partner in crime, Laurentini di Udolpho, capitulate to their desires and so commit horrible crimes. For the warning implied by their weakness to be meaningful, however (Laurentini to Emily St. Aubert: " '[B]eware of the first indulgence of the passions; beware of the first!' "), these characters must remain recognizably like the heroine: they can be erring, that is, but they cannot be utterly alien. In *Dracula*, by contrast, the Count is repeatedly referred to as a "thing," a "monster," a creature of a different order of being from those upon whom he preys. The scene of his death, achieved by two men wielding hunting knives, confirms Dracula's identity as inhuman, perhaps as an animal. By the same token, however, that scene cannot help but suggest the animalism of his killers as well. They, and indeed all the characters with whom he comes into contact, are bestialized, made monstrous themselves by virtue of contamination – a fate rendered possible only by their own Jekyll-like susceptibility to atavism, a susceptibility actualized by the Count's presence as much as by his bite.

And what of that bite, which is surely the most memorable feature of the novel? As we have seen, it allows Dracula to feed upon men without actually having to touch them; further, it signals his animalism even as it provides the means for turning others into animals. But none of this gets to the heart, as it were, of the Count's odd culinary habits, which are most remarkable insofar as they enable his equally odd relation to history. For, like Victorian Gothic itself, Dracula is nothing if not a parasite: an absurdity or impossibility that exists only by battening upon the real; a piece of the past that stays alive by feeding upon the present. And so, again like Victorian Gothic, Dracula must also be seen as a paradox: by all rights dead and gone, he refuses to be left behind, living on as an ambulatory relic amid a remorselessly up-to-date nineteenth century replete with the latest technologies (cameras, telegraphs, phonographs, typewriters) as well as the latest incarnations of humanity (Jonathan Harker, upwardly mobile middle-class professional; Mina Harker, "new woman"). Foreign in his origins but self-schooled in Englishness so successfully as to be nearly indistinguishable from a native (and in this, too, like the Gothic), Dracula figures not simply the persistence of the past but also the insistence of an otherness in Englishness, permanently threatening to erupt. Even as Britain appears to move further away from the feudal and the feral along the path toward modernity and rationality, *Dracula* insists (the Gothic insists) that such otherness remains or returns: in out-of-the-way corners of London, in legacies, in the blood. The history of the Gothic romance in the Victorian period, of *Dracula* as well as of Dracula, of textuality as well as of vampirism, is the history not so much of how such a story comes to be (although it is partly that) as of how such a story comes to be told – and told again, without cease, as irrepressible as its own living dead.

See also VICTORIAN PSYCHOLOGY; EMPIRE, RACE AND THE VICTORIAN NOVEL; SCIENTIFIC ASCENDANCY; TECHNOLOGY AND INFORMATION; GENDER POLITICS AND WOMEN'S RIGHTS; NEWGATE NOVEL TO DETECTIVE FICTION; THE SENSATION NOVEL; VICTORIAN SCIENCE FICTION.

REFERENCES

Allott, Miriam (1974), *The Brontës: The Critical Heritage* (London and Boston: Routledge).

Bakhtin, M. M. (1981), "Forms of Time and Chronotope in the Novel," in *The Dialogic Imagination: Four Essays*, ed. Michael Holquist, trans. Caryl Emerson and Michael Holquist (Austin: University of Texas Press), 84–258.

Brantlinger, Patrick (1988), *Rule of Darkness: British Literature and Imperialism, 1830–1914* (Ithaca: Cornell University Press).

Chorley, H. F. (1866), "New Novels," *Athenaeum*, 29, 732–3.

Darwin, Charles (1981), *The Descent of Man, and Selection in Relation to Sex* (Princeton: Princeton University Press). (First publ. 1871.)

Heilman, Robert B. (1958), "Charlotte Brontë's 'New' Gothic," in Robert C. Rathburn and Martin Steinmann, Jr, eds., *From Jane Austen to Joseph Conrad: Essays Collected in Memory of James T. Hillhouse* (Minneapolis: University of Minnesota Press), 118–32.

James, Henry (1865), "Miss Braddon," *The Nation*, 9 Nov., 593–5.

Jameson, Fredric (1981), *The Political Unconscious: Narrative as a Socially Symbolic Act* (Ithaca: Cornell University Press).

Page, Norman, ed. (1974), *Wilkie Collins: The Critical Heritage* (London and Boston: Routledge & Kegan Paul).

Sedgwick, Eve Kosofsky (1985), *Between Men: English Literature and Male Homosocial Desire* (New York: Columbia University Press).

Wordsworth, William (1991), "Preface," in R. L. Brett and A. R. Jones, eds., *Lyrical Ballads* (London and New York: Routledge), 241–72. (First publ. 1800.)

FURTHER READING

Auerbach, Nina (1982), *Woman and the Demon: The Life of a Victorian Myth* (Cambridge, Mass.: Harvard University Press).

Baldick, Chris (1987), *In Frankenstein's Shadow: Myth, Monstrosity, and Nineteenth-Century Writing* (Oxford: Oxford University Press).

Duncan, Ian (1992), *Modern Romance and Transformations of the Novel: The Gothic, Scott, Dickens* (Cambridge: Cambridge University Press).

Halberstam, Judith (1995), *Skin Shows: Gothic Horror and the Technology of Monsters* (Durham and London: Duke University Press).

Heller, Tamar (1992), *Dead Secrets: Wilkie Collins and the Female Gothic* (New Haven and London: Yale University Press).

Hughes, Winifred (1980), *The Maniac in the Cellar: Sensation Novels of the 1860s* (Princeton: Princeton University Press).

Hurley, Kelly (1996), *The Gothic Body: Sexuality, Materialism, and Degeneration at the Fin de Siècle* (Cambridge: Cambridge University Press).

Malchow, H. L. (1996), *Gothic Images of Race in Nineteenth-Century Britain* (Stanford: Stanford University Press).

Massé, Michelle A. (1992), *In the Name of Love: Women, Masochism, and the Gothic* (Ithaca and London: Cornell University Press).

Mighall, Robert (1999), *A Geography of Victorian Gothic Fiction: Mapping History's Nightmares* (New York and Oxford: Oxford University Press).

Milbank, Alison (1982), *Daughters of the House: Modes of Gothic in Victorian Fiction* (Basingstoke: Macmillan).

Milligan, Barry (1995), *Pleasures and Pains: Opium and the Orient in Nineteenth-Century British Culture* (Charlottesville: University Press of Virginia).

Moers, Ellen (1976), *Literary Women: The Great Writers* (Garden City: Doubleday).

Punter, David (1980), *The Literature of Terror: A History of Gothic Fictions from 1765 to the Present Day* (London: Longman).

Schmitt, Cannon (1997), *Alien Nation: Nineteenth-Century Gothic Fictions and English Nationality* (Philadelphia: University of Pennsylvania Press).

Sedgwick, Eve Kosofsky (1986), *The Coherence of Gothic Conventions* (New York: Methuen).

Wilt, Judith (1980), *Ghosts of the Gothic: Austen, Eliot, and Lawrence* (Princeton: Princeton University Press).

18

The Provincial or Regional Novel

Ian Duncan

I

Three nineteenth-century novelists invite us to reflect upon the distinctive regions of Great Britain colonized by their fiction: the Ayrshire of John Galt's "Tales of the West," Anthony Trollope's Barsetshire, and Thomas Hardy's Wessex. The Revd. Micah Balwhidder, the narrator of Galt's *Annals of the Parish* (1821), looks back on the pattern of change in his community from 1760 to 1808:

> Through all the wars that have raged from the time of the King's accession to the throne, there has been a gradually coming nearer and nearer to our gates, which is a very alarming thing to think of. In the first, at the time he came to the crown, we suffered nothing. Not one belonging to the parish was engaged in the battles thereof, and the news of victories, before they reached us, which was generally by word of mouth, were old tales. In the American war, as I have related at length, we had an immediate participation, but those that suffered were only a few individuals, and the evil was done at a distance, and reached us not until the worst of its effects were spent. And during the first term of the present just and necessary contest for all that is dear to us as a people, although, by the offswarming of some of our restless youth, we had our part and portion in common with the rest of the Christian world; yet still there was at home a great augmentation of prosperity, and every thing had thriven in a surprising manner; somewhat, however, to the detriment of our country simplicity. By the building of the cotton-mill, and the rising up of the new town of Cayenneville, we had intromitted so much with concerns of trade, that we were become a part of the great web of commercial reciprocities, and felt in our corner and extremity, every touch or stir that was made on any part of the texture. (ch. 49)

Balwhidder, up until now a naïve narrator, unfolds a complex vision of the changing structural relations between a local society, bounded by personal experience, and a larger political and economic system that is not just national but global in its extent.

The historical processes of British modernization – the imperialist expansion of trade, the "industrial revolution" – have changed the very terms of space and time by which locality is constituted. Balwhidder describes a "coming nearer and nearer" of remote contingencies until they penetrate the everyday life of the parish; events that were once "old tales" have become immediate and personal. Strikingly, he specifies this historical process as a diffusion of the conditions of *war*; and in the chapter of *Annals of the Parish* that follows, we see how the war comes home to destroy local lives, not by military violence, but by one of those spasmodic contractions to which the new economy is prone. Balwhidder and his readers witness the collapse of a traditional distinction between horizons of knowledge – one of them immediate, proximate, concrete, present to the senses, measured by the pace of daily life; the other temporally as well as spatially distant, invisible and intangible, abstract. Province and world are inextricably enmeshed together in a "great web" – the image stays close here to its source in the industrializing work of weaving.

Next, Trollope's narrator surveys his domain in the opening pages of *Doctor Thorne* (1858):

> There is a county in the west of England not so full of life, indeed, nor so widely spoken of as some of its manufacturing leviathan brethren in the north, but which is, nevertheless, very dear to those who know it well. Its green pastures, its waving wheat, its deep and shady and – let us add – dirty lanes, its paths and stiles, its tawny-coloured, well-built rural churches, its avenues of beeches, and frequent Tudor mansions, its constant county hunt, its social graces, and the general air of clanship which pervades it, has made it to its own inhabitants a favoured land of Goshen. It is purely agricultural; agricultural in its produce, agricultural in its poor, and agricultural in its pleasures. There are towns in it, of course; dépôts from whence are bought seeds and groceries, ribbons and fire-shovels; in which markets are held and county balls are carried on; which return members to Parliament, generally – in spite of Reform Bills, past, present, and coming – in accordance with the dictates of some neighbouring land magnate: from whence emanate the country postmen, and where is located the supply of post-horses necessary for county visitings. But these towns add nothing to the importance of the county; they consist, with the exception of the assize town, of dull, all but death-like single streets. Each possesses two pumps, three hotels, ten shops, fifteen beer-houses, a beadle, and a market-place. (ch. 1)

Trollope lets us know that he is setting his territory apart from the currents of modernization. The industrial revolution, a process understood by Galt's narrator Balwhidder as involving his parish in a global "web of commercial reciprocities," is now represented as contained in a particular region – "the north" – as well as (implicitly) in a particular literary genre, the industrial or condition of England novel of the 1840s and 1850s. Trollope's opening line echoes, instead, the opening of Fielding's *Tom Jones* ("In that part of the western division of this kingdom, which is commonly called Somersetshire"); the self-conscious reversion to an earlier style signals that the problems of modernity have been bypassed. This unnamed western county maintains its "purely agricultural" character "in spite of Reform Bills" as well as the repeal of the Corn Laws (1846); its towns, the narrator reassures us, remain social and economic accessories of the country, unlike those towns elsewhere that have gained a manufacturing or commercial predominance. Trollope's admission of these historical realities, in order to deflect them, informs his vision with its arch, lightly ironical stylization. The writing acknowledges that in certain ways this is an imaginary and nostalgic rather than a real territory ("a favoured land of Goshen"), with its old-fashioned way of life removed to an archaic, anthropological past ("general air of clanship"). The narrative of *Doctor Thorne* will make it clear that we are reading about an endangered culture, something we might soon find in a museum, with its tale of property rescued for traditional landlords from a disreputable class of new men. Meanwhile, the narrator's insistence on the "all but death-like" character of the towns falls in with his representation of the county as "not so full of life": it is a curiously depopulated landscape, devoid of particular people doing particular work, rendered instead as a catalogue of properties. Only, the green pastures, waving wheat, rural churches, Tudor mansions, and so on of the countryside have the advantage of an archetypal dignity over the two pumps, three hotels, ten shops and fifteen beer-houses of the town, where the numerical specification mocks the petty labor of accounting that goes on there.

In the last of these examples, the protagonist of Hardy's *Jude the Obscure* (1895) goes to work in the fields:

> The fresh harrow-lines seemed to stretch like the channellings in a piece of new corduroy, lending a meanly utilitarian air to the expanse, taking away its gradations, and depriving it of all history beyond that of the few recent months, though to every clod and stone there really attached associations enough and to spare – echoes of songs from ancient harvest-days, of spoken words, and of sturdy deeds. Every inch of ground had been the site, first or last, of energy, gaiety, horse-play, bickerings, weariness. Groups of gleaners had squatted in the sun on every square yard. Love-matches that had populated the adjoining hamlet had been made up there between reaping and carrying. Under the hedge which divided the field from a distant plantation girls had given themselves to lovers who would not turn their heads to look at them by the next harvest; and in that ancient cornfield many a man had made love-promises to a woman at whose voice he had trembled by the next seed-time after fulfilling them in the church adjoining. But this neither Jude nor the rooks around him considered. For them it was a lonely place, possessing, in the one view, only the quality of a work-ground, and in the other that of a granary good to feed in. (ch. 2)

Hardy divides the scene between two kinds of perspective. One, brought into focus at the end of the passage, belongs to the natives – Jude and the rooks – who must make their living from this piece of ground. (Although the final sentence seems to mock these perspectival identifications and distinctions: how far, really, does Jude see the field as the rooks see it?) The other, unspecified as to ownership, evokes a detailed knowledge of the local history and customs of the place. In contrast to Jude and the rooks, intent on the materiality of what lies before them, this perspective has access to absent sights and sounds – an invisible, inaudible wealth of "associations enough and to spare." Such a perspective suggests a leisured or professional acquisition of omniscience, detached from the exigencies of the scene, belonging perhaps to the gentleman antiquary of an earlier era or else to a new breed of professional ethnographer, scouring the countryside in search of "folkways."

With whose perspective, though, does the passage open? The "utilitarian" fixation on the ground would seem to find its viewpoint with Jude and the rooks at the end of the passage. Yet this viewpoint is far more alienated than the antiquarian or ethnological one, which is able to immerse itself, if only by association, in the warm currents of work, play and lovemaking that have constituted the life of the community. This view is "lonely," it holds itself to an austere refusal of that communal life, it defines itself in a starkly aesthetic attention to the form of the landscape, abstracted and metaphorized. "Meanly utilitarian" suggests the programmatic reduction of a Benthamite political economy. The striking simile, "channellings in a piece of new corduroy," makes us think of mechanized, sweatshop production. Most startlingly, the harrowing of the field appears to have erased from it "all history beyond that of the few recent months." Far from evoking an immemorial seasonal cycle of agricultural labor (as, for instance, throughout Hardy's earlier *Far From the Madding Crowd*), the description of the ground makes it seem as though it has been broken for the first time – turned into that paradigmatically modern space, a tabula rasa or taxonomic grid. Even the most "traditional" kind of work, in short, partakes of the radical, categorical discontinuities of a modern temporality and political economy. The reader recalls the account, at the end of Hardy's previous chapter, of the demolition of the ancient church of Marygreen in favor of a new mock-Gothic structure, put up "by a certain obliterator of historical records who had run down from London and back in a day." But now that rather easily satirical distinction has become complicated. Jude the worker is bound to the dispossessed view, while the antiquarian–ethnographic narrator can enjoy the luxury of sympathetic identification with the life of the local community – as the members of that community, perhaps, no longer can themselves, since they are evoked as ghosts, figures in a romantic reverie. An organic relation to place is not available to anybody. Hardy summons a set of conventional distinctions – between native and alien, traditional and modern, pastoral and georgic – but in order to scramble them, unsettling the reader into the relentlessly ironical narrative that follows.

II

Literary historians and critics agree that a kind of fiction distinguished by its regional or provincial setting flourished in the nineteenth century. The characteristics of this setting are that it is *distinctive*, differentiated from the metropolis or from other regions within the nation, and that it is at the same time *familiar*, a more or less spacious version of what Raymond Williams (1973) has called the "knowable community" (see also Edwards 1988). Familiar, even though the reader comes from outside it; from the beginning this kind of space is framed in an elegiac relation between imaginative or sympathetic belonging and historic exile. The region or province represents a concentrated version of the "imagined community," the term with which Benedict Anderson (1983) has characterized the modern nation; and it will always be set, tacitly or not, against the larger horizon of the nation, to which it occupies a critical relation. The province or region may represent an authentic site or source of national identity – a distillation of the nation; or it may take the place of a larger national identity that has failed; or it may register a wholesale disintegration of the categories of home: origin, community, belonging.

In some cases a series of novels by a particular author covers a broadly regional territory, typically a county (Trollope's Barsetshire; George Eliot's Loamshire) or a former kingdom absorbed into the modern state (the Scotland of Walter Scott's *Tales of My Landlord*; Hardy's Wessex). But individual works tend to focus on a smaller space, typically a parish or county town and its outlying countryside, in which the inhabitants are known to one another: Trollope's Barchester or Framley, Elizabeth Gaskell's Cranford, Margaret Oliphant's Carlingford, Hardy's Casterbridge. While most critical definitions emphasize a rural setting, a recent study argues that regionalism also encompasses urban and even metropolitan locations (see Snell 1998), and Raymond Williams's insistence on the dialectical historical relation between country and city should always be kept in mind. Nor can the regional simply be mapped on to the category of the "peripheral," in the terms of Immanuel Wallerstein's world-system topology (Wallerstein 1974), since a number of novelists regionalize London itself, the imperial core, in a variety of ways. (Dickens is the outstanding example.) Some kind of rural setting is, however, the norm, and I shall focus my discussion on it, although I shall also look at urban regional fiction, in the industrial or condition of England novel, since it crucially affects other developments.

Most commentators recognize a distinction between the categories of "regional" and "provincial" in nineteenth-century fiction (for an extended discussion, see Gilmour 1989; see also Keith 1988). The distinction is valid for heuristic purposes, although the relation between the categories is more variable, because historically produced, than the commentary tends to allow. Regional fiction specifies its setting by invoking a combination of geographical, natural-historical, antiquarian, ethnographic, and/or sociological features *that differentiate it from any other region*. A provincial setting is defined more simply by its *difference from the metropolis* – by the fact that it is not London (or, secondarily, not Edinburgh or Manchester). Thus, while "regional" implies a neutral or even positive set of multiple local differences, "provincial" connotes a negative difference, based on a binary opposition, expressed as a generic or typical identity, within which any particular provincial setting may take the place of any other. The fictional names of Victorian provincial towns and counties express their archetypal, rather than local-specific, character: Cranford, Barchester and Barsetshire, Carlingford, Loamshire and Middlemarch. These places occupy a more or less abstract orientation and distance, although they are usually found (vaguely, implicitly) within a hundred and fifty miles of London, in the aptly named "home counties" or non-industrial "midlands." Anywhere very much farther afield starts to acquire specific signifiers of difference and turn into a region. Regional settings are more closely tied to a real historical geography, locatable on the map of Victorian Britain, even when – as in the case of Hardy's Wessex – the places have been renamed and even (*The Wood-landers*) recombined. The more tenuous associations of Gaskell's and Eliot's fiction with Cheshire and Warwickshire are sustained by biography and tourism, rather than by the fiction itself.

The region, then, is a place in itself, the source of its own terms of meaning and identity, while the province is a typical setting defined by its difference from London. The hierarchy implicit in this latter difference by no means necessarily subordinates the province. Gilmour notes the rise of a derogatory association of "provincialism" with inferiority and backwardness in the periodical criticism of the 1860s. Strikingly, though, that usage coincides with the splendid zenith of mid-Victorian fiction, from *Cranford* to *Middlemarch*, in which "provincial life" assumes the burden of national representation. In the great novels of Gaskell, Trollope, and Eliot the provincial county town or parish becomes the generic and typical setting of a traditional England, responsive to the pressures of modernity (politics, debt, fashion, crime) that have overwhelmed metropolitan life, but resisting or absorbing them – if only ambiguously, if only for a time. The symbolic relations between nation and region, premised on the latter's irreplaceable singularity, work differently, as we shall see.

The critical literature pursues a further distinction, between a regionalist approach to representations of a geographically particularized local society (e.g. Keith 1988; Snell 1998), and studies of a more exclusively "pastoral" or "idyllic" kind of fiction (e.g. Hunter 1984; Edwards 1988). These approaches roughly follow the still-useful classical distinction between georgic and pastoral modes of writing. Georgic represents a local scene of (usually) agricultural production, in which human labor is the force that binds together the natural order (the land and seasons) and the social order (the family, the state). Pastoral represents a leisured fantasy of country life on the part of property-owners, as a condition of privileged retirement from political and economic struggle. Thus, georgic represents the integration of local work and larger world within a complex economy, while pastoral represents a sentimental opposition between idealized country and alien city. It is by no means always the case that the regional is georgic and the provincial pastoral. When provincial life becomes the dominant topos for representing national identity, in the third quarter of the nineteenth century, it assumes a georgic attention to the interrelations between local work and customs, natural settings, and the larger temporal and political frames of history and the nation.

These categories, and the relations between them – regional and provincial, pastoral and georgic – are defined, above all, by their relation to an accelerated rate of historical change, registered both at the particular level of everyday life and as an abstract, universal process. Historical change – modernization – is the condition through which the province or region becomes narratable: as an island, or reef, in a rising tide of wholesale economic and social transformation. A new, linear, open-ended impetus of historical time rushes against a traditional, closed, repetitive temporal order, marked by a double chronology of everyday life and the seasons. Not for nothing does regional fiction fully emerge in the historical novels of Scott, committed to the historical geography of uneven development. The view from the imperial metropolis, dictating the terms of modernization, measures the relative backwardness of the regions, consigning them to a graduated series of pasts. So regional fiction sets itself to the elegiac task of recording extinct or vanishing ways of life: from Maria Edgeworth and Scott, resuming the antiquarian and romance-revival projects of the late Enlightenment, to Hardy, attuned to Victorian domestic archeological and ethnographic enterprises such as the London Folklore Society. The crucial distinction falls between those representations that make the region or province the site of an inquiry into the process and effects of historical change, and those that make it a site that escapes change; between a georgic exploration of the transformations and resistances that constitute local history, and the pastoral imagining of a place where history is suspended. That these are tendencies, historically variable and often working together, rather than absolute distinctions, should be clear from the examples read in the first part of this essay: Galt's account of a local community gradually invested by world history, Trollope's of a "land of Goshen" outside it, Hardy's of a historical transformation so thorough that all distinctions between modernity and tradition have been subverted, in that they are the discursive products of that very process.

In his 1902 preface to *Far From the Madding Crowd* (1874), Hardy issues a conventional lament for the "break of continuity in local history, more fatal than any other thing to the preservation of legend, folk-lore, close inter-social relations, and eccentric individualities"; he identifies as its principal cause "the recent supplanting of the class of stationary cottagers, who carried on the local traditions and humours, by a population of more or less migratory labourers." Critics as well as novelists have addressed "the break of continuity in local history" through which the region falls into narrative, and have identified an array of historical causes and correspondences: the massive social disruptions brought about by the agricultural and industrial revolutions; associated technological transformations; the 1832 Reform Bill, the repeal of the Corn Laws, and other legislative enactments. The advent of the railways, from the late 1830s, has appeared especially decisive. The mechanization and acceleration of transport technology, Wolfgang Schivelbusch's "industrialization of time and space" (Schivelbusch 1986), provides for one of the key tropes of modernity, the production of speed; and a corresponding attention to places traversed and left behind, glimpsed from the window of the hurtling vehicle, in a stark dramatization of the slash of progress across an inert countryside.

The railway concretized a theme already at work in the culture. Scott's *The Heart of Mid-Lothian* (1818) opens with a meditation on the mail-coach, a conveyance which upsets everything (including itself) in its career across ancient communities. Less than twenty years later, in Dickens's *Pickwick Papers* (1837), a new technology has relegated the mail-coach to the quaint old England – the provincial England – of Muggleton

and Dingley Dell. Dickens went on to make the railway the emblem of change, smash-
ing up old neighborhoods, in *Dombey and Son* (1848); later, the steam engine would
also take its place in that nostalgic scenery. A *locus classicus*, the "Author's Introduction" to George Eliot's *Felix Holt* (1866), rehearses a view from the passing coach in
a nod to the tale's historical setting (1832): "Five-and-thirty years ago the glory had
not yet departed from the old coach-roads." The lapse of historical time allows the
narrator to imagine, in turn, the obsolescence of the present: "Posterity may be shot,
like a bullet through a tube, by atmospheric pressure from Winchester to Newcastle"
– so that Winchester and Newcastle will become arbitrary designations, like the
names on the London Underground. Such motion completes the abolition of the
spatial and temporal coordinates by which place is secured: all regions dissolve into
an undifferentiated screen for the flow of capital.

Accordingly, the nineteenth-century provincial setting is imagined as an area a
person can traverse on foot or horseback, from the narrator of Mary Russell Mitford's
Our Village (1823), inviting the reader along on her walk, to those well-mounted gentlemen in Trollope and Eliot who assist our views of Barsetshire and Loamshire.
Walking is a semiotically loaded activity, especially for women, whose problematic
occupancy of outdoor space it measures. Female pedestrianism evokes fallen women,
and trials of maternity and sisterhood, in a loss of domestic space, from Jeanie Deans's
heroic hike from Edinburgh to London in *The Heart of Mid-Lothian* to the forlorn pere-
grinations of Gaskell's Ruth and Eliot's Hetty, and, drawing all the tropes together,
Hardy's Tess. Now the fallen woman shares the lot of that figure for the "break of
continuity in local history," the migrant worker, as she wanders across a Wessex grown
as geographically various, immense, and strange as (say) Oregon.

III

The rough typological distinction between province and region follows a historical
scheme, also rough and susceptible to exceptions and contradictions. Lucien Leclaire
(1954) divides the development of British regional fiction into three chronological
stages, marked at 1800, 1830, and 1870; I prefer to identify the crucial turning-
points at ca. 1850 and 1875. A regionalist discourse is established, in the early decades
of the nineteenth century, in national and historical novels by Irish and Scottish
authors. These narrate the regional constitution of the British nation through the
historical process that Michael Hechter (1975) has called "internal colonialism," in
an era of national (and global) crisis and consolidation: the defeat of revolutionary and
Bonapartist France, the securing of British imperial supremacy abroad, but also the
internal destabilization of national society in the postwar recession and industrialization. The intensification of this social crisis through the 1840s provokes a critical
resurgence of regional fiction at the end of the decade, focused on the industrial
north and midlands, in which, however, regionalism decisively loses its ideological
capacity to stabilize the figure of the nation. The economic prosperity and imperial

confidence of the decades from 1850 through the early 1870s accommodate, instead, a new invention, the fiction of provincial life. The imaginary province of the mid-Victorian era represents a traditional England that selectively absorbs the forces of modernization.

The third stage of this scheme, from the mid-1870s until the end of the century, falls under the gloom of a worldwide economic depression – among the effects of which are a collapse of British agricultural prices and the loss, between 1875 and 1895, of two-thirds of the land devoted to wheat production. The novel in this period abandons the stabilizing equation of provincial with national life and resumes a variety of regionalisms, all of which articulate a centrifugal relation to the historical form of the nation. Some of these provide imaginary refuge from contemporary conditions, while others confront and test them. The former tendency includes a nostalgic and idyllic saturation of regionalist difference (in the Scottish "Kailyard" writers) and a proliferation of historical romances devoted to an escapist rather than critical invest-ment of regional difference in the past. The outstanding example is R. D. Blackmore, who though best known for his romance of seventeenth-century Exmoor, *Lorna Doone* (1869), colonized large tracts of (mainly southern) England in a series of novels. The major figure in this regionalist revival is of course Hardy, whose own novels perform the turn from mid-Victorian provincialism to an increasingly critical account of regional and national forms of cultural identity.

Regionalism, with its insistence on local grounds of identity, thus represents the ideological crisis of a national history, whether the nation is a project still to be assem-bled or one that is falling apart. The region first emerges to solve the categorical problem of nationality posed by the modern imperial state. Once that national for-mation can be taken for granted, in an era of expansion, it invests the great fictions of provincial life. When the imperial nation again undergoes internal crisis, region-alism returns, its local specificity providing sentimental refuge from historical change or else a critical view of it. In the rest of this chapter, rather than attempt an even coverage of this historical development, I shall examine its points of transition: the emergence of regionalism in romantic-era Irish and Scottish fiction, its crisis and replacement by an ideologically enlarged provincialism at midcentury, and the criti-cal return to the region in Hardy.

IV

Although there are eighteenth-century precursors, notably Smollett's fictional tour through Great Britain in *The Expedition of Humphry Clinker* (1771), the regional novel is effectively invented by Maria Edgeworth in *Castle Rackrent* (1800), and developed in regional historical fiction by Scott, Galt, and their Irish and Scottish contempo-raries (see Trumpener 1997). Anomalous historical conditions at the periphery of Britain's domestic empire, notably a categorical discrepancy between nation and state, make the relation between region and nation an Irish and a Scottish project before it is an English one. Scotland and Ireland had fallen, by different historical routes, from national to provincial status with their political absorptions into the United Kingdom in 1707 and 1801 respectively; the loss of a national identity based on sovereignty required the narration of a new kind of nationality, for which regionalism became the figure. Irish and (especially) Scottish regionalism are invoked as the antidotes to provincial degradation, preserving or restoring national status in the form of local cultural differences. The peculiar manners and traditions of Ayrshire, or the Scottish Borders, are able to represent British nationhood precisely because they distinguish these places from England, and from each other, in a multinational – not English – constitution. The essence of national belonging is to be grasped here, in the dense, vital differences of the regional periphery, rather than at the metropolis, with its denatured spaces and its commodified temporality of "fashion."

Castle Rackrent installs the key conventions of regional writing: an ethnographic "thick description" of manners and traditions, a written imitation of dialect, an attention to landscape and natural forms, an analytic account of a local economy and its relation to a wider horizon of historical change, and – decisively – the relegation of all this to the past. Edgeworth assures the reader "that these are 'tales of other times;' that the manners depicted in the following pages are not those of the present age: the race of the Rackrents has long since been extinct in Ireland." This is the crucial problem: the very elements that make the region an organic site of belonging in the imperial nation are doomed to vanish under its modernizing political economy. While Edgeworth applauds the passing of bad old Rackrent ways, the obliteration of local manners and traditions is mourned by other authors, notably Scott, whose novels exploit the ideologically fertile terrain between a comic affirmation of progress and an elegiac sense of loss.

Scott's historicization of the difference between metropolitan modernity and regional tradition highlights the temporal instability of the bond between region and nation in the modern geopolitical frame of empire. The Waverley novels find a solution to the historical contradiction between nation and state in the domain of *culture*, specified as a ground of identity apart from the political regime of the state: loss of sovereignty need not vex a national identity that consists in autonomous local cultural forms. Scott (and Edgeworth), following Scottish Enlightenment social theory, locate that autonomy, however, in the private sphere of economic activity: which is – precisely – the engine that drives historical change, restructuring local societies and eroding their traditions. The equilibrium of "culture" thus remains inherently unstable, its associations subject to reinterpretation. Far from being fixed and dead in their museum-like preservation, cultural properties may at any moment come back to life, the figures of a militant, politicized difference, as economic and social inequities remain intact or are produced anew – as, for instance, rural communities are displaced into a migrant or industrial workforce, subject to underdevelopment or economic downturn. The repoliticization of (ancient) regional difference as (modern) class difference becomes the theme of the "condition of England" novels of the 1840s, and the process is revisited in the later novels of Hardy. The romantic historical novels and national tales recognize the crux very clearly, notably by their recursion to the theme of civil conflict, which Scott makes the canonical topos of historical fiction: as though the nation is always to be narrated through its crisis of violent dissolution, whether in local riot, regional rebellion, or full-scale civil war.

Both Irish and Scottish regionalism are unable to bear the burden of national representation as the century goes on. Scotland became a Victorian province. The most militantly regional Scottish novel after the 1830s, William Alexander's *Johnny Gibb of Gushetneuk*, circulated in the *Aberdeen Free Press* (1869–70) but was not much read further south. Margaret Oliphant began her literary career with Scottish regional domestic tales and historical romances, and occasionally returned to a Scottish setting (*Kirsteen*, 1890); but she established her reputation with the series of "Chronicles of Carlingford" (1863–76), making it clear that provincial life would have to be English for it to represent the life of the nation. In the last decades of the century the so-called Kailyard school (J. M. Barrie, S. R. Crockett, John Watson) infused Scottish regionalism with a nostalgic idyllicism. Scotland's fate shows starkly through the lens of two English novels. In *The Duke's Children* (1880) Trollope describes the Highland estates of Crummie-Toddie and Killancodlem, one of which is devoted exclusively to grouse-shooting, the other to picturesque tourism. The rationalization and commodification of these settings is complete, with their differences specialized to service the consumer requirements of different sectors (gentry and "cockney") of the British ruling classes. In *The Mayor of Casterbridge* (1886) Hardy relates the career of the emigrant Scot Donald Farfrae: passing through Casterbridge on his way to Canada, he decides to settle there instead, and makes his fortune. We first encounter him charming the local inhabitants by singing the sentimental songs "of his dear native country that he loved so well as never to have revisited it." The Scotsman, at the end of the century, personifies the inauthenticity of a regionalism exported for nostalgic consumption – and acts as the foil to Hardy's true Wessex version.

Irish regionalism becomes still more problematic, for the opposite reason: that of a catastrophic failure of national integration. Ireland remains the site of an intractable colonial difference between the Protestant landlord class and the rest of the population, expressed not only in persistent outbreaks of repression and rebellion but, far more grievous, genocidal famine: an event that destroyed the material (georgic) base of regional representation in the 1840s. The famine confounded the careers of John and Michael Banim, Charles Lever, and Samuel Lover, invested in comic Irish picaresque and national tales. Attempts to represent it, including William Carleton's *The Black Prophet* (1847) and Trollope's *Castle Richmond* (1860), underscore the famine's subsequent status as an unrepresentable trauma, a blank figure for the impossibility of modern Irish history. The most famous of Victorian Anglo-Irish novels, Bram Stoker's *Dracula* (1897), represents post-famine Ireland in antiregionalist disguise, through the looking-glass of Gothic: the land of a great hunger is a nation of the undead, sinisterly reoriented to the eastern instead of western limit of Christian Europe.

V

Provincial fiction emerges as a minor literature, dialectically contemporaneous with the historical novels of Scott and the other Romantic regionalists, in Mary Russell Mitford's *Our Village* (1823). Much as Edgeworth established the tropes of regionalism, Mitford establishes those of provincialism. "Of all situations for a constant residence, that which appears to me most delightful is a little village far in the country." Mitford's real-life model lay just outside Reading, close enough to London, so that "far in the country" denotes the province's archetypal alterity rather than a measurable geographical distance. Mitford characterizes her setting as

> a little world of our own, close-packed and insulated like ants in an ant-hill, or bees in a hive, or sheep in a fold, or nuns in a convent; where we know every one, are known to every one, interested in every one, and authorised to hope that every one feels an interest in us . . . Even in books I like a confined locality, and so do the critics when they talk of the unities. Nothing is so tiresome as to be whirled half over Europe at the chariot-wheels of a hero, to go to sleep at Vienna, and awaken at Madrid; it produces a real fatigue, a weariness of spirit. On the other hand, nothing is so delightful as to sit down in a country village in one of Miss Austen's delicious novels, quite sure before we leave it to become intimate with every spot and every person it contains.

Mitford's pastoral recension of Austen's "three or four families in a country village" (paving the way for the later cult of "Jane") installs a conception of neighborhood quite alien to her model. "Neighbours in Jane Austen are not the people actually living nearby," writes Raymond Williams; "they are the people living a little less nearby who, in social recognition, can be visited. What she sees across the land is a network of propertied houses and families, and through the holes of this tightly drawn mesh most actual people are simply not seen. To be face-to-face in this world is already to belong to a class" (1973: 166). In this respect, at least, Austen's major Victorian heir is Trollope, whose Barsetshire and Palliser novels map a ruling-class apparatus of institutions, estates, and benefices which renders the nation as a political topology rather than a geography. The specific location of a given estate or county town is unimportant, except in such matters as convenience of access to London or the provision of suitable conditions for game.

Mitford imagines a "little world of our own" in which internal familiarity, a closed system of mutual sentimental surveillance, is predicated on isolation and seclusion. The village is not just "far in the country," but – in striking contrast to Galt's Ayrshire parish – disconnected from a global historical economy and its transforming pressures. Cosmetic alterations, such as the macadamization of the road, highlight the village's existence outside history, out of the world. When the narrator returns to her village two years later, she is happy to confirm its "trick of standing still, of remaining stationary, unchanged, and unimproved in this most changeable and improving world." She opens the third series by reassuring an Indian correspondent that there is still "no change in our village."

Elizabeth Gaskell's *Cranford* (1853) performs the exemplary task of opening up the pastoral provincialism of *Our Village* for the major, georgic treatment afforded in the Victorian novels of provincial life. *Cranford* revises Mitford's provincialism in dialectical response to, rather than denial of, the crisis of historical change, as this was addressed in the new genre of the industrial novel, of which Gaskell herself had produced an outstanding example (*Mary Barton*, 1848). In fact, Gaskell's literary career tracks the dissolution of regionalism and its replacement by a transformed provincialism with exemplary clarity. Although based on Knutsford in Cheshire, Cranford too is a typical rather than a local setting; but already its opening lines ironize the gendering of the idyll implicit in Mitford: "In the first place, Cranford is in possession of the Amazons." Gaskell takes up the tropes of provincialism as instruments of critical inquiry into the imaginary condition of sentimental refuge from the modern world. *Cranford* tests the relation of the little town to the wider world, to modernity and change, to sexuality and patriarchy and capital; the fiction reflects upon its own cultural function, its ideological appeal, its conditions and limits. Like *Our Village*, *Cranford* at first poses its setting in a negative relationship to London, as in the arch questions, "Do you ever see cows dressed in grey flannel in London?", "Do you make paper paths for every guest to walk upon in London?" But the narrative quickly establishes a more proximate and urgent antithesis: "the great neighbouring commercial town of Drumble," source of those modern systems – the railway, finance capitalism – with which the local community must come to terms.

"Drumble," the modern world of business and industry, had already been regionalized in the industrial novels of the 1840s, notably by Gaskell herself in *Mary Barton: A Tale of Manchester Life*. Hailed by reviewers as a radical updating of Scott's regional historical romance, *Mary Barton* is better described as postregional, since it narrates the displacement of rural communities into an industrial regime which systematically disables the principles upon which community is sustained. The industrial novel deconstructs the regionalist figure of the nation, in effect, by reducing geography to a function of political economy. Benjamin Disraeli's title, *Sybil, or The Two Nations* (1845: "the RICH, and the POOR") identifies a calamitous splitting of the nation along the new faultline of class produced by industrialization. Gaskell's later title, *North and South* (1855), sketches a regional mapping of this faultline, although the starkness of the division marks an abstraction of local specificity. The region fails in its ideological task of containing the dislocating forces of industrial and finance capitalism. Regionalism's late-1840s crisis is nowhere more vivid than in its militant, muscular reassertion in the novels of the Brontë sisters. Charlotte Brontë's *Shirley* (1849) defends the regional integrity of its setting against the threat of provincial degradation by subsuming the topic of the industrial novel, reversing its generic priority. Brontë vehemently directs the charge of provincial difference back on to London, investing the metropolitan core with the stigmata of locality and lowness: "cockneys" are represented as ignorant and uncivil, their "southern accent" robbed of normative neutrality when channeled through "northern ears." Yorkshiremen, by contrast, maintain their own standards of gallantry, sagacity, and courage. Even rioting workers express not some cockney class *ressentiment* but an autochthonous truculence: "A yell followed this demonstration – a rioters' yell – a North-of-England – a Yorkshire – a West-Riding – a West-Riding-clothing-district-of-Yorkshire rioters' yell. You never heard that sound, reader?"

Shirley seems to have been the Brontë novel that most impressed Gaskell, who opens her *Life of Charlotte Brontë* (1857) with two whole chapters devoted to Keighley, Haworth and the West Riding, deemed necessary "for a right understanding of the life of my dear friend." "Even an inhabitant of the neighbouring county of Lancaster [Gaskell herself] is struck by the peculiar force of character which the Yorkshiremen display": Gaskell pays tribute to the regionalist project in this distinction, well after the symptomatic move to a provincial representation in her own career. The Manchester of *Mary Barton* had become the offstage, allegorical Drumble of *Cranford*, and when Gaskell revisits the setting, and the industrial novel genre, in *North and South*, both the schematizing title and the abstraction of Manchester as "Milton Northern" reflect the hegemony of a provincial mode – indeed, the novel's heroine grows up in a Mitford-like rural idyll. In *Sylvia's Lovers* (1863) Gaskell restored regionalism, but (anticipating a later development) under the glass of historical distance; and in *Wives and Daughters* (1866) she abandoned it altogether, for a full-scale essay in the novel of provincial life.

The mid-Victorian provincial novel emerges, then, in dialectical reaction to the industrial novel, subsuming its problematic (the condition of England) in an era of relaxed economic and social tensions, and infusing an earlier, minor and idyllic provincialism with the critical ambition of national representation. These novels recognize, rather than deny, the historicity of their provincial setting, but in order to domesticate history as a manageable, orderly, morally accountable process. Far from being set outside "the world," the province *is* the world: the authentic site of an imperial England able to select and absorb the forces of change, renewing rather than surrendering its traditional properties. Eliot's title, *Middlemarch: A Study of Provincial Life* (1872), expresses the synecdochal function of this setting at its most ambitious. The province is peripheral ("march," a border territory) and at the same time central ("middle"); it represents an England of which the center is everywhere and the circumference nowhere.

Eliot brings the provincial novel to its fullest development and beyond, to its mid-1870s point of dissolution. If the Loamshire of the early chapters of *Adam Bede* (1859) seems very close to Barsetshire, the famous defense of realism in the seventeenth chapter is itself a regionalist convention. (Brontë's formula at the beginning of *Shirley*, "unromantic as Monday morning," alludes to the opening rubric – "*Monday morning*" – of *Castle Rackrent*.) Eliot goes on to enrich the ideology of provincialism with a burden of philosophical and literary allusion: in her hands the provincial novel enlarges the project of Scott's historical fiction, drawing on the Wordsworthian discourse of a moral resource of "common life" found amid natural forms and traditional associations. Eliot's last novel, *Daniel Deronda* (1876), states the doctrine:

> A human life, I think, should be well rooted in some spot of a native land, where it may get the love of tender kinship for the face of the earth, for the labours men go forth to, for the sounds and accents that haunt it, for whatever will give that early home a familiar unmistakable difference amidst the future widening of knowledge.

The narrative context gives this meditation an ironic as well as elegiac cast. The heroine's upbringing, the opposite of "well rooted," makes her immune to the influences of a timeless provincial England (which Eliot here calls "Wessex"). The novel goes on to unfold a crisis of national representation, as it narrates the failure of the genre associated with provincial and country-house settings, the female bildungsroman. The novel engineers a catastrophic split between its domestic plot of courtship and provincial life, and its world-historical plot directed to an alien nation, Israel.

The ideological failure of provincial life had already received programmatic treatment in the antithetical genre of the 1860s, the so-called "sensation novel." Sensation novels vengefully apply the Gothic-revival tropes of the urban mysteries genre (as in Dickens) to provincial and country-house settings. An especially virtuosic example, Wilkie Collins's *The Moonstone* (1868), exposes the province's complicity not just with metropolitan corruption but with the crimes of empire; while Dickens's unfinished last novel, *The Mystery of Edwin Drood* (1870), goes a step further in making its setting (in effect) Trollope's Barchester, rather than a country house. The hallucinatory superimposition of distinct settings in the opening paragraphs – squalid London, a fantasmagoric orient, and the "ancient English Cathedral town" – grasps the occult connections among province, metropolis, and empire, to be unwound, presumably, in the unfinished plot. No more than the city can the province now claim to represent a pure, true, archetypal England.

VI

Hardy's attention to the complex specificity of local place makes him an authentic successor to Scott and Galt, reworking their historical regionalism towards a rigorous irony. In particular, Hardy develops the historical formula of romantic regionalism – the synchronization of different layers of temporal difference – in order to move his narratives through and outside history, not back into the timeless enclosure of pastoral, but radically outside, to the windswept *mise-en-scène* of tragedy. In his late novels Hardy empties regional being into a posthistorical, postgeorgic (and certainly antipastoral) condition of loss and alienation; his protagonists (Henchard, Tess, Jude) may enter the archetypal domain of myth, but as sacrificial victims. The reassertion of archaic patterns of identity, in suffering and destruction, is mocked by the absence of any theodicy that will give them human meaning.

Hardy's earlier novels explore the provincial mode, evoked in their pastoral titles: *Under the Greenwood Tree: A Rural Painting of the Dutch School* (1872); *Far From the Madding Crowd* (1874). The great set-pieces of seasonal labor and feasting in *Far From the Madding Crowd* align its narrative with the cyclical time of traditional society, reassuring us of a comic containment of any local catastrophes. The sheep-shearing in the tithe barn at Weatherbury discloses a setting where "for once mediaevalism and modernism had a common stand-point." According to Anderson, the imagined community of the modern nation takes the form of a temporal synchronization across its different regions: all subjects mentally inhabit the same historical moment in a scheme of "homogeneous, empty time." At the sheep-shearing, "modernism" is the temporal contingency that sinks ("for once") into the recurrent, timeless "mediaevalism" of provincial life. Elsewhere in *Far From the Madding Crowd* Hardy glosses the historical geography of uneven development, in which region and metropolis occupy different time-zones:

> In comparison with cities, Weatherbury was immutable. The citizen's *Then* is the rustic's *Now*. In London, twenty or thirty years ago are old times; in Paris ten years, or five; in Weatherbury three or four score years were included in the mere present, and nothing less than a century set a mark on its face or tone. Five decades hardly modified the cut of a gaiter, the embroidery of a smock-frock, by the breadth of a hair. Ten generations failed to alter the turn of a single phrase. In these Wessex nooks the busy outsider's ancient times are only old; his old times are still new; his present is futurity.

It is not simply the case that a premodern temporal experience is still to be found in the provinces. Hardy's comparison between London and Paris, pursuing the trope of "fashion," introduces relative differences into the metropolitan core, destabilizing its claim on standard time. In *Tess of the D'Urbervilles* (1891) Hardy discovers different synchronous states within the same region – within the same family:

> [B]etween the mother with her fast-perishing lumber of superstitions, folk-lore, dialect, and orally-transmitted ballads, and the daughter, with her trained National teachings and Standard knowledge under an infinitely Revised Code, there was a gap of two hundred years as ordinarily understood. When they were together the Jacobean and the Victorian ages were juxtaposed.

This takes up a famous passage in the last chapter of Scott's *Waverley* (1814): "The gradual influx of wealth, and extension of commerce, have since united to render the present people of Scotland a class of beings as different from their grandfathers as the existing English are from those of Queen Elizabeth's time." The teleology explicit in Scott is implicit in Hardy: the mother represents the (regional) cultural past, the daughter the (national) future.

But *Tess of the D'Urbervilles* tells a different story. Victorian metropolitan culture, promised here in the Arnoldian trope of standardized literacy, fails to provide Tess with a future. In the person of Angel Clare, it betrays her as thoroughly as does the "ancient" habit of predatory exploitation enacted by Alec – whose role out of the old ballads is in fact a reactionary modern facsimile. Tess's ancient misfortunes are at the same time representatively modern; Hardy dissolves these pseudohistorical distinctions into a different kind of temporality, in his rhetorical insistence on the recurrence of primordial, mythic events, embedded in the structure of the cosmos. In stark contrast to the provincial idyll, this temporality of eternal recurrence belongs to the mode of tragedy. Tess's wanderings end at Stonehenge, a site that belongs to a past deeper than local history. The archetypal pattern of sacrifice recurs in a temple from which the gods have long since departed – along with the cultural system, the communal memory, that would give the sacrifice some meaning. Just so, the Aeschylean "President of the Immortals" invoked at Tess's hanging has nothing at all to do with Wessex rural tradition; the narrator's appeal, for the last time, to an Arnoldian register of "culture" mocks the incapacity of either to provide explanatory comfort.

REFERENCES

Anderson, Benedict (1983), *Imagined Communities: Reflections on the Origin and Spread of Nationalism* (London: Verso).

Edwards, P. D. (1988), *Idyllic Realism from Mary Russell Mitford to Hardy* (New York: St. Martin's).

Gilmour, Robin (1989), "Regional and Provincial in Victorian Literature." In R. P. Draper, ed., *The Literature of Region and Nation* (New York: St Martin's Press), 51–60.

Hechter, Michael (1975), *Internal Colonialism: The Celtic Fringe in British National Development, 1536–1966* (Berkeley: University of California Press).

Hunter, Shelagh (1984), *Victorian Idyllic Fiction: Pastoral Strategies* (London: Macmillan).

Keith, W. J. (1988), *Regions of the Imagination: The Development of British Rural Fiction* (Toronto: University of Toronto Press).

Leclaire, Lucien (1954), *Le roman regionaliste dans les Iles Britanniques, 1800–1950* (Paris: Société d'Edition "Les Belles Lettres").

Schivelbusch, Wolfgang (1986), *The Railway Journey: The Industrialization of Time and Space in the Nineteenth Century* (Berkeley: University of California Press).

Snell, K. D. M. (1998), "The Regional Novel: Themes for Interdisciplinary Research," in K. D. M. Snell, ed., *The Regional Novel in Britain and Ireland 1800–1990* (Cambridge: Cambridge University Press), 1–53.

Trumpener, Katie (1997), *Bardic Nationalism: The Romantic Novel and the British Empire* (Princeton: Princeton University Press).

Wallerstein, Immanuel (1974), *The Modern World-System* (New York: Academic).

Williams, Raymond (1973), *The Country and the City* (New York: Oxford University Press).

FURTHER READING

Bakhtin, M. M. (1981), "Forms of Time and the Chronotope in the Novel," in *The Dialogic Imagination: Four Essays*, ed. Michael Holquist, trans. Caryl Emerson and Michael Holquist (Austin: University of Texas Press), 84–258.

Barrell, John (1998), "Geographies of Hardy's Wessex," in K. D. M. Snell, ed., *The Regional Novel in Britain and Ireland 1800–1990* (Cambridge: Cambridge University Press), 99–118.

Craig, Cairns (1998), "Scotland and the Regional Novel," in K. D. M. Snell, ed., *The Regional Novel in Britain and Ireland 1800–1990* (Cambridge: Cambridge University Press), 221–256.

Crawford, Robert (1992), *Devolving English Literature* (Oxford: Clarendon).

Darby, H. C. (1948), "The Regional Geography of Thomas Hardy's Wessex," *Geographical Review*, 38, 426–443.

Eagleton, Terry (1995), *Heathcliff and the Great Hunger: Studies in Irish Culture* (London: Verso).

Enstice, Andrew (1979), *Thomas Hardy: Landscapes of the Mind* (London: St. Martin's).

Moretti, Franco (1998), *An Atlas of the European Novel 1800–1900* (London: Verso).

19

Industrial and "Condition of England" Novels

James Richard Simmons, Jr.

During the nineteenth century, questions about the lives and labors of the populace were of great interest to British citizens; it was under the broad rubric of the "condition of England" that these questions came to be addressed. From the late 1830s on, with issues such as the "factory question," the "hungry forties," the repeal of the Corn Laws, and the Chartist uprisings as rich ground from which to mine subject-matter, novels about problems of class conflict and capitalism became one of the most significant subgenres of Victorian literature. Such fiction has been variously labeled, but the "condition of England novel" seems most inclusive.

To understand how and why the condition of England novel originated, it is important to understand the laws that by the 1830s compelled the public to feel there were many victims in a society in which Benjamin Disraeli's concept of "The Two Nations," rich and poor, was a reality. Debates leading to passage of the New Poor Law of 1834 revealed the extent of pauperism, even as the Revd. Thomas Malthus's *An Essay on the Principle of Population* (first published in 1798) argued that population pressure made poverty for the "lower classes" inevitable. Industrialization and explosive urbanization gave public prominence both to pauperism and to the proletariat and its discontents. As a result, the middle and upper classes began to realize how little they knew about the lives of their less fortunate compatriots. Most shocking of all was the realization that hundreds of thousands of people in Britain, including men, women, and children, labored like slaves ("factory slaves" became a widely used metaphor). To limit the ages and daily working hours of children employed by the factories was the aim of the Ten Hours Movement, which inspired Charlotte Elizabeth Tonna's *Helen Fleetwood* and Frances Trollope's *The Life and Adventures of Michael Armstrong, the Factory Boy*. As the appetite for knowledge about the condition of England was whetted, novelists found an audience interested in learning more about the plight of the working classes, and the novel became a method of teaching the middle and upper classes about the "real" condition of England. Reform was on the minds of all of England, and the novel was the apparatus by which many matters of concern would be presented to the public in a manner and language not suited only for lawyers and politicians, but for the common man and woman as well.

Paramount among the types of condition of England novels was the industrial novel, in part because by the midcentury as much as 38 percent of the working population of England was employed in factory work (Bairoch 1968: 191). Contributing to the appeal of the industrial novel was the further element of pathos and helplessness that the large numbers of children and women working in the factories provided. Women worked for lower wages and were found to be easier to manage than men; thus by the middle of the century more than a million women worked in factories. Furthermore, most factory work could be performed equally as well by children as by adults, and usually at half the wages. It is conservatively estimated that no fewer than 100,000 children under fourteen worked in English factories at midcentury, and if one includes all teenagers, the number rises to as much as half a million. Despite these substantive numbers, by the 1840s legislation had mandated that only a very few children over a certain age could legally be employed in factories, and only under strictly supervised hours of work and working conditions which had slowly (if sometimes marginally) improved since the beginning of the century. Considering that in the early 1800s there were few regulations governing the ages at which children were employable or the hours that children could work, the numbers of children working in the factories in the early 1800s must have been staggering. Thus, because large numbers of women and children did in fact work in industry, and because the plight of these workers was sympathetic, many industrial novels take as their central characters individuals who are children, females, or both.

To understand fully, however, how and why these large numbers of working people were deserving of sympathy, it is first necessary to examine the legal, economic, and literary influences that brought about the condition of England novel. These elements of realism would ultimately ensure that the condition of England novel was one of the most popular subgenres of Victorian fiction.

The "Factory Question"

The practice of using child laborers had originated during the Renaissance with the Elizabethan poor law of 1601, which empowered parish officials to apprentice paupers and orphans to industries so that they might learn a trade. Yet what began as a well-intentioned attempt to teach orphans and poor children useful skills by which they might earn a living had, by the late eighteenth century, become an abomination. Up until that point the public had remained for the most part ignorant of the conditions under which children worked, and apparently the first widely publicized indication that abuses existed in the mills occurred when an "infectious fever" broke out in a cotton works in Radcliffe in 1784. When health officials investigated, they were appalled to find that hundreds of children were crowded together in cramped rooms, working long hours in highly unsanitary conditions. Similar outbreaks of "malignant fever" in Manchester and Liverpool during the 1790s led to comparable discoveries, and investigations revealed that children as young as three and four years old were employed in the factories, often working sixteen- and eighteen-hour days (Hutchins and Harrison 1911: 1–3).

As the deplorable working conditions in the factories were publicized, child labor in the mills, hours of work per day and week, the mistreatment and abuse of workers, diet, education, and lodging all came under the rubric of the "factory question," and enlightened social reformers such as Sir Robert Peel and Robert Owen pushed for improved working conditions through legislation, one of the most significant measures being the Factory Act of 1802 (the Health and Morals of Apprentices Act). This Act called for reforms which included limiting the working hours of factory children to twelve a day, the eventual discontinuation of night work, and the provision of some form of education. The Act passed with little opposition, no doubt because it did not attempt to regulate the ages of employees, and furthermore, because even if the factory owners chose not to abide by the new law, noncompliance would result in a meager fine of two to five pounds. The next significant Factory Act, passed in 1819 (the Act for the Regulation of Cotton Mills and Factories), did attempt to regulate the age of child factory workers; it outlawed more than a total of twelve working hours a day for anyone under sixteen and prohibited the employment of children under the age of nine in cotton mills.

Yet even with these gains, the laws under which the factories were allowed to operate still seem appalling in their laxity. Owen, Peel, and others were attempting to do even more, but the powerful factory lobby was actively fighting the laws, and conditions in the factories improved only marginally, if at all. Despite the passage of further Factory Acts in 1820, 1825, and 1831, little substantial improvement in conditions for factory workers actually resulted, no doubt because the need to compromise to get the measures passed diluted their effectiveness. While these early Acts did help by making illegal the all-too-common employment of children five and six years old and even as young as three or four, in some cases the laws were ignored, and even when factory owners adhered to the law, by modern standards the conditions in which these children continued to work were squalid and their treatment in the factories was ghastly.

It was obvious to anyone paying attention that, notwithstanding the efforts of the reformers, conditions in the factories improved only marginally, and the indifference exhibited by the upper and middle classes seemed to indicate that factory children were victims of the popularity of the principles of Malthusian economics: they were regarded as an insignificant part of the surplus population. Thus, as the nineteenth century began, factory workers and factory children in particular had no voice and few official representatives to champion their cause.

Two voices did, however, emerge from the throng to decry the inherent evils of the factory system, from two men reared in widely different circumstances and with extremely different intellectual backgrounds. One was the man who Malthus himself claimed was "greatly erroneous," the radical philosopher William Godwin. The other, a factory child himself, was an illiterate orphan from the St. Pancras workhouse whose name would come to symbolize the horrors of the factories, Robert Blincoe. Godwin and Blincoe were two of the first to publish accounts of the lives of factory children. While Godwin's brief episodic narrative of the life of a factory child would pass almost unnoticed, Blincoe's personal account would become one of the most controversial and influential pieces of prose to be written about the new "factory system." Both, however, were influential in establishing the Victorian industrial novel.

Godwin, the husband of Mary Wollstonecraft and father of novelist Mary Shelley, was one of the leading novelists and philosophers of the late eighteenth century. Though his *Fleetwood: or, the New Man of Feeling* (1805) contains only a few chapters in which he presents children doing factory work, it is the earliest novel to give any extended treatment to the factory question. In chapter 11, Kasmir Fleetwood's godfather, Ruffigny, tells his godson about his experiences as a factory child in a silk mill, and the wretched and inhumane monotony of day-to-day life. Ruffigny explains that, as an orphaned boy, he was left in the care of an uncle. The uncle, anxious to appropriate the boy's inheritance for himself, had Ruffigny apprenticed to a silk mill owned by Vaublanc. In an effort to justify his calling and the need for child labor, Vaublanc explains "what an advantage these mills are." He goes on to say that rather than children being a burden to their families, by being put to work in the mills "they learn no bad habits; but are quiet, and orderly, and attentive, and industrious. What a prospect for their future lives! God himself must approve and bless a race who are thus early prepared to be of use to themselves and others" (Godwin 1805: 94–5).

Though the naïve Ruffigny is interested in an enterprise which does so much good for so many, when he enters the mill he notes a situation far different from that described. Rather than the healthy, happy workers he had been led to expect, he finds that "not one of the persons before me exhibited any signs of vigour and robust health. They were all sallow; their muscles flaccid, and their form emaciated. Several of the children appeared to me, judging from their size, to be under four years of age – I never saw such children" (pp. 96–8).

Even though Godwin's novel is set in France and not England, *Fleetwood* is nevertheless an important early indictment not only of the mills themselves, but of the justifications advanced by the factory owners themselves for child labor. Although Godwin only briefly addresses the factory question before moving on to other events more central to the plot, an individual who would provide a more detailed account of his own real-life sufferings in the factories was, during that same year Godwin's novel was published, being beaten, starved, and compelled to sleep in a sackcloth bed full of maggots in the Lowdham Cotton Mill. Where Godwin's account would only briefly confront his readers with the wretched realities of the factories, Robert Blincoe's account would be a rallying cry for the working classes for years to come.

There is no doubt about the political aims of John Brown's *A Memoir of Robert Blincoe* (1828), arguably the most famous account by a factory child ever published and generally considered to be the first example of nineteenth-century life-writing which substantially dealt with abuses within the factories. Though journalist John

Brown served as amanuensis for the illiterate Blincoe and therefore the *Memoir* is not technically an autobiography, the account was important because of the legislation and the fiction which it inspired. As Richard Carlile, publisher of the radical paper *The Lion* in which Blincoe's story first appeared, noted, "such a memoir as this has been much wanted, to hand down to posterity, what was the real character of the complaints about the treatment of children in our cotton mills" (1828: 146). Indeed, perhaps the best way to judge the *Memoir*'s impact is to note that after Carlile published it, trade union leader John Doherty reissued it in 1832, and Blincoe was named a star witness before the Select Committee Investigating the Employment of Children in Manufactories in 1833. Even as late as the early twentieth century Blincoe's story was seen as one of the most significant works of its day, and in 1911 Hutchins and Harrison's *A History of Factory Legislation* alluded to Blincoe's account as an accurate representation of the horrors of factory life by referring readers to "the revolting personal cruelties to be read of in Robert Blincoe's memoirs" (p. 19). Blincoe's detailed account of the beatings, starvation, and abuses suffered at the hands of the factory masters served as propaganda for the Ten Hours Movement. It also inspired one novelist in particular, Frances Trollope, who would borrow from Blincoe's narrative quite heavily when writing her novel *Michael Armstrong, The Factory Boy* (1840). The widely read *Michael Armstrong* itself served as propaganda for the Ten Hours Movement, which led finally to the Ten Hours Act of 1847.

The First Victorian Industrial Novels

Literary works which detailed the lives of factory operatives appeared throughout the 1830s. These include John Walker's *The Factory Lad* (1832), a dramatic interpretation of the factory controversy, and Caroline Bowles's *Tales of the Factories* (1833) and Caroline Norton's *A Voice From the Factories* (1836), both of which offered poetic representations of the misery of factory life for adults as well as children. Like *Michael Armstrong*, Tonna's evangelical novel or "tract," *Helen Fleetwood*, also condemned working conditions in the factories and supported the Ten Hours Movement. While these works emphasized the horrors of factory work with reform as the ultimate goal, their melodramatic plots allowed critics to dismiss them as the products of the overworked imaginations of their writers. In contrast, proponents of the factory system could point to seemingly nonfictional examinations of the system such as Edward Baines's *History of the Cotton Manufacture in Great Britain* (1835) and Andrew Ure's *The Philosophy of the Manufactures* (1835) as proof that the factories were not injurious to workers, but in fact beneficial. Baines, a journalist, offered a historical approach in a volume complete with illustrations that tended to soften and idealize the factory system. Ure, a Scottish professor of chemistry and natural philosophy, repudiated the claims of critics who protested that factory work was bad for children by insisting on the cheerfulness of the operatives and the wholesomeness of their work. He noted that the children were

cheerful and alert, taking pleasure in the light play of their muscles, – enjoying the
mobility natural to their age. The scene of industry, so far from exciting sad emotions
in my mind, was always exhilarating. It was delightful to observe the nimbleness with
which they pieced the broken ends . . . The work of these lively elves seemed to resemble a sport, in which habit gave them a pleasing dexterity. (1967: 301)

If there was a literary war over the factory system, up until 1839 it appeared that
writers such as Ure, who obviously supported the system, were winning it. It was
Trollope's novel, *The Life and Adventures of Michael Armstrong, The Factory Boy*, that
would bring the plight of the factory worker to mainstream Victorian audiences. In
what Catherine Gallagher calls "a deliberately shocking piece of propaganda" (1985:
127), *Michael Armstrong* was, according to Trollope, an attempt to open the eyes of
readers to "the hideous mass of injustice and suffering to which thousands of infant
labourers are subjected, who toil in our monster spinning mills" (1840: iii). Michael
Armstrong lives with his well-meaning but somewhat naïve mother and his crippled
brother in Ashleigh, a factory town controlled by the evil industrialist Sir Matthew
Dowling. Sir Matthew takes Michael into his home to impress Lady Clarissa
Shrimpton with his benevolence, although his motives are entirely selfish. He considers Michael a "dirty little dog," and he asks his overseer Parsons for more information about the boy. Parsons tells him that Michael takes care of his brother, "who
is but a poor rickety, shriveldy sort of a child," and his mother, who is a "bedridden
woman, and ought to be in the workhouse; but she's uppish, and can't abide it."
Parsons tells Dowling that, crippled or not, Michael's brother should have to work
because "his fingers is just as able to handle the reels and handle the threads as they
ever was; and in course, a little dwarf like him, with his legs like crooked drumsticks,
can't look for any but the youngest wages, so after all, he's one of them as answers
best" (pp. 33–4).

No doubt Trollope hoped that the malignancy of the factory owner and his
overseer would strike a nerve with her readers, as would her presentation of the
Armstrongs as abused but honest, hardworking British citizens. In order to make a
claim for verisimilitude, Trollope spent several weeks in Manchester interviewing
factory workers, and she also drew heavily upon Brown's *A Memoir of Robert Blincoe*.
According to Ivanca Kovačević (1975: 99), Trollope was introduced to *A Memoir of
Robert Blincoe* by trade union leader John Doherty, who had republished that *Memoir*
himself. While there are many similarities between settings and incidents in the two
works, in terms of the characters and their personal situations, the only resemblance
is that Blincoe and Armstrong are both children. The setting of the Deep Valley Mill
where Michael works is much like the Lowdham Mill where Blincoe worked, and
individual incidents, such as fighting with the hogs for scraps, were unquestionably
patterned after Blincoe's *Memoir* with only slight alteration. Due to the repeated
republishings of Blincoe's work, informed readers would have had little trouble connecting the two stories, and, by association, readers may have accepted Trollope's
fiction as fact. Thus, Trollope's combination of melodrama and veracity made *Michael*

Armstrong one of the first widely read works of industrial literature. Though many critics savaged the book as being unrealistic – Trollope's fairytale ending has benefactress Mary Brotherton adopting Michael, his brother, and another child, and making them prosperous, educated, and wealthy – the novel sold well and gained support among factory reform advocates, and particularly among the Chartists. As John Cobden noted in *The White Slaves of England*, *Michael Armstrong* was a novel that was "a fiction merely in construction, a truthful narrative in fact" (1853: 162).

Tonna's *Helen Fleetwood*, also published in 1839–40, was one of the first industrial novels to make use of the "exploitation of women" by a "social-problem novelist" (Wheeler 1985: 19). Tonna would also go beyond Trollope's use of mere melancholy and pity to appeal to readers' sympathies, and to this mix she would also add the appeal to readers' empathy for fellow Christians.

Helen Fleetwood has been called the "first novel completely devoted to the life of English proletarians" (Kovačević 1975: 101), and indeed, whereas a large portion of *Michael Armstrong*'s action takes place in the homes of the novel's wealthy villains, the main setting of *Helen Fleetwood* is among the poor. The Widow Green leaves her rustic village to find jobs for her family (including the pious Helen Fleetwood) in the Godless town of M. (a thinly disguised Manchester), where other members of her family already live. The widow's son-in-law and daughter, the Wrights, have been as corrupted by the factory system as the factory owners themselves, but perhaps the most marked contrast between the people from the country and those from the city is in the children. Factory children Phoebe and Charles Wright are vicious and hard-hearted, inured to pain, greed, and poverty by an industrial system that thrives on all three factors. Tonna suggests that as a result Phoebe is destined to become a prostitute and Charles an alcoholic. The Wrights' other daughter, Sarah, is a good child, but her body is twisted and crippled from hours of labor in the factory. She is so deformed, in fact, that the Wrights initially try to hide her in the attic so that the Widow Green and her grandchildren won't see her.

Tonna's novel eschews the standard happy ending – the Widow Green ends up in a workhouse, and Helen Fleetwood dies – but there is a religious message from which readers can take heart. Through Christianity and devotion to God, the widow and her grandchildren are able to maintain their dignity and goodness and, even though some of the good characters die, their reward will come in heaven. This ending, unlike that of *Michael Armstrong*, was at least something many working-class readers could actually relate to: they were much more likely to die while still "factory slaves" than be rescued by a rich benefactress. Further, Tonna's Christian call to action is quite clear, as the last lines illustrate:

> We should pray for those men who are trying to make the factory children less miserable; and whenever you speak to the great folks, put in a word: for I can't help thinking that God must be angry with them while they take so much care about their own little ones, and have no thought, no feeling for the perishing children of the poor. (Tonna 1841: 328–9)

A similar didacticism, but in defense of the factories, is evident in Frederic Montagu's 1839 novel *Mary Ashley*. Montagu emphasizes that a job in the factory has saved the titular heroine from a life of destitution. In contrast to illustrations in Trollope's novel that showed tattered children working exhaustedly in cramped spinning-rooms, illustrations in Montagu's novel depict a few clean, cheerful children working in large, airy rooms that look much like the interiors of cathedrals. Even the mill-owner stands in contrast to characters such as Trollope's Dowling and Parsons; he is a soft-spoken, kind-hearted, and intelligent man who doesn't mind if Mary sings a psalm or two while she works. In short, *Mary Ashley* is as much propaganda as are Trollope's and Tonna's novels, different only in that *Mary Ashley* argues the cause of the mill-owners, while *Michael Armstrong* and *Helen Fleetwood* present the opposite case.

Later Factory Acts and the Regulation of the Labor of Children

While the first significant Act to address the labor of children in the factories, the Factory Act of 1833 (introduced as an Act to Regulate the Labour of Children and Young Persons in Mills and Factories) was passed before these novels were written, mill-owners were constantly attempting to have the Acts overturned or amended to lessen their severity. As a result, the laws under which the factories were allowed to operate up until 1833 were appalling in their laxity. For example, though the Act of 1819 originally called for the working hours for all aged under eighteen to be less than ten and a half hours a day, the *Leeds Mercury* reported in 1830 that children in Bradford were working thirteen hours a day with a respite of only half an hour for a meal, and went on to note that in some other manufactories children worked from five in the morning until nine o'clock at night. In 1830, under the heading "Slavery in Yorkshire," Richard Oastler wrote a series of letters denouncing the abuses of the factory system to the *Mercury* as well as the *Leeds Intelligencer*, and soon the Ten Hours Campaign was underway. The campaign was bipartisan, with both Tories such as Oastler and Michael Sadler and Radicals such as John Fielden calling for the introduction of still more laws regulating the labor of children.

The first result was the Factory Act of 1833, which disallowed night work (between 8.30 p.m. and 5.30 a.m.) for all people under eighteen in cotton, hemp, worsted, flax, silk, linen, tow, or woolen mills, and mandated that a person under eighteen could not work more than twelve hours a day or sixty-nine hours a week. It further forbade the employment of children under nine in any but silk mills, and decreed that no child under eleven could be employed more than forty-eight hours in a week or nine in a day (the second year after the passing of the Act the age was increased from eleven to twelve, and the third year to thirteen).

Despite the 1833 Act and the Ten Hours Act of 1847, conditions in the factories, in mines, and in other workplaces continued to occupy reformers into the 1840s and beyond. For literature, one result was the flourishing of condition of England writing, as in Thomas Carlyle's *Past and Present* (1843), Douglas Jerrold's novel about rich versus poor, *St. Jiles and St. James* (1845), and such poems as Thomas Hood's "The Song of the Shirt" (1843) and Elizabeth Barrett Browning's "The Cry of the Children" (1844). With some legislative success in improving the lot of factory children, by the late 1840s attention was shifting to the issue of the poor law and the working class in general. While the Factory Act of 1844 included women under the same regulations as children, the first significant gains for adult males came through the Ten Hours Act of 1847, passed in the midst of the "hungry forties." According to Hutchins and Harrison, when the Act came into effect that year, trade was so bad that of the 179 mills in Manchester only 92 were working full-time. When one also considers that of the 41,000 mill employees in Manchester about 50 percent were only working part time or were unemployed, the Ten Hours Bill was, as the Report of Inspectors of Factories for 1847–8 noted, only "very partially felt." While legislation was finally improving working conditions, unemployment was so high that initially few workers benefited from the changes. Many of those whom the legislation would have helped were now unemployed, while those who worked were still living in poverty.

The Chartists were still doing what they could to call attention to the problems of unemployment and poverty among the working classes. The Chartist movement, founded in 1838 when William Lovett drafted the "People's Charter," had been campaigning for change since the Reform Act of 1832 in an attempt to improve conditions for the working classes. While the Chartists' petitions to Parliament for changes were denied in 1839, 1842, and 1848 – the final failure resulting in the collapse of their movement – they did bring England's attention to working-class problems. Nor did the failure of the Chartist movement mean that the plight of the working classes would henceforth go unnoticed. During the 1840s and 1850s, with the ill-used factory child now essentially a figure of the past, sympathetic writers turned to adults as the focus of their industrial novels. This posed a new problem, however, as novelists now had to produce works that would interest readers through other means than merely appealing to their sympathy: a dirty, cold, poor child living in the streets excites sympathy, while a dirty, cold, poor adult living in the streets is a ne'er-do-well who needs to get a job. Then, too, the industrial novels of this later period were more complex and significant as works of literature, because they aimed at portraying and understanding the condition of England question in all its complexity, and not merely at getting the Ten Hours Bill passed.

From Working-Class Child to Working-Class Adult

Elizabeth Stone's *William Langshawe the Cotton Lord* (1842) took a different approach to the factory question from earlier novels about factory life. Her vignettes of Manchester life and events depict the town as a center for culture and commerce. Stone (who was the daughter of John Wheeler, owner of the *Manchester Chronicle*) approaches the textile industry as a flawed but valuable system, and so she is understandably concerned with pointing out the good that the factory system offers; but she does so in a fashion that is secondary to the plot. The novel tells the story of a factory-owner's son murdered by a trade unionist (loosely based on the murder of Thomas Ashton in 1831), and also addresses the adversity in the lives of a middle-class woman (Edith Langshawe) and of working-class characters (Jem Forshawe and Nancy Halliwell). Further, the plot elements of murder, seduction, and women's struggles offer greater complexity than the good versus evil conflict confronted by factory children in some earlier industrial novels. Indeed, *William Langshawe* foreshadows Elizabeth Gaskell's better-known *Mary Barton* (1848), although the theme of a young woman exploited by society harkens back to Tonna's *Helen Fleetwood* and prefigures Stone's own later novel *The Young Milliner* (1843) as well.

The focus on adult characters and issues also extends to Benjamin Disraeli's *Sybil, or, The Two Nations* (1845), which detailed the Chartist agitation and the class conflict that beset Britain from 1839 to 1842. It was Disraeli who stressed the widening gap between the "two nations," rich and poor, "between whom there is no intercourse and no sympathy; who are . . . ignorant of each other's habits, thoughts, and feelings . . . who are formed by a different breeding, are fed by different food, are ordered by different manners, and are not governed by the same laws" (bk 2, ch. 50). In *Sybil* the squalor and desperation pervasive in the lives of the poor sharply contrast with the lives of the rich. Chartist leader Walter Gerard represents the noble possibilities within the working class, and Walter's daughter Sybil is an "angel" (bk 2, ch. 14) who forgoes a life as a nun to marry the aristocrat Egremont. While Disraeli's sympathy is clearly with the working class, he nevertheless has a somewhat patronizing attitude towards them; it is still in their best interest, he believes, to defer to the aristocracy and the assumption that the blue-bloods truly know what is best for the nation. Indeed, Sybil herself turns out to be of aristocratic lineage and heir to a title, and thus the message seems to be that this superior being who has risen to the top of her class by good deeds and intelligence succeeds because of her noble lineage. *Sybil* was the second of Disraeli's Young England trilogy; along with *Coningsby* (1844) and *Tancred* (1847), it explores the condition of England question in depth, and makes the case that its solution lies in a rejuvenated aristocracy.

Certainly *Sybil* illustrates that condition of England novels were becoming better and more complex. While novelists such as Stone, Trollope, Montagu, and Tonna were all marginally successful, few of them are well known today, and the same might be said of their works. However, by the late 1840s more serious and better-known novelists began to address the condition of England in their novels, and as a result the works that best represent industrial fiction and that are best known today were all published a decade or two after the subgenre originated.

Elizabeth Gaskell's *Mary Barton: A Tale of Manchester Life* (1848) takes place in the midst of the unrest of the "hungry forties." Mary's father, John Barton, is a working-class man with a meager income; he is also an active trade unionist, and in the union meetings he finds solace, as the oppressed workers commiserate and unite against their oppressors. The unionists feel that they are not only ignored by the factory-owners, but mocked and despised, and as a result they decide to murder Harry Carson, the son of Barton's employer. John Barton draws the lot to do the deed, but to complicate matters, his daughter Mary has been receiving attention from Harry Carson, which has led her to spurn her working-class lover Jem Wilson. After the murder the suspicion naturally falls on Wilson, and it is Mary who faces the task of how to clear Wilson without implicating her father, whom she knows to be the murderer. She manages to do this, and on his deathbed her father confesses his crime to Harry Carson's father, who forgives him.

Readers then and now have observed that the ending tends to undercut the novel's effectiveness, although, as the *British Quarterly Review* said, it "serve[s] the didactic purpose of the author" (1848: vol. 9, 128; cited in Gallagher 1985: 67). The oppression and misery of the workers, who are driven by despair to the extreme measures they adopt, seem to be almost forgotten in the Christian forgiveness between John Barton and Mr. Carson. Yet despite the ending, *Mary Barton* offers a stark look at the brutality, poverty, and oppression of working-class life. Gaskell is careful to point out differences between what the workers *think* is their lot in life and what is actually the case, even if the truth may actually be different from what it seems. The result is that she presents what appears to be an unbiased account, showing how and why both employer and employee think and act as they do, in what is almost a fictionalized literary case study. Thus, despite its flawed ending, *Mary Barton* remains a first-rate industrial novel, and one of the first written to remain even today a highly regarded account of factory life.

Charlotte Brontë's *Shirley* (1849) is another such novel. Unlike Gaskell, Brontë was at the height of her fame when she published *Shirley* as the follow-up to her acclaimed first novel, *Jane Eyre*. *Shirley* was no *Jane Eyre*, however; rather, it was both an historical novel and an industrial novel in which Brontë said she was trying not to "make even a more ridiculous mess of the matter than Mrs. Trollope did" (quoted in Wise and Symington 1932: vol. 2, 184). In *Shirley*, Brontë presents a tale of the Luddite machine-breaking riots which occurred in the north of England in 1811–13. Mill-owner Robert Moore decides to upgrade his mill with new machinery, and workers fear that this mechanization will put them out of work. The workers attempt to destroy the mill and later to kill Moore, but Moore is eventually able to overcome adversity and at the end of the Napoleonic wars he gains financial stability. The heroine, Shirley Keeldar, herself a mill-owner, braves the threats of the Luddites, rejects Moore's proposal of marriage (which would have provided financial security for him and his factory), and instead ends up marrying his brother Louis. While Brontë doesn't quite make "the mess" of the topic that she believed Frances Trollope did, her industrial novel takes industry and industrial matters mainly as a backdrop for its action; the middle-class characters' lives and romances are the centerpiece.

Another condition of England (but not technically industrial) novel is Charles Kingsley's *Alton Locke: Tailor and Poet* (1850). Just as Chartism and Owenism were issues in Disraeli's novel, so Chartism and Christian socialism are issues in Kingsley's. Alton Locke is apprenticed to a tailor and works in sweatshop conditions that could be considered only slightly better than factory work. He becomes a Chartist, while his talent for poetry allows him to begin to interact with individuals such as Eleanor and Lillian Staunton, as well as with the working-class intellectual bookseller Saunders Mackaye, Kingsley's portrait of Thomas Carlyle. In an effort to please Lillian and her father, prompted partly by his own aspirations to move upward socially, as well as by his having fallen in love with Lillian, Alton tones down his vituperative verse about working-class life. As a result he is subsequently seen as one who has sold out and is spurned by his Chartist associates. To show that he is still true to their cause, he goes to the country to preach Chartism to farm laborers. There, he unintentionally incites the audience to riot. He is sentenced to a prison term, and in the meantime Lillian marries another man. Eleanor, however, remains devoted to him, nurses him through an illness, and eventually convinces him that Christian socialism is the means by which working conditions in England can be changed. Alton subscribes to this view, and in the end dies while on his way to the United States.

Not surprisingly, Kingsley himself was a Christian socialist. This movement, which spurned violence and instead espoused education and interclass cooperation (but not the abolition of private property), was led by Frederick Denison Maurice and John Malcolm Ludlow. Only a few years before *Alton Locke*, Kingsley had expressed a similar belief in Christian socialism as a tool for change in his novel *Yeast* (1848), which deals with issues of the poor and sanitary reform, particularly concentrating on the fouled water, filth, and raw sewage that affected the poor even more than the other classes. In that novel too religion plays a part, from the pointing out of the evils of the Catholic Church to the harm done by the atheist Lancelot Smith. Both *Yeast* and *Alton Locke* emphasize that the transformation of individuals and society as a whole must be based upon principles of Christian goodness if it is to be successful. Like some earlier novels such as *Helen Fleetwood*, the tone of *Alton Locke* (as well as *Yeast*) tends to be preachy and didactic, but it offers a more complex, interesting analysis of the condition of England than that in the earlier factory-child novels.

Charles Dickens, the most important novelist of the Victorian period, had shown an early interest in the condition of England genre; *Oliver Twist* (1838) had been and remains one of the best-known novels of its time. Though not an industrial novel, *Oliver Twist* addressed such social problems as the New Poor Law of 1834, crime, and poverty. Despite its popularity, Dickens abstained from writing an industrial novel for quite some time. In response to a letter in 1839 from Samuel Laman Blanchard concerning the subject of his forthcoming novel *Barnaby Rudge*, Dickens was clearly dismissive about factory novels, saying his upcoming novel "has nothing to do with factories, or Negroes – white, black, or parti coloured. It is a tale of the riots of Eighty, before factories flourished as they did thirty years afterwards, and containing – or intended to contain – no allusion to cotton lords, cotton slaves, or anything that is cotton" (House and Storey 1965: 507). This disclaimer might lead one to suspect that Dickens felt that there was enough literature on the market about factory workers.

While Dickens would never devote an entire novel to the factory-child controversy, it is perhaps ironic that, despite the many volumes dedicated to the plight of child laborers in industrial settings, it is a brief section of *David Copperfield*, depicting young David's brief stint in Murdstone and Grinby's warehouse, that may be the most familiar of all nineteenth-century factory narratives. Through his experience at Murdstone and Grinby's, while not subjected to the beatings or to the unhealthy diet endured by many real-life child laborers, David does convey the drudgery and misery of the factory child. Dickens had himself briefly been a child laborer in a blacking warehouse, and thus *David Copperfield*'s account has a poignancy that many novels about factory children lack. By dint of being the most popular author of his time, and by inserting this brief episode into one of the greatest novels of any time, Dickens achieved a visibility for the plight of factory children that perhaps surpassed the more protracted factual accounts by many of his contemporaries.

When Dickens published *Hard Times* (1854), his one truly industrial novel, it may have come as a surprise to readers that he avoided the issue of factory children altogether. Dickens is interested in other topical issues – the strikes and lockouts at factories in Preston in 1853–4. He is even more interested in the educations of his middle-class characters – Louisa and Tom Gradgrind – and the circus girl, Sissy Jupe. Further, his attitude toward the trade union and the strike in *Hard Times* is clearly no more sympathetic than his attitude toward the factory-owner and banker, Josiah Bounderby.

Early in the novel, Dickens sets the tone for life in Coketown, by noting that

> it was a town of red brick, or of brick that would have been red if the smoke and ashes had allowed it . . . It was a town of machinery and tall chimneys, out of which inter-minable serpents of smoke trailed themselves for ever and ever . . . It had a black canal in it, and a river that ran purple with ill-smelling dye, and vast piles of building full of windows where there was a rattling and a trembling all day long, and where the piston of the steam-engine worked monotonously up and down, like the head of an ele-phant in a state of melancholy madness. (1854: 28)

Through descriptions such as these, Dickens brilliantly displays the sense of hope-lessness and monotony that pervades Coketown. This hopelessness is not limited only to the factory workers; Dickens tells the stories of a number of characters, most of whom, such as Sissy Jupe, have little to do with the factories. The principal charac-ter who is concerned with the factories is Stephen Blackpool, an honest, hardworking man who works in the mill owned by Josiah Bounderby. It is Blackpool's honesty, causing him to refuse to join the trade union, that leads to his ostracism by his fellow factory workers; in contrast, it is Bounderby's dishonesty that leads to the latter's ruin. Yet Dickens's novel doesn't identify either character as good or bad simply because he is a worker or a factory-owner. While Stephen and the woman who loves him, Rachel, are positively portrayed, long-suffering characters, Stephen's wife, a former factory worker, is a drunken prostitute, and Stephen's co-workers who ostracize him and the trade-union organizer Slackbridge certainly are not admirable individuals. Gone is the moral simplicity of a novel such as *Michael Armstrong* where the good factory worker is pitted against the evil factory-owner. Dickens presents a more complex situation, and one which no doubt more realistically mirrors the complexities of life.

Dickens serialized *Hard Times* in his periodical *Household Words*, and to immediately follow it he secured the services of Elizabeth Gaskell, who serialized her next industrial novel, *North and South*, there in 1855. Like Dickens, and unlike so many of the earlier industrial novels, Gaskell does not equate the factory owner with evil; indeed, one of the novel's heroes, John Thornton, is a factory-owner, and a loving son and brother as well. Owner of a factory in the town of Milton-Northern (yet another thinly disguised representation of Manchester), Thornton meets the heroine Margaret Hale, a woman who has been brought to the town by her father, who desires to teach mill-owners who want an education. Margaret dislikes industry and what it does to people and the environment, and, seeing the depressed conditions in the area she soon takes the side of the mill-workers in their struggles to gain better working conditions. Margaret advocates that Thornton take a more humane approach to the workers' problems, which Thornton initially rejects. However, he eventually comes to see that Margaret is right; after Margaret protects him from rioting strikers, the two very different characters come together at the end of the novel.

In literary terms, *North and South* may be the best of all industrial novels. It is neither preachy nor didactic; the factory question is intrinsic to the action of the novel, yet the story can stand on its own; it does not rely entirely on melodrama; and the characters are vividly portrayed rather than stock villains or angels. Gaskell attempts to deal with the issues surrounding the factory in an even-handed, adult manner, and she presents both sides of the question quite well. The result is a novel that is both readable and enjoyable whether one is interested in the factory question or not. Ironically, however, just as novelists such as Dickens and Gaskell seemed to have finally brought the condition of England novel to a state of high art, the genre itself became all but superfluous.

The End of the Condition of England Novel

As legislation enacted reforms and factory work became less dangerous and exploitative, there was quite naturally less antifactory literature written. The ways in which factory workers were perceived was undergoing a change, and by the 1860s the melodramatic factory novel was seen as *passé*. As the *Edinburgh Review* noted in an article of 1862 entitled "Modern Domestic Service," factory work was by then preferable even to domestic service, which had once been seen as the most genteel of working-class professions. The article claimed:

> Servant-girls and foot-boys cannot dress as the factory lads and lasses may — [they have] not the daily stimulus and amusement of society of their own order . . . The maidservant must have "no followers," while the factory-worker can flirt to any extent.

Servant-girls rarely may marry, while factory-girls probably always may, whether they do or not . . . Public opinion among the class is in favour of the independence of factory and other day-work . . . In one word, it is *independence* against *dependence*. (Anon. 1862: 414)

Employment in the factories had become more normalized, and while abuses still existed and there were still some concerns about working conditions for both children and adults, clearly the widespread problems that had existed fifty years before had been improved or even, in many cases, eradicated.

As Peter Mathias notes in *The First Industrial Nation: An Economic History of Britain 1700–1914*, prior to 1853 "no limitations were imposed on adult males in the mills" (1969: 204), and thus in order to equalize the working conditions for all factory operatives, subsequent Factory Acts began to repeal or emend former Acts, and additionally they began to address issues other than those dealing with hours of work, such as questions of safety: for example, the fencing of shafts. Obviously, the regulation of labor in factories is a process that has continued since, but for the most part the period after 1850 introduced legislation that provided workers with a system of laws more uniform in their application, ensuring that all factory workers, be they men, women, or children, were subject to reasonably fair treatment. As Frances Gillespie notes in *Labor and Politics in England, 1850–1867*, after midcentury "the upper and middle classes [were] aware of the wage-earning classes with a distinctness that left no debate as to the latent power residing in the labouring classes" (1967: 4); and so, their message having been heard, industrial novels ceased to have a topical political message that readers were willing to pay to read. Consequently, other than the occasional novel such as Mary Elizabeth Braddon's *The Factory Girl* (1869) or Herbert Glyn's *The Cotton Lord* (1862), as a subgenre the condition of England novel disappeared. Arguably the last significant work in the subgenre was George Eliot's *Felix Holt, The Radical* (1866). In the early 1830s, Felix Holt keeps a watch and clock shop in North Loamshire. As an intelligent young man, Felix longs to expand his vistas and enter the political life, not only for his own benefit but also for the education and improvement of his working-class colleagues. Another man, Harold Transome, also has his sights set on a political career, intending to enter Parliament as a Liberal. Both Holt and Transome are interested in Esther Lyon, daughter of a Dissenting minister. As it turns out, Esther has a claim to the Transome estate, though she relinquishes her interest before she marries Felix. The backdrop of the novel is the political intrigue of the period, including the political corruption so prevalent at the time, just after the passage of the First Reform Bill of 1832. As *Felix Holt* illustrates, much of the subject matter in the condition of England novel during the latter part of the century relied on anachronism, as the abuses and concerns addressed involved events that had happened decades before. Indeed, who could write a novel with a Chartist uprising or a starving factory child at its center when such things, for all practical purposes, no longer existed?

In a sense, the condition of England novel became a victim of its own success, because as legislation enacted reforms and the working class enjoyed improving conditions, other issues such as socialism and feminism (as in the "new woman" novel of the 1890s) came to the fore. Nevertheless, the condition of England novel played an important part in the development of Victorian literature, and more generally in Victorian politics and culture.

REFERENCES

Anon. (1862), "Modern Domestic Service," *Edinburgh Review*, 65/235, April, 409–39.

Bairoch, Paul (1968), *The Working Population and its Structure* (New York: Gordon & Breach).

Carlile, Richard, ed. (1828), *The Lion*, 1/5, February 1, 1828.

Cobden, John C. (1853), *The White Slaves of England* (Buffalo: Derby & Miller).

Dickens, Charles (1854), *Hard Times: For These Times* (London: Bradbury & Evans).

Forster, John (1872), *The Life of Charles Dickens* (London: n.p.).

Gallagher, Catherine (1985), *The Industrial Reformation of English Fiction: Social Discourse and Narrative Form, 1832–1867* (Chicago: University of Chicago Press).

Gillespie, Frances (1967), *Labor and Politics in England, 1850–1867* (New York: Octagon).

Godwin, William (1805), *Fleetwood: or, The New Man of Feeling* (London: n.p.).

House, Madeline, and Storey, Graham, eds. (1965), *The Letters of Charles Dickens* (Oxford: Clarendon).

Hutchins, B. L. and Harrison, A. (1911), *A History of Factory Legislation*. (London: P. S. King).

Kovačević, Ivanka (1975), *Fact into Fiction: English Literature and the Industrial Scene, 1750–1850* (Leicester: Leicester University Press).

Malthus, Thomas (1798), *An Essay on the Principle of Population* (London: n.p.).

Mathias, Peter (1969), *The First Industrial Nation: An Economic History of Britain, 1700–1914* (London: Methuen).

Tonna, Charlotte Elizabeth (1841), *Helen Fleetwood* (London: Seely & W. Burnside). (First publ. 1839–40 in *The Christian Lady's Magazine*.)

Trollope, Frances (1840), *Michael Armstrong, the Factory Boy* (London: Colburn).

Ure, Andrew (1967), *The Philosophy of the Manufactures; or, an Exposition of the Scientific, Moral, and Commercial Economy of the Factory System of Great Britain* (London: Cass). (First publ. 1835.)

Wheeler, Michael (1985), *English Fiction of the Victorian Period, 1830–1890* (New York and London: Longman).

Wise, T. J. and Symington, J. A., eds. (1932), *The Brontës: Their Lives, Friendships, and Correspondence*, 4 vols. (Oxford: Blackwell).

FURTHER READING

Braddon, Mary Elizabeth (1869), *The Factory Girl; Or, All Is Not Gold That Glitters: A Romance of Real Life* (New York: Dewitt).

Brontë, Charlotte (1849), *Shirley: A Tale* (London: Smith, Elder).

Brown, John (2002), *A Memoir of Robert Blincoe*, in James R. Simmons Jr., ed., *Factory Lives: Four Nineteenth-Century Working Class Autobiographies* (Toronto: Broadview). (First publ. 1828.)

Cook, Chris and Keith, Brendan (1975), *British Historical Facts, 1830–1890* (New York: St. Martin's).

Disraeli, Benjamin (1845), *Sybil; or, the Two Nations* (London: Colburn).

Eliot, George (1866), *Felix Holt, the Radical* (London: William Blackwood & Sons).

Gaskell, Elizabeth (1848), *Mary Barton: A Tale of Manchester Life* (London: Chapman & Hall).

Gaskell, Elizabeth (1855), *North and South* (London: Chapman & Hall).

Gilmour, Robin (1993), *The Victorian Period: The Intellectual and Cultural Context of English Literature, 1830–1890* (London: Longman).

Gray, Robert (1996), *The Factory Question and Industrial England, 1830–1860* (Cambridge: Cambridge University Press).

Hopkirk, Mary (1949), *Nobody Wanted Sam: The Story of the Unwelcome Child, 1530–1948* (London: John Murray).

Joyce, Patrick (1990), "Work," in F. M. L. Thompson, ed., *The Cambridge Social History of Britain, 1750–1950*, vol. 2: *People and their Environment* (Cambridge: Cambridge University Press), pp. 131–94.

Kingsley, Charles (1848), *Yeast: A Problem* (London: Colburn).

Kingsley, Charles (1850), *Alton Locke, Tailor and Poet* (London: n.p.).

Knott, John (1986), *Popular Opposition to the 1834 Poor Law* (London: Croom Helm).

Marshall, J. D. (1968), *The Old Poor Law, 1795–1834* (London: Macmillan).

Martineau, Harriet (1855), *The Factory Controversy: A Warning Against Meddling Legislation* (Manchester: printed by A. Ireland for the National Association of Factory Occupiers).

Montagu, Frederick (1839), *Mary Ashley, The Factory Girl, or Facts Upon the Factory* (London: n.p.).

Rose, M. B. (1996), *The Lancashire Cotton Industry: A History since 1700* (Preston: Lancashire County Books).

Stone, Elizabeth (1842), *William Langshawe, the Cotton Lord* (London: n.p.).

Thesing, William B., ed. (2000), *Caverns of Night: Coal Mines in Art, Literature, and Film* (Columbia: University of South Carolina Press).

Ward, James (1962), *The Factory Movement, 1830–1855* (New York: Macmillan).

20

Children's Fiction

Lewis C. Roberts

At the conclusion of *Alice's Adventures in Wonderland*, Lewis Carroll contrasts fantasy with reality, and childhood with adulthood. Alice's elder sister reclines alone in the grass and imagines that the noises she hears are not the everyday sounds of the countryside, but rather the fading strains of Wonderland itself. As she drifts into a dream-like state of contemplation, she imagines what the story of Wonderland will mean to Alice in her adult years:

> she pictured to herself how this same little sister of hers would, in the after-time, be herself a grown woman; and how she would keep, through all her riper years, the simple and loving heart of her childhood; and how she would gather about her other little children, and make their eyes bright and eager with many a strange tale, perhaps even with the dream of Wonderland of long ago; and how she would feel with all their simple sorrows, and find a pleasure in all their simple joys, remembering her own child-life, and the happy summer days.

This passage illustrates several important ways in which the Victorians tended to define childhood and to understand the purposes of children's fiction. Perhaps most importantly, Carroll makes a clear demarcation between child and adult – adulthood is the "after-time," which implies that childhood (here Alice's "own child-life") is the most important phase of life. Becoming an adult seems to involve a kind of death, a falling away from an ideal, and Alice, her sister predicts, will spend this "after-time" attempting to recapture the ideal of her childhood through memory and storytelling. According to Catherine Robson, "such retrospective imaginings of the early years of life as a paradise of innocence and purity . . . placed an absolute line of division between childhood and adulthood" (2001: 8). It also dictated the relationship between adult writers and child readers. This need to keep the "simple and loving heart" of childhood, to relive this most significant of life's stages, can be found throughout Victorian children's fiction. The desire to reconnect to childhood, and fiction's potential to enable such a remembrance, as well as the suspicion that actual childhood could not abide such tremendous symbolic weight, underlie many Victorian discussions and practices of children's fiction. For many Victorians, childhood was an idealized life quite apart from the corruptions of adulthood, and for that very reason, childhood and children represented an ideal to strive for, and to protect, especially through the medium of children's literature.

Children's literature is a unique literary category which is based on a specific power relationship. This is a class of texts generally defined by its readership and yet seldom produced by those readers. Simply put, adults write, publish, distribute, and buy books for children. Why a particular book finds its way into the hands of a particular child at a particular historical moment has much to do with how childhood is understood at that moment. For our purposes, it also has much to do with the prevailing notions about fiction and its perceived effects (both desirable and dangerous) on Victorian child readers.

Victorian narratives were often obsessed with images of children and childhood, and this obsession had its roots in the prior history of childhood and children's literature. While it is an exaggeration to say that the Victorians "invented" childhood, it can be argued that the Victorians inherited a growing concern about children, and that childhood came to be seen as the most significant phase of life. The sheer overwhelming attention shown to children in Victorian narratives bears witness to this importance – whether we look at Little Nell or Oliver Twist, Heathcliff and Catherine running wild on the moor, Jane Eyre shut up in the red room, Alice in pursuit of the White Rabbit, Jim Hawkins in pursuit of the pirate's treasure, case studies and horror stories of child labor, Sarah Ellis's advice to the *Daughters of England*, or W. T. Stead's shocking stories of child prostitution, the Victorians strove to measure their own morality and improve their society by telling stories about and to children.

This focus on childhood is often traced to eighteenth-century concerns over education and the accompanying recognition of childhood as an ideally separate and unique phase of human life. John Locke and Jean Jacques Rousseau promoted educational philosophies which defined all children as capable of developing into rational, enlightened human beings through a nurturing system of education based on experience and observation rather than rote memorization or harsh, punitive discipline. Seeing the child as a tabula rasa, a blank slate, Locke argued that educators must carefully evoke the desire to learn in each individual child. Rousseau argued that children were born in a state of innate innocence, not original sin, and that social institutions corrupted such childhood virtue.

In Britain, these notions were heavily influential on educators such as Richard Edgeworth and his novelist daughter Maria, and on other romantic writers and poets such as William Blake, William Wordsworth, Samuel Taylor Coleridge, and Charles and Mary Lamb. The Victorian era began with two separate, but not wholly incompatible, notions of childhood deriving from these earlier writers. On the one hand, the romantic ideal became central through the poetry of William Wordsworth, especially his "Intimations of Immortality" ode. On the other, the evangelical revival insisted that childhood was centrally important as a site for redeeming individual souls and reforming society. Within both romantic and evangelical perspectives, competing notions of childhood as embodying either innate innocence or original sin helped to position childhood itself as a period of great spiritual and sentimental significance.

In a line that would be echoed by educators and writers for the rest of the century, Wordsworth wrote that children come into the world "trailing clouds of glory . . . from God, who is our home." This romantic notion drew a sharp distinction between what it meant to be a child and what it meant to become an adult. Not only did this ideal child show up throughout Victorian fiction, but the concomitant idea of adulthood as a degenerate phase, a falling away from the innocence and virtue of childhood, meant that children (and especially fictional children) carried great symbolic weight as near-angelic beings who had to be protected and preserved, rather than educated and cultivated into adults. The romantic child became the site for the exploration of the self, the measure of morality and human perfection, and the standard for the evaluation of Victorian society. The evangelical view offered a seemingly obverse notion of childhood based on doctrines of original sin and innate depravity, and often insisted that children needed strict discipline, austere conditions, and regular, enforced prayer within the context of home and family. Nevertheless, as Claudia Nelson has written, such strongly Puritan doctrine faded, largely in response to the crisis of belief suffered by many evangelicals at midcentury, to be replaced by the romantic notion of children as embodying innocence (Nelson 1991: 11). In this view, children offered world-weary adults access to the light and comfort of God. As the century progressed, both the romantic and the evangelical child came to embody purity, innocence, virtue – indeed, all those good characteristics which adults, supposedly, had lost. However, another view of childhood was simultaneously being explored and exposed: narratives of the working-class child, the laboring child, suggested that for many real children, childhood was experienced as a time not of innocence, but rather of nightmarish exploitation at the hands of adults. Many commentators have seen Victorian social reforms as an attempt to support and reaffirm the special nature of children by extending to all levels of society the right to a protected and carefree childhood.

Far from seeing children's books as innocent, harmless, or simpleminded, the Victorians inherited a rising concern that reading could have a profound effect on childhood innocence. If the eighteenth century saw the development of important notions about childhood and education, it also accompanied these philosophical concerns with the gradual development of books intended specifically for children. Such pre-Victorian children's literature was often heavily didactic in nature, whether it came from the rational school of writers such as John Locke or was primarily religious in nature. At the beginning of the nineteenth century, writers such as Sarah Trimmer sought to combat the influence of romanticism (and Rousseau) by producing books for children which stressed religion and morality. In 1802, Trimmer founded the periodical *The Guardian of Education*, which for the first time offered thorough reviews of contemporary books for children aimed at informing (and cautioning) parents and educators. Trimmer warned against the taint of much children's literature and advised parents "to be very cautious what books they put into their hands." Similar attitudes on the function of children's reading are found throughout the nineteenth century. A commentator in 1855 warned that reading fiction would "inevitably enervate their vigour," while in 1867, Horace Scudder, editor of the *Riverside Magazine for Young People*, argued against too much reading in terms that will seem very familiar to modern parents of television-addicted children:

> Children have too much reading, and the fault is not theirs but their elders' . . . it serves our indolence . . . to still their noise with a book, and relieve ourselves of a burden by placing them under the care of some livelier, though silent companion. A child's mind is awaking into a restless inquiry, and we administer a soothing draught in the shape of an entertaining story. The spell works for a time, we get comfort; and so we always keep the *book* by us, just as a lazy and foolish nurse is never without a mysterious bottle.

The notion that children could be corrupted and enervated by their reading was balanced by the opposing view, deriving from the romantic privileging of the imagination, that reading fiction awakened children to an awareness of their individuality and developed their emotional and intellectual faculties. A commentator in the *Quarterly Review* in 1860 wholly agreed with this sentiment: "the great purpose of children's books is not so much to impart instruction, as to promote growth. We must not think of a child's mind as of a vessel, which it is for us to fill, but as a wonderfully organized instrument, which it is for us to develop and set in motion." It is important to note that the dichotomy of entertainment versus instruction which is frequently applied to children's literature is here overturned. As Victorian's children's fiction developed, an ideal of clothing didacticism in amusement, and justifying amusement as a necessary part of a happy, fulfilling childhood, came to be generally accepted.

The desire to protect children from potentially corrupting fictions (and in many cases, such corruption was seen in terms of a too-early awareness of adulthood) can also be seen in the developing subgenres of children's fiction. The Victorians' division of child/adult and their privileging of childhood as a prelapsarian phase of life are crucial to understanding the protective and the wistful feelings of adult writers for their child characters and readers. Similarly, we must recognize that the child often depicted in Victorian fiction (whether for adult or child readers) and the (often working-class) child who was "discovered" in government reports on child labor and other social issues created a growing tension in Victorian views of childhood. This tension can be seen in the many efforts to legislate reforms to protect children throughout the nineteenth century, and it can also be seen in the growing significance of children's literature as both an educative and an entertaining strategy for defining and maintaining the child/adult distinction. This is especially true in the development and use of categories of children's fiction. In addition to being part of an increasingly subtle mechanism for marketing books and creating specialized readerships, such categorization helped to place Victorian children in relation to adults and adulthood, and so served to reinforce the prevailing definitions of childhood which were growing unstable as the nineteenth century proceeded.

Rather than undertaking a chronological survey of Victorian children's fiction, this chapter maps several important subgenres and their associate texts and authors, along with some key cultural issues and views of childhood associated with each type. After mapping this textual territory, I will summarize recent alternative views of Victorian children's fiction which complicate such a strictly generic survey. The categories I will briefly examine (all of them inextricably interrelated to one another) are fairytales and fantasy literature; didactic, moral and religious books; school stories and adventure tales; and stories of home and family life.

Fairytales and Fantasy

The Victorians inherited a long tradition of the fairytale, dating at least from the middle ages. However, the nineteenth century saw a new attitude toward these wonder tales, which stemmed largely from popular reception of the work of the Brothers Grimm in a Britain which had previously voiced suspicion of fantasy stories and their influence on British writers of fantasy and collectors of folk tales. As Jack Zipes has written (2001), the fairytale, which had been regarded as an element of oral folk traditions, had developed into a literary form, culminating in the Grimms' collection. The Grimms' fairytales were first published in Britain in 1823 in a translation by Edgar Taylor entitled *German Popular Stories*. This proved so popular that hundreds of editions were published over the course of the century. The fairytale form had entered British literature in full force, and as stories meant for children.

Folklorists such as Vladimir Propp have sketched out a common structure of fairytales which identify recurring patterns and plot functions. Fairytales commonly depict a protagonist who has violated a boundary or prohibition in some way and so must perform a task, which in turn becomes part of the protagonist's characterization. Eventually, the protagonist will encounter enemies, usually in the form of witches or monsters, or friends whose magical gifts enable the protagonist to deal with a new task or test. Sometimes the protagonist must experience a temporary setback, but finally achieves success in the form of marriage, wealth, or power. Significantly, the fairytale suggests that worthy characters have the ability to transcend class boundaries, and that powerless characters can potentially achieve great power. This fairytale paradigm not only influenced fantasy works, but appears throughout Victorian fiction for both children and adults, not merely providing "happy-ever-after" endings, but also heavily influencing the interactions and desires of characters, the use of iconic characterizations and symbolic settings, and the relationship between wishes and wish fulfillment in the stories' plots. Just a few examples of British fairytale writers and texts will show the impact and popularity of the form: John Ruskin's *The King of the*

Golden River (1850), George Cruikshank's *Fairy Library* (1853–4), William M. Thackeray's *The Rose and the Ring* (1855), Frances Browne's *Granny's Wonderful Chair* (1857), George MacDonald's *The Light Princess* (1867), Juliana Horatia Gatty Ewing's *Old Fashioned Fairytales* (1882) Andrew Lang's *The Blue Fairy Book* (1884) and eleven subsequent color-coded volumes, Oscar Wilde's *The Happy Prince* (1888), Joseph Jacobs's *English Fairytales* (1890).

But why were fairytales considered appropriate for children? The sudden notion that fairytales were children's fare has much to do with the changing attitudes toward childhood emanating from the work of the romantics. The romantic child had access to both a divine innocence and the power of the imagination. Thus both the fantastic elements, and the themes of justice, redemption for the innocent and punishment for the guilty, made fairytales appropriate for children. David Sandner writes, "Romanticism's new view of the imagination as a positive creative force . . . and, especially, its new view of childhood as sacred, all promoted the legitimacy of fantasy for children" (1996: 8). In "Frauds on the Fairies," Charles Dickens argued that fairytales helped to reinforce and maintain children's natural virtues:

> It would be hard to estimate the amount of gentleness and mercy that has made its way among us through these slight channels. Forbearance, courtesy, consideration for the poor and aged, kind treatment of animals, the love of nature, abhorrence of tyranny and brute force – many such good things have been first nourished in the child's heart by this powerful aid.

John Ruskin's contribution to the British fairytale was the 1850 *The King of the Golden River*, which is often called the first English literary fairytale. Ruskin's attitude toward child readers and fairytales was similar to that of Dickens. U. C. Knoepflmacher has pointed out that Ruskin's stance toward children's literature was dependent on his own investment in and attraction to the "unquestioning innocence" of children. For Ruskin, fairytales should not be "retouched" to emphasize moral messages, but rather should "naturally" convey their themes to their "unsullied" young readers (Knoepflmacher 1998: 41). This innocence, on the part of the tales and the readers, is complicated by Ruskin's own relationship to his audience, for he wrote this fairytale in 1841 at the request of Euphemia Gray, then a thirteen-year-old girl, who in 1848 would become Ruskin's bride. The story's insistence on childhood innocence and incorruptibility, and Ruskin's insistence that child readers should not be sullied by "premature glimpses of uncomprehended passions," seem to anticipate his inability ever to see Effie Ruskin as anything but an innocent child, and his eventual dismissal of his story as "totally valueless."

Ruskin's story serves as a finely wrought example of the fairytale form as it was used by many Victorian children's writers, with some curious and telling distinctions. In *King*, Ruskin deployed the fairytale paradigm to create a familiar romantic child-hero, a boy of innocence, honesty, and charity. Gluck is a young boy who lives with his two greedy and abusive older brothers in the Treasure Valley. Schwartz and Hans force Gluck to work as a servant and rarely feed him anything but table scraps, but such ill-treatment does nothing to diminish Gluck's goodness. He is not only generous to the disguised magical strangers who visit his home, but even works hard to bail one of his wicked brothers out of prison. Eventually, the brothers' greed and ill-temper bring their fertile Treasure Valley to ruin, and in their selfish attempts to gain the treasure of the King of the Golden River, they are both turned to stone. Gluck then undertakes the perilous journey to the Golden River, where he must "cast into the stream at its source three drops of holy water." Encountering on his way three thirsty figures who beg him for a drink, he charitably shares his holy water, giving the last drops to a dying dog with the words, "Confound the King and his gold too." The King, who of course had been disguised as the dying dog, immediately reveals himself to commend Gluck for his selflessness and mercy and to restore the wasted Treasure Valley. "And thus the Treasure Valley became a garden again," wrote Ruskin, "and the inheritance which was lost by cruelty was regained by love."

Knoepflmacher comments that the character of Gluck is not only heavily romanticized, but indeed feminized in a way that removes almost all traces of the aggression or sexuality which are commonly found in fairytale heroes; Ruskin has, moreover, removed the father figure whose power the protagonist generally achieves and the princess figure who stands as a reward and confirmation of the hero's achievement (Knoepflmacher 1998: 55). Gluck's ability to endure the abuse of his brothers and the trials of his journey seems wholly a part of his innocence and virtue, never the result of masculine strength or adult power. In the end we get no sense that Gluck will grow up – he simply remains the ideal child within the edenic Treasure Valley. Here Ruskin creates an extreme example of the Victorian desire to separate childhood from adulthood and to preserve a space free from adult greed and power in which the romantic child can live forever young and innocent.

This desire is qualified in many other Victorian fairytales, which follow the traditional paradigm in allowing the protagonist to grow up and achieve power, wealth, and marriage. Thackeray's *The Rose and the Ring*, for example, takes a much more ironic view of the fairytale form, using it to comment on social mores as well as the unrealistic coincidences of the fairytale plot itself, while the stories of writers such as Margaret Scott Gatty and Juliana Ewing adhere to what they perceived as an oral, folk-tale tradition. In "Amelia and the Dwarfs" (1870), Ewing invokes her "godmother's grandmother" as the source for the tale. Amelia, unlike Gluck, is hardly a model of childhood virtue – she is a spoiled child who has a "strong, resolute will, and a clever head of her own" and enjoys engaging in "constant wilful destruction." When she is kidnapped by the dwarves and "pushed underground" to repair all that she has destroyed, she becomes such a good and repentant girl that the dwarves decide to keep her for ever. Amelia, however, has retained her cunning and tricks the dwarves into taking her above ground so she can dance in the moonlight. She makes good her escape, returns home, and grows up to be "good and gentle, unselfish and considerate." Her experience has taught her good behavior, Ewing says, but it has also made her "unusually clever." Indeed, the narrator seems to take a special delight in Amelia's destructive outwitting of both her parents and the dwarves. The narrator's insistence that Amelia retains her cleverness, even as she gives up her destructiveness, suggests that Amelia has not been tamed by her experience, but perhaps has learned to better conceal her strength from the adults around her. Many women fairytale writers seemed suspicious of notions of an eternally innocent childhood. Sandner suggests that such disruptions of the child–adult relationship in tales by women connote "a scathing commentary on the static children of much nineteenth-century children's literature by men" (1996: 140).

Fairytales provided an initiation into imaginative literature for Victorian readers and writers, but fantasy fiction is said to have its distinctive origins in Lewis Carroll's *Alice's Adventures in Wonderland* (1865) and his later *Through the Looking-Glass* (1871). From the 1860s onward, fantasy novels for children were produced in abundance: Charles Kingsley's *The Water Babies* (1863), George MacDonald's *At the Back of the North Wind* (1871) and *The Princess and the Goblin* (1872), Rudyard Kipling's *The Jungle Book* (1894), E. Nesbit's *The Book of Dragons* (1900), J. M. Barrie's *Peter Pan* (1906), Kenneth Grahame's *The Wind in the Willows* (1908).

Alice is often described as *the* definitive work of children's literature (past and present), the turning point at which fantasy and imagination banished dry didacticism, and the moment when children's fiction gained a complexity and literary value to equal adult literature. Carroll's *Alice* books have always attracted both adult and child readers, and from their initial publication have inspired thousands of fictional imitations and critical analyses. Indeed, *Alice* constituted a paradigm which other writers of fantasy eagerly followed, one which included a unique and intelligent child protagonist who leaves the world of reality to travel through a fantasy realm and meet strange creatures. Such stories often utilized nonsense language and engaged with questions of identity, morality, and social conventions.

Alice has been variously read as an example of childhood innocence and as a rejection of childhood innocence. The richness of the *Alice* texts and the *Alice* phenomenon generally gave rise to a new view of children's fiction as predominantly a fiction of fantasy and unreality, setting it apart from the trend towards realism in other aspects of Victorian and modern fiction. It is usual in this regard to view *Alice* in conjunction with other fantasy works such as MacDonald's *At the Back of the North Wind*. Fantasy works opened up troubling questions for many Victorians. How much reality could children be exposed to before they begin to lose their innocence? Conversely, how could fantasy be balanced with realism so as not to over-excite children's sensibilities with a too-illusionary view of the world? Would imaginative fiction sustain or poison childhood?

Alice herself is a character who never gives a clear answer to such questions. She is variously polite and rude, naïve and shrewd as she interacts with the inhabitants of Wonderland, and her uncertainty in the face of the madness and nonsense around her has the curious effect of making her seem more like the harried adult than the ingenuous child. James Kincaid has written that "we find no child at home" in Wonderland – Alice is "the false child, resisting the play, telling us coldly at every turn in the game that we are being silly, that we must wake up, grow up" (1992: 289). To the contrary, Jackie Wullschläger (1995) suggests that the *Alice* books demonstrate Carroll's use of "the Child as Muse," and from its first publication reviewers have praised Alice as more realistic than most fictional children precisely because she seems to be struggling with her identity as a child attempting to grow up in a world which often makes no sense to her.

MacDonald's *At the Back of the North Wind* presents a more typically romantic child. Diamond is a boy who is taken on fantastic journeys by the North Wind, a powerful force of nature who shows him not just fantastic and wonderful landscapes, but also grimly realistic views of the world. Diamond responds to both the fantastic and the harshly realistic with an angelic belief in providence which causes some to suspect that he is a simple-minded, foolish "God's baby." MacDonald, however, assures us that Diamond is a potential genius who sees the truth of God's love in even the meanest of situations and has the power to inspire those adults who listen to him to live better lives. As he comforts the crying baby of a drunken cabman, Diamond appears to be sent from heaven, "as if he has been an angel with a flaming sword, going out to fight the devil."

Many fairytales and fantasy novels tended to invoke uncertainty and to frame the fantastic in terms of the real, offering reassurance and affirmation in the figure of the romantic child or in the certainty of God's love. Fantasy might have signaled a significant shift away from purely moralizing fiction, but the didactic impulse was still operative. When moralists objected to this preoccupation with the imagination, writers would respond, as did George MacDonald, that "the imagination of man is made in the image of the imagination of God."

Evangelical and Moral Books

David Sandner writes that in Victorian children's fiction, "the fairytale and the moral tale move towards one another." Writers of moral tales in the latter half of the nineteenth century, "in imitation of the runaway success of fantasy fiction," used fairytale materials "in such a dry and didactic way as to drain any magic out of [them] in service of moral instruction" (1996: 138). There is a tendency to view Victorian moral and religious fiction as too dull and preachy, especially in the face of the supposedly liberating power of fantasy. The moral tale as a genre thrived in the eighteenth century, and throughout the Victorian period books such as Sarah Trimmer's *The History of the Robins* (1786), Hannah Moore's *The Shepherd of Salisbury Plain* (1798), and Mary Sherwood's *The Infant's Progress, from the Valley of Destruction to Everlasting Glory* (1821) were still commonly read, as was John Bunyan's perennial *Pilgrim's Progress*.

Bunyan's work was the "inspiration, justification, model, and source of perpetually recurring motifs" for a group of nineteenth-century tract writers whose works were promulgated through the Religious Tract Society and evangelical publishers and were often intended to be given as rewards in Sunday schools and other educational institutions (Bratton 1981: 69). Many evangelical writers used allegories and fairy-tale formats to make their morals more attractive, as did Charlotte Tucker, who wrote under the pseudonym ALOE (A Lady of England). Mary Sherwood, in the popular *The History of the Fairchild Family* (1818), wedded family drama to her sermons and catechisms and paved the way for the evangelical domestic novel. Others, such as Sara Smith (Hesba Stretton), wrote about the conditions of children living with poverty and abuse in books such as *Little Meg's Children* (1868) and *Max Kromer* (1871). Much of this fiction was part of a larger evangelical effort to reform Victorian society, and evangelical writers intended to educate and convert the young through the use of fic-tional narratives. Early Victorian tracts had to find a way to use imaginative writing while also countering religious prejudices against fiction itself in order to "establish [fiction's] respectability and its value as a vehicle of moral teaching" (Cutt 1979: 186). The address to child readers likewise had to be kept strictly focused on the child's relationship to God, and this often caused such evangelical and tract fiction either to present the stereotypically "bad" child as an example of how not to behave, or to indulge in a form of romanticism in which the "good" (and often dying) child stood as an example of virtue and salvation to children and adults alike.

Just as writers of tract fiction had often to balance their employment of fictional forms with their general repudiation of fiction itself, the efforts of the evangelicals to establish schools and promote literacy for the children of the working class could iron-ically lead to the kinds of reading which they opposed – that is, of secular fiction, fantasy, and penny dreadfuls, rather than of the Bible and religious tract reading. In order to counter the possibility that literacy might further endanger the souls of their child readers, these writers sought to define and tightly control the kind of reader they were addressing; evangelical writing attempted to regulate both child readers and the reading material available to them. Potential readers were defined as essen-tially lacking in both spiritual and material well-being, which the tract narratives tried to remedy through stories of either a model or a disobedient fictional child.

However, as Patricia Demers has noted, we should not necessarily regard tract writers as "joyless, grim, Bible-quoting isolationists," nor tract fiction itself as lacking in literary value or interest. The best of these stories, which were very popular and well received by many Victorian readers, dealt with important issues of education, child-rearing, and the relationship between art and religion. While they were often fraught with contradictions about the role of fiction in religious education and the role of literature in the life of working-class children, these works also possessed "a consciously double vision, glimpsing the eternal in the natural, the sublime in the quotidian" (Demers 1991: 131).

School Stories and Adventure Tales

The school story and the adventure tale (or imperial fantasy), primarily associated with boys' fiction, were also especially concerned with education, both the institutional and the pragmatic. Fictional accounts of schooling existed in children's literature previous to Thomas Hughes's 1857 *Tom Brown's Schooldays* – for instance, Harriet Martineau's *The Crofton Boys* (1841). Hughes's book, however, exemplified the Victorian novel of school life, and it precipitated many imitators, such as Henry Cadwallader Adams, Thomas Street Millington, and many writers for the *Boys' Own Paper*, especially Talbot Baines Reed, until it was overturned in Rudyard Kipling's harshly unsentimental *Stalky and Co.* (1899). F. W. Farrar's *Eric, or Little by Little* (1858) is much more in the evangelical tradition, demonstrating "the vivid inculcation of inward purity and moral purpose." *Tom Brown* too contains scenes of boys wrestling with "moral purpose," but Hughes was more interested to show how Tom matures from a self-involved, pleasure-seeking child into a civilized young man. Hughes used school sports and the relationships among masters, prefects, and boys to demonstrate the necessity of finding one's place and knowing one's duty, both morally and socially.

Hughes based his novel on the Rugby of Thomas Arnold, which he had attended from 1833 to 1842, and his book did much to popularize both Arnold's notion of the role of the British public school in the education of boys and the picture of public-school life which subsequent school stories would present as authentic. Though the book was enthusiastically received (*The Times* called it "a most faithful and interesting picture of our public schools"), it presented an accurate account neither of Rugby school life in the 1850s nor of Arnold's educational theories. Arnold's interest in civilizing the "sinful nature" of boys entailed the hierarchization of previously unruly school life by the introduction of prefects and strict lines of moral authority on the one hand, and of ideals of "muscular Christianity" and chaste masculinity on the other. However, Hughes's focus on the importance of team sports rather than Arnold's educational theories came to structure both the school story and the school experience for many Victorian boys as they prepared to become builders of the British Empire.

The school was thought of as a world in miniature, an enclosed society in which boys could test themselves and learn to become part of the larger world outside the school's walls. School stories performed a similar function by presenting boys with an advance notion of the school world – Hughes wrote his novel in order to prepare his own sons for school. Yet such an education also entailed a separation from home and all the civilizing values Victorians associated with the hearth. Peter Stoneley argues that school stories enacted the ambivalence of such separations by turning away from episodes of sport to the sickroom, which "becomes the scene . . . of a resurgent familialism. . . . It serves as . . . a metaphoric opportunity to mend or to simulate some of the patterns of love and desire that the fact of school disrupts" (1998: 70). This concern for family can be seen in the opening of *Tom Brown*, in which Hughes carefully enumerates the Brown family's contributions "wherever the fleets and armies of England have won renown."

Such efforts to unite family, school, and empire suggest how both school stories and adventure tales worked to "support the culture of imperialism" (Kutzer 2000: xv). Critics such as Perry Nodelman and M. Daphne Kutzer have noted that children's literature is itself an imperialist project. Writers used fiction to acculturate child readers to the belief that empire was itself a natural good. Kutzer writes that "children are colonized by the books they read" (p. xvi). For Victorian writers of adventure tales and imperialist fantasies, *Robinson Crusoe* provided the model of the brave Englishman setting out into the world, surviving harsh conditions and savage natives in order to win land and wealth for Britain and for himself. In the Victorian adventure tale, this model hero was likely to be the product of a "school story" education, a "public school boy making a full-blooded and glorious contribution to the development and expansion" of the British Empire (Mangan 1989: 174).

The Victorian adventure tale had its roots in many earlier fictional forms: Defoe's novel, stories of missionary work in evangelical tracts, historical novels such as the works of Sir Walter Scott. The adventure tale also owes much to the fairytale paradigm: "the valiant but unrecognized hero travels to strange realms, overcomes obstacles and villains, all in order to reach the pot of gold (or ivory, or spices, or oil, or rubber, or diamonds) at the end" (Kutzer 2000: 1). Such stories were popular with adolescent boys and adults alike, as the British Empire's presence in India and Africa provided potential access to real-life wonderlands, populated by strange beings in need of the civilizing influence learned at English public schools, and offering treasures and glory for those brave enough to take them. Novels such as Frederick Marryat's *Mr. Midshipman Easy* (1836), W. H. G. Kingston's *Mark Seaworth* (1852), R. M. Ballantyne's *The Coral Island* (1858), Charles Kingsley's *Westward Ho!* (1858), Robert Louis Stevenson's *Treasure Island* (1883), H. Rider Haggard's *King Solomon's Mines* (1885), G. A. Henty's *With Clive in India* (1884), and Rudyard Kipling's *Kim* (1901) opened up the world for boy readers, suggesting that it was rightfully theirs to explore, possess, and rule. The hundreds of adventure novels by Marryat, Ballantyne, Henty and others attest to the popularity and pervasiveness of this form and the notions of empire it persuasively taught.

The adventure novel, like the school story, occupied a complex relationship toward Victorian notions of childhood. The romantic and the evangelical child were seen as distinct from adulthood, but adventure and school stories problematized such a division by presenting childhood in transition. These types of stories attempted to mediate between boyhood and adult masculinity. Whereas other categories tended to focus on the innocent perfection of childhood, these works purported to show how children could become successful adults. Nevertheless, the themes of education, maturation, and adventure were imbued with the ethos of empire in these stories more as a myth of male identity than as a guide to growing up. Only within such narratives, writes Joseph Bristow, could "all the problematic elements of male identity . . . cohere" (1991: 226), and such cohesion depended on the stories' ability to enshrine an ideal boyhood in the midst of impending masculinity. Mangan sees this "British image of imperial manhood in the making" as the conjunction of the public-school cult of athleticism with a moral chivalric code which identified the British hero as superior to those he conquered on the playing field and the battlefield (1989: 175). This can be seen in the heroes of Ballantyne's novels, who "retain a childlike purity even amid the slings and arrows of adulthood" (Nelson 1991: 124). Likewise, Kipling's Kim, rather like the author himself, preferred adventures in India to life in Britain precisely because the colonies provided an "escape . . . from adult responsibilities and adulthood itself" (Kutzer 2000: 23). The adventure novel often reversed the process of growing up, showing men playing at being boys rather than boys learning to become men, although the virtues ascribed to British boyhood were seen as precisely those necessary for governing the Wonderland, or perhaps the Neverland, of empire.

Stories of Home and Family Life

Just as imperial themes can be found throughout Victorian children's fiction, issues of home and family were also pervasive. Such domestic fiction, aimed primarily at girl readers, evolved from evangelical fiction's focus on the spiritual significance of family and the role of religion in the home, but under the influence of adult domestic fiction such as *Jane Eyre* and the imported works of Americans Susan Warner and Louisa May Alcott, especially *The Wide, Wide World* (1850) and *Little Women* (1868), these novels increasingly focused on social matters and the maturation of girls into women. Whereas school stories involved the separation of their child heroes from home life, domestic fictions placed their young heroines wholly within the context of home and family, often suggesting that girls must (gladly) give up certain opportunities and interests in order to become wives and mothers. Domestic fiction, like adventure fiction, was heavily gendered in terms of its audience, and such gender orientations acculturated child readers to the separate, gendered spheres of public and private, work and home. However, we should not automatically assume that girls read only those books intended for them. Furthermore, such apparent divisions of social spheres, fictional forms, and readerships belie the ways in which domesticity and Victorian notions of childhood served as part of the culture of empire, providing important symbols of virtue and civilization to justify the extension of British political and military power.

The move toward a more secular domestic fiction is first evident in the novels of Elizabeth Sewell and Charlotte Yonge, each of whom broke with tract-writing traditions to concentrate on more realistic stories. Writing under the influence of the Oxford Movement, both Sewell and Yonge rejected the stock evangelical plots of sudden religious conversions in favor of a detailed depiction of the role of Anglican beliefs in middle-class family life. Sewell's *Experience of Life* (1853) and Yonge's *The Heir of Redcliffe* (1853) and *The Daisy Chain* (1856) gained great popularity among both child and adult, and evangelical and non-evangelical, readers. Yonge's novels often focused on the need for women to learn self-control and sacrifice, and her vividly realistic stories suggest that such self-denial is a realistically attainable virtue. While she can be easily attacked as antifeminist, we should also recognize that Yonge's fiction complicated the received notion of childhood innocence. Rather than holding up the child as an ideal of virtue for which adults should yearn, Yonge suggested that childhood is a state during which the child's sense of self must be controlled, even quashed, in order that he or she may become a useful and successful adult. This approach certainly drew on religious notions of original sin, but in showing her characters' often painful struggles to master themselves and to accept the predominance of family in their lives, Yonge poignantly depicted the conflict many of her girl readers were undergoing. Talia Schaffer observes that Yonge's fiction contains "some of the most vivid (and heartrending) accounts of intellectual girlhood in Victorian England – the struggle to keep up with brothers' education, the desperate need for meaningful work, the frustration at the accumulation of petty but exhausting tasks" (2000: 244).

Indeed, in Yonge's novels, as in much of the domestic fiction in the mid- and late Victorian period, the girl rebel played a prominent role. While Yonge always showed the eventual, inevitable reform of girls who rebelled against their predestined domestic roles, such reformation was not achieved without a painful sense of loss. Reynolds explains that the typical pattern involved the "use of temporary paralysis to bring about the reform of the central 'rebel' character" (1990: 128). An injury or emotional crisis would restrain the rebellious conduct and allow the girl to unlearn her "masculine" behaviors and embrace conventional femininity (pp. 128–9). It is impossible to tell how effective these fictions were in urging their girl readers to emulate such characters, but the depiction of female rebellion and female intellect must have been powerfully attractive.

Toward the end of the century, the increasing salience of girls' schools and especially colleges allowed for the portrayal of even more rebellious characters and situations. L. T. Meade's novels attempted to reconcile the expanding opportunities for girls with the conventional ideologies of writers such as Yonge. In *A Sweet Girl Graduate* (1891) and *Girls New and Old* (1896), for example, Meade demonstrated the changing reality while using girls' school fiction "as the means of new and greater opportunities for self-denial" (Reynolds 1990: 135). The impulse toward self-restraint in these novels, as in the works of Yonge, suggests that for girls growing up and assuming the role of "angel in the house" implied an arrested maturation. Such domestic angels functioned much like the romantic child, bringing innocence and peace, upholding virtue, symbolizing morality. However, girls' fiction could also counter this notion by presenting a more practical, capable, and "adult" notion of the mature woman. Maiden aunts, household managers, intellectually curious schoolgirls, and courageous girls fallen from their class offered alternatives for girl readers. Such alternative role models found their culmination in the character of Sara Crewe in Frances Hodgson Burnett's *A Little Princess* (1905). Burnett drew on fairytale motifs and domestic fiction as well as adventure stories and imperial fantasies in order to tell the story of a girl whose fortunes are made, taken away, and restored by empire. As Kutzer notes, the domestic realm Sara inhabits, both as student and then as servant, in Miss Minchin's school can be read as a poorly governed colony, while Miss Minchin's incompetent rule is the result of her "unmotherly" nature. Burnett's fiction turns not on Sara's eventual submission to feminine ideals (she is already superior to Miss Minchin as a woman and a potential mother), but rather on Sara's strength of character, her refusal to submit. Her relationship with the exotic and mysterious Indian servant Ram

Dass, whose respectful submission to Sara Burnett never questions, replaces the magical devices of the fairytale with the reality of Sara's place in the culture of empire. In novels such as *A Little Princess* and *The Secret Garden*, Burnett insisted on children's strength of imagination and determination to overcome temporary evils and assert control over their own lives. This control is eventually subsumed within the conventions of domesticity and empire, but Burnett's use of so many Victorian fictional forms – fairytale and fantasy, religious narratives, school stories and imperial fantasies, domestic fiction – signals not only the extent to which children's fiction entered into the culture of empire, but also the extent to which it enabled childhood to serve as a potent symbol for so much that the Victorians held dear.

Alternative Views and Explorations

The categories presented above are not mutually exclusive – many authors worked in several subgenres, and many readers did not confine themselves to texts aimed only at boys or girls. Additionally, many authors, texts, and views of Victorian childhood and children's reading are omitted from the traditional adult canon, particularly women writers and girls' fiction. Issues of gender, nostalgia, empire, domesticity, and religion overdetermined the Victorians' categorizations of "children's fiction." These same issues also tend to influence how we map out that territory retrospectively. James Kincaid suggests that we need to "unglue" the binaries involved in the way we think about children so that we can examine our own assumptions about childhood, starting with the division between child and adult (1992: 6). Victorian children's literature is also seen in terms of such divisions and dissociations: child/adult, boy/girl, romantic/evangelical, innocence/experience, purity/sinfulness, obedience/disobedience, nature/civilization, nostalgia/innovation, ignorance/education, submission/subversion. If we can separate these dyads in our views of childhood and children, we may find that new understandings of Victorian childhood can have profound effects on our interpretations and valuing of Victorian children's fiction.

Some recent inquiries into matters of gender, of empire, of new biographical perspectives and cultural studies have given us new insights into the importance of children's fiction for understanding Victorian literature and culture. Catherine Robson's *Men in Wonderland* examines the "male myth of feminized origin" in order to explain Victorian gentlemen's fascination with and nostalgic investment in the "idealization and idolization of little girls" (2001: 3). Karoline Leach's *In the Shadow of the Dreamchild* (1999) attempts a new biographical appraisal of Lewis Carroll in light of newly read archival materials. Roderick McGillis's *A Little Princess: Gender and Empire* (1996) and M. Daphne Kutzer's *Empire's Children* (2000) examine the role children's literature played in normalizing and transmitting imperialist values. Laura C. Berry's *The Child, the State, and the Victorian Novel* (1999) looks at the interconnections among cultural images of children, writings for children, and adult fiction in the nineteenth century. Romanticists are re-evaluating influences of romantic thought on Victorian and twentieth-century children's literature, as in James McGavran's collection *Literature and the Child: Romantic Continuations, Postmodern Contestations* (1999). The study of Victorian children's fiction has the potential to open up these and many other rich areas of inquiry.

Just like the Victorians, we too have inherited a cultural concern for children, a curiosity about the nature of childhood and the role of reading in child development. At the outset, we saw Alice's sister fantasizing about the adult Alice as a teller of stories to children. However, what Carroll actually gives us is a picture of the child Alice telling her own story to her grown-up sister. The question of audience for children's fiction is necessarily fraught with such contradictions, for in a sense we all try to read children's stories from the point of view of the child even as we rely on personal and cultural memories in order to imagine such a child reader. As we construct our own views of Victorian children's fiction, we need to ask how we are selecting and grouping texts and imagining readerships, and we need to keep asking questions about our own investment in this literature. How can we distinguish between fictions for children and fictions about children? How do our cultural assumptions about childhood determine our assessment of these texts? Would we share these stories with our own children?

REFERENCES

Berry, Laura C. (1999), *The Child, the State, and the Victorian Novel* (Charlottesville: University Press of Virginia).

Bratton, J. S. (1981), *The Impact of Victorian Children's Fiction* (London: Croom Helm).

Bristow, Joseph (1991), *Empire Boys: Adventures in a Man's World* (London: HarperCollins).

Cutt, Margaret Nancy (1979), *Ministering Angels: A Study of Nineteenth-Century Evangelical Writing for Children* (Wormley, Herts: Five Owls).

Demers, Patricia (1991), "Mrs. Sherwood and Hesba Stretton: The Letter and the Spirit of Evangelical Writing of and for Children," in James Holt McGavran, ed., *Romanticism and Children's Literature in Nineteenth-Century England* (Athens: University of Georgia Press), pp. 129–49.

Kincaid, James R. (1992), *Child-Loving: The Erotic Child and Victorian Culture* (New York: Routledge).

Knoepflmacher, U. C. (1998), *Ventures into Childland: Victorians, Fairytales, and Femininity* (Chicago: University of Chicago Press).

Kutzer, M. Daphne (2000), *Empire's Children: Empire and Imperialism in Classic British Children's Books* (New York: Garland).

Leach, Karoline (1999), *In the Shadow of the Dreamchild: A New Understanding of Lewis Carroll* (London: Peter Owens).

McGavran, James Holt, ed. (1999), *Literature and the Child: Romantic Continuations, Postmodern Contestations* (Iowa City: University of Iowa Press).

McGillis, Roderick (1996), *A Little Princess: Gender and Empire* (New York: Twayne).

Mangan, J. A. (1989), "Noble Specimens of Manhood: Schoolboy Literature and the Creation of a Colonial Chivalric Code," in Jeffrey Richards, ed., *Imperialism and Juvenile Literature* (Manchester: Manchester University Press), 173–94.

Nelson, Claudia (1991), *Boys Will Be Girls* (New Brunswick: Rutgers University Press).

Reynolds, Kimberly (1990), *Girls Only? Gender and Popular Children's Fiction in Britain, 1880–1910* (Philadelphia: Temple University Press).

Robson, Catherine (2001), *Men in Wonderland: The Lost Girlhood of the Victorian Gentleman* (Princeton: Princeton University Press).

Sandner, David (1996), *The Fantastic Sublime: Romanticism and Transcendence in Nineteenth-Century Children's Fantasy Literature* (Westport: Greenwood).

Schaffer, Talia (2000), "The Mysterious Magnum Bonum: Fighting to Read Charlotte Yonge," *Nineteenth-Century Literature*, 55, 244–76.

Stoneley, Peter (1998), "Family Values and the 'Republic of Boys': Tom Brown and Others," *Journal of Victorian Culture*, 3, 69–93.

Wullschläger, Jackie (1995), *Inventing Wonderland: The Lives and Fantasies of Lewis Carroll, Edward Lear, J. M. Barrie, Kenneth Grahame, and A. A. Milne* (London: Methuen).

Zipes, Jack (2001), "Cross-Cultural Connections and the Contamination of the Classical Fairytale," in Jack Zipes, ed., *The Great Fairytale Tradition: From Straparola and Basile to the Brothers Grimm* (New York: Norton), 845–69.

FURTHER READING

Cadogan, Mary and Craig, Patricia (1986), *You're a Brick, Angela! The Girls' Story 1839–1985* (London: Gollancz).

Manlove, C. N. (1983), *The Impulse of Fantasy Literature* (Kent: Kent State University Press).

Musgrave, P. W. (1985), *From Brown to Bunter: The Life and Death of the School Story* (London: Routledge).

Quigly, Isabel (1982), *The Heirs of Tom Brown: The English School Story* (London: Chatto & Windus).

Vallone, Lynne (1995), *Disciplines of Virtue: Girls' Culture in the Eighteenth and Nineteenth Centuries* (New Haven: Yale University Press).

21

Victorian Science Fiction

Patrick Brantlinger

The increasing explanatory power and hegemony of the sciences affected Victorian fiction in two main ways. First, novelistic realism took scientific objectivity and epistemology as its analogue, model, or even method (see chapter 7 by John Kucich in this volume). Second, what has come to be called "science fiction" emerged, partly in response to scientific and technological developments, but not within the realist paradigm. Rather, science fiction was from the beginning closely related to the Gothic romance and to other forms of nonrealistic narrative such as the imaginary voyage (for example, Swift's *Gulliver's Travels*).

Ironically, therefore, narratives ordinarily included in the rubric of science fiction are typically more fantastic than realistic. They are also often highly critical of science, or at least of too-rigid applications of scientific rationality and techniques. The novel most frequently claimed as the first work of modern science fiction is Mary Shelley's *Frankenstein* (1818). With its source in the author's nightmares, its ghost-story analogues, its emphasis on homicide and horror, and its schizophrenic "divided self" or doppelgänger protagonists (the mad scientist and his demonic alter ego), *Frankenstein* belongs to the genre of Gothic romance or horror tale rather than to that of social and psychological realism. And the same is true of the other narrative by Mary Shelley which is often also cited as a forerunner of modern science fiction, *The Last Man* (1826) – as its title indicates, an apocalyptic, end-of-the-world fantasy.

From the romantic period to World War I, the production of science fiction was huge. Darko Suvin writes that, when he began to map the terrain, he thought that he was surveying a mostly submerged "iceberg," but instead discovered an entire "occulted continent" (1983: xi). "Occulted" is apt, because the Victorian dominance both of realism and of its major format, the triple-decker novel, overshadowed alternative modes of fiction. Toward the end of the century, this dominance weakened. Several factors facilitated the renewed interest in romance and fantasy in the 1880s and 1890s. Among these factors, the rise of mass-circulation newspapers and magazines and, in 1894, the demise of the triple-decker system encouraged the writing of shorter, often nonrealistic stories, including science fiction.

Well before the 1890s, Darwin's *Origin of Species* (1859) had inspired various responses among novelists, some of whom wrote, instead of works of evolutionary realism or naturalism such as George Eliot's *Middlemarch* (1871), stories now recognized as science-fiction classics. These include Edward Bulwer-Lytton's *The Coming Race* (1871) and Samuel Butler's *Erewhon* (1872). Several tales of future wars and dystopias also appeared in the 1870s, such as George Chesney's *The Battle of Dorking* (1871). And in that decade, Jules Verne's works began to appear in translation (*Twenty Thousand Leagues under the Sea*, for instance, in 1873).

After summarizing standard definitions of science fiction, this chapter examines four major types of narrative: stories like *Frankenstein* that deal with mad scientists and their destructive creations; imaginary voyages or journeys that typically follow the conventions of imperialist adventure romances even as they move into outer space; utopias and dystopias; and apocalyptic, "terminal vision" fantasies like *The Last Man*. These four types often overlap, as in several of H. G. Wells's novels. Thus, *The Time Machine* (1895) is one highly influential work that combines features of all four types.

Definitions

Coined by William Wilson in 1851, the phrase "science fiction" is an oxymoron, and so is the somewhat more specific label that Wells applied to his nonrealistic stories in the 1890s and after: "scientific romances." That phrase in turn seems first to have been applied to the English translations of Verne's *voyages extraordinaires*. Wells also occasionally spoke of his "less plausible" tales as "scientific fantasies" (James 1995: 28). Edward James notes that late Victorian stories now categorized as science fiction often carried such subtitles as "A Romance" or "A Romance of the Future"; he cites some other labels including, in the 1920s, "pseudoscientific stories" (p. 29).

Both "science fiction" and "scientific romances" express the antithesis, central to romanticism, between reason and imagination. Attempts to define the genre and to account for its historical emergence range between these two poles: at one extreme, definitions and theories that stress its apparently rational, scientific, or "cognitive" aspect; at the other, acknowledgments that it is not possible to distinguish it rigorously from other types of romance or fantasy. Perhaps today's bookstores get it right: science fiction and "sword and sorcery" fantasies are usually shelved side by side or simply mixed together.

In his study of the "scientific romance" in Britain between 1890 and 1950, Brian Stableford argues that in both fiction and essay-writing, the genre emerged in response to the "ongoing war of ideas whereby men of science were trying to displace the dogmas of religion" – hence, for example, secular versions of apocalypse as in Wells's *The Time Machine*, but also something like the reverse in the Revd. Edwin Abbott Abbott's amusing, seemingly scientific allegory about religious transcendence,

Flatland (1884). Stableford continues: "A scientific romance is a story which is built around something glimpsed through a window of possibility from which scientific discovery has drawn back the curtain" (1985: 8). One problem with this definition is that, in many instances, "scientific discovery" seems to have little or nothing to do with what is revealed behind "the curtain." Stableford continues: "The point of identifying some romances as *scientific* is not to make them into a species of scientific speculation to be judged by scientific standards, but rather to separate them from other kinds of imaginative fiction . . . The distinguishing characteristic is not that scientific romances are scientific, but that they pretend to be" (p. 8).

Stableford's suggestion that stories need only "pretend to be" scientific to qualify as science fiction renders nugatory the many attempts to claim for the genre some definitive link to science. For example, Suvin's definition of science fiction as "the literature of cognitive estrangement" suggests an at least quasi-scientific "mapping of possible alternatives" to reality (1979: 12). In *Victorian Science Fiction*, Suvin writes that the genre "is distinguished by the narrative dominance of a fictional novelty (novum, innovation) validated both by being continuous with a body of already existing cognitions and by being a 'mental experiment' based on cognitive logic" (1983: 86). Suvin uses this "cognitive" definition to draw up extensive lists of nineteenth-century stories that, in his estimation, both do and do not qualify as science fiction. A difficulty with this procedure, though, is that there are almost as many borderline cases as there are clear examples either of "cognitive" science fiction or of non-science fiction that other bibliographers have placed in the genre. Another, more serious difficulty is that, as Stableford notes, the element of science is often more imaginary than rigorously "cognitive." In *New Maps of Hell*, Kingsley Amis writes that science fiction "is that class of prose narrative treating of a situation that could not arise in the world we know, but which is hypothesised on the basis of some innovation in science or technology, or pseudo-science or pseudo-technology, whether human or extra-terrestrial in origin" (1960: 18). Amis's addition of "pseudo" of course begs the question; he goes on to acknowledge that "most of the science is wrong anyway, and its amount is such that one might as well be reading Westerns in the hope of finding out about ranching methods" (p. 63).

Wells recognized that his science fiction stories were not necessarily dependent on science. In the preface to a 1933 anthology of his stories, *Scientific Romances*, Wells declared:

Hitherto, except in exploration fantasies, the fantastic element was brought in by magic. Frankenstein, even, uses some jiggery-pokery magic to animate his artificial monster. There was some trouble with the thing's soul. But by the end of last century it had become difficult to squeeze even a momentary belief out of magic any longer. It occurred to me that instead of the usual interview with the devil or a magician, an ingenious use of scientific patter might with advantage be substituted . . . I simply brought the fetish stuff up to date, and made it as near actual theory as possible. (quoted in Aldiss 1974: 8–9)

Wells's odd phrase "the fetish stuff" perhaps points both to the aptness of psychoanalytic approaches to his stories (highlighting something powerfully infantile and uncanny about them) and also toward imperialism and imperialist adventure romances ("fetish" comes, via Portuguese, from early exploring and slave-trading along the west coast of Africa).

In *The Language of the Night*, contemporary American science-fiction writer Ursula K. Le Guin insists that her chosen genre is a type of fantasy closely allied to dreaming: "The great fantasies, myths, and tales are indeed like dreams: they speak *from* the unconscious *to* the unconscious, in the *language* of the unconscious – symbol and archetype" (1979: 62). For Le Guin, the identification of science fiction with fantasy, myth, and dreams does not diminish the significance of the genre, but is a key source of its power, both cognitive and aesthetic: "Those who refuse to listen to dragons are probably doomed to spend their lives acting out the nightmares of politicians. We like to think we live in daylight, but half the world is always dark; and fantasy, like poetry, speaks the language of the night" (p. 11).

Mad Scientists and their Monsters

From *Frankenstein* through Robert Louis Stevenson's *Dr. Jekyll and Mr. Hyde* (1886) down to Wells's *The Island of Dr. Moreau* (1897), *The Invisible Man* (1897), and beyond, the Gothic, nightmarish plot of the mad scientist concocting monsters suggests that science fiction, rather than celebrating science or investigating how its discoveries affect everyday life, more often illustrates the dangers of scientific overreaching. In more realistic narratives, there are occasional portrayals of scientists as heartless overreachers or fanatics, as in Charles Dickens's account of Thomas Gradgrind's ruthlessly repressive, scientific system of education in *Hard Times* (1854), and in the depiction of Dr. Benjulia's sadistic experiments in Wilkie Collins's antivivisection novel, *Heart and Science* (1883).

Among scientific overreachers in realist novels, Tertius Lydgate in George Eliot's *Middlemarch* (1871) aspires to discover, through his research, "the primitive tissue of life." But his scientific and medical-reform ambitions are undermined by his "spots of commonness" and his hasty marriage, and Lydgate comes to recognize that he has failed. He offers a younger parallel to Edward Casaubon, the pedant whom Dorothea Brooke myopically marries, and who is engaged in the similarly ambitious, overreaching project of constructing "The Key to All Mythologies." Both Lydgate's and Casaubon's scientific and scholarly ambitions are contrasted to the much more pragmatic, down-to-earth, but gradually improving activities of Caleb Garth, whose main ambition is to do his humble work well.

Of all the great Victorian realists, Eliot was, perhaps, the most sophisticated about science. *Middlemarch* may not be science fiction, but it is, by Victorian standards, scientific fiction. The narrative persona that Eliot adopts often assumes the guise of scientific experimenter, and the novel itself is a web of biological, optical, and other scientific metaphors. In 1876, Eliot published her last work, *The Impressions of Theophrastus Such*, which contains the brief chapter, "Shadows of the Coming Race." In it, Theophrastus and his friend Trost speculate, as both Bulwer-Lytton and Butler had done, about the future evolution of the human species. Butler's *Erewhon* (and its 1901 sequel, *Erewhon Revisited*) depicts an ambivalent utopia/dystopia whose citizens, having realized that "machines were ultimately destined to supplant the race of man" (Butler 1970: 97), have abolished them. Bulwer-Lytton's *The Coming Race* depicts the subterranean world of the Vril-ya, creatures much superior to humans, who are perhaps preparing to extinguish and replace *homo sapiens*. According to Theophrastus, "one sees that the process of natural selection must drive men altogether out of the field," supplanted by "the immensely more powerful unconscious race" of machines. He echoes Butler, but also Bulwer-Lytton, whose Vril-ya with their mechanical wings and mysterious energy source are at least cyborgian. While Theophrastus thinks "a parliament of machines" might be a distinct advance in politics, his prophecy also figures all humanity as mad scientist, and all machinery as the monster that will one day destroy its maker.

There is an evolutionary edge as well to Stevenson's 1886 "shilling shocker," which recasts the *Frankenstein* divided self motif by internalizing the monster. As in Bram Stoker's *Dracula* (1897) and many other *fin de siècle* horror stories, the monster – Hyde – seems to be an evolutionary throwback or atavism (he is also a stereotypical Irish hooligan). While there was much post-Darwin speculation that evolution was progressive and that humankind and life in general were developing "higher" forms (as Darwin himself suggested in the last two paragraphs of the *Origin*), there was at least as much speculation about other possibilities, including devolution or regression; and the idea of atavistic degeneration became central to a number of at least quasi-scientific discourses, including criminology, "scientific racism," and eugenics (see chapter 4 by Athena Vrettos in this volume).

Otherwise, as in *Frankenstein* so in *Dr. Jekyll and Mr. Hyde*: Stevenson's horror story has little to do with science. In his at-home laboratory, Jekyll has concocted certain "powders" that, when he swallows them, transform him into Hyde. Even though Stevenson "moralized" his first version, turning what had been a mere nightmare into an allegory of good versus evil, he worried about the popular, mass-cultural status of his bestseller. The bestial, blasphemous, violent Hyde, hideous incarnation of the masses, overcame the rational, professional, upper-class Jekyll in more ways than one: the popular success of Stevenson's neo-Gothic romance bested his own ambition to write what he saw as more serious, higher-quality, realistic literature. As in Mary Shelley's account of the nightmare genesis of *Frankenstein*, Stevenson's frettings about his own literary success placed him, in relation to what he saw as a sort of literary monstrosity, in the situation of the mad scientist – the unruly victim of his own vivid imagination.

Besides Dr. Jekyll, the other two best-known mad scientists in Victorian fiction are Wells's Dr. Moreau and Invisible Man; the latter's story is an obvious reworking of Stevenson's classic. Like Jekyll, Griffin has discovered a chemical formula that conjures up the repressed monster within. But his transformation appears to take two stages: Griffin is, perhaps, rational enough when he first becomes invisible; it is not possible to say whether the formula or the invisibility renders him mad. Wells supplies little evidence about what Griffin was like before his discovery, though Griffin tells Dr. Kemp that "I am just an ordinary man" (Wells 1987: 70). He adds that Kemp might remember him from their university days together, when he was "a younger student, almost an albino, six feet high, and broad, with a pink and white face and red eyes, – who won the medal for chemistry" (p. 70). This brief description, however, does not explain "the reign of terror" Griffin tries to establish once events get out of hand. "'He is mad,' said Kemp; 'inhuman. He is pure selfishness . . . He has wounded men. He will kill them unless we can prevent him . . . Nothing can stop him' – except, of course, his own madness" (p. 116).

In *The Invisible Man*, Wells leaves the connections between science and madness, invisibility and homicidal rampage, undermotivated and unexplained. A much more original, powerful version of the mad scientist–monster narrative is *The Island of Dr. Moreau*. Wells here identifies the madness with scientific rationality as such. As Moreau tells the narrator, Prendick, "The study of Nature makes a man at last as remorseless as Nature" (Wells 1994: 85). Moreau is trying to remake "Nature" through surgery to carve higher attributes into his "Beast-People," much as imperialists with their "civilizing mission" were attempting to turn "savages" into supposedly higher selves. As in Collins's *Heart and Science*, in *The Island of Dr. Moreau* the scalpel and vivisection underscore the absence of "heart" intrinsic to scientific objectivity and experimentation. In this case, Moreau's coolly rational sadism *is* the reign of terror, until one of his supposedly improved creatures slays him. Moreau can be read not just as a scientist trying to play God, but also as a parody of God himself, installing the often cruel processes of evolution – "Nature red in tooth and claw," in Tennyson's famous phrase – as reign of terror. According to Wells's biographers, to some of its first readers and reviewers the story "seemed overtly blasphemous, as if Wells were implying that the Divine Purpose which had rough-hewn humanity from the instinctual animal had employed suffering for its instrument in the way that Moreau had used the scalpel" (MacKenzie and MacKenzie 1973: 125).

Imaginary Voyages and Journeys

Through Buck Rogers and Flash Gordon, *Star Wars* and *Star Trek*, and also through incessant fantasizing about UFOs, science fiction today is commonly associated with space flight in both directions – human explorations of the beyond, and alien explorations of Earth. But space exploration fantasies have a lengthy history, back to Francis Godwin's 1638 *The Man in the Moone* and beyond. Related to these are other sorts of exploration and discovery stories, including the hundreds of imperialist adventure romances in which the heroes discover "lost worlds" or previously unknown societies and cultures. These in turn were inspired by the actual filling in of the last "blank spaces on the map" in central Africa, Australia, and elsewhere, through the often heroic work of explorers, geographers, naturalists, and archaeologists. Stories of Atlantis (back to Plato) and of "lost" or buried civilizations thriving at the center of the Earth, as in *The Coming Race*, also belong to the imaginary journey tradition. *Erewhon*, too, follows the paradigm of imperialist exploration of uncharted terrain (Butler based his satirical fantasy in part on his sheep-farming years in New Zealand in 1860–4).

Other blends of imperialist adventure and scientific romance range from American Edgar Allan Poe's *Narrative of A. Gordon Pym* (1838) to Sir Arthur Conan Doyle's *The Lost World* (1912). In Doyle's romance, Professor Challenger and his intrepid crew discover a Jurassic Park in South America, a land in which time has stalled and the dinosaurs still roam and prey. In his *Principles of Geology* (1830–3), Sir Charles Lyell had speculated about the possible return of the dinosaurs and other extinct creatures. Lost race or world romances are related to fantasics about "prehistory," typically inspired by geology and archaeology. These include, for example, Stanley Waterloo's *The Story of Ab: A Tale of the Time of the Cave Man* (1897).

Also inspired by both archaeology and Darwin, H. Rider Haggard produced one of the most influential lost world romances in *She* (1887). Haggard set out to rival Stevenson's *Treasure Island* when he wrote *King Solomon's Mines* (1885); aimed primarily at boy readers, it became an immediate bestseller. Its British protagonists discover the ruins of a lost civilization in south-central Africa. The Kukuanas dwelling in the region have no knowledge of their predecessors, who, Haggard implies, must have been a white or semitic people (sub-Saharan Africans, Haggard believed, were incapable of creating civilizations). Haggard repeats the pattern in later romances, including *She* and *Allan Quatermain* (1887). In the former, the mysterious Ayesha or "She-Who-Must-Be-Obeyed" has discovered "the pillar of fire" that seems to confer immortality and has ruled for at least two thousand years over the brown-skinned Amahaggers, waiting for the incarnation of her dead lover to appear. Ayesha dwells among the ruins of Kôr, a civilization of such antiquity it may be even older than that of the Pharoahs. As Allienne Becker notes, "All the stock conventions [of] the Lost Worlds Romance . . . are found in *She*." These include "a beautiful white queen" ruling over cannibals, a "preoccupation with death and the grotesque," and "archaeological ruins . . . among others" (1992: 34–5).

Most of these conventions are peripheral to science fiction, and yet Haggard's African quest romances were often imitated and could easily be transposed to other planets and galaxies. Brian Aldiss notes the frequency with which Ayesha's horrific death in the pillar of fire, which shrivels her into the atavistic form of a monkey, has been copied by science fiction writers: "From Haggard on, crumbling women, priestesses, or empresses – all symbols of women as Untouchable and Unmakeable – fill the pages of many a scientific 'romance'" (1974: 139). The misogynistic traits of *She* and more generally of imperialist adventure fiction also characterize much science fiction. One of Haggard's most successful imitators was William Le Queux, better known for his espionage and invasion-scare novels, but whose *The Great White Queen* (1896) is, according to Becker, "one of the most interesting of the early imitations of Haggard's fiction" (1992: 44). Another successful imitator is American Edgar Rice Burroughs, author both of the Tarzan-of-the-Apes stories and of several interplanetary romances, including *A Princess of Mars* (1917).

By the time of Burroughs's Martian romance, space-flight stories had become a staple of science fiction. The 1877 discovery by an Italian astronomer of "canals" on Mars produced a burst of speculation about life on the Red Planet that included such romances as Percy Greg's *Across the Zodiac: The Story of a Wrecked Record* (1880), Robert Cromie's *A Plunge into Space* (1890), and Edwin Pallander's *Across the Zodiac: A Story of Adventure* (1896). While human explorers voyaged to Mars and the other planets, extraterrestrials voyaged to Earth – notably in George du Maurier's *The Martian* (1897) and Wells's *The War of the Worlds* (1898). Du Maurier's visitor from outer space has angelic attributes, and like the Vril-ya suggests the links among early science fiction, the conventions of Gothic romance, and late Victorian interest in the occult. (To cite another example, Marie Corelli's 1886 *A Romance of Two Worlds* blurs the line between spiritualism and fantasizing about life on other planets so completely that it is hard to know whether to categorize it as science fiction or spiritualist potboiler – see Suvin 1983: 93–4.)

Wells's invasion-scare fantasy, in contrast, is a thoroughly Darwinian tale of survival of the fittest (who turn out to be *homo sapiens*, not the Martians). It is also an apocalyptic, end-of-the-world romance that, in its reworking of Mary Shelley's "last man" and extinction-of-humanity themes, serves also as a critique of imperialism. Wells declared that the inspiration for *War of the Worlds* came from a conversation with his brother Frank about "the discovery of Tasmania by the Europeans – a very frightful discovery for the native Tasmanians!" (quoted in Bergonzi 1961: 124). The narrator of *War of the Worlds* says that, before judging the Martian invaders "too harshly,"

> we must remember what ruthless and utter destruction our own species has wrought, not only upon animals, such as vanished bison and the dodo, but upon its own inferior races. The Tasmanians . . . were entirely swept out of existence in a war of extermination waged by European immigrants, in the space of fifty years. Are we such apostles of mercy as to complain if the Martians warred in the same spirit? (Wells 1988: 4–5)

Utopias and Dystopias

In the English literary tradition, portrayals of ideal societies look back to Sir Thomas More's *Utopia*, which first appeared in Latin in 1516, and sometimes also to earlier works such as Plato's *Republic*. During the Victorian era, many works combined utopian and dystopian features. In novels characterized by their social realism, a time of troubles often leads to reconciliation, renewed community, or emigration. Dickens's dystopian vision of Coketown in *Hard Times* is countered by the partially utopian features of Sleary's circus. And in Eliot's *Daniel Deronda* (1876), selfish, narrow-minded versions of community and nationalism are contrasted to the ideal, transnational self-lessness that Daniel discovers in Judaism.

Both *The Coming Race* and *Erewhon* belong in the ambivalent category; the societies they portray are as much dystopian as the reverse. Thus, the Vril-ya have surpassed human morality, although they still use money and also view aliens in terms that can only be described as racist: "Nations which, not conforming their manners and institutions to those of the Vril-ya, nor indeed held capable of acquiring the powers over the vril agencies . . . were regarded with more disdain than citizens of New York regard the negroes" (Bulwer-Lytton n.d.: 725). And the Erewhonians are both better than mere Victorian mortals (in their leniency toward criminals, for example, and their "musical banks") and worse, or at least no better (in their treatment of disease as criminal, their colleges of "unreason," and their worship of Ygrund – Mrs. Grundy's name with the syllables reversed). Satirically, Butler wanted to have his cake and eat it, too.

A number of the other works mentioned so far also have utopian or dystopian features. The empire of Haggard's *femme fatale*, for instance, is a reign of terror that She threatens to transplant to England, the British Empire, and the world. *Flatland* is not precisely a dystopia, but the penetration of its two-dimensional world by a Sphere opens up religious possibilities that are also in a general way utopian. Depictions of extraterrestrial societies, like Abbott's account of Flatland or Bulwer-Lytton's of the Vril-ya underworld, frequently satirize or offer pointed contrasts to Victorian mores, politics, and society. In the preface to his utopian romance, *A Crystal Age* (1906), W. H. Hudson writes: "Romances of the future, however fantastic they may be, have for most of us a perennial if mild interest, since they are born of a very common feeling – a sense of dissatisfaction with the existing order of things, combined with a vague faith in or hope of a better one to come" (1906: v).

Much the same can be said, of course, of romances of the past, or historical fiction. Tennyson's *Idylls of the King* (1842–72) is a case in point, and so too are other examples of Victorian medievalism, from Thomas Carlyle's semi-novelistic *Past and Present* (1843) through John Ruskin's famous "Nature of Gothic" chapter in *Stones of Venice* (1851–3) to William Morris's *A Dream of John Ball* (1888) and most of his prose romances. Typically these works construct an ideal middle ages, in which chivalry, courtly love, feudal obligation and duty, and unquestioned religious faith are contrasted to their modern absences or paltry counterparts. Both Ruskin and Morris, however, emphasize conditions of labor rather than chivalric or religious ideals. For Ruskin, the Gothic workman was an artist, taking pleasure in his work, in contrast to modern factory workers, slaves to their machines. And Morris's *John Ball* takes as its subject a peasant rebellion that foreshadows the necessity for a communist revolution in the modern era.

Morris's odd fusion of romantic medievalism with Marxism underlies the most important utopian romance produced during the Victorian era, his *News from Nowhere* (1890). Written in part as a critique of American Edward Bellamy's technophilic

Looking Backward (1888), Morris's utopia depicts a postrevolutionary, communistic, pastoral society whose inhabitants lead the simple life and engage in labor only if it pleases them. Though machinery is still used for performing tasks that would be "irksome" to humans, it is unobtrusive. London has faded into the countryside. The denizens of Nowhere relate to each other as family and community members, sharing everything from the raising of children to the enjoyment of nature. In this ideal "arts and crafts" world, art and artistic activity are no longer the privilege and possession of the rich, but are identical, or nearly so, with everyday life. There is no need for money. Though crimes of passion still occasionally occur, other sorts of crime have disappeared, along with private property and poverty. Class conflict has also disappeared into communal harmony. It is, as Morris's subtitle has it, an "Epoch of Rest," one in which history itself seems to have drawn to an edenic close.

In his first major "scientific romance," *The Time Machine* (1895), Wells critiques both Bellamy's *Looking Backward* and Morris's *News from Nowhere*. The wonderful invention named in its title is an obvious symbol for progress through technology. At this level, Wells appears to be chiming in with Bellamy's technology worship. But the machine also allows its inventor to follow progress to its bitter, dystopian end, first in the world of the Eloi and Morlocks, and then, some 30 million years hence, to the outer limit, where the Time Traveller almost witnesses the heat death of the sun and the planets. After he comes back to narrate his voyage into the future, the Time Traveller goes on another journey, perhaps into the remote past, and does not return. His disappearance suggests behavior bordering on the suicidal; he seems, at the end of the story, to be another case of a mad scientist who has created the thing that destroys him.

The Time Machine also parodies and critiques Morris's "Epoch of Rest." At first, the Time Traveller thinks that he has arrived at a "social paradise" (Wells 2001: 91); the world of the Eloi appears to be another Eden. He calls them "exquisite creatures" and "pretty little people," and likens their "prettiness" to "Dresden china" (p. 82). He also notes the beautiful simplicity of their clothes and behaviors. Both their aesthetic effeminacy and the Time Traveller's first hypothesis about their manner of living – " 'Communism,' said I to myself" (p. 88) – point to Morris, as does the idea that they are the result of "a perfect conquest of Nature. For after the battle comes Quiet" (p. 92) – an evident allusion to Morris's "Epoch of Rest." That the Eloi are illiterate and can manage only the simplest utterances seems also to be an extension of what Morris has to say about books, literacy, and education in *News from Nowhere*. In the communist future as Morris envisions it, books and reading are of interest only to those who find them interesting. The stories his Nowhereians care about are archetypal ones – fairy tales and folklore – and explicitly not Victorian novels rooted in bourgeois values and neuroses. And the education of children in Nowhere is, to say the least, relaxed – they learn what gives them pleasure; they don't learn what doesn't.

Wells's critical extrapolations of Morris underscore the central theme of *The Time Machine* that progress will be its own undoing. Even before he encounters the Morlocks, the Time Traveller has begun to puzzle about the end of humanity:

> It seemed to me that I had happened upon humanity upon the wane . . . The work of
> ameliorating the conditions of life – the true civilising process that makes life more and
> more secure – had gone steadily on to a climax. One triumph of a united humanity over
> Nature had followed another . . . And the harvest was what I saw! (p. 90)

Effeminacy, illiteracy, loss of intelligence – no matter how aesthetically pleasing the
Elois seem, they are at best a degenerate version of humanity. This dystopian aspect
of utopia is magnified, to say the least, when the Time Traveller discovers the underground "human rats" who feed on the Elois – the demonic Morlocks.

The Time Traveller's further speculations about the two symbiotic types of creatures he discovers in the far future invoke Darwin's theory of evolution:

> But, gradually, the truth dawned on me: that Man had not remained one species, but
> had differentiated into two distinct animals: that my graceful children of the Upper
> World were not the sole descendants of our generation, but that this bleached, obscene,
> nocturnal Thing [a Morlock], which had flashed before me, was also heir to all the ages.
> (p. 107)

Social progress has gone so far that it has turned into its opposite, and so in a sense
has evolution. Despite Darwin's comment at the conclusion of *Origin of Species* about
the "grandeur" of the idea of nature's production of "higher animals," there is nothing
in his theory of organic change through natural selection that mandates a progressive,
"higher" outcome; on the contrary, as Wells's fantasy illustrates, remove most of the
causes of the struggle for existence, and the result is apt to be regression.

The Time Traveller, moreover, adds to the critique of *News from Nowhere* when he
speculates that the division of humankind into two symbiotic but inimical species
has resulted from the division of labor: "the gradual widening of the present merely
temporary and social difference between the Capitalist and the Labourer, was the key
to the whole position" (p. 109). Instead of the communist revolution that Marx,
Engels, and Morris hoped would lead to a harmonious, classless society, the conflict
between capital and labor has instead, the Time Traveller supposes, ossified into a virtually eternal opposition. Though all else evolves and changes in Wells's imaginative
version of history and the future, one item, consonant with the conventions of Gothic
romance, remains unchanged: the manichean division of the world between good and
evil, heaven and hell, light and darkness. This is not to say that the Elois are angelic
and the Morlocks demonic in any more than a superficial way. On the contrary, the
two opposed species, outcome of humanity's progress, are merely the random creations
of an implacable but definitely not anthropomorphic nature.

Apocalypse Now

The Time Traveller escapes the clutches of the cannibalistic Morlocks, and throttles
full speed ahead to, apparently, the very edge of existence. In this ultimate future, he

nearly witnesses the end of everything through the heat death of the sun, an idea based on the Second Law of Thermodynamics. Discovered and codified by a number of physicists, notably James Clerk Maxwell and Lord Kelvin (James Thomson), this law entails the concept of entropy, according to which every substance and phenomenon in nature has a finite quantity of energy to expend, until it reaches its heat-death. Applied to the world or the universe, entropy entails the inevitable, if far-distant, end of everything. In his 1862 papers "On the Age of the Sun's Heat" and "On the Secular Cooling of the Earth," Kelvin in particular theorized that all of the stars, including the sun, must gradually dissipate their energy, until the universe itself reaches the point of absolute darkness and absolute zero. This is a theory that distressed even Darwin.

In all "last man" fantasies, the final witness to the apocalypse must find a way to communicate the grand catastrophe backward in time, out of the ultimate abyss, or across the vast reaches of space. Wells's Time Traveller has his convenient, superclock vehicle on which to make his escape back to the comfortable present of 1895 suburban London. There is less convenience and less logic in a number of other *fin de siècle* novels and short stories, including several by Wells himself. Among those by other writers are George Griffith's *The Angel of the Revolution: A Tale of the Coming Terror* (1893) and its sequel, *Olga Romanoff: or, the Syren of the Skies* (1894). Griffith's tales of terror and future warfare are replete with predictable or already existing technological marvels. But in the midst of the worldwide combat in the second romance, a perfectly natural comet crashes into Earth, almost ending everything.

Comparable in its vision of ultimate destruction is Edward Fawcett's *Hartmann the Anarchist: or, The Doom of the Great City* (1893). Set in 1920, and narrated by a socialist who at first has some sympathy for Hartmann's plan to "regenerate" humankind by razing civilization, the story features a monstrous "aëronef," the *Attila*, created by Hartmann from a superlight material. The anarchists use their huge flying-machine to bombard London with dynamite and burning petroleum. Hartmann nearly succeeds in destroying "the great city," "ventricle of the heart of civilization, that heart which pumps the blood of capital everywhere." "Paralyze this heart," the chief anarchist tells the narrator, "and you paralyze credit and the mechanism of finance almost universally." But the hoped-for revolution on the ground sputters and fails, and this, plus the news of the death of his mother in the midst of the conflagration he has caused, prompts Hartmann to blow up his marvelous weapon and himself with it (another mad scientist bites the dust). No, Fawcett was not an anarchist, but yes, he believed the anarchists were sufficiently threatening in the early 1890s to turn them into fictional, doomsday fodder. Joseph Conrad would later desensationalize both espionage and anarchist-apocalyptic fantasies with his tragic *The Secret Agent* (1907), in which he revisits an actual – botched – anarchist attempt to bomb Greenwich Observatory in 1894.

A number of utopian fantasies involve cataclysms, sometimes political and sometimes natural, that bring the late Victorian or Edwardian world of capitalism, imperialism, industrialism, and urbanization to an end. Besides the revolution that leads to the communist future in Morris's *News from Nowhere*, Hudson's comparable idyll in *A Crystal Age* depicts "a remotely future Europe" that, as Warren Wagar says, emerges "after unspecified disasters . . . put an end to the ugly urban sprawl of the nineteenth century" (1982: 19). Following the similarly unspecified catastrophe that destroys civilization in Richard Jefferies' *After London* (1885), the society that emerges is barbaric and wild rather than idyllic (part one is called "The Relapse into Barbarism," and part two, "Wild England"). But barbarism is, the naturalist Jefferies suggests, better than the begrimed, polluted, overcrowded present – an opinion that Morris also expresses in *The House of the Wolfings* (1888), for example, with its idealization of the freedom-loving Germanic barbarians, as opposed to the tyranny of the Roman Empire. Narratives of future warfare such as Wells's *The War in the Air* (1908) are often also what Wagar calls "terminal visions." And both M. P. Shiel's *The Purple Cloud* (1901) and Conan Doyle's *The Poison Belt* (1913) depict world-ending cataclysms via massive air pollution, one by volcanic eruption and the other by the Earth's entry into a toxic band of ether.

Fred T. Jane, who authored major reference works on military hardware such as *Jane's Fighting Ships* as well as other works of science fiction such as *The Incubated Girl* (1896) and *To Venus in Five Seconds* (1897), published *The Violet Flame: A Story of Armageddon and After* in 1899. This oddly jaunty, parodic novella features "lunatic" Professor Mirzarbeau, "a quaint little Anglo-French scientist," who invents a machine that can read the thoughts of the world-brain but that doubles as a death-ray capable of destroying everything. After distintegrating Waterloo Station and a large chunk of China with his death ray, Professor Mirzarbeau holds Britain hostage for a while, and poses as its absolute ruler. The rather breezy, amusing relationships among himself, the narrator, a young American woman named Landry Baker, and a few other characters, spiced by meetings of the *Finis Mundi* society and many references to the Beast of the Apocalypse (Mirzarbeau is the Beast, apparently), are brought to an end when the Professor accidentally disintegrates himself. However, the "violet flame," now identified with the crash-course of a comet, proceeds to devastate the world anyway. After this almost final *finis mundi*, the narrator and Landry Baker find themselves the Adam and Eve in a new Eden, with an empty world all before them.

That *The Violet Flame* can be read as a parody of doomsday stories such as *Hartmann the Anarchist* (which Jane illustrated, as he did his own stories) bespeaks the *fin de siècle* familiarity of the genre. In *Terminal Visions: The Literature of Last Things*, Wagar points out that between "1890 and 1914 . . . almost every sort of world's end story . . . was written, published, and accepted by a wide reading public":

> Great world wars that devastated civilization were fought in the skies and on imaginary battlefields dwarfing those of Verdun and Stalingrad. Fascist dictatorships led to a new Dark Age, class and race struggles plunged civilization into Neolithic savagery, terrorists armed with super-weapons menaced global peace. Floods, volcanic eruptions, plagues, epochs of ice, colliding comets, exploding or cooling suns, and alien invaders laid waste to the world. (1982: 20)

Whether this flourishing of apocalyptic fantasy was a result of end-of-century, millennialist dreaming or, more accurately, prophetically foreshadowed "the real-life cataclysm of 1914," writers of such "terminal visions," Wagar notes, "did not miss their chances" (p. 20).

Coda

In the conclusion to *The Wonderful Century: Its Successes and Failures* (1898), the codiscoverer of the theory of evolution by natural selection, Alfred Russel Wallace, lists the achievements of nineteenth-century science and technology and finds them much more numerous and impressive than those "of all preceding ages." Most Victorian writers of science fiction would not dispute Wallace's basic observation, but their stories often contradict his conclusion that these achievements are necessarily tending toward utopia or the future perfection of civilization. On the contrary, from *Frankenstein* on, as Carl Freedman (2000) contends, science fiction often expresses versions of what Theodor Adorno and Max Horkheimer called "the dialectic of enlightenment" – that is, the use of reason and science for irrational, destructive, dystopian purposes. A genre of storytelling that typically takes the form of secular prophecy, science fiction seems often to be retelling versions of the Tower of Babel and the fall of Babylon, Armageddon and Judgment Day. It does not question the validity and power of science and scientific discoveries, but it deeply distrusts how that power will affect the shape of things to come.

REFERENCES

Aldiss, B. W. (1974), *Billion Year Spree: The True History of Science Fiction* (New York: Schocken).
Amis, K. (1960), *New Maps of Hell: A Survey of Science Fiction* (New York: Harcourt, Brace).
Becker, Allienne R. (1992), *The Lost Worlds Romance: From Dawn Till Dusk* (Westport: Greenwood).
Bergonzi, B. (1961), *The Early H. G. Wells: A Study of the Scientific Romances* (Manchester: Manchester University Press).
Bulwer-Lytton, E. (n.d.), *The Works of Edward Bulwer-Lytton*, vol. 2: *The Coming Race* (New York: Collier).
Butler, Samuel (1970), *Erewhon* (Harmondsworth: Penguin).
Freedman, Carl (2000), *Critical Theory and Science Fiction* (Hanover, Conn.: Wesleyan University Press).
Hudson, W. H. (1906), *A Crystal Age* (London: T. Fisher Unwin).
James, E. (1995), "Science Fiction by Gaslight: An Introduction to English-Language Science Fiction in the Nineteenth Century," in D. Seed, ed., *Anticipations: Essays on Early Science Fiction and its Precursors* (Liverpool: Liverpool University Press), 26–45.
Le Guin, U. K. (1979), *The Language of the Night: Essays on Fantasy and Science Fiction*, ed. Susan Wood (New York: G. P. Putnam).
MacKenzie, N. and MacKenzie, J. (1973), *H. G. Wells* (New York: Simon & Schuster).
Stableford, B. (1985), *Scientific Romance in Britain 1890–1950* (New York: St. Martin's).
Suvin, D. (1979), *Metamorphoses of Science Fiction* (New Haven: Yale University Press).
Suvin, D. (1983), *Victorian Science Fiction in the UK: the Discourses of Knowledge and Power* (Boston: G. K. Hall).

Wagar, W. (1982), *Terminal Visions: The Literature of Last Things* (Bloomington: Indiana University Press).
Wallace, A. R. (1898), *The Wonderful Century: Its Successes and its Failures* (London: Swann Sonnenschein).
Wells, H. G. (1987), *The Invisible Man* (New York: Bantam).
Wells, H. G. (1988), *The War of the Worlds* (New York: Bantam).
Wells, H. G. (1994), *The Island of Dr. Moreau* (New York: Bantam).
Wells, H. G. (2001), *The Time Machine* (Peterborough, Ont.: Broadview).

FURTHER READING

Alkon, P. (1994), *Science Fiction before 1900: Imagination Discovers Technology* (New York: Twayne).
Bleiler, E. F. (1990), *Science Fiction: The Early Years. A Full Description of more than 3,000 Science-Fiction Stories from Earliest Times to the Appearance of the Genre Magazines in 1930* (Kent: Kent State University Press).
Clarke, I. F. (1979), *The Pattern of Expectation: 1644–2001* (New York: Basic).
Franklin, B. (1978), *Future Perfect: American Science Fiction of the Nineteenth Century* (New York: Oxford University Press).
Gerber, R. (1973), *Utopian Fantasy: A Study of English Utopian Fiction since the End of the Nineteenth Century* (New York: McGraw-Hill). (First publ. 1955.)
Ketterer, D. (1974), *New Worlds for Old: The Apocalyptic Imagination, Science Fiction, and American Literature* (Bloomington: Indiana University Press).
Parrinder, Patrick (1995), *Shadows of the Future: H. G. Wells, Science Fiction, and Prophecy* (Syracuse: Syracuse University Press).
Punter, David (1980), *The Literature of Terror: A History of Gothic Fictions from 1765 to the Present Day* (London: Longman).
Ruddick, N. (1993), *Ultimate Island: On the Nature of British Science Fiction* (Westport: Greenwood).

PART III
Victorian and Modern Theories of the Novel and the Reception of Novels and Novelists Then and Now

22

The Receptions of Charlotte Brontë, Charles Dickens, George Eliot, and Thomas Hardy

Elizabeth Langland

Reception implies a reader and a concern with that reader's relationship to literature. Any discussion of reception will have at least two significant foci. The first is to identify the various and differing ways in which readers and critics have responded to individual writers or texts over time. That is what we might mean when we speak of undertaking a critical study of a work's or an author's reception. On the other hand, we might address reception from another perspective, one that undertakes a metacritical analysis of how various literary theories position the reader in relation to writers and texts. The first approach is comprehended in the second, in the sense that the second allows us an overarching view of how dominant theories have influenced a particular period's reception of particular works. Peter Widdowson has defined this metacritical approach to reception as a *critiography* or literary sociology; that is, a definition of the main constitutive discourses within which a writer is produced and reproduced (1989: 6).

This chapter will look at three dimensions that round out our understanding of the reception of Victorian novels. It will, as one aspect, provide an overview of the critical and popular receptions of four prominent novelists – Charlotte Brontë, Charles Dickens, George Eliot, and Thomas Hardy – beginning with their initial receptions and coming down to the present. I have selected these four because their receptions by audiences over the past century and more have traced different and distinctive trajectories, yet, as we begin the twenty-first century, each now enjoys critical renown and some popular esteem, due, in part, to recent screen and television adaptations.

Before we begin with the discussions of particular novelists, however, we need to lodge those analyses within a larger framework that defines shifting critical emphases from the mid-nineteenth century through the end of the twentieth century. That discussion will comprehend a second aspect of this analysis. The third dimension, more speculative, considers the process of canonization and queries how the canon of major Victorian fiction was formed and has been maintained. The chapter begins, then, by developing an overview within which to understand reception, then turns to the reception of particular authors and texts, and finally undertakes a more theoretical analysis of aesthetic valuation.

Reception and Literary Criticism

Broadly, I share Terry Eagleton's account of the history of modern literary theory, which identifies three general phases: first, a preoccupation with the author (romanticism and the nineteenth century); second, an exclusive concern with the text ("new criticism"); and third, in recent years a marked shift of attention to readers (1983: 74). Each of these emphases, even those that downplay the reader's role, has substantial implications for the reception of particular novels, which is determined by how well an individual work answers the critical demands placed upon it.

That is to say, changing critical standards sweep writers in and out of fashion. At the same time, however, there is always some resistance to change because reputations linger. Thus, despite change, it may be difficult to "rescue" an author from a critical niche he or she has long occupied. Accumulated critical responses to individual novels will generate a significant resistance to attempts to re-estimate a writer, even though the critical focus has changed. For example, examined through the lens of fidelity to reality, Hardy was early acclaimed as a "lyrical and tragic annalist of the English rural community" (Widdowson 1989: 27). Although critical emphases have shifted dramatically since that early evaluation, it nonetheless continues to haunt critical estimations of Hardy today. As a result, the thrust of some recent reception studies, like Widdowson's of Hardy, is to challenge the niche of "good little Thomas Hardy" in which this writer resides and to encourage readers to perceive "a rather more spirited figure" (p. 226).

Certain broad critical dispositions have shaped our receptions of whole bodies of work. In the Victorian age generally, novels were valued for being a fictitious meditation on and mediation of reality. In Eagleton's words, "As religion progressively ceases to provide the social 'cement,' affective values and basic mythologies by which a socially turbulent class-society can be welded together, 'English' is constructed as a subject to carry this ideological burden from the Victorian period onwards" (1983: 24). Certain works of English literature were to be the vehicle to carry this ideology; its central proponent was Matthew Arnold, who argued in "The Study of Poetry" that these timeless texts belong to the "class of the truly excellent," and they provide us with "short passages, even single lines" that are an "infallible touchstone for detecting the presence or absence of high poetic quality" (Buckler 1958: 507).

Arnold's standards for evaluating poems and even single lines also influenced assessments of novels and partly determined the nineteenth century's predilection for realistic representation in the service of humanistic inquiry, which found its critical apotheosis in F. R. Leavis's *The Great Tradition*. There, Leavis defined the heritage that made up the "Great Tradition" of English literature, those works "made for life." One Victorian novelist continuously in the main line was George Eliot, but Charles Dickens was initially out and then in, while Emily Brontë, but not Charlotte, had a marginal status (Eagleton 1983: 33).

Leavis had the distinction not only of summarizing what had been a dominant critical tendency of the nineteenth century but also of ushering in a new mode that focused more exclusively on the text itself, ignoring cultural and historical contexts. As Eagleton notes, there is really no conflict here, rather a logical progression: "if literature is 'healthy' when it manifests a concrete feel for immediate experience, then you can judge this from a scrap of prose as surely as a doctor can judge whether or not you are sick by registering your pulse-beat or skin-colour" (1983: 43). The tradition of "practical criticism" in England, associated with I. A. Richards, who wrote a study by that name, found an echo and further development in the United States in the evolution of "new criticism." Both emphasize "close reading" of texts, a phrase that seemed to imply that previous reading had been a somewhat lax affair. The new insistence that readers concentrate exclusively on the words on the page and treat the aesthetic artifact as a self-sufficient object made contexts virtually irrelevant to the critical enterprise. Its goal was, in part, achieving an analytical rigor that emulated that of the sciences.

Paul Lauter (1991) has pointed out that the standards and emphases of new criticism ensured that many, perhaps most, works by women or the working classes or ethnic others would be marginalized. Without access to formal education, they were writing outside of the dominant literary traditions and conventions, often in ignorance of them. We may note, for example, that Leavis's tradition had room for only two and a half women: Jane Austen and George Eliot plus Emily Brontë, whose *Wuthering Heights* was put within the special category of "a sport."

The new critical mode privileged works that invited detailed explication, ones that were integrated wholes: stylistically complex, imagistically rich, and formally unified. George Eliot and Charles Dickens held their own in the world of the novel, but these critical conditions did not favor the emergence of Charlotte Brontë. Thomas Hardy, who had claimed a major place among the minor novelists, continued to attract interest. However, aspects of his novels formerly deplored for their lack of realism were now criticized for disrupting formal unity.

Deconstruction emerged in the late 1960s and early 1970s as a practice that called into question the possibility of unity itself and, presumably, undermined the whole new critical tradition. However, many scholars were quick to point out that deconstruction relied for its examples on the canon of texts established by new criticism. In short, it changed the reading practice without altering the object of interest. Paul Bové effectively summarized this critique:

> The similarities in technique between New Criticism and deconstruction produce a critical impasse not easily broken. Since neither New Criticism nor deconstruction bothers to account for its own function and position historically in society – precisely because

they are both radically anti-historicist – even the most sophisticated employment of the latest reading techniques merely repeats and extends a power formation already in place. (1983: 4)

Other critical strands were developing that gave the reader prominence for the first time. Emerging in Germany as a development of hermeneutics, "reception aesthetics" or "reception theory" focused on the reader's role in literature. Recognizing the role of the reader in completing a text, reception theory argued that literary works are "processes of signification materialized only in the practice of reading. For literature to happen, the reader is quite as vital as the author" (Eagleton 1983: 74). Reception theory thus took as fundamental that every work of art had "gaps" that the reader "concretized" in the process of reading.

Despite its apparent open-endedness, reception theory as articulated by Hans Georg Gadamer, Roman Ingarden, and Wolfgang Iser often, in Eagleton's words, surreptitiously relied on "doctrines of the unified self and the closed text" (1983: 80). No doubt Eagleton is right in his general observation; however, it also seems true that these varied critical modes that understood literary works as incomplete without the reader, or as marked by a tendency to undo or deconstruct their own meanings, helped to dislodge the aesthetic premium on integrated, complex textual wholes. In so doing, they cracked open the door to valuing texts for being and doing other kinds of things.

Recent critical theory has been marked by its attention to the contexts in which literature is written, produced, disseminated, consumed, and valued. New historicist, Foucauldian, feminist, and cultural criticism are some of its most notable manifestations. Feminist critique, for example, has re-evaluated and revalued both male and female novelists, such as George Eliot and Charles Dickens, even as it has helped to break Thomas Hardy out of the mold of rural annalist and brought Charlotte Brontë into new prominence and importance.

The Reception of Victorian Novelists

The novel as an art form was still struggling to establish its aesthetic stature in early Victorian England. The British novel is generally agreed to have emerged as a genre only recently, in the eighteenth century, a consequence of the rise of Protestantism, capitalism, and industrialism. All of these "isms" privileged the individual and made possible works that focused on the lives of ordinary individuals and that secured our interest through the device of a narrator who could provide psychological depth and social breadth. In its early days as a young and emerging genre, when the novel had roughly the aesthetic status that we accord to television and film today, novelists felt pressured to justify its seriousness. Henry Fielding famously compared the novel to the epic as a way of dignifying its artistic reach and aesthetic achievement. In short, there was a real question about whether one should read novels at all, and they certainly did not figure in any educational curriculum.

The early readers of novels, like today's audiences for film and television, came from all of the literate classes and included both men and women. However, middle-class women were becoming an increasingly significant portion of the novel-reading public because they had fewer opportunities for advanced education and gainful employment. There were frequently expressed concerns about the advisability of making novels too readily available to young girls, who might be adversely influenced by them. But, generally, by the dawn of the Victorian age, novel-reading was an established activity for women, especially because a domestic ideology that discouraged women's "work" and the increasing wealth generated by the industrial revolution produced many leisure hours for middle-class women to fill. Not only did expanded leisure encourage women's reading, but the bar erected against women's profitable employment in all but a few areas – of which writing was one – encouraged many women to pen novels. And, by and large, they penned novels in preference to poetry or drama. In *A Room of One's Own*, Virginia Woolf queries this predilection, pondering the "strange force" that "compelled [women], when they wrote, to write novels" (1929a: 69). She explains that "it would be easier to write prose and fiction [in the common sitting room available to them] than to write poetry or a play. Less concentration is required" (p. 70).

At the same time that women picked up pens, they just as readily adopted male pseudonyms. Charlotte, Emily, and Anne Brontë published their novels as Currer, Ellis, and Acton Bell. Charlotte explained the rationale of their pseudonyms: "The ambiguous choice being dictated by a sort of conscientious scruple at assuming Christian names positively masculine, while we did not like to declare ourselves women, because . . . we had a vague impression that authoresses are liable to be looked on with prejudice" (Wise and Symington 1932: vol. 2, 70–80). This same concern with how her works would be perceived if known to be from the hand of a woman perhaps motivated Marian Evans, who adopted the pseudonym George Eliot. In Evans's case, there was also concern that the reception of her work would suffer from her reputation as the woman who had eloped to the continent with a married man. Even women of impeccable reputations had to worry that they would be accused of having lived the lives they only imagined.

One of the major moral guardians standing at the gates of culture was Charles Edward Mudie, tycoon of the Victorian circulating libraries (see chapter 1 by Kelly Mays in this volume). Mudie began lending books in his Bloomsbury shop in 1842 and rapidly expanded throughout the country and abroad. After paying a fee of a guinea per year, readers were entitled to borrow one volume at a time. Thus, readers unable to afford expensive "triple-deckers" – the three-volume novels, priced by publishers at a guinea and a half each – could subscribe to this circulating library and sate their appetite for adventure and romance. Known as Mudie's Select Library, or "Mudie's" for short, the business anticipated the enormous success of Blockbuster Video today, where what is available for inexpensive rental helps set canons of taste in film. Guinevere Griest notes that "Readers who wanted recent novels were driven to the powerful circulating libraries, which exerted a significant . . . influence in the

Victorian library milieu" (1970: 2). At the same time, readers were helping to mold what the circulating libraries stocked. Griest adds, "In the Victorian era, publishers, authors, and the public all recognized the might of the libraries, and the structure and contents of novels conformed to their wishes. That this was possible indicates the extent to which they were satisfying the demands made by their customers, so that their policies in effect mirror the attitudes and desires of the novel-reading public" (p. 5). Whether one's new novel was offered by Mudie's could make or break the fortunes of an aspiring writer. The couple of hundred copies Mudie's would order for its clientele often meant the difference between a promising career and instant oblivion.

At the same time that Charles Mudie offered affordable books with an eye to his own profit margin, he also used his commercial dominance to become an arbiter of public taste and morality. Mudie's evaluation – and the responsiveness of his company to irate letters from clergymen or fathers – had the power to shape an author's ongoing reception. Like his chief rival, W. H. Smith, Mudie was "convinced that, with a few dangerous exceptions, the public did not want books which questioned the generally accepted Victorian standards, a judgment verified by the increasing numbers of satisfied subscribers" (Griest 1970: 33). Small wonder, then, that Wilkie Collins, whose sensation novels sometimes offended readers, dubbed Mudie and Smith the "twin tyrants of literature." And Thomas Carlyle, who met Charles Edward Mudie in 1850 commented, "So, *you're* the man that divides the sheep from the goats! Ah! It's an *awfu'* thing to judge a man. It's a *more* awfu' thing to judge a book." Mudie simply responded: "In my business I profess to judge books only from a commercial standpoint, though it is ever my object to circulate good books and not bad ones" (Quoted in Carlyle 1884: 11).

So large was Mudie's establishment and his influence that he was dubbed a "leviathan." That magnitude stemmed directly from the public's enthusiasm for what the business offered. Anthony Trollope, a prolific novelist himself, memorably declared that "We have become a novel-reading people, from the Prime Minister down to the last-appointed scullery-maid . . . Poetry also we read and history, biography and the social and political news of the day. But all our other reading put together hardly amounts to what we read in novels" (1938: 108).

Despite the well-nigh universal hunger for novels from all segments of the population, we must not assume that everyone was reading the same novels. As Richard Altick has demonstrated, one must exercise care when generalizing about Victorian readers, about popular versus educated audiences, or the *vox populi* versus the *vox critici* (1989: 120). Nonetheless, the population's reception of novels in the early decades of the Victorian age was much more seamless than in later decades. In general, as the Victorian age advanced, there emerged an increasing distinction between popular and cultured audiences, an increasing stratification of readers by education, and a decline in the quality of popular literature.

Just as the educated and popular audiences were not necessarily congruent, so, too, the critical and the popular receptions often differed, especially in the early years of a novel. However, it was hard for anyone critical of Mudie's policies and practices to stem the tide of public taste and commercial profit. In the last two decades of the nineteenth century, George Moore, whose novels were banned by Mudie's, launched his own campaign against the leviathan:

> At the head, therefore, of English literature sits a tradesman who considers himself qualified to decide the most delicate artistic question that may be raised, and who crushes out of sight any artistic aspiration he may deem pernicious. And yet with this vulture gnawing at their hearts writers gravely discuss the means of producing good work; let them break their bonds first. (Moore 1884: 1)

Although Moore was confident that his attacks had helped to cripple the circulating library empire, it was the economics of publication that determined its ultimate demise. The demise of the triple-decker in 1894 and the increasing availability of inexpensive one-volume editions ended the system of profit that had sustained a Mudie's and a Smith's.

Following the Victorian age, the critical and popular estimations continued to differ; however, to the extent that republication and reprinting of novels was determined by their adoption in school curricula, the critical reception significantly influenced which texts were available and helped to shape a public's perception of what was "popular." And a novel that had enjoyed vigorous sales among a popular audience could, for any number of reasons, fall out of the public consciousness and gradually disappear from print.

Charlotte Brontë

Charlotte Brontë's first published novel, *Jane Eyre*, enjoyed an immediate popular success and set the stage for the success of her subsequent novels. Complicating Charlotte Brontë's early popular reception, however, was the critical concern about her book's immorality and a confusion between herself and her sisters. As noted above, the three women had adopted the pseudonyms Currer, Ellis, and Acton Bell to preserve their anonymity and to ensure that their works' reception did not suffer from an audience's prejudice against women writers. When Emily and Anne subsequently published *Wuthering Heights* and *Agnes Grey* with the publisher Thomas Newby, he unscrupulously sought to generate a wider readership for his new publications by claiming they were from the same hand that penned *Jane Eyre*. Charlotte and Anne rushed to London to confront Newby with his lie. Nonetheless, the confusion among the three writers persisted, and when Anne published *The Tenant of Wildfell Hall*, which chronicles, in part, one man's drunken, immoral, and brutal career, critics were quick to recollect the tendency of earlier "Bell" novels to focus on depraved and dissolute behavior.

After the early deaths of her two sisters, Charlotte was eager to clarify the differences among the three novelists when she wrote the preface to a new edition of *Wuthering Heights*. Her negative comments on her sister Anne's novel suggest Charlotte's additional concern to limit an association that might produce a more negative reception of her own works. Charlotte's refusal to republish *The Tenant* during her own life ensured the demise of her youngest sister's reputation. Whether it bolstered her own is questionable; however, fewer than ten years after the publication of her first novel, Charlotte too was dead and the country was mourning the loss of a distinctive genius.

The publication in 1855 of Elizabeth Gaskell's *Life of Charlotte Brontë* intervened in the critical debate and, by revealing circumstances of the life, advanced an image of Charlotte Brontë as a model of Victorian womanhood. By the end of the 1850s, the hagiography of Brontë was well under way, sympathy for the life trumping criticism of the work. Typical, perhaps, was this confession in the *Eclectic Review* (1857): "Now that we have finished the strange, sad story, we have no heart for mere literary criticism . . . others may criticize her writings – we are unable to think of anything but her life." The focus on the woman over the works led, over time, to a tendency "to love her more than her books."

The tendency of critics to focus heavily on biographical concerns persisted up to the early 1960s. In his summary for the second edition of *Victorian Fiction: A Second Guide to Research*, Herbert Rosengarten notes that the "criticism of the novels often took second place to the theories of amateur psychologists or to debates about such matters as . . . authorship" (1978: 172). Only in the 1960s did professional academics begin to turn criticism firmly toward consideration of the works themselves, and scholarly interest in style, theme, and technique of Charlotte Brontë's novels accelerate.

In the 1970s, with the advent of feminist criticism, Charlotte Brontë began what has been a steady march from minor to major status as Victorian novelist. Early aesthetic concerns about Charlotte's inability to distance herself from her protagonists, voiced by Henry James and echoed by Virginia Woolf, have been challenged by other critics who have found evidence of great artistry in her handling of narrative technique. And scholars such as Terry Eagleton, examining the social and political implications of Charlotte Brontë's work (Eagleton 1975), have taken their place alongside feminist critics interested in this author's quintessential representation of the disadvantages against which women and women writers fought in the Victorian age. The decade opened with the publication in 1970 of Kate Millett's *Sexual Politics* and concluded with Sandra Gilbert and Susan Gubar's *The Madwoman in the Attic* (1979), in which Brontë's Bertha Mason from *Jane Eyre* provided both title and central image for a study of female rage against the constrictions of women's lives in patriarchy. Gayatri Spivak linked a feminist to a postcolonial reading of *Jane Eyre* and sparked significant scholarly interest in Charlotte Brontë's representation of race, class, and nationality, an interest that has only intensified with the development in the past decades of cultural studies.

Current critical interest is mirrored in a continuing popular audience, particularly for *Jane Eyre*, because directors never tire of undertaking yet another filmic interpretation of this early Brontë novel, beginning memorably with Orson Welles starring as a dark and brooding Rochester. However, Brontë's other major novels, *Villette* and *Shirley*, have never enjoyed that kind of attention in film and television adaptations.

Of the four writers whose receptions we are examining here, Charlotte Brontë is the one whose reputation and estimation have changed the most dramatically. From being a popular novelist, of minor stature in the English canon, unmentioned in F. R. Leavis's *Great Tradition*, she has emerged at the end of the twentieth century as one of the most significant writers of the Victorian age and a major canonical figure among novelists.

Charles Dickens

The phenomenal popularity of Charles Dickens in his own day led early reviewers "decade after decade" to speak "glibly and repetitiously, of Dickens's unique appeal to 'the million.'" Amplifying this truism, Richard Altick points out: "There were . . . other millions who were disqualified from reading him on the twin counts of illiteracy and poverty" (1989: 117). Altick cautions us, from our distance of a century and a half, not to take literally the words of a reviewer like this one, writing for the *English Review*: "Dickens, affectionate, earnest, at times sublime, speaks to rich and poor, high and low; to all, perhaps, save some of the middle classes, who think him 'vulgar.' His sphere of operation is almost boundless; he may be said to write for all, and work for all" (quoted in Altick 1989: 117–18). Helen Small has suggested an important reason for a perception that Dickens was accessible to the entire population, which is that Dickens's public readings from his novels formed an important cultural extension of the contemporaneous political debates: "Dickens's readings were not, as might have been expected, aimed purely or even primarily at the middle classes. They were conceived and promoted as occasions which would bring together readers from widely differing social backgrounds as one reading public" (1966: 266).

A more accurate assessment of the actual, contemporaneous *readers* of Dickens, suggests Altick, is the tempered opinion of another periodical writer who claimed that Dickens's works had "a peculiar appeal in language and subject to the middle classes – *we had almost written*, the masses of society" (quoted in Altick 1989: 118; emphasis in original). As Altick's studies confirm, Dickens's early audiences came overwhelmingly from the middle classes, but across that great mass his popularity was enormous and unrivalled by any other novelist of his day. W. M. Thackeray avidly read new numbers of his rival's *Dombey and Son* as they appeared and, describing his own plight as a contemporary of Dickens's, exclaimed after the fifth number, "There! Read that. There is no writing against such power as this – no one has a chance" (quoted in Ray 1958: 427). When his own first Christmas book was published in 1846, Thackeray was "satisfied with a sale of 1,500 copies, even though Dickens's . . . sold 25,000" (Ray 1958: 426).

Even as he enjoyed a broad popular readership, Dickens has also garnered critical praise, and his cultural cachet has tended to remain high. But, argues Simon Dentith, he may be "unique among canonical writers in retaining some element at least of a popular readership" (1992: 79). I would augment this observation by reminding readers of this chapter that Charlotte Brontë's novels, particularly *Jane Eyre*, have also kept a popular readership. Unlike Dickens's novels, however, they have only recently gained canonical status.

It is, perhaps, the very breadth of Dickens's representations and the range of genres upon which he calls – from romance, to Gothic, to realism, to moral fable, to melo-drama and sensationalism – that have kept him popular with audiences and critics alike, who find in his works a trove of styles, images, techniques, and themes to answer the demands of changing critical fashion. Still, Dickens's critical reputation has varied in the twentieth century. As noted above, F. R. Leavis was uncertain of whether to include him in the "Great Tradition," and concluded by focusing on what most readers would see as one of Dickens's lesser works, *Hard Times*, which Leavis praised as a concise "moral fable." When the aesthetic standard of excellence was derived from fidelity to reality and moral seriousness, it was relatively easy for critics to fault Dickens's major novels, despite their popularity among readers.

In fact, the earlier failure of critics to appreciate Dickens's versatility led scholars of the mid-twentieth century to embrace him as a "contemporary." Responsible for summarizing Dickens's critical reception in the first *Victorian Fiction: A Guide to Research* (1964), edited by Lionel Stevenson, Ada Nisbet contended: "The twentieth century is more like Dickens' world than the nineteenth" (quoted in Collins 1978: 35). And Philip Collins adds, "there are special features of Dickens's genius that have lately made him seem increasingly attractive, important, and explicable, his work having chimed, for instance, both with critical developments away from mimetic assumptions about the novel and with the nature of much important recent fiction" (p. 34). By 1970, George Ford computed that Dickens had lately been the subject of "well over twice as many scholarly books and essays as any other Victorian author" (quoted in Collins 1978: 35).

In the past thirty years, Dickens has retained his hold on both popular and critical audiences; he remains today one of a select few Victorian authors read for pleasure. In the 1990s, the BBC undertook dramatizations of several of the major novels, including *Our Mutual Friend, Bleak House, Little Dorrit*, and *David Copperfield. Oliver Twist* and *Great Expectations* have come to life on the musical stage and in recent major film productions (see chapter 26 in this volume by Joss Marsh and Kamilla Elliot). And the list goes on. Recent cultural studies critics have found in Dickens's novels an immense tapestry of a world undergoing rapid social and intellectual change. The richness of the picture, drawing as it does from all aspects of Victorian life, provides a seemingly endless resource for understanding issues of class, gender, race, and nationality in Victorian England and for examining the fitful processes through which change is effected or stalled.

George Eliot

Although Marian Evans early felt that her reputation as a "fallen" woman in Victorian England might compromise the readership for and reputation of her fiction, she rose quickly in her lifetime to become one of the most revered figures in late Victorian England. The critical approbation and fervid speculation about authorship that greeted the publication of her first work, *Scenes of Clerical Life*, and the willingness of a certain clergyman to let speculation settle on him as the pseudonymous George Eliot, led Marian Evans to lift the veil on her identity with the publication and enormous popular success of *Adam Bede*. She continued, of course, to sign her novels as George Eliot, but she was widely known and quickly lionized by an adoring audience.

Eliot hewed more consistently to the dictates of realism than did the other novelists we are examining here and her concept of realism was highly sophisticated. Not satisfied with mere "*detailism* which calls itself realism," that is, a preoccupation with ordinary details, George Eliot set out to capture all truth and beauty by "a humble and faithful study of nature, and not by substituting vague forms, bred by imagination on the mists of feeling, in place of definite substantial reality" (Eliot 1856: 626).

This understanding of realism makes clear why George Eliot's novels modeled a high moral seriousness that led F. R. Leavis to place her prominently in the "Great Tradition." In an 1859 letter to a friend, Eliot early claimed this high ground in describing the reception with which her work had met: "I have written a novel [*Adam Bede*] which people say has stirred them very deeply – and *not a few* people, but almost all reading England . . . I think you will believe that I do not write you word of this out of any small vanity: – my books are deeply serious things to me, and come out of all the painful discipline, all the most hardly-learnt lessons of my past life" (Haight 1985: 230). The near cult status she would come to enjoy as Britain's most revered living novelist is clearly anticipated in Eliot's own words.

Despite their enormous popularity during her lifetime, George Eliot's novels suffered a significant (some would say, precipitous) decline in readership during the decades following her death in 1880, until a resurgence of interest in the late 1940s. In 1948, the same year that Leavis published *The Great Tradition*, Samuel C. Chew, in *A Literary History of England*, wrote of George Eliot: "No other Victorian novelist of major rank is so little read today," and he linked her to Margaret Oliphant for their presumed resemblance to one another (quoted in Knoepflmacher 1978: 234). Eliot's reputation had suffered in the wake of attacks by post-Jamesian critics, who deplored the "presumably ponderous and intrusive effect of her authorial interventions" (Knoepflmacher 1978: 235). Percy Lubbock's *Craft of Fiction* (1921), which celebrated Henry James's narrative innovations, contributed significantly to that low estimate.

What W. J. Harvey described as a "post-1945 phenomenon" burgeoned into, in Knoepflmacher's words, "an even more impressive 'post-1960 phenomenon'" (1978: 234). And we can confidently say today that there appears no sign of any slackening of critical interest in George Eliot; further, with the BBC's productions in the 1990s of *Middlemarch*, *The Mill on the Floss*, and *Silas Marner*, there is a renewed popular interest in this novelist.

In 1978, Knoepflmacher attributed George Eliot's reinstatement as "a major writer and seminal thinker" to "a variety of causes: among them the general resurgence of interest in all things Victorian, the new attention given to the female imagination, and the higher respect paid to the mixture of 'honest doubt' and religious yearning found in her work" (1978: 234). The development of feminist criticism and theory and the advent of post-structuralist criticism and recent developments in cultural studies have further fueled that interest, which shows no signs of abating. *Middlemarch*, established by Leavis as integral to the canon of English realist fiction, has solidified its canonical position by proving amenable to post-structuralist deconstructors. Feminist critics have added to their focus on *Middlemarch* a revitalized interest in *The Mill on the Floss*, which chronicles a young girl's development to womanhood within a restrictive, patriarchal milieu. In turn, cultural studies approaches have reinvigorated attention to *Daniel Deronda*, which develops the idea and possibility of founding a Jewish state.

Thomas Hardy

Thomas Hardy's reception has never suffered a serious decline since the days "when he was universally revered as the Grand Old Man of English letters" (Millgate 1978: 308). And, like the current interest in Brontë, Dickens, and Eliot, the current interest in his novels seems inexhaustible. Michael Millgate attributes a "spectacular increase in the specifically academic study of Hardy beginning in the 1960s to a general interest in the Victorian period and the ongoing revaluation of the 'modern.'" In addition, he cites the "extent to which the formal characteristics of both Hardy's fiction and his verse seem especially accessible to current critical approaches" (Millgate 1978: 308). In this renewed popularity in the last decades of the twentieth century, Hardy's reception parallels that of Charlotte Brontë, Charles Dickens, and George Eliot.

In the modernist era, which valued subtle and unobtrusive narrative effects – a legacy of Henry James – and, then, following Leavis, an emphasis on realism coupled to moral seriousness, Hardy's artistry was never fully appreciated. His novelistic strengths emerged once critics became interested in multiple literary effects and grasped the rhetoric of fiction in more complex ways. To some extent, however, Hardy studies have remained in the grip of an early image of "good little Thomas Hardy." Just as Peter Widdowson struggled in 1989 to create the picture of a more spirited figure by bringing the so-called "minor" fiction into relationship with the "major," so, too, Michael Millgate in 1978 called for just such a realignment. Despite the noble efforts of both, critical work on Hardy still suffers from a bifurcation of his novels into the two camps of major and minor. Brontë, Dickens, and Eliot have not suffered from this same tendency, despite the fact that some novels of each are read more often than others.

By World War I, when he had turned from writing novels to poetry, Thomas Hardy the novelist had been cast as "a great modern tragic humanist and rural annalist, flawed by perverse tendencies, but whose five or six major 'novels of character and environment' represent his 'true' achievement" (Widdowson 1989: 24). His so-called "flaws" (flaws within a critical mode that valued realism enhanced by narrative subtlety) had been identified: "pessimism, preaching, clumsy style, melodrama, coincidence" (Widdowson 1989: 25). The characterization of Hardy as a great but faulty writer persisted, even as he was celebrated, first, as an elemental tragedian and, later, as elegist of a passing order. Leavis, as we have seen, barely gave Hardy a nod, referring to him as a "provincial manufacturer of gauche and heavy fictions" (1948: 32–3, 139–40). Widdowson summarizes this period: "Largely ignored by Leavis and the New Critics in the mid century when 'Anglo-Saxon criticism [was] increasingly controlled by formalist, organicist and anti-theoretical assumptions', Hardy is recovered in the fifties by a sentimental sociological criticism which regards him as the apologist of the passing rural order" (1989: 21).

As Leavis's influence waned and the critical reception of Hardy waxed, possible approaches to Hardy's fiction multiplied. Eagleton wittily summarizes the post-1960 critical reception of Thomas Hardy: "the sixties and seventies witness a steady recuperation of his texts by formalist criticism. Hardy has been phenomenologized, Freudianized, biographized, and claimed as the true guardian of 'English' liberal-democratic tendencies against the primitivist extremism of emigré modernists" (1981: 127–8). In Widdowson's estimation, however, the essential reception of Hardy did not significantly change under this critical attention. Formalist approaches remain informed by a humanist ideology: " 'Thomas Hardy of Wessex' has simply become a larger and denser figure than hitherto" (1989: 29).

Beginning in the 1970s and continuing more vigorously in the last two decades of the twentieth century, critics attended more fully to Hardy as a social novelist engaged with rural economy and with class, property, and gender relations. In 1970, Raymond Williams set the stage for a different critical estimation of Hardy in *The English Novel from Dickens to Lawrence*. Eagleton followed in 1974 with a Marxist introduction to the "New Wessex" edition of *Jude the Obscure*. Subsequently, feminist criticism has continued to challenge the dominant reception of Hardy, in part because its critique of the political/ideological nature of critical perspectives has enabled it to be freer of the old ideologies governing earlier readings. Feminist critics have examined not only the representation of women, but also, subsequently, the construction of gender – masculinity and femininity – and the sexual/textual politics of the novels. And, as it has for the other novelists examined here, the recent advent of cultural studies has opened up Hardy's novels to much more detailed analyses of the cultural and social politics he so tellingly details. Furthermore, filmic and television adaptations of Hardy's novels have ensured a continuing popular interest in his fiction. Roman Polanski's *Tess*, which used Hardy's novel as an occasion to explore the director's feelings about Charles Manson's murder of his pregnant wife, Sharon Tate, helped to renew the readership for Hardy's novels, particularly *Tess of the D'Urbervilles*.

Canons and Aesthetic Value

Finally, in considering reception of the Victorian novel, I wish to pose a broad question about how canons are constituted – that is, about how certain novels are received as aesthetically superior to others. Generally, in examining receptions of these four different Victorian novelists, we have been analyzing those factors that helped to shape their inclusion in the canon of Victorian fiction. I would now like to consider a novelist who in the middle of the twentieth century was linked closely to George Eliot in her reception and fate: Margaret Oliphant. Whereas F. R. Leavis's interest in Eliot's realism returned that novelist's works to the centrality they had enjoyed at the time of their publication, Oliphant's novels, equally heralded in their day, now "rest in unvisited tombs." What factors have contributed to that different reception?

Theorist Pierre Bourdieu has developed concepts through which we might propose one answer. Distinguishing among different kinds of "capital" or value that objects may accrue, Bourdieu defines cultural capital as an "elaborated taste for the most refined objects," and he traces how "art and cultural consumption are predisposed, consciously and deliberately or not, to fulfill a social function of legitimating social differences" (1984: 7). Particularly, Bourdieu pinpoints the corollary relationship between economic and cultural capital, or money and aesthetic taste. He explains that the aesthetic disposition is dependent on "past and present material conditions of existence" or "distance from necessity" (p. 53). In short, the aesthetic disposition depends on economic power, or a "power to keep economic necessity at arm's length" (p. 55). Thus, the accumulation of cultural capital is built on a withdrawal from economic necessity (p. 54). In addition, cultural capital is derived through education, which depends not only on economic wherewithal but also on access to an entire system of schooling. For these reasons, in part, taste – or the ability to make aesthetic distinctions between one object and another – functions to validate social, class, and gender distinctions. Hence, although often unrecognized, class and gender figure prominently in aesthetic evaluation, a point to which I alluded earlier in citing Paul Lauter's critique of the "new critical" standard of excellence, which tended to exclude fiction and poetry by the working classes and many women.

Margaret Oliphant and George Eliot, as I noted earlier, have been frequently linked, not only in their posthumous fates but in their subject matters. Q. D. Leavis, F. R. Leavis's wife, read Oliphant and Eliot in relationship to each other, and, ironically, claimed Oliphant's text as an influential precursor of Eliot's and found Oliphant's protagonist in *Miss Marjoribanks*, Lucilla Marjoribanks, much more attractive and likable than Eliot's Dorothea Brooke in *Middlemarch*. However, Eliot's *Middlemarch* fits much more comfortably within the evaluative standards of realism and moral seriousness that F. R. Leavis established for his "Great Tradition," in part because certain class and economic issues are obscured. The very qualities that Q. D. Leavis found attractive in Oliphant's work – especially her pragmatic representation of women's economic sophistication and class management – are precisely those that are muted in George Eliot's realism that focuses on higher truth. As I noted earlier, Widdowson suggested that F. R. Leavis had to exclude Thomas Hardy because he jeopardized Leavis's reading of English literature. Oliphant, too, jeopardizes that reading. Specifically, George Eliot's *Middlemarch* minimizes or even erases women's roles as household managers, protoprofessional positions that demanded the skills required to run any small business: acumen in hiring, supervising, and disciplining workers along with financial accountancy expertise. Little of this is represented in *Middlemarch*, where a lady like Dorothea Brooke finds only ennui in the idleness and triviality of her life as it is depicted by Eliot.

In contrast to Eliot, Oliphant represents middle-class women as class managers who relish their positions. Eliot's heroines chaff under the social restrictions that keep them confined to the home; Oliphant's pragmatically gather into their hands the reins that allow them to control local society and effect class management. Eliot's heroines are, if anything, deemed too good, too idealized in their ultimate self-abnegation and resignation to the status quo; Oliphant's are termed "hard" and "unpleasant" for calculating strategies through which to amass power and influence, disdaining romantic love in favor of shrewd political alliances.

The contrasts are even more marked as we consider the ways Eliot and Oliphant represent aesthetic practice both inside and outside their novels. If we follow Bourdieu's logic that cultural capital derives principally from social capital and certain kinds of educational capital, then it should be obvious that women writers are, from the beginning, seriously disadvantaged. Bourdieu's analyses allow us to deepen our grasp of what it means for a woman to employ a male pseudonym. Cultural distinction is not simply a generic refinement of manner that is coded as the outward manifestation of inner taste; it is also gendered masculine, as Eliot's narrator in *Middlemarch* succinctly and ironically alleges: "A man's mind – what there is of it has always the advantage of being masculine, – as the smallest birch-tree is of a higher kind than the most soaring palm, – and even his ignorance is of a sounder quality" (Eliot 1956: 16). Presumably his ignorance is of a sounder quality because it is educated ignorance.

George Eliot fashioned an aesthetic practice that underwrote a conventional logic of culture. Obviously, those who produce high culture have a fund of educational capital on which to draw. A level of education might be generally conceded for a man of a certain class, but could never be assumed in a woman. Thus, Eliot's *Middlemarch*, our test text here, demonstrates from chapter to chapter the extraordinary bank of educational capital on which its author can make generous drafts. Epigraphs are drawn not only from Cervantes, Milton, Spenser, Chaucer, Dante, Pascal, and Shakespeare but also from Blake, Ben Jonson, Goldsmith, Beaumont and Fletcher, Burton, Donne, Alfred de Musset, Italian proverbs, and so forth. A knowledge of Italian art, classical music, German higher criticism, and philosophy in general, French, German, and Italian languages, contemporary science, and the literatures of several nationalities constitutes only a part of the erudition that informs the narrator's commentary.

Social or class capital also has its subtle but pervasive presence. As Bourdieu points out, individuals of a superior class will always disdain the pleasures of the class or classes beneath them. Thus, the "Keepsake" album that Ned Plymdale proudly presents to Rosamond Vincy as the "very best thing in art and literature" can be sneeringly dismissed by Lydgate as "sugared invention" (1984: 198–9). It is the narrator who places each participant in this comic social drama of cultural distinction, and yet that narrator already has one up on Lydgate, who is "so ambitious of social distinction" that the "distinction of mind which belonged to his intellectual ardour," cannot save him from confusing the acquisition of substantial material possessions with the attainment of true culture (p. 111).

Bourdieu's theories, then, offer some plausible explanations for George Eliot's achievement of canonicity. This is neither to fault nor to criticize her works; rather, it simply foregrounds some factors that have contributed to their elevation. On Oliphant's claims to cultural distinction, in contrast, we can be rather brief. She does not bank on any educational capital of the kind found in Eliot. Indeed, Margaret Oliphant has had her cultural capital fixed at a low estimate: bourgeois woman's novelist, who focuses on inconsequential domestic details and eschews the kind of moral seriousness that is a touchstone of Eliot's novels.

Middlemarch strategically lays out its claims to high culture, just as representations of the author's life lay claim to a social and economic distinction free from the worries of getting and spending. We know, in fact, that Eliot supported herself with income produced from her writing, but portrayals of her life often suggest a principled withdrawal from such monetary concerns. She termed novel writing her "true vocation," spoke of her books as "deeply serious things to me," "something worth living and suffering for," and celebrated her success in writing a novel that "people say has stirred them very deeply." Contrasting her own life with Eliot's, Oliphant picks up on this narrative, complaining, "How I have been handicapped in life! Should I have done better if I had been kept, like her, in a mental greenhouse and taken care of?" (1988: 5).

Oliphant's story of her own life, recounted in her *Autobiography*, differs dramatically from Eliot's. And here I will touch only on the received truisms about that life because, as I wish to argue, it is precisely those truisms that have contributed to her aesthetic capital – or lack thereof – as a writer. The key details are these: Oliphant wrote too fast and too much because she needed money. The mercenary motive, Oliphant's obsession with her income, and the fact that she claims that "it was necessary for me to work for my children" (1988: 4) seem to disqualify her from artist's status and to turn her into a hack writer. Perhaps Virginia Woolf led the way, memorably encapsulating Oliphant's career in *Three Guineas*: "Mrs. Oliphant sold her brain, her very admirable brain, prostituted her culture and enslaved her intellectual liberty in order that she might earn her living and educate her children" (1929b: 91–2). Strains of that "incandescence" Woolf rated so highly in *A Room of One's Own* return in this assessment linking material, educational, and cultural capital. Thereafter, the anecdotal Margaret Oliphant became a figure who "wrote her way out of debt" (Trela 1990: 32), was "addicted to the trappings of a genteel style of life" (O'Mealy 1992: 247), "never travelled other than first class . . . [and] always wore silk" (Haythornthwaite 1988: 39), and continually hounded her forbearing publishers for advances. Not surprisingly, we arrive at this final estimate: "all her books are flawed by speedy and careless writing" (Haythornthwaite 1988: 38).

Each of the writers whose reception I have examined in this essay wrote, in part, to support him or herself. But when a writer was seen to let economic exigency take precedence over aesthetic considerations, then the aesthetic estimate of the work tended to suffer. Returning to Hardy's reception over the past century, we might understand the persistent categorizing of his novels as "major" and "minor" as one consequence of the public's response to his open avowal of the economic difficulties he faced. Like Oliphant, he frequently confessed to writing for money.

*

In this chapter, I have set out to provide readers not only with a history of the receptions of four Victorian novelists, but also with a grasp of the metacritical contexts shaping the particular reception of particular works at particular times. The two together help us also to understand some of the forces shaping both the shifting status of works over time and the complex relationship between popular and critical audiences. Finally, too, as I have demonstrated in the last section, we need to ask what forces beyond critical fashion might limit or enhance receptiveness to an individual literary work. In short, we need to think generally about how aesthetic value is constituted and shapes the range of works that come under a critical purview. With the advent of feminist, postcolonial, and cultural studies, these questions about value have recently become more prominent. As a result, the landscape of Victorian fiction continues subtly to shift as more works by women and the working classes are being unearthed and examined.

References

Altick, Richard (1989), *Writers, Readers, and Occasions: Selected Essays on Victorian Literature and Life* (Columbus: Ohio State University Press).

Anon. (1857), "Charlotte Brontë", *Eclectic Review*, 1, 630–42.

Bourdieu, Pierre (1984), *Distinction: A Social Critique of the Judgment of Taste* (Cambridge, Mass.: Harvard University Press).

Bové, Paul (1983), "Variations on Authority: Some Deconstructive Transformations of the New Criticism," in Jonathan Arac et al., eds., *The Yale Critics: Deconstruction in America* (Minneapolis: University of Minnesota Press; Theory and History of Literature, 6).

Buckler, William E., ed. (1958), *Prose of the Victorian Period* (Boston: Houghton Mifflin).

Carlyle, Thomas (1884), "A Visit to Mudie's," *Pall Mall Gazette*, 39.

Collins, Philip (1978), "Charles Dickens," in George H. Ford, ed., *Victorian Fiction: A Guide to Research*, 2nd edn. (New York: Modern Language Association), 34–113.

Dentith, Simon (1992), "How Popular Was *Dombey and Son?" The Dickensian*, 88/2, 69–81.

Eagleton, Terry (1975), *Myths of Power: A Marxist Study of the Brontës* (New York: Barnes & Noble; London: Macmillan).

Eagleton, Terry (1981), *Walter Benjamin or Towards a Revolutionary Criticism* (London: Verso).

Eagleton, Terry (1983), *Literary Theory: An Introduction* (Minneapolis: University of Minnesota Press).

Eliot, George (1856), "Art and Belles Lettres," *Westminster Review*, 9, 625–50.

Eliot, George (1956), *Middlemarch* (Boston: Houghton Mifflin).

Ford, George H., ed. (1978), *Victorian Fiction: A Guide to Research*, 2nd edn. (New York: Modern Language Association).

Griest, Guinevere L. (1970), *Mudie's Circulating Library and the Victorian Novel* (Bloomington and London: Indiana University Press).

Haight, Gordon S., ed. (1985), *Selections from George Eliot's Letters* (New Haven: Yale University Press).

Haythornthwaite, J. (1988), "A Victorian Novelist and her Publisher: Margaret Oliphant and the House of Blackwood," *The Bibliotheck: A Scottish Journal*, 15, 27–50.

Knoepflmacher, U. C. (1978), "George Eliot," in George H. Ford, ed., *Victorian Fiction: A Guide to Research*, 2nd edn. (New York: Modern Language Association), 243–73.

Lauter, Paul (1991), "Caste, Class, and Canon," in Robyn R. Warhol and Diane Price Herndl, eds., *Feminisms: An Anthology of Literary Theory and Criticism* (New Brunswick: Rutgers University Press), 227–48.

Leavis, F. R. (1948), *The Great Tradition* (London: Chatto & Windus).

Leavis, Q. D. (1969), "Introduction," in Margaret Oliphant, *Miss Marjoribanks* (London: Zodiac), 1–24.

Lubbock, Percy (1957), *The Craft of Fiction* (New York: Viking). (First publ. 1921.)

Millgate, Michael (1978), "Thomas Hardy," in George H. Ford, ed., *Victorian Fiction: A Guide to Research*, 2nd edn. (New York: Modern Language Association), 308–32.

Moore, George (1884), "A New Censorship of Literature," *Pall Mall Gazette*, 40.

Oliphant, Margaret (1988), *The Autobiography of Mrs. Oliphant*, ed. Mrs. Harry Coghill (Chicago: University of Chicago Press).

O'Mealy, Joseph H. (1992), "Mrs. Oliphant, *Miss Marjoribanks*, and the Victorian Canon," *The Victorian Newsletter*, 44–9.

Ray, Gordon N. (1958), *Thackeray: The Uses of Adversity (1811–1846)* (New York: McGraw-Hill).

Rosengarten, Herbert J. (1978), "The Brontës," in George H. Ford, ed., *Victorian Fiction: A Guide to Research*, 2nd edn. (New York: Modern Language Association), 172–203.

Small, Helen (1966), "Dickens and a Pathology of the Mid-Victorian Reading Public," in James Raven, Helen Small, and Naomi Tadmor, eds., *The Practice and Representation of Reading in England* (Cambridge: Cambridge University Press), 263–90.

Stevenson, Lionel, ed. (1964), *Victorian Fiction: A Guide to Research* (New York: Modern Language Association).

Trela, D. J. (1990), "Jane Welsh Carlyle and Margaret Oliphant: An Unsung Friendship," *The Carlyle Annual*, 11, 31–40.

Trollope, Anthony (1938), "On English Prose Fiction as a Rational Amusement," *Four Lectures*, ed. Morris L. Parrish (London: Constable).

Widdowson, Peter (1989), *Hardy in History: A Study in Literary Sociology* (London: Routledge).

Wise, T. J. and Symington, J. A., eds. (1932), *The Brontës, Their Lives, Friendships, and Correspondence*, 4 vols. (Oxford: Blackwell).

Woolf, Virginia (1929a), *A Room of One's Own* (New York: Harcourt Brace & World).

Woolf, Virginia (1929b), *Three Guineas* (New York: Harcourt Brace & World).

FURTHER READING

Altick, Richard (1998), *The English Common Reader: A Social History of the Mass Reading Public, 1800–1900*, 2nd edn. (Columbus: Ohio State University Press).

Fish, Stanley (1980), *Is There a Text in This Class?: The Authority of Interpretive Communities* (Cambridge, Mass.: Harvard University Press).

Flint, Kate (1993), *The Woman Reader, 1837–1914* (Oxford: Clarendon).

Ford, George H. (1955), *Dickens and his Readers* (Princeton: Princeton University Press).

Gilbert, Sandra and Gubar, Susan (1979), *The Madwoman in the Attic: The Woman Writer and the Nineteenth-Century Literary Imagination* (New Haven and London: Yale University Press).

Guillory, John (1993), *Cultural Capital: The Problem of Literary Canon Formation* (Chicago: University of Chicago Press).

Harman, Barbara Leah and Meyer, Susan, eds. (1996), *The New Nineteenth Century: Feminist Readings of Underread Victorian Fiction* (New York and London: Garland).

Ingarden, Roman (1973), *The Literary Work of Art*, trans. George G. Grabowicz. (Evanston: Northwestern University Press).

Iser, Wolfgang (1978), *The Act of Reading: A Theory of Aesthetic Response* (Baltimore: Johns Hopkins University Press).

Iser, Wolfgang (1989), *Prospecting: from Reader Response to Literary Anthropology* (Baltimore: Johns Hopkins University Press).

Iser, Wolfgang (2000), *The Range of Interpretation* (New York: Columbia University Press).

Jauss, Hans Robert (1982), *Aesthetic Experience and Literary Hermeneutics*, trans. Michael Shaw (Minneapolis: University of Minnesota Press).

Jauss, Hans Robert (1982), *Toward an Aesthetic of Reception*, trans. Timothy Bahti (Minneapolis: University of Minnesota Press).

Kincaid, James R. and Kuhn, Albert, eds. (1984), *Victorian Literature and Society: Essays Presented to Richard D. Altick* (Athens: Ohio State University Press).

Langland, Elizabeth (1995), *Nobody's Angels: Middle Class Women and Domestic Ideology in Victorian Culture* (Ithaca and London: Cornell University Press).

Lauter, Paul (1991), *Canons and Contexts* (New York: Oxford University Press).

Leavis, Q. D. (1969), "Introduction," in Margaret Oliphant, *Miss Marjoribanks* (London: Zodiac), 1–24.

Malone, Catherine (1996), "'We have learnt to love her more than her books': The Critical Reception of Brontë's *Professor*," *Review of English Studies*, 47, 175–87.

Perkin, J. Russell (1990), *A Reception History of George Eliot's Fiction* (Ann Arbor: UMI Research Press).

Poovey, Mary (1995), *Making a Social Body: British Cultural Formation, 1830–1864* (Chicago: University of Chicago Press).

Robinson, Lillian S. (1978), *Sex, Class, and Culture* (Bloomington: Indiana University Press).

Schweickart, Patrocinio P. and Flynn, Elizabeth A., eds. (1986), *Gender and Reading: Essays on Readers, Texts, and Contexts* (Baltimore: Johns Hopkins University Press).

Skilton, David, ed. (1993), *The Early and Mid-Victorian Novel* (London: Routledge).

Spivak, Gayatri Chakravorty (1984), "Three Women's Texts and a Critique of Imperialism," *Critical Inquiry*, 12, 243–61.

Stewart, Garrett (1996), *Dear Reader: The Conscripted Audience in Nineteenth-Century British Fiction* (Baltimore and London: Johns Hopkins University Press).

Terry, R. C. (1983), *Victorian Popular Fiction, 1860–1880* (London: Macmillan).

Trela, D. J. (1995), *Margaret Oliphant: Critical Essays on a Gentle Subversive* (London: Associated University Presses).

Wheeler, Michael (1985), *English Fiction of the Victorian Period, 1830–1890* (New York and London: Longman).

23

Victorian Theories of the Novel

Joseph W. Childers

It is no secret that many of the great novelists of the early Victorian period looked back to the eighteenth century for literary guidance and models. Dickens, for instance, was especially fond of the novels of Tobias Smollett, and his works are riddled with references to *Peregrine Pickle* and *Humphry Clinker*. Samuel Richardson's influence is clearly discernible in novels such as *The Tenant of Wildfell Hall*, while Thackeray's works display more than a passing acquaintance with the novels of Henry Fielding and Laurence Sterne. Walter Scott and Jane Austen, of course, also stand as important figures whose influence projects well into the nineteenth century and can be seen in novels by George Eliot, Robert Louis Stevenson, Anthony Trollope, and H. Rider Haggard.

By the beginning of the nineteenth century, the subgenres of the English novel had established themselves along fairly regular lines. Dominant were the historical romances of Scott, the realist novels of Austen, and – perhaps the most popular – the Gothic romances of authors such as Ann Radcliffe and Gregory "Monk" Lewis. Critics of the novel had found the Aristotelian approach that had predominated criticism during most of the century to be woefully inadequate for evaluating these works. And though they agreed on the division between realistic and idealistic fiction – a distinction that for many was the difference between novels and romances – it would fall to the critics of the Victorian era to formulate coherent theories of realism and idealism. Further, it would be the aesthetic and economic competition (and sometimes collaboration) between these two varieties of the novel that would engender so many of the theories of fiction of the Victorian period.

Novelists as Critics

In the 1853 preface to the first edition of *Bleak House*, Dickens defends the spontaneous combustion of Krook, the proprietor of the fictional rag and bottle shop located across from Chancery. Dickens adduces a number of recorded cases of the pheno-menon, the most famous being that of "the Countess Cornelia de Bandi Cesenate" which in 1731 was "minutely investigated" by a prebendary of Verona. In all, he says, there have been "about thirty" recorded cases of spontaneous combustion, and he offers "general reference to the authorities which will be found at page 329, the recorded opinions and experiences of distinguished medical professors, French, English, and Scottish." Such overwhelming "evidence," apparently, is irrefutable, for he avers that he will not "abandon the facts." Immediately after that Gradgrindian pronouncement, he writes that "[I]n Bleak House [*sic*] I have purposely dwelt upon the romantic side of familiar things" (Dickens 1985: 42–3). Apart from the narrative oddity of Krook's conflagration, which bedeviled Dickens's contemporaries as well as subsequent gen-erations, what strikes today's reader of the preface to *Bleak House* is how Dickens seems to be pulled between two contradictory impulses. On the one hand, he is determined to justify as rational and *real* the possibility of someone literally going up in smoke. On the other, he asks his readers to believe that someone can instantly, and without any obvious cause, burst into flames; he may as well have directed them to believe that a character can fly – or is a ghost.

The alacrity of Dickens's move from fact-wielding authority to devotee of "the romantic side" of experience is indicative of the state of the theory of the novel in the mid-nineteenth century. The specter of Sir Walter Scott still exerted considerable power in the 1850s. Realism had begun to assert itself in important ways by then, but the author of *Waverley* had been dead only since 1832, and the romantic legacy he bequeathed to his literary heirs, even those as original and expansive as Dickens, demanded attention. There had been attempts to displace Scott's influence, especially by Thomas Carlyle and Edward Bulwer-Lytton, and to some extent the standards he set had come to seem outmoded to the aesthetic sensibilities of the mid-Victorians. Nevertheless, both novelists and critics continued to find Scott's work the touchstone of novel-writing – for good or ill – long into the century. After all, it was Scott who had made the novel "respectable," calling on the form to do more than offer salacious thrills or recount the manners of the wealthier classes. He had placed it alongside history, asking it to do the work at a personal and fictive level that history claimed to do on a much grander scale. For a critic like Carlyle, fiction's attempt to compete descriptively with history could lead only to failure for the novelist. Carlyle, himself a professional historian at a time when history was just beginning to coalesce into a self-conscious discipline, often argued for the primacy of the historical over the fictive, even as he recognized the difficulty – if not impossibility – of providing anything like a complete account of any historical event. While history-writing, when done correctly, is "a real prophetic Manuscript" attempting to represent multidimensional, multi-temporal "Action," narrative, in contrast, is one-dimensional, traveling only in one direction. Thus, as important as narrative is, and must be even for history, it is, writes Carlyle, "linear," while "action is solid" (1980: 55). Such is Carlyle's general view of the limits of narrative as a mode of unraveling the mysteries entailed in history. But his specific comments on Scott, though damning, do compare the novelist with other writers who produce literature which "has other aims than that of harmlessly amusing indolent, languid men" (Carlyle 1979: 207). Scott may not fare well against the likes of Shakespeare or Goethe, but Carlyle compares him to those writers, and in doing so helps to set a literary standard for the novel. Likewise, Bulwer-Lytton's essay "Art in Fiction" draws similar implicit conclusions about Scott, arguing that his novels fail to excite the passions and the intellect, relying instead on the effects they produce on the "fancy." Yet again, like Carlyle, Bulwer-Lytton places fiction within the realm of great literature, contending that the effects it produces should be judged as one would judge the effects of great comedy or tragedy.

One result of these early essays by Carlyle and Bulwer-Lytton was partially to reduce Scott's reputation as a novelist. But they were also important in helping to place the novel at the center of a discussion about aesthetic standards. As the novel became the dominant literary form in the Victorian period, theories of what novels should be and do, how they should be composed and for whom, began to be formulated. At first many of the most important critics of the novel were novelists themselves. They wrote in the wake of Scott and his particular style of romance, moving easily from the aristocratic intrigues of "silver-fork" novels, or the derring-do of larger-than-life criminal protagonists in Newgate fiction, to essays discussing the standards and goals of novels and novelists. Bulwer-Lytton himself was among these novelist-critics. As a writer of fiction, he was often castigated by reviewers for the overblown quality of his prose and the outlandishness of his plots. As a critic, ironically, he held up very high standards for the novel. In Bulwer-Lytton's opinion, the novelist must take great care in composing his or her work; writing a novel demands the same care and consideration a painter must use in composing a picture. And, like a painter, the novelist must learn and master the rules guiding his art. Bulwer-Lytton, however, was not interested in delineating these rules; rather, he believed they should be absorbed. Novelists should do as "sculptors do – gaze upon all the great masterpieces of our art till they sink into us, and we are penetrated by the secret of them. Then and not till then, we write according to rules without being quite aware of it" (Lytton 1913: vol. 1, 460). Further, for Bulwer-Lytton, the narrator of a novel – and therefore the author – "must be as thoroughly in earnest as if he were the narrator of facts" (Bulwer-Lytton 1862).

As does Dickens in the preface to *Bleak House*, Bulwer-Lytton the critic suggests both a romantic and a realistic aspect to novel-writing. The rules of the novel, even the very aesthetic qualities that would allow one to call it a masterpiece, cannot be taught as though they were a formula. Like most of the early critics of the novel, the critical apparatus that Bulwer-Lytton employed depended heavily upon taste – his own taste (which was often at odds with the tastes of his readers). Foremost among those standards was the responsibility of the novelist to be convincing. At bottom, implies Bulwer-Lytton, it is not enough for the novelist to merely instruct or entertain; he or she must attempt to convey the tale as though it were not a fiction at all but the truth. And here, he does not mean a transcendental truth in the way a romantic like Carlyle might describe the "truth" of Shakespeare or Goethe; rather,

Bulwer-Lytton is referring to an approximation of empirical veracity. Successful, artistic fiction must be told as though the narrator herself believes the tale.

While this does not translate directly into a call for the realism of someone like George Eliot, it certainly places a special onus on the novelist. However fantastic or improbable a story may be, the novelist must make it believable. Thus, from the outset, the theory of the novel sets a nearly impossible task for the genre. The author must understand that what he is producing is a tale, a fiction: "clothing," as Carlyle would have it. Simultaneously, the work should not be recognizable as a fiction. It should belie the fact of its contrivance and enter into the consciousness of the reader as though it were a fact or a report. One might easily argue that it is with the Victorian fetishization of the "fact" that the oxymoron of "realist fiction" can emerge.

Furthermore, when the novel comes to be characterized as a kind of seamless performance, it takes on a greater array of responsibilities, for it is a product of the imagination that may well have the force of the "real." The outcry over the death of Little Nell in Dickens's *The Old Curiosity Shop* is a good example. The political possibilities of this aesthetic also became increasingly evident. Less successful than Dickens, but acceding in practice to the theory that novels must be told as if they were fact, novelists such as Elizabeth Gaskell, Harriet Martineau, and Charles Kingsley, among others, used their works to advocate social reforms during the 1840s.

By no means should we understand this early formation of a theory of the novel to be systematic, especially in the hands of the novelists themselves. It was much more a kind of piecemeal process, with statements appearing in reviews and prefaces and shared privately in letters. Nor should we think of the novelists as particularly singleminded in their approaches either to their own fiction or to others'. William Makepeace Thackeray, for instance, was a vituperative critic of Bulwer-Lytton's fiction; he found it stylistically overwrought and conventional in its melodrama. Nor did he always seem to agree with Bulwer-Lytton's edict that the novelist should take his art seriously. More than once Thackeray pooh-poohed any notion of artistic "triumph," and insisted that novel-writing was his work and that he wrote for money. Yet, like many of his contemporaries, he lived a vivid life of the mind, coming to know his characters intimately, as though they were indeed real and possessed an agency of their own. "They must go a certain way, in spite of themselves," he writes in *The Roundabout Papers* (1899: 370). And despite the cynicism of a novel like *Vanity Fair*, Thackeray retained enough of his romantic antecedents to declare that "the writer is like a Pythoness on her oracle tripod" (1899: 374–5), essentially a tool for a power greater than himself. For Thackeray, it was imperative to tell the truth as he saw it, even if it made his readers uncomfortable. Indeed, the power of fiction for Thackeray rested in its ability to unsettle the reader, to challenge orthodox habits of mind. He writes of *Vanity Fair* that he "wanted to leave everybody unhappy and dissatisfied at the end of the story – we ought all to be with our own and all other stories"(1945–6: 423).

Other novelists had different concerns as they struggled both to articulate the theories that governed their own approach to writing novels and to conceive of more general aesthetic standards by which fiction could be judged. Some, like Charlotte Brontë, equated the novel with poetry; like the romantic poets, she believed that writers are not always masters of their powers, that often the creative force "strangely wills and works for itself" (1985: 40). Dickens had similarly romantic conceptions of his art, believing that he must be willing to give himself up to it, allow it to take complete possession of him. Yet as he progressed in his career and became amazingly successful, he was also aware that the novelist must exercise a certain control over his creative powers. By 1857, he was advising other novelists to discipline themselves in their writing (1938: vol. 2, 850). As for novels themselves, he took them quite seriously as art, but he did not believe that the best work necessarily dwelt in obscurity. Good novels are meant to be read, and – as his did – should have large audiences. Further, while he took as great a delight in his own works as his readers did, he also believed that novels had social functions, that they could do important work by changing public opinion and opening the eyes of the public to social and political abuses.

Although Dickens's commentaries on the novel as an art form and his own compositional processes are valuable for our understanding of Victorian theories of fiction, Anthony Trollope, George Meredith, and George Eliot are also particularly notable for their contributions to literary criticism and theory. Of the three, Trollope's work as a critic is perhaps best-known, primarily because of the pronouncements about fiction he makes in his *Autobiography* (published in 1883; Trollope 1947), but also because of his book-length study of Thackeray. Trollope found the English to undervalue the novel as an art form; and though he never made the claims for his art that Dickens and George Eliot made for theirs, he did wish to claim for novelists "a just appreciation of their calling" (Trollope 1947: 183–4). But the standards by which novels should be judged, apparently, were not the same as those of the poet or other artists. Novels were inferior to poetry: "By the common consent of all mankind who have read, poetry takes the highest place of literature" (p. 181). Nor is the novel an artifact for the ages: "I fear," he writes, "that the novelist can expect no centuries of popularity. But the poet adapts himself to all ages, by the use of language and scenes which are not ephemeral" (p. 181). The novelist, in contrast, is a creature of his age, and the best tailor themselves to their age. In their own time, they might indeed have great effect, but not as great artists – more as crafters of superior forms of amusement. For Trollope, then, entertainment was a major function of the novel, but novelists must recognize that their works should also instruct. Trollope often writes of the novel as a form of conduct book, from which young women may learn "what is expected from them and what they are to expect when lovers come," while young men learn that thrift, industry, and honesty are the qualities needed to get on in the world (p. 186). As to which is the greater responsibility of the novel – to amuse or to instruct – Trollope sometimes seems at variance with himself, even within the same work. In *Thackeray*, for instance, he writes that "the object of the novel should be to instruct in morals while it amuses" (1879: 107); yet a few pages later he urges a different view: "a novel, if it fatigues, is unpardonable. Its only excuse is to be found in the amusement it affords" (1879: 187).

Such ambivalence is characteristic of much of Trollope's criticism. Despite his own diffidence about the novel as art, he berates Thackeray for failing to take his work seriously enough, accusing him of "little confidences" with his readers, which lead to "an absence of the dignity to which even a novel may aspire" (1879: 197–8). For Trollope, the novel may never be able to reach the sublime heights of poetry; nevertheless the novelist, like the poet, who "can deal adequately with tragic elements is a greater artist, and reaches a higher aim than the writer whose efforts never carry him above the mild walks of everyday life" (1947: 190).

Placing the tragic at an artistic height above the everyday, or the comic, is in direct opposition to the theorizing of George Meredith. One of Meredith's stated goals as a novelist was to use comedy, "finely tempered, showing sunlight of the mind," to expose those who are "out of proportion, overblown, affected, pretentious, bombastical, hypocritical, pedantic, fantastically delicate." The novel should show such people what they truly are "whenever it sees them self-deceived or hoodwinked, given to run riot in idolatries, drifting into vanities . . . planning short-sightedly, plotting dementedly, whenever they are at variance with their professions, and violate the unwritten but perceptible laws binding them in consideration one to another" (1980: 13–14). Meredith also believed, however, that novels should aspire to the level of art and that those aspirations are undercut when they become too didactic. He labeled Kingsley's *Two Years Ago* as just such a failure, for "Mr. Kingsley is always in the pulpit" (1857a: 609). On the other hand – and quite unlike most of his contemporaries – he praised *Madame Bovary* precisely because Flaubert allows Emma's "wickedness" to become manifest without an attending homily. He found similar merit with Trollope's first two Barchester Chronicle novels, singling out *The Warden* and *Barchester Towers* for their reluctance to "harangue and scold," and for the author's entrusting of the moral to "the individual of his story" and for successfully interweaving his satire (1857b: 601).

Meredith did find fault with Trollope in that review, however, for "wanting in certain of the higher elements that made a novelist. He does not exhibit much sway over the emotional parts of our nature" (1857b: 595). For Meredith, this power of emotion must arise from the characters. Furthermore, they should not be "in hopeless subjection to purpose" (1857a: 610), but the plot should arise from their interactions as characters. Thus, it was to this end that Meredith insisted that examining the interiority, the psychology, of characters must be as important as the intricacies of plot. For him, the real "subject matter of novels is the human mind, 'internal history'" (1910: 17–19). It was this proclivity toward psychological analysis that underlay Meredith's admiration for Stendhal, and which caused him to label George Eliot the greatest of female writers.

Despite the differences in tone and subject matter between George Eliot's and Meredith's novels, they shared one important belief about the function of art. As she articulates it, "the greatest benefit we owe to the artist . . . is the extension of our sympathies . . . a picture of human life such as a great artist can give, surprises even the trivial and the selfish into that attention to what is apart from themselves, which may be called the raw material of moral sentiment" (1856: 54). For Eliot the value of art lies precisely in its ability to connect the subjectivities of disparate beings. Her goal as a novelist was to help her readers to be better able to imagine and feel "the pains and joys of those who are different from themselves in everything but the broad fact of being struggling erring human creatures" (1954–78: vol. 3, 111). For her, in both form and content, a novel should offer a moral standard for human interaction without stooping to didacticism. She believed that a novel's situations should arise from "some natural combination of character with circumstances" and not because the "men and women speak and act in order to prove a moral or to rouse some sentiment in the reader" (1855: 612). As much as she detested the unapologetic didacticism of many of her contemporaries, she held the more sentimental novels of the period in equal contempt. In perhaps her most famous essay on the novel, "Silly Novels by Lady Novelists," published in the *Westminster Review* in October 1856, Eliot scathingly ridicules "mind and millinery" novels for their utter disregard for the novel as art, asserting that "in the majority of women's books you see that kind of facility which springs from the absence of any high standard" (1979: 297). She also takes exception to these novels for their failure to attend to the details of representation: "if their peers and peeresses are improbable, their literary men, tradespeople, and cottagers are impossible, and their intellect seems to have the peculiar impartiality of reproducing both what they *have* seen and heard and what they have *not* seen and heard with equal unfaithfulness" (1979: 281).

For Eliot, that attention to detail was precisely what the novel calls for in its composition – since it is only then that characters and their situations are believable. That is, it is only then that the novel becomes realistic. In her own first novel, *Adam Bede*, Eliot makes her famous justification of realism in chapter 17, in which the "story pauses a little." There she writes, "I aspire to give no more than a faithful account of men and things as they have mirrored themselves in my mind" (1985: 221). She is "content to tell [her] story without trying to make things seem better than they were; dreading nothing indeed, but falsity" (p. 222). She would not, she writes, even if she had the choice, create a world better than the one in which we "get up in the morning to do our daily work," nor would she people such a world with the exceptional. Rather, "these fellow mortals, every one, must be accepted as they are" (p. 222). This is what art is meant for; it should "always remind us" of the common people, the everyday. "Therefore let us always have men ready to give the loving pains of a life to the faithful representing of commonplace things" (p. 224).

Another major novelist of the latter part of the century who was also deeply invested in realism was Henry James. Early in his career, James wrote dismissively of Dickens's last complete novel, *Our Mutual Friend*, finding fault with it as a work peopled with eccentrics and unbelievable characters: "What a world were this world if *Our Mutual Friend* were a reflection of it." For James, the community Dickens creates is no community at all. It is precisely at odds with the sort of world that Eliot was striving to represent in her novels. For James, the characters in *Our Mutual Friend* have "nothing in common with each other except that they have nothing in common with mankind at large" (1865: 786). His stance toward realism evolved, however, and by 1884 he could write that "the measure of reality is difficult to fix . . . The reality of Don Quixote or of Mr. Micawber is a very delicate shade; it is a reality so coloured by the author's vision . . . one would hesitate to propose it as a model" (1979: 294). The essay containing that somewhat qualified pronouncement on realism, "The Art of Fiction," sets forth James's apologia for the "new fiction" that emerged in the early 1880s, and of which he and William Dean Howells were proclaimed the major practitioners. Arthur Tilley, in 1883, found their novels comparable

> in the elaborate analysis of character, in the absence of plot, in the sparing use of incident, in the studied realism, in the conscientious subordination of the artist to his art, in the acute powers of observation, and in the humor, which never forced or obtrusive, seems to exist, not because the writer's own gifts lie specially in that direction, but because as a healthy and impartial observer of human life, he cannot fail to take note of its humorous side. (1979: 255)

For James, the early 1880s were opening new vistas for the novelist, who should consider him or herself to have much in common with both the painter and the philosopher. The form of the novel must be considered after the fact (of composition), for it is then that "we can estimate quality, we can apply the test of execution" (1979: 292). A novel is "a personal impression of life," and it is the "intensity of the impression" that helps to "constitute its value" (p. 292). Further, argues James, criticism of a novel that takes up character or plot or form to the exclusion of its other aspects misses one of the most fundamental characteristics of the novel – that it is an "organic whole." "A novel is a living thing, all one and continuous," he writes, "in each of the parts there is something of each of the other parts" (p. 296).

James's essay helped to establish a new arena for the novelist and to once again insist on the importance of the novel as art. In James's view, the novel searches for and reveals truth as much as does history or philosophy. But the moral didacticism that found its way into earlier novels no longer has pride of place in fiction. As James puts it, "the only classification of the novel that I can understand is into the interesting and the uninteresting" (1979: 297). The moral qualities that so many earlier critics insisted upon in fiction, for James are not a matter of art: "questions of art are questions (in the widest sense) of execution; questions of morality are quite another affair" (p. 304). Consequently, the subject-matter of novels need only meet the condition of being interesting, though, as James points out, "no good novel will ever proceed from a superficial mind" (p. 302). The result of views like James's was an increase in novels that focused on the interiority of characters, providing much more detailed examinations of the motivations, desires, and fears of those populating works of fiction. Often carefully structured and finely wrought, these works became the touchstones of literary taste from the mid-1880s through the end of the century. Works by Scott and Dickens fell out of critical favor and were often characterized as out of proportion aesthetically and too dependent on conventional plot devices to rise to the level of "art."

The Emergence of the Critics

While literary critics *qua* critics began to exert considerable influence during the last two or three decades of the nineteenth century and found an increasing number of venues in which to express their views, criticism as a profession was taking shape much earlier in the century in such venerable periodicals as the *Edinburgh Review*, the *Quarterly Review*, and, toward midcentury, the *Westminster Review*. These journals were remarkable primarily for their political and social criticism (the *Edinburgh Review* was Whig, the *Quarterly* Tory or Conservative, and the *Westminster* the organ of the Philosophic Radicals or Utilitarians); but, as novels became an undeniable part of Victorian culture, they began to review contemporary fiction in their pages. In 1853 the *Edinburgh Review*, oldest of the quarterlies, announced that fiction could not be considered "an insignificant or trivial province of literature" (Anon. 1853: 380). Two years later the *Quarterly Review* declared that the very best works of fiction were "in a very high rank among the achievements of the human intellect" (Elwin 1855: 350). Partly as a result of this newfound respectability, novels came under increasing scrutiny by these quarterlies. Articles reviewing novels often were anonymous, and in many instances the critics have passed into relative obscurity. In some cases writers whose expertise lay primarily in other fields, such as history or political economy, turned their hand to literary criticism. Nassau Senior, for instance, the political economist who co-authored the 1834 New Poor Law, reviewed fiction and even wrote a book on fiction. The issues that confronted the critics were myriad. Many believed criticism of fiction should be expressed from a morally didactic standpoint; others contended that the very best novels achieved artistic merit only when they grappled with tragedy in the grand manner of classical Greek drama or the plays of Shakespeare. Still other critics focused on the literary merits of sentimentality and melodrama, features characteristic of many of the most popular novels of the day. And some attempted to evaluate novels on their own terms while simultaneously holding them to high artistic standards.

Three important but now lesser-known critics of the novel during the 1850s and 1860s were W. C. Roscoe, Walter Bagehot, and Richard H. Hutton. All three were associated with the *National Review*, which ran from 1855 to 1864 and which became such an important organ for literary criticism that Matthew Arnold published "The Function of Criticism at the Present Time," "Joubert," and "Eugénie de Guérin" in its pages, despite the rather meager remuneration he received for the essays. In an 1856 essay on Defoe, Roscoe attributed the rapid growth in popularity of the novel to the rise of political democracy. As individual liberties increased, he argued, there was a concomitant increase in interest both in the ability of a person to shape his or her own character and in "the individual character of others." This had been the purview of drama, which was now found to be lacking. As a result, "an intimate union of the dramatic and narrative modes of delineation has been contrived to give scope to the new requirements of art." As external forces on men and women are reduced by democracy, however, the differences between people become less obvious, thus demanding a more subtle and "delicate expression . . . to delineate [the] diversities" among them (quoted in Stang 1959: 51–2). Thus the responsibilities of the novelist increase: he or she must be prepared to represent "the actual interior life and individual character of a living soul" (Roscoe 1856: 180). According to Roscoe, those like Defoe, as well as Thackeray and Bulwer-Lytton, were too content to dwell on the "surface of things" and thus failed to live up to the demands of their art.

Roscoe also took issue with the style of many of the novels of his own day. Writing of Bulwer-Lytton, he suggested that the failure of that novelist's imagination was directly related to his rhetorical and linguistic inaccuracies. As a result, Bulwer-Lytton's characters are merely superficial types, and do not reflect "universal and essential characteristics" (1859: 288–9). Bagehot was of the same opinion about Scott. Despite his important place as an innovator, Scott gives us nothing more than "the exterior delineation of character" without any "delineation of the soul" (1858: 468–9). Further, for Bagehot, Scott had major defects in style. On those "great occasions" when "there should be passages in which the words seem to cleave to the matter," Scott was satisfied with "the first sufficient words that came uppermost" (pp. 471–2). The "exquisite accuracy and inexplicable appropriateness" that characterize a great style for Bagehot always eluded Scott (p. 471). For examples of the possibility of greatness in the novel, one must look to George Eliot, who upon the publication of *Adam Bede* (1859) became, for the *National Review*, "the greatest living writer of fiction" (Bagehot 1864: 533).

Notably, the *National Review* critics greatly emphasized characterization over plot. These critics were particularly put off by those works that relied on "artificial enhancements of interest which do not arise fairly out of the moral constitutions of the characters" (Bagehot 1860: 192). When Hutton became editor of the *Spectator* in 1861, he maintained similar literary standards. For instance, his essays on Trollope's Barchester series indicate that he admired Trollope's ability to take his readers "into an interior almost beyond the artist's sight," getting to "a deeper passion in the depths in which he sounds" (1862: 1136–7). Nevertheless, he also sometimes found Trollope lacking in willingness to incur the responsibilities of "delineating the darkest features" [of tragedy] (1865: 422). In comparison, Hutton had very little good to say about the sensation fiction of writers such as Braddon, Wood, Collins, or Ouida (see chapter 15 by Winifred Hughes in this volume). And while much of the contemporary hubbub over such works tended toward moral condemnation, Hutton found them artistically deficient. Their recourse to melodrama, "the use of illegitimate means to produce an effect upon a reader," he found to be little more than a cheap parlor trick (1868: 931). He also condemned Dickens for retreating into heavy-handed and self-indulgent sentimentality, despite praising the author for his ability to draw "powerfully . . . the mood of a man haunted by a fixed idea, a shadowy apprehension, a fear, a dream, a remorse" (1894: vol. 1, 89).

In the writing of these critics, as in much of the rest of the criticism composed during the Victorian period, once again the issue often comes down to one of realism.

Even Thackeray, who was frequently hailed in the periodicals as one of the most accomplished of the early realists, did not escape the *National Review* critics' demand for characters fully and deeply drawn and for novels whose plots were driven by the plausible actions and foibles of its characters. It was at the hands of these critics that the sensation novelists received much of their roughest usage, and where Dickens's repute as an artist, despite Hutton's occasional praise, began a decline through the last third of the nineteenth century and well into the twentieth. By the mid-1850s, realism seems to have won the day as the preferred representational mode of the "serious" novelist. One of its most ardent and eloquent champions was George Henry Lewes.

It is difficult to overestimate Lewes's contribution to theories of the novel in the nineteenth century. Extraordinarily prolific, he was one of the most influential of all the critics; his reviews were far-ranging, and many of his critical judgments have been borne out by subsequent generations of readers and critics. He was among the very first to identify the artistic mastery evident in *Moby Dick*, and his famous review of *Jane Eyre* in *Fraser's Magazine* in 1847 helped to make the career of Charlotte Brontë. Even that early, Lewes was formulating a conception of realism that he would share with his companion, George Eliot, and which would become his critical watchword. He notes that Brontë's novel is rife with "melodrama and improbability which smack of the circulating library." Nevertheless, and much more importantly, the author was "unquestionably setting forth her own experience." What is important here is not so much the autobiographical aspect Lewes detects, but his contention that "unless a novel be built out of real experience it can have no real success," a sentiment that looks forward to the full-blown realism he was to advocate from the 1850s forward (1979: 692).

The notion of the novelist drawing on his or her own experience lies at the heart of Lewes's conception of realistic representation. "A novel," for Lewes, "must fuse one's own personal experience and observation" (quoted in Stang 1959: 171). But as Lewes's ideas about realism became more complex, he was careful to point out that experience need not necessarily be empirical. In reviewing John Ruskin's *Modern Painters*, he affirms Ruskin's admonition not to paint what one does not see as applicable to the fiction writer as much as to the painter. He amplifies this remark, however, explaining that this does not mean that "only actual visible objects, or events actually experienced" should be chosen for representation. The imagination makes it possible to feel and see much more. One should not "feign to see or feel what he does not see or feel," of course. Rather, the artist's goal should be to communicate the depth of his or her imagination to the work's readers (1856: 545). For Lewes, realism is the basis for all art; art is "a representation of reality" and should not be an attempt to "elevate the public by 'beautifying' life" (1858: 493). At the same time, however, Lewes felt that realism loses its force when it concentrates on the mundane or the trivial, that it fails when it confuses the familiar with the true. Verisimilitude, he contended, should not be an end in itself. Realism, thus, is not distinctive merely by its attention to details. It calls on the reader to look closely at an unadorned view of life – "real life" – and in so doing reveals something of the ideal as well, something of the truth of existence.

At heart in many of the discussions of realism in the 1850s and beyond was its opposition to "idealism." In his 1851 essay *"Pendennis* and *Copperfield*: Thackeray and Dickens," David Masson draws from the language of art criticism to refer to real and ideal styles in fiction. He uses the two literary giants of the midcentury to emphasize that dichotomy. Unlike so many of the other critics of the period, and in direct contradistinction to Lewes, Masson thought realism was the death knell of the novel. For him, realism was necessarily bounded by sameness and monotony; it dampened the imagination and forced an uninspired attention to the unexceptional. For him, the best literature lay in the realm of the "ideal," characterized by Dickens's work. The ideal is less concerned with the veracity of the representation of quotidian life than with the possibility of "taking the mind out of itself into a region of higher possibilities, wherein objects shall be more glorious, and modes of action more transcendent, than any we see, and yet shall see in nature" (Masson 1979: 16). Eight years later, in *The British Novelists and Their Styles*, Masson goes much further in his taxonomy of the novel, though he retains realism and idealism as opposing styles. He ranks the novel with the very highest of literary achievements, declaring that at its very best a novel is a prose epic. Further, the capabilities of prose fiction are equivalent to those of narrative poetry, and indeed the novel can "concern itself more intimately than Verse with what is variable in time and place" (Masson 1859: 16). Although in his early *British Review* essay Masson had found Thackeray's talent more constrained, a product of a "closer and more compact" mind than Dickens's, he had praised it according to the criteria of the "real" style it exemplified. By 1859, however, Masson had become more disenchanted with realism, especially as a dominant novelistic style, calling for novelists to take up "the grand, the elemental, the ideal," subjects that he deemed "large, comprehensive, primitive, impressive, enduring" (1859: 296, 298).

Late Victorian Criticism: Realism, Idealism, and Aesthetic Form

In some ways the war waged over realism and idealism was a series of misfires and misunderstandings. Especially around midcentury, proponents of realism often simply considered the job of the novel as to reflect as accurately as possible a world and characters recognizable to its readers. For the idealists, this was seen as an abdication of literature's responsibility to be elevating and morally improving. Leslie Stephen, for instance, writing in 1877, epitomizes some of these attitudes. In his famous collection of essays, *Hours in a Library*, he derides Trollope's fiction for its fidelity to the real. For him, an "actual illusion" should not be the "object of a really good novelist" (Stephen 1904: vol. 1, 88). Too much of the particular, not enough of the universal, such as the characterization of Paul Emmanuel in *Villette*, means there is "too much of the temporary and accidental – too little of the permanent and essential" (vol. 3, 295–6) – and, consequently, one must presume, too little of the "embodiment of one answer to a profound and enduring problem" (vol. 3, 296). For Stephen, and many other critics of the last quarter of the century, an over-attention to detail keeps the novelist from penetrating to a realm of truth and beauty, miring him instead in the grime of "reality."

John Ruskin, whose theories of aesthetics and representations in *Modern Painters* helped to galvanize the realist theories of G. H. Lewes and George Eliot, was often especially repulsed by the practice of literary realism, and its later avatar, naturalism. In *Fiction, Fair and Foul* (1880–1), he takes issue not only with the representational practices of contemporary fiction, but with its choice of subject-matter as well. Ruskin lambasts the novelists of his day for their use of "the reactions of moral disease upon itself, and the conditions of languidly monstrous characters developed in an atmosphere of low vitality" (1908: 268). It should be pointed out, however, that Ruskin objects equally to realism and romance, finding most contemporary novels to be salacious: images of the tumult of city life pandering to readers' need for excitement. As he puts it, "the monotony of life in the central streets of any great modern city . . . especially London . . . leaves the craving for a sincere, yet changeful interest." For the "thoroughly trained Londoner," the excitement that lessens his monotony is "by varying to his fancy the modes, and defining for his dulness the horrors, of Death" (1908: 270–1). Few of Ruskin's contemporaries escape his disdain: Thackeray and Dickens alike are infected by the disease of the modern infatuation with the foulness of urban life. George Eliot fares no better. He writes of *The Mill on the Floss* that it is "perhaps the most striking instance extant of this study of cutaneous disease. There is not a single person in the book of the smallest importance to anybody in the world but themselves, or whose qualities deserved so much as a line of printer's type in their description" (1908: 377).

The implications of Ruskin's argument are important, even if his novel criticism seems a bit old-fashioned for its time. Ruskin's distaste for the fiction of his era is grounded in his conception of the artist's organic relation to the world, to nature, and ultimately to some sense of the divine. The fact of the increasing urbanization of modern life was a symptom of a falling away from the beauty and truth with which Ruskin believed the artist should connect. Later critics such as Arthur Symons may well have repudiated Ruskin's aesthetics for its romanticism, but Symons's and others' responses to Emile Zola's brand of naturalism at the end of the century indicate that late Victorian critics were still heavily invested in the personal intuition of the artist. They typically assessed Zola's "scientific method" on one of two fronts. Some critics found that he was unable to fulfill the objectivity called for by his method – that in the act of observing, the temperament of the writer must intercede. On the other hand, the intensity of his "nature through formula" observations lead to a kind of hyperrealism which can exist only in the author's mind, and which thus succumbs to the ideal. For critics like George Moore, J. A. Symonds, and Havelock Ellis, Zola, despite his insistence on realism, is always, finally, about the ideal: Zola's selection and formal organization of his material support their assertion that the novel is ordered to sustain a central idea, which is always an enduring, everlasting problem in the same sense that Stephen describes.

This movement away from realism to the "subjective" or "ideal" is partly, if perhaps less loftily, realized in the resurrection of the romance by such late Victorian writers as H. Rider Haggard, Robert Louis Stevenson, and Rudyard Kipling. Elaine Showalter suggests that the deluge of adventure romances at the end of the century can be read as a reaction to the death of George Eliot and her influence over the novel during the 1860s and 1870s. Further, as Showalter points out, it was during those years that the number of women authors rose dramatically, and the emergence of the "new woman" helped to reshape the social roles of women (1990: 75–80). By 1880 and the death of George Eliot, however, men began to assert themselves as masters of the romance genre. As Showalter puts it, "now that Queen Realism was dead, King Romance might recover his virility and power" (p. 79). Certainly writers such as Stevenson and Haggard led the way critically. In his "A Humble Remonstrance," Stevenson argues against James's "The Art of Fiction," insisting that no art can "compete with life"; thus the writer "in this age of the particular" should attempt "a simplification of some point of life" rather than a copy of it (1979: 343, 349). And, like the critics who championed idealism, Stevenson emphasized the selection and organization of the material that the author uses for his work. For Stevenson, "the life of man is not the subject of novels, but the inexhaustible magazine from which subjects are to be selected," and "with each new subject . . . the true artist will vary his method and change the point of attack" (p. 345). Haggard's manifesto, "About Fiction" (1887), also pits the romance squarely against realism, offering to rescue readers from French naturalism and "the laboured nothingness" of writers like James and Howells. The implication is that romance will remasculinize literature. Finally, in his 1890 essay, "The New Watchwords of Fiction," Hall Caine offers what may well be the most striking, if not most strident, articulation of the romance writers' theory of fiction: *"Fiction is not nature, it is not character, it is not imagined history; it is fallacy, poetic fallacy, pathetic fallacy, a lie if you like, a beautiful lie, a lie that is at once false and true – false to fact, true to faith"* (1979: 477; emphasis in original).

This statement clearly echoes Oscar Wilde's dictum from "The Decay of Lying" that the aim of art should be "the telling of beautiful untrue things." Wilde's essay, along with Caine's diatribe, may well have helped to hammer the last nail into realism's coffin in the 1890s. Although realism certainly survived, and continues to flourish, the impressionism and symbolism that led to modernist experiments in the novel were well on their way by the *fin de siècle,* and the morally invested realism epitomized by George Eliot and practiced by Meredith and Trollope was on the wane. Even Thomas Hardy, whose work is often connected to the naturalist movement, emphasized the transcendental ends of art. He likened the novel to poetry in its ability to "irradiate" nature's defects " 'with the light that never was' on their surface but is seen to be latent in them by the spiritual eye" (quoted in Hardy 1928: 150–1).

It is particularly interesting to note the social implications of the trajectory of the modes of the novel and the shifts in critical favor during the Victorian era. Again, in the early years of the period, Scott's was by far the most influential voice. Yet even in the 1830s and 1840s, the social and aesthetic value of romance was being questioned. By the late 1850s and certainly throughout the 1870s, realism became the mode of the "serious" novel, the work that aspired to the status of art. Despite the resistance of novelists such as Dickens and Bulwer-Lytton to what they perceived as the despotism of realism, it was not until the 1880s that romance reasserted itself as the dominant representational mode for the novel. As we have seen, by that time the arguments of the idealist–romantics had effectively coopted even the naturalism of Zola. One upshot of this turn was to underscore the importance of the novel in arguments about aesthetics, giving it an increasingly predominant role in such discussions. This increased importance, coupled with the novel's relative ubiquity and availability (as, say, in comparison with painting or even music during this period), afforded late Victorian critics of the novel the opportunity to shape cultural tastes in ways that did not extend to critics and practitioners of other arts.

The success of the efforts of these late Victorian critics, however, is at best ambiguous. Despite the broad audience that still existed for the novel, and the resulting consequence that, whether promoting realism, romance, or an idealized form of naturalism, critics and novelists alike had the opportunity to continue the tradition of the social mission for fiction that had begun asserting itself in earnest in the 1840s, criticism at the end of the century increasingly turned to technical analyses of novels. It is only in our own time that literary historians have taken up issues that touch upon both the form of the novel and the culture it participated in – and helped produce. For instance, a modern critic may well consider the gendering of romance as masculine, the effects of pitting boys' novels against the "teapot conversation" novels of Howells and James, or the place of the new woman fiction of authors like Olive Schreiner and Charlotte Mew. Such expansive thinking about the novel was not necessarily available to late Victorian critics. As John Charles Olmsted has pointed out, by the mid-1890s "no great consensus about the novel had emerged" (1979: vol. 3, xix). Even as late as 1894, Hubert Crackanthorpe could write that "the popular mind" is "persuaded that in order to produce good fiction, an ingenious idea or 'plot,' as it is termed is the one thing needed. The rest is a mere matter of handwriting" (Crackanthorpe 1979: 544). However true his observation was, for nineteenth-century critics of the novel, the battle that was fought over the status of fiction was vital to their understanding of art and its claims. And Crackanthorpe's cynicism about the taste of common readers illustrates how seriously critics took their responsibility to those readers: to teach and morally improve them, to allow access to truth and beauty, to make them conversant with "the best that has been thought and said," to provide them with what Arnold called "culture." It remains to twenty-first century critics to appraise their success, the forms such culture might take, and the role of criticism in the formation of that culture.

REFERENCES

Anon. (1853), "Recent Novels: *Agatha's Husband*," *Edinburgh Review*, 97, 380–90.

Bagehot, Walter (1858), "The Waverley Novels," *National Review*, 6, 442–72.

Bagehot, Walter (1860), "The Novels of George Eliot," *National Review*, 11, 191–219.

Bagehot, Walter (1864), "Sterne and Thackeray," *National Review*, 18, 523–53.

Brontë, Charlotte (1985), "Editor's Preface to the New Edition of *Wuthering Heights*," in Emily Brontë, *Wuthering Heights* (Harmondsworth: Penguin). (First publ. 1850.)

Bulwer-Lytton, Edward (1862), "Preface," *A Strange Story*. (London: S. Low, Son & Co.).

Caine, Hall (1979), "The New Watchwords of Fiction," in J. C. Olmsted, ed., *A Victorian Art of Fiction: Essays on the Novel in British Periodicals*, 3 vols. (vol. 1: 1830–1850; vol. 2: 1851–1869; vol. 3: 1870–1890) (New York: Garland), 469–80. (First publ. 1890.)

Carlyle, Thomas (1979), "Lockhart's *Life of Scott*," in J. C. Olmsted, ed., *A Victorian Art of Fiction: Essays on the Novel in British Periodicals*, 3 vols. (vol. 1: 1830–1850; vol. 2: 1851–1869; vol. 3: 1870–1890) (New York: Garland), 203–14. (First publ. 1838.)

Carlyle, Thomas (1980), "On History," in Alan Shelston, ed., *Thomas Carlyle: Selected Writings* (Harmondsworth: Penguin). (First publ. 1830.)

Crackanthorpe, Hubert (1979), "Reticence in Literature: Some Roundabout Remarks," in J. C. Olmsted, ed., *A Victorian Art of Fiction: Essays on the Novel in British Periodicals*, 3 vols. (vol. 1: 1830–1850; vol. 2: 1851–1869; vol. 3: 1870–1890) (New York: Garland), 537–44. (First publ. 1894.)

Dickens, Charles (1938), *The Letters of Charles Dickens*, ed. Walter Dexter, vols. 10–12 of *The Nonesuch Dickens* (London: Nonesuch).

Dickens, Charles (1965), *The Letters of Charles Dickens*, 11 vols., ed. Madeline House and Graham Storey (Oxford: Clarendon; Pilgrim Edition).

Dickens, Charles (1985), *Bleak House* (Harmondsworth: Penguin). (First publ. 1853.)

Eliot, George (1855), "Belles Lettres," *Westminster Review*, 64, Oct., 596–615.

Eliot, George (1856), "The Natural History of German Life," *Westminster Review*, 66, 51–79.

Eliot, George (1954–78), *The George Eliot Letters*, ed. Gordon S. Haight, 9 vols. (New Haven: Yale University Press; London: Oxford University Press).

Eliot, George (1979), "Silly Novels by Lady Novelists," in J. C. Olmsted, ed., *A Victorian Art of Fiction: Essays on the Novel in British Periodicals*, 3 vols. (vol. 1: 1830–1850; vol. 2: 1851–1869; vol. 3: 1870–1890) (New York: Garland), 277–98). (First publ. 1856.)

Eliot, George (1985), *Adam Bede* (Harmondsworth: Penguin). (First publ. 1859.)

Elwin, Whitwell (1855), "*The Newcomes*," *Quarterly Review*, 97, 350–78.

Haggard, H. Rider (1979), "About Fiction," in J. C. Olmsted, ed., *A Victorian Art of Fiction: Essays on the Novel in British Periodicals*, 3 vols. (vol. 1: 1830–1850; vol. 2: 1851–1869; vol. 3: 1870–1890) (New York: Garland), 377–88. (First publ. 1887.)

Hardy, Florence E. (1928), *The Early Life of Thomas Hardy, 1840–1891* (London: Macmillan).

Hutton, Richard Holt (1862), "*Orley Farm*," *Spectator*, 35, 1136–8.

Hutton, Richard Holt (1865), "*Can You Forgive Her?*," *Spectator*, 38, 978–9.

Hutton, Richard Holt (1868), "Sensation Novels," *Spectator*, 41, 931–2.

Hutton, Richard Holt (1894), *Criticisms on Contemporary Thought and Thinkers*, 2 vols. (London: Macmillan).

James, Henry (1865), "*Our Mutual Friend*," *The Nation*, 21 Dec., 786–7.

James, Henry (1979), "The Art of Fiction," in J. C. Olmsted, ed., *A Victorian Art of Fiction: Essays on the Novel in British Periodicals*, 3 vols. (vol. 1: 1830–1850; vol. 2: 1851–1869; vol. 3: 1870–1890) (New York: Garland), 285–306. (First publ. 1884.)

Lewes, George Henry (1856), "Imaginative Artists," *The Leader*, 7, 545–6.

Lewes, George Henry (1858), "Realism in Art: Recent German Fiction," *Westminster Review*, 70, 488–518.

Lewes, George Henry (1979), "Recent Novels: French and English," in J. C. Olmsted, ed., *A Victorian Art of Fiction: Essays on the Novel in British Periodicals*, 3 vols. (vol. 1: 1830–1850; vol. 2: 1851–1869; vol. 3: 1870–1890) (New York: Garland), 686–95. (First publ. 1847.)

Lytton, Earl of (1913), *The Life of Edward Bulwer, First Lord Lytton*, 2 vols. (London: Macmillan).

Masson, David (1859), *British Novelists and their Styles* (London: Macmillan).

Masson, David (1979), "*Pendennis* and *Copperfield*: Thackeray and Dickens," in J. C. Olmsted, ed., *A Victorian Art of Fiction: Essays on the Novel in British Periodicals*, 3 vols. (vol. 1: 1830–1850; vol. 2: 1851–1869; vol. 3: 1870–1890) (New York: Garland), 1–36. (First publ. 1851.)

Meredith, George (1857a), "Belles Lettres," *Westminster Review*, 67, April, 602–20.

Meredith, George (1857b), "Belles Lettres," *Westminster Review*, 68, Oct., 586–604.

Meredith, George (1910), *Diana of the Crossways*, memorial edn. (New York: Scribner's & Sons).

Meredith, George (1980), "An Essay on Comedy," in Wylie Sypher, ed., *Comedy* (Baltimore: Johns Hopkins University Press). (First publ. 1879.)

Olmsted, John Charles (1979), "Introduction," to vol. 3 of *A Victorian Art of Fiction: Essays on the Novel in British Periodicals*, 3 vols (vol. 1: 1830–1850; vol. 2: 1851–1869; vol. 3: 1870–1890), xiii–xix.

Roscoe, William Caldwell (1856), "W. M. Thackeray, Artist and Moralist," *National Review*, 2, 177–213.

Roscoe, William Caldwell (1859), "Sir E. B. Lytton, Novelist, Philosopher, and Poet," *National Review*, 8, 279–313.

Ruskin, John (1908), *Fiction, Fair and Foul*, in *The Works of John Ruskin*, library edn. (London: George Allen), vol. 34.

Showalter, Elaine (1990), *Sexual Anarchy: Gender and Culture at the Fin de Siècle* (New York: Penguin).

Stang, Richard (1959), *The Theory of the Novel in England 1850–1870* (New York: Columbia University Press).

Stephen, Leslie (1904), *Hours in a Library*, 4 vols. (New York: Putnam).

Stevenson, Robert Louis (1979), "A Humble Remonstrance," in J. C. Olmsted, ed., *A Victorian Art of Fiction: Essays on the Novel in British Periodicals*, 3 vols. (vol. 1: 1830–1850; vol. 2: 1851–1869; vol. 3: 1870–1890) (New York: Garland), 339–350. (First publ. 1884.)

Thackeray, William Makepeace (1899), *The Roundabout Papers*, in *The Works of William Makepeace Thackeray*, biographical edn, 13 vols. (New York and London: Harper Brothers), vol. 12.

Thackeray, William Makepeace (1945–46), *The Letters and Private Papers of William Makepeace Thackeray*, ed. Gordon N. Ray, 4 vols. (Cambridge, Mass.: Harvard University Press).

Tilley, Arthur (1979), "The New School of Fiction," in J. C. Olmsted, ed., *A Victorian Art of Fiction: Essays on the Novel in British Periodicals*, 3 vols. (vol. 1: 1830–1850; vol. 2: 1851–1869; vol. 3: 1870–1890) (New York: Garland), 253–66. (First publ. 1883.)

Trollope, Anthony (1879), *Thackeray* (New York: Harper).

Trollope, Anthony (1947), *An Autobiography*, ed. Bradford A. Booth (Los Angeles: University of California Press). (First publ. 1883.)

Wilde, Oscar (1889), "The Decay of Lying," *Nineteenth Century*, 25, 35–56.

Further Reading

Arnold, Matthew (1987), "The Function of Criticism at the Present Time," in *Selected Prose*, ed. P. J. Keating (Harmondsworth: Penguin).

Baldick, Chris (1983), *The Social Mission of English Criticism* (Oxford: Clarendon).

Dale, Peter Allan (1977), *The Victorian Critic and the Idea of History: Carlyle, Arnold, Pater* (Cambridge, Mass.: Harvard University Press).

Graham, George Kenneth (1965), *English Criticism of the Novel, 1865–1900* (Oxford: Clarendon).

Nadel, Ira Bruce, ed. (1986), *Victorian Fiction: A Collection of Essays from the Period* (New York: Garland).

Orel, Harold (1984), *Victorian Literary Critics: George Henry Lewes, Walter Bagehot, Richard Holt Hutton, Leslie Stephen, Andrew Lang, George Saintsbury, and Edmund Gosse* (London: Macmillan).

Parrinder, Patrick (1991), *Authors and Authority: English and American Criticism 1750–1990* (Basingstoke: Macmillan).

Senior, Nassau W. (1864), *Essays on Fiction* (London: Longman, Green).

Small, Ian (1991), *Conditions for Criticism: Authority, Knowledge and Literature in the Late Nineteenth Century* (Oxford: Clarendon).

Tillotson, Geoffrey (1951), *Criticism and the Nineteenth Century* (London: Athlone).

Tuchman, Gaye and Fortin, Nina E. (1989), *Edging Women Out: Victorian Novelists, Publishers, and Social Change* (New Haven: Yale University Press).

Wellek, Rene (1965), *A History of Modern Criticism, 1750–1950*, 8 vols.: vols. 3–4 (New Haven: Yale University Press).

Williams, Raymond (1983), *Culture and Society, 1780–1950*, new edn. (New York: Columbia University Press). (First publ. 1958.)

24
Modern and Postmodern Theories of Prose Fiction
Audrey Jaffe

In twentieth-century criticism, the novel appears most frequently as a genre whose significant features are its attention to circumstantial detail and empirical experience – its "realism" – and its ostensible freedom from and rebellion against the constraining conventions of other genres, including previous forms of the novel and, especially, poetry. Its origins and ideological commitments are said to lie with the middle class, its preoccupations with bourgeois modes of perception and action. For a long time, the generally accepted view of the novel's development was that articulated by Ian Watt in *The Rise of the Novel* (1957). Watt argued that the novel arose in the eighteenth century along with other social, economic, and philosophical expressions of individualism, most significantly capitalism and the modern philosophical tradition of Descartes and Locke. Long unchallenged, Watt's scenario relies on the novels of Defoe, Fielding, and Richardson and on what appeared to him to be the seamless connection between social, economic, and philosophical forms of individualism and the novel's attention to empirical experience. In the 1970s and 1980s, however, in the wake of Michel Foucault's revisionist histories and the insights of feminism, deconstruction, Marxism, and the "new historicism," Watt's scheme was challenged on a number of grounds. In contrast to Watt's view of the novel's masculine origins, for instance, critics have recovered a significant tradition of female authorship. The novel has been re-examined as a capitalist genre, structured by the writer's relation to the marketplace and the development of modern advertising. These revisions of novel history have been accompanied by a wide-ranging rereading of the Victorian novel – a form whose position at the early stages of mass culture and concern with social issues has in recent years positioned it as a kind of ur-novel: a test case for understanding the genre per se. The novels of the Victorian period have invited revisionary discussions of the nature of novelistic realism; of the novel as an exemplary commodity form; of female authorship and the status of women; and, in general, of the novel's role in structuring readers' relations to ideologies of class, gender, national identity, and race.

In American universities in the 1940s and 1950s, in keeping with the new-critical emphasis on the unity, totality, and isolation of the aesthetic object, poetry was the premier object of literary study. Gradually, the new critics widened their analytical framework to include the novel, aided in the case of Victorian fiction by the intervention of the Leavises, who included George Eliot in their definition of a "Great Tradition" in English literature. After an initial attempt to squeeze the novel into a new-critical format – to evaluate fiction solely according to criteria of unity and aesthetic coherence – critics began to deal with novels in more expansive terms, considering, for instance, the relevance of biographical material and social context.

Even so, however, Victorian novels tended to be held distinct from Victorian society and culture – often seen as "reflecting" or attempting to reproduce it, they were generally treated as isolated aesthetic objects. But the theoretical movements of the 1960s and 1970s gave critics powerful tools with which to describe the novel's integral role in Victorian society and culture, encouraging them to explore its capacity not only to "reflect" but also to shape that culture. These discussions have led to a dissolution of disciplinary boundaries: a shift from literary to cultural studies in which criticism of the Victorian novel has played a major role. They have also led to a dissolution of critical boundaries, such that the divisions that structure this chapter become, as the chapter advances toward the present day, less and less meaningful. The critic who writes about gender, for instance, may also be a Marxist and a feminist; and her readings may, at the same time, not be inconsistent with psychoanalytical or reader-response criticism. And if asked to define herself, this critic might indeed invoke none of the above categories, possibly claiming instead the all-encompassing title of "cultural critic."

Except in the case of feminist criticism, it is difficult to claim the particular appropriateness of a particular theoretical approach to Victorian fiction (as is the case, for instance, in the close connection between romanticism and deconstruction). The relation of Victorian novels to theory is almost always (as in the case of theoretical interpretations generally) not one of essential connection but rather one of exemplar, in which the novel becomes a vehicle for demonstrating a theoretical concept, and the theoretical concept sheds light on the novel. The feminist connection works so well because of the large numbers of women who both wrote and read Victorian fiction, and because of the centrality of "women's issues" in Victorian life and in the novel. The advent of new-historical criticism led to a more explicit concern with the specific Victorianness of the Victorian novel, in which the emphasis often seems to fall on the novel as medium rather than message: on the ways in which the juxtaposition of novels with other kinds of cultural documents produces insights about Victorian culture.

The Modernist Critique

Early twentieth-century critiques of the Victorian novel tended to focus on two issues: what the modernists claimed were their predecessors' conventional assumptions about character; and, following Henry James's assessment of Victorian novels as "loose, baggy monsters," form – or, more precisely, what was perceived as the absence thereof. Though some of these writers offered particular theories of the novel, their critiques tend not to be made explicitly; rather, they have been derived from the novels of the canonical modernists – James Joyce, Virginia Woolf, and Joseph Conrad – themselves. In one of the few manifestoes, Woolf's "Mr. Bennett and Mrs. Brown," the novelist assails Edwardian writers in general and Arnold Bennett in particular for a method that, in its reliance on external details to convey the "real," fails to support what Woolf considered her own, more internal brand of realism. Despite their acute powers of observation, Woolf asserts, the Edwardians have looked not at the character of her Mrs. Brown, but rather at the material world that surrounds her: they have looked "very powerfully, searchingly, and sympathetically, out of the window; at factories, at Utopias, even at the decoration and upholstery of the carriage; but never at her, never at life, never at human nature."

This emphasis on what Woolf called "human nature" – on individual perception or impression rather than the ostensibly objective representation of external details – is an important feature by means of which the modernists distinguished their work from that of their Victorian predecessors. According to this view, character in modern fiction is less a construct delivered in descriptive form by an omniscient narrator than a collection of elements readers glean from interior monologues and "streams of consciousness." And the stability of readers' knowledge is called into question as the single omniscient narrator of what has since been called the "classic realist novel" is replaced by the multiple perspectives of various characters (as in the layered voices of *Heart of Darkness*, for instance) – so that a reality shared either between characters themselves, or between characters and readers, cannot be taken for granted. Though twentieth-century critics have shown that the Victorian omniscient narrator is a less unitary and less assured construct than it once seemed, the modernists deliberately sought to dismantle the structures of authority associated with it: the dominating narrative voice that, typically, guides the reader and, in a manner that has been likened to divine providence, lends a comforting assurance that the events of the novel are firmly in hand. Ideas of plot and time are similarly reconfigured as, for instance, Woolf and Joyce (in *Mrs. Dalloway* and *Ulysses*) focus on the events of a single day as filtered through the consciousnesses of separate characters. In addition, what had been seen as the relatively transparent language of Victorian fiction gives way to an assertive linguistic play, calling attention to the self-reflexive quality of language and the novelistic "world."

The modernist emphasis on individual psychology and critique of conventional assumptions about perspective or point of view occurred as colonial empires foundered in the late nineteenth century and Freudian psychoanalysis posited the discontinuity of the individual self, the primacy of the unconscious, and the threat to civilization posed by repressed instincts. Indeed, modernism characteristically values "primitive" irrationality over bourgeois rationality. Thus the earliest psychoanalytic theories of the novel might be said to exist in works such as *Heart of Darkness*, which both lend themselves to Freudian interpretation and associate the Freudian unconscious with the "dark" continent of Africa. But criticism of the immediate postwar period tended, with some exceptions, to ignore the possible psychological meaning of texts in favor of an approach that, drawing on the new-critical tradition, sought to elaborate the novel's distinctive formal features.

New Criticism

"The novel," wrote Philip Stevick in 1967, "has no poetics" (1967: 1). The new critics of the 1930s and 1940s founded their theoretical practice on criteria derived from the study of poetry, but in the 1950s and 1960s they brought their interest in form and strategies of close reading to bear on the novel, in an attempt to construct its ostensibly missing poetics. Much of the work that followed was devoted to the question of form, as a way of distinguishing the novel from other genres; this emphasis had the result of transforming what had long been considered an inferior genre into one that could be deemed worthy of serious study.

The new-critical impulse made itself felt in an emphasis on classification, as in the study of "style," "narrative technique," "character," "symbol," and "plot." Critics working in this mode tended to see the novel not only as self-divided but also as self-contained: an attempt to reproduce the real which had in itself no particular communication with the social world. Indeed, criticism of this type often took a phenomenological turn, arguing that novels produced aesthetically self-contained "worlds" of their own. In *The English Novel: Form and Function*, for instance, Dorothy Van Ghent sought to demonstrate the aesthetic coherence of a variety of novels, and her discussions of *Great Expectations*, *Vanity Fair*, and other Victorian novels consider the way the formal strategies of each novel forge a "world" that "hangs together" and possesses "individual character": "its own tensions, physiognomy, and atmosphere" (1953: 66–7). A similar though more explicitly biographical emphasis on "the world of the novel" occupies J. Hillis Miller in *Charles Dickens: The World of his Novels*, which draws on the phenomenological work of Georges Poulet to convey what Miller calls the unique quality of Dickens's imagination, and to show how relations between characters are structured from the novelist's distinct point of view ("For all the works of a single writer form a unity, a unity in which a thousand paths radiate from the same center": 1958: ix).

Some critics of this period, notably Harry Levin and Lionel Trilling, address the novel's social and ethical dimensions; Trilling's influential discussion of the prison motif in Dickens's *Little Dorrit*, for instance, links this novel's concerns and its form with the structure of Victorian society. And in *The Rhetoric of Fiction* (1961), Wayne Booth combines an Aristotelian emphasis on form with an interest in the novel as a vehicle of communication. Unlike the new critics, Booth emphasized the novel's communicative or rhetorical function, arguing that new-critical precepts isolated the novel from its audience and assigned to it qualities of "realism" and "objectivity" it did not in fact possess. Within what Booth calls "impersonal narration," for instance, he claims that signs of authorial presence, or "rhetorical attitude," are always present. Booth located "point of view" firmly at the center of novel criticism, and his discussions of "reliable" and "unreliable" narrators and "implied" authors gave novel critics a new and useful lexicon. Despite the extent to which critics of fiction have generally made use of his categories and adopted his terminology, however, the Victorians do not figure largely in Booth's account, which concentrates on those authors – especially Austen and James – whose work seems to him emphatically concerned with the author's rhetorical control of the audience.

Feminist Criticism

Criticism of the Victorian novel and feminist criticism have been strongly linked from the movement's beginnings; indeed, it often seems that they have a natural affinity for one another, not least because of the Victorian novel's concern with domestic life and with the topics of marriage and female sexuality, as well as the pertinence of "the woman question" in Victorian life. The interrogation of these and related issues constituted – and constitutes – a vast and continuing project: one of rereading canonical novels and re-evaluating the roles of female characters in them; of unearthing and re-evaluating noncanonical novels and authors, and of questioning the meaning of the established canon as a hierarchy founded on patriarchal values. It also involves, in ways that have become aligned with Michel Foucault's revision of the repressive hypothesis, a new understanding of women's roles and of feminine authority both inside and outside the household, and – in ways that have become aligned with the new historicist project – re-evaluations of key figures and concepts in Victorian fiction and Victorian life.

Kate Millett's *Sexual Politics*, a crucial text published at the beginning of the feminist movement, anchors its argument in part in a powerful reading of Charlotte Brontë's *Villette* – a novel Millett terms "too subversive to be popular" (1970: 140). "In Lucy," Millett wrote, "one may perceive what effects her life in a male-supremacist society has upon the psyche of a woman" (p. 140). "Escape is all over the book; *Villette* reads like one long meditation on a prison break" (p. 146). And for many feminist critics of the 1970s and 1980s, in keeping with the movement's interest in linking the personal and the political, re-interpreting the Victorian novel that had most influenced their own emotional and intellectual development – Brontë's *Jane Eyre* – became a necessary gesture. In this context, and for the subsequent history of feminist criticism, M. Jeanne Peterson's essay on the socially and economically ambiguous position of the Victorian governess ("The Victorian Governess: Status Incongruence in Family and Society") articulated what now stands as an indispensable context for the novel and for Victorian feminist criticism as a whole, paving the way as it does for rereadings based on new understandings of the interrelations between class and gender and a new awareness of the importance of social context for novelistic interpretation.

In its early stages, feminist criticism was generally concerned with images of women in literature. Critics tended to universalize what was termed "female experience," elaborated around such traditionally feminine themes as sexuality, maternity, and domestic life. The attempt to define what was uniquely feminine in literature continued as criticism of the 1970s echoed the masculine model, seeking to define an alternative "Great Tradition," as in Ellen Moers' *Literary Women* (1976) and Elaine Showalter's *A Literature of Their Own* (1977). While neither book focused solely on the novel, both offered readings which have since become classics, the best known of which is probably Moers' reading of Mary Shelley's *Frankenstein* as a "phantasmagoria of the nursery." Nina Auerbach's *Communities of Women* (1978) sought to define the ways in which Victorian novels by women, including *Cranford* and *Villette*, produced images of women's collective visions: communities governed by women. While some early feminist criticism was founded on critics' identification with female characters in fiction, later criticism tended to take a more distanced approach, concerning itself with the way such images structured the identities of female readers and analyzing the implications of such identification for women, as in Rachel Brownstein's *Becoming a Heroine*. Early feminist criticism tended to rely on an unbroken continuity between reading and social experience, in which a woman inevitably reads "as" a woman. Later, following Judith Fetterley's work on American literature, feminist critics worked to expand their models of reader-response criticism.

In 1979, Adrienne Rich described *Jane Eyre* as a radical response to the powerlessness of Victorian women. In the same year Sandra Gilbert and Susan Gubar published *The Madwoman in the Attic*, a revisionist literary history with Brontë's madwoman, *Jane Eyre*'s Bertha Mason, as its paradigmatic figure. Invoking and revising Harold Bloom's theory of literary influence, Gilbert and Gubar argue for the existence of a feminine tradition in which a recurring Bertha Mason figure embodies feminine anger against patriarchal oppression, and trace the appearance of this figure in works by Emily Dickinson, Jane Austen, Emily Brontë and others.

In an influential essay, "Three Women's Texts and a Critique of Imperialism," Gayatri Chakravorty Spivak took Gilbert and Gubar to task for failing to consider Bertha Mason's status as a Creole. In claiming to uncover "a common, female impulse to struggle free from social and literary confinement through strategic redefinitions of self, art, and society" (1985: xii), argues Spivak, Gilbert and Gubar – white, middle-class female critics – unselfconsciously confine themselves to, and reproduce as a universal critical paradigm, a white, middle-class perspective. For Spivak, Bertha Mason represented another kind of rage from that articulated by *Madwoman*: the rage of the marginalized non-European "other" against a pervasive colonialist mentality. A wave of criticism – soon to be classified as postcolonial criticism – followed Spivak's lead, and generally took the form of identifying the imperialist attitudes implicit in canonical texts. The postcolonial inflection of feminist criticism was significant because it called into question the assumption of a universal "female" experience by showing how the "community of women" was itself structured and fractured by class and race; it also identified connections between the oppression of women and the subjugation of non-Western peoples (see the section below on postcolonial criticism).

Feminist criticism of the Victorian novel often turns on the central issue of whether female characters in novels support or subvert the period's dominant paradigms of women's behavior. Some critics, following Foucault, argue that women are necessarily subjected to patriarchal norms, while others (such as Auerbach in *Woman and the Demon*, 1982) insist that literary images of women subvert, and women in narrative take a "deviant" path that subverts, masculine prerogatives and desires. Feminist criticism has also become linked with Foucauldian criticism and the new historicism in studies that articulate the Victorian novel's role in supporting dominant ideologies about womanhood and gender difference. Following the example of Nancy Armstrong's *Desire and Domestic Fiction* (1987), for instance, contemporary students of Victorian fiction pursue these issues by reading novels alongside Victorian essays on the nature of women, such as Sarah Stickney Ellis's *The Women of England*.

Reader-Response Criticism and Studies of Readers

The feminist emphasis on reading as a woman drew upon a more general emphasis on the reader's experience that had been pioneered by Wolfgang Iser, Hans Robert Jauss, Stanley Fish, and Norman Holland. Iser, who led the way to reader-response criticism of the novel, argued for a tradition in which meaning is mutually constructed by authors and readers. Though he demonstrates his method with reference to texts from various historical periods, he makes specific use of Victorian fiction, arguing that the narrator of *Vanity Fair* considers the reader a "partner" in constructing the text's meaning, deliberately leaving "gaps" in the text for a reader to fill in. Also concerned with the way readers respond to a Victorian text is Susan Horton, who in *The Reader in the Dickens World: Style and Response* (1981) explores the effect Dickens's work produces in readers. Garrett Stewart theorizes the way readers are both hailed by and represented within Victorian novels: in *Hard Times*, for instance, Stewart finds that "a socially mobilized audience [is] conscripted from within narrative as a telos of the story's own omniscient plotting" (1996: 302). In another mode, some critics of Victorian fiction, such as Kate Flint (1993), follow the influential example of Richard Altick's *English Common Reader* – which attempted to "systematically analyse and document" (1957: 1) the growth and nature of the mass reading public in England – by fleshing out our knowledge of actual readers of the period.

Marxist Criticism

In *The English Novel from Dickens to Lawrence* (1970), Raymond Williams sought to trace what he terms a "new kind of consciousness" produced in the wake of the industrial revolution and along with the rise of urban culture, especially in the years

1847–8. Here, as in his *The Country and the City* (1973), Williams is concerned with the way the industrial revolution destroyed confidence in the "knowable community" on which novels tend to rely: their attempt to "show people and their relationships in essentially knowable and communicable ways" (Williams 1970: 14).

Perhaps the first study of Victorian fiction to give priority to class relations in the novel was Terry Eagleton's *Myths of Power*. Objecting to a "Marxist" criticism that consists merely of "relating empirical literary facts to empirical social facts" (1975: 3), Eagleton argued for a method that identified the ideological structure of the Brontës' works. In the novels of Charlotte and Emily Brontë he found fictional resolutions, or "myths," that appeared to resolve conflicts between the emergent bourgeoisie and the aristocracy. Arguing in a similar fashion that structure creates apparent resolution but also reveals contradiction is Pierre Macherey's *A Theory of Literary Production* (1978). Macherey – who could also be located in the "critique of realism" section (below) – attempts to demonstrate that the intelligibility of the classic realist text is inevitably troubled by tensions between ideology and literary form. Like Eagleton before him and Jameson after, Macherey relies not only on Marx but also, crucially, on Louis Althusser, whose theory of interpellation provides a powerful model for the way novels function as institutions of the state. In this view, as in Eagleton's, the novel's apparent resolution of contradiction and its ability to "suture" its readers – to enable them to identify with characters – accommodates them to the contradictions of capitalist society, making society's dominant fictions (of, for instance, class, gender, nationality, and race) seem natural. For Macherey, as for Fredric Jameson in *The Political Unconscious* (1981), the gap between a text's ideological project and the attempt to fit that project to a literary form produces a textual "unconscious."

Similarly concerned with the novel's resistance to and exposure of the limitations of systems is the work of M. M. Bakhtin, whose *Dialogic Imagination* (1981) altered the critical landscape once again. Bakhtin's arguments about the way the novel stages struggles among different social voices – what he calls "dialogism" or "heteroglossia" – fit within both Marxist and post-structuralist contexts (in its claim, for instance, that "all transcription systems . . . are inadequate to the multiplicity of meanings they seek to convey": 1981: xx). In the essay "Discourse in the Novel," Dickens's *Little Dorrit* figures as an illustrative example because of the mixed language that, Bakhtin argues, characterizes the text: it is impossible to establish firm boundaries between language held to be, respectively, professional, authorial, or impersonal.

Deconstruction and the Realist Critique

The new-critical emphasis on form – and its accompanying valorization of unity in form and theme – finds its opposing tendency in the deconstructionist fissuring of the novel, as well as in other, related work of the 1970s and 1980s in which what criticism newly discovers, and newly values, is tension and "difference" rather than unity and resolution. This work takes as its model Bakhtin's work on dialogical form, which emphasizes the irreconcilability of opposing voices in the novel as figures for opposing and discontinuous social consciousnesses. Peter Garrett (1980), for instance, extends Bakhtin's model to novelistic structure, arguing that the multiple plots of Victorian novels offer divergent and not necessarily reconcilable perspectives on the world. In *Narrative and its Discontents* (1981) D. A. Miller takes this emphasis on discontinuity further, arguing that narrative is enabled by the very condition of disequilibrium it inevitably seeks to erase.

Twentieth-century critics had for a long time associated the Victorian novel with a naïve realism of plot and character: with unquestioned assumptions about the correspondence between words and things. In the 1960s, however, Ferdinand de Saussure's critique of the status of the sign not only undid the major assumptions of realism, but also exploded the idea that realism could remain undeconstructed; because of the unstable nature of language itself, critics soon began to argue, any text purporting to be "realistic" (and any readers who accepted a novel's account of its own realism) was merely in the grip of an illusion. From this perspective, the novel – and particularly the Victorian novel, with its critical tradition of constructing a totality or "world" – begins to appear in criticism as the exemplar of what Roland Barthes dubbed "classical realism": the genre that, in attempting to reproduce empirical experience, to convey the solidity of the material world, in its identification of representation with reality solidifies the relationship between readers and the ideological institutions in which they dwell. The epistemological tenets of realism were further undermined by semiotics, as in Roland Barthes' *S/Z* (1970), and by feminism and deconstruction, as in the arguments of Catherine Belsey (see Belsey 1980). *S/Z* provided a crucial model for rereading the Victorian novel, and realist fiction in general, by dividing Balzac's *Sarrasine* into numerous "codes" in order to uncover the strategies by means of which texts sustain an illusion of realism. *S/Z* divides texts into two categories – the "readerly" and the "writerly" – though, as Barthes' own example demonstrates, these might also be described as two modes of reading. Most Victorian fiction would come under the heading of the readerly, or "classic realist" text: the text whose ostensibly transparent language constructs a passive reader who simply consumes the text. Here and elsewhere in his work, notably *Mythologies*, Barthes – by defining realism in literature, and realistic "transparency" in cultural artifacts, as bourgeois illusion – led the way to the cultural criticism of the 1980s and beyond.

In the wake of the Saussurean critique, critics of Victorian fiction were soon demonstrating how assumptions embedded in Victorian novels were undone by the novels' very language; how, in short, Victorian novels self-deconstructed. Edward Said explored Derrida's conclusions about the impossibility of origins by demonstrating, in *Beginnings*, how novelistic authority is always "molested," or troubled, by knowledge it must exclude; in *Great Expectations*, for example, Said argues, Pip's identity and his connections to criminality are a form of compensation for the absence of an authorizing agency – in Pip's case, the absence of parents. Novelistic identity, claims Said, includes a recognition of the self's "hideous, molesting foundations" (1975: 99).

While John Romano's *Dickens and Reality* (1978) anticipated the deconstructive criticism of the 1980s by arguing that Dickens's realism foregrounds the failures of representation to capture the real, some of the most important work of this kind appeared in individual essays on George Eliot, whose complex use of metaphor provided it with ready material. Defining the classic realist text, Colin McCabe used Eliot to illustrate "a narrative discourse [that] simply allows reality to appear and denies its own status as articulation" (1985: 36). In "Narrative and History" (1974) and "Optic and Semiotic in *Middlemarch*" (1975), J. Hillis Miller argued that Eliot's reliance on metaphor undermines the supposedly objective narration of *Middlemarch*, and refers to Eliot's "recognition of the deconstructive powers of figurative language" (1975: 144), while Neil Hertz, in "Recognizing Casaubon" (1985), described the way "signs of textuality" cluster around the name and character of Casaubon. And somewhat notoriously, Cynthia Chase (1978) deconstructed the causal narrative of *Daniel Deronda*, arguing that for Eliot's hero not to have known he was Jewish he must "never have looked down."

A number of influential works on Victorian realism appeared during this time. George Levine's *The Realistic Imagination* continued the deconstructionist revision by arguing that realism is founded on uneasiness rather than stability: "Despite its appearance of solidity, realism implies a fundamental uneasiness about self, society, and art" (1981: 12). Levine discerned a "Frankenstein pattern" in realist fiction in which "monstrous, unnameable possibilities" (p. 38) inhabit the fringes of a genre whose primary concern is to make language "conform" to social reality (p. 35). These possibilities ultimately emerge, in a version of the return of the repressed not unlike Bersani's "hero of desire" (see section below on psychoanalytic criticism).

Foucauldian Criticism

The work of Michel Foucault, especially *The History of Sexuality*, vol. 1 (1978) and *Discipline and Punish* (1977), had a tremendous impact on the interpretation of Victorian fiction. Foucault's idea of discourse paved the way for both new historicism and cultural studies, encouraging a redefinition of literature not as a form distinct from other forms of cultural production but rather as an institution that, like other institutions, is complicit in the construction and perpetuation of ideologies. For Foucault, social structures include multiple discourses, or bodies of thought that define social institutions, assist in the construction of subjectivities, and encode ideological structures and values. These discourses – such as law, medicine, religion, education, and literature – like the ideologies they reflect, intersect with and overlap with one another. Critics used Foucault's unsettling of the repressive hypothesis, for instance – which argued that, rather than "repressing" sexuality, as the term is commonly understood, Victorian discourse actively produced both sexuality and gender – to argue for a similar productivity in novelistic discourse. And Foucault's analysis of the disciplinary strategies of modern society as extensions of Jeremy Bentham's panopticon, in which the modern subject is "subject" to a monitoring, internalized gaze, allowed for a radical revision of both the Victorian novel's form and its cultural role. The most influential Foucauldian rereading of the Victorian novel, D. A. Miller's *The Novel and the Police* (1988), argues that characters in novels by Dickens, Trollope, Braddon, and others enact and embody Victorian society's disciplinary functions. For Miller, as for Foucault and Althusser, the novel functions as an interpellating institution like the school, the hospital, or the prison, and its disciplinary techniques habituate readers to the divisions of labor and regulated rhythms of a capitalist economy.

Building on Foucault's work on sexuality, and attempting to move feminist criticism in a more political direction – an explicitly Marxist–feminist one – Nancy Armstrong in *Desire and Domestic Fiction* defines a novelistic tradition whose emphasis on character and interiority psychologizes and domesticates the political. Thus in *Jane Eyre*, as in other novels of the period, she argues, desire both authorizes and subordinates other aspects of social life. Like Catherine Gallagher (see section on "new historicism" below), Armstrong aligns her readings of novels with readings of other cultural documents; in a widely imitated gesture, her readings of novels alongside eighteenth- and nineteenth-century conduct books build a case for understanding novels of the period *as* conduct books, aimed at producing gender-differentiated forms of behavior. Armstrong drew upon the new-historical use of documents originated by Greenblatt and further developed by Gallagher and, along with Mary Poovey and others, turned it in the direction of gender criticism.

New Historicism

Catherine Gallagher's *The Industrial Reformation of English Fiction* (1985) brought new historicism to criticism of the Victorian novel and assisted in a general shift toward interdisciplinarity – away from Victorian literature and towards Victorian studies – in academic criticism. In the model of Stephen Greenblatt's work in Renaissance studies, which itself builds upon Foucault's work on culture as a series of overlapping and intersecting discourses, Gallagher constructs a series of mutually informing readings of texts in different genres. Her readings of these texts – including Harriet Martineau's seamstress tales, Elizabeth Gaskell's *Mary Barton*, Arnold's *Culture and Anarchy*, and Dickens's *Hard Times* – position both traditionally literary works and traditionally nonliterary or noncanonical ones as cultural documents, examining similar issues and impulses in each and showing how constructions of cultural meaning transcend conventional generic differences. In *Uneven Developments: The Ideological Work of Gender in Mid-Victorian England*, Mary Poovey employs a similar methodology, situating *Jane Eyre* alongside Victorian commentaries on the position of the governess and *David Copperfield* in the context of contemporary ideas about the professionalization of writing. This parallel reading of texts – which seeks to avoid the "old" historical method, in which history serves as a backdrop for literary texts – is behind Poovey's claim that "the kind of linear narrative that many literary critics and historians employ necessarily obscures the critical complexity of social relations" (Poovey 1988: 18). Both Armstrong and Poovey use new-historical methodology explicitly in the service of what has since been termed, more generally, gender criticism. And because these projects involve the rereading and reinterpretation of Victorian culture, and argue that novels play a key role in shaping that culture, they also belong to the category of cultural criticism.

Psychoanalytic Criticism

Though there is no consistent school of psychoanalytic criticism devoted to the Victorian novel, several critical works stand out as touchstones. Freud's influence is evident in Edmund Wilson's *The Wound and the Bow*, which emphasizes Dickens's traumatic childhood and its influence on his subsequent development. Helen Moglen emphasizes development somewhat differently in *Charlotte Brontë: The Self Conceived* (1976), using the novels as clues to the growth of Brontë's feminist sensibility – in keeping with a feminist interest in the light psychoanalytic models shed on the woman's "point of view." In the 1980s and 1990s interest in such models shifted away from Freud and Erikson toward object-relations theory, including new work on female development by Melanie Klein and Nancy Chodorow emphasizing the importance of the child's separation from the mother. Meredith Skura includes enlightening readings of Dickens's novels in her survey of the field, *The Literary Uses of the Psychoanalytic Process*.

In a manner that anticipated cultural criticism of the 1980s and beyond, psycho-analytic reading was moved in a new direction by Steven Marcus's essay on Freud's *Dora*, which takes as its project the analysis of the case study "from the point of view of literary criticism." Characterizing Freud as a novelist, and pointing out the strategies whereby the narrative of this case study constructs its "truths," Marcus calls *Dora* a "tribute" to the culture that produced "the great bourgeois novels of the nineteenth century," and "the beginning and the end of that tradition and its authority." Marcus's analysis of the means by which "reality," in this text, "turns out to be something that for all practical purposes is indistinguishable from a systematic fictional creation," paved the way not only for Stanley Fish's deconstruction of Freud's "Wolf Man" case, but also for the numerous critiques of realism discussed above.

"Desire" became a key term in psychoanalytically oriented criticism of the novel in the 1970s and 1980s, serving as a metonym for a psychoanalytic approach that escapes that method's potentially reductive tendencies. In *A Future for Astyanax: Character and Desire in Literature* (1976), Leo Bersani argues that the nineteenth-century realist novel's emphasis on significant design, which trains readers to find meaning in every detail, serves the desire to render character and society significant and coherent and thereby perpetuates what Bersani calls "the literary myth of a rigidly ordered self" (1976: 16). In fact, Bersani argues, the realist novel reveals a "terror" of desire, as novels expel the disruptive feeling that exposes the self's incoherent, fragmentary nature, usually in the form of an alien and alienated yet glamorous hero such as *Wuthering Heights*'s Heathcliff. Aligning psychological desire with narrative rather than character, Peter Brooks in *Reading for the Plot* relies on the idea of an ordering principle embodied in plot, and proposes that readers rely on plot to discover meaning in texts: we "conceive of the reading of plot as a form of desire that carries us forward, onward, through the text" (1984: 37). For Brooks, the "fort-da" dynamic of *Beyond the Pleasure Principle*, in which moments of quiescence at beginning and end are interrupted by deviance or digression, is Freud's "masterplot." Brooks's reading of *Great Expectations* follows Said in emphasizing the importance of Pip's search for origins, or authority; it outlines the progression of the plot in terms of a series of four double plots, each with an "official" plot whose function it is to "bind" or constrain the energies of a "repressed" plot.

Critics of Victorian fiction also make use of the theories of Jacques Lacan, in particular the splitting and fragmentation of the self involved his formulation of the mirror scene, to investigate self-divided characters such as Dickens's Esther Summerson. A Lacanian emphasis also informs what is sometimes called "gaze theory," in which (following and adapting Laura Mulvey's influential essay on women in cinema) critics make use of Foucault, gender theory, and psychoanalytic theory to discuss the function of the disciplinary gaze in Victorian novels. Defining the general deployment of the male gaze as a powerful device for constructing women as objects of masculine desire – as objects but not subjects – critics of Dickens, the Brontës, Hardy, and numerous other novelists complicate Foucault's work on surveillance. Criticism in this mode raises such issues as the subjection of female characters to a masculine gaze; the internalization by characters of this gaze; and the way the narrative voices of particular novels align readers with a masculine view, inviting them to identify with its structures of desire and appropriation.

Gender and Queer Theory

Gender criticism of Victorian fiction may be said to have begun with Eve Sedgwick's *Between Men* (1985). By means of a radically revisionist reading of Dickens's *Our Mutual Friend*, among other texts, Sedgwick established a theory of male homosociality in literature. Her reading of Dickens's novel traces a pattern of same-sex desire in the rivalry between Bradley Headstone and Eugene Wrayburn, and of "traffic in women" (Gayle Rubin's phrase) as patriarchal power is routed through, but never resides in, the figure of Lizzie Hexam. Elaborating on Rubin's theories about gender relations and René Girard's model of triangular desire, Sedgwick's demonstrations of the way Victorian fiction reproduces the gendered structure of capitalist society had a profound influence on criticism of the Victorian novel, and also demonstrated the particular relevance of queer reading and gender theory for a period in which the patriarchal model was being extended externally, in the form of colonialism, while it was under attack internally, in challenges to traditional masculine authority both in the workplace (as women occupied positions traditionally held only by men) and in the legal system (in, for instance, the Married Women's Property Act). Sedgwick's theory of male homosexual panic shows how Victorian society required, for the perpetuation of its power structures, both intense emotional bonding between men and conventional heterosexual marriage. Her work here, as in her later *Epistemologies of the Closet* (1990), became a reference point for numerous critics who continued to develop the fields of queer theory and gender studies, notably D. A. Miller, Ed Cohen, and Christopher Craft. Both books made available a methodology and language for what have become known as queer readings of novels, whose project generally involves disrupting the automatic association of texts with normative, heterosexual sexuality, and uncovering or decoding homosocial or homosexual subtexts. An important early essay in this context is Craft's rereading of *Dracula* (1984). Critics have produced numerous rereadings of *The Picture of Dorian Gray*, as well as of less obvious candidates for queer reading such as *Great Expectations* and *Silas Marner*. Much of this work outlines the relationship between economic structures and ideologies of gender and sexuality, and serves to demonstrate the particular relevance of Victorian fiction to an understanding of homosocial structures in Victorian society. Even as critics underscore the way in which constructions of subjectivity and structures of interpellation in Victorian novels tend to support cultural models of normative sexuality, the readings they offer also render visible other forms of sexuality embedded in the novels' language and imagery. These critics decode and unravel the dominant ideological structures that Victorian novels have long been assumed to support. Relevant to the category of gender criticism as well is the development of a substantial branch of critical writing on the topic of masculinity in Victorian fiction.

Gender criticism, new historicism, and deconstruction meet in Poovey's *Uneven Developments*, which seeks to dismantle the binary construction of gender in mid-Victorian England. Poovey's goal, as she describes it, is to "reveal the other face" of gender ideology: to demonstrate "the extent to which what may look coherent and complete in retrospect was actually fissured by competing emphases and interests" (1988: 3).

Cultural Criticism

The term "cultural studies" or "cultural criticism" with reference to work on the Victorian novel covers a wide range of topics; indeed, the term is so all-encompassing and so compelling (for who would not want to be an authority on "culture"?) that few critics writing in the 1990s and beyond choose to see themselves as not practicing some form of cultural criticism. The claim to be "doing" cultural criticism sees all aspects of Victorian culture, including literature, *as* culture. For those who wish to narrow the field, however, the term "cultural criticism" has been used more specifically to refer to work that sees the Victorian novel as a form of cultural production and an early example of mass culture, associated with and sometimes in competition with other cultural forms. Thus cultural criticism includes work such as

D. A. Miller's, which explicitly considers the novel as a shaping force in culture, and Armstrong's, which reads Victorian novels alongside, but also as, conduct books. An early and influential example of work fitting this narrower definition is Tania Modleski's *Loving with a Vengeance* (1982), which makes a claim for continuity between canonical fiction (especially *Pride and Prejudice* and *Jane Eyre*) and twentieth-century popular romance forms such as Harlequin fiction and contemporary soap opera. Modleski argues, against conventional wisdom, that these mass-cultural genres subvert dominant constructions of feminine identity, and she analyses their ideological implications as forms of cultural discourse and mass entertainment aimed specifically at women. Terry Lovell (1995) also argues for the centrality of the relationship between women and consumer culture to the Victorian novel, while Jennifer Wicke (1988) discusses the dialectic between the Victorian novel and "its shadow partner, the mass communication form that constitutes its matrix." Also situating women at the center of her argument, Ann Cvetkovich (1992) considers sensation fiction as a form of mass culture and discusses the "politics of affect" the form embodies.

Postcolonial Criticism

Postcolonial criticism of the Victorian novel is overwhelmingly indebted to Edward Said's *Orientalism* (1978), which uses Foucault's concept of discourse to demonstrate the ways in which "the Orient" has been constructed as a projection of Western fears and desires. Spivak's essay, as well as work by Patrick Brantlinger, Mary Louise Pratt, Ann McClintock, and others, unearths the imperialist contexts and colonialist metaphors deployed by Victorian novels. Such arguments involve, for instance, uncovering a text's reliance on colonial metaphors and discussing the way its use of such metaphors reveals the text's, and the culture's, reliance on the political structures of colonization. They may also demonstrate – as in the case of Susan Meyer's discussion of *Jane Eyre* – the ways in which a Victorian novel's ostensibly enlightened liberal stance is compromised by its characters' acceptance of, in the form of their direct or indirect participation in, imperialist ventures; thus the inheritance that renders Jane economically independent and makes it possible for her to return to Rochester as his equal is problematic in its derivation from the West Indian estate of her uncle, Mason, just as Rochester's wealth is the product of the labor of slaves.

The New Nineteenth Century

The most recent development in criticism of the Victorian novel has been an attempt to widen the canon: to bring back into print, and make available for critical interpretation, "underread" novels, especially those by women. As John Sutherland writes in the introduction to *The New Nineteenth Century*, "Generalizations about 'the Victorian novel' . . . are often hobbled by being restricted to the dozen writers designated as 'major' by the *New Cambridge Bibliography of English Literature* – writers whose extraordinary literary distinction renders them necessarily unrepresentative" (Harman and Meyer 1996: xi). Attention to the numerous unstudied and largely (now) unread practitioners of the novel form during the Victorian period, Sutherland writes, alters the historical, critical, and generic lansdscape dramatically, since these works reveal what we call "the novel" to be a more varied and internally differentiated form than is commonly assumed in academic criticism. The Harman–Meyer volume addresses itself chiefly to women writers, on the basis of the fact that so much of Victorian fiction was written and read by women; given the tendency of literary canons to be dominated by men, unearthing the noncanonical is almost by definition a feminist project. But the category of the underread includes male novelists as well, and this volume includes essays on Wilkie Collins, Charles Reade, and Walter Besant as well as Mrs. Oliphant, Anne Brontë, and Mrs. Humphry Ward.

References

Altick, R. (1957), *The English Common Reader: A Social History of the Mass Reading Public (1800–1900)* (Chicago: University of Chicago Press).

Armstrong, N. (1987), *Desire and Domestic Fiction: A Political History of the Novel* (Oxford: Oxford University Press).

Auerbach, N. (1978), *Communities of Women: An Idea in Fiction* (Cambridge, Mass.: Harvard University Press).

Auerbach, N. (1982), *Woman and the Demon: The Life of a Victorian Myth* (Cambridge, Mass.: Harvard University Press).

Bakhtin, M. M. (1981), *The Dialogic Imagination: Four Essays*, ed. M. Holquist, trans. C. Emerson and M. Holquist (Austin: University of Texas Press).

Barthes, R. (1970), *S/Z* (New York: Hill & Wang).

Belsey, C. (1980), *Critical Practice* (New York: Methuen).

Bersani, L. (1976), *A Future for Astyanax: Character and Desire in Literature* (Boston: Little, Brown).

Booth, W. (1961), *The Rhetoric of Fiction* (Chicago: University of Chicago Press).

Brooks, P. (1984), *Reading for the Plot: Design and Intention in Narrative* (New York: Vintage; Oxford: Clarendon).

Chase, C. (1978), "The Decomposition of the Elephants: Double-Reading *Daniel Deronda*," *Publications of the Modern Language Association of America*, 93, 215–27.

Craft, Christopher (1984), "Kiss Me with Those Red Lips: Gender and Inversion in Bram Stoker's *Dracula*," *Representations*, 8.

Cvetkovich, A. (1992), *Mixed Feelings: Feminism, Mass Culture, and Victorian Sensationalism* (New Brunswick: Rutgers University Press).

Eagleton, T. (1975), *Myths of Power: A Marxist Study of the Brontës* (New York: Barnes & Noble; London: Macmillan).

Flint, K. (1993), *The Woman Reader 1837–1914* (Oxford: Clarendon).

Foucault, M. (1977), *Discipline and Punish*, trans. Alan Sheridan (New York: Vintage).

Foucault, M. (1978), *The History of Sexuality*, vol. 1, trans. Robert Hurley (New York: Pantheon).

Gallagher, C. (1985), *The Industrial Reformation of English Fiction: Social Discourse and Narrative Form, 1832–1867* (Chicago: University of Chicago Press).

Garrett, P. (1980), *The Victorian Multiplot Novel: Studies in Dialogical Form* (New Haven: Yale University Press).

Gilbert, S., and Gubar, S. (1979), *The Madwoman in the Attic: The Woman Writer and the Nineteenth-Century Literary Imagination* (New Haven and London: Yale University Press).

Harman, B. L., and Meyer, S., eds. (1996), *The New Nineteenth Century: Feminist Readings of Underread Victorian Fiction* (New York and London: Garland).

Hertz, N. (1985), "Recognizing Casaubon," in *The End of the Line: Essays on Psychoanalysis and the Sublime* (New York: Columbia University Press).

Horton, S. (1981), *The Reader in the Dickens World: Style and Response* (Pittsburgh: University of Pittsburgh Press).

Iser, W. (1974), *The Implied Reader* (Baltimore: Johns Hopkins University Press).

Jameson, F. (1981), *The Political Unconscious: Narrative as a Socially Symbolic Act* (Ithaca: Cornell University Press).

Levine, G. (1981), *The Realistic Imagination* (Chicago: University of Chicago Press).

Lovell, T. (1995), *Consuming Fiction* (London: Verso).

Macherey, P. (1978), *A Theory of Literary Production* (Boston: Routledge & Kegan Paul).

McCabe, C. (1985), *Tracking the Signifier. Theoretical Essays: Film, Literature, Linguistics* (Minneapolis: University of Minnesota).

Miller, D. A. (1981), *Narrative and its Discontents* (Princeton: Princeton University Press).

Miller, D. A. (1988), *The Novel and the Police* (Berkeley: University of California Press).

Miller, J. H. (1958), *Charles Dickens: The World of His Novels* (Cambridge, Mass.: Harvard University Press).

Miller, J. H. (1974), "Narrative and History," *English Literary History*, 41, 455–73.

Miller, J. H. (1975), "Optic and Semiotic in *Middlemarch*," in Jerome Buckley, ed., *The Worlds of Victorian Fiction* (Cambridge, Mass: Harvard University Press), 125–45.

Millett, K. (1970), *Sexual Politics* (New York: Doubleday).

Modleski, T. (1982), *Loving with a Vengeance* (Hamden: Archon).

Moers, E. (1976), *Literary Women: The Great Writers* (Garden City: Doubleday).

Moglen, H. (1976), *Charlotte Brontë: The Self Conceived* (New York: Norton).

Peterson, M. Jeanne (1972), "The Victorian Governess: Status Incongruence in Family and Society," in M. Vicinus, ed., *Suffer and Be Still: Women in the Victorian Age* (Bloomington: Indiana University Press).

Poovey, M. (1988), *Uneven Developments: The Work of Gender in Mid-Victorian England* (Chicago: University of Chicago Press).

Rich, A. (1979), *On Lies, Secrets, and Silence* (New York: Norton).

Romano, J. (1978), *Dickens and Reality* (New York: Columbia University Press).

Said, E. (1975), *Beginnings: Intention and Method* (Baltimore: Johns Hopkins University Press).

Said, E. (1978), *Orientalism* (New York: Pantheon).

Sedgwick, E. (1985), *Between Men: English Literature and Male Homosocial Desire* (New York: Columbia University Press).

Sedgwick, E. (1990), *Epistemology of the Closet* (Berkeley: University of California Press).

Showalter, E. (1977), *A Literature of their Own: British Women Novelists from Brontë to Lessing* (Princeton: Princeton University Press).

Spivak, G. (1985), "Three Women's Texts and a Critique of Imperialism," *Critical Inquiry*, 12, 243–61.

Stevick, P. (1967), *The Theory of the Novel* (London: Free Press).

Stewart, G. (1996), *Dear Reader: The Conscripted Audience in Nineteenth-Century British Fiction* (Baltimore and London: Johns Hopkins University Press).

Van Ghent, D. (1953), *The English Novel: Form and Function* (New York: Rinehart).

Watt, I. (1957), *The Rise of the Novel* (London: Chatto & Windus).

Wicke, J. (1988), *Advertising Fictions* (New York: Columbia University Press).

Williams, R. (1970), *The English Novel from Dickens to Lawrence* (Oxford: Oxford University Press).

FURTHER READING

Adams, J. (1995), *Dandies and Desert Saints: Style of Victorian Masculinity* (Ithaca: Cornell University Press).

Althusser, L. (1971), *Lenin and Philosophy*, trans. Ben Brewster (New York: Monthly Review Press).

Brantlinger, P. (1988), *Rule of Darkness: British Literature and Imperialism, 1830–1914* (Ithaca: Cornell University Press).

Brownstein, R. (1982), *Becoming a Heroine* (New York: Viking).

Fetterley, J. (1978), *The Resisting Reader* (Bloomington: Indiana University Press).

Lacan, Jacques (1977), *Ecrits: A Selection*, trans A. Sheridan (New York: Norton).

Leavis, F. R. (1954), *The Great Tradition* (New York: Doubleday).

McClintock, A. (1995), *Imperial Leather: Race, Gender, and Sexuality in the Imperial Conquest* (New York: Routledge).

Marcus, S. (1975), *Representations* (New York: Random House).

Said, E. (1993), *Culture and Imperialism* (New York: Knopf).

25

The Afterlife of the Victorian Novel: Novels about Novels

Anne Humpherys

> "'Everything has been said. These lines aren't my writing.'"
>
> Kathy Acker, *Great Expectations*

Many if not most readers, when asked to name a late twentieth-century novel based on a previous one, will think of John Fowles's *The French Lieutenant's Woman* (1969), or Jean Rhys's *Wide Sargasso Sea* (1966), or perhaps A. S. Byatt's *Possession* (1990). All three of these use, in different ways, the Victorian novel as source, and this fact generates the topic of "the afterlife of the Victorian novel" that is the subject of this chapter. My purpose is both to describe this literary phenomenon and also to speculate why many twentieth-century writers have turned to the nineteenth-century novel as the generative source for their work.

A word at the beginning about terminology. Critics writing about these "afterings" of the Victorian novel frequently refer to them as "postmodern." This term is a significantly controversial one: it can describe a historical movement (what comes after and is opposed to modernism); a continuation or extension of modernism (intertextuality); a way of reading (against the text); and a cultural phenomenon in all the arts involving quotation and self-reflexiveness. The term has generated many theoretical and critical studies, some in opposition to each other and all offering varying perspectives. It is beyond the scope of this chapter to enter into the debates about postmodernism in general or about whether the texts under review here can indeed be called "postmodern." I have instead coined the word "aftering" to describe the "writing over" of Victorian novels that has been such a distinctive part of the late twentieth-century literary scene. But many of the characteristics of this aftering have also been identified as part of the postmodern project; therefore, I will use the term "postmodern" occasionally, though always with a recognition of its slipperiness.

While there is a popular sense that there is something special about the relationship of the late twentieth-century novel to the Victorian period, there are plenty of texts which use non-Victorian sources in a similar way: to mention a few, consider John Gardner's *Grendel* (1971), based on *Beowulf*; Michael Cunningham's *The Hours* (1999), based on Virginia Woolf's *Mrs. Dalloway*; Sena Jeter Naslund's *Ahab's Wife* (1999), based on *Moby Dick*; and John Updike's *Gertrude and Claudius* (2000), based on *Hamlet*.

Furthermore, from the very beginning of the Western literary tradition, narratives have been parasitical on previous narratives: Greek drama is based on well-known myths, as are the *Iliad* and the *Odyssey*. Though the romantic linking of the value of art to originality initiated a shift in the way readers judge works of art, and the perception of the novel – as indicated in the very word "novel" – was that it was new in form and told the "news" in content, novels in fact have always responded to and often revised earlier texts. The arguably first modern novel, Cervantes' *Don Quixote*, is a response to hundreds of previous chivalric romances. (And one of the foundational postmodernists, Jorge Luis Borges, in "Pierre Menard, Author of *Quixote*" [1939], tells the story of a man who spends his life writing Cervantes' novel, which will be, despite a word-for-word identity, a different novel because written by a different writer and in a different time.) So, too, Daniel Defoe's founding English novels take the forms of previous texts: narratives of travel (*Robinson Crusoe*) and lives of criminals (*Moll Flanders*); Samuel Richardson's *Pamela* grows out of his efforts both to write a book of model letters and to counteract earlier "romances." And Henry Fielding's first novels, *Shamela* and *Joseph Andrews*, famously "rewrite" *Pamela*.

In the early nineteenth century, Jane Austen begins by parodying novels of sensibility, and Walter Scott's historical novels turn to the past for their inspiration. Dickens returns to *Don Quixote* for his first narrative, *Pickwick Papers*, and to *The Newgate Calendar* for his second, *Oliver Twist*. In its own time, *Jane Eyre*, itself integrating the conventional Gothic story of the demon lover into a realist novel, spawned a raft of imitations and revisions. And finally a founding text of modernism, James Joyce's *Ulysses*, links Homer's work with a day in the life of modern Dubliners.

Further, the Victorian novelist Anthony Trollope essentially invented the novel sequel and the novel series or sequence; that is, the carrying over of the characters and setting of one novel into another or into a series of other novels. Trollope's Barsetshire series of six novels includes one intentional sequel (*The Warden* and *Barchester Towers*), while the Palliser series of six novels includes one sequel (*Phineas Finn* and *Phineas Redux*; a pair which Trollope referred to in his *Autobiography* as "in fact, but one novel" [1980: 60]). Trollope's sequels grow out of similar impulses to the afterings, namely the desire to undermine closure, not just to prolong the pleasure of reading about a created world but also more closely to represent the contingency and disorder of "real life." In fact, one major theoretical treatment of the sequel makes no distinction between what Trollope does and what these twentieth-century Victorian afterings do (Budra and Schellingberg 1988: introduction).

In general, the novel fuels desire, specifically for more narrative and more information about the world created by a particular novel. Thus, built into the novel as a form is a strong tendency to use prior texts as the basis for a new work. We might even go so far as to say that the novel from the beginning was engaged in an "after-ing," even a postmodern project.

So what if anything *is* special about the twentieth-century novels that write over the Victorian novel, such as those by Fowles, Rhys, Byatt – or those by Kathy Acker (*Great Expectations*, 1982), David Lodge (*Nice Work*, 1988), Valerie Martin (*Mary Reilly*, 1990), Carole Nelson Douglas (*Good Night, Mr. Holmes*, 1990), William Gibson and Bruce Sterling (*The Difference Engine*, 1991), Peter Carey (*Jack Maggs*, 1997), and Maryse Condé (*Windward Heights*, 1999), to name only a few of dozens?

Though most readers probably will have read at least one of these novels, I want to begin by summarizing the action of one of the most famous so that the theoreti-cal parts of this essay can be grounded in specifics. *Wide Sargasso Sea* by Jean Rhys tells the story of the first Mrs. Rochester in the novel *Jane Eyre* by Charlotte Brontë. Rhys's novel gives a history to Brontë's mad Bertha Mason, who in the Victorian novel is incarcerated in the attic of her husband's estate, Thornfield. Renaming Bertha Antoinette, Rhys recounts her troubled childhood and girlhood in Jamaica, where she was shaped by historical changes in both racial relationships and gender expectations. She also recounts Antoinette's arranged marriage to Edward Rochester and its col-lapse in a maze of cultural misunderstandings, followed by her descent into madness when she is ripped from all she knows and loves and imprisoned in a cold, dark cell in an alien country. Rhys's novel ends just before Antoinette/Bertha sets the fire that, in *Jane Eyre*, results in her death and Rochester's mutilation.

With this paradigmatic relationship between pretext and aftertext, Victorian novel and sequel in mind, we can begin to contemplate the phenomenon of the "aftered" Victorian novel. The Victorian novel has been used by twentieth-century writers in a number of different ways, and though the impulse to return to the Victorian period in all these uses probably stems from similar late twentieth-century notions of Victorian culture, some are merely "retro." For example, the many recent historical novels, such as those by Charles Palliser (*The Quincunx* [1989] and *The Unburied* [2000]) or Sheri Holman's *The Dress Lodger* (2000), use both the Victorian period and a certain kind of Victorian multiplot structure, but they are quite conventional and nostalgic novels in both form and content. They return to the Victorian period and the Victorian novel because of a sense of that period's contradictory richness and simplicity, a period of modern complexities but also of seeming confidence that the novel can represent these complexities. Thus, they tend to treat Victorian England as though it were stranger and darker than we ordinarily think because, as a critic writing about *The Difference Engine* has speculated, "a rejigged Victorian London seems to serve as a favourite kind of artificial unconscious, where anxieties can be condensed and discharged on the understanding that this lurid place is definitely *other*" (Spufford 1996: 277). However, these historical novels do not raise questions about intertextu-ality, nor call attention to the significant gaps and omissions of the Victorian novel.

Similar in their sentimental relationship to the Victorian period are twentieth-century novels which, though not set in the Victorian period, are clearly influenced by Victorian novels. These include the many works by Angela Thirkell which are derivative of Anthony Trollope's cathedral novels (they are actually set in a county called "Barshetshire"), but which take place in contemporary times. Robert Polhemus has speculated that this nostalgic use of Trollope is due to "the longing for the supposed sureties of physical community. . . . In times of urban anonymity and social turbulence, Barchester feeds a hunger for images of solidity and 'home'" (1980: 203). This nostalgia also accounts in large part for the popularity of the many film and television adaptations of nineteenth-century works. It is even part of the postmodern project.

The aftered Victorian novel is nonetheless something quite different from the "costume drama" adaptations and the returns to Barshetshire. If we turn to a number of terms which have been used to describe the phenomenon of aftering, we can begin to distinguish its crucial characteristics: sequel, historical metafiction, parody, pastiche, appropriation, intervention, rewrites, alternative history. They all point, though indirectly, to a sense of belatedness: that is, to a recognition that there is nothing new, that we are all caught up in repeated conventions and old stories. They underline the fact that novelistic texts are always in an endless discussion with other texts. Further, each calls attention to one or more of the ways a novel might create its intertextuality with its Victorian original, and describes a different mode of aftering it.

But more important, all these terms suggest that the reader must read the texts in a particular way, that is *doubly*. The reader must interpret two texts at once – the pretext which exists in memory and the aftertext which exists on the page. In the case of novels like those by Fowles and Byatt, which are not parasitical on a single work but instead on Victorian culture as well as the genre of Victorian fiction as a whole, the text demands a knowledge of the Victorian novel in general. For example, we must remember *Jane Eyre* in order to make sense of *Wide Sargasso Sea*; in particular, there is no way we can understand the ending of Rhys's novel without knowing the ending of Brontë's. The relationship between the endings of the two texts exemplifies perfectly the tension in these double readings: Bertha's story in *Jane Eyre* is closed definitively by her death, but in *Wide Sargasso Sea* Antoinette/Bertha's story is always unfinished.

This double reading, which results in the satisfactions of recognition and a sense of special, even privileged knowledge, is a source of much of the pleasure of these texts. This does not mean that a reader ignorant of *Jane Eyre* cannot enjoy *Wide Sargasso Sea* or that a reader who has never read a Victorian novel cannot enjoy *The French Lieutenant's Woman* or *Possession*, but such a reader would not be able to make even rudimentary meaning of the narrative strategies employed in any of these texts without knowledge of the pretexts.

The next general characteristic that distinguishes these novels is also a function of this double reading. The interplay between the two (or more) texts results in a relationship between the pretext and the aftertext which is *ironic*: that is, it brings to light a reality different from the appearance. More importantly, the recognition of this difference between appearance and reality, between what is present and what is absent usually results in a *critique* of the pretext, even as *Wide Sargasso Sea* criticizes the attitude of *Jane Eyre* toward the Creole woman specifically and more generally the Victorian attitudes toward race and empire that are implicit in *Jane Eyre*. But the relationship between what is present and what is absent is complex, for the absent is inevitably present in the pretext, even as the "madwoman in the attic" is present in *Jane Eyre*, though marginalized, hidden, or implied. The project is to bring the margin to the center.

Because of this interest in the marginal, the unrepresented, the rejected, the other, most of the ironic critiques in these afterings of Victorian novels focus on what is perceived to be missing or fudged or misrepresented in the pretext – the story of the Creole Bertha Mason for Rhys, Magwitch's Australian experience for Peter Carey in *Jack Maggs*, the woman's perspective in Stevenson's *Dr. Jekyll and Mr. Hyde* for Valerie Martin (*Mary Reilly* [1990], who, since the central character is a servant also brings out issues of class repressed in the pretext), and race in *Wuthering Heights* for the Caribbean writer Maryse Condé. The aftertext moves into a perceived gap and expands the pretext to include the missing element, whether through providing a "prequel" as in *Wide Sargasso Sea*, a sequel as in many of the Jane Austen afterings, or, most frequently, an expansion of the pretext through an additional perspective, for example as Carole Nelson Douglas retells the Sherlock Holmes story "A Scandal in Bohemia" from the point of view of "the woman," Irene Adler (*Goodnight, Mr. Holmes*). In doing this, the aftertext does not destroy the pretext. In Douglas's work, the insistently homosocial world of Sherlock Holmes remains, but the text expands this world to include the woman's point of view. The resulting ironic double reading succeeds in pointing out not only the misogyny of the Holmes stories specifically but also general Victorian attitudes toward women. It does not, however, question the teleology of the conventional detective novel structure.

The aftering of the Sherlock Holmes stories is a minor industry in itself; few of the texts, however, are self-conscious about the detective novel genre. Most grow out of the impulse of sequels: to continue for ever the life and adventures of a charismatic character. Douglas is unusual in this first of her Irene Adler series (though not in the subsequent ones) in actually aftering a specific Victorian text, demanding a double reading. Valerie Martin's *Mary Reilly* works similarly with *Dr. Jekyll and Mr. Hyde* by presenting the story of the pretext from the first-person point of view of a female servant in Jekyll's house. The double reading and ironic relationship make visible the homosocial world of Stevenson's novel as well as its class bias.

The gaps in the Victorian novel into which the aftered Victorian novel moves most persistently, then, are those of gender, race, sexuality, and sometimes class. Thus, the aftered Victorian novel parallels developments in critical perspectives, from feminism to structuralism and post-structuralism, to postcolonialism, to queer studies. Indeed, one could almost say cynically that the purpose of these novels in terms of the Victorian novel is simply "to put the sex in." But beyond the obligatory sex scenes that are always part of the expansion of the pretexts (and surely this need to include explicit descriptions of sexual acts says as much about the late twentieth century as it does about the nineteenth), the next most frequent expansions involve women's experiences and consciousness, and then those of race, ethnicity, and imperialism. Finally, at a deeper level, the acknowledgment of these gaps in the pretexts frequently results in a questioning of the very possibility of representation, narration, and history.

Undoubtedly part of the pull of the Victorian novel for these writers, with their postmodern skepticism about absolutes and their denial of the transparency of language which is hopelessly compromised by culture and history, is the desire to challenge several implicit claims of the Victorian novel: first, that the novel as a form and the Victorian novel in particular can "represent reality"; second, that this representation can give us some fundamental truth about human experience; and third, that the novel reinforces the idea of a unified identity.

Clearly, the novel as a form is too selective to represent reality completely. No novel can tell everything; further, the story must be mediated through a narrator or narrators (as drama or film does not need to be), which inevitably limits the representation; and the elements of plot give an order and coherence to human experience that simply do not exist in "real life." The novel's focus on the individual's development suggests a unity and linearity that postmodernism has challenged. So what better way to undermine these claims than to demonstrate their falseness in the very texts that make them?

In the effort to represent the unrepresentability of reality and to critique the claims of the novel as well as the specific gaps in the Victorian novel's representation, one type of aftered Victorian novel self-consciously and overtly calls attention to its aftering. This type has been called "historical metafiction" – fiction about fiction. Though the action is located in a realistically rendered historical past, the text questions the possibility and the truth of such a representation, both of its pretext and of itself. One way of doing this is to undermine the narrator's authority, as when the narrator of *The French Lieutenant's Woman* asks, "Who is Sarah? . . . I do not know. This story I am telling is all imagination" (Fowles 1969: 94–5). Such a novel also tries to undermine closure and hence the teleology of plot which suggests that it is possible to have a final summing up, a final meaning-making.

John Fowles's *The French Lieutenant's Woman* was not the first such work to burst on the scene in a highly visible way, but it was the one that posed these narrative issues most overtly. (In "The Literature of Exhaustion" in 1967, John Barth was also one of the first to write about the phenomenon.) Fowles's novel is set in England in 1867 and tells the story of Charles Smithson, a member of the gentry and an amateur scientist who is engaged to Ernestina, the pretty daughter of the rich owner of a large emporium. Charles meets and is attracted to Sarah Woodruff, an intelligent and passionate woman who is reputed to have been the mistress of a French lieutenant who abandoned her. The novel traces the development of the relationship between Charles and Sarah, though there are many other strands of interest – the rise to power of the capitalist class, the impact of Darwin, nascent psychology, and the lives and thoughts of the servant class. While Fowles does not base his novel on one particular Victorian novel, it calls to mind the novels of Thomas Hardy and self-reflexively employs the Victorian narrative techniques of omniscient narration, plot, and multiple stories. The narrator also makes overt analyses of the differences between the Victorian period and the late twentieth century.

The novel thus invites a double reading, and the resulting ironic commentary is directed mainly at the novel's claims to authority, though, as a discussion in *Victorian Studies* pointed out, one could also read the novel as a characteristic "sixties" move to "put the sex in" in order to show both the sexual repression of the Victorians and the more open modern response to the body (Brantlinger et al. 1972).

In a tactic characteristic of many later afterings, Fowles focuses his story on a remarkable woman who is silenced and oppressed by a society governed by narrow-minded religion and genderized science. (We must remember that many English novels from *Moll Flanders* to *Tess of the D'Urbervilles* have had a similar woman as the central character.) Though, as the title suggests, the story is focused on Sarah, it is seen through Charles, the man who desires her, and it is from his perspective that we experience the story. As a result, feminists have objected to the novel's mystification of woman, including its reinforcement of the stereotypes of woman as unknowable, passionate, devious, and untrustworthy.

Fowles's aftering also parodies aspects of the Victorian novel. Parody is "the imitation of a peculiar or unique, idiosyncratic style, the wearing of a linguistic mask, speech in a dead language" (Jameson 1991: 17). Fowles parodies the Victorian novel's omniscient narrator by giving his narrator a self-consciousness about his activity similar to that which Thackeray gives his "puppeteer" persona in *Vanity Fair*. More directly than Thackeray, however, Fowles's narrator admits that knowledge is limited, that the novel's realism is a deception, and that the reader is complicitous.

The result in Fowles's novel is an undermining of the kind of narrative authority the Victorian novel took for granted. The most notorious aspect of the narrator's subversion of the novel is his refusal to bring the story to a conventional end. Instead, he provides three different endings and invites the reader to choose which he likes best: one a conventional Victorian ending in which the hero represses his desire for the fatal woman and returns to his fiancée, and then two variations of the results of his not doing that. Both of these two endings involve his disgrace and the loss of his fiancée; in one version he ultimately gets Sarah, the girl of his dreams, and in one he does not. But in a final turn of the screw (and Henry James's novella of that name is a precursor to these efforts to undermine the omniscient authority of fiction), since the narrator must present the three endings one after another (words on a page must follow each other linearly), the final ending – in which Charles does not get Sarah – has a kind of authority that the other two do not.

It turns out not to be so easy to undermine the authority of narrative, though novel after novel tries. (The post-postmodern phenomenon of hypertext may finally achieve that.) Another narrative tactic is to conclude with an epilogue to the effect that the foregoing story was found in an archive the reliability of which is in doubt. Both *Mary Reilly* and *Jack Maggs* end this way. In the former, the epilogue introduces a skeptical narrator/editor who undercuts the authority of Mary's diaries on which the preceding story has been constructed, and in the latter the reader is told that the narrator has based the story on [fictitious] documents in the "Mitchell Library of Sydney" (Carey 1997: 357).

One novelist who is unquestionably postmodern by anybody's definition dispenses with irony and attacks the Victorian novel (among much else) head-on: the punk novelist Kathy Acker. Her fiction overall involves a fierce challenge to all received notions and conventions, including the premises of the nineteenth-century novel. As she herself declares, her texts are constructed of bits and pieces of other novels in a technique of "pastiche," which Jameson says differs from parody by its absence of ironic critique – it is "a blank parody" or "appropriation." One of these fictions is *Great Expectations* (1982), in which Acker appropriates not only one of the greatest titles in English fiction and many sentences from Dickens's novel, but also the three-part structure of Pip's expectations (childhood, which she entitles "Plagiarism" and which contains the subsections "I Recall My Childhood" and "I Journey to Receive my Fortune"; then "The Beginnings of Romance", and finally "The End"). Acker updates a number of themes in Dickens's novel: betrayed desires; hidden forces; the orphan and the family; money and love; repressed and displaced violence. And she "puts the sex in" with shocking realism.

"What a writer does, in nineteenth-century terms," Acker has said in an interview, "is that he takes a certain amount of experience and he 'represents' that material. What I'm doing is simply taking text to be the same as the world, to be equal to non-text, in fact to be more real than non-text and start *representing* text" (1991: 13). Of her novel *Great Expectations* she says it "has no beginning nor end, but there's a cumulative effect . . . I thought that I didn't need a centralized plot or centralized characters, so I would take Dickens and grid him, do a structural analysis . . . So I started doing my version of *GREAT EXPECTATIONS*, cutting it up, not even rewriting, just taking it and putting it together again, like playing with building blocks" (1991: 15–16). The overall effect of this work is multiple, but in terms of the issues here, Acker thoroughly undermines any notion of narrative authority or originality at the same time that she critiques, through the forced double reading, nineteenth-century ideas of a unified identity, representation, and gender and other hierarchies.

Jack Maggs (1997) by the Australian writer Peter Carey engages all these devices in a novel that is not quite an intervention into *Great Expectations* but rather a parallel to it. In an earlier novel, *Oscar and Lucinda* (1988), Carey described the adventures of a couple of Victorian immigrants to Australia, and in doing so wrote a twentieth-century evaluation of Victorian values. As he has said in an interview, "Australia kept on being Victorian long after the British stopped being Victorian. People arriving in Australia many years after the Victorian era well and truly ended would see its vestiges there. In the outposts of the Empire these exiled people were still keeping up the standards, unaware that they were no longer the standards. Things like that happen when people feel they are exiled from where the centre is, or from where home is" (Wachtel 1993).

In *Jack Maggs*, however, the criminal exile, a parallel to Magwitch in Dickens's novel, goes "home" after making a fortune in Australia to settle some scores and to make contact with Henry Phipps (Pip), who in Carey's aftering turns out to be an unredeemable cad. Pip's guilt and shame, which save him in Dickens's novel, are transferred to Maggs in Carey's. Though there is a potentially unreliable narrator, the novel is focused on Maggs; as Rhys did for Bertha, Carey gives Magwitch a history. In fact, the novel is concerned mainly with all the varieties of people marginalized by the bourgeois Victorian novel – servants, petty tradesmen, and criminals, the lower classes in general.

Carey "puts the sex in" and the violence; there are two abortions and the Pip character is engaged in several unpleasant homosexual affairs. (In the latter, Carey brings to the surface the repressed homosocial element in Dickens's novel.) The double reading calls attention to the bourgeois base of the Victorian novel as well as to the marginalization of the colonies, and the notion of development in the conventional bildungsroman.

Carey's parallel text also raises the issue of nineteenth-century notions of the novelist through his Dickens character, Tobias Oates, a devious and manipulative man, who gains access to Maggs's mind through mesmerism but can only turn what he finds into popular convention – a Newgate novel. The issue is: Who is to control the story of a life? Maggs is writing his own version of his life in a series of ultimately undelivered letters to Henry Phipps. The narrative uncertainty in this novel results from the four layers of narrative – the narrator's telling of the tale, Maggs's story of his life in letters, Oates's novel of the "criminal mind" as represented by Maggs, and the embedded story of Phipps/Pip's homosexual exploits. Further stories are the narratives of Mercy the maid and also of Oates himself, in particular of his incest with his wife's sister. In a twist at the end, a version of the postcolonial "empire striking back," Maggs lives happily ever after with Mercy back in Australia, while Oates dies in a fire very similar to the one he had written as the end to his version of Maggs's story.

Not all aftering texts, however, concentrate on the novel as a form. Some appear to accept the claims of the novel in terms of representation but want certain "charismatic texts" (the term is Terry Castle's in her discussion of sequels [1986: 133]) to become "more representative" through the expansion of point of view and the addition of neglected or misrepresented stories. Some of these, such as *Nice Work* (1988) by David Lodge, update a Victorian novel without necessarily attacking its gaps and absences. Lodge's novel appropriates the plot of Elizabeth Gaskell's *North and South* (1855) in which a genteel southern Englishwoman, Margaret Hale, learns about the industrial north by falling in love with a factory owner, John Thornton, and he with her. She teaches him to respect his workers and old cultural values, and he teaches her to respect the new industrial energy and creativity. The novel emblematizes this synthesis by a marriage between the two.

Lodge puts this plot into Margaret Thatcher's England of the 1980s and reproduces certain structural features of the pretext – for example, the use of epigraphs. Now the woman is a feisty English professor consumed by trendy theory, Robyn Penrose. She is as contemptuous of industry as Margaret Hale was. But Robyn too learns to respect the problems and contributions of the managing director of Pringle's engineering firm, Vic Wilcox (an allusion to *Howard's End*, perhaps?). But in this "postromantic" era (Robyn suggests it is actually a post-sex era), she does not marry him, though she does sleep with him. The novel is not really an intervention in Gaskell's text, but it does call into question the conventional Victorian novel's resolution of social problems by marriage. In Lodge's version the heroine remains single and a successful academic; the hero returns to his wife and family, loses his job, and becomes a start-up capitalist. The last paragraph is a vision of a socialist utopia where worker and manager and professional unite to make everyone's life good: this vision is certainly implied by Gaskell, but the uncertainty about narrative authority means that in Lodge's novel we are uncertain whether Lodge is mocking this utopian vision or providing it as a norm for his satire.

Recent novelists who accept the claims of the novel but want to open up "charismatic texts" to be more representative frequently turn to two novels by Emily and Charlotte Brontë, namely *Wuthering Heights* and *Jane Eyre*. No texts, other than those of Jane Austen, have generated more afterings in the twentieth century than these two. Before looking more closely at some recent versions of them, we might pause to speculate about the reasons why the novels of Austen, in particular *Pride and Prejudice*, and these two novels of the Brontës have generated so many sequels. (The Brontës' biography has also been a source for a number of twentieth-century novels, like May Sinclair's *The Three Sisters* [1914].)

The bibliography of aftertexts for these three novels and their writers is immense – close to a hundred for Austen, and for the Brontës enough for an entire book to be devoted to listing them (Stoneman 1996) – and it is growing all the time. Most of these afterings do not qualify as postmodern interventions; the impulse behind all of them is a nostalgic one. The desire to after these texts is a desire to prolong the stories either by providing sequels or by projecting them into different times, different locations, different cultures; only in a few cases is it a desire to correct something that is perceived to be wrong or missing in the pretext.

Surely some of the draw of these novels for later writers is the immensely attractive heroines – independent, self-realizing, and, in the case of Austen's and Charlotte Brontë's texts, lucky in love and life. Also a draw, though in many cases a negative one, is the powerful success in all of them of romantic love, whether the later impulse is to reproduce that success or to debunk it.

As I have said, novels fulfill our fantasies and desires, and in doing so create further desire for more narrative. These archetypal stories of women's struggles and triumph create more desire for more narrative than do most stories. But this desire to prolong in turn creates a resistance in a culture self-conscious about ideology and convention, and so the more postmodern afterings couple nostalgia with a critique of the pretexts. They usually both admire the texts and criticize them by inserting what has been ignored, diminished, mis-stated, or distorted.

Part of the reason for the popularity of the Brontë texts is the barely suppressed eroticism in the stories, a reason for condemnation in their own time and for obsessive aftering in the twentieth century. They are easy texts "to put the sex in." However, *Jane Eyre* has always been a popular source for aftering. First published in 1847, it generated a number of imitations in the nineteenth century, as Margaret Oliphant noted as early as 1855. Most were versions of Jane's story introduced into different contexts, such as Diana Maria Craik's *Olive* (1850), where Jane's plain looks are replaced by a kind of physical deformity and the heroine converts a Byronic agnostic to Christianity and marriage. But there are some, like Mary Elizabeth Braddon's *Lady Audley's Secret* (1862), which are more critical of Jane's story. Braddon combines the Jane character and the Bertha character and makes her the bigamist; in the process she takes a more negative position about both the "angel in the house" and the fairytale of the plain girl who gets the prince.

These reworkings of the Jane Eyre story continued for decades; there were adaptations in film, television, and prose fiction. The most popular of the written texts is probably Daphne du Maurier's *Rebecca* (1938). But in the 1960s and 1970s, creative and critical attention became diverted from Jane to the marginalized characters, specifically to the mad Bertha, and the novel was not merely adapted, it was aftered. Jean Rhys says she was shocked when she first read *Jane Eyre* at age seventeen. "I thought, why should she think Creole women are lunatics, and all that? What a shame to make Rochester's first wife, Bertha, the awful madwoman . . . She seemed such a poor ghost. I thought I'd try to write her a life" (Vreeland 1979: 235). She, coupled with feminist critics such as Sandra Gilbert and Susan Gubar (*The Madwoman in the Attic*), changed the way we read the pretext for ever.

Wuthering Heights was much slower entering popular consciousness. Published in the same year as *Jane Eyre*, it was generally reviled in its own time and not until the end of the century did critical opinion begin to change. In the twentieth century, du Maurier wrote a romantic version of it in *Jamaica Inn* (1936), and it has been adapted in film and television, the most crucial version being William Wyler's 1939 film that created the popular perception that *Wuthering Heights* is mostly a great love story.

The serious afterings of this novel appeared after 1960. Of these I will consider three: Lin Haire-Sargeant's *Heathcliff: The Return to Wuthering Heights* (1992), which fills in the blanks of Heathcliff's life; Alice Hoffman's *Here on Earth* (1997), which not only recasts the story in a contemporary small town in Massachusetts, but continues Brontë's story by imagining what might have happened had Cathy and Heathcliff actually lived together (it is not pleasant); and Maryse Condé's *Windward Heights* (1999 in English translation; first published 1995), which sets the story in the late nineteenth-century Caribbean and substitutes for the class differences in Brontë's novel the issue of race. (Condé said in a WNYC radio interview with Leonard Lopate in January 2000 that when she first encountered *Wuthering Heights* it was in French and she thought it was a Caribbean novel.) As one of Condé's characters says, "the tropical humus produced a society whose roots and branches were so intertwined, so twisted and interlocked that falling in love and sharing a bed with a half-brother or an unknown first cousin was no surprise" (1999: 312). The original title for her novel, which was written in French, was *La migration des cœurs*, which calls attention to the story of crossings – racial, physical, and textual – whereas the English title simply refers the novel back to *Wuthering Heights*.

Haire-Sargeant's novel is intertextual with both *Jane Eyre* and *Wuthering Heights*, its secret being that Heathcliff is the son of Rochester and Bertha. The novel brings both the sex and the violence inherent in both the pretexts to the surface, and probably this is the main import of its aftering. But, like most of the aftertexts under review here, it also tries to undermine the closure. In the last chapter the claim that Heathcliff was a real person and a friend of Emily Brontë's allows the text to suggest that Cathy did not die and that Heathcliff and she went to America. When Charlotte asks Emily, "is that true?" Emily ends the novel by saying, "you will never understand" (Haire-Sargeant 1992: 291).

Both Hoffman and Condé focus their afterings of *Wuthering Heights* on the second half of Brontë's novel. Both see the original's representation of passionate love lasting beyond death and the implied happy ending of young Cathy and Hareton's marriage and inheritance of the two estates as untenable. As the dustjacket blurb for Hoffman's book has it: "in heaven and in our dreams, love is simple and glorious. But it is something altogether different here on earth." Condé, unlike Hoffman, puts the story into a historical context, giving it a broader range than the psychological.

Both novels begin in the belief that the second generation would be for ever negatively marked by their parents' lives. Hoffman said in an interview that she remembered the Wyler movie version of *Wuthering Heights* as not having "a lot of the darkness about the second generation, so I think it started from there." In Condé's novel the narrator says, "It would be too simple if death avenged us for all the failures we accumulate while on earth; if, once in the other world, we could possess everything we wanted. Losers we are when alive, losers we remain in eternity" (1999: 281). But because Condé's novel has such an involuted narrative structure, similar to that in the pretext but far more complex, it is not clear who is speaking here. As the last page asserts, "Who would ever know the truth behind this somber love story? Who would know the fruit it had borne?" (1999: 348)

Heathcliff is the center of the moral confusion in Brontë's novel; Hoffman keeps the ambiguity in his character but demonstrates that the devastating impact he has on all around him, including the young Cathy, cannot be reversed. Condé also focuses part of her story on Heathcliff, calling him Razyé, meaning "wildlands"; he is half black, half white. The older Cathy is also a mulatta; only the Lintons or the de Linsseuils are pure white. The second generation, the young Cathy and Hareton (Razyé II, who fulfills the roles of both Linton Heathcliff and Hareton Earnshaw), are probably brother and sister. So Condé writes into *Wuthering Heights*, the ultimate charismatic text of passionate enduring love, its secret issues of race and of incest, and revises its overt issues of inheritance, violence, and betrayal – in Condé's case though not in Brontë's, the betrayal of romantic love.

But the aftering of a Victorian novel does not need a charismatic text like *Wuthering Heights* in order to pose its challenge to the assertions of the novel and the cultural equipoise of the Victorian period. William Gibson and Bruce Sterling take the most unlikely of Victorian novels to after, namely Benjamin Disraeli's social problem novel *Sybil, or the Two Nations* (1845). In the pretext, the aristocratic hero Egremont discovers the nation of the industrial and agricultural poor and falls in love with a working-class radical's daughter, Sybil. The action climaxes in a Chartist riot and ends with the marriage of Egremont and Sybil and, through them, a triumphant conservative vision of a new aristocracy which will unite the two nations of rich and poor.

Gibson and Sterling's intervention in this Victorian text is to write an "alternative history," an imagining of a "what if?" Though alternative history is a term used to describe a kind of science fiction, its postmodern elements are seen in the way it emphasizes the "extent to which history is chance-made, and therefore turns on accidents and on choices as opposed to laws or necessities" (Spufford 1996: 280). In the case of *The Difference Engine* (1991), the question posed is: "What if the nineteenth-century mathematicians Charles Babbage and Ada Byron had succeeded in building the first computer, the difference engine, in 1827?"

The answer is that Victorian Britain would have been a cyberculture where the machine took over the work of human beings and the scientists took over the government; where Disraeli became a journalist and Keats "wrote for" a kind of television. As Herbert Sussman says, "the novel asks us to redefine the Victorian period as the age of emergent information technology, as the historical site of the dissolution of the boundary between the human and the machinic in the intelligent machine" (1998: 5).

Thus, Gibson and Sterling after Disraeli's novel by reversing its value system. Egremont, with his antitechnological and conservative preference for the agrarian, feudal world, is the villain. The riot at the end, which in Disraeli's text is wrong and a failure, in the alternative history is one of liberation from the misuse of technology. For the potential of a society dominated by the machine is not seen negatively. The action of the novel charts the successful effort to wrest control of the machine and information from those who would use it to oppress through surveillance and control rather than to liberate new forms of autonomy. Gibson and Sterling thus not only reverse the roles of some of the characters and situations in the pretext, but also, through the double reading that results, critique the antitechnological thrust of Western culture from the Victorians until today in general and the conservative agrarian vision of Disraeli's *Sybil* in particular. If they are nostalgic, they are so, as Sussman says, "for the heroism of Brunel and Babbage, for the delight in invention, for the joy in working at the interface of the organic and mechanical to dissolve the boundaries of the human and machine" (1998: 17); theirs, in other words, is a nostalgia that is in opposition to and hence an implied criticism of all the other nostalgia at work in the aftering of Victorian novels.

The more usual form of nostalgia for the Victorian novel and the Victorian period is fundamental to the works of A. S. Byatt. As a reviewer of *Jack Maggs* said, in contrasting Carey's novel to Byatt's *Possession*, a novel which tells one story of passionate love in the Victorian period and several others about the more anxiety-laden love today, "the most passionate lovers are the author and the imagined Victorian past"

(Diedrick 1998). Byatt's double readings do not point to the gaps in the Victorian novel so much as suggest that it is we who have lost something important in moving away from the Victorians. *Possession* can be seen as an ironic commentary not on the Victorian novel so much as on the postmodern project itself.

The novel's action involves the pursuit by a number of American and British academics of evidence of a secret love affair between two major Victorian poets, R. H. Ash and Christabel LaMotte, very loosely based on Robert Browning and Christina Rossetti. While the story of the Victorian lovers is gradually revealed, the twentieth-century academics fall in and out of relationships with each other. The postmodern element in Byatt's novel lies mainly in its questioning of the basis of knowledge: everything the characters and the readers can know about the Victorian lovers is based on texts – biased, incomplete, indirect, and necessitating interpretation. The "truth" of texts is forever receding. We are always at a distance from "the real thing"; we are always entrapped by language. For example, the hero Roland gets the first clue to the Victorian story when he is reading about the Victorian poet Ash reading about Milton reading Genesis. To emphasize this structurally, Byatt's novel is made up of many different texts: letters, poems, journals, fairytales, criticism, biographies. Though right at the opposite end of the scale of twentieth-century fiction from Kathy Acker in terms of readability, Byatt's novel accepts Acker's premise that we have only texts, written words by which we can make contact with history – even perhaps with experience itself.

Byatt has said that what she wants is what she finds in George Eliot's novels: "not parody, not pastiche, not plagiarism – but a good and greedy reading." But the result of such a reading would inevitably "look different in modern novels – because of the pressure of the past, because of the accumulation of literary criticism and because of the weight of anxiety as it shows itself in modern form" (Byatt 1991: 149). Byatt does not criticize the Victorians; however self-conscious her narrator is, the irony is not there. Instead, what is under attack is postmodernism's skepticism and the aridness of postmodern literary criticism, including most powerfully the late twentieth century's ironic stance toward romance. *Possession* reflects a desire for both the Victorian belief in romance (the subtitle of *Possession* is "A Romance") and its trust that the novel can capture the totality of a society's experience. But it is a late twentieth-century novel, so self-consciously Byatt's text recognizes its own nostalgic desire, though it does not critique that desire. The ending of the novel invokes both nineteenth- and twentieth-century novelistic practice. While the story of the Victorian poets has a modern ending – the two poets misunderstand each other, and the letter and the message that would help them know the truth are undelivered – the narrator intervenes at the end and, through a scene that only she can "know," brings the story of the two poets to a Victorian kind of closure. The plot reinforces the twentieth-century skepticism, but the narrator's intervention supports the Victorian view that the novel can indeed reveal truth.

Byatt's critique of the postmodern project would seem to bring us to a kind of full circle. While some late twentieth-century novels continue to write into and over older texts, and while there is still a sense of belatedness in some novels, it would seem that the project of revisioning and expanding the Victorian novel is pretty much over. The drive to put into the Victorian novel the sex, the women, the lower classes, and the colonial subject, and to undermine the novel's claims of authority and truth-telling, itself feels belated now. For, as this volume testifies, we have never lost our appreciation of or our desire for the pleasures of the Victorian novel. But these afterings of the Victorian novel have for ever changed the way we read their pretexts; although the Victorian novel can recapture us again and again, our rereadings can never be innocent of what is not there.

See also THE RECEPTIONS OF CHARLOTTE BRONTË, CHARLES DICKENS, GEORGE ELIOT, AND THOMAS HARDY; THE VICTORIAN NOVEL IN FILM AND ON TELEVISION.

REFERENCES

Acker, Kathy (1982), *Great Expectations* (New York: Grove).

Acker, Kathy (1991), "Devoured by Myths: An Interview with Sylvère Lotringer," in *Hannibal Lecter My Father* (New York: Semiotext(e)).

Barth, John (1984), "Literature of Replenishment" and "The Literature of Exhaustion," in *The Friday Book: Essays and other Nonfiction* (New York: Putnam's). (First publ. in *Atlantic Monthly*, 1967.)

Borges, Jorge Luis (1962), "Pierre Menard, Author of *Quixote*," trans. E. Irby, in *Labyrinths* (New York: New Directions). (First publ. 1939.)

Brantlinger, Patrick, Adam, Ian and Rothblatt, Sheldon (1972), "*The French Lieutenant's Woman*: A Discussion," *Victorian Studies*, 15, 339–56.

Budra, Paul and Schellenberg, Betty A., eds. (1988), *Part Two: Reflections on the Sequel* (Toronto: University of Toronto Press).

Byatt, A. S. (1990), *Possession* (London: Chatto & Windus).

Byatt, A. S. (1991), *Passions of the Mind* (London: Chatto & Windus).

Carey, Peter (1997), *Jack Maggs* (London: Faber).

Castle, Terry (1986), *Masquerade and Civilization: The Carnivalesque in Eighteenth-Century English Culture and Fiction* (Stanford: Stanford University Press).

Condé, Maryse (1999), *Windward Heights*, trans. Richard Philcox (New York: Soho Press). (First publ. in French as *La migracion des cœurs*, 1995.)

Diedrick, James (1998), "Magwitch Refulgent," *About.com*, http://authors.miningco.com/arts/authors/library/arb/okcarey.htm

Douglas, Carole Nelson (1990), *Goodnight Mr. Holmes* (New York: Tor).

Fowles, John (1969), *The French Lieutenant's Woman* (New York, Boston, and London: Little, Brown).

Gibson, William and Sterling, Bruce (1991), *The Difference Engine* (New York: Bantam).

Haire-Sargeant, Lin (1992), *Heathcliff: The Return to Wuthering Heights* (London: Century).

Hoffman, Alice (1997), *Here on Earth* (New York: Berkley Books/Penguin).

Hoffman, Alice (n.d.) Interview with amazon.com, http://www.amazon.com/exec/obidos/subst/features/h/hoffman/hoffman-.../104–6690340–037880

Jameson, Frederic (1991), *Postmodernism, or, the Cultural Logic of Late Capitalism* (Durham: Duke University Press).

Lodge, David (1989), *Nice Work* (London: Penguin). (First publ. 1988.)

[Oliphant, Margaret] (1855), "Modern Novelists Great and Small," *Blackwood's Edinburgh Magazine*, 77, May, 554–6.

Polhemus, Robert (1980), *Comic Faith: The Great Tradition from Austen to Joyce* (Chicago: University of Chicago Press).

Rhys, Jean (1966), *Wide Sargasso Sea* (New York: Norton).

Spufford, Francis (1996), "The Difference Engine and *The Difference Engine*," in Jenny Uglow and Francis Spufford, eds., *Cultural Babbage* (London: Faber).

Stoneman, Patsy (1996), *Brontë Transformations: The Cultural Dissemination of* Jane Eyre *and* Wuthering Heights (London and New York: Harvester Wheatsheaf/Prentice Hall).

Sussman, Herbert (1998), "Cyberpunk Meets Charles Babbage: *The Difference Engine* as Alternate Victorian History," *Victorian Studies*, 38, 1–23.

Trollope, Anthony (1980), *An Autobiography* (Oxford: Oxford University Press). (First publ. 1883.)

Vreeland, Elizabeth (1979), "Jean Rhys: The Art of Fiction LXIV," *Paris Review*, 76, 218–37.

Wachtel, Eleanor (1993), "'We can really make ourselves up': An Interview with Peter Carey," Australian and New Zealand Studies in Canada, http://www.arts.wo.ca/~andrewf/anzsc9/Carey9.htm

FURTHER READING

Baudrillard, Jean (1988), "Simulacra and Simulations," in *Selected Writings*, ed. Mark Poster (Stanford: Stanford University Press).

Benjamin, Walter (1969), "The Task of the Translator," in *Illuminations*, ed. Hannah Arendt, trans. Harry Zohn (New York: Schocken).

Bloom, Harold (1973), *The Anxiety of Influence: A Theory of Poetry* (London: Oxford University Press).

Eco, Umberto (1986), *Travels in Hyperreality*, trans. William Weaver (New York: Harvest/Harcourt Brace Jovanovich).

Eliot, T. S. (1950), "Tradition and the Individual Talent," in *Selected Essays* (New York: Harcourt, Brace and Co.).

Felber, Lynette (1995), *Gender and Genre in Novels Without End: The British Roman-Fleuve* (Gainesville: University of Florida Press).

Foucault, Michel (1977), "What Is an Author?" in *Language, Counter-Memory, Practice*, ed. Donald F. Bouchard, trans. Donald F. Bouchard and Sherry Simon (Ithaca: Cornell University Press).

Ganner-Rauth, Heidi (1983), "'To be Continued?' Sequels and Continuations of Nineteenth-Century Novels and Novel Fragments," *English Studies*, 64, 129–43.

Gilbert, Sandra M. and Gubar, Susan (1979), *The Madwoman in the Attic: The Woman Writer and the Nineteenth-Century Literary Imagination* (New Haven and London: Yale University Press).

Glavin, John (1999), *After Dickens: Reading, Adaptation and Performance* (Cambridge: Cambridge University Press).

Hutcheon, Linda (1998), *The Poetics of Postmodernism: History, Theory, Fiction* (London: Routledge).

Kershner, R. B. (1997), *The Twentieth-Century Novel: An Introduction* (Boston and New York: Bedford).

Kiely, Robert (1993), *Reverse Tradition: Postmodern Fictions and the Nineteenth Century Novel* (Cambridge, Mass.: Harvard University Press).

Kucich, John and Sadoff, Dianne F., eds. (2000), *Victorian Afterlife: Postmodern Culture Rewrites the Nineteenth Century* (Minneapolis and London: University of Minnesota Press).

Morris, Robert K. (1972), *Continuance and Change: The Contemporary British Novel Sequence* (Carbondale: South Illinois University Press).

Schwartz, Hillel (1996), *The Culture of the Copy: Striking Likenesses, Unreasonable Facsimiles* (New York: Zone).

Serres, Michel (1982), *The Parasite* (Baltimore: Johns Hopkins University Press).

Stewart, Susan (1991), *Crimes of Writing: Problems in the Containment of Representations* (Durham: Duke University Press).

Woodmansee, Martha and Jaszi, Peter, eds. (1994), *The Construction of Authorship: Textual Appropriation in Law and Literature* (Durham: Duke University Press).

26

The Victorian Novel in Film and on Television

Joss Marsh and Kamilla Elliott

Cinema, born in 1895, grew out of many nineteenth-century arts and technologies, from stage plays and tableaux vivants to narrative paintings and magic lantern shows, optical toys, city tram-rides, waxwork exhibits, and three-dimensional photographs. In only its first twenty years it burgeoned from a showground and nickelodeon "attraction" into a narrative medium capable of complex expression. It has since established itself as the world's dominant storytelling medium. And no source has been more credited in film's transformation than the Victorian novel.

The novel almost certainly did not hold the privileged position in this development that its advocates claim, and its overvaluation has allowed critics to shake off other ancestors: painting and still photography, from which film inherited techniques from framing to the psychological use of color; dance and mime, which taught how to make stories from movement in space; and, most complexly, theater, from which film learned its languages of gesture and *mise-en-scène*.

But the Victorian novel still remains an important origin for film, and there are four main strands to consider in its persisting influence: its value as a quarry for plots and characters; the social function it transmitted to cinema; its role as narrative model; and the cultural prestige it lent the new medium. This chapter weaves those strands together, while keeping in view the fairly complex chronologies of film's development and the development of the film–novel relationship, and considers significant adaptations of specific novels, including *East Lynne*, *Vanity Fair*, *Dr. Jekyll and Mr. Hyde*, *Alice in Wonderland*, *Wuthering Heights*, *Jane Eyre*, and (as an extended case study) *Dracula*. Subjects examined include: fantasy and realism; melodrama and the mediation of theater in novel–film relations; adapting the text as against adapting the author; cultural adaptation and the film-maker as secondary *auteur*; story, history, fidelity, and authenticity; adaptation as modernization, translation, and criticism; Victorian fiction's impact on film genres; novel/film audiences, production, and censorship; Anglo-American tensions; adaptation for children; "adult" adaptation; and international/intercultural variations.

As this list implies, the very term "adaptation" covers a variety of approaches, and the century's worth of novel adaptations that have come down to us (erratically, in part because film is a volatile and perishable medium) constitutes an extraordinary record of interpretation and cultural recycling. For as long as we continue to read Victorian novels – whether we envision them as personal holy books (as Christine Edzard, a shy feminist with a background in economics and opera, did her version of *Little Dorrit* [1987]), or as the engines for creative change (as Alan Bleasdale saw *Oliver Twist* [1999], sympathetically disinterring Monks's submerged story of epilepsy and childhood rejection), or as fodder for the industrial film machine – we will continue to adapt them to the screen. For adaptation is a form of reading, one that offers texts the possibility of vivid incarnation, and one that opens up startling gaps among our different visions of them.

I

The cultural legacy of the Victorian novel was immeasurably lengthened by its role as source material, particularly during cinema's formative decades – for the vast majority of the 1,500 or more film adaptations of Victorian prose fiction were made before 1930, though those made before the early 1910s (when movies began to push toward feature length and complexity) were scenes and cameos rather than full adaptations. Some of the materials film raided were richly nostalgic, enabling a "peering into the past" (*Variety* reviewer, 29 Oct. 1915: 22) that seemed more affecting by dint of the medium's capacity to embody its fictions. The new medium blurred the boundary between fictional story and actual history: as a review of Vitagraph's 1910 *Uncle Tom's Cabin* expressed it, a film version seemed like "the real thing in every respect – real ice, real bloodhounds, real negroes, real actors, real scenes from real life as it really was in the antebellum days!" (quoted in Blum 1953: 17). Meanwhile, a strong current of reaction against our nineteenth-century grandparents quickly developed, whether in the form of modernized, pornographic, or children's adaptations, post-Freudian adaptations claiming to "out" sexuality, films incorporating contemporary biographical and literary criticism (on all of which, see below), or parodies (like *Dr. Jekyll's Hide* [1932]).

The novel's legacy extends into the imaginative operations of everyday twentieth-century life. The classical Hollywood feature film took – "relay fashion," as in a race – the "historical place" and "social function," as Christian Metz memorably puts it, of the "grand-epoch, nineteenth-century novel," which "the twentieth-century novel, less and less diegetic and representational, tends partly to abandon." It inherited fiction's burden of social commentary, community-building, and the dramatization of values. And film's history as a cultural formation revealingly parallels its predecessor's. Both Victorian novel and narrative film, for example, offer audiences (as Metz has it) behavioral blueprints and "libidinal prototypes" (1977: 110). Both lay structural stress on endings that return the story world to order, marriage, and family:

thus, no less than Braddon's 1862 sensation novel *Lady Audley's Secret*, a postwar *film noir* like *Mildred Pierce* (1945), starring "independent" Joan Crawford, seeks to neutralize at the close the threats (female power, desire, and autonomy) unleashed in the course of the narrative.

While much remains to be done on these subjects, there has already been much impressive work on film's more formal inheritance from Victorian fiction. Some powerful narrative models like the adventure and detective stories, which throve on physical action and the concrete presentation of evidence – made their way into film without regard to particular progenitors. Fundamental to film's development was the diffused influence of classic realist narration, from which the medium may have derived scopic (that is, highly visual) narration, as in Hardy's opening to *The Return of the Native*, which descends slowly on Egdon Heath from an aerial perspective; the mingling of melodramatic convention with realistic settings, as in the sleepwalking scene of his *Tess of the D'Urbervilles*; sudden shifts between scenes (montage or "editing"), as in the movement back and forth between Bathsheba, Troy, and Boldwood as they prepare for the fatal party in the seven-part chapter (52) entitled "Converging Courses" in *Far from the Madding Crowd*; attention to telling empirical detail, like Tess's boots or Jude's dog-eared books; and shifting points of view, for example from Bathsheba's to her suitors'.

The role of American director D. W. Griffith in this development looms large. His technique of "cross-cutting" or "parallel editing" (switching back and forth between two simultaneous lines of action) may well have owed much to Dickens, as the director protested (perhaps mythically) to his baffled producers at the Biograph studio in 1908; it structures even the founding epic of Western cinema, Griffith's adaptation of 1903/1905 novels by white supremacist Thomas Dixon, *The Birth of a Nation* (1915). In a seminal essay of 1944, Soviet director and film theorist Sergei Eisenstein traced cross-cutting and other innovations in editing "syntax" to Griffith's encounter with Victorian fiction, especially Dickens. But Griffith made equally creative use of the era's poetry (notably Tennyson's *Enoch Arden*) and drama. Despite Griffith's and Eisenstein's stress on Dickens, there is no single novelistic Victorian "father" of film – not Hardy (film's one living link to the Victorian novel, who even wrote program notes for the 1915 British film of *Far from the Madding Crowd*); not George Eliot, whose work has been extensively discussed in terms of visual art; not Robert Louis Stevenson or Bram Stoker, whose *Dr. Jekyll* and *Dracula* (as we shall see) have proved more fertile ground for adaptation than any other Victorian fiction; not Dickens, though his popularity, his theatricality, his larger-than-life mythic characters, and the intensity with which place, sensation, vision, and the material world are rendered in his fiction make him the best candidate for the role.

Between novel and film also lies the crucial influence of Victorian melodrama, which the example of Mrs. Wood's blockbuster weepie *East Lynne* (1861) may begin to unravel. The book was filmed as early as 1902, and again in 1910 (twice), 1913, and 1922. A catalogue entry for the 1910 British Precision Films version succinctly captures its appeal for early audiences: "Lady elopes with murderer, is abandoned, and poses as nurse to dying son." But even the more ambitious 1913 version, the first British six-reel feature, demonstrates the importance of melodramatic content in triggering formal development. For it was *East Lynne*'s very requirements of suspense, emotion, and intrigue that suggested, for example, the close-up visual miscue – the initials "RH" on a gun – that convicts an innocent man of a killing; large-scale camera panning that allows lascivious villain Francis Levison (literally) to mislead Lady Isabel; and dynamic composition in depth, as in a scene where he stalks her as she plays blind man's buff with her children, a perfect visual translation of the heroine's unseeing vulnerability.

But we misunderstand both the Victorian novel's relations with film, and film's relations with its other ancestors, if we do not also consider that *East Lynne* had long been a standard warhorse of the Victorian stage. Its multiple theatrical manifestations mediated Wood's text for film. (We could multiply similar examples: Griffith's 1909 film of Dickens's Christmas tale, *The Cricket on the Hearth*, for example, was based on a theatrical version of Dickens's text by Victorian showman Albert Smith; and his *Way Down East* [1920] incorporated scenes from stage versions of *Tess* and *Uncle Tom's Cabin*.) The stage mediated relations between the Victorian novel and cinema through the 1930s, a fact which has been alternately repressed and overstressed, depending on the type of theater in question.

Thus, credits for the 1913 *East Lynne* list only the film's novel source, not its popular stage antecedents; disreputable early film quickly began (as the British *Kinematograph Monthly Film Record* put it) to take its melodrama "mellowed by a little literary tradition" (quoted in Low and Manvell 1950: 204). The melodrama-repressing maneuver also obliterated the complicating fact of widespread theatrical borrowings by novel-writers from Brontë and Dickens to James. One reason for historical overemphasis on film's novelistic inheritance thus lies in the medium's craving for legitimacy.

Another way to achieve that desired end, however, was affiliation with highbrow theater. This is the message of the unusual filmic preface to the 1917 *Masks and Faces*. Through title cards, distinguished members of the "Council of the Academy of Dramatic Art" discuss how to clear off a debt.

> *Sir James Barrie.* Why not an All-star film – say "MASKS AND FACES"?
> *Sir Arthur Pinero.* A most excellent suggestion, too. The "Pictures" owe much to the stage.
>   It [*sic*] shall repay.
> *Sir John Hare.* There shall be no caste prejudice. The film is the sister of the stage.

The "legitimate" stage – or so its luminaries believe – lends prestige to the screen, its natural (though subordinate) "sister" art, so that the film version of a stage play rep(l)ays a debt.

However, many film scholars have seen such deference to theater as a growth-retarding incubus on early film, limiting it to a proscenium-arch view of screen action, perpetuating a confusion of shot with scene as the natural "unit" of film, and so forth. By this logic, cinema secured its aesthetic future only by its turning to the novel; the more film adopted prose fiction's techniques, the further it moved from filmed theater (what the luminaries of 1917 call "a worthy memory" of stage production) to an independent art. While this theater phobia has been overstated, the history of novel adaptation and early film in general does evidence a distinct shift from a flat theatrical mode to a more kinetic filmic narrative over the 1910s and 1920s. The change is apparent in three silent films of *Vanity Fair*.

Vitagraph's 1911 version, for example, positions the viewer in the stalls of an imaginary theater, sticking resolutely to a static camera in long or three-quarters shot (a variation one review denounced as a "pernicious habit" of "cutting the characters off at the knees" [*Moving Picture World*, 16 Dec. 1911: 887]). Scenes generally begin with entrances and end with exits; there is no cross-cutting between scenes and few outdoor shots. In the near-absence of dialogue, the film creates a series of tableaux vivants held together by a thin narrative thread; title cards take the form of scene headings – "In Vauxhall Gardens" – or brief plot summaries – "The Marquis schemes to rid himself of Rawdon."

By contrast, an Edison version of 1915 bristles with dialogue: "God forgive me, Mr. Sedley, but you are no better than a coward!"; "Tell father-to-take-care-of . . . -Amelia." While this development may have evidenced a minor element of theatrical motivation, the camera's movement into the action emphatically did not. Here, the actors' bodies are more frequently seen in medium shot, though (as *Variety* tartly speculated), "[p]rofiting by the mistake of several years ago when Mrs. Fiske was picturized in 'Tess of the D'Urbervilles' and showed the 'ravages of time,' there are no [facial] close-ups" (29 Oct. 1915: 22). (The film does have close-ups of objects.) The camera is freer, moving within shots, and we cross-cut suspensefully between a praying Amelia, a dying George, a fleeing Jos, and a machinating Becky as the war presses toward its climax.

But it is not until a 1922 British version of *Vanity Fair* that we see the variety of shot sizes and camera angles that mark the more mature silent film. Though the adaptation never escapes stilted homage to its source text, it nevertheless creates a spatial sense of the romantic triangle between Becky, Rawdon, and Lord Steyne. Rawdon does not strut full-length on to a set stage as he does in the earlier versions, but is introduced in a midshot cameo mask, which opens to show him in characteristic context, playing cards. Similar introductions to Becky and Steyne follow, and it is only as the shot widens that we become aware that the three characters inhabit adjoining spaces. Thus, through clever use of editing, *mise-en-scène*, and camera angle, the actors are both separated and brought together.

Besides their obvious debts to theater, the two earlier films of *Vanity Fair* also dramatize a fraught relationship of written text to visual image. The films are full of letters, bills, notes of hand, battle orders, invitations, calling cards, newspapers, and paper money, which have power to move bodies to battle, to prison, to parties, and into the maelstrom of emotion. Meanwhile, however, characters also fetishize pictures and the pictorial. The 1915 *Vanity Fair* in particular pits picturesque Amelia (worshipper of her dead husband's portrait) against textual tyrant Mr. Osborne, who suffers a (literal and figurative) heart attack when he catches sight of her in an affecting maternal pose with her son, and falls to the ground – after writing a new will in their favor.

Such interplay of visual and verbal reminds us that the Victorian novel was itself a mixed, illustrated medium. Both the 1911 and 1915 films of *Vanity Fair* play to their audience's familiarity with Thackeray's illustrations: the plate "Mr. Joseph Entangled," for example, becomes a filmic tableau vivant in 1911; the 1915 Edison version adapts an endpiece of George and Amelia at the piano. Other films – like the 1914 London Film version of George du Maurier's 1894 *Trilby* – seem to exist for the pure pleasure of animating much-loved illustrations. (Du Maurier's drawings were more romantically approachable than Thackeray's semiotically complex illustrations.) Book illustration historians have thus argued that the cinema displaced Victorian illustrated fiction (James 1947: 9; Harthan 1981: 279). In fact, the new medium may have shouldered aside not only illustration, but also the art form which flourished at its side throughout the nineteenth century, the theatrical tableau vivant. It was precisely the tableau vivant interlude which early film shorts replaced on vaudeville and music hall programs; and films like the 1902 *East Lynne* were explicitly presented in catalogues and publicity as tableaux from well-known texts: "Elopement – Abandoned – Home Again – Little Willie – Death of Lady Isabel."

The British may have been constitutionally prone to view film as "illustration" in a secondary sense, since the Victorian novel was their inheritance, and British versions of Victorian fiction were more artistically inhibited by respect, patriotism, and cultural pride. But all adaptations found prestige and promotional value wherever they could. Cultural capital funded, for example, the Gaumont company's "Novels in a Nutshell" in the early 1900s, and a constant tension endures between the economic value and wider audiences that film brings literature and the prestige that literature, reciprocally, lends to film. Significantly, 73 percent of best-film Oscars between 1927 and 1995 went to adaptations. More copies of *Wuthering Heights* were sold in a single year after MGM's 1939 film version was released than in the nearly one hundred years since its publication; there were similar dramatic increases in the readership of *David Copperfield* and of *Pride and Prejudice* in 1935 and 1940 (Bluestone 1971: 4). More recently, a 1985 study found that 46 percent of viewers had bought or borrowed a novel directly as a result of seeing a television adaptation (Giddings et al. 1990: 22–3); the "tie-in" paperback classic is a lucrative publishing phenomenon, and any glance at a bestseller list reveals the ongoing influence of film and television adaptations on popular literary consumption.

In 1911, Vitagraph located prestige in title, author, and literary respectability: "VANITY FAIR . . . Based on the Classic Novel . . . by William Makepeace Thackeray" (opening title). In 1915, studio identity and star value outweighed the novel's claims: "The Thomas A. Edison Studios . . . Present . . . Mrs. Fiske . . . as . . . Becky Sharp . . . in Vanity Fair." The opening sequence of the 1922 British *Vanity Fair* (one of the series "Tense Moments with Great Authors") piled on the claims to audience attention, from theatrical prestige (shot 1), through scholarly accuracy (shot 2), to prideful sense that the story happened "here" (shots 4 and 5):

1. Credits card – theatrical review of cast.
2. Close-up-cover of the original monthly parts, 1846.
3. Cameo portrait – author Thackeray.
4. Close-up-plaque: "L.C.C. [London County Council] W. M. Thackeray. 1811–1863. Novelist. Lived Here."
5. Pull back to long shot – whole house front. Fade to:
6. Title card – "Colonel Rawdon Crawley C. B. [Clive Brook] – the distinguished Waterloo officer . . ."

Embedded in such claims to respect and attention was the insinuation that fiction's realization on screen can invite us into the living presence of an author, while the film (by implication) flows straight from his pen. Edison pledged that a "prologue" to its 1915 *Vanity Fair*, for example, "will show Thackeray, in all verity, in his study starting to write the novel" (*Motography*, 10 July 1915: 51). The film's prefatory shot, of course, shows not Thackeray but an actor impersonating him (as the celebrity of later photographs, moreover, not the man who wrote *Vanity Fair*); it concludes with an image of him placing the final period on the text's last handwritten page, as if Thackeray has "written" the film. So, too, autobiographical readings of Dickens's *David Copperfield* inspired intense filmic fantasies of proximity to an embodied author. The final shots of the 1923 Nordisk Films "authentic version" show:

1. Medium long shot – the young David and Agnes embrace.
2. Title card – "Fifteen years later we find a famous author in the happiest period of his life. He calls himself . . . David Copperfield."
3. Long shot – bearded middle-aged gentleman with his family in a sunny park.
4. Title card – ". . . But his real name is . . . CHARLES DICKENS."
5. Close-up oval cameo portrait – David Copperfield/Charles Dickens.

The immobile face of the actor finally blinks, as if to reassure us that the filmic embodiment is indeed "real." Television Dickens has continued the intimate trajectory: the 1999 BBC *David Copperfield*, for example, substituted "accurate" details of Dickens's childhood misery in a blacking factory for his fictional account of David's drudgery. Mary Shelley's maternal traumas and Emily Brontë's moorland wanderings have been similarly credited with the inspiration of *Frankenstein* (dir. Branagh, 1994; see also *Gothic*, dir. Polanski, 1986) and *Wuthering Heights*.

II

Some of the greatest film adaptations of Victorian fiction, however, have had little to do with the embodiment of Victorian authors or the identification of authors with their characters. And if the history of film has been a long series of alternations between the founding traditions of the brothers Louis and Auguste Lumière – film's ancestral documentary-makers – and Georges Méliès – the magician–showman who invented special effects, the era before talkies (1895–1928) inclined to Méliès and to magic. This was true even of the full-grown silent feature: it was an international entertainment, romantic, fantastical, and proletarian; it traded on the enabling distance from real life granted by silence. Eliot, Trollope, Thackeray, and the rest had little impact on the film genres that established themselves by the 1920s. What most attracted cinema – besides melodrama – in these days before the coming of synchronized sound was not classic Victorian realism but the fiction of the adventurous and decadent 1880s and 1890s, when most early film-makers were young. And nothing lured more than late Victorian Gothic. Bram Stoker's *Dracula* (1897) and Robert Louis Stevenson's *The Strange Case of Dr. Jekyll and Mr. Hyde* (1886) remain the most-filmed texts of all time, beating out – at more than 200 versions, revisions, and loose adaptations each – Rider Haggard's 1887 adventure *She* (whose exoticism was a more expensive proposition), *Frankenstein* (whose female authorship thwarted Hollywood's gendered sense of genre), and even Dickens's *Christmas Carol* and *Oliver Twist* (each repeatedly filmed, but only one-quarter as often as *Dracula* and *Dr. Jekyll*). What factors account for the special status of these two texts?

As we might expect, both were popular stage properties; and both made play of theatrical conventions – the dark double and the Gothic specter. More crucially, both texts refigured Christian material (resurrection, communion, possession) and condensed period fears about the human body (disease, degeneration, and post-Darwinian animalism) into narratives with startling clarity of mythopoeic action, whose fearfulness has remained current. Both were nonrealist texts, and neither entered the canon of Victorian fiction before the last quarter of the twentieth century – factors which muted objection to creative departures in their cinematic versions. And both texts were libidinally saturated.

Dracula may be the more perfect test case for the critical claim that nineteenth-century Gothic fiction has functioned (and continues to function) as the Freudian id or lurid subconscious of film. "I'm going below," says the first mate, the last of his crew left alive, to the captain of the doomed ship *Demeter* in F. W. Murnau's 1922 version, "I want to look in the hold." In the *Dracula* adaptation and its film descendants (as in *Jekyll and Hyde*, where psychic geography admits the dark self through the doctor's "back door"), the night-time and shadowy fears and desires that belong "down there" rise like the vampire from his grave into consciousness. Stoker's fiction allowed cinema access to decadence without risk of censorship, though there was an obvious relationship between vampires and "vamps" (the term dates from Theda Bara's 1915 film *A Fool There Was*): Dracula's conversion of sex into violence, and its displaced pornographic fixation on the dead and rotting (as opposed to the ecstatic and tabooed) body, have become standard tropes of film horror.

The film history of Dracula opens doors on the transforming exigencies of directorial styles and production methods, and on the creative interchanges between adapter and text. The first major version, the 1922 *Nosferatu* by Murnau (who had made a version of *Dr. Jekyll* two years before – now lost, as is 80 percent of silent film), was an illegal as well as a loose adaptation. Stoker's widow prosecuted for copyright infringement, but her husband's text owes its long cinematic afterlife to the film she tried to destroy. *Nosferatu* is a masterpiece whose artistic shadow falls across all subsequent adaptations; like the novel it adapts, the film entwines itself with the cultural history of the uncanny, the horrible, the camp, and the queer.

The film proclaims independence in its very title: the more exotically alien name "Nosferatu" (a Romanian variant for "vampire") appears only once in the novel (Stoker 1983: 237). And *Nosferatu* is shaped by its director's obsessions as much as by Stoker's – Murnau's fascination with two seventeenth-century ancestors accused of witchcraft, his complex about his great height (which he projects on to his spindly Count Orlok), and his self-knowledge as a homosexual dandy (Murnau does not shrink from the implications of the Count's relations with Harker, here renamed Hutter). Parts of the film are even narrated in first-person titles, with no basis in Stoker's text.

But the peculiar force of *Nosferatu* owes as much to its German origin as to Murnau's imaginative self-investment. On the one hand, distance from Britain brought creative freedom; on the other, transposition to a German setting allowed Stoker's borrowings from uncanny German romantic sources like Goethe's *Faust* and Wagner's *Flying Dutchman* to come fruitfully to the surface. Film adaptation thus also became cultural translation and national cooption. *Nosferatu*'s impact certainly owes much to its location within the broad movement of German expressionism, which turned eagerly from poetry and drama to the alternative new medium of film in the face of the horrors and generational betrayals of World War I: the movement found a charged vehicle in *Dracula*'s myth of mass carnage and bloodsucking old aristocracy. The novel's bodily mutations and eerie settings, meanwhile, appealed vividly to an artistic vision which projected angst on to the material world.

Thus, through Murnau (and his gifted designer, spiritualist Albin Grau), the Gothic settings of Stoker's *Dracula* – the castle courtyard across which falls the vampire's shadow, the pointed archway that frames him – entered the vocabulary of mainstream world cinema with redoubled Gothic intensity. *Nosferatu* remains an extraordinary example of how film works to transform the words and images of literary texts into objective and affective visual worlds. Tod Browning spent most of his budget for the 1931 *Dracula* recreating at Universal Studios the monumental staircases and crypts that Murnau found on location; Browning's *Dracula* learned the lesson that adaptations should adapt previous adaptations, and deteriorates badly when it stops imitating Murnau's *Nosferatu*. Films as different as Leni Riefenstahl's propaganda masterpiece *Triumph of the Will* (1935) went so far as to replicate individual shots, like Murnau's bird's-eye perspective on the empty street of a medieval town. In *Nosferatu*'s plague sequence the street slowly fills with coffins and bearers; in *Triumph*, with a different sense of fulfillment, it is overrun by a slow-marching procession of Hitler-saluting Nazi troops.

Regrettably, it was not only the style of *Nosferatu* that proved grist to the Nazi mill. The film's content – and thus, obliquely, the content of Stoker's *Dracula* – was also perversely useful. Though Stoker was certainly xenophobic, Murnau was not antisemitic: his film locates its horrors not in another country (Stoker's demonized

Transylvania), but in a more amorphous "Land of Shadows" or "Phantoms." But *Nosferatu* brought intensely into being a chalk-white, stick-thin, obscurely foreign vampire, with rat-like teeth, pointed ears, and claw-like nails – all features culled from a few pages of Stoker's text (1983: 17–18), but magnified by film realization; Orlok/Dracula brings the plague to Wisborg as surely as the rats who arrive with him in the hold of the ship *Demeter*. This Count proved not only the founding type of the monster we see in film's mirror, but also a model for the subhuman, alien Jew of "documentary" Nazi hate films like *The Eternal Jew* (1938), which prepared the way for the Final Solution. Moreover, it has been argued that expressionist film nourished a debilitating sense of dread in the German people that made them fatally susceptible to authoritarian suggestion (see Kracauer 1947, passim). And textual undercurrents of helpless impotence and male hysteria are certainly brought uppermost by Murnau's version of Dracula: the agent of the Count's downfall, for example, is not Stoker's strong band of male vampire-hunters but Mina (renamed Ellen), who defeats him only by surrendering herself to him. Shifts like these had incalculable but troubling real-world consequences.

Hollywood had a different sense of otherness, and different models to impose on Stoker's text. In *Nosferatu*, a considerable intellectual ("Herr Doktor" to his crew) and film *auteur* met a popular Victorian author, with disturbing and beautiful results. In Tod Browning's *Dracula* (1931), a still-risky literary property met the studio system, by way of a cliché- and box-set-bound stage production, under the nominal directorial control of an alcoholic ex-circus clown. Browning's 1931 *Dracula* is a resolutely mass-market product, though one almost as rich as Stoker's text in popular-cultural interest.

While *Nosferatu* had fulfilled Stoker's fear of contamination and social disorder, in the capitalist studio system's *Dracula* everything is predicated upon the individual, and nothing is put down to the state. It is not London that is threatened by the vampire's presence – just a few flower-sellers. Hollywood's industrial process flattens out ambiguities that Murnau's film had heightened – like the confusion of reference and meaning in Ellen/Mina's anticipatory cry (as both husband and vampire approach): "He is coming!" The 1931 film contains and sensationalizes the gender disturbance of Stoker's myth through an open format of misogynistic rape fantasy: Mina is straightforward prey; Lucy – and, with her, active female desire – is cut down to small size; Harker is never unmanned by going to Transylvania (the trip instead drives Renfield mad); and patriarchal authority is neatly reasserted by giving Mina a father, and giving Seward (Stoker's madhouse doctor) the paternal role. Meanwhile, Browning's *Dracula* revels in its ethnographic tourist trappings of Transylvanian peasants. The film has no truck with Murnau's "Land of Shadows"; here, the uncanny remains safely exoticized. *Dracula* fulfills, in fact, all the promise of the abortive 1930 sound reissue of *Nosferatu*, *Die Zwoelfte Stunde* (The Twelfth Hour), in which – courtesy of re-editing, out-takes, and stock footage – Ellen/Mina survives her encounter with the Count for a classically inappropriate happy ending, her (delayed) wedding to Hutter/Harker.

What most turned the 1931 *Dracula* into a cult classic was its Count's un-American otherness. The weird conviction that screen unknown Bela Lugosi brought the role lends camp depth to his poppycock lines (learned phonetically, and heavily accented by his native Hungarian). Browning's *Dracula* rapidly became the secondary source of a decadent Stoker lineage: Hammer Horror's long string of "sex vampire" B-movies (1957–), shot in bloodily lurid Technicolor; Harry Kumel's 1971 lesbian *Daughters of Darkness*; Roman Polanski's gay parody *Dance of the Vampires* (a.k.a. *The Fearless Vampire Killers*, 1967); the Warhol Factory's flat-footed *Blood for Dracula* (1974); a clutch of pornographic films; and Werner Herzog's return to Murnau and Stoker, *Nosferatu, the Vampyre* (1979), which experimented with group hypnotism in filming the townspeople's plague-dance of death. A related and perverse admiration for the Count's celebrity "aura," together with a post-1960s youth-culture appreciation of the horror of aging incarnated by Stoker's Count (who "grow[s] young" while Harker ages overnight [p. 172]) strongly marks numerous films more distantly related to the original text, including *Martin* (1976), *The Hunger* (1981, starring rock idol David Bowie), *The Lost Boys* (1987), *Nadja* (1992), and Neil Jordan's screen version of Anne Rice's *Interview with the Vampire* (1994), which imagines the vampire Lestat as a rock star ("For [Anne Rice's] vampires," writes Nina Auerbach, "spectacle is the only credible substance" [1995: 155]). The proliferation is startling, though its trajectories trace the same lines as two generations of *Dracula* criticism.

It is no wonder that Francis Ford Coppola felt the need to distinguish his *Bram Stoker's Dracula* (1992) by trumpeting the author's name, and thus his version's claim to "faithfulness" and "authenticity," despite its intrusion of a previous-life "undying" love story between Mina and Dracula, variously plagiarized from a 1974 TV movie *Dracula*, Haggard's much-filmed *She*, and Jean Cocteau's classic 1946 film of the fairy-tale *Beauty and the Beast*. (The ploy bred other titular co-options of authors: Branagh's 1994 *Mary Shelley's Frankenstein*, and the 1998 television productions *Thomas Hardy's Tess of the D'Urbervilles* and *Emily Brontë's Wuthering Heights*.) Nevertheless, it is no longer possible to make a direct adaptation of *Dracula*; in filming the text, one also films a tradition coterminous with the horror film, even with cinema itself. Hence the kaleidoscopic inclusiveness of Coppola's operatic extravaganza, in which the hypnotic eyes of Bela Lugosi meet the detachable demonic shadow of Murnau's Count Orlok, Tod Browning's Gothic castle is inhabited by Hammer vamps, *The Hunger*'s blood disease mimics the absinthe addiction of Stoker's *fin de siècle*, and – above all – Mina and the Count enter their vampiric love relationship by entering a "kinematograph" exhibition.

For Coppola's version is not only a "testimonial to the glories of film making as an end in itself" (Vincent Canby, *New York Times*, 13 Nov. 1992: B1); it is also a film in which cinema acknowledges and returns to its origins, as a medium possessed not only with the power to titillate (Mina and the Count watch a naked lady in flickering black-and-white on the screen), but with the "animating" powers of that machine to bring stillness to movement and death into life – a phenomenon which should rightly remind us of *Dracula*'s original title, "The Un-Dead." Film and film spectatorship may even be forms of vampirism, Murnau would have us suspect: the shadow of his *Nosferatu* repeatedly falls before "us" across his victims, as if it were our own; and the text's motif of hypnotism was uncannily insinuated in one of Grau's production sketches, in which "monstrous beams, projected outwards" from the Count's burning eyes, "transfix [the] spectator/victim" (Skal 1990: 45), a rich suggestion crudely capitalized upon in Browning's film and lurid promotion of Lugosi as Dracula.

Thus, Stoker's *Dracula* was both conceived at exactly the same time as the new medium of film, and in some sense also imagined its advent. The text itself tells how its night-time fears play on the screen of the mind, as the vampirized Lucy describes it, like "bad dreams" (1983: 125), a line transferred to the bloodsucking asylum inmate Renfield in Tod Browning's 1931 version, and delivered several times over with eye-popping relish. What makes Stoker's text – like *Dr. Jekyll* – so attractive to film is that its emphases on transformation and materialization are peculiarly and perfectly realizable by film, with that medium's capacity (thanks to Méliès-like trickery) to make the fantastic seem as solidly real as the railroads and factories of the Lumières' prosaic universe.

III

Realism did not slumber through the 1920s and the heyday of the silent feature. For while, on the one hand, film presents itself as specter, on the other, the fleeting mental images inspired by the symbolic signs of texts also seem to cry out for incarnation in more phenomenological sign systems. From the mid-nineteenth century, as one period reviewer wrote, "the desire for realization" – which Martin Meisel glosses as "both literal re-creation and translation into a more real, that is more vivid, visual, physically present medium" – "gr[ew] almost a passion with our young artists and poets." And the desire extended naturally into a boundless appetite for film adaptations of fiction. On screen, as on stage or in paint, as Meisel puts it, "Always . . . the effect depended on the apparent literalness and faithfulness of the translation, as well as the material increment" (Meisel 1983: 30, 36).

Fidelity of realization expressed itself partly in commitment to historical authenticity. In the case of Henry King's 1925 production of *Romola* this was "attested by DR. GUIDO BLAGI, Director of the Laurentian Library, FLORENCE, ITALY." Yet sometimes authenticity conflicted with textual fidelity. So, in a 1923 interview, "Hugo Ballin Edits 'Vanity Fair,' Cutting the Anachronisms," the adapter proudly announces that "the costumes in the pictures are more correct than those described in the book," as are the facial hair, smoking practices, and use of envelopes (*New York Tribune* 6 May 1923: VI: 3; there are no known surviving copies of this film).

At the other end of this corrective spectrum lies the imposition of twentieth-century ideologies and values on Victorian texts. This was most honestly achieved in modernizations of the text, which are common from the earliest days of cinema: 1906 witnessed Vitagraph's *A Modern Oliver Twist; Or, The Life of a Pickpocket*, 1908 Selig Company's *The Modern Dr. Jekyll*. Other adaptations update appearance, speech patterns, and character psychology. A 1918 flapper version of *Jane Eyre* makes perky Jane so evidently and sighingly in love with Rochester that even Bertha (renamed Pauline) quips: "I am not so mad as not to see you are trying to get him from me." George Edwardes Hall's 1920 *Dr. Jekyll and Mr. Hyde* (less well-known than John S. Robertson's Gothic version of the same year) casts Jekyll as a jet-set golfer, diner, and opera-goer. His greatest crime in this film is neglecting his social duties to attend to the lower classes. And the atrocities he commits as Hyde turn out to be only a dream: as he writhes in the electric chair, turning from Jekyll to Hyde and back again before the horrified gaze of his captors, the scene dissolves to show him seated in a comfortable armchair, wriggling as his fiancée tickles him with a feather. They will live happily ever after, we infer, so long as he fulfills his class role correctly.

In a similar vein, though with opposite political aims, the BBC's 1985 *Oliver Twist* aims at leftist social realism combined with historical public-health accuracy in its depiction of lower-class characters. Noah Claypole, for example, sports a runny nose and facial sores; even Nancy has a large mole. But the attempt at realism paradoxically overemphasizes the grotesque element in Dickens's and George Cruikshank's depictions. For while it reflects Victorian reality, we are left with a still more problematic class contrast than author and illustrator created: on film, the execrable gentleman in the white waistcoat does not affront us with his face; the less reprehensible Artful Dodger does.

Other films adapt literary criticism as much as they do literature. Patricia Rozema added postcolonial and gender critiques of slavery and patriarchy to her 1999 *Mansfield Park*, in which Sir Thomas Bertram features as arch-villain, equally violent to sons and slaves, and hedonistic, late twentieth-century morality displaces Austen's own austere analysis: in the novel, Sir Thomas rightly puts down a theatrical entertainment of which Fanny and Edmund both disapprove; in the film, he is simply a killjoy, a crime an entertainment medium will hardly forgive.

Nowhere, however, are corrections of our Victorian ancestors more relentlessly relished than in attempts to restore the sexuality we believe they repressed. Those borderline Victorians, Jane Austen and Henry James, are particular favorites of revisionism. Rozema's *Mansfield Park* adds touches of lesbian eroticism between Mary Crawford and Fanny (refigured as a feisty feminist version of author Austen herself); the BBC's 1995 *Pride and Prejudice* parades a handsome, bathing Darcy ("Tonight's the night, ladies!" ran newspaper headlines when the déshabillé episode was about to be aired). Peter Bogdanovich's *Daisy Miller* (1974) features nudity; Iain Softley's *The Wings of the Dove* (1997) contains sex scenes. But the works of both borderline and bona fide Victorians were more generally eroticized after the collapse of old film censorship codes in 1969. A 1970 *Wuthering Heights* exhibits a post-coital Cathy and Heathcliff; Joseph tells the latter (who smirks) that Edgar is "waiting to see the color" of Cathy's baby's eyes; and Heathcliff asks Isabella, in one decidedly un-Victorian exchange, "Do you fancy a tumble?"

Not all post-Freudian revisions are outings of sexuality. Some adaptations transpose hero and villain in the psychoanalytic belief that it is repression rather than unbridled libido that destroys. In both Jane Campion's *The Piano* (1993), which she has called her "tribute" to *Wuthering Heights*, and a 1979 episode of the television series *Fantasy Island*, "Wuthering Heights/House of Dolls," it is the civilized, decorous Edgar (or his surrogate) who violently threatens to rape (and, in Campion's film, ultimately dismembers) Cathy; Heathcliff, meanwhile, is reshaped as a harmless Harlequin romancer, and (on Fantasy Island) Edgar's efforts to have him certified insane backfire, as a wise onlooker summarizes: "Perhaps the wrong gentleman was considered for the asylum." Rouben Mamoulian's 1931 *Jekyll and Hyde* revises on all fronts, replacing Stevenson's war of good and evil with a battle between id and superego, and swapping a craving for sexual knowledge for Jekyll's quest for philosophical–moral perfection. Thus he suggestively tells his fiancée: "You've opened a gate for me into another world . . ."

Title cards are a thing of the past in Mamoulian's early synchronized sound film; we hear the tension and desire in Jekyll's voice. While, for many film-makers, sound reinforced film's propensities toward the real, Mamoulian used it to derealize his adaptation and to bring forward (as Murnau did through *Nosferatu*'s expressive locations) the psychological dimensions of the text. The film's most famous sound sequence is Jekyll's first transformation into Hyde, an "incredible reality" Mamoulian suggested through "a mélange of sounds that do not exist in nature" (as he remembered in a 1973 interview), like the light of a candle (photographed and transformed into sound), the beat of a gong (with the impact cut off, and run backwards), and (since "the whole thing lacked rhythm"), the noise of the director's own heartbeat (*Film Journal*, 2: 2 [March 1973]: 42).

Psychological shots and Freudian symbolism proved invaluable in getting around another new development: the Hayes Production Code, which brought formal censorship to film in 1931. Like the prudish dictates personified by Victorian novelists and publishers as "Mrs. Grundy," this was a censorship voluntarily self-imposed with an eye to holding onto the industry's single, unified, family-dominated audience. It proved equally literal-minded: just as Victorian critics missed the phallic import of Louisa Gradgrind's fiery smokestacks in Dickens's *Hard Times*, so film censors blanked out the implications of a pot boiling over on a stove in Mamoulian's *Jekyll and Hyde*, and even of a cliché-laden dream sequence in MGM's 1941 remake, in which Ingrid Bergman's laughing head bursts like a cork from an orgasmic champagne bottle.

Like sound, color brought both greater phenomenological veracity and heightened fantasy to film. Depression audiences hungry for screen glamor and luxurious surroundings lapped up adaptations like Mamoulian's 1935 *Becky Sharp* (*Vanity Fair*), the first feature-length Technicolor film, and a classically anachronistic blend of historical authenticity and Hollywood fashion. While bustlines, uniforms, and minor characters' costumes bear some resemblance to Regency dress, pencil-thin arched eyebrows, darkly painted heart-shaped lips, side curls, cloche hats, hip-hugging bias-cut dresses, bare backs, polka dots, bright colors, and metallic fabrics all declare the

1930s. The habit of deference to modern conceptions of glamor has continued through recent BBC and Merchant–Ivory productions, despite their reputation for being correct to the point of distraction: even today, the vanities of the star system balk at authentically flawed skin, unplucked eyebrows, and unwashed hair, oiled to accommodate elaborate Victorian hairstyles.

As the preoccupation with glamor indicates, adaptations of the 1930s and 1940s were largely aimed at female audiences, a fact which participated in the broad contemporary condemnation of "feminine" Victorianism. Thus MGM's 1940 *Pride and Prejudice* opens with giggling scenes of shopping, to the accompaniment of arch synchronized music (the technique known as mickey-mousing), while also emphasizing the strong female character at its center (Greer Garson as Elizabeth Bennett), exactly as Mamoulian's *Becky Sharp* had foregrounded its titular character (Miriam Hopkins). But neither glamorization nor a more rational focus on women prevented antifeminist adaptations. William Wyler's 1939 *Wuthering Heights* turns Cathy into the archvillain of the piece. Erotically greedy as well as money-grubbing, she dies in sheer frustration that she cannot have both Edgar and Heathcliff (whose viciousness is simply written out), though her misogynist denigration is offset by the film's equal villainization of Hindley and its sanctification of Isabella. The shifts are certainly due in part to censorship rules, which precluded most of Heathcliff's violence, and to the star system, which could not let Laurence Olivier enact it.

The 1940s saw a further maturing of the novel–film relationship, best exemplified by David Lean's *Great Expectations* (1946) and *Oliver Twist* (1948), in which innovative design and camerawork (trick perspective, forced focal lengths) sought to capture the nightmare realism and child's-eye qualities of the originals. In contrast, the 1944 version of *Jane Eyre* exemplifies the baroque degree to which literary and filmic reference could be layered on one another. Directed by Robert Stevenson, and improbably featuring the young Elizabeth Taylor as Helen Burns, the film evidences the influence not only of Orson Welles, who plays Rochester, but of Alfred Hitchcock's 1940 adaptation of Daphne du Maurier's *Rebecca*, whose star (Joan Fontaine) plays Jane. The *Rebecca* connection made Stevenson's *Jane Eyre*, in fact, a kind of inspired back-formation, since du Maurier's fable – shy poor girl weds Byronic hero with a marital skeleton in his closet – obviously derived from Brontë's romance. And more broadly, the Brontë model of transgression and curiosity – whereby a woman penetrates the secrets of a locked room, a gendered variation on the Gothic's handling of space – is important not just for Hitchcock's whole œuvre, but for film horror and the thriller generally (as is the Jane/Bertha doubling).

The same quirk of cultural relationship that turned *Rebecca* back into *Jane Eyre* uncovered Brontë's novel (as well as her sister's *Wuthering Heights*) behind Jane Campion's *The Piano* (1993) fifty years later. Eleven-year-old Anna Paquin moved naturally from her Oscar-winning role as Flora, Ada/Jane/Cathy's daughter and double, to her incarnation as the young Jane Eyre in Zeffirelli's 1996 adaptation. But it was not casting alone that revealed the *Jane Eyre/Piano* relationship. At the heart of Campion's film, pointedly enacted by hapless New Zealand settlers for the edification of baffled Maori, lies the same text-within-a-text that is repeatedly and uneasily referenced by *Jane Eyre*, and by Hitchcock's *Rebecca* – Bluebeard, folklore's ur-myth of spousal violence. Thus film brings to the surface the often troubling fairytale underpinnings of Victorian fiction, and adaptation lays bare realism's repressed fantastic device.

Conversely, the adult Victorian novel (and with it our Western cultural heritage) has been filmically repackaged as edu-tainment for children, a process which involves not only cuts but plot simplification, emphasis on childhood sections, and the imposition of adapters' values. The 1967 McGraw-Hill *Wuthering Heights*, released in their "Classical Literature Series," thus excises the sex and violence, and normalizes the more bizarre psychological elements: Cathy's cry "I *am* Heathcliff!" thus becomes the flat statement "I am *like* Heathcliff."

More disturbing is the modern cultural censorship imposed on Victorian childhood classics. In Harry Harris's 1985 television adaptation of *Alice in Wonderland*, for example, Carroll's nonsensical dream-world is subjected to the conventions of earlier children's films – with Alice as a hybridized Shirley Temple/Judy Garland trying to find her way "home" from Oz/Wonderland – and magical events are explained in terms of scientific cause and effect, so that her soliloquies serve as captions for the logically impaired portions of the film ("It was the fan that was making me shrink"; "These are my tears from when I was nine feet tall"). This Alice (unlike Carroll's) primly invokes the legal drinking age when offered wine, and warbles moralistic ditties about "golden rules" and universal kindness. Particularly miscast is cultural icon Ringo Starr as the Mock Turtle, trapped in pink tights and a maundering song that bluntly contradicts Carroll's "nonsense" critique of the tyrannical rules of language that prepare the child for injustice and social oppression.

Harris's sequel, *Alice Through the Looking Glass* (also 1985), further pop-psychologizes away the text's fear of the objective world by turning the dreaded Jabberwock into Alice's personal demon, and exorcizing him. Similarly, in the NBC special of 1999 (with Whoopi Goldberg as the Cheshire Cat and Ben Kingsley as the Caterpillar), Alice must overcome a phobia about singing in public to emerge as a performer: thus Carroll's Alice is reduced to an entertainment-industry coming-of-age parable. Far more in keeping with the text are Walt Disney's whimsical, animated version of 1951, which plays as delightfully with sounds and images as Alice does with words, and Jan Svankmajer's disturbing surrealist animation of 1988, which upsets the laws of physics much as Carroll does the laws of language.

Svankmajer's version opens with the words: "Now you will see a film for children . . . perhaps." But there is no "perhaps" about another strain of adaptation: pornographic films of Victorian fiction made for adults only. While the majority appear in the horror genre – *Dracula Sucks* (a.k.a. *Lust at First Bite*, 1979); *Dr. Sexual and Mr. Hyde* (1971) – one that provides a sinister continuity with the moralizing strain that marks adaptations for children is the 1976 Playboy version of *Alice in Wonderland* (a.k.a. *The World's Greatest Bedtime Story*). Here, a frigid teenaged librarian finds a copy of Carroll's classic, and vows to grow up all over again – as the ingénue sexual apprentice of a top-hatted but trouserless Mad Hatter, an incestuous Tweedle Dee and Tweedle Dum (a brother–sister pair, courtesy of Playboy homophobia), an impotent Humpty Dumpty (whom Alice does put together again), and a ferocious lesbian Queen (who keeps screaming "Give me some head!"). Duly instructed in the art of pleasing men, the heroine is rewarded with marriage to the beau she rebuffed at the opening, plus children, a home, and a dog.

The colonizing of Victorian texts and the propagation of the cultural values they embodied was most frankly undertaken by the Hollywood Dream Factory in its heyday. Industry heads hoped to "lessen sales resistance" in foreign countries, as a producer told Harvard business students in 1927, by "drawing on their literary talent, taking their choicest stories, and sending them back into the countries where they are famous" (quoted in Chanan 1983: 56). As regards British material, the strategy extended to Victorian tales of imperial adventure, so that the Spielberg blockbuster *Raiders of the Lost Ark* (1981) may be said to descend not only from American Saturday-morning serials but from Rider Haggard's *She* (filmed by RKO in 1935) and *King Solomon's Mines* (MGM, 1950). Britain competed for the same texts not only as a matter of national pride (Hammer filmed *She* in 1965; Gainsborough mined the *Mines* in 1937), but as a means of survival: as early as mid-1916, claimed the *Bioscope* trade magazine, adaptation accounted for all but 5 percent of the home film industry's output.

The imperial power flow has reversed in television adaptations. British penetration of the "quality" TV drama market since the 1960s – with the worldwide success, for example, of the 1995 BBC *Middlemarch* – makes a powerful implicit claim for British capacity to understand and represent the world, if no longer to rule it, a claim that Eliot's pose of authorial omniscience very amply fostered. The export of stories is big business, and on the television front Britain dominates that business as once it dominated the English-speaking world of the Victorian novel: the American contribution to UK/US coproductions of the 1990s appears to have been exclusively monetary. International collaboration sometimes produces genuinely intercultural adaptations, however, like the 1989 Anglo-French mini-series *A Tale of Two Cities*, whose French director, British screenwriter, and French actors playing French characters gave the Revolution a far more sympathetic spin than Dickens's account.

Television adaptations often also mark collaborations of arts and technologies – radio and theater, film and television drama. The BBC shifted easily from radio play and serialized dramatic readings to televised dramatizations of Victorian novels, often running to more than ten episodes; the Corporation's prodigious output of adaptations peaked at over fifty airings per decade in the 1970s. It was not uncommon for the same novel to be re-adapted with a different cast and crew every decade or so, as if the story needed to be continually refreshed in the public imagination. In the 1980s and 1990s, a larger selection of channels and shifting audience tastes led to shorter, film-length adaptations, a change that mirrors the move from eagerly awaited magazine or part-issue serializations to single-volume novels in the Victorian period. The change has further fostered changes in videography and televised sound. Earlier television adaptations stuck rigorously to British theatrical modes: characters conversed indoors on period sets under static cameras. Later ones add more filmic lighting, camerawork, high-budget location shooting, and a mixed soundtrack (often including the once eschewed extra-diegetic musical score).

Finally, though Hollywood film and British television dominate, cultural transmission has not been entirely unidirectional, as we saw in the case of Murnau's German reworking of *Dracula*. Foreign film-makers who adapt Victorian novels inevitably imbue them with other cultural heritages. Luis Buñuel's *Abismos de Pasion* (Mexico, 1953) and Kiju Yoshida's *Arashi ga oka* (Japan, 1988), intercultural adaptations of *Wuthering Heights*, both turn the Yorkshire moors into volcanic slopes, settings with the potential to erupt as violently as any of the novel's characters, and date the story (originally set in the 1700s) to appropriately "primitive" eras: Buñuel's low-budget feature film, shot in stark black and white, is set in the desert mountains of nineteenth-century Mexico; Yoshida's high-budget color film is set on Mount Fuji in medieval Japan. Buñuel explores a witchcraft-tinged Catholicism, as José (Joseph) sacrifices live frogs to exorcise the house; Yoshida recasts the Earnshaws as Yamabe Shinto priests shunned and eventually stoned by fearful villagers. Both unfamiliar religious contexts ground the confused passion and ethics of Brontë's novel far more effectively than do British and American adaptations, which have all too often reduced it to a tale of domestic abuse.

Buñuel's *Abismos* is celebrated for its surrealistic privileging of sadism, madness, and *l'amour fou*, as well as for a shock ending (which influenced other adaptations, including Yoshida's), in which Hindley survives to shoot Heathcliff/Alejandro as he embraces the bridal corpse of Cathy/Catalina, thus disturbingly merging the genres of Western shoot-out, romantic wedding, and *Liebestod* (Wagnerian love-in-death). The last twist to Buñuel's cinematic revision of Brontë's text is the word "Fin," superimposed over the slamming doors of Cathy/Catalina's burial vault. As the word enlarges on the screen, it seems to move toward the viewer with an in-your-face gesture, as if to say, "Yes, this is the ending!" As the vault doors bang shut, they look astonishingly like the closing covers of a book.

Yoshida's *Arashi ga oka* fulfilled Geoffrey Wagner's 1975 prophecy that only the Japanese could make a good adaptation of *Wuthering Heights* (236). Blending principles of Japanese art, theater, and painting with Western cinematic techniques, Yoshida maintains a delicate balance between compelling beauty – every shot is an exquisite work of visual art: mountainscapes, gauzy mists, figures like hieroglyphic characters – and the repellent violence that other (Western) adaptations mitigate. Characters who die from illness in Brontë's novel meet violent deaths in Yoshida's film: Hidemaru (Mr. Earnshaw), is killed by soldiers, his white robe daubed red by their arrows; Shino (Frances) is robbed, stripped, raped, killed, and her body splayed like litter on the unsympathetic landscape; raped and abandoned by Onimaru (Heathcliff), Tae (Isabella) hangs herself. Japanese art in general views the human figure as a small, integral part of the landscape, while Western art centers it, and sees it large; Yoshida's complementary alternation of Western close-ups and Eastern extreme long shots exacerbates the viewer's sense of being both pulled into and pushed away from the text, as well as torn between two cultures, Brontë's and Yoshida's. Tensions within the film thus combine to create a compelling spectatorial experience that is far closer to the Victorian reading experience than Western films of this novel.

*

"Last night," wrote Maxim Gorky after his first encounter with film, 4 July 1896, "I was in the Kingdom of Shadows" (quoted in Leyda 1960: 408). The phrase recalls Murnau, whose cinematic transformation of Stoker's Transylvania into a "Land of Shadows" or "Phantoms" brilliantly capitalized – in superimpositions, negative–positive sequences, stop-motion, shadow-play, and the deathly dissolve that announces the Count's vaporization by sunlight – on the text's own density of visual imagery and ghostly, photographic ("shadow-picture") reference, from Harker's Kodak camera to his experience of the Count's "materialization" as an optical effect. But the phrase also suggests the whole project of film's incorporation of Victorian fiction. For in adapting Victorian novels to film – like Heathcliff, yearning for the dead Cathy to haunt him – we deliberately haunt ourselves with our ancestors; we return to these texts not only as cinematic origins but as the origins of our own modern era, impelled by our master-narrative, the Freudian imperative to uncover what has been hidden and repressed. Often, we project our values and fictions on to our Victorian forebears – like Wyler, cleaning up *Wuthering Heights* to the standards of 1939. But the old ghosts continue to haunt us, through all our modernizations and containments. Like the icy hand of Cathy's ghost attaching itself to the warm hand of Lockwood, the past's encounter with the present, film's encounter with Victorian fiction, can still produce the chill of an encounter with otherness.

REFERENCES

Auerbach, Nina (1995), *Our Vampires, Ourselves* (Chicago: University of Chicago Press).

Bluestone, George (1971), *Novels into Film: The Metamorphosis of Fiction into Cinema* (Berkeley: University of California Press). (First publ. 1957.)

Blum, Daniel (1953), *A Pictorial History of the Silent Screen* (New York: Grosset & Dunlap).

Chanan, Michael (1983), "The Emergence of an Industry," in James Curran and Vincent Porter, eds., *British Cinema History* (London: Weidenfeld), 39–58.

Eisenstein, Sergei (1944), "Dickens, Griffith, and the Film Today," repr. in *Film Form: Essays in Film Theory*, ed. and trans. Jay Leyda (New York: Harcourt, Brace, 1949).

Giddings, Robert, Selby, Peter and Wensley, Chris (1990), *Screening the Novel: The Theory and Politics of Literary Adaptation* (London: Macmillan).

Harthan, John (1981), *The History of the Illustrated Book: The Western Tradition* (London: Thames & Hudson).

James, Philip (1947), *English Book Illustration 1800–1900* (London: Penguin).

Kracauer, Siegfried (1947), *From Caligari to Hitler: a Psychological History of the German Film* (Princeton: Princeton University Press).

Leyda, Jay (1960), *Kino: A History of the Russian and Soviet Film* (London: Allen & Unwin).

Low, Rachel and Manvell, Roger (1950), *The History of the British Film*, vol. 3 (London: Allen).

Meisel, Martin (1983), *Realizations: Narrative, Pictorial, and Theatrical Arts in Nineteenth-Century England* (Princeton: Princeton University Press).

Metz, Christian (1977), *The Imaginary Signifier: Psychoanalysis and the Cinema*, trans. Celia Britton, Annwyl Williams, Ben Brewster, and Alfred Guzzetti (Bloomington: Indiana University Press).

Skal, David J. (1990), *Hollywood Gothic* (New York: Norton).

Stoker, Bram (1983), *Dracula*, ed. A. N. Wilson (Oxford: Oxford University Press; World's Classics). (First publ. 1897.)

Wagner, Geoffrey (1975), *The Novel and the Cinema* (London: Tanting).

FURTHER READING

Andrew, Dudley (1981), *Concepts in Film Theory* (New York: Oxford University Press).

Beja, Morris (1979), *Film and Literature* (New York: Longman).

Bordwell, David (1985), *Narration in the Fiction Film* (Madison: University of Wisconsin Press).

Bordwell, David (1997), *On the History of Film Style* (Cambridge, Mass.: Harvard University Press).

Cartmell, Deborah and Whelehan, Imelda, eds. (2000), *Adaptations: From Text to Screen, Screen to Text* (New York: Routledge).

Charney, Leo and Schwartz, Vanessa R., eds. (1995), *Cinema and the Invention of Modern Life* (Berkeley: University of California Press).

Chatman, Seymour (1978), *Story and Discourse: Narrative Structure in Fiction and Film* (Ithaca: Cornell University Press).

Cohen, Keith (1979), *Film and Fiction: The Dynamics of Exchange* (New Haven: Yale University Press).

Corrigan, Timothy, ed. (1999), *Film and Literature: An Introduction and Reader* (Upper Saddle River, NJ: Prentice-Hall).

Fell, John L. (1974), *Film and the Narrative Tradition* (Norman: University of Oklahoma Press).

Gledhill, Christine, ed. (1987), *Home is Where the Heart Is: Essays on Melodrama and the Woman's Film* (London: British Film Institute).

Klein, Michael and Parker, Gillian, eds. (1981), *The English Novel and the Movies* (New York: Ungar).

Kozloff, Sarah R. (1985), "Where Wessex Meets New England: Griffith's *Way Down East* and Hardy's *Tess of the D'Urbervilles*," *Literature/Film Quarterly*, 13/1, 35–41.

McFarlane, Brian (1996), *Novel to Film: An Introduction to the Theory of Adaptation* (Oxford: Clarendon).

Marsh, Joss (2001), "Dickens and Film," in John Jordan, ed., *The Cambridge Companion to Dickens* (Cambridge: Cambridge University Press), 204–23.

Merritt, Russell (1983), "Melodrama: Postmortem for a Phantom Genre," *Wide Angle*, 5/3, 24–31.

Naremore, James, ed. (2000), *Film Adaptation* (New Brunswick: Rutgers University Press).

Orr, Christopher (1984), "The Discourse on Adaptation," *Wide Angle*, 6/2, 72–6.

Tibbetts, John C. and Welsh, James M. (1998), *Encyclopedia of Novels into Film* (New York: Facts on File).

Index

Index compiled by Randy Miller